D0820881

GARDENS AND GHETTOS

The Art of Jewish Life in Italy

This volume is published in cooperation with

THE JEWISH MUSEUM

The Jewish Museum is under the auspices of
The Jewish Theological Seminary of America

COSPONSORS OF THE EXHIBITION

Comune di Ferrara
Cassa di Risparmio di Ferrara
Istituto per i Beni Artistici, Culturali e Naturali della Regione Emilia-Romagna
Istituto per i Beni Culturali della Giunta Regionale del Lazio
Soprintendenza Archeologica di Ostia
Soprintendenza Archeologica di Roma
Unione Comunità Israelitiche Italiane

GARDENS AND GHETTOS

The Art of Jewish Life in Italy

Edited by
Vivian B. Mann

UNIVERSITY OF CALIFORNIA PRESS
Berkeley Los Angeles Oxford

Gardens and Ghettos: The Art of Jewish Life in Italy has been published on the occasion of the opening of the exhibition organized by the Jewish Museum, New York. The exhibition dates are September 17, 1989 to February 1, 1990. Exhibition staff: Vivian B. Mann, Curator; Emily Braun, Consulting Curator (for modern section); Diane Lerner, Exhibition Coordinator; Gabriel M. Goldstein, Research Assistant; Meg Shore, Anna Farkas, Raymond Rosenthal, Translators.

University of California Press
Berkeley and Los Angeles, California

University of California Press, Ltd.
Oxford, England

Library of Congress Cataloging-in-Publication Data

Gardens and ghettos: the art of Jewish life in Italy / edited by Vivian B. Mann.
p. cm.
Catalog of an exhibition organized by The Jewish Museum, New York, held in New York, Sept. 17, 1989 to Feb. 1, 1990.
Bibliography: p.
ISBN 0-520-06824-6 (alk. paper).
ISBN 0-520-06825-4 (pbk. alk. paper)
1. Jews—Italy—Exhibitions. 2. Italy—Ethnic relations—Exhibitions. I. Mann, Vivian B. II. Jewish Museum (New York, N.Y.)
DS135.I8G37 1989
945'.004924'00747471—dc20
89-5015
CIP

Printed in Japan

9 8 7 6 5 4 3 2 1

C O N T E N T S

Lenders to the Exhibition vi
Donors to the Exhibition viii
Advisory Committee x
Honorary Committee xi
Tullia Zevi Foreword xii
Primo Levi Preface xv
Joan Rosenbaum Acknowledgments xviii

David Ruderman At the Intersection of Cultures: The Historical Legacy of Italian Jewry 1
Mario Toscano The Jews in Italy from the Risorgimento to the Republic 25
Vivian B. Mann The Arts of Jewish Italy 45
Richard Brilliant Jewish Art and Culture in Ancient Rome 67
Evelyn Cohen Hebrew Illuminated Manuscripts from Italy 93
Dora Liscia Bemporad Jewish Ceremonial Art in the Era of the City States and the Ghettos 111
Emily Braun From Risorgimento to the Resistance: A Century of Jewish Artists in Italy 137
Allen Mandelbaum A Millennium of Hebrew Poetry in Italy 191

Catalogue of the Exhibition 209
Biographies of Painters and Sculptors 329
Glossary 341
Selected Bibliography 345
Contributors to the Catalogue 353
Photo Credits 356

Gloria Abrams of Atikoth, New York
N. M. de' Angelis, Rome
Archivio di Stato di Reggio-Emilia, Reggio-Emilia
Giovanni Audoli, Turin
Beinecke Rare Book and Manuscript Library, Yale University, New Haven
Biblioteca Apostolica Vaticana, Vatican City
Bibliothèque Nationale, Paris
B'nai B'rith Klutznick Museum, Washington, D.C.
Eredi Cagli, Rome
The Carpi Family, Milan
Civica Galleria d'Arte Moderna, Milan
Comunità Israelitica di Bologna, Bologna
Comunità Israelitica di Ferrara, Ferrara
Comunità Israelitica di Firenze, Florence
Comunità Israelitica di Livorno, Livorno
Comunità Israelitica di Padova, Padua
Comunità Israelitica di Roma, Mostre Permanente, Rome
Comunità Israelitica di Torino, Turin
Comunità Israelitica di Venezia, Venice
Philippe Daverio Gallery, New York
Piero Dini, Montecatini
Ermes Drago, Marostica
Michael Ehrenthal, New York
Peter Ehrenthal, New York
Franco Evangelisti, Rome

LENDERS TO THE EXHIBITION

Dr. and Mrs. Solomon Feffer, New York
Piero and Naomi Foà, Detroit
Fondazione Carlo Levi, Rome
Daniel M. Friedenberg, Greenwich
Jacobo and Asea Furman, Santiago
Galleria Civica d'Arte Moderna, Palazzo dei Diamanti, Ferrara
Galleria d'Arte Moderna, Palazzo Pitti, Florence
Galleria degli Uffizi, Florence
Galleria Nazionale d'Arte Moderna, Rome
Garrett Collection of Medieval and Renaissance Manuscripts, Princeton University, Princeton
Yosef Goldman, New York
Gross Family Collection, Tel Aviv
Hebrew Union College, Jewish Institute of Religion, Cincinnati
Hirshhorn Museum and Sculpture Garden, Smithsonian Institution, Washington, D.C.
The Israel Museum, Jerusalem
Istituto Centrale per il Catalogo e la Documentazione, Rome
Jewish National and University Library, Jerusalem
Ovidio Jacorossi, Rome
Judah L. Magnes Museum, Berkeley
Mrs. Alexander Lewyt, New York
Library of The Jewish Theological Seminary of America, New York
Los Angeles County Museum of Art, Los Angeles
Daisy Nathan Margadonna, Rome
Metropolitan Museum of Art, New York
Alfred Moldovan, New York

Monumenti Musei e Gallerie Pontificie, Vatican City
Museo Civico-Galleria Civica d'Arte Moderna, Turin
Museo Civico "G. Fattori," Livorno
Museo Civico Revoltella-Galleria d'Arte Moderna, Trieste
Museo Nazionale Romano, Rome
Museo Sacro, Vatican City
Museum of Modern Art, New York
Franco Muzzi, Rome
National Museum of American History, Smithsonian Institution, Washington, D.C.
New York Public Library, New York
Henry and Rose Pearlman Foundation, Inc., Princeton
Philadelphia Museum of Art, Philadelphia
Private Collections
R.A.I., Radiotelevisione Italiana, Sede Regionale, Friuli-Venezia Giulia, Trieste
Giorgio di Raimondo, Rome
Irene Roth, New York
Giuseppe Selvaggi Collection, Rome
Mark Sonnino, New York
Soprintendenza Archeologica di Ostia, Ostia
Judy and Michael Steinhardt, New York
Studio Paul Nicholls, Milan
Trustees of The Victoria and Albert Museum, London
Netta Vespignani, S.r.l. Galleria d'Arte, Rome
The Sir Isaac and Lady Edith Wolfson Museum, Hechal Shlomo, Jerusalem
Benjamin Zucker, New York

DONORS TO THE EXHIBITION

"Gardens and Ghettos: The Art of Jewish Life in Italy" has been made possible, in part, by grants from the National Endowment for the Humanities, a federal agency.

Major funding for the exhibition has been provided by The Horace W. Goldsmith Foundation, the Comune di Ferrara, The Joe and Emily Lowe Foundation, The J. M. Kaplan Fund, S. H. and Helen R. Scheuer Family Foundation and the National Endowment for the Arts. Other significant funds have been contributed by Israel Discount Bank of New York, The Morris S. and Florence H. Bender Foundation, the Provincia di Roma and New York State Council on the Arts. Additional support has been provided by the New York City Department of Cultural Affairs, Enichem Americas, Inc., Maurice Amado Foundation, Harry DeJur Foundation and Netta Vespignani, S.r.l. Galleria d'Arte.

The catalogue is being published with the generous assistance of the Lucius N. Littauer Foundation and the Region of Lazio.

The international conference on the Cultural Legacy of Italian Jewry is partly supported by the Istituto per i Beni Artistici, Culturali e Naturali della Regione Emilia-Romagna.

Special considerations have been provided by Alitalia Airlines.

ADVISORY COMMITTEE

Charles Avery
Paolo Baldacci
Roberto Bassi
Paola Jarach Bedarida
Dora Liscia Bemporad
Carlo Bertelli
Father Leonard Boyle
Richard Brilliant
Bonnie Burnham
Nicola Caiola
Guido Calabresi
Beniamino Canarutto
Philip Cannistraro
David Cassuto
Evelyn Cohen
Shaye J. D. Cohen
Maria Teresa Contini
Bernard Cooperman
Philippe Daverio
Maurizio Fagiolo Dell'Arco
Piero Dini
Dario Durbé
Oreste Ferrari
Giuseppe Gentile
A. Bartlett Giamatti
Rafi Grafman
Rabbi Raffaele Grassini
Samuel Gruber
Carole Herselle-Krinsky
Elliot Horowitz
Adriano La Regina
Tullio Levi
Gianclaudio Macchiarella
Miriam Mafai
Allen Mandelbaum
Giuliano Matteucci
Leonard Meiselman
Augusta Monferini
Giuliano Montenero
Rosanna Morozzo
Paul Nicholls
Gastone Ortona Orefice
Celestina Ottolenghi
Carlo Pietrangeli
Mayer Rabinowitz
Paolo Ravenna
Giovannina Reinisch
David Ruderman
Giacomo Saban
Shalom Sabar
Vittorio Sacerdoti
Menahem Schmelzer
Paul Schwartzbaum
Jerry Schwarzbard
Elisabetta Seeber
Lela Titonel
Rabbi Elia Toaff
Mario Toscano
Netta Vespignani
Rabbi Achille Viterbo
Martin Weyl
Anna Gallina Zevi
Fausto Zevi
Susan Zuccotti

HONORARY COMMITTEE

Sergio Balanzino

Direttore Generale Relazione Culturali
Ministero Affari Esteri, Roma

Renzo Carella

Assessore Culturale, Provincia di Roma

Francesco Corrias

Console Generale d'Italia, New York

Mario M. Cuomo

Governor of the State of New York

Giuseppe Gherpelli

Presidente dell'Istituto per i beni artistici, culturali
e naturali della Regione Emilia-Romagna

Elisabetta Kelescian

Consigliere
Direzione Generale Relazioni Culturali
Ministero Affari Esteri, Roma

Bruno Landi

Presidente della Giunta Regionale del Lazio

Emilio Manara

Assessore alla Cultura, Comune di Ferrara

Rinaldo Petrignani

Ambassador of Italy to the United States

Aldo Rivela

Segretario Amministrativo della Presidenza
della Giunta Regionale
del Lazio

Elisabetta Seeber

Istituto Nazionale Servizi Culturali Enti Locali, Rome

Carla Sepe

Assistente Giuridico del Presidente della Repu Italiana
Presidente I.N.S.C.E.L.

Roberto Soffriti

Sindaco Comune di Ferrara

Tullia Zevi

Presidente Unione Comunità Ebraiche Italiane

"C'mon, there's no Jews in Italy!" the Jewish immigrants from eastern Europe would say in the early forties to this young refugee from Italy, buying her groceries in their stores in lower Manhattan. As proof of my not being a Jew, they cited the fact that I spoke no Yiddish, the language that was then still the living and lively *koiné* of first-generation Ashkenazic Jews in the United States.

Further downtown the inhabitants of Little Italy regarded me with equal suspicion: how could anyone claim to be *both* Italian and Jewish? And why was I planning to go back to Italy at the end of the war? "You're safe here!" they said, "and free!" Why go back?

How to explain to these people, whose passage from poverty and persecution to the unlimited opportunities of America had been one-way and definitive, that I was answering other needs, obeying a call that even I understood only dimly? It had to do with my having been born into a tradition of Jews living on Italian soil since the era of ancient Rome, a tradition of seventy generations that Mussolini and Hitler had failed to destroy. My need was to bear witness that the tradition was still alive.

My double identity, Italian and Jewish, suspect to both Italo-Americans and Jews in the United States, lived on as I returned to Italy and became increasingly involved in Jewish communal life. But something new had been added: the memory of my years in the United States replete with affection and gratitude for my having been granted refuge along with those others fortunate enough to have escaped war-torn Europe.

The fusion of these three elements present in me gave birth to an urge to share this triple inheritance with others, and this led to contacts with the Jewish Museum in New York and the suggestion that it undertake to tell the story of the Jews of Italy. Why the Jewish Museum of New York? Because it is an outstanding center for a much-needed cultural dialogue between European and American Jewry, and a pioneer in presenting to the American public the many facets of Jewish history and tradition.

After a few months (or was it years?) of incubation, Director Joan Rosenbaum and Curator Vivian Mann decided that the Jewish Museum would undertake to tell the story of the first two thousand years of Jewish art and life in Italy. And so the collaboration among the efficient "Americans"; the quiet, subdued world of Italian-Jewish families and communities proud of their heritage but reluctant to display it; scholars and artists; members of the Italian government; mayors of Italian towns; and high Vatican prelates began. Once the complexities of Italian bureaucracy were unraveled, the exhibition slowly took shape. The result is the first overall visual history of the Jews of Italy presented anywhere.

F O R E W O R D

The intelligence, courage, hard work, and financial support that went into this project have brought to life a faithful and stimulating picture of what we Italian Jews were and are: a community that through the centuries has managed to maintain both a distinctive character and a high degree of integration with the rest of Italian society. A community that is both very Jewish and very Italian: faithful to its archetypes and traditions, engaged in an ongoing osmotic process, a fertile symbiosis even in times of segregation and—it must be said—of persecution.

This exhibition helps reveal the secret of our heritage, identity, and survival: tolerance. Tolerance and a flexible, resilient brand of orthodoxy have kept us united through the centuries, sparing us schisms, religious strife, and the proliferation of conflicting hues of Judaism. We seem to have always managed to keep under the same communal roof Ashkenazim and Sephardim, natives rooted in Italy and Jews from other lands, who brought with them the wealth of their specific cultures.

Ours were and still are *kehilloth,* easy to leave and easy to return to with the expectation, seldom disappointed, of being welcomed back *besever panim yafot,* with benevolence. Ours is a Judaism in which the majority always shunned both ultraorthodoxy and hypersecularism, where the zealots, the *kannaim,* never prevailed, a community that sought to tread the *shevil ha-zahav,* the golden path of moderation Maimonides preached.

The Jews of Italy would not have developed their distinctive character had they not shared common traits with fellow Italians, who were and are comparatively tolerant and humane, generally curious and respectful of the mores of the person next door, and endowed with the virtue of disobedience when afflicted by unjust rulers. Our communities seldom found themselves in a situation of isolation or estrangement from their surroundings. Even our ghettos were never airtight shtetls. In their houses of worship, ritual objects, and life-styles, Jews and Gentiles in Italy over the centuries have revealed a shared love for beauty and harmony, formal order, pride in good craftsmanship, intellectual curiosity, and humor.

This exhibition is much more than a "Jewish story." By presenting the bimillennial history of a community that developed in a country both European and Mediterranean, that is at the crossroads of east and west, of north and south, it also points to a new dimension of the Jewish presence at the very roots of European civilization.

Warm thanks to Joan, Vivian, and their precious collaborators, to American and Italian private institutions, and to all those who made this event possible. I defy anyone seeing this exhibition to say, "There's no Jews in Italy!"

Tullia Zevi
President
Unione Comunità Ebraiche
Italiane

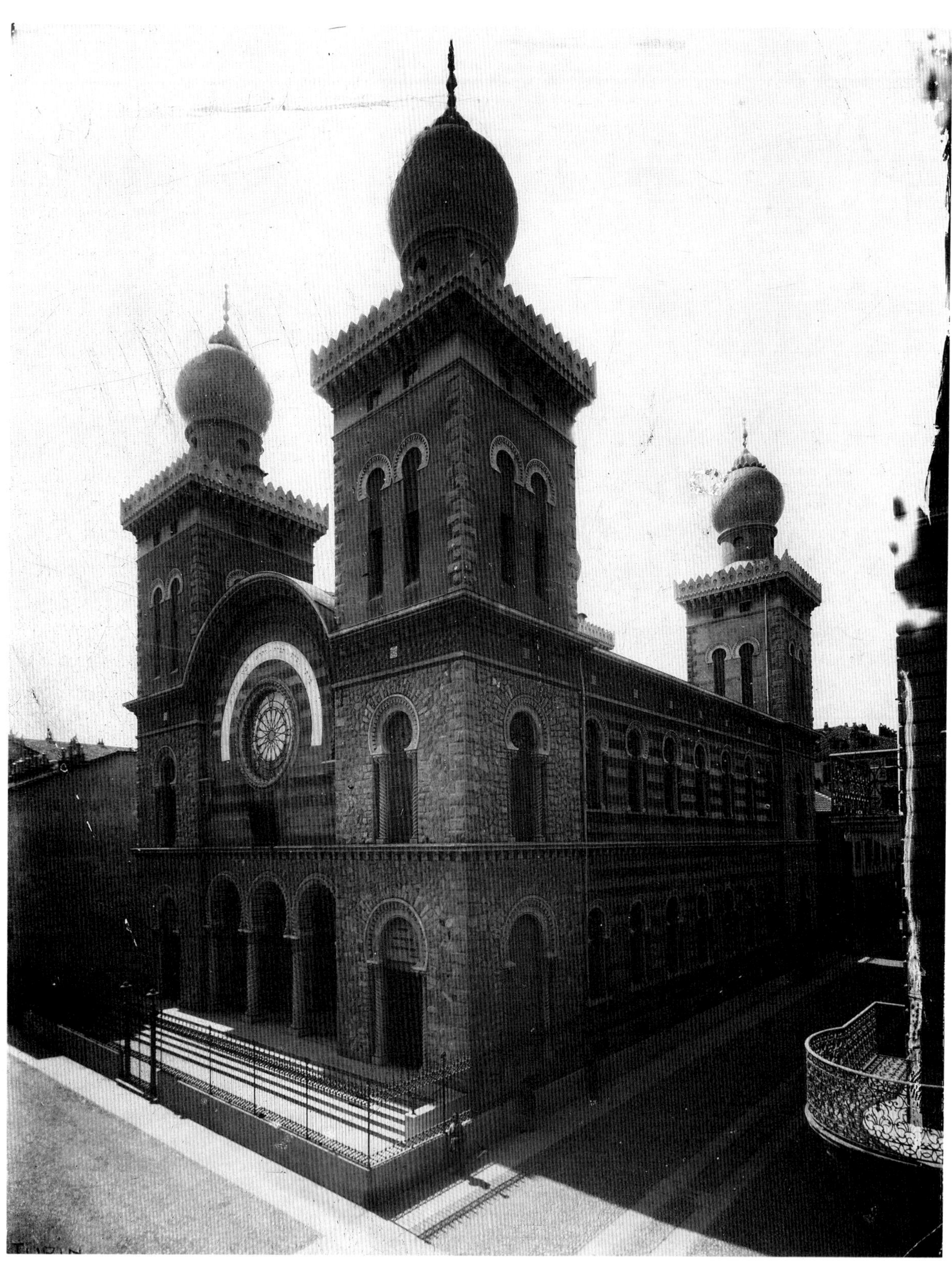

Fig. 1. Exterior of the Tempio Israelitico, Turin, 1880–1884

P R E F A C E

On the occasion of the centennial of our synagogue's inauguration, which took place on February 16, 1882, we Jews of Turin have decided to abandon for once our traditional twofold reserve. It is this well-known Piedmontese reserve, tied to geographical and historical roots (leading some to see in us the least Italian among Italians) superimposed on the millennial reserve of the Jews of the Diaspora, accustomed from time immemorial to live in silence and suspicion, to listen much and speak little, to keep from being noticed because, as is said, "one never knows."

We've never been numerous, little more than four thousand in the 1930s—and indeed that was the highest number we ever attained—little more than one thousand today. And yet we do not believe that we exaggerate if we affirm that we have counted for something, and still count for something, in the life of this city. Paradoxically our history as quiet, modest people is connected with Turin's most important monument, which certainly is not modest or in tune with our essential temperament. Indeed, as Alberto Rachelli tells us in detail . . . , we ran the serious risk of sharing with Alessandro Antonelli the responsibility for the presence of the Mole Antonelliana, that enormous exclamation point right in the center of our city. Obviously as Turinese we too have a certain affection for the Mole, but it is an ironic and polemical affection that does not blind us. We love it as one loves the walls of one's home, but we know that it is ugly, presumptuous, and not very functional; that it involved an extremely bad use of public money; and that after the 1953 cyclone and the 1961 restoration, it was kept erect by a metal prosthesis. In short, it is quite some time now that it has no longer deserved even a mention in the Guinness *Book of Records,* it is no longer, as they taught us in school, "the tallest brick construction in Europe." We therefore offer our posthumous gratitude to the municipal assessor Malvano, our coreligionist, who in 1875 had the cleverness to resell the commissioned and unfinished money-devouring edifice to the city. If his operation had not succeeded, today we would be forced to witness a melancholy spectacle: the few hundred Jews who go to temple on high holidays and the few dozen who go there for daily ceremonies would be almost in-

* Editor's note: This preface was originally printed in *Ebrei a Torino* (Turin, n.d.), published in conjunction with an exhibition celebrating the centenary of the Turin Synagogue in 1984. References to the exhibition in Dr. Levi's preface are to that one; the Rachelli essay that he mentions is in *Ebrei a Torino*. Shortly before his untimely death Dr. Levi gave the Jewish Museum permission to translate this preface into English and to print it in the present volume as his contribution to the exhibition and its catalogue.

visible in the enormous space enclosed by Antonelli's cupola.

Nevertheless, as I was saying, if we hadn't been there, the city would have been different, and this exhibition intends to prove it. When our ancestors (most of them not Turinese but residing mainly in Piedmont's smaller communities) became urbanized toward the end of the last century, they brought with them the great, perhaps the only, special gift that history has linked to the Jews: literacy, culture, religious and lay, felt as a duty, a right, a necessity, and a joy of life. And all this at a time when in Italy the great majority of the population was illiterate. Therefore emancipation did not catch them unprepared, as is shown by the histories of the many families outlined on the panels. Within one or two generations the Jews out of the ghetto easily moved from crafts and small commerce to the newly born industries, to administration, high public office, the armed forces, and the universities. Indeed, it is precisely in the academic environment that the Jews of Turin have left illustrious traces, completely disproportionate to their numbers, and their presence is still conspicuous both in quantity and in quality. In this ascent of theirs, which indeed paralleled that of much of the Christian middle class, they were favored by the fundamental tolerance of the population. It has been said that every country has the Jews it deserves: post-Risorgimento Italy, a country of ancient civilization, ethnically homogeneous and uncontaminated by serious xenophobic tensions, has made of its Jews a class of good citizens, respectful of the laws, loyal to the state, and alien to corruption and violence.

From this point of view the integration of Italian Jewry is unique in the world, but perhaps even more unique is the equilibrium of Turinese-Piedmontese Jewry, which easily became integrated without, however, renouncing its identity. Save for rare and peripheral cases, such as the Yemenite Jews of the Caucasus, all Jewish communities in the world bore (and still bear) the marks of the tortured history of the people of Israel, a fabric woven of slaughters, expulsions, humiliating separations, excessive and arbitrary taxation, forced conversions, and migrations. The Jews expelled from one country (from England in 1290, from France all through the fourteenth century, from the Rhineland at the time of the Crusades, from Spain in 1492, all the way down to the recent migrations to the Americas) sought refuge elsewhere, attaching themselves to the existing communities or founding new ones. They therefore were doubly alien, because of their religion and their provenance. Thus the greater part of the communities are stratified and internally composite, with occasional tensions and fractures. Of this Israel Zangwill has given us a lively picture in his famous story "The King of the Schnorrers," which recounts the clash between a scholarly, arrogant beggar who is a "Spanish" Jew and an integrated, rich, and naive "German" Jew in the London of the early 1800s. In Amsterdam the local Jews of German origin sheltered the Jews expelled from the Spanish peninsula, although these two components did not merge to any extent. In Venice there are still as many as five synagogues, originally meant for Jews of different rites and provenances. The present situation in Paris, where Jews of old French origin live together with Jews of Algerian, Egyptian, Polish, Russian, and German origin is similar. The case of the highest complexity and greatest historical weight is notoriously that of Israel, where the simultaneous presence of Jews belonging to all the branches of the Diaspora constitutes to this day an intricate problem of internal politics, and the most recent instance is that of the Milan community, in which the massive influx of refugees from the Arab states and Iran is causing unrest and friction along with an unforeseen numerical growth.

By contrast the Jews of Turin, of distant Franco-Provençal and Spanish origin, have never had substantial additions from other regions. Of course there were infiltrations at various epochs, attested to by a number of surnames of proven German origin (Ottolenghi, Diena, Luzzati, Morpurgo, and, obviously, Tedeschi) and the solitary dialectal and liturgical term *ij ursai,* the anniversary of a death, which is a corruption of the Yiddish *yahrzeit,* "time of the year." But they were rapidly absorbed into a social fabric that has remained ethnically stable until the forty-year period (1880–1920), indeed, to this day, in strident contrast to what happened in Milan, which during the period of the economic boom swallowed up five or six thousand immigrants in two or three years, with profound changes to all its structures and superstructures.

That we are dealing with a small nation conscious of its identity and endowed with a consolidated physiognomy, almost a village set within the capital of the Savoys, is demonstrated by the prevalent endogamy, rarely extended beyond the region's confines, and by the curious Judeo-Piedmontese speech, today a subject of study for linguists and sociologists, but already described by such an acute observer of things Piedmontese as Alberto Viriglio. For this linguistic hybrid to be born and survive a number of conditions were indispensable: a profound integration with the majority population, an adequate memory of the liturgical tongue (the single channel by which Hebrew and Aramaic have followed the currents of the Diaspora), and a climate devoid of strong tensions between majority and minority. Hybrid languages cannot be born when such tensions exist; for instance, there never arose a Judeo-Polish dialect, nor are there Italo-German hybrids in the Alto Adige, whereas Italian immigrants to the United States, despite limited phonetic compatibility, have from the very beginning developed a specific speech of their own, cleverly used by Pascoli in a famous poem.

Our fathers, and above all our mothers, daily and with great naturalness, used Judeo-Piedmontese; it was the language of the family and the home. They were nevertheless conscious of its intrinsic comic charge, which sprung from the contrast between the fabric of the discourse, which was the rustic and laconic Piedmontese dialect, and the Hebrew inlay, drawn from the language of the patriarchs, remote but enlivened every day by public and private prayer and the reading of the books, polished by the millennia like the bed of a glacier. But this contrast mirrored another, the essential contrast of Judaism dispersed amidst the "peoples," the *gentes* (the *gentiles,* precisely), torn between divine vocation and quotidian misery, and it mirrored yet another, much vaster contrast, that intrinsic to the human condition, since man is twofold, an impasto of celestial afflatus and earthly dust. After the Diaspora the Jewish people have dolorously lived this conflict and have drawn from it, together with their wisdom, also their laughter, which in fact is absent in the Bible and the Prophets.

To these ancestors of ours, industrious and witty, not heroic, neither saints nor martyrs, not too distant in time and space, this exhibition is dedicated. We are conscious of its limitations, which we have deliberately kept within certain bounds. As for the history of the Jews of Turin during the following decades, there would have been other things of a different import to be noted: their early anti-Fascist commitment, paid for by long years of jail and forced relocation and house arrest, all the product of that thirst for liberty and justice that runs through all of Jewish history; the exemplary lives of men such as Umberto Terracini; Leone Ginsburg; Emanuele and Ennio Artom; Giuseppe, Mario, and Alberto Levi; the fallen partisans Sergio, Paulo, and Franco Diena; Jewish participation in the Resistance, once again much larger than their numbers would imply; the eight hundred deportees, of whom nothing is left but a tablet in our cemetery. On this occasion we do not want to speak of victories, defeats, struggles, and slaughters. It is our intention here to remember, to invite people to remember, and to make ourselves known before it is too late. In fact there exists for every human group a critical mass, below which stability ceases; at that point it tends toward an ever more excessive dilution and toward a silent and painless dissolution. Our community, except for unforeseeable events, seems to have started down this road. With this exhibition it is our intention to perform a work of filial piety, to show our Turinese friends and our children who we are and where we come from.

Primo Levi

Translated from the Italian by
Raymond Rosenthal

The Jewish Museum often investigates the cultural interaction of Jews with other religions and polities. But the art and life of Italian Jews offer an especially fascinating opportunity: the peninsula of Italy is the scene of two thousand years of unbroken history; and in this exhibition we can examine and delight in objects that are among the most consummate and compelling in all of Jewish art.

Gardens and Ghettos traces the evolution of the Jewish community on the Italian peninsula from the Roman republic through the modern era. This vista offers great scope, quality, and variety in the works exhibited, from the archaeological remains of an ancient synagogue to the paintings of little-known artists. Thanks to the work of the curators and scholars and the graciousness of lending institutions and collectors, we have been able to capture both the narrative of an important phase of history and the incomparable beauty of Jewish art created in the context of Roman and Italian art.

The challenge of creating this exhibition was prompted by Tullia Zevi, President of the Italian-Jewish Community. It is to her that the museum owes its first debt of gratitude, for her inspiration and also for her voice in this catalogue, as she so perfectly articulates the historical associations and identity of a modern Italian Jew. Dr. Vivian Mann, the Museum's Curator of Judaica, has been the project's director and guide since its inception. She not only has contributed her expertise in the areas of medieval art history and her knowledge of Jewish ceremonial art, she has exhibited extraordinary energy, vision, and complete dedication in expanding the boundaries of what is possible in an exhibition that examines Jewish history from the perspective of its art and artifacts. I thank her for undertaking the many years of planning and research and her willingness to take responsibility for every aspect of this complex and ambitious project. Guest curator Emily Braun has contributed her unique understanding of twentieth-century Italian art to bring to light a group of artists unknown to the American public. Although she has worked with the Jewish Museum for the first time on this project, she has shown exceptional sensitivity to the Museum's cultural context, bringing her skills to bear in a way that has provided a contribution to both art history and Jewish history.

The development, planning, and execution of this exhibition and catalogue involved the commitment and support of the Museum's Trustees and donors. Board Chairman Morris Offit and Development Committee Chairperson Susan Lipton took major roles in pursuing sources of funding and promoting the project.

The first financial contribution to the exhibition came from the National Endowment for the Humanities, which provided essential planning money. This was succeeded by major implementation grants from The Horace W. Goldsmith Foundation, The Joe and Emily Lowe Foundation, and the National Endowment for the Humanities. Additional vital support came from

ACKNOWLEDGMENTS

many sources including government agencies, with grants from the National Endowment for the Arts, the New York State Council on the Arts, and the New York City Department of Cultural Affairs. From Italy we were very kindly rewarded with help from the Foreign Ministry and the City of Ferrara as well as the Region of Lazio, the City of Rome, and the Istituto per i Beni Artistici Culturali e Naturali della Regione Emilia-Romagna. Several other donors participated in the project and they are listed on page viii of this catalogue. I thank all of the individuals, corporations, foundations and government agencies whose generosity provided the means to create, in *Gardens and Ghettos,* new scholarship, a catalogue of lasting value, and a unique exhibition experience.

In undertaking a project of such large scope the Museum forged a number of new partnerships with a variety of institutions, individuals, and municipalities. Among them we extend our gratitude for the critical collaboration of the Istituto Nazionale Servizi Culturali Enti Locali for facilitating the presentation of the exhibition in Italy, to Adriano La Regina, Soprintendenza di Archeologia of Rome; Mayor Roberto Soffriti; Cultural Commissioner Emilio Manara both of the city of Ferrara; the Director of the Archive of the Scuola Romana, Netta Vespignani; Augusta Monferini, the Director of the Museum of Modern Art in Rome; and the following rabbis and heads of Jewish communities in Italy: Rabbi Eli Toaff and Giacomo Saban of Rome; Rabbi Raffaele Grassini and Roberto Bassi, Venice; Igina Liscia Leoni, Florence; Rabbi Achille Viterbo and Vittorio Sacerdoti, Padua; Bianca Colbi Finzi, Bologna; and Tullio Levi, Turin.

The Jewish Museum staff working most directly with this exhibition has handled an enormous quantity of work with deftness and intelligence. My gratitude is expressed to Exhibition Coordinator Diane Lerner; Research Associate Gabriel Goldstein; and Administrative Assistant Erica Granetz. In Italy we were given invaluable assistance with travel coordination by Elisabetta Seeber, and with administration and conservation by Paul Schwartzbaum, Renata Rossani, Diana Della Venezia, and Patricia Miracola. The modern section of the exhibition and catalogue research would not have been possible without the gracious and invaluable assistance of Francesca Morelli of Rome. We are also grateful for the generous cooperation of the Archivio della Scuola Romana, Rome. All the Jewish Museum staff have been involved in one way or another in creating the exhibition and publication. While all the names cannot be mentioned in this space, I want to give a special word of appreciation for the tireless and excellent work of Diane Fyrnyk, Exhibitions Administrator; Ward Mintz, Assistant Director of the Museum; Rita Feigenbaum, Registrar; Susan Palamara, Assistant to the Registrar; Al Lazarte, Director of Operations; Judith Siegel, Director of Education; Jean Rosensaft, Assistant Director of Education; Philip Meranus, Director of Public Affairs;

Barbara Perlov, Development Associate; Anne Scher, Director of Public Relations; Ruth Dolkart, Administrator; and Carole Putter, Financial Administrator.

Designers Lynne Breslin and Shauna Mosseri wed their considerable talents to develop a beautiful exhibition installation. Stanley Holwitz, Shirley Warren, and Steve Renick of the University of California Press offered patient and professional guidance at difficult moments as did the copy editors Karen Jacobson and Deborah Birns. Catalogue authors Richard Brilliant, Allen Mandelbaum, Dora Liscia Bemporad, Evelyn Cohen and David Ruderman aided the project well beyond their scholarly contributions. Meg Shore, Raymond Rosenthal and Anna Farkas worked diligently to provide excellent translations.

There are more than three hundred works from ninety-four different collections included in this exhibition, and these loans would not have been possible without the confidence and enthusiasm of many private and public lenders, all listed on page vi. Their cooperation has been extraordinary, and the Museum gives its sincerest thanks for the willingness of these institutions to send their works both to the Jewish Museum and to the exhibition's subsequent venue in Italy.

Many other individuals provided moral support, research ideas, introductions, fund-raising advice, and intellectual stimulation. Among these people, I thank Sally Fischer, George Pavia, Richard Menschel, Alfredo de Marzio, Renaldo Petrignani, Francesco Corrias, Bernard Cooperman, and Mayer Rabinowitz.

Joan Rosenbaum
Director, The Jewish Museum

Fig. 2. The Arch of Titus, Rome, 81 C.E.

DAVID B. RUDERMAN

AT THE INTERSECTION OF CULTURES: THE HISTORICAL LEGACY OF ITALIAN JEWRY

Among the precious artifacts included in the Jewish Museum's exhibition on Italian-Jewish life is a work of singular importance. It is a lexicon of rabbinic literature called the *Arukh,* written by Nathan ben Jeḥiel of Rome (1035–c. 1110) at the beginning of the twelfth century (cat. no. 61). Why so modest a work, a mere dictionary of words and phrases, should elicit special attention requires some elucidation.

Nathan headed the Talmudic academy of Rome, a post he held with his two brothers and one that had earlier been held by his father, who died in 1070. Nathan apparently belonged to the well-known Anau (Anav) family, an ancient clan that, according to its tradition, descended from one of four aristocratic families that Titus brought from Jerusalem to Rome after the destruction of the Temple in 70 C.E. That his family were no mere newcomers to the glorious city of the popes but claimed an ancestry that even predated the emergence of Rome as the center of Western Christendom was not an insignificant fact for either Nathan's coreligionists or his other Italian neighbors. For Jews it underscored their long-standing and uninterrupted residence in the first important beachhead of Jewish settlement in Europe in the aftermath of Jerusalem's defeat at the hands of Rome. For non-Jews it suggested that the longevity of Jewish residency in Italy for some one thousand years should not be taken for granted, for it entitled them to a place of honor in the political and cultural life of their community.

Nathan's *Arukh* was a work of prodigious scholarship, a glossary of encyclopedic proportions. The author presented both the meaning and etymology of difficult or unusual terms found in the Talmud and Midrashim, drawing on his impressive knowledge of Hebrew, Aramaic, Latin, Greek, Persian, and Arabic. Nathan's most significant achievement was his amalgamation of the individual exegetical and legal traditions of his day: first and foremost, that of the Babylonian Talmud and the legal decisions of the gaonate of Baghdad. He also incorporated the Palestinian Targum, Tosefta, Midrashim, and Talmud; the rabbinic commentary of Hananel ben Hushi'el of Kairouan (d. 1055–56), who had quoted extensively from the Palestinian Talmud and compared it with its Babylonian counterpart; and finally, the emerging rabbinic scholarship of northern Europe, especially Germany and Provence, in particular the commentaries of Rabbenu Gershom (960–1028) and "the scholars of Mainz." Nathan even occasionally consulted the latest books on mathematics and medicine.

In correlating and fusing all of these diverse traditions and sources in the pages of his massive compendium, Nathan initiated a creative process that was to become the most consistent and characteristic feature of Italian-Jewish scholarship for centuries to come. It is no coincidence that one of the most significant products of Italian-Jewish culture in the early modern era was also a Talmudic encyclopedia, the *Pahad Yiẓḥak* of Isaac Lampronti (1679–1756) of Ferrara, written in the eighteenth century. In their efforts to integrate and mediate disparate traditions, to reconcile and accommodate conflicting legal opinions and religious ideals, in short, to tolerate, to cultivate, and even to be enlivened by diversity, a long line of Italian-Jewish writers from Nathan to Isaac adopted the genre of the encyclopedia. Accordingly one might argue that Nathan's literary undertaking came to represent the most typical and unique signature of Italian-Jewish culture.[2]

One additional facet of the *Arukh* should be mentioned: its publication date. A good indication of its enduring popularity and usefulness to students of Talmudic and Jewish civilization was the fact that it was one of the first books to be printed by a Hebrew press, fittingly in the same city in which it was written, between 1469 and 1472. From the fifteenth century on, the work enjoyed wide circulation through numerous editions. Furthermore a number of authors saw fit to enlarge and emend the original work. For example, Menahem de Lonzano (1550–c. 1624) and Benjamin Mussafia (1606–1675) both published important expansions of the *Arukh*. Through Nathan's writing, particularly in its printed versions, the study of rabbinic texts, of comparative philology, customs, and legal traditions has been stimulated in communities outside Italy until the present day.

Through the assumed ancestry of its author, the *Arukh* testifies to the longevity of Italian Jewry's residency on the European continent. Moreover, as a mediator and harmonizer of disparate and even conflicting traditions and values, it embodies the characteristic mode of Italian-Jewish civilization, at least until the threshold of the modern era. And finally, it underscores the importance of Italy as a nerve center, as a conduit, and as a critical disseminator of knowledge to Jewish communities throughout the continent and beyond. In exemplifying these three major themes of Jewish cultural history in Italy, Nathan's *Arukh* offers a fitting introduction to the subject of this essay.

The Modest Beginnings of Italian-Jewish Culture in the Roman Empire

Among the stereotyped Latin and Greek epitaphs of the Jewish catacombs of Rome is the personalized poem of a husband to his wife:

> Here lies Regina, covered by such a tomb, which her husband set up as fitting to his love. After twice ten years she spent with him one year, four months, and eight days more. She will live again, return to the light again, for she can hope that she will rise to the life promised, as is our true faith, to the worthy and the pious, in that she has deserved to possess an abode in the hallowed land. This your piety has assured you, this your chaste life, this your love for your people, this your observance of the Law, your devotion to your wedlock, the glory of which was dear to you. For all these deeds your hope of the future is assured. In this your sorrowing husband seeks his comfort.[3]

The poem to Regina provides one of the few individual portraits of Jews who lived in the environs of Rome during the period of the empire. Her husband, in recalling the more than twenty years of marriage to his beloved wife, is confident of her immortality in light of her good deeds, her love of her people, and her faithful observance of Jewish law. Beneath the pleasant pieties of the husband's verse emerges the faint sense of a Jewish woman devoted to her religious heritage and her community and deserving of life after death in the estimation of her loved one. But the stamp of her individuality remains all too faint, and since this epitaph has been called the longest and most elaborate inscription found in the Roman Jewish catacombs,[4] the promise other inscriptions hold for reconstructing Italian-Jewish life in the period of the empire is disappointingly limited. More typical of the hundreds of epitaphs is the standard phrase: "Be of good courage; no one is immortal."[5]

In the absence of more concrete documentation of Jewish life in ancient Italy, only the bare outlines are discernible.[6] As early as the Hasmoneon era in the second century B.C.E., Jewish delegations from Palestine visited Rome, and perhaps some individuals remained to settle there. A more substantial presence of Jews in Rome and southern Italy is visible in the middle decades of the next century, consisting primarily of slaves deposited in Rome and probably also of merchants from the East. Jews flourished under the protection

Fig. 3. Sarcophagus Cover of Faustina with Theatrical Masks and Funerary Inscription, Rome, second half of the third century C.E., Museo Nazionale Romano, Rome (cat. no. 14)

of Julius Caesar and Augustus, who allowed them to practice their ancestral laws. Despite occasional disruptions and murmurings of certain intellectuals and public figures, Jewish life was generally unmolested during the first Christian centuries.

A large number of Jewish prisoners were deported to Rome after the failure of the revolt in Judaea. The majestic Arch of Titus in Rome still bears the sculpted record of Roman triumph and Jewish humiliation. Despite the continued insurrections of Jews throughout the empire, culminating in the defeat of Bar Kochba in Palestine in 135 C.E., the emperors generally treated their Jewish subjects in Italy benevolently. Even with the adoption of Christianity as the official religion of the empire by the fourth century, the passage of discriminatory legislation in the name of Theodosius and Justinian in the fifth and sixth centuries, and periodic expressions of public hostility by individual church leaders, Jewish life in Italy apparently remained surprisingly stable, to the extent that it is known. In Rome itself many Jews were engaged in humble occupations and hardly attained prominence economically or socially.

There is even less to say about the status of Jewish cultural and intellectual activity in ancient Italy. With the exception of the Jewish historian Josephus, who settled in Rome after the revolt, and the mention of a Palestinian rabbi, Mattiah ben Ḥeresh, who lived in Rome in the second century, one is struck by the sheer absence of literary activity and intellectual life among Italian Jews before the ninth century C.E. With the lack of writings, there remain only synagogue ruins and tombstone inscriptions offering testimony of Jewish settlement in Ostia, Naples, Salerno, Bari, Otranto, Taranto, Venosa, Reggio, and elsewhere, but little more. More telling is the language of the inscriptions: either Greek or Latin, interspersed occasionally with simple Hebrew words (*shalom, shalom al Yisrael,* etc.), and decorated with pagan symbols or a simple figure of a menorah, testifying to a low level of Hebraic literacy and a high degree of assimilation.

In the Orbit of Byzantine Influence: Jewish Culture in Southern Italy in the Ninth and Tenth Centuries

From the time of the stoic Latin epitaph "No one is immortal," consistently repeated through the seventh and eighth centuries, to that of the celebratory Hebrew pronouncement paraphrasing Isaiah 11:3: "For out of Bari shall go forth the Law, and the word of the Lord from Otranto," associated with the ninth century and beyond, a dramatic transformation in the culture of Jews residing in southern Italy had obviously taken place.[7] The transition can best be gauged by the language in which tombstone inscriptions appear from the beginning of this period until its close. Initially all the epitaphs, as we have seen, are written in Greek and Latin; gradually they are mixed with Hebrew ones; and finally they are all in Hebrew.[8]

The Hebrew revival of the ninth century reveals the end product of a long political and cultural development that is shrouded in considerable obscurity. The steady disintegration of the western Roman Empire, the barbarian incursions into Italy, and the gradual isolation of western Europe as a result of the Muslim hegemony in the East all play a part in this transition.

The fate of this miniscule Jewish minority in Italy could not have been unaffected by these larger upheavals. Certainly the apparent arrival of North African Jews in Italy as a result of the Muslim raids into Italy may have constituted one important factor in the subsequent rise in Hebrew literacy.

Whatever the precise cause of this mutation, the small communities of Jews living in southern Italy under Byzantine rule in the ninth century were of a different character than those who had earlier left their cryptic messages on tombstones in Rome, Venosa, and elsewhere. Their economic life had not radically changed, to the extent that it can be reconstructed. They were artisans and merchants, dyers and silk weavers, and even landowning farmers. In the sphere of culture and intellectual creativity, however, they were profoundly different. Literary sources opaquely describe the existence of institutions of rabbinic learning in Rome and Lucca, in Bari, Otranto, Venosa, and Oria. After a complete absence of Hebrew writings for centuries, Italian Jewry suddenly and dramatically rediscovered its link with the language of scripture and the rabbis.

What is striking about the Hebrew revival of the ninth and tenth centuries is not only its seeming "creation out of nothing" but also its variegated and colorful nature. While Italian rabbis were presumably engaged in the teaching of Torah in a manner similar to their counterparts in the centers of Israel, Baghdad, and North Africa, they left little trace of their scholarship prior to the lexicon of Nathan of Rome. What remains instead is a small but innovative literary output in such diverse fields as ancient and local family history, liturgical poetry, medicine and science, and even a faint echo of early Jewish mystical traditions.

Only a small number of works survive, but they reveal in their totality the existence of a highly complex society, receptive to the strains and influences of powerful Jewish centers outside Italy and stimulated by cultural contacts with the non-Jewish world. At the crossroads between Palestinian and Babylonian rabbinic spheres of domination, between Eastern and Western Christendom, and between Christianity and Islam, these fledgling Jewish communities could hardly be immune to intense cultural stimulation, confusion, and even conflict.

Among the most important literary products of this age was *Sefer Josipphon,* a historical narrative composed in Hebrew describing the later biblical period and that of the Second Temple.[9] The work is usually dated to 953 C.E. and is attributed to an anonymous author living in southern Italy who utilized a Latin manuscript based on Josephus' *Antiquities of the Jews* and *The Jewish War,* called the *Hegessippus.* Among the interpolations found in the narrative is a description of ancient Italy and the founding of Rome as well as a listing of the boundaries of the world more appropriate for the tenth century than for antiquity. While celebrating the glorious history of ancient Israel, the work appears to betray little or no rabbinic cultural influence, especially that emanating from the Talmudic centers of Baghdad and North Africa. Throughout the Middle-Ages *Sefer Josipphon* enjoyed enormous popularity. Its earliest printed edition appeared in Mantua around 1480, testifying to the continued fascination with this book among Italian-Jewish circles.

A historical work of a different sort is that of the eleventh-century chronicler Aḥimaaz ben Paltiel, generally called *Megillat Aḥimaaz.*[10] The author, a resident of Capua and Oria in southern Italy, compiled in rhymed Hebrew prose a genealogy of his family from the ninth century on. The author's ancestors, such as Amittai, Silano, and Shephatiah, known through the liturgical poems they also composed, lived colorful and active lives and engaged in magic and wonder-working miracles. Given the author's penchant for telling fabulous tales of his family heroes, the work has often been discounted as an unreliable historical source and perceived as an unsophisticated product of the early medieval historical imagination. More recently the imaginative stories of Aḥimaaz have been deemed significant in revealing vividly the transition from the Palestinian sphere of influence to the Babylonian. Treating especially the story of the scholar Abu Aaron of Baghdad, who arrived in Italy, one recent scholar has attempted to focus on the Palestinian cultural substrate that existed in Italy prior to the introduction of the Babylonian influence, and then to show how the latter ultimately engaged and overtook the former in Italy and eventually throughout Europe.[11]

The Palestinian layer of Italian-Jewish culture is particularly prominent in the religious poetry composed during this period. The early liturgical creations of Silano and Amittai, for example, dwell on the memory of Israel's glorious past and are heavily indebted to the Palestinian *piyyut* form and to midrashic materials centering in the land of Israel. Yet they also reflect their own ambiance in their use of Latin, Greek, Italian, and even Arabic words. From the tenth century on, the writing of poetry extended beyond southern Italy to Rome and to Lucca in the north. In Rome Solomon ha-Bavli in the late tenth century composed a number of major poems that entered the hymnology of the Ashkenazic service. In Lucca members of the famous Kalonymus family also actively pursued the writing of liturgical poems for the synagogue.[12]

The most extraordinary Jewish intellectual figure of southern Italy in the tenth century was surely Shabbetai Donnolo, the pharmacist, physician, and commentator on the ancient mystical text the *Sefer Yeẓirah*. Well versed in rabbinic literature, in Greek and Latin medical and scientific writings, conversant in colloquial Italian, and even an occasional poet of Hebrew verse, Donnolo fully embodied the multifaceted character of Italian-Jewish culture long before its efflorescence in the Renaissance period. Donnolo's *Sefer ha-Mirkaḥot* (The Book of Remedies), a treatise on pharmacology, and his commentary constitute his principal extant works. In interpreting the mystical cosmology of the *Sefer Yeẓirah* within the context of the scientific knowledge of his day, Donnolo prefigured a major preoccupation of later Italian-Jewish thinkers in correlating and harmonizing potentially competing and conflicting epistemologies.[13]

Donnolo's fascination with a text of mystical speculation underscores the importance of Italy as a point of origin and dissemination of Jewish mysticism and pietism throughout Europe. According to a tradition preserved by the later Ashkenazic pietists, the Kalonymus family, who left Lucca for Mainz in the ninth century, was supposedly well versed in esoteric lore. In German pietistic circles Abu Aaron, considered to be the principal representative of Babylonian rabbinic learning in *Megillat Aḥimaaẓ,* was also held to be simultaneously a master of secret names and a progenitor of early Jewish mysticism. The contradictory images of this sage of Baghdad illustrate, at the very least, how conflicting ideologies and values competed for legitimization in the fertile soil of early medieval Italy.[14]

The importance of Italy as a conduit of ancient Jewish mysticism to northern Europe constitutes only a part of the larger cultural role this Jewish community was to play in the creation of other European centers of Jewish culture. The Kalonymus family was also well known for its rabbinic scholarship and for its leadership role in the Rhine communities in a later period.[15] The ultimate product of the dialectical encounter between Palestinian and Babylonian traditions in Italy was thus eventually transmitted to the north. And if a twelfth-century account of the ransoming of four rabbinic captives to North Africa and Spain can be seen to reflect the reality of a power shift of Jewish authority from the East to the West, its casual mention of Bari as the port of embarcation of the rabbis suggests an Italian cultural role in the transmission of Jewish culture to the West as well.[16] Whatever the case, the substantial repercussions of the creative processes of self-definition emerging within the tiny Italian communities of the ninth and tenth centuries were to be felt far beyond Italy and for centuries to come.

A Shift Northward: The Late Middle Ages

When the Spanish-Jewish traveler Benjamin of Tudela visited Italy in the 1160s and 1170s, his itinerary was predominantly towns in southern Italy. He reported on Jewish communities in Taranto, Capua, Brindisi, Trani, Naples, and Palermo while referring to only two important settlements north of Rome: Lucca and Pisa.[17] To all appearances the demographic distribution of Italian Jews in the twelfth century, notwithstanding the Norman conquest in the previous century, was not radically different from that of the Byzantine era. Nor was the economic life of Italian Jews dissimilar to that of earlier times. Benjamin reported on Jewish crafts, especially dyeing and weaving. And well into the thirteenth century, Emperor Frederick II, king of Sicily and Apulia, extended special protection to the Jews in his realm and offered them a virtual monopoly on their traditional industries related to the manufacture of silk products.

When the Angevin rulers conquered the region in 1265, there appears to have been a general decline in Jewish fortunes. The church began to exert more conversionist pressure on Jewish residents, a blood libel against the Jews of Trani endangered the welfare of Jewish communities in the region, and by the end of

Fig. 4. View of the Jewish Quarter, Trapani, twelfth century

the century many Jews had either been killed, fled for their lives, or converted to Christianity. By the fourteenth century Jewish life in southern Italy, with the exception of Sicily, was severely depressed and never regained its former élan and cultural significance despite its thousand-year history. Jewish life was shifting northward.

The Jewish community of Rome, notwithstanding periodic setbacks, continued to flourish throughout the Middle Ages and constitutes the one continuous thread in Jewish settlement in Europe from antiquity to the modern era. By the time of Rabbi Nathan ben Jeḥiel of Rome, in the late eleventh and early twelfth centuries, Jewish intellectual life was certainly thriving. Benjamin of Tudela reported on a sizable Jewish community there later in the twelfth century, and despite certain setbacks in the thirteenth century, Jewish residence remained constant.

The real change in Jewish settlement took place in the northern communities. Before the thirteenth century only a handful of Jews were allowed to live north of Rome. The northern Italian communities had initially prohibited Jewish merchants and artisans from settling in their neighborhoods out of a fear of economic competition. This situation was gradually altered in the thirteenth and fourteenth centuries by the simultaneous rise to prominence of Jewish moneylending, spurred by the church's campaign against Christian usury, and by the burgeoning populations and economies of the northern Italian communes, which created an increasing need for capital. With the gradual decline of Jewish life in the south, and the eventual removal of Jews from trade and the textile industry, increasing numbers of Jews emigrated from the area and invested in pawnbroking banks in cities throughout northern and central Italy.[18]

Subject to the vagaries of an agrarian economy and constantly in need of cash to support their standing militia and public projects, the petty city-states of northern and central Italy were predisposed to invite individual Jewish bankers to settle in their communities. Usually such Jews were offered a *condotta* (charter) by the civic authorities for a limited number of years with the possibility of extensions of residency. The arrival of relatively affluent Jews in cities such as Ancona, Urbino, Perugia, Forlì, Padua, Bologna, Milan, and Ferrara eventually paved the way for the entrance of their coreligionists. Jewish moneylenders thus be-

Fig. 5. House of Salamon Ebreo, Monteveglio, fifteenth century

Fig. 6. Inscription from the house of Salamon Ebreo, Monteveglio, fifteenth century

came the economic mainstay of the small Jewish settlements sprouting up north of Rome and the chief source of communal leadership. When their economic power and position were threatened, the welfare of every member of the Jewish community was adversely affected.

Jewish cultural and intellectual life during the era of these developments is difficult to characterize precisely given the incomplete nature of our sources. The lines of continuity with cultural achievement in earlier periods, especially in the orbit of Byzantine civilization of the ninth and tenth centuries, are also most difficult to assess. Undoubtedly the political and economic disruptions described above, the decline of the south, and the steady shift to the north affected the patterns of cultural activity that emerged from the thirteenth century on. What appears most certain is the gradual impact that the concentration of economic power in the hands of a small number of relatively affluent banking families eventually had on Jewish cultural life. Not surprisingly the major luminaries of Jewish culture—rabbinic scholars, poets, physicians, astrologers, or philosophers (quite often the same individual)—usually aligned themselves with these families. Their intellectual activities were supported by those privileged patrons of higher culture in a manner not unlike that of their counterparts in the Christian world of letters. This system of Jewish patronage, which continued to expand during the Renaissance, could not help but broaden the range of cultural interests pursued by an intellectual class directly dependent on the personal whim and will of economic magnates and their families.

The new demographic and economic order influenced Jewish cultural life in two other ways. In the first place the primary immigration of Jews to northern and central Italy was initially an internal one from the south. Despite the cultural differences they surely encountered, the majority of the new Jewish residents were still Italian speaking. They traced their origins to imperial Rome or to other ancient communities in the south, and in some ways they saw themselves as Italian as much as Jewish. The opportunities for social, economic, and cultural interaction with their Christian neighbors were enhanced given the relative ease in which they adjusted to their new surroundings. With the later immigration of Jews from France, Germany, and Spain from the fourteenth century on, the alien character of the Jewish minority was more pronounced. Nevertheless the Italian indigenous element was still the dominant one, and it continued to set the tone for dialogue with the majority culture.

In the second place the relatively small size of the political states and their Jewish neighborhoods also facilitated maximum interaction between Jews and Christians. Individual Jews lived in close proximity not only to their Christian neighbors but also to the local duke or public officials. Under such circumstances Jews naturally felt an integral part of their surroundings to a greater degree than in most other communities in Christian Europe. In sum the stimulus of the Christian cultural environment was profoundly felt by individual Jews because of the personal position of Jewish bankers, because most Jews spoke and read Italian, and because of their constant and unavoidably close contacts with their Christian neighbors.

Yet it would be wrong to infer from the above that Italian Jews were not often violated spiritually and physically by the Christian majority. Jewish existence was still precarious in the central and northern communities: moneylenders were constantly subjected to

Fig. 7. Ornamental page, "Keter Malkhut," *The Rothschild Maḥzor,* Florence, 1492, The Library of The Jewish Theological Seminary of America, New York (cat. no. 43)

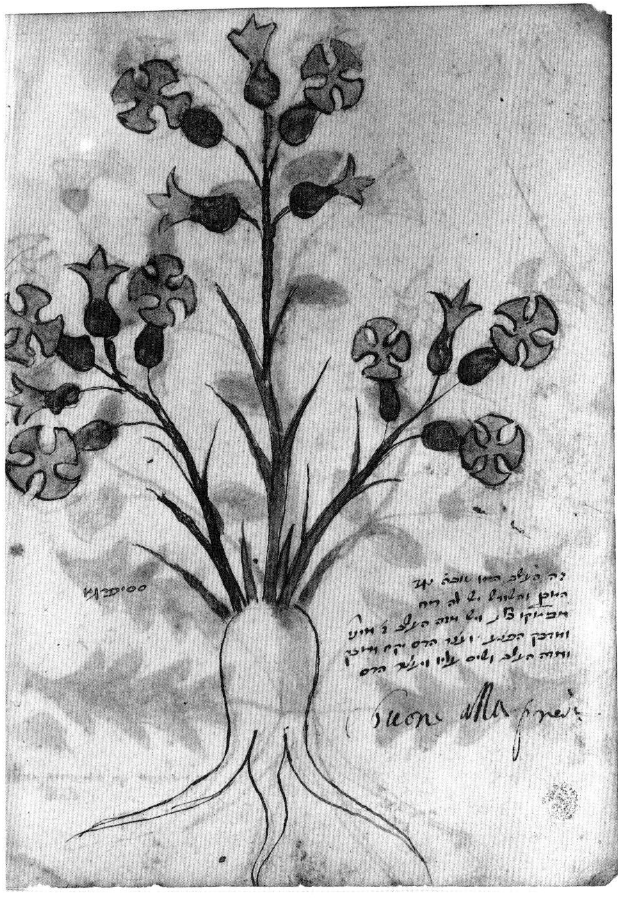

Fig. 8. *Medical Herbal,* Italy, second half of the fifteenth century, Bibliothèque Nationale, Paris (cat. no. 45)

vilification and physical harm, and conversionist activities often threatened to undermine Jewish morale, even under the special conditions of the new surroundings. Nevertheless it should be emphasized that in this most intense period of Christian assault against Judaism throughout most of western Europe, the Jews of northern and central Italy fared better than most of their coreligionists elsewhere.

In considering the cultural creativity of Italian Jews in the thirteenth and fourteenth centuries, one is struck by its vitality and diversity and its profound interaction with the outside world. From at least the time of Nathan ben Yeḥiel, rabbinic learning in Italy flourished, producing a number of well known exegetes and codifiers. The most famous Italian halakhist of the thirteenth century was Isaiah ben Mali di Trani the elder (c. 1200–c. 1260), whose most important works were his *Pesakim* on the Talmud, summaries of the Talmudic discussions and resolutions of various issues raised in the discussions. Isaiah ben Elijah di Trani the younger (d. c. 1280), his grandson, also wrote important novellae on the Talmud. And Zedekiah ben Abraham of the famous Anau family composed his well-known halakhic compendium on the liturgy and the holidays, entitled the *Shibbolei ha-Leket* (The Gleaned Ears), also in the thirteenth century.[19]

Under the stimulus of first the Norman, then the Hohenstaufen, and finally the Angevin kings of the south, a number of individual Jewish savants were specifically employed in translating the important philosophic and scientific works of the Muslim world from Arabic to Hebrew and sometimes directly into Latin. This critical work of cultural intermediation not only left its mark on Latin culture from the twelfth century on; it also stimulated Jewish intellectual life through its encounter with Arabic philosophy and science. At the invitation of Frederick II, for example, Jacob Anatoli left France and arrived in Naples around 1230, where he served as a physician and translated some of the commentaries of Averroës and the *Almagest* of Ptolemy, among other works. Moses of Palermo (c. 1275) came to Naples and Salerno at the behest of Charles of Anjou. His most famous translation from Arabic to Latin, which was later rendered in Italian, was a treatise of Hippocrates on the healing of horses. Charles also invited Faraj da Agrigento to serve as physician and translator at his court. Among his translations was that of the medical encyclopedia of Rhazes into Latin, containing an illumination depicting Faraj handing over his finished product to his grateful mentor. During the rule of Robert of Anjou, Kalonymus ben Kalonymus of Arles was invited to the court to translate several commentaries of Averroës.[20]

The scholars who had undertaken translations were clearly engaged in a larger cultural process far weightier than the mere technical function for which they had been commissioned. Their renderings into Hebrew and Latin were an integral part of a more intense *translatio scientiae* engendered by the encounter of Arabic culture with the West. Jewish scholars in Italy were hardly immune to this deeper "translation" process. Jacob Anatoli, for example, imbibed the new philosophic spirit in his own homiletic work called *Malmad ha-Talmidim* (A Goad to Scholars). He often quoted Aristotle, Plato, Averroës, and even his contemporary Michael Scot; he defended Maimonides and argued for an allegorical-philosophical understanding of the biblical text.

The intellectual achievements of Hillel ben Samuel (c. 1220–c. 1295), who lived in Naples and Capua, reflect a further stage of the translation process, the rendering of Latin scholastic culture into Hebrew. Hillel was both an active translator of Latin works into Hebrew and a philosophic writer in his own right. His most important work is *Tagmulei ha-Nefesh* (The Rewards of the Soul), dealing with the nature of the soul and the intellect and the soul's ultimate retribution. Hillel generally followed Averroës but was also indebted to Thomas Aquinas on the question of the immortality of the soul. Hillel was also a major defender of Maimonides but nevertheless was fully aware of the dangers of philosophic speculation regarding matters of faith.[21]

Zeraḥiah ben Isaac ben Shealtiel Gracian emigrated to Italy at the end of the thirteenth century, lived in Rome, and like Hillel, was engaged in translations and philosophical exegesis. Another member of the same circle was Judah ben Moses ben Daniel Romano, who translated philosophical works, wrote philosophical commentaries, and even composed a Hebrew-Italian glossary of philosophical terms.[22]

The most illustrious member of this group of philosophical exegetes was certainly Immanuel ben Solomon of Rome (c. 1260–c. 1328), who wrote commentaries on most of the books of the Bible. Although born in Rome, he was part of the northern migration of the thirteenth and fourteenth centuries, living in such communities as Perugia, Gubbio, Ancona, and Verona while probably serving as a tutor in the home of wealthy banking families. His most important work was the *Maḥberot* (Compositions; cat. no. 65), a large collection of poems structured within a loose narrative framework. His style and imagery are reminiscent of Spanish-Jewish precedents, but the Italian influence of the sonnets of Petrarch and Dante on Immanuel's poems is unmistakable, and so is their licentious spirit. The last composition in his long work, entitled *Tofet and Eden,* is an account of an imaginary journey to heaven and hell closely modeled on Dante's *Divine Comedy*. The heaven of Immanuel, however, is a Judaized one teeming with patriarchs, rabbis, contemporary Jews, and righteous Gentiles. Immanuel apparently never knew Dante, but he did correspond with the poets Bosone da Gubbio and Cinco da Pistoia and was highly appreciated by them both. Immanuel was undoubtedly the most original of the Italian-Jewish writers of his day and the most brilliant representative of the fusion of Latin, Italian, and Jewish cultures. Clearly affiliated with the philosophical world of the southern Jewish translators and exegetes, Manuel da Gubbio, as he was known in the Christian world, introduced a new literary genre to Hebrew writing and accordingly moved Jewish culture in Italy in altogether novel directions.[23]

The philosophical coloring of Italian-Jewish thought in the thirteenth and fourteenth centuries also produced its dissenters. Abraham ben Samuel Abulafia (1240–c. 1291) had come to Italy from Spain via Palestine and Greece and studied Maimonidean thought with Hillel ben Samuel. But he was dissatisfied with the conventional manner of understanding Maimonides's *Guide to the Perplexed* and was moved by a prophetic vision that he divulged to a devoted circle of his followers. He then wandered throughout Europe, composed numerous works based on his particular mystical outlook, eventually returned to Italy, and even attempted to speak with the pope in Rome in 1280. In contradistinction to the regnant theosophic kabbalah, with its emphasis on the elaborate structure of the divine world and the human means of attaining harmony by relating to that world, Abulafia taught a highly anthropocentric form of kabbalah that came to be called prophetic or ecstatic kabbalah. Instead of the ideal of divine harmony, his primary concern was

Fig. 9. *Madonna and Child Enthroned with Saints and Donors* (the Norsa family), end of the fifteenth century, Church of Sant'Andrea, Mantua. In 1496 Daniel Norsa, head of the prominent Jewish banking family, acquired a house in Mantua whose façade was decorated with a Christian image. With the approval of the bishop, Norsa removed the image, an action that provoked the populace. The house was torn down, and the Church of Santa Maria della Vittoria was built on its site. Norsa was required to pay for the painting of an image of the Madonna and Child by Mantegna placed in the new church. The painting reproduced here is a copy by an anonymous artist and one of the few Renaissance portraits of Italian Jews.

the mystical experience of the individual. He stressed the importance of isolation and the centrality of letter combination in reaching the mystical state and considered the discussion of the divine *sefirot* as a lower form of kabbalah. Abulafia's prophetic and messianic activity engendered considerable opposition from kabbalists and others but had a profound impact on later kabbalistic schools.[24]

A younger contemporary of Abulafia was Menaḥem ben Benjamin Recanati, who was heavily indebted to the theosophic stream of kabbalah that had developed in Spain. His influence as a popularizer of kabbalah was particularly strong because of his widely read kabbalistic commentary on the Torah, which was first printed in Venice in 1524. Two sixteenth-century kabbalists, Mattathias Delacrut and Mordecai Jaffe, both of eastern Europe, even wrote their own commentaries on it.

In short the culture of Italian Jews in the thirteenth and fourteenth centuries reflected profound changes in their environment: the stimulus of the enlightened monarchs of the south in promoting the translation of Arabic culture in the Latin West, the eventual deterioration of Jewish life in those regions, the steady movement to and settlement of the north, the rise of Jewish loan banking, the stimulation of new forms of Latin and Italian literature, and the impact of philosophic and mystical currents from Spain and Provence. Jewish intellectual life remained multifaceted and energized by these new developments. Individual writers excelled in rabbinics, philosophy, medicine and science, poetry, homiletics, and kabbalah. And all of this creative activity was in some ways a mere prelude to the cultural efflorescence of the Renaissance.

Jewish Culture in Renaissance Italy[25]

By the fifteenth century Jewish loan bankers were a noticeable element in the major urban centers of northern and central Italy and in many of the smaller towns as well. In a few instances Jewish families such as the Da Pisa or Norsa had succeeded in amassing a considerable fortune and had established a rather intricate network of loan banks in several communities. Jewish loan banking was well entrenched in such cities as Florence, Siena, Ferrara, Mantua, Pesaro, Reggio, Modena, Padua, and Bologna.

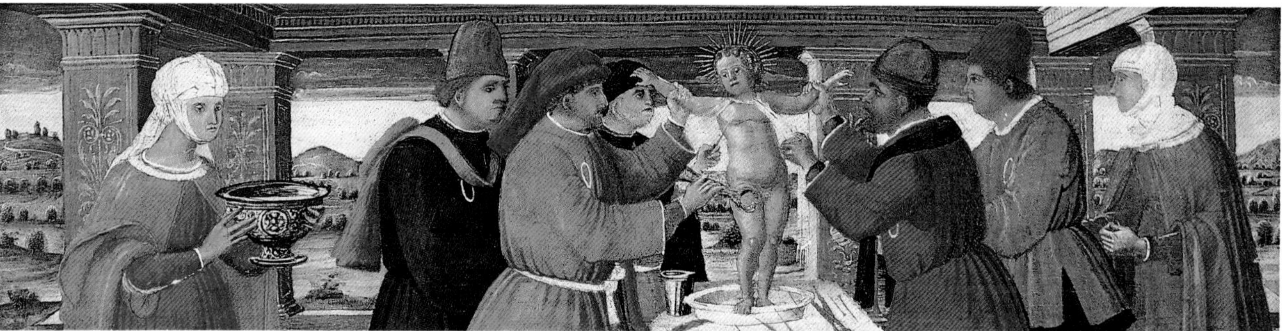

Fig. 10. Gandolfino di Roreto d'Asti, *Martyrdom of Simon of Trent,* late fifteenth century, The Israel Museum, Jerusalem (cat. no. 245)

With the gradual increase of Jewish residents in these cities, encouraged by economic opportunities engendered by the loan bankers, recurrent signs of organized Jewish communal activity became more visible by the fifteenth century. One notes the appearance of cemeteries, synagogues, community schools, and later, voluntary associations to maintain basic social services for the community. In this same era immigrants from Germany and southern France joined the original native Italian element in settling these regions. The expulsion of the Jews of Spain resulted in a new influx of Sephardic Jews, who arrived in Italy as early as 1493. They were later joined by a steady stream of Marrano immigrants throughout the sixteenth century, fleeing the Iberian peninsula in search of more tolerant surroundings. The new Italian communities became more international in flavor, and understandably the process of political and social self-definition and differentiation that these increasingly complex communities underwent was sometimes accompanied by considerable stress, internal conflict, and even bitter struggles over religious and political authority.

The infusion of larger numbers of Jews into these regions evoked hostile reactions from elements of the local populace as well. The concentrated and conspicuous presence of Jewish moneylenders was particularly offensive to churchmen, especially members of the Franciscan order. The most vigorous attacks against Jewish usury in the fifteenth century came from such preachers as Bernardino of Siena and Antonino of Florence, who openly deplored the economic basis of the Jewish community and its supposed cancerous effect upon the local Christian populace. Others, like Bernardino of Feltre, launched the drive to establish *Monti di Pietà,* public free-loan associations with the avowed purpose of eliminating Jewish usury in Italy altogether. Such campaigns often had painful consequences for Jewish victims: riots, physical harrassment, even loss of life. In some cases Jews were expelled from various cities, although these measures were often temporary. Sometimes the results of such provocations were more disastrous. Bernardino of Feltre's charge of ritual murder in the city of Trent in 1475 had serious repercussions for Jews not only in that city but throughout northern Italy (cat. no. 245; fig. 10).

If there was a safety valve from such disasters, it was to be found in the fragmented political nature of the Italian city-states. The Jewish victims of persecution often sought refuge in neighboring communities and on occasion even succeeded in returning to their original neighborhoods when the hostilities had subsided. An outburst in one locality, however, could easily trigger a similar explosion in another contiguous with it. The friars' inflammatory sermons, accompanied by severe public pressure against the local Jewish citizenry, usually traveled from town to town with the same predictable results. Yet such disruptions, no matter how harmful, lacked the finality and drastic consequences associated with anti-Semitism elsewhere in western Europe. Because of the localized and circumscribed nature of the outbursts, Jewish life in Italy was never fully suppressed and continued to flourish through the modern era.

Incessant hostility was also counterbalanced by the relatively benign relations that existed between certain Jewish and Christian intellectuals in Italy at the height of the Renaissance and long after. The new cultural intimacy could not dissipate the recurrent animosities between Jews and Christians, but it did allow some Jews greater access to Christian society than before, and accordingly their impact on certain sectors of the majority culture was more profound. This intense interaction between intellectuals of different faiths would have significant impact on the cultural concerns of both communities.

An illuminating example of the dialogue between Renaissance and Jewish culture is the case of Judah Messer Leon, a Jewish physician, rabbinic scholar, and master of Aristotelian philosophy, who lived in a number of cities in north-central Italy in the second half of the fifteenth century. Sometime before 1480 Messer Leon composed a Hebrew book entitled *Nofet Ẓufim* (The Book of the Honeycomb's Flow), in which he introduced to his Jewish readers a new genre of rhetorical writing, placing himself squarely in the center of a new and ultimately dominant expression of Renaissance culture, that of Italian humanism. As early as the fourteenth century, with the revival and imitation of classical antiquity, the humanists had reclaimed rhetoric as a significant and independent part of the new *studia humanitatis,* which also included grammar, poetry, history, and moral philosophy. As a reaction to the more technical philosophical interests of Aristotelian scholars, the humanists revived the ideal of the ancient Latinists Cicero and Quintilian, believing that the integration of rhetoric with philosophy would shape a new breed of educated persons endowed with both wisdom and eloquence.

Messer Leon's rhetorical compendium likewise projected to its Hebrew readers the ideal of a good and righteous man, gifted in the oratorical art, who thus combined his knowledge and noble character to produce a new and effective leadership for the Jewish community. Furthermore, in grafting the Ciceronian ideal onto Judaism, Messer Leon boldly attempted to portray his new image of leadership as an intrinsic part of Jewish tradition in the first place. He designated his new Jewish leader the *ḥakham kolel* (a direct Hebrew translation of the expression *homo universalis*), a person obliged to lead his community by virtue of a unique combination of broad and substantive learning together with good character. As Messer Leon Judaized the civic orator, so too did he treat the entire field of rhetoric. The model of classical oratory initially was conceived not in Greece or Rome but in ancient Israel itself, so he claimed. If indeed the entire Hebrew Bible, especially its prophetic orations, was the font and exemplar of the rhetorical art, it followed not only that rhetoric was a subject worthy for Jews but also that it was incumbent upon them to appreciate and to master a discipline that had been theirs in the first place. Moreover the idea that rhetoric had been perfected first by the Hebrews offered to Jews of the fifteenth century a satisfying reassurance regarding the intrinsic worth of their own cultural legacy.

Messer Leon's effort to inspire Jewish humanist interests was not without success. As one of the earliest Hebrew books in print, the *Nofet Ẓufim* was studied as a handbook of rhetorical art by Jewish students and helped to inspire the writing of Hebrew rhetorical compositions, letters, and sermons for a number of generations. Especially in the sixteenth and seventeenth centuries, Italian rabbis such as Judah Moscato (c. 1530–1593), Azariah Figo (1579–1647), and Leone Modena (1571–1648) imbibed directly the Ciceronian ideal by perfecting the art of oratory in both their oral sermons delivered in Italian and in their later written versions published in Hebrew.

Even more decisive than the impact of humanism on Italian-Jewish culture was that of the encounter of Giovanni Pico della Mirandola (1463–1494), the famous Florentine philosopher, and his colleagues with a number of contemporary Jews. Out of a mutually stimulating interaction between Pico and his Jewish associates and a prolonged study of Jewish texts emerged one of the most unusual and exotic currents in the intellectual history of the Renaissance, the Christian kabbalah. While in the case of humanism the encounter between Renaissance and Jewish culture was generally one-sided, wherein Jews were primarily recipients of cultural forms that they absorbed from the outside, the interaction with Pico's circle was substantially different since it was mutual. In a relatively unprecedented manner a select but influential group of Christian scholars actively desired to understand the Jewish religion and its sacred texts in order to penetrate their own spiritual roots more deeply. Such a major reevaluation of contemporary Jewish culture by Christians would leave a noticeable mark on both Christian and Jewish self-understanding in this and later periods.

Pico and his intellectual circle were drawn to Jewish study partially out of a sincere devotion to missionary activity, as were earlier Christians before them, especially in Spain. But Pico's attraction to Jewish texts in general and to the kabbalah in particular had more to do with the philosophical and theological currents among his Florentine contemporaries. From Marsilio Ficino (1433–1499), the leading Neoplatonist in Florence, Pico derived the vital concept of ancient theology, the notion that a single truth pervades all periods and all cultures, and that among the ancient writers—pagan, Jewish, or Christian—a unity and harmony of religious insight can be discerned. By universalizing all religious knowledge, Ficino and Pico fashioned a more open and tolerant Christian theology. In searching for truth in cultural and religious settings distant from their own, they ultimately came to appreciate the centrality and priority of Hebraic wisdom in Western civilization.

While ancient theology led Pico back to the biblical beginnings of Western culture, his employment of the concept of "poetic theology" led him to the kabbalah. Pico believed that the ancient pagan religions had concealed their sacred truths through a kind of "hieroglyphic" imagery of myths and fables. Moses had similarly addressed the Israelite nation in a veiled manner called the kabbalah. The kabbalah then constituted that part of the Jewish tradition where the essential divine truths could be located; it was the key to lay bare the secrets of Judaism, to reconcile them with the mysteries of other religions and cultures, and thus to universalize them. Kabbalah also represented a higher power to Pico, a means of enhancing man's ability to control his destiny. It was a superior form of licit magic, superior to the magical practices taught by the ancient pagans, establishing a direct link between heaven and earth.

In order to study Jewish sources systematically, Pico engaged three notable Jewish scholars, among others: Elijah Delmedigo (c. 1460–c. 1493), a scholastic philosopher, translator, and authority on the commentaries of Averroës; a Sicilian convert who called himself Flavius Mithridates (fifteenth century), who translated some forty works of Hebrew exegetical, philosophical, and kabbalistic works into Latin for Pico; and an erudite and prolific Jewish writer and physician named Yoḥanan Alemanno (c. 1435–1505). Through the instruction he received from his teachers and through his own synthetic powers, Pico became the pioneering figure in the gradual penetration of contemporary Jewish thought into European culture. His Christianization of kabbalistic techniques and his fusion of magic and Jewish mysticism, while officially condemned by the church, were enthusiastically endorsed by a significant number of Christian thinkers throughout the Continent well into the eighteenth century. Through the count of Mirandola, Christian kabbalah left its mark on Renaissance culture with its integration with Neoplatonic philosophy. It also influenced both the Catholic and Protestant Reformations through its impact on such thinkers as Johannes Reuchlin, Egidio Viterbo, and Cornelius Agrippa. Its remarkable persistence as a thread in post-Renaissance culture—in art, in literature, and even in scientific thought—has also been well observed.

Pico's syncretistic theology also noticeably affected contemporary Jewish thought. Yoḥanan Alemanno, like Pico, recast the kabbalah in a magical and Neoplatonic framework. Judah, the son of the Spanish philosopher and exegete Isaac Abrabanel, known to the Christian world as Leone Ebreo (c. 1460–c. 1521), composed a Neoplatonic treatise on love called the *Dialoghi di amore,* which became a classic of Renaissance literature. Other Jewish writers of the sixteenth and seventeenth centuries, such as Abraham Yagel (1553–c. 1628), Joseph Delmedigo (1591–1655), and Abraham Cohen de Herrera (c. 1570–c. 1635), displayed the marked influence of the Florentine school; still others followed Flavius Mithridates by accepting Pico's universal faith and converting to Christianity.

The interaction between the new Christian Hebraists such as Pico and Italian Jews was significant in offering Jews a novel challenge to their own national existence. It introduced the image of a universal culture transcending both Christianity and Judaism in their present forms. Renaissance culture, of course, was still pervaded by traditional religious values; it was neither as secular nor as rational as some earlier historians had conceived it to be. Nor was Jewish communal life, its long-standing educational and social institutions, and its strong commitment to the traditional study of rabbinic texts, on the whole, radically different from what had existed in previous eras. And as we have seen, some Christians still attacked Jews, publicly ridiculed their faith, and sought to convert them. But perhaps in one respect the dialogue between Judaism and Christianity was different in the Renais-

Fig. 11. *Frontispiece, Historia de riti hebraici,* Venice, 1638, The Library of The Jewish Theological Seminary of America, New York (cat. no. 79)

sance era. In sensing a greater urgency to justify their own particularity before an intellectual community increasingly ecumenical in spirit if not in practice, a certain number of Jews were offered a preview of the intellectual and spiritual challenges their descendents would face with growing regularity and intensity in the centuries to come.

The Age of the Ghetto

The relatively tolerant climate Italy had offered its small Jewish community during the Renaissance was short-lived. As a result of the oppressive policy of Pope Paul IV (1476–1559) and his successors, the Italian-Jewish communities of the papal states as well as the rest of Italy experienced a radical deterioration of their legal status and physical state. Italian Jews suddenly faced a major offensive against their community and its religious heritage, culminating in the public burning of the Talmud in 1553 and in restrictive legislation leading to increased impoverishment, ghettoization, and expulsion. Jews had been expelled from the areas under the jurisdiction of Naples in 1541. In 1569 they were removed from the papal states, with the major exceptions of Ancona and Rome. Those who sought refuge in Tuscany, Venice, or Milan faced oppressive conditions as well. The only tolerable haven was in the territory controlled by the Gonzaga of Mantua or that of the Estensi of Ferrara.

The situation was aggravated further by increasing conversionary pressures, including compulsory appearance at Christian preaching in synagogues and the establishment of transition houses for new converts, which were designed to facilitate large-scale conversion to Christianity. Whether motivated primarily by the need to fortify Catholic hegemony against all dissidence, Christian and non-Christian alike, or driven by a renewed missionary zeal for immediate and mass conversion, the papacy acted resolutely to undermine the status of these small Jewish communities in the heart of Western Christendom.[26]

The most conspicuous phenomenon associated with these changes was the erection of the ghetto itself. The word was probably first used to describe an island of Venice supposedly once the site of a foundry (*getto*), selected in 1516 as the compulsory residential quarter for Jews. The real impetus for the proliferation of the ghetto throughout Italy, however, came only in 1555,

Fig. 12. Interior of the Scuola Canton, Venice, sixteenth century (with later additions)

when Pope Paul IV ordered that all Jews living within the papal states be confined to one street or to a few adjacent ones, and that the new quarter should have no more than one entrance and one exit. The Jews of Rome were the first to relocate to a compulsory quarter, and numerous other Italian communities soon followed Rome's example: Florence and Siena in 1571, Verona in 1600, Mirandola in 1602, Padua in 1603, Mantua in 1612, Rovigo in 1613, Ferrara in 1624, and so on, continuing until the end of the eighteenth century.[27]

The period of the ghetto, extending well into the beginning of the nineteenth century, has usually been described as a radical break with a more tolerable past, an era of economic and political decline, and of the growing cultural isolation of Italian Jewry. No doubt Jews confined to a heavily congested area surrounded by a wall shutting them off from the rest of the city, except for entrances bolted at night, were subjected to considerably more misery, impoverishment, and humiliation than before. And clearly the result of ghettoization was the erosion of ongoing liaisons between Christians and Jews, including intellectual ones. But the social and cultural results of this new confinement were indeed more paradoxical than one might initially assume.

Jewish cultural priorities did in fact shift considerably by the second half of the sixteenth century; a kind of "turning in," an internalization of Jewish culture, did emerge among certain sectors of Italian Jews. But

Fig. 13. Giovanni del Pian, *Scene of a Jewish Funeral: Transport of the Body to the Cemetery,* Venice, ca. 1784, The Library of The Jewish Theological Seminary of America (cat. no. 89)

it is unclear whether the imposition of the ghetto was its primary cause. Even before the 1550s, a growing insecurity and spiritual crisis over the inadequacy of philosophical speculation was felt among some Jews. And by the end of the century a pervasive Jewish mysticism, with its emphasis on practical acts of piety, came to challenge and supplant the crumbling edifice of Jewish scholasticism of the previous age.[28] Also, with the erection of the ghetto, there was a dramatic proliferation of pious confraternities (*ḥevrot*) in every major Italian town, providing Jewish men and women an opportunity to engage in charity, the care of the sick and the growing number of indigent Jews, as well as the burial of the dead. No doubt these voluntary associations were partially stimulated by similar Christian sodalities, but they were also an expression of internal Jewish needs, both economic and religious. They provided an outlet for enhanced public prayer, even innovations in times and texts of liturgy, and intense spiritual fellowship. They were particularly receptive settings for the new pietistic and mystical trends emanating from Israel into Italy.[29]

At the same time, within the ghetto walls themselves, Jewish intellectual life displayed a remarkable openness to external culture. Ironically, Jewish writers and official communal scribes expressed themselves more frequently in Italian than they had done during the Renaissance. Jewish intellectuals, to an even greater extent than before, studied Latin and Italian literature (a few even Greek), rhetoric, history, music, and art; read and wrote poetry in Hebrew and Italian; and especially mastered medicine and the sciences. Conventional Jewish history textbooks usually offer the erudite Azariah de' Rossi (c. 1511–1578) or the prodigious Leone Modena as the most typical exemplars of Renaissance Jewish culture. The first penned the most significant work of Jewish historiography among Italian Jews called the *Me'or Einayim* (Enlightenment to the Eyes), a critical historical evaluation of Talmudic chronology correlated with non-Jewish sources of late antiquity, in 1575 (cat. no. 74). The second was a prolific writer, a gifted preacher, and skillful polemicist who served the Venetian Jewish community in the early seventeenth century (cat. no. 79).[30] Yet both pursued their "Renaissance" interests in a post-Renaissance age, or more precisely within the cultural world of the counter-Reformation and emerging ghetto environment. Similarly, Salamon de' Rossi (c. 1570–c. 1630) composed his famous "Renaissance" madrigals within the confines of the Mantuan ghetto (cat. no. 78; fig. 14). Leone de Sommi Portaleone (1527–1592), the dramatist and stage director, who wrote and staged plays for the Gonzaga court theater some years earlier, also wrote Hebrew plays, which were performed by his coreligionists well into the ghetto period. Abraham Portaleone (1542–1612), Tobias Cohen (1652–1729), Isaac Cardoso (1604–1681), Joseph Delmedigo, and Jacob Ẓahalon (1630–1693) all composed integrative "Renaissance" encyclopedias of knowledge in the segregative ambiance of their ghetto domiciles. And within identically enclosed walls Deborah Ascarelli (late sixteenth century) and Sarah Coppio Sullam (c. 1592–1641) emerged as two gifted poets in the Italian language.

The limitations of ghetto life do not appear to have inhibited numerous Jews from attending Italian medical schools, especially in Padua, in unprecedented numbers in the sixteenth through eighteenth centuries (cat. no. 53).[31] In fact, during the ghetto era more rabbis and communal leaders than ever before possessed medical educations, were literate in a variety of scientific literatures in addition to rabbinics, were conversant with Italian literature and music, and enjoyed writing and reading poetry. Such luminaries of seventeenth- and eighteenth-century Italian rabbinic culture as Solomon Conegliano, Isaac Cantarini, Isaac Cardoso, Jacob Ẓahalon, Isaac Lampronti, or Solomon

Fig. 14. Salomone de' Rossi, *Canti ha-shirim asher li-Shlomo,* Venice, 1624, The Library of The Jewish Theological Seminary of America, New York (cat. no. 78)

Morpurgo, to name only a few, all fit this profile of a Jewish intellectual and communal leader. Despite the apparent intentions of the planners of the ghetto, its ultimate products were hardly isolationists. On the contrary, the enclosure in a restricted space might even have accentuated the desire of many Jewish intellectuals to engage more intensely in the enticing cultural world just beyond the suffocating walls of their enclosed neighborhoods.[32]

Most paradoxical of all is the role of the kabbalah in this cultural engagement with the outside world. The study of kabbalah among Italian Jews did not necessarily impede their scientific or literary involvements; it may even have encouraged them.[33] Students of the kabbalah such as Abraham Yagel, Joseph Delmedigo, or Solomon Aviad Sar Shalom Basilea (c. 1680–1749) were highly conversant with contemporary science. Moses Zacuto (1625–1697) and Moses Ḥayyim Luzzato (1707–1746) composed full-length plays in the style of their Christian contemporaries while they meditated on the secrets of the divine.

The ghetto ironically became the setting for an explosive diffusion of Jewish culture of all varieties—rabbinic, kabbalistic, moralistic, scientific, and literary—through the agency of the printing press. Despite the threat of church censorship, the Italian-Jewish communities of the late sixteenth to eighteenth centuries, especially Venice, became publishing capitals of the Jewish world (cat. nos. 77–79). Indeed many of the first great publishers of Hebrew books were Christians, and because of the pressing need for literary competence in typesetting and proofreading, their collaborators were usually Jews. The publishing houses were yet another example of how the church's attempt to impoverish Jewish life and erect a barrier between Jews and the outside world had manifestly failed.[34]

In addition to disseminating culture through books, the Italian-Jewish communities of the ghetto period performed a similar function in an even more tangible way, as a hospice for Jews from outside Italy. In this respect the Jewish minority simply mirrored their majority culture. Merchants from Amsterdam and Hamburg, medical and rabbinic students from Cracow and Prague, Sephardic emissaries from Salonica, Constantinople, Jerusalem, and Safad traversed the Italian peninsula in search of markets, education, or charity. The closed ghetto was to them an open marketplace of goods and ideas.

In sum, long before the coming of emancipation, the Risorgimento, and the demolishing of the ghetto walls by the mid-nineteenth century, the Jews of Italy were prepared for the transition out of the ghetto. While faithfully entrenched in the Jewish traditions of their past, they had long accepted worldly culture as a natural part of that heritage and were constantly engaged in harmonizing the old with the new and in reconciling the disparate elements of a richly complex Jewish cultural environment.[35]

Epilogue

Having surveyed some eighteen hundred years of Jewish life in Italy, we finally are obliged to reflect on the lines of continuity in this vast cultural legacy and on its significance for Jewish and general history. We opened this essay by describing Nathan ben Yeḥiel's *Arukh* as a kind of signature of Italian-Jewish culture because it exemplified three recurrent themes: the longevity of Jewish residence and culture in Italy, the role this community played in the mediation and correlation of Jewish and non-Jewish cultures, and its function as a channel of ideas and values to other Jewish communities.

These same themes are also central to a critical appraisal of Italian-Jewish civilization written by the late historian Isaiah Sonne more than sixty years ago.[36] In this seminal Hebrew essay Sonne arrived at the negative conclusion that Italian Jewry was unique among Jewish communities in lacking a clear definition of itself and a unified character. Throughout its long history it was always a hostelry or satellite for the development of cultural forms that had originated elsewhere, in such communities as Palestine, Babylonia, or Spain. Thus Italy was primarily a receptacle, a dumping ground, and at best, a mosaic of diverse Jewish life-styles and ideologies. It was consistently passive and dependent on other cultural centers for the infusion of new ideas; it could never stand on its own two feet. And because it could never assert its independence or leave its individual stamp on Jewish civilization, it was thoroughly tolerant of everything. In Italy there was never extremism or fanaticism among Jews. Since Italian-Jewish culture was essentially formless and directionless, individual writers and thinkers were left the license to create as they saw fit. In a community lacking a coherent collective identity, multiple expressions of individual creativity naturally abounded.

Sonne's stimulating and repercussive essay is certainly in need of some modification and reformulation as we reflect on the legacy of Italian Jews more than a half-century later and with the hindsight of an abundance of new historical research in Italy, Israel, England, and the United States on that legacy. By way of a general conclusion to this essay, only two comments are in order: the first, historical; the second, a rumination on contemporary Jewish culture.

To the contemporary historian Sonne's perceptive analysis lacks sufficient perspective. It underestimates the most banal observation that the cultural life of any minority was simultaneously shaped by its own internal traditions and by the forces of its external environment. Jewish culture emerged differently in Italy because Italy was different from other European communities. Italian Jews in some respects were simply a smaller reflection of a larger cultural configuration shaped by its geography, its political instability, its centrality as a marketplace of goods and services, its relatively poor agricultural resources, and its linguistic and cultural diversity. In almost every respect Sonne emphasizes cultural, social, and political traits of Italian Jews that were shared by their Italian neighbors. This should not imply that Italian-Jewish history can be reduced to a mere bisection of Italian history without due consideration of its uniquely Jewish religious and cultural patterns.[37] Since Sonne laid greater emphasis on the internal connections of Italian Jewry to other Jewries, however, a more solid anchoring of his subject in Italian history might sharpen the focus of the essay.

My second reaction is of a different sort. Sonne's negative evaluation of the cultural legacy of Italian Jewry betrays, at least to this observer, a value judgment on his part. Sonne obviously admired strong-willed, independent, homogenous, and well-defined Jewish cultures: the clarity of the Babylonian legal tradition or the originality of Hispanic-Jewish culture. Dependence, disunity, and variety undermine the cohesive energy that makes a vibrant culture for Sonne. Undoubtedly such a rigorous assertion reveals something other than a descriptive reading of the historical past. Alternatively might we define these unique qualities of Italian Jewry in a positive rather than a negative light? In absorbing diverse Jewish and non-Jewish cultural forms and creatively molding them into constantly novel configurations, in patiently tolerating diversity and discord, in channeling ideas and values from one place to another as an entrepôt and clearinghouse of merchandise, and in allowing individuality to blossom within a framework of communal consensus, Italian Jewry was expressing its own vitality, its own creativity. Perhaps the function of mediating and correlating, of translating one universe of discourse into another, is not so passive, so unspectacular an achievement as Sonne would have it. From the perspective of the postmodern world in which we live, one of diverse cultural life-styles and values where no single ideology reigns supreme but where bitter acrimony and extremism hold sway, the image of Italian Jewry seems refreshingly appealing. Perhaps in its quiet sanity and dignified restraint, in its mutual respect and tolerance for competing and dissenting parties, and in its harmonizing and integrative capacities, can be located not only the essential legacy of Italian-Jewish civilization but also its enduring significance for contemporary culture.

Notes

1. I have kept bibliographical references to a minimum in this essay. The two basic surveys of Italian-Jewish history are C. Roth, *The History of the Jews in Italy* (Philadelphia, 1946); and A. Milano, *Storia degli ebrei in Italia* (Turin, 1963). Standard histories of some of the major local communities include U. Cassuto, *Gli ebrei a Firenze nell'età del rinascimento* (Florence, 1918, 1965); H. Vogelstein and P. Rieger, *Geschichte der Juden in Rom,* 2 vols. (Berlin, 1896); S. Simonsohn, *History of the Jews in the Duchy of Mantua* (Jerusalem, 1977). For further references the reader should consult A. Milano, *Bibliotheca historica Italo-Judaica* (Florence, 1954); idem, *Bibliotheca historica Italo-Judaica: Supplemento 1954–63* (Florence, 1964) (a supplement for the years 1964–1966 was published in *Rassegna mensile di Israel* 32 [1966]); and D. Carpi, A. Luzzatto, and M. Moldavi, *Biblioteca Italo-Ebraica: Bibliografia per la storia degli ebrei in Italia 1964–73* (Rome, 1982). A further installment of these guides is presently in preparation. I wish to thank Professors Elliot Horowitz and Benjamin C. I. Ravid for reading a draft of this essay and offering me their constructive comments.
2. Compare G. Sermoneta, "Encyclopedias in the Medieval Hebrew World," and A. Melamed, "The Hebrew Italian Renaissance and Early Modern Encyclopedias," both in *Rivista di storia della filosofia* 40 (1985): 7–50, 91–112.

3. The full inscription is found in H. Leon, *The Jews of Ancient Rome* (Philadelphia, 1960), pp. 334–335.
4. Ibid., pp. 248–249.
5. A rich sampling of epitaphs is found in ibid., pp. 263–346.
6. Recent surveys of Jewish life under Roman rule that touch upon ancient Italy include M. Grant, *The Jews in the Roman World* (New York, 1973, 1984); and M. Smallwood, *Jews under Roman Rule, from Pompey to Diocletian* (Leiden, 1976).
7. The latest and most comprehensive treatment of this period is found in the proceedings of a recent conference: *Atti della XXVI settimana di studio del Centro Italiano di Studi sull'Alto Medioevo: Gli ebrei nell'alto medioevo* (Spoleto, 1980). See also the comprehensive essays by C. Roth, B. Blumenkranz, H. J. Zimmels, and J. Dan, in C. Roth, ed., *The World History of the Jewish People: The Dark Ages,* 2d ser., vol. 2 (Ramat Gan, Israel, 1966).
8. See R. Bonfil, "Between Eretz Yisrael and Babylonia" (Hebrew) *Shalem* 5 (1987): 20, nn. 69–70, for recent bibliographical references. Bonfil's essay was originally published in Italian as "Tra due mondi: Prospettive di ricerca sulla storia culturale degli ebrei dell'Italia meridionale nell'alto medioevo," in *Italia Judaica: Atti del I convegno internazionale* (Rome, 1983), pp. 135–158. See also S. Simonsohn, "The Hebrew Revival among Early Medieval European Jews," in *Salo W. Baron Jubilee Volume* (Jerusalem, 1975), pp. 831–858.
9. The work was published in two volumes with a thorough introduction and notes by D. Flusser (Jerusalem, 1979–1981).
10. B. Klar published a critical edition (Jerusalem, 1944), which was reissued in 1973. An English translation was prepared by M. Salzmann, *The Chronicle of Aḥimaaz* (New York, 1924). R. Bonfil's essay (see note 8 above) is the most recent and imaginative treatment of the book.
11. I refer to the essay by R. Bonfil mentioned in note 8 above.
12. See the essay by J. Shirmann, in Roth, *The Dark Ages,* pp. 249–266, for a succinct overview.
13. See A. Sharf, *The Universe of Shabbetai Donnolo* (New York, 1976).
14. See the essay by J. Dan in Roth, *The Dark Ages,* pp. 282–290.
15. See A. Grossman, *Ḥokhmei Ashkenaz ha-Rishonim* (Jerusalem, 1981), pp. 29–78.
16. See G. D. Cohen, "The Story of the Four Captives," *Proceedings: American Academy for Jewish Research* 29 (1960–1961): 55–131.
17. M. N. Adler, *The Itinerary of Benjamin of Tudela* (London, 1907), pp. 5–9.
18. On these new economic opportunities of the thirteenth century and after, see S. W. Baron, *A Social and Religious History of the Jews,* 18 vols. to date (New York, 1952–1983), esp. vol. 12 (1967), pp. 159–165; L. Poliakov, *Jewish Bankers and the Holy See,* trans. M. L. Kochan (London, Henley, and Boston, 1977); J. Larner, *Italy in the Age of Dante and Petrarch, 1216–1380* (London and New York, 1980), pp. 206–208.
19. On rabbinic scholarship in medieval Italy, see I. Twersky, "The Contributions of Italian Sages to Rabbinic Literature," in *Italia Judaica,* pp. 383–400.
20. The work of the translators is summarized in C. Roth, *The Jews in the Renaissance* (Philadelphia, 1959), pp. 64–88.
21. See Hillel ben Shemuel of Verona, *Sefer Tagmule ha-Nefesh,* ed. J. Sermoneta (Jerusalem, 1981). A second volume is forthcoming.
22. See J. Sermoneta, "Judah ben Moshe Daniel Romano, traducteur de Saint Thomas," in *Hommage à Georges Vajda,* ed. G. Nahon and C. Touati (Louvain, 1980).
23. A critical annotated edition of the *Maḥbarot* was published in Jerusalem in 1957 by D. Jarden (2 vols.).
24. See M. Idel, *The Mystical Experience in Abraham Abulafia* (Albany, 1988).
25. For a considerable expansion of this section, with full bibliography, see D. B. Ruderman, "The Italian Renaissance and Jewish Thought," in *Renaissance Humanism: Foundations and Forms,* ed. A. Rabil, Jr., vol. 1 (Philadelphia, 1988), pp. 382–433.
26. See K. R. Stow, *Catholic Thought and Papal Jewry Policy, 1555–1593* (New York, 1977).
27. See especially B. C. I. Ravid, "The Religious, Economic, and Social Background and Context of the Establishment of the Ghetti of Venice," in *Gli ebrei e Venezia,* ed. G. Cozzi (Milan, 1987), pp. 211–259.
28. See R. Bonfil, *Ha-Rabbanut be-Italyah bi-Tekufat ha-Renesance* (Jerusalem, 1979), pp. 173–206.
29. See, for example, E. Horowitz, "Jewish Confraternal Piety in the Veneto in the Sixteenth and Seventeenth Century," in *Gli ebrei e Venezia,* pp. 301–314.
30. Joanna Weinberg is preparing a critical edition and English translation of de' Rossi's work for the Yale Judaica series. On Leon Modena, see M. Cohen, ed. and trans. (with introductory essays and historical notes by other scholars), *The Autobiography of a Seventeenth-Century Venetian Rabbi: Leon Modena's Life of Judah* (Princeton, 1988).
31. See D. B. Ruderman, "The Impact of Science on Jewish Culture and Society in Venice (with Special Reference to Jewish Graduates of Padua's Medical School)," in *Gli ebrei e Venezia,* pp. 417–448.
32. For an imaginative discussion of ghetto culture in Italy, see R. Bonfil, "Change in Cultural Patterns of Jewish Society in Crisis: The Case of Italian Jewry at

Fig. 15. Haggadah (Judeo-Italian Issue), Venice, 1609, The Library of The Jewish Theological Seminary of America, New York (cat. no. 77)

the Close of the Sixteenth Century," in *Jewish History* (forthcoming).

33. On this subject, see D. B. Ruderman, *Kabbalah, Magic, and Science: The Cultural Universe of a Sixteenth-Century Jewish Physician* (Cambridge, Mass., and London, 1988).
34. There is an extensive literature on Jewish printing in Italy. See, for example, the useful collection of reprinted essays in C. Berlin, ed., *Hebrew Printing and Bibliography* (New York, 1976); and the standard work of D. Amram, *The Makers of Hebrew Books in Italy* (Philadelphia, 1909).
35. For a similar conclusion, see L. C. Dubin, "Trieste and Berlin: The Italian Role in the Cultural Politics of the Haskalah," in *Toward Modernity: The European Jewish Model,* ed. J. Katz (New Brunswick, N.J., and Oxford, 1987), pp. 189–224.
36. See I. Sonne, *Ha-Yahadut ha-Italkit: Demutah u-Mekomah be-Toledot Am Yisrael* (Jerusalem, 1961) (first printed in *Ha-Tekufah* 22 [1924]).
37. This point is well developed in R. Bonfil, "The Historian's Perception of the Jews in the Italian Renaissance: Towards a Reappraisal," *Revue des études juives* 143 (1984): 59–82.

Fig. 16. Interior of the Tempio Israelitico, Florence, 1874–1882

MARIO TOSCANO

THE JEWS IN ITALY FROM THE RISORGIMENTO TO THE REPUBLIC

In the two-thousand-year history of the Jewish presence in Italy, the relatively brief period bracketed by the final phase of the Risorgimento and the birth of the Italian republic is unique. It contains memories and experiences accumulated over a long period of historical development and clearly conveys an image of the problems faced by the unified state during its first century of existence.

The emancipation of Italian Jewry has always been judged an unprecedented success, an effective phenomenon of social integration, but one that by no means resulted in the negation of the Jewish identity of its participants.[1] An analysis of this emancipation's premises, its causes and its forms, makes it possible to focus more clearly on the particular characteristics of the relationship between Italian society and the Jewish minority. During the first half of the twentieth century, this association was severely harmed by the anti-Jewish politics of fascism, which left a deep, lacerating mark on the course that had been delineated during the early years of Italian unification.

The rapidity of Jewish integration into the social fabric of a unified Italy was clearly favored by the coincidence of the Jewish emancipation with the Risorgimento. In Italy, unlike other European countries, the formation of a national consciousness by Jews paralleled the formation of a national consciousness by the rest of the population. This resulted in a convergence of objectives between the liberal bourgeoisie and Jewish groups and the avoidance—on a political, economic, and ethnic level—of the identification of Jews as a group extraneous to the national community, the usual premise for anti-Jewish suspicion, hostility, and prejudice.[2]

The specific process that, between the end of the eighteenth century and the middle of the nineteenth century, led to the granting of equal rights to Jews was complex and sometimes contradictory. The arrival of French troops in 1796 did away with civil limitations imposed on Jews, and some ghetto gates, first erected in the sixteenth century, fell. But as early as 1799, with the French withdrawal from Italy, there were abrupt and dramatic reversals. Jews were the chosen victims of the *sanfedista,* the antirevolutionary, traditionalist, and Christian reaction. Anti-Jewish violence in 1799 was the result of the inherently limited nature of the first emancipation of Italian Jewry, which was imposed on Italian society by the French and lacked solid roots in the country's social fabric.

With the return of Napoléon in 1800, and until his fall some fifteen years later, the approximately thirty thousand Jews residing in the north-central regions of the peninsula enjoyed a climate of substantial liberty as a result of his tolerant policies toward Jews. During this period Jews increased their participation in general activities and public life, setting in motion the

Fig. 17. Ghetto, Florence, late nineteenth to early twentieth century

first transformations of their social and economic life.[3] Despite its limitations and its brief duration, this was a historical phase of great importance. Although restoration of the old regime, which began with the Congress of Vienna, signified the revival of prerevolutionary conditions and a return to the ghettos, the memory of the freedom that had been so recently attained could not be erased. The states composing preunified Italy adopted different attitudes toward their Jewish communities; compared with the rigors of the Papal States and the kingdom of Sardinia, the conditions of Jewish life in the grand duchy of Tuscany and the duchy of Parma were much more tolerable. Above all, the process of transformation that had begun gradually soon became unstoppable, both for Jews and for Italian society as a whole.

The then still small ranks of the liberal nobility and the bourgeoisie perceived the economic and political necessity of unification and therefore displayed greater sensitivity to liberal ideals. They were the initial core group that, together with former military figures allied with Napoléon and the more advanced liberals of the lower classes, formed the first secret societies and patriotic movements. In this environment legal and civil recognition of Jews as equals became one aspect of a more general aspiration to Italy's independence and liberty. The Jews, distressed by the return to servitude after a brief period of freedom, quickly gave their full support to nationalist objectives. Slowly a new phase in the history of Italian Jewry began, one destined to intertwine its goals with the attainment of national independence. This phase would continue almost undisturbed until the promulgation of the Racial Laws on the part of the Fascist regime in 1938.

For Jews emancipation took the form of a dialectical process, oscillating between conscious integration and unconscious assimilation, leading them to question their own traditional heritage. In the end Jews did indeed become Italians among Italians, adhering to and participating in the struggles, movements, and political debates of the Risorgimento. Beginning in 1815 a Jewish presence became increasingly significant in the secret society known as the Carboneria, in the Piedmontese movements of 1821, in the Giovine Italia movement of Giuseppe Mazzini, and in the Modenese movement of 1831. At the same time the status of Jews became a central issue for some of the principal participants in the cultural and political debate of the Risorgimento, including Gabriele Pepe, Carlo Cattaneo, Vincenzo Gioberti, Niccolò Tommaseo, Ugo Foscolo, and Cesare Balbo. The struggle for the freedom of Jews in Italy became more and more closely tied to the struggle for the freedom and independence of the entire nation.[4]

Eighteen forty-eight, a crucial year in the history of the Risorgimento, was also of great importance for the fate of Jews on the peninsula. On March 29 the Piedmontese sovereign, Carlo Alberto, granted civil rights to Jews, fifty days after the granting of statutory concessions and forty days after the extension of equality to the Waldensian minority. It was the beginning of a new historical phase, and little by little equal rights were accorded to Jewish communities in the various states of Italy. These advances were cut short, however, by the defeat suffered by the Italian democratic and liberal movement in 1849. Only in Piedmont did statutory guarantees remain intact. Still the prevailing sentiments throughout Italy made it impossible to turn back the clock. The legal and civil emancipation of Jews was an integral part of the Risorgimento, and its realization was closely linked to the movement's victorious stages, the second war for Italian independence in 1859 and the proclamation of the kingdom of Italy in 1861. The only communities to remain outside this process were Venice (until 1866) and Trieste (until 1918), where, however, Hapsburg rule had mandated Jewish emancipation since 1782. Until 1870 the policies of the Catholic church had brought bitter disappointment to the Jews of Rome. Ancient theological condemnation of the Jewish population combined with more recent attacks on the dangers of liberalism. The results were the harshest of measures, from persistent closings of the ghetto to forced baptisms. In 1858, for example, the little Edgardo Mortara was taken away from his family in Bologna.

The effects of this varied pattern of Jewish emancipation were felt for decades. The Piedmontese, Emilian, and Tuscan communities saw important economic and social transformations, the foundations of which had been laid some years earlier. The poverty and underdevelopment of the Roman Jews remained particularly grave, however, as admirably described in the writings of the Piedmontese author and political figure the Marchese d'Azeglio and in the observations of the German historian Ferdinand Gregorovius. In Rome liberation came late and fostered the persistence of a broad-based proletariat, which would continue to be characteristic of the social structure of Roman-Jewish life.[5]

Fig. 18. Ghetto, Rome, late nineteenth century

In the decade that preceded Italian independence (1849–1859), Jewish participation in the struggles of the Risorgimento intensified, with members of the community attaining important political positions. To cite just one example, Isacco Artom assumed the role of secretary to Camillo Benso, the count of Cavour, the Piedmontese prime minister and one of the principal architects of Italian unity. During the outburst of patriotism of 1859–1860, Jews shared the experience of other Italians in the struggle for the attainment of common goals. Numerous Jews volunteered to fight alongside Garibaldi. Clearly, in many areas, especially in the south of Italy, where there had been no Jewish presence for about four hundred years, Jews were an unknown entity. Vast pockets of prejudice persisted, essentially Catholic in origin. Nevertheless Jewish emancipation in Italy was accomplished as an integral part of the formation of a unified nation.

Through the granting of equal rights, the Risorgimento ushered in a new phase in the history of Italian Jews and their relationship to the majority. In comparison with their coreligionists in other European countries, Italian Jews did not meet significant obstacles. Jews entered a society that accepted the principles of their equality and that, in keeping with its liberal orientation, made no issue of their cultural specificity, a theme that seemed of little interest, even to Italian Jews themselves. With emancipation the Jews of Italy saw an entire, ancient world of traditions and values vanish along with its limitations and hardships, necessitating the invention of a new self-image, a new projection of their role in society. Their earlier experiences seemed to offer little direction, partly because there arose the new question of defining the role of what had once been considered a dispersed and exiled people in the nineteenth-century reality of national and liberal states.

With the achievement of national unity and independence, the ghetto system came to an end. In addition to being a symbol of legal and civil discrimination, the ghetto had also represented a specific and all-encompassing way of life that touched upon the legal, economic, social, cultural, and religious activities of the community. In Italy, as elsewhere, a new type of Jew was born along with emancipation. He was characterized by his religion[6] in an epoch in which traditional religious values were being questioned and gradually being supplanted by laic culture, with its new national and socialist myths. The entry of Jews into Italian society set in motion, encouraged, or brought to maturation processes of acculturation that tended to modify Jewish identity radically. The confrontation between majority society and the Jewish minority essentially opened two paths: that of social integration, characterized by the persistence, albeit slight, of a Jewish identity, and that of full assimilation, to the point of total negation of Jewish origins and identity. In post-1861 Italy, society did not demand the abandonment of one's heritage to obtain entry into social life, and Jews were left free to choose either path.

The peaceful and productive life of Italian Jews during the first fifty years of the unified state seems wrapped in a gray cloud of mediocrity[7] and has for the most part been ignored by historical research. The relative obscurity surrounding this period has helped strengthen the formation of unsubstantiated clichés that extol the integration of Italian Jewry as the most successful known. In reality the very first attempts to deal with this period, which remains to be fully studied, seem to focus upon the unique characteristics of the incorporation of the Italian-Jewish community into the social fabric of the nation.

The integration of Jews into Italian society was successful, not only because it occurred at the same time as the process of unification and independence but also because of other fundamental factors. There was an absence of linguistic barriers between Gentiles and Jews (Jewish-Italian dialects cannot really be considered as such). Additionally the ancient coexistence of several rituals (Italian, Sephardic, Ashkenazic) within Italian Judaism introduced a beneficial awareness of religious pluralism and contributed to an internal climate of religious tolerance and to a weakening of the reformist movements that had animated other European communities. The Italian-Jewish community, especially the more intellectual element, peacefully regarded the waning of its religious feelings as it grew more distant from tradition yet managed to perceive that its religious crisis was too deep to be resolved by incidental reforms. Traditional religious culture, while neglected, still remained intact and constituted a spiritual patrimony of great scope and wealth, to be drawn upon whenever Italian Jews might desire it.

Rather than expressing decided choices, Italian Jews demonstrated a vocation for cultural and religious compromise, an autonomous search for solutions to problems faced by world Jewry. They were drawn to the banner of tolerance, of pluralism, of the denial of reformist codifications and renunciations.[8] But it was precisely this tendency that delineated the true problem to be resolved. In an identity enriched and torn by the encounter between two cultures, the Jewish side, in addition to being the minority, also seemed decidedly to come out the loser in the long run.

The evidence to support this reconstruction is not substantial. In fact, on the basis of the few extant studies and reports, one can state that at the end of the nineteenth century and until the beginning of World War I, Italian Judaism continued to be characterized by the observance of principal religious holidays and of ceremonies connected to rites of passage. Mixed marriages were still few in number, and social life continued to be limited to the family. The observance of dietary codes was on the decline, however. Italian Jews were brought into society primarily through their entry into civil administration and university positions, professional activities that had a political impact.[9]

Integration into Italian society brought with it important social, economic, and cultural transformations within the Jewish community. The opening of the ghetto gates resulted in a new mobility for Italian Jews, who tended to migrate from the small centers where they had lived for centuries to major cities, where they reinforced ancient communities or gave strength to newer ones. This phenomenon of urbanization was accompanied by a tendency for the Jewish community to grow at a rate considerably lower than that of the overall Italian population, further diluting its numerical weight in the country. Increased contact with the surrounding environment favored the weakening of traditional culture and sense of identity. Integration was accompanied by a dissolution of cultural and historical patrimony, the adaptation of traditional structures and modes of expression to new values emanating from a different social context, and the consequent assumption of elements typical of Italian national culture in place of traditional Jewish ones.[10]

One obvious, striking example of these tendencies was the construction of monumental temples in Turin, Florence, Milan, Rome, and Trieste at the turn of the century (figs. 15, 19). These "synagogue-cathedrals" replaced the *scole* of the ghettos with buildings addressed to both the Jewish world within and the Gentile world without. Indeed these buildings came to represent both a proud exhibitionism and, with their imposing presence and location, a reaffirmation of the historical roots of the communities. The temples symbolized a new definition of religion in terms of the group as a whole. They were the expression of a tendency to support an increasingly uncertain religious identity with ostentatious display.

Pockets of emptiness could already be seen in these new, grandiose spaces. The challenge of the surrounding society encouraged the beginning of secularization, the adoption of laic values, and modernization. In this context Judaism was reduced to a mere religious dimension and took on negative, archaic, backward, restrictive connotations. Traditional values were replaced by "newer," more "modern" ones. The anxious awaiting of messianic redemption was replaced by the palingenetic myths of socialism; the sense of belonging to a small community of the larger Jewish world was replaced by the reassuring certainty of patriotic, ethical, and ideological identification with the national state. In short, there came about an ever deeper and fuller adherence to the values and ideals that were current and prevalent in Italian society.[11]

This incorporation of Jews into the life of the nation was also encouraged by the weakness of anti-Semitism in postunification Italy. Even if there were islands of prejudice and isolated instances of suspicion, those economic, social, and political factors that might have stimulated the diffusion of active anti-Semitism were lacking. In Italy Jews were few in number, they had no external traits that distinguished them from the rest of the population, and they had relegated the practice of their religion to their homes. Italian culture of this period lacked a racist tradition, and anti-Semitism was not a tool for politically mobilizing the masses. It survived in Catholic circles as an expression of a traditionalism that identified the Jew as a symbol of modernity, of liberalism, of capitalism, and of socialism. Anti-Jewish ideas were not absent from the nascent nationalist movement and also surfaced in the socialist camp. At the turn of the century, however, criticism and prejudice, rather than focusing on racism and anti-Semitism, were directed more toward Zionism, which was seen as a threat to the patriotic fidelity of Italian Jewry and as an undesirable instrument of Jewish penetration into lands held sacred by the Catholic church.[12]

Within the larger picture these were limited phenomena that did not prejudice the full participation of Jews in all aspects of Italian life. In fact, during the fifteen years preceding World War I, Jews were present

Fig. 19. Interior of the Tempio Israelitico, Rome, 1901–1904

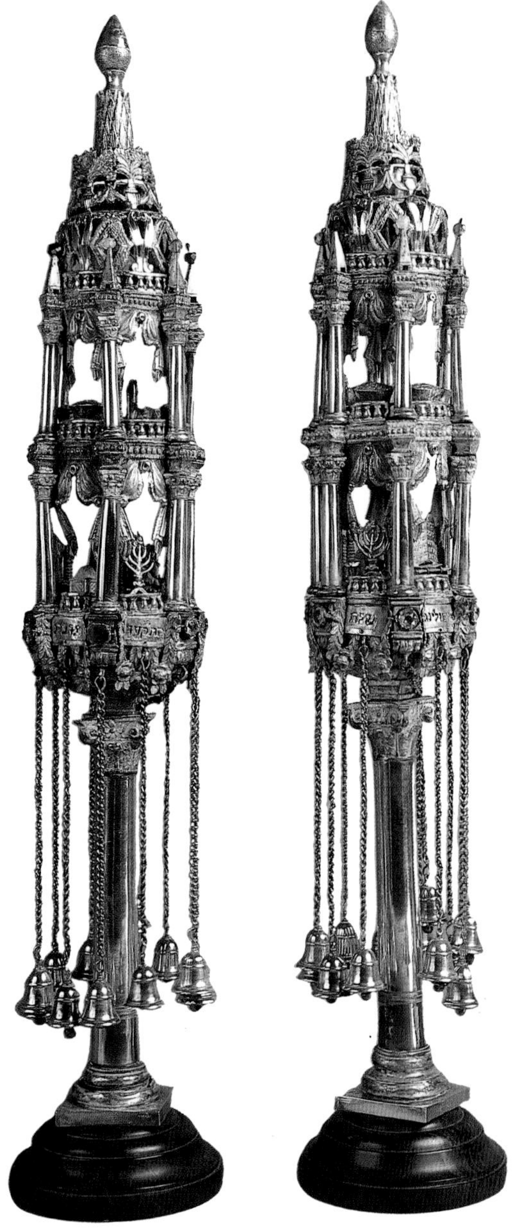

Fig. 20. Torah Finials, Turin, 1814–1850, The Jewish Museum, New York (cat. no. 199)

in all professions and in some cases became particularly prominent. In 1902 General Giuseppe Ottolenghi was named minister of war (cat. no. 199; fig. 20); in 1910 Luigi Luzzatti became prime minister; Senator Vittorio Polacco was appointed tutor to the king; between 1907 and 1913 Ernesto Nathan, leader of a laic-Masonic coalition, supplied the city of Rome with an efficient administration; Claudio Treves and Giuseppe Emanuele Modigliani were important leaders of the Socialist party. Just a few years after emancipation, a great many Italian Jews were prominent in the arts and sciences, with men of letters such as Angiolo Orvieto, Italo Svevo, Alessandro D'Ancona; philologists such as Graziadio Isaia Ascoli; artists such as Amedeo Modigliani and later Cesare Lombroso, Vito Volterra, Tullio Levi-Civita, Guido Castelnuovo, and Edoardo Weiss, to name just a few.[13]

The counterpart to this broad Jewish participation in national life was a weakening of the great tradition of Italian-Jewish culture, which had still represented an important point of reference during the nineteenth century. Major figures were Samuel David Luzzatto and Elia Benamozegh. But at precisely the moment when the crisis of Jewish identity seemed greatest, with the decline of traditional culture within the liberal climate of the nation, a significant movement toward revival and reawakening began to make itself felt. This Jewish movement was in keeping with the general development of the country in the Giolittian age and echoed the idealistic reawakening and cultural debate that animated the liveliest sectors of society.

The center of this movement of Jewish cultural revival was the rabbinical college of Florence, enlivened by the figure of Rabbi Samuel Zeví Margulies. In 1907 he and his young students founded the Pro Cultura movement, the objective of which was to link traditional Jewish studies with scientific methods that would render them appropriate to the cultural needs of the time. Although this was the most obvious element, other factors contributed to the success of this spiritual revival. During these same years the philosophy of Zionism, in the spiritual rather than political sense, spread among some of these youths and was seen as a tool for recovering Judaism, its language, culture, and history. At the same time there occurred a revival of Jewish journalism in Italy thanks to Dante Lattes and Margulies of the *Corriere Israelitico* in Trieste. In 1910, assisted by young students from the rabbinical college, Margulies promoted the establishment of *Settimana Israelitica,* considered "the first true newspaper to come out in Jewish Italy," a newspaper of young people, which had as its goal the reawakening and cultural renewal of Italian Judaism. Thus, amid the cultural desert of Italian Judaism, an ideology began to emerge that had the capacity to mobilize certain student sectors and some of the more sensitive bourgeois intellectuals. There arose leaders capable of linking this ideology to the traditional culture in a scientific manner, making it attractive to young intellectuals and providing the means for the diffusion and discussion of new ideas.[14]

On the basis of these developments the principal problems that distressed the Jewish community, its organizational frailty and its intellectual depression, slowly came to light. The young Florentine group attempted to remedy this situation. Its initiative achieved unexpected success and brought to light the numerous, previously unexpressed Jewish needs of a significant group of young intellectuals and members of the bourgeoisie.

On July 14, 1911, *Settimana Israelitica* launched an editorial "Appeal to young people," inviting them to a "simple, friendly, affectionate conference . . . an occasion for meeting and for debate," so that young Italian Jews could feel themselves to be "a vital force, not an anachronism, an active virtue, not a prejudice." Within just a few weeks the initiative met with unexpected success, culminating in a conference in Florence in late October 1911, attended by figures destined to play a prominent role in Italian Judaism for years to come, including Alfonso Pacifici and Elia S. Artom. The conference attempted to reappropriate the rich cultural tradition of Italian Jewry and the teachings of its great leaders, such as Luzzatto and Benamozegh, who had exalted the beauty of Judaism and who spoke of the "indescribable figure of that Messiah who has not come and who will not come in the future, but who is coming now."

Thus began a process of cultural and organizational renewal, the fruits of which would nurture Italian Judaism until after World War I. At this point the efforts of and contacts between young intellectuals of various communities were pursued at conferences held in Turin (1912) and Rome (1914). The significant debates held at these conferences were fueled by new, notable contributions on the part of Pacifici, Artom, Umberto Cassuto, and Lattes.

While this movement of spiritual reawakening and cultural renewal had enormous merit and overall historical importance, it was limited by its intellectual and elitist nature. It involved only a narrow segment of young people and excluded the "masses" of the Jewish population and those proletarian groups that still dominated various communities, particularly Rome. With the outbreak of World War I in the summer of 1914, these same youths, while conscientiously fulfilling their duty as citizens after Italy's entrance into the war in May 1915, also immediately understood the dramatic dimension of the human and Jewish tragedy that was unfolding. They distinguished themselves from the vast majority of Italian Jews who, from the moment that Italy entered the conflict, were excited by fervent patriotism, expressed in passionate, significant terms, especially by *Il Vessillo Israelitico,* a periodical that was emblematic of the transformation of the Jewish community in the fifty-year span between the liberation of Rome and the advent of fascism.[15]

Thus World War I appears as a fundamental stage in the history of Italian Jewry after the emancipation. The ways in which Jews joined the national war effort effectively express the degree to which their identity was transformed. Indeed, for the majority of Italian Jews this period saw the conclusion of the process of Jewish "denationalization" and Italian nationalization. The global conflict constituted the trial and the ratification of the process of emancipation that had begun with the Risorgimento. Indeed *Il vessillo,* evidently expressing the sentiments of the majority of the Jewish community, maintained that the moment had arrived for demonstrating gratitude to the motherland and to the house of Savoy, which with great benignancy had granted equal rights to Jews. Sacrifice in war became the ethical sanction of the national integration that had occurred, a sense of belonging now sealed with spilled blood. Thus it is no accident that Jewish expressions of support for the national war effort were characterized by a rationale related to the ideals of the Risorgimento. In this light it was possible to see the Great War as a fourth war of Italian independence, which brought the unredeemed lands of Trento and Trieste, where the important Jewish communities had long been characterized by strong feelings of Italian identity, back to Italian soil.

Fig. 21. Umberto Boccioni, *Ritratto di Margherita Sarfatti* (Portrait of Margherita Sarfatti), 1912, Private Collection (cat. no. 293)

During these years, as the events of the war brought about important transformations in the self-image of Italian Jews, other international events also influenced the community, in particular, the approval of the Balfour Declaration by Italy in 1918, which was viewed by the few Italian Zionists as an authentic watershed in the long history of the Jewish people. Despite the weight and the implications of the declaration, Italian identity clearly prevailed over Jewishness for most Italian Jews when they made political choices, as was demonstrated by the attitudes they assumed toward the dramatic events that stirred the country following the war.

In Italy the masses exploded in a context made more dramatic by Italy's long, consuming commitment to war. The fragile structure of the liberal state was beset by difficulties: the need to meet the demand for social advancement of the working and peasant classes, who were galvanized by the example of the Bolshevik revolution; the necessity of channeling ex-combatants' requests to have places found for them in society again; to protect the petite bourgeoisie from inflation; to satisfy the aspirations of the middle classes whose lives had been overturned by the circumstances of war; to encourage new, productive changes in industrial operations and the rationalization of an often archaic agrarian sector. The postwar period was marked by the electoral and organizational explosion of the Socialist party, by the entry of organized Catholics into the national government, by the formation of anti-Bolshevik groups, by the establishment of new political forces (from the Communist party to Benito Mussolini's militant Fascist groups), and by the eruption of violence in political struggles. Within this context Jews took positions analogous to those of the rest of the population, and as a rule their choices stemmed not from their Jewishness, but from their social positions and political ideals. Although they moved in socialist and liberal circles, their numbers also included representative and militant Fascists (for example, Margherita Sarfatti was a codirector of the political journal *Gerarchia* (cat. nos. 294–297; fig. 21), while Umberto Terracini was one of the founders of the Communist party).

In any case there were moments of continuity in events of a more frankly Jewish nature, in particular in the vigorous cultural revival movement initiated by young people on the eve of World War I. In 1924 this development reached a high point with the Livorno

Convention, the Fourth Youth Convention, and the First Cultural Convention, a crucial moment in the history of Italian Zionism and a watershed in the history of Italian Jewry.[16] There was an awareness of new conditions brought about by the Balfour Declaration and the impetus it gave to Zionism and by the changes brought about by the Fascists' accession to power in Italy. In late 1924 the Fascist movement was going through a difficult phase following the assassination of the socialist Giacomo Matteotti.

The significance of the Livorno Convention can be seen in the themes debated there and in the exemplary personalities who participated. They were concerned with the problems of the affirmation of an integral Judaism, of the relationship between Judaism and liberty, and of socialist Zionism. Delegates to the convention expressed a new self-awareness and the necessity of moving as Jews in society. Even though the convention expressed the attitudes of an intellectual elite and not those of the Jewish majority, absorbed in everyday matters rather than in political developments, it came to symbolize the destiny of a significant part of Italian Jewry during the Fascist years. Outstanding participants included Pacifici, who, despite the evils evident in the violent society of the time, maintained the necessity of returning to the idea of the unity of God and his moral law, and Nello Rosselli, who, joining Italian identity with Jewishness, proposed his Jewishness as the heart of Benedetto Croce's "religion" of liberty. Enzo Sereni, in keeping with his image as the representative of new ideas, argued for the necessity of manual labor in Palestine, for the reinforcement of a Jewish national home, and for the social normalization of diaspora Judaism, which he claimed was disproportionately bourgeois and commercial. Joseph Colombo asserted that it was necessary to build Jewish schools to foster Jewish awareness and Jewish culture, both for their own value and for the benefit of majority society. Colombo's initiative was a response to the innovations of Giovanni Gentile, who introduced Catholic religious instruction in Italian schools in 1923.

Lively ideals emerged from the Livorno Convention, as did the future leaders of Italian Jewry under fascism, who would later manage to rise above the difficult predicaments resulting from the enactment of the Racial Laws and the dark months of German occupation. But the history of Italian Jewry under fascism is more complex than the participation of elite groups in the Livorno Convention would indicate.[17]

It is not easy to define Mussolini's position toward Judaism and the Jews when he first came to power. Certainly he harbored prejudices that were typical of nationalistic leaders; he tended to believe in the idea of a global Jewish power. But on the whole racist ideologies were foreign to him, and his prejudices did not prevent him from being interested in political collaboration and personal relationships with Jews. Unlike similar movements in Europe between the two wars, Italian fascism was not characterized by the myth of race or by political, economic, or religious anti-Semitism. It was a varied, composite movement, in which many positions, traditions, and different attitudes converged, but except in specific cases, it was not an anti-Semitic movement. Thus most Jews had the same attitudes toward Mussolini as other citizens, basing their political choices on social interests and on convictions, ideals, and morals.

Jews experienced the violence and convulsions of the immediate postwar period along with other Italians. After the Fascists came to power, Jews were subjected to the consequences of an unstable political climate and to the actions of a regime that attempted to crush all forms of dissent. In any case, during the first half of the 1920s there existed mutual suspicion between the nascent regime and the Jewish community. Yet, overall, Italian-Jewish life did not undergo changes different from those experienced by the general population. A few facts can be chosen to illustrate this: 230 Jews received certificates attesting to their participation in the October 1922 Fascist march on Rome; Aldo Finzi, who had a Jewish background, was Undersecretary of the Interior in Mussolini's first government; in 1932 Guido Jung was named to the Ministry of Finance. Once the new regime had completed the first phase of its consolidation in the mid-1920s, there were signs of a reciprocal relaxation in relationships with the Jewish community. From time to time there were unpleasant attacks by certain organs of the press, but for the most part Italian-Jewish life went on without any particular anxiety.

Beginning in the second half of the 1920s, encounters between Mussolini and important Italian Jews and Zionist organizations were symbolic of a new relationship between the regime and Italian Jewry. In September 1926 Mussolini met with Chaim Weizmann; in May 1927 he met with Rabbi David Prato, who was

Fig. 22. Interior of the Livorno Synagogue

about to leave for Alexandria, Egypt, to assume the position of grand rabbi; in June he met with Victor Jacobson; in October, with Nahum Sokolow, who acknowledged that fascism was free of anti-Semitic prejudices.[18]

These encounters responded to a double need. They were the effective manifestation of the easing of tensions between the regime and the Jewish world, and they expressed fascism's interest in Zionism as an international political movement that could become a useful weapon against the British presence in the Mediterranean. This attention and openness to international Zionism were, however, countered by reservations and suspicions about the participation of Italian Jews in a movement whose philosophy was considered separatist and an alienating force within the fascist state.

Yet these prejudices did not make deep inroads into the lives of Italian Jews, who were increasingly integrated into the country and the regime. Indeed some Jews even exhibited indifference or hostility toward that small group of Jews who, with their attachment to ancestral traditions and to the idea of a return to Zion, placed their well-being as Italians and Fascists at risk.

In 1929 there was a brief flurry of concern among sensitive Jews in the circle around the weekly publication *Israel* as a result of the Concordat between the Italian state and the Catholic church, which encouraged fears for the future autonomy of non-Catholic cults. Within a few months, however, statements by Alfredo Rocco, the minister of justice, and by Mussolini himself put these doubts to rest. At the same time work was completed on a new legal arrangement for the Jewish communities.

After the formation of a united Italy, these local communities had varying legal statuses, tied to the traditions and norms of the preunification states. This heterogeneous condition paralleled a lack of organization on the national level, a situation that changed only with the cultural reawakening at the beginning of the twentieth century. In 1911 the Committee of Italian-Jewish Universities was established; in 1914 a consortium of communities was set up, which in 1920 was made into an official body. Its organizational structure remained weak because of limitations resulting from legal conditions, economic difficulties resulting from the impossibility of imposing contributions on members, and to a confusion of roles between the rabbinate and the lay administration.

During the second half of the 1920s, the Fascist restructuring of the state furnished the occasion to review the legal status of the Jewish communities. A commission was established to study the situation, three of whose six members were Jews (Angelo-Raphael Sacerdoti, Angelo Sereni, Mario Falco). The result was Law 1731, enacted on September 30, 1930, with further modifications in September and November of 1931. The new law standardized the legal situation of the Italian-Jewish communities. It obliged them to join a central representative body, the Union of Italian-Jewish Communities, and defined the criteria for participation. It also established mandatory contributions, required the elections of internal leaders, defined the role of rabbis who were entrusted with the spiritual direction of their communities, and decreed that the communities and the Union were subject to the supervision and protection of the state.

For the most part the law responded to some long-standing requests by Italian-Jewish leaders, who lamented the difficulties resulting from the lack of organization in their communities and from the scarcity of voluntary financial contributions. The regulation concerning local elections seemed remarkable, but in practice it affected only individual communities, since national congresses of the Union were composed of delegates nominated by local community councils.[19] The parameters of state intervention in Jewish life remained open, but at the beginning of the 1930s this was not cause for concern. The life of Italian Jews, the relationship between the Fascist state and Jewish communities, seemed at this point to be absolutely tranquil, and the attitude of Italy seemed exemplary in contrast to events unfolding in numerous other European countries. In the 1932 interview with the journalist Emilio Ludwig published by Mondadori, Mussolini confirmed the full integration of Jews into Italian society, the nonexistence of anti-Semitism in the country, and his complete rejection of racism. Yet these positions were destined to disappear by the latter half of the decade due to the influence of international events on Fascist Italy and on the internal evolution of the regime.

The January 1933 rise to power of National Socialism in Germany brought about significant changes in Italian fascism. Clearly, neither then nor later, at least not until 1943, did the Germans pressure Italy to adopt anti-Jewish policies, yet the rise of nazism was nevertheless fraught with repercussions. Indeed, from the time of the earliest manifestations of German anti-Semitism, Mussolini attempted to present himself as a mediator between the German regime, which proclaimed its affinity with Italian fascism, and the Jewish world, which according to obsolete stereotypes was considered a homogeneous and organized whole. In reality the Jewish community was extremely diversified, lacked adequate organization, and in any case could not be compared with the institutions of a sovereign state. But apart from these difficulties, Mussolini's attempts at mediation, which in some cases brought concrete advantages to certain Jewish communities, and whose aim was to increase the international prestige of the duce, were carefully directed so as not to prejudice the developing relationship between the two regimes.

In the meantime the consolidation of Nazi power in Germany promoted a realignment of Italian Fascists and gave new prominence to the pro-German and anti-Semitic wing of the regime. One symptom of this new situation was the bitter anti-Zionist and anti-Semitic campaign unleashed in January 1934 by the Roman daily paper *Il Tevere,* edited by T. Interlandi and backed, if not actually promoted, by Mussolini. In March of that year, when the paper was about to fold, it found new strength in the arrest of a group of anti-Fascists, for the most part Jews, belonging to the Giustizia e Libertà movement. This was reported on March 31 with a venomous editorial background piece entitled "Lascianà abbà Biruscilaim ('l'anno prossimo a Gerusalemme'): Quest'anno al Tribunale Speciale." Despite the progressive decline of this campaign, in large part a journalistic stunt, it expressed a new situation and provoked grave consequences. Anti-Semitism began to take shape in Italy, as it had in Germany, as a tool of political struggle. Italian Jews, confronted by a harsh attack on their patriotism, their Fascist and anti-Zionist feelings, split into factions, encouraged by groups such as La Nostra Bandiera in Turin. Only with the enactment of the Racial Laws in 1938 would this rift begin to heal.[20]

Although Italian Zionists continued to be regarded with little sympathy by the authorities and became the object of ferocious attacks by the regime's extremist fringes, Mussolini still gave considerable heed to international Zionism, particularly of a revisionist, anti-English slant. This was the framework for his encounters with Weizmann on April 26, 1933, and February 17, 1934, and with Nahum Goldmann on November 13 of the same year, during which the duce assumed the role of intermediary with Germany and reached an agreement allowing the Jews of the Saar, about to come under German rule, to leave the country with their possessions. The high point of this political negotiation was the collaboration between Italian Fascists and revisionist Zionists, with both sides taking a decidedly anti-British stance and boasting ideological affinities. In December 1934, against the background of this collaboration, the Italian maritime school of Civitavecchia began to teach revisionist Zionists. It operated until 1938,[21] when both internal and international factors brought about a complete rupture between fascism and the Jewish world and Zionism, a break that had been in the works for some years and one that pushed the regime toward the adoption of anti-Jewish policies.

There were at least four factors of varying significance that came together during this period to change the perspective of the regime and its attitude toward Jews: (1) its progressive rapprochement with Nazi Germany, (2) changes in Italy's political prospects in the Mediterranean, (3) the emergence of a racial problem in Africa following the conquest of Ethiopia, and (4) the Mussolinian myth of a new civilization and anxiety about creating a "new Italian."[22]

Internal and international consequences of the wars with Ethiopia and Spain played a central role in this turn in Fascist policies during the second half of the 1930s. These wars moved Italy away from the Western democracies and closer to Nazi Germany. Between 1936 and 1939 political contacts between the leaders of the two regimes intensified and led to the proclamation of a Berlin-Rome axis around which the reconstruction of Europe was to turn, through Italy's adherence to the Anti-Comintern Pact and to the "Pact of Steel" that committed Italy and Germany to reciprocal assistance in case of war. The relationship between the two countries became increasingly close. The ambition of creating a "totalitarian" alliance imposed the need to eliminate all elements of dissonance between the two regimes. In the late summer of 1938, without any pressure from Germany, Fascist Italy proceeded to set forth anti-Jewish legislation, thereby contradicting previous governmental positions and overturning the tradition established by united Italy without appreciable internal resistance or reaction.

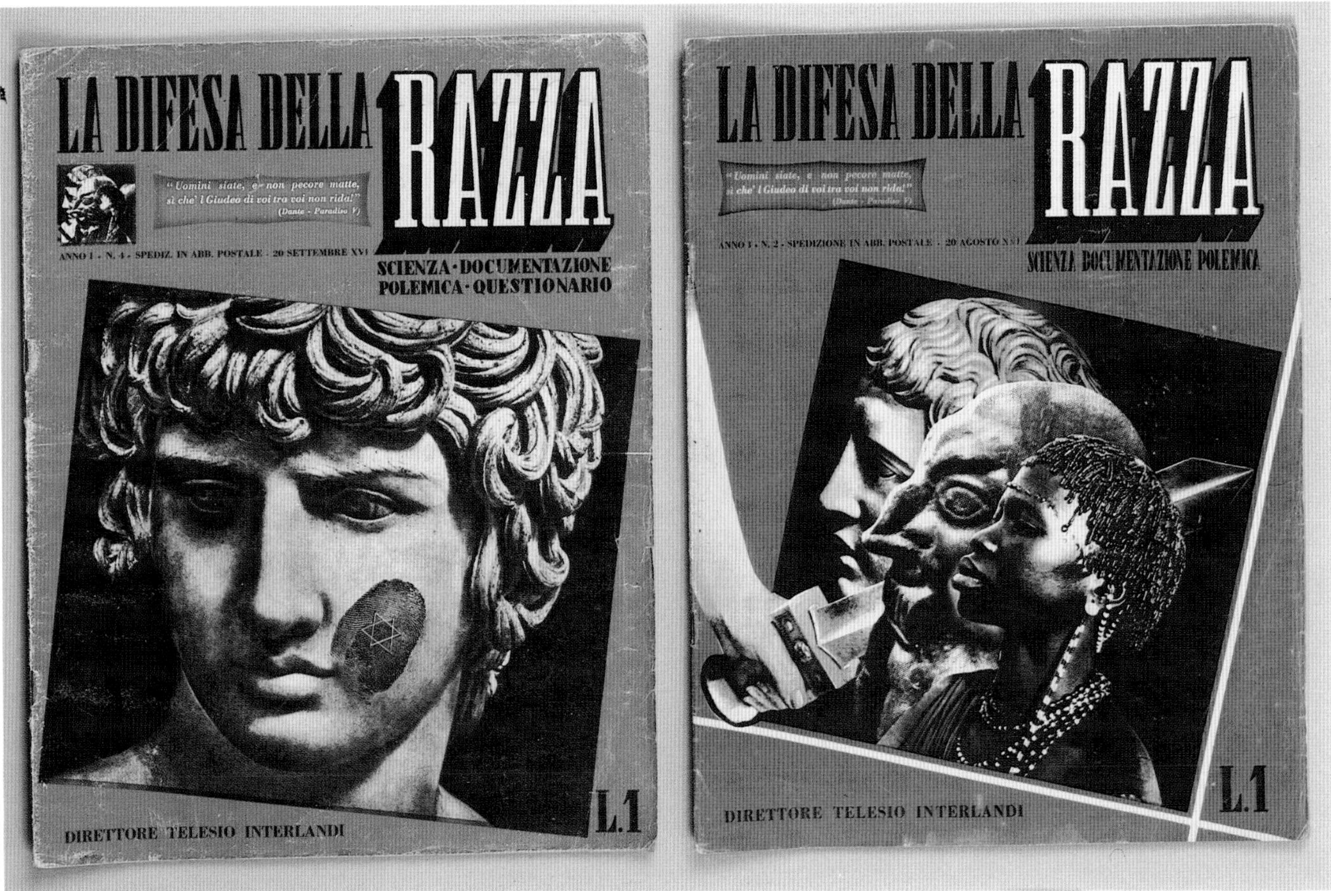

Fig. 23. *La Difesa della Razza,* Italy, 1938–1943, The Library of The Jewish Theological Seminary of America, New York (cat. no. 331)

If the relationship with Nazi Germany represented a sufficient reason for the adoption of state anti-Semitism, new prospects in the Mediterranean opened by the 1938 accord with Great Britain and new interest in the Arab world proclaimed by Mussolini in Tripoli on March 18, 1937, made Zionism a useless factor in Italian foreign policy. The Italian government was already disturbed by the democratic nature of Zionism and by recent anti-Fascist positions taken by Jews in democratic countries. But other factors also helped bring about this change in perspective. The conquest of Ethiopia presented the problem of a relationship with indigenous peoples, in this case, blacks. As far as the Fascist regime was concerned, Italian civilian and military personnel in the colonies were not assuming a stance suitable to a colonizing power. It was necessary to prevent the growth of interracial marriage and to furnish the Italians with the mentality of conquerors, awareness of their racial dignity and superiority. To this end, Law 880 was enacted on April 19, 1937, prohibiting conjugal relationships between Italian citizens and subjects in Italian East Africa.

The creation of this new Italian consciousness was not only tied to the situation in the colonies. During the second half of the 1930s Mussolini's objectives went further, toward a fascist takeover of Italian society capable of shaping his people's character and rendering them worthy of the imperial destiny that lay ahead, capable of creating a new, hard, ruthless race of Italian conquerors and dominators. Therefore it was necessary to combat negative bourgeois virtues, the

Fig. 24. Corrado Cagli, *Veduta di Roma* (View of Rome) or *Trionfo di Roma* (Triumph of Rome), 1937, Eredi Cagli, Rome (cat. no. 306)

cosmopolitanism and pacifism that were regarded as typical Jewish traits. Racism and anti-Semitism were part of a political operation aimed at hardening the Italian character in order to support the totalitarian direction of the regime and to go along with its international allies.

In this complex combination of international and domestic political motives can be seen the causes of the racist and anti-Semitic direction taken by Italian fascism, a radical deviation from the traditional relationship between the Risorgimento state and the Jewish minority. Behind the ideological cover furnished by racism was a political design that emerged with increasing force and clarity in the second half of the 1930s. After the sporadic anti-Zionist and anti-Jewish press campaigns of preceding years, propaganda activities and the priming of public opinion gained new impetus in 1936 and especially 1937, in keeping with political developments. During the course of 1938 this press campaign was strengthened by the regime's new political positions, by theoretical enunciations, and finally by legislative measures.

On February 16, 1938, the *Informazione diplomatica* number 14, notwithstanding its ambiguous tone, announced measures against foreign Jews in Italy, indicated quotas for Jews in public life, and supported the creation of a Jewish state, but not in Palestine. While attacks in the press continued, lower-level administrative decisions that presaged the marginalization of the Jews in Italy were silently adopted. Official ostracization did not occur until July 14, 1938, when the racist *Manifesto degli scienziati* (scholars' manifesto) was published. Its ten points proclaimed, among other things, that the Italian population was Aryan in origin, that a pure Italian race existed to which Jews did not belong, and that this race had to be defended from possible contamination.

As these aberrant racist positions slowly began to attract some youths and intellectuals, on August 5, 1938, the *Informazione diplomatica* number 18 announced the introduction of quotas for the participation of Jews in national life. Only one month later the first anti-Jewish measures were adopted. On September 2 and 3, major steps were taken against foreign Jews, prohibiting them from permanent residence in Italy, revoking the citizenship of all foreign Jews obtained after January 1, 1919, and decreeing their expulsion within six months. At the same time Jewish students and teachers were expelled from all schools. On October 6 the meeting of the Fascist Gran Consiglio ratified, with the opposition of only Italo Balbo, Emilio De Bono, and Luigi Federzoni, further anti-Jewish measures to be put into effect by November. On the basis of these provisions, intermarriage between Italian citizens and people of other races was prohibited and Jews were excluded from civil and military administrative positions and from local and state-controlled enterprises. Strict limitations were placed on their property rights, and their right to practice their professions was limited to the narrow field of fellow Jews. Traditional practices of the Jewish faith, such as the ritual slaughter of cattle, were prohibited.

Along with these rulings, which relegated Italian Jews to the humiliating position of second-class citizenship, came attempts at mitigation, resulting in grotesque consequences and further moral oppressions. Thus, for example, discriminatory measures were established to favor Jews considered well deserving of the Fascist cause, or those in possession of high patriotic titles. An immoral standard was established, whereby the interior minister was able to declare that certain Jews were Aryans, even in opposition to the outcome of civil rulings.

These anti-Semitic measures, which upset the lives of Jews and their identity as Italians, were received without substantial opposition. Many Fascist leaders were zealous in applying the new laws. The king was acquiescent, and Vatican opposition was limited to an attempt to protect mixed marriages and respect for the Concordat of 1929. Even the cultural world—with few exceptions, such as Benedetto Croce, Giovanni Gentile, Filippo Tommaso Marinetti, Massimo Bontempelli, and Giorgio La Pira—remained inactive when it was not applauding the tragic political turn taken by the regime. The majority of the populace, substantially ignorant not only of the existence of a "Jewish problem" but sometimes also of the very existence of Jews, was overwhelmed by more immediate and concrete personal problems, soon to be overshadowed by the drama of the world war.[23]

In the autumn of 1938 life continued unchanged for the majority of "Aryan" Italians. While antifascists abroad saw the Racial Laws as yet another abomination of fascism, supporters of the regime in Italy saw the new racist and anti-Semitic line as a means to give new impetus to the "Fascist revolution" and cement the alliance with Germany. In contrast the approximately forty-seven thousand Italian Jews, cut off and bewildered, were for the most part forced to seek solutions to more mundane problems. During those months a high percentage of university professors, public officials, clerks, and merchants had to find new ways to survive. Those who could, nearly six thousand, decided to go elsewhere to try to rebuild their lives and fortunes; these were primarily intellectuals and members of the middle and upper middle classes who went to Argentina, the United States, Palestine, England, and Brazil, where they defended their Jewish identity, honored their Italian origins, and made important contributions to the anti-Fascist cause. Some of the more prominent figures among this group were Emilio Segré, Edoardo Weiss, Emilio Servadio, Rodolfo Mondolfo, Tullio Ascarelli, Enzo Joseph Bonaventura, Umberto Cassuto, Dante Lattes, Bruno Rossi, Renato Treves, Franco Modigliani, and Bruno Zevi. Some three thousand others, weaker or more assimilated, hoped to avoid persecution by converting to another religion.[24]

For Italian Jews the Racial Laws represented an extremely serious material blow and an even deeper moral wound, since it upset a historical, cultural, and ethical identity that had been peacefully assembled over time. Clearly, from the autumn of 1938 until September 8, 1943, Italian Jews did not face the perils of deportation and extermination that threatened their coreligionists in countries under the dominion of Nazi Germany. Given the seriousness of what happened after September 8, 1943, however, any minimization of the gravity of the condition of Jews in Italy between 1938 and 1943 would be misleading.

Furthermore, while the Office for Demography and Race of the Ministry of the Interior continued to study new measures to make the living conditions of Italian Jews even harsher, the Ministry of Foreign Affairs attempted to protect those Jews residing abroad. After June 1940 Italian armed forces in the occupied zones of France, Greece, and Yugoslavia worked to rescue Jews from the Germans and their local collaborators.[25]

The fall of fascism on July 25, 1943, did not change the condition of Italian Jews. Despite solicitations from some democratic intellectuals, the Badoglio government, fearful of arousing the suspicions of its German ally, took great care not to do away with the Racial Laws or to neutralize their more dangerous effects with silent, shrewd administrative measures. For Jews all limitations established by Fascist laws remained in force, including registration at the commissioner's office, which would furnish precise information for future raids. Yet a strange, optimistic climate spread among Jews and non-Jews alike, heightening their unawareness of danger and their unpreparedness for the events that would follow. After September 8, 1943, armistice with the allies and the flight of the king and Badoglio to Brindisi brought about the collapse of the country and its division into two sections, with the Nazis occupying the north-central region.

In the regions occupied by Germans, where the Italian Social Republic was established, new laws were enacted between November 1943 and January 1944 declaring Jews foreigners, dispossessing them of their property, and ordering their internment in camps. Even before these new measures were adopted, Germans personally hunted down Jews, at times with the collaboration of Fascist forces. In September 1943 massacres and deportations began, which would affect more than eight thousand Italian Jews before they were over.[26]

In the south, liberated by the allies, the laborious task of repealing the Racial Laws began with the approval of two decrees on January 20, 1944.[27] But laws alone could not heal the wounds inflicted by Fascist anti-Semitism. A profound political and moral renewal of the country was required for the full reintegration of Jews into Italian society. Italian Jews themselves made an important direct contribution to this goal through the struggle for liberation from the Nazis and Fascists, in which they participated as Italians among Italians. This solidarity was essential in helping them achieve their reintegration into Italian life, but clearly the events that had shattered their existence from the autumn of 1938 until the summer of 1943 and then between 1943 and 1945 had not left their identity unscathed. Immediately following liberation, in the material and moral ruins of the defeated country, the wounds suffered by Jews were very prominent. Emigration, conversions, and deportations had reduced the Italian-Jewish community by a third and had deprived it of some of its most outstanding members.[28] Now it was necessary to rebuild the identity of the survivors within the context of the moral, political, and material reconstruction of the country.

Between 1944 and 1947 great efforts were made in this regard by the new anti-Fascist government and by some Italian-Jewish leaders. They were determined to restore the political, civil, and patrimonial conditions of which Jews had been so harshly deprived. These restorations proceeded with some difficulty, however. While liberation signified the Jews' return to the state of equality that had been sanctioned and confirmed shortly after the birth of the republic by the enactment of the Constitution on January 1, 1948, a full return to the past was not possible. The Racial Laws had impinged directly on all aspects of Italian-Jewish life, and the community was demographically, culturally, and economically impoverished. It was necessary for Italian society to go beyond the promotion of the legislative reintegration of Jews as citizens and to undertake a deep search of its conscience and a detailed analysis of its recent history, of which fascism and the Racial Laws were an integral part.

These were the political, cultural, and historical themes of debate in the Republic that was created in 1946 and in which Jews slowly began to participate fully. New problems resulted from the difficult process of reinforcing democratic institutions and from the anxiety inherent in the reconciliation of the right to equality with the right to diversity. Soon another problem emerged, one that has been at the crux of Jewish identity both in modern times and throughout the ages: the necessity of reconciling the memories and experiences of the recent past with a historical interpretation that should neither neutralize nor exorcise the recent past, but create an identity suitable for the future.[29]

Translated from the Italian by Meg Shore

Notes

1. See, for example, M. Michaelis, *Mussolini e la questione ebraica* (Milan, 1982), p. 25; H. Stuart Hughes, *Prigionieri della speranza alla ricerca dell'identita ebraica nella letteratura italiana contemporanea* (Bologna, 1983), pp. 7–8. For a general historical background, see A. Milano, *Storia degli ebrei in Italia* (Turin, 1963); lively evidence is offered in A. Segre, *Memorie di vita ebraica,* preface by R. De Felice (Rome, 1979), p. 464.
2. A. Momigliano, review of C. Roth, *Gli ebrei in Venezia,* in *Pagine ebraiche,* ed. S. Berti (Turin, 1987), pp. 237–239.
3. See Milano, *Storia,* pp. 342–351; S. Foa, *Gli ebrei nel Risorgimento italiano* (Assisi and Rome, 1978), p. 11ff.
4. See Milano, *Storia,* pp. 351–357; Foa, *Gli ebrei,* p. 28ff.; B. Di Porto, "Gli ebrei nel Risorgimento," *Nuova Antologia* 2136 (October–December 1980): 256–272; A. M. Canepa, "L'atteggiamento degli ebrei italiani davanti alla loro seconda emancipazione: Premesse e analisi," *Rassegna mensile di Israel* 43 (September 1977): 419–436.
5. Milano, *Storia,* p. 372; see also F. Gregorovius, "Il ghetto e gli ebrei a Roma (1853)," in *Passeggiate romane* (Rome, 1965), p. 51ff.; M. D'Azeglio, *Sulla emancipazione civile degli israeliti* (Florence, 1848), p. 57.
6. Milano, *Storia,* p. 371.
7. Milano, "Gli enti culturali ebraici in Italia nell'ultimo trentennio (1907–1937)," *Rassegna mensile di Israel* 4 (February–March 1938): 253–254.
8. Milano, *Storia,* p. 374; Hughes, *Prigionieri,* pp. 16–18, 24, 32; M. Toscano, "Gli ebrei in Italia dall'emancipazione alle persecuzioni," *Storia contemporanea* (October 1986): 907–908.
9. See, for example, L. Allegra, "La comunità ebraica di Torino attraverso gli archivi di famiglia," in *Ebrei a Torino: Ricerche per il centenario della sinagoga 1884–1984* (Turin, 1984), pp. 31–36; A. Momigliano, "Gli ebrei d'Italia," in the same volume, p. 138.
10. Milano, *Storia,* pp. 377–378; Toscano, "Gli ebrei," p. 911.
11. See A. M. Racheli, "Architettura e architetti delle sinagoghe italiane del periodo eclettico," in *Italia Judaica: Atti del I convegno internazionale* (Rome, 1983), pp. 483–497; "Il centenario del Tempio Israelitico di Firenze," in *Atti del Convegno* (Florence, 1985), p. 78.
12. See R. De Felice, *Storia degli ebrei italiani sotto il fascismo,* 4th ed. (Turin, 1988), p. 27ff.; see also A. Canepa, "Emancipazione, integrazione, e antisemitismo in Italia: Il caso Pasqualigo," *Comunità* 29 (June 1975): 166–203; idem, "Cattolici ed ebrei nell'Italia liberale (1870–1915)," *Comunità* 32 (April 1978): 43–109; idem, "L'immagine dell'ebreo nel folclore e nella letteratura del postrisorgimento," *Rassegna mensile di Israel* 44 (May–June 1978), pp. 383–399; G. Tortorelli, "L'affare Dreyfus e i socialisti italiani," *Società e storia* 9 (January–March 1986): 105–132.
13. A. Milano, *Storia,* p. 383ff.; G. Bedarida, *Ebrei d'Italia* (Leghorn, 1950), p. 324.
14. Milano, *Gli enti,* pp. 254–257; M. Toscano, "Fermenti culturali ed esperienze organizzative della gioventù ebraica italiana (1911–1925)," *Storia contemporanea* 13 (December 1982): 915–961.
15. M. Toscano, "Ebrei ed ebraismo nell'Italia della Grande Guerra: Note su una inchiesta del Comitato delle comunità israelitiche italiane del maggio 1917," in *Israel—Saggi sull'ebraismo italiano,* ed. F. Del Canuto (Rome, 1984), pp. 349–392; on *Il vessillo,* see A. Milano, "Un secolo di stampa periodica ebraica in Italia," *Rassegna mensile di Israel* 4 (April–June 1938), pp. 107–108.
16. See De Felice, *Storia degli ebrei,* pp. 88–91; Toscano, "Fermenti," pp. 949–959.
17. For a discussion of these themes, see De Felice, *Storia degli ebrei,* upon which this discussion is based, unless otherwise indicated. See also Michaelis, *Mussolini.*
18. De Felice, *Storia degli ebrei,* pp. 92–93.
19. See ibid., pp. 101–108; for more general information, see G. Fubini, *La condizione giuridica dell'ebraismo italiano,* intro. by A. C. Jemolo (Florence, 1974), pp. xxvii–129; interesting documentation of the organization of the communities and their relationships with the state, from the law of 1930 to the new agreement laid out in article 8 of the Constitution of the Republic, can be found in *Rassegna mensile di Israel* 51 (September–December 1985), 52 (January–April 1986), 53 (January–August 1987).
20. De Felice, *Storia degli ebrei,* p. 140ff.
21. For more on the relationships between fascism and Zionism, see ibid., pp. 132, 135–138, 165–166, 169ff.
22. Ibid., p. 237ff.; see also Michaelis, *Mussolini,* pp. 128–138.
23. See De Felice, *Storia degli ebrei,* esp. pp. 216, 309, 313–315, 319, 385–396.
24. Ibid., pp. 334–335, 367, 436–440.
25. Ibid., p. 402ff. and the ample bibliography given there.
26. In addition to ibid., chap. 8, see G. Mayda, *Ebrei sotto Salo* (Milan, 1978), p. 274; Centro di documentazione ebraica contemporanea, *Ebrei in Italia: Deportazione, resistenza* (Florence, 1975), p. 61.
27. M. Toscano, "Dall' 'antirisorgimento' al postfascismo: L'abrogazione delle leggi razziali e il reinserimento degli ebrei nella società italiana," in *L'abrogazione delle leggi razziali in Italia (1943–1987)* (Rome, 1988), pp. 21—65.
28. Milano, *Storia,* p. 409; Momigliano, *Gli ebrei d'Italia,* p. 141; S. Della Pergola, *Anatomia dell'ebraismo italiano,* (Assisi and Rome, 1976), pp. 54–55, 92.
29. For the most recent developments in Italian Judaism, see Della Pergola, *Anatomia*; L. Tas, *Storia degli ebrei italiani* (Rome, 1987), pp. 171–234; E. Campelli and R. Cipollini, *Contro il seme di Abramo* (Milan, 1984), p. 324; M. Toscano, "Tra identità culturale e partecipazione politica: Aspetti e momenti di vita ebraica italiana (1956–1976)," in *Annuario di studi ebraici 1985–1987,* vol. 11 (Rome, 1988), pp. 293–325.

Fig. 25. Curtain for the Torah Ark, Padua(?), c. 1550, Comunità Israelitica, Padua (cat. no. 141)

VIVIAN B. MANN

THE ARTS OF JEWISH ITALY

לזכרון הורי הורים האהובים הרב אהרן ראובן טשארני והרבנית מרים ז״צל

Working on *Art and Jewish Life in Italy* has been, since its inception, inspiring and challenging. From the first meeting in Rome with communal leaders in January 1985 to the mounting of the exhibition at the Jewish Museum in New York in September 1989, the road has been long, but rewarding.

At that meeting in Rome I, as curator, spent a lot of time listening to the concerns of leaders of the Unione Comunità Ebraiche Italiane. Although our ancestors had taken such different paths centuries ago, we were twenty Jews sitting in one room planning a project that would present a culture that is our common heritage (since Italian-Jewish thought and art have had profound influence on other Jewries) and yet was the particular patrimony of a small community whose history stretches over two millennia. What most impressed me was my colleagues' pride in being the oldest continuous Jewish community in Europe. We agreed that the proposed exhibition would have to tell a story that is two thousand years long and that it would begin in the Roman period. With the gracious cooperation of the Soprintendenza Archeologica di Roma, the Soprintendenza Archeologica di Ostia, the Vatican Museums and Library, the Library of the Jewish Theological Seminary of America, the Jewish communities of Bologna, Ferrara, Florence, Padua, Rome, Turin, and Venice, plus major public and private collections, we have been able to do just that.

The art of the first section demonstrates a major theme of *Gardens and Ghettos: The Art of Jewish Life in Italy,* the creative ability of a Jewish community to adapt the conventions and styles of a dominant culture to its own contents and purposes. This can be seen in sarcophagi such as the Front of a Sarcophagus with Menorah (fig. 72; cat. no. 13), and in the gold glass (see figs. 68–69; cat. nos. 34–36). Both are Roman art forms decorated with modeled figures arranged in centralized compositions. The sarcophagus also bears abundant imagery drawn from the Greco-Roman tradition: representations of the Four Seasons, Victories holding aloft a *clipeus* (shield), and Dionysiac putti trampling grapes, symbolic of belief in the afterlife. At the same time the Jews of ancient Rome incorporated into these and other works of art a language of symbols commonly held with Jews under imperial rule elsewhere: the menorah and other implements of the Temple in Jerusalem (which often expressed belief in a messianic age when that ancient center of Jewish life would be rebuilt); and the Torah ark, which represented both the Temple and the synagogue, the then relatively new center of Jewish communal and religious life. All of these symbols appear on the gold glasses, the tomb inscriptions, and the synagogue reliefs in this exhibition (cat. nos. 10, 19, 34, 36; figs. 56, 60, 68, 69).

A unique and interesting find is the late antique bronze amulet inscribed with the priestly blessing re-

corded in Numbers 6: 24–26 (cat. no. 24, fig. 26). The discovery in Jerusalem a decade ago of two similarly inscribed amulets that date to the seventh century B.C.E.[1] is a powerful reminder of the continuity of Jewish culture and of the common core of texts and traditions that link Jewish communities through time and space.

The amulet from Rome dates to the sixth century, a period that marked both the end of the Roman Empire and the dawn of the Middle Ages. Later expulsions and destructions led to the disappearance of nearly all the Jewish material culture dated to the centuries that immediately followed. Only scattered building fragments and tombstones remain[2] and, of course, the texts that lived on in later manuscript copies and printings. For example, *Megillat Aḥimaaz,* written around 1054, is a vivid chronicle of Jewish life in southern Italy from the ninth through the eleventh centuries and should be read for knowledge of a period of Italian-Jewish history that cannot be well represented in an exhibition.[3]

A new age in the artistic history of Italian Jewry began in the late thirteenth century, the era of the city-states. The earliest extant illuminated Hebrew texts date from this period,[4] as do new literary works.[5] Some of these, such as the *Maḥberot* of Immanuel ben Solomon of Rome (cat. no. 65), introduce novel genres into Hebrew literature, some based on Italian models. In this same period Jewish patrons, attracted by the dazzling achievements of Italian culture, began to commission works that blend contemporary artistic modes with Jewish content, just as the Jews of Roman times had done centuries before. Hebrew manuscripts

Fig. 26. (opposite, left) Amulet with Hebrew Inscription, Rome, sixth century, Museo Nazionale Romano, Rome (cat. no. 24)

Fig. 27. (opposite, right) Prayer Book, Italy, 1460–1470, The Library of The Jewish Theological Seminary of America, New York (cat. no. 38)

Fig. 28. (left) Book of Emblematic Vignettes Presented to Pope Clement XIV, Rome, 1769, Beinecke Library, Yale University, New Haven (cat. no. 56)

whose frontispieces bear the coats of arms of their owners embedded in lush foliate and animate borders and whose interior folios are enlivened by narrative scenes set in three-dimensional spaces inhabited by fully modeled figures moving gracefully and assuredly, are one example of this marriage of Italian style and Jewish content (cat. nos. 40, 43, 44, 46; figs. 7, 77, 80, 82–84).

Initially the art of Hebrew manuscript painting in Italy paralleled the development of the same art form in Iberia.[6] Because of the expulsions from Spain and Portugal in the late fifteenth century, however, the Iberian development was cut short, while in Italy manuscript illumination continued to flourish after the invention of printing and indeed never died out. Presentation volumes (cat. no. 56; fig. 28), record

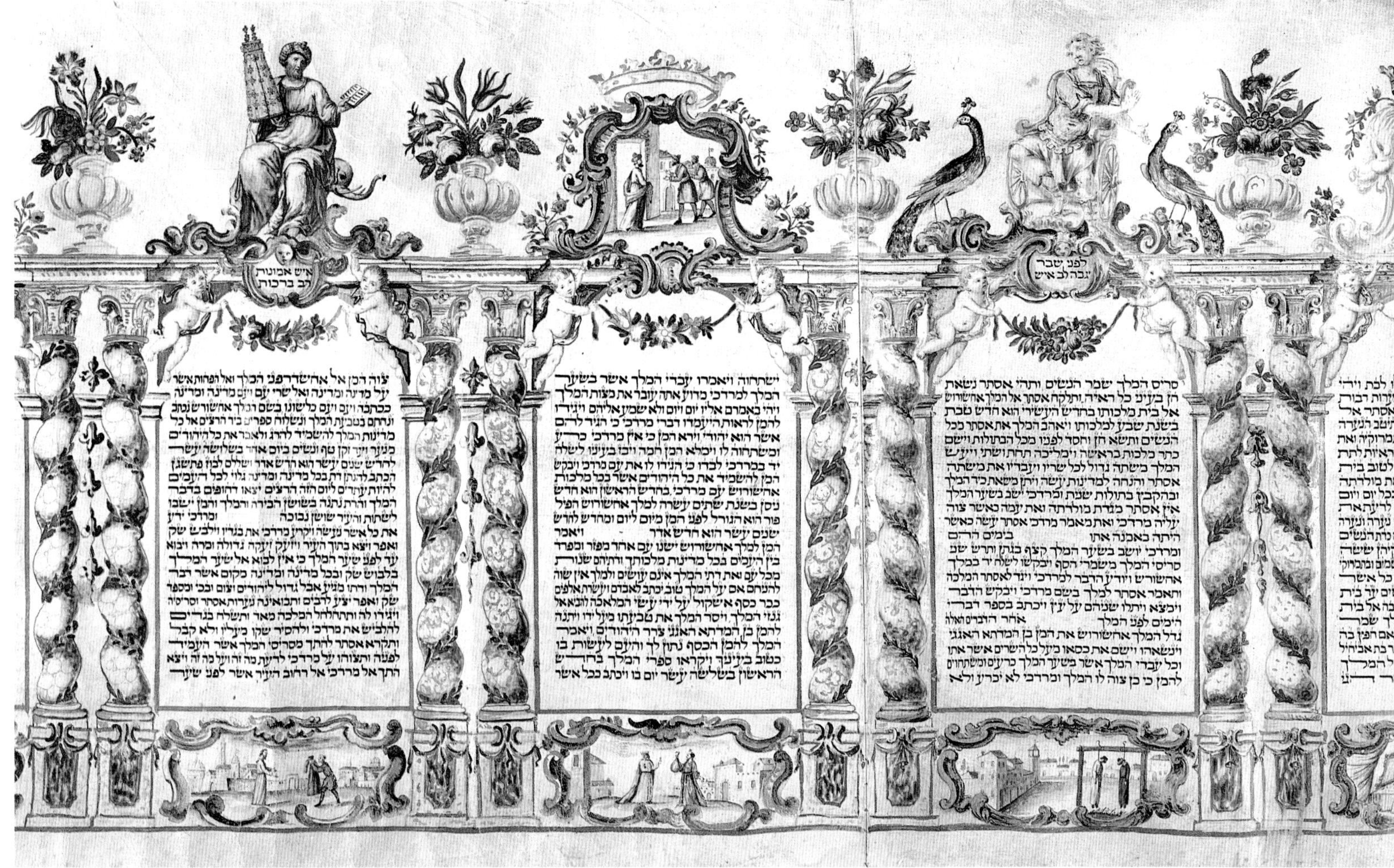

books of synagogues and societies (cat. no. 50), Esther scrolls (cat. nos. 54, 55, 57; fig. 29), omer books (cat. no. 58), and documents such as marriage contracts and medical diplomas (cat. nos. 53, 103–107, 110–111) are late examples of an art form patronized by Jews for centuries.[7]

We know much less about another area of Jewish artistic endeavor during the Renaissance, ceremonial art, as few works survive from the fourteenth and fifteenth centuries. Additional examples are known from literary descriptions, for example, the Torah ark curtain with coat of arms in relief embroidery which Hertz Wertheim of Padua placed in the synagogue despite the objections of Rabbi Judah Minz (1408–1506), the leading rabbinic authority of his time.[8] But although written sources inform us that the curtain bore the figure of a deer executed in relief by means of pearl embroidery, we know nothing of its supporting material or composition. We are therefore fortunate to have in the Jewish Museum's collection the Torah ark from Urbino that dates from about 1500 (cat. no. 114; fig. 30). Created as a type of "built-in" furniture that spread across one side of the synagogue,[9] the ark was modified over the centuries as the taste and fortunes of the Jewish community of Urbino changed.[10] Its original stained wood, fluted pilasters, and gilt frieze inscriptions (reminiscent of the late fifteenth-century *studioli* in both the Urbino and Gubbio palaces of the dukes of Urbino) were painted over in 1623. A new teal color, painted Tablets of the Law, and a rhymed

Fig. 29. (opposite) Scroll of Esther, northern Italy, late eighteenth century, Collection of Michael and Judy Steinhardt, New York (cat. no. 57)

Fig. 30. (above) Torah Ark from the Urbino Synagogue, Urbino, c. 1500 (repainted 1622–1623), The Jewish Museum, New York (cat. no. 114)

Fig. 31. (top) Frontispiece, *D'rashot ha-Torah* of Shem Tov ben Shem Tov, Padua, 1567, The Library of The Jewish Theological Seminary of America, New York (cat. no. 73)

Fig. 33. (above) Frontispiece, *Pesiktah Zutarta,* Venice, 1546, The Library of The Jewish Theological Seminary of America, New York (Heb. K)

verse inscription accorded well with baroque taste and the growing practice in the Jewish community of writing poetry for special occasions.[11] When the ark was first created, in the period when Urbino was a flourishing city-state under Montefeltre rule, biblical verses had been inscribed in the frieze.

Another work of ceremonial art of the era of the city-states, the ark curtain from the Padua Synagogue (cat. no. 141; fig. 25), exemplifies the mingling of three cultures on Italian soil (Jewish, Muslim, and Christian) and is an elegant reminder of the important historical role played by Italian Jewry in transmitting learning and culture from areas under Muslim domination to those under Christian hegemony.[12] The curtain is a knotted pile rug whose border is composed of Mamluk medallions, but whose center incorporates Ottoman motifs such as the tulip-shaped flowers on the branches of the menorah and on the brazier below.[13] At the same time the framing element, an arch, is drawn from the architectural vocabulary of Renaissance Italy and must have been based on the frontispiece of a printed book such as the *D'rashot haTorah* of Shem Tov ben Shem Tov, printed in Padua between 1520 and 1527 (cat. no. 73; fig. 31).[14]

The Padua rug is the earliest work to demonstrate the profound impact of the new art of printing on traditional forms of Jewish artistic expression.[15] The compositions of later Torah curtains show other influences from the art of the printed book. For example, the additive organization of the field as a series of discrete segments, as on a curtain dated 1643, recalls the decoration of early printed books by means of separate woodblocks (see cat. nos. 72, 143; fig. 32), while the spiral columns and framed vignettes of the Ottolenghi curtain repeat common motifs of baroque title pages (see cat. nos. 145, 68; figs. 42, 33).

Hebrew printing in Italy began around 1470, a scant eight years after the introduction of printing technology from Germany.[16] In 1512 the Gersonides family of Hebrew printers from northern Italy went to Prague, establishing the first Hebrew press north of the Alps,[17] while the Soncino family (who took their name from the northern Italian city in which they settled) expanded to southern Italy, Greece, Turkey, North Africa, and perhaps even to the Iberian peninsula.[18]

Another Renaissance art form eagerly embraced by Jews was the small bronze. In the fifteenth and sixteenth centuries Renaissance artists—some, like Donatello, of major status—created bronze statuettes as well as useful works of the decorative arts. These pieces

Fig. 32. Curtain for the Torah Ark, Italy, 1643–1644, The Jewish Museum, New York (cat. no. 143)

were composed of motifs adapted from classical art, such as putti, wreaths, mythical beings (centaurs and sirens), and the like, and of others drawn from the "fine" arts of sculpture and painting, such as Judith with the Head of Holofernes.[19] Of all the Renaissance bronzes that survive, the most easily attributable to Jewish ownership and patronage are the Hanukkah lamps, whose arrangement of eight lights in a single row is characteristically Jewish.[20] Their overall form and decoration, however, are not specific (cat. nos. 177–180; figs. 34,38,180). Many of the motifs found on Renaissance door knockers, mortars, and bells appear on the backplates of bronze Hanukkah lamps, including coats of arms.[21] The large number of these lamps that survive testifies to the popularity of this medium among Italian Jews of the city-state and ghetto periods (sixteenth to nineteenth centuries) and to the prestige accorded bronzes as an art form in Renaissance Italy.[22]

Two other types of Renaissance bronze can definitely be associated with Jewish ownership, and both are secular: the medal and the mortar. During the era of the city-states men and women of culture sought to re-create ancient art forms, among them the antique coins struck in honor of Roman emperors. Four medals of Jewish subjects are known; examples of three are included here (cat. nos. 167–169; figs. 35–36). The

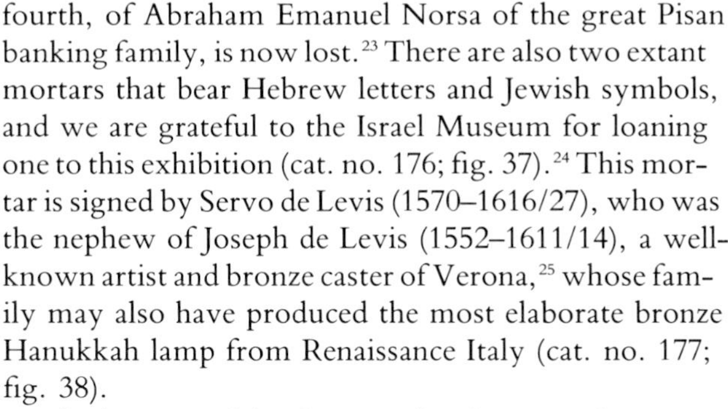

fourth, of Abraham Emanuel Norsa of the great Pisan banking family, is now lost.[23] There are also two extant mortars that bear Hebrew letters and Jewish symbols, and we are grateful to the Israel Museum for loaning one to this exhibition (cat. no. 176; fig. 37).[24] This mortar is signed by Servo de Levis (1570–1616/27), who was the nephew of Joseph de Levis (1552–1611/14), a well-known artist and bronze caster of Verona,[25] whose family may also have produced the most elaborate bronze Hanukkah lamp from Renaissance Italy (cat. no. 177; fig. 38).

The history of the de Levis family raises the issue of Jews functioning as artists in Italy during the eras of the city-states and the ghettos. Joseph was probably born a Jew and appears to have remained one,[26] which did not prevent his receiving numerous church commissions.[27] His children, however, were all baptized, as were his nephews (except for Servo).[28] The story of the younger de Levis is paralleled by those of other Jewish artists and artisans active before the granting of civil rights in the nineteenth century. Guglielmo Ebreo, one of the most influential dance masters of the fifteenth century and the author of seven of the nine surviving Renaissance treatises on the dance (in which he established the theoretical basis of dance as an art form), whose career flourished at the courts of Ferrara, Pesaro, Naples, and other ducal capitals, ended his life as Gugli-

Fig. 34. (opposite, right) Ḥanukkah Lamp, Italy, sixteenth century, Israel Museum, Jerusalem (cat. no. 172)

Fig. 35. (opposite, left, top) Medal of Elijah de Latas and His Mother, Rica (obverse), Rome, 1552, The Jewish Museum, New York (cat. no. 168)

Fig. 36. (opposite, left, bottom) Medal of Elijah de Latas and His Mother, Rica (reverse), Rome, 1552, The Jewish Museum, New York (cat. no. 168)

Fig. 37. (above) Servo de Levis, Mortar with Hebrew Inscription, Verona, early seventeenth century, Israel Museum, Jerusalem (cat. no. 176)

Fig. 38. (above, left) Workshop of Joseph de Levis(?), Ḥanukkah Lamp with Judith Beheading Holofernes, Italy, late sixteenth to early seventeenth century, Sir Isaac and Lady Edith Wolfson, Hechal Shlomo, Jerusalem (cat. no. 177)

ſto. diſſoluto. & corrotto eſſer proſumptu
oſi & temerari oltra il douere. et queſti
ſon quegli che di arte dignissima la fano
ritornar uile & diſhoneſta, magiormente
non eſſendo bene doctrinati & acoſtuma
ti & honeſti nel parlare & ſobrij nellor
mangiar & bere, per che la diſſolutio
ne & ebrieta ſonno deſtruttrici dogni
uirtu. Pero dato che haueſſero tutte le
degne parti predicte & non obſeruaſſe
ro queſto nuouo precepto nongli uarre
bono nulla. Et coſi facendo ſerano ama
ti. honorati. & reueriti in ogni parte.
et queſto baſti. Segue adoncha La
praticha.,

Fig. 39. Guglielmo Ebreo da Pesaro, *De pratica seu arte tripudii vulgare opusculum,* Italy, 1463, Bibliothèque National, Paris (F. ital. 973, f. 21v.)

elmo de Pesaro, a Catholic (see cat. no. 38 and fig. 39).[29] Santo Seraphin (1699–1748), who made violins for both Christian and Jewish patrons in Venice and was considered one of the finest violin makers of his generation, was originally a Jew from Udine (cat. no. 117; fig. 40).[30]

While in many principalities baptism was perceived as the price of success,[31] in other locales artists flourished who remained faithful to Judaism.[32] Individual decisions were no doubt influenced by the relative tolerance of the local community.[33] Documentary records of painters' guilds in Perugia and of silversmiths in Mantua and Turin, as well as records of court commissions from several cities, mention Jewish artists.[34] Unfortunately none of their works survives. In the field of manuscript illumination, where one would most likely expect Jewish participation, only a few artists can be identified, such as Joel ben Simeon and Abraham Farissol, who were both active in the fifteenth century, and they were not necessarily the most skilled (see cat. nos. 37, 46, 48, 49; figs. 77–81).[35] The talented engraver Salom d'Italia, born to a family of printers in Mantua in 1619, created most of his oeuvre in Amsterdam.[36]

It is obvious from the works of art that survive that Jews patronized both Jewish and Christian artists during the Renaissance and baroque periods, which partly explains Jewish acculturation to the art of the majority. One of the Renaissance medals, that of Gracia Nasi the younger (cat. no. 169), dated 1558, was created and signed by Pastorino di Pastorini (c. 1508–1592), a well-known Ferrarese medalist. Silver ceremonial objects dating from the late seventeenth century on often bear the hallmarks of Christian silversmiths.[37] Other, anonymous silver works should probably be attributed to Jewish artists, whose careers are known only from archival records.[38]

Some of the synagogue and home textiles for ceremonial use were signed and dated by Jewish women, for example, the early Torah binder created by Honorata Foa in 1582–1583 (cat. no. 124; fig. 108). The important role of women in the creation of textiles for the synagogue is signaled in the liturgy of the Italian rite. Among those blessed for sustaining the congregation are "every daughter of Israel who makes a mantle or cover in honor of the Torah." Simḥah Meshullami and Leah Ottolenghi signed the extraordinary Torah curtains bearing representations of Judaism's holiest sites that they created in 1680–1681 and 1698–1699, respectively (cat. nos. 144–145; figs. 41–42). Meshullami's work is modeled on a curtain still in Venice that was

Fig. 40. Sanctus Seraphin, Violin with Hebrew Inscription, Venice, c. 1725–1744, The Jewish Museum, New York (cat. no. 117)

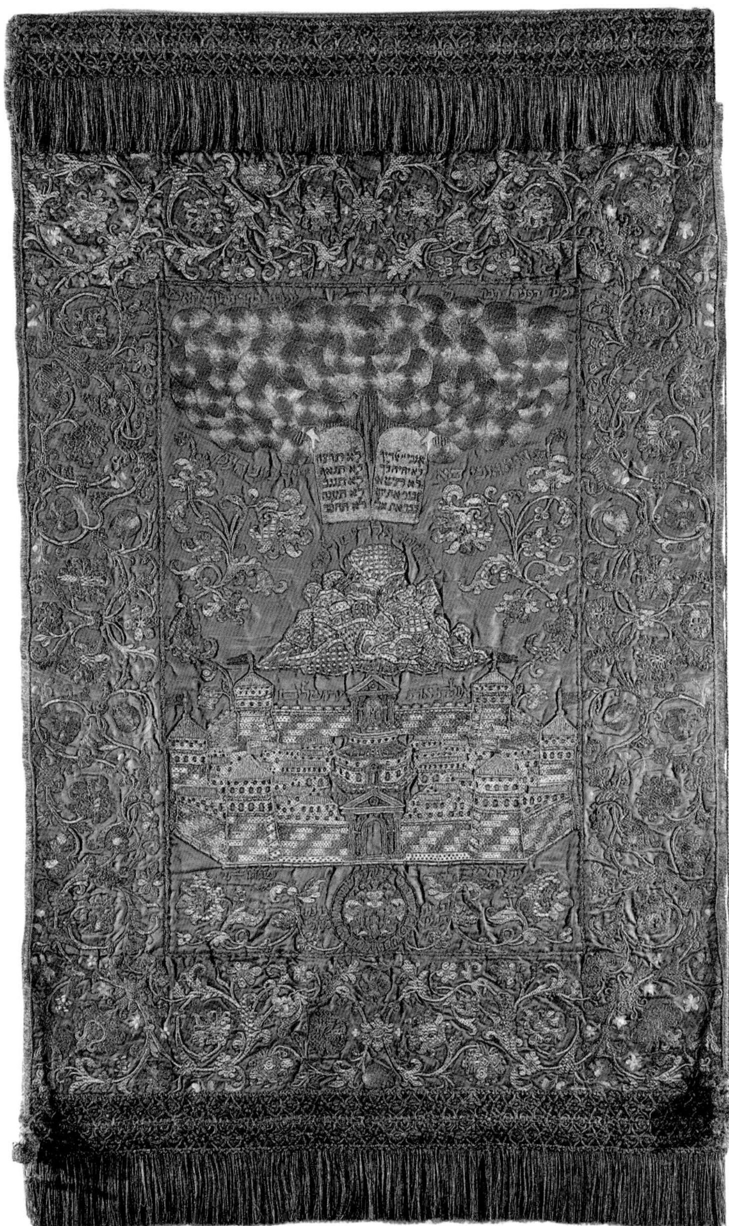

Fig. 41. (right) Simḥah, wife of Menaḥem Levi Meshullami, Curtain for the Torah Ark, Venice, 1680–1681, The Jewish Museum, New York (cat. no. 144)

Fig. 42. (opposite) Leah, wife of Ḥananiah Ottolenghi, Curtain for the Torah Ark, Venice, 1698–1699, The Jewish Museum, New York (cat. no. 145)

created by Stella Perugia in 1672, an achievement mentioned on the latter's tombstone in the Lido cemetery.[39] The most frequently signed textiles are the Torah binders. They were sometimes dedicated in honor of male relatives, for example, a beautiful lace binder from Padua dated 1630 whose inscription mentions the maker's husband, her father, and father-in-law (cat. no. 125; fig. 110). Far more numerous are the hundreds, if not thousands, of textiles made for synagogue and home whose authorship is unknown.

Fig. 43. (above) Torah Shield with Musical Insignia, Venice(?), 1740–1741, Comunità Israelitica, Padua (cat. no. 212)

Fig. 44. (opposite) Leonora Colorni, Torah Binder with Shofrot and Trumpets, Italy, 1692–1693, National Museum of American History, Washington, D.C. (cat. no. 129)

Another outstanding characteristic of Italian Judaica of the ghetto era is its incorporation of musical symbols, testimony to the importance of music in Italian-Jewish life. Many Jews were well-known music and dance masters during the Renaissance, with the result that the church repeatedly issued injunctions against their employment by Christians.[40] Despite these bans Jews gained prominence in music, dance, and drama, especially in Mantua, where court performances by Jewish troupes were scheduled around Sabbaths and holidays.[41]

With the establishment of ghettos in Italian cities during the sixteenth century and the subsequent isolation of their inhabitants, Jewish interest in music turned inward.[42] As Israel Adler has stated, "The Jewish musician, whose flourishing activity of the Renaissance period came to a standstill because of segregation, being prevented from exercising his art in gentile society, from that time on turned toward the synagogue."[43] As a result, by the end of the sixteenth century or, at the latest, the beginning of the seventeenth century, Jewish musicians were creating art music for the synagogue.

The most famous Jewish musician in all of Italy was Salamon de' Rossi, a contemporary of Monteverdi and the writer of numerous secular madrigals.[44] In 1623 he published the *Canto Ha-Shirim Asher li-Shelomo,*[45] the first attempt to adapt musical notation to a Hebrew text (cat. no. 78). This work was published in Venice in 1623, edited by Leone Modena (1571–1648), rabbi of the Venetian community, who also wrote an introduction to the volume in which he justified the writing of annotated music for the synagogue.[46] Modena's musical activities went further than his association with Rossi; he served as *maestro di capella* for a synagogue choir in Ferrara early in the seventeenth century and later for the musical academy formed in the Venetian ghetto by Mantuan musicians and performers.[47] Both groups performed in the synagogue on Sabbaths and holidays as well as on special occasions such as weddings.

The significance of music in the cultural life of Italian Jewry is reflected in the iconography of ceremonial objects such as the shields from Padua, the crown from Venice, and the Torah binder of 1693 (cat nos. 212, 209, 129; figs. 43, 44). It is also reflected in the decoration of synagogues,[48] and in the portrait of Isaac Hayyim de Medina of Livorno, who edited a book

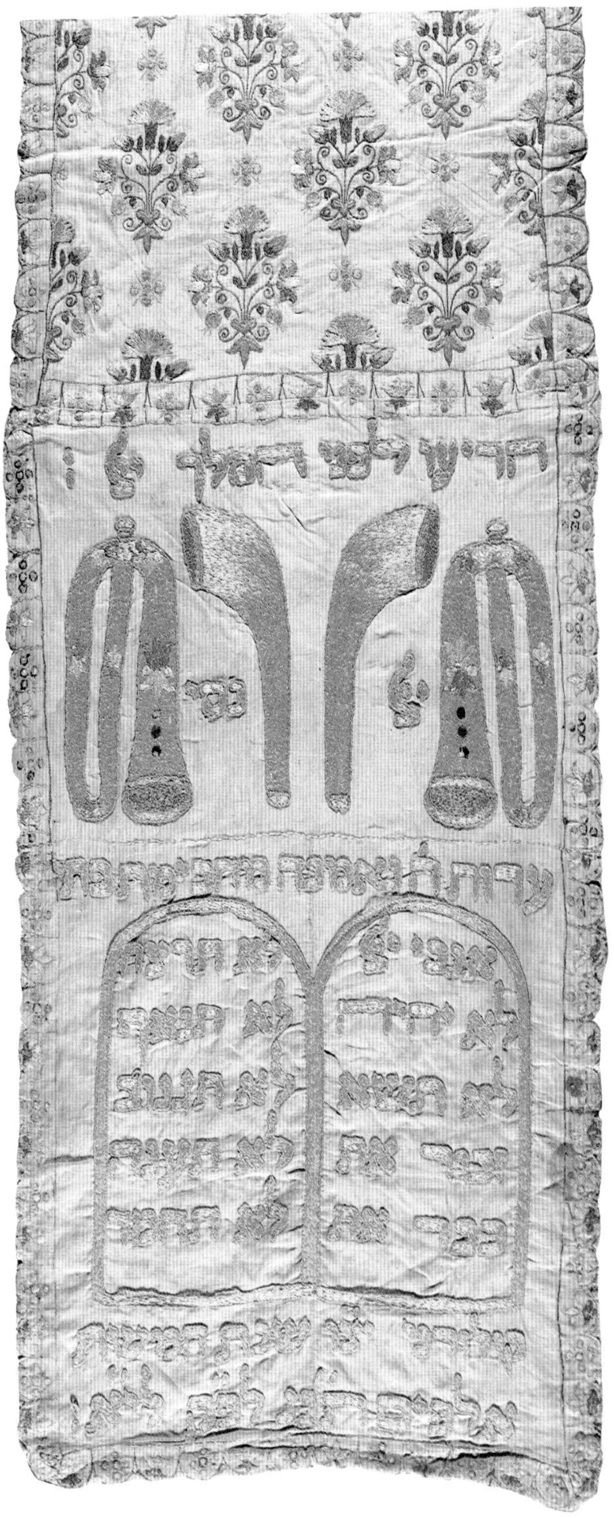

Fig. 45. (above) Anonymous, *Isaac Ḥayyim di Medina,* Italy, second half of the eighteenth century, Comunità Israelitica, Livorno (cat. no. 248)

Fig. 46. (below) Moise Segre, Pair of Crown-Form Torah Finials, Turin, 1828, Comunità Israelitica, Turin (cat. no. 203)

of songs for the synagogue in 1748 (cat. no. 248; fig. 45).[49] Isaac Hayyim chose to be represented with a recorder and viol, a sheet of music spread before him, in the manner of famous composers such as Vivaldi.[50]

Another Mantuan Jew, Leone de Sommi Portaleone, was a playwright who wrote secular plays in Italian as well as the first Hebrew drama, *Ẓaḥut Bediḥuta de-Kiddushin* (An Eloquent Marriage Farce), in 1557 and was the author of a pioneering work on the theater and stagecraft, the *Dialoghi in materia di rappresentazione sceniche* (c. 1560).[51] De Sommi's Jewish colleagues were actors who formed their own theatrical troupe; other Mantuan Jews were performing musicians and singers at court. After the plundering of their native city by the Germans in 1628, many of these creative artists settled in the Venetian ghetto and participated in theatrical presentations there.[52]

The flight of artists previously active at court to the Venetian ghetto is emblematic of the turning inward of artistic impulses that resulted from the repression of the Counter-Reformation period. Forced residence in the ghettos of Italy did not, however, mean an end to acculturation. Leone Modena's writings, for example, his *Riti hebraica* (cat. no. 79) and his autobiography, attest to a profound knowledge of contemporary cultural life.[53] Still the restrictions of this era could not help but curtail the activities and development of Jewish artists. Only with the fall of the ghettos in the Napoleonic era could Jewish artists flourish and gain prominence.

The beginnings of widespread Jewish activity in the visual arts were modest and centered in Piedmont, birthplace of the modern Italian state, where ideas of civic equality first took hold. A group of Jewish silversmiths active in and around Turin in the eighteenth and nineteenth centuries represent the first identifiable community of Jewish artists.[54] Familial relationships between artists such as Moise and Benaje Segre no doubt played a part in the sharing of styles and motifs (compare, for example, cat. nos. 202–203; fig. 46). By the mid-nineteenth century Jewish painters of stature had emerged in the same region. Vito D'Ancona (fig. 47) and Serafino De Tivoli were part of a group called the Macchiaioli, whose members fought for the unification of Italy and whose works emphasize a deep attachment to the land.[55]

With the passage of time and the spread of emancipation and the libertarian ideals of a unified Italy, Jewish artists emerged in other centers: Livorno, Florence, Trieste, and Rome. They joined movements such as the

Fig. 47. Vito D'Ancona, *Donna dormiente* (Sleeping Woman), c. 1870s, Israel Museum, Jerusalem (cat. no. 261)

Novecento and Scuola Romana, in which they worked, for the most part, alongside Christian artists and rarely displayed any Jewish concerns. Only the shock of the Racial Laws of 1938 forced all these artists to confront their origins and to examine their relationship to the Jewish community of Italy, whose millennia-long history and receptivity to outside influences had made their previous assimilation possible.

Their dilemma was intensified by the Holocaust. Although the war years were relatively kind to Italian Jewry in comparison with other communities, no Italian Jew escaped their impact.[56] For some, such as the writer Primo Levi, Holocaust experiences inspired brilliant creativity. But in other areas of artistic endeavor, outstanding achievements seem to belong to the past. The loss of 15 percent of the Jewish population of Italy to death and emigration, together with the secularization of modern life and the prior existence of an immense artistic patrimony from past generations, decreased the need for new ceremonial objects. Other areas of Jewish cultural life have seen a resurgence of activity in the last two decades, however; perhaps the next decades will see its further extension into the realm of the visual arts.[57]

Notes

1. On the Jerusalem amulets, the oldest inscribed biblical texts in existence, see Israel Museum, *Ketef Hinnom: A Treasure Facing Jerusalem Walls,* exh. cat. (Jerusalem, 1986), pp. 29–30 (English text), ills. pp. 35–36 (Hebrew text).
2. On material remains in Southern Italy, see C. Colafemmina, "Archeologia ed epigrafia ebraica nell'Italia meridionale," in *Italia Judaica: Atti del I convegno internazionale* (Rome, 1983), pp. 199–210.
3. An English translation by M. Salzman has been published (*The Chronicle of Ahimaaz,* Columbia University Oriental Studies, no. 18 [New York, 1924]). On the significance of the text, see R. Bonfil, "Tra due mondi: Prospettiva di recerca sulla storia culturale degli ebrei dell'Italia meridionale nell'alto medioevo," *Italia Judaica,* pp. 135–157. See also David Ruderman's essay above.
4. On the reasons for the appearance of this art form among Jews in the late thirteenth century, see E. M. Cohen, "The Decoration of Medieval Hebrew Manuscripts," in *A Sign and a Witness: Two Thousand Years of Hebrew Books and Illuminated Manuscripts,* ed. L. S. Gold (New York and Oxford, 1988), p. 47.
5. See David Ruderman's essay above and Allen Mandelbaum's essay below.
6. For brief overviews of the history of Hebrew manuscript illumination in Italy, see J. Gutmann, *Hebrew Manuscript Painting* (New York, 1978), pp. 27–31; B. Narkiss, *Hebrew Illuminated Manuscripts,* 3d ed. (Jerusalem, 1978), pp. 36–39; U. and K. Schubert, *Judische Buchkunst,* pt. 1 (Graz, 1983), p. 96ff. See also L. M. Ottolenghi, "Miniature ebraiche italiane," in *Italia Judaica,* pp. 211–227.
7. There is a dispute in the scholarly literature as to the date of the first illuminated Hebrew manuscripts. According to one opinion, the frescoes of the Dura Europos Synagogue, which predate the destruction of that city in 256 C.E., attest to the existence of a tradition of manuscript illumination in antiquity. (E.g., G. Sed-Rajna, *The Hebrew Bible in Medieval Illuminated Manuscripts* [New York, 1987], p. 8.) J. Gutmann, however, disputes this assertion (*Hebrew Manuscript Painting,* p. 10.) The earliest extant illuminated Hebrew codex dates to 895 and was written and decorated in Tiberius (Gutmann, *Hebrew Manuscript Painting,* fig. VI).
8. The dispute over the curtain is recorded in J. Caro, *Shealot u-teshubot Evkat Rokhel* (Jerusalem, 1960), no. 65 (Hebrew).
9. For the plan of the synagogue and the position of the ark, see U. Nahon and G. Sarfatti, eds., *Sefer Ha-Maftir di Urbino: Manoscritto ebraico del 1704* (Jerusalem, 1964) (Italian and Hebrew).
10. For a complete discussion of the transformation of the ark, see V. B. Mann, "The Recovery of a Known Work," *Jewish Art,* 12–13 (1986–1987), pp. 269–278.
11. On this practice, see Dan Pagis, *Change and Tradition in the Secular Poetry: Spain and Italy* (Jerusalem, 1976), p. 256ff. (Hebrew).
12. See David Ruderman's essay above.
13. This curtain has only become widely known in recent scholarly literature. See A. Boralevi, "Un tappeto ebraico italo-egiziano," *Critica d'arte,* 49 no. 2 (1984): 42ff.; idem., "Three Egyptian Carpets in Italy," *Oriental Carpet and Textile Studies,* vol. 2, *Carpets of the Mediterranean Countries* (London, 1986), pp. 211–220; W. B. Denny, "The Origin and Development of Ottoman Court Carpets," *Oriental Carpet and Textile Studies,* vol. 2, p. 255; V. B. Mann, "Jewish-Muslim Acculturation in the Ottoman Empire: The Evidence of Ceremonial Art," *Proceedings of the Brandeis Conference on the Jews of the Ottoman Empire* (in press).
14. This comparison was first made in B. Yaniv, "Sixteenth–Eighteenth Century Bohemian and Moravian Parochot with an Architectural Motif" (Ph.D. diss., Hebrew University, 1987), vol. 1, p. 96 (Hebrew).
15. On the general influence of printing on art history, see E. L. Eisenstein, *The Printing Press as an Agent of Change* (London, New York, and Melbourne, 1979), p. 83ff. On its influence on Jewish ceremonial art, see R. Wischnitzer-Bernstein, "Von der Holbeinbibel zur Amsterdamer Haggadah," *Monatsschrift für Geschichte und Wissenschaft des Judentums* 7 (1931): 269–286; V. B. Mann, "Community Life," in *The Precious Legacy: Judaic Treasures from the Czechoslovak State Collections,* ed. D. Altshuler (New York and Washington, 1983), pp. 150–152; idem, "Forging Judaica—The Case of the Italian Majolica Seder Plates," *Studies in Contemporary Jewry* 6 (in press).
16. On early Hebrew printing in Italy, see M. Glatzer, "Early Hebrew Printing," in *A Sign and a Witness,* pp. 80–91. On later printing, see M. N. Rosenfeld, "The Development of Hebrew Printing in the Sixteenth and Seventeenth Centuries," in *A Sign and a Witness,* p. 92; D. W. Amram, *The Makers of Hebrew Books in Italy* (Philadelphia, 1909; reprint, London, 1963).
17. Mann, "Community Life," p. 152, nos. 277–278, figs. 57–58, 135, 161; Rosenfeld, "The Development of Hebrew Printing," p. 93.
18. Glatzer, "Early Hebrew Printing," pp. 86, 89.
19. For examples, see Kunstgewerbemuseum Berlin, *Bronzen und Plaketten vom ausgehenden 15. Jahrhundert bis zur Mitte des 17. Jahrhunderts: Katalog des Kunstgewerbemuseums Berlin,* vol. 3, ed. K. Pechstein (Berlin, 1968), nos. 52–121.

20. For a brief summary in English of the laws relating to Hanukkah lamps, see S. Ganzfried, *Code of Jewish Law,* trans. H. Golden (New York, 1963), 139: 5–10.
21. See Israel Museum, *The Joseph Stieglitz Collection: Masterpieces of Jewish Art,* exh. cat., ed. C. Benjamin (Jerusalem, 1987), nos. 121–123; M. Narkiss, *The Hanukkah Lamp* (Jerusalem, 1939), pl. 12, nos. 34–35.
22. In contrast to Italian-Jewish practice, the rabbis of Germany stressed the importance of silver, a reflection of the premium placed on that material in Frankfurt, Nuremberg, Berlin, and other centers of Jewish life. In his *Yosef 'Ometz,* a book on Jewish customs, Rabbi Joseph Juspa Hahn Nordlingen (c. 1570–1637) recommends having a silver Hanukkah lamp or, at the very least, a lamp incorporating one silver light ([Frankfurt, 1723], fol. 1322).
23. The Norsa medal was created in 1557 (A. Milano, *Storia degli ebrei in Italia* [Turin, 1963], fig. 55).
24. The second mortar with Hebrew inscription is in a private collection.
25. On the history and activity of the de Levis family, see L. Franzoni, ed., *Fonditori di campane a Verona dal XI al XX secolo* (Verona, 1979), pp. 10–11, 71ff. For an overview of de Levis's entire oeuvre, see C. Avery, "Giuseppe de Levis of Verona, Bronze Founder and Sculptor," in *Studies in European Sculpture* (London, 1981), pp. 45–78.

    I want to express my appreciation to Charles Avery, who first broached the idea of an exhibition of de Levis bronzes at the Jewish Museum. The discussion here reflects the many informative conversations we have had on the topic.
26. For information on the de Levis family drawn from archival records, see L. Rognino, "I Levi," in *Fonditori di campane a Verona,* p. 71ff. Rognino presents archival evidence concerning the baptism of Joseph's sons and other relatives, but not for Joseph himself, nor for Servo, who created the mortar on exhibition (p. 75, nos. 3, 17).

    Another indication of Joseph's religion is his name. He signed his works either Joseph de Levis or Josepho di Levi, but never Giuseppe. The latter was considered by Italian Jews to be a Christian reference to Jesus' father (V. Colorni, "La correspondenza fra nomi ebraici e nomi locali nella prassi dell'ebraismo italiano," in *Italia Judaica,* p. 72; C. Roth, *The Jews in the Renaissance* [Philadelphia, 1959], p. 198).

    In a recent publication C. Benjamin attempted to date the Mortar with Hebrew Inscription by Servo (cat. no. 176) to the late fifteenth century, but her interpretation of the Hebrew letters as a chronogram for the year 1480 is contradicted by both the stylistic and iconographic evidence (Israel Museum, *The Stieglitz Collection,* p. 279).
27. For a listing of known works by Joseph de Levis, see Avery, "Giuseppe de Levis."
28. Rognino cites baptismal records for Joseph's sons and two of his nephews, but not for Servo, the oldest son of Joseph's brother Santo ("I Levi," p. 75, nn. 3, 17).
29. On the career of Guglielmo, see Comune di Pesaro, *Mesura et arte del danzare: Guglielmo Ebreo de Pesaro e la danza nelle corti italiane del XV secolo,* exh. cat. (Pesaro, 1987). I want to acknowledge the many stimulating discussions I have had with Barbara Sparti of Rome, who is writing a book on Guglielmo's life and career.
30. On Seraphin, see W. H. Hill, *The Violin-Makers of the Guarneri Family (1626–1762): Their Life and Work* (London, 1965), pp. 140–141; W. Henley, *Universal Dictionary of Violin and Bow Makers* (Brighton, 1973), p. 1057.
31. Many more examples of apostate Jewish artists could be given. See C. Roth, "Jewish Art and Artists before Emancipation," in *Jewish Art: An Illustrated History,* ed. B. Narkiss (Greenwich, Conn., 1971), pp. 178–180. Roth includes in this discussion Ercole dei Fedeli (p. 178), who was originally known as Salomon da Seso Ebreo (active 1487–1518), a sword maker and goldsmith at the court of Ferrara (see C. Yriarte, *Autour des Borgia* [Paris, 1891], p. 302). Recent scholarship questions the definitive attribution of any known works to this documented artist (C. Blair, "Cesare Borgia's Sword-Scabbard," *Victoria and Albert Museum Bulletin* 2, no. 4 [1966]: 125–136). I want to thank Stuart W. Phyrr of the Arms and Armor Department of the Metropolitan Museum of Art for this reference.

    Roth also discusses families of majolica makers in northern Italy, supposedly active during the Renaissance. On the making of these plates in the late nineteenth century, see my forthcoming article, "Forging Judaica."
32. F. Landsberger, "Jewish Artists before the Period of Emancipation," *Hebrew Union College Annual* 16 (1941): 353ff.
33. J. Newman notes that none of the Jewish musicians of Mantua converted to Catholicism, while the leading musicians at Pope Leo X's court were apostates. The behavior of the Mantuan musicians may have been partly due to the relatively high level of religious tolerance at the Gonzaga court ("The Madrigals of Salamon de' Rossi" [Ph.D. diss., Columbia University, 1962], p. 9).

34. For example, U. Gnoli, in his *Pittori e miniatori nell'Umbria* (Spoleto, 1923), notes an "Angelo di Elia pittore ebreo in Perugia," who paid dues to the *arte dei pittori,* the painter's guild, and his contemporary Giacobbe di Vitale, who paid dues to the guild in 1507 and 1508 (pp. 29, 130).

    For Jewish silversmiths active in Piedmont prior to their admission to the guild in the early eighteenth century, see P. Gaglia, "Gli argenti," in *Ebrei a Torino* (Turin, 1984), p. 146. See also S. Simonsohn, *History of the Jews in the Duchy of Mantua* (Jerusalem, 1983), pp. 263, 274.

    For musicians, see I. Adler, "The Rise of Art Music in the Italian Ghetto," in *Jewish Medieval and Renaissance Studies,* ed. Alexander Altmann (Cambridge, Mass., 1967), p. 341; Newman, "Madrigals of Salamon de' Rossi," p. 6ff.
35. On Joel ben Simeon, see M. Fooner, "Joel ben Simeon, Illuminator of Hebrew Manuscripts in the Fifteenth Century," *Jewish Quarterly Review* 27 (1937): 217–232; F. Landsberger, "The Washington Haggadah and Its Illuminator," *Hebrew Union College Annual* 21 (1948): 73–103; J. Gutmann, "Thirteen Manuscripts in Search of an Author: Joel ben Simeon, Fifteenth Century Scribe-Artist," *Studies in Bibliography and Booklore* 9 (1970): 76–95; M. Beit Arie, "Joel Ben Simeon's Manuscripts: A Codicologer's View," *Journal of Jewish Art* 3–4 (1977): 25–39; S. Edmunds, "The Place of the London *Haggadah* in the Work of Joel ben Simeon," *Journal of Jewish Art* 7 (1980): 25–34.

    On Farissol as an artist, see E. M. Cohen, "The Illustrations in Abraham Farissol's Haggadah of 1515," *Jewish Art,* 12–13 (1986–1987): 89–95.
36. M. Narkiss, "The Oeuvre of the Jewish Engraver Salom ben . . . Mordecai Italia," *Tarbiz,* 25 (1956): 441ff.; 26 (1957): 87ff.; The Jewish Museum, *Danzig 1939: Treasures of a Destroyed Community,* exh. cat. (New York, 1980), no. 48; E. Bilski, "Scroll of Esther . . . ," in Jewish Museum, *Treasures of the Jewish Museum,* exh. cat., ed. Norman L. Kleeblatt and Vivian B. Mann (New York, 1986), pp. 64–65.

    Recently, S. Simonsohn published documentary evidence that d'Italia returned to Mantua by 1664 (*History of the Jews,* p. 654), but it is not known if he produced any works there.
37. See essay by Dora Liscia Bemporad below.
38. Roth makes this point and cites some of the documentary evidence (*Jews in the Renaissance,* pp. 195–197).
39. A. A. Piattelli, "Un arazzo veneziano del XVII secolo," *Rassegna mensile di Israel,* 36 (1970): 315–322. D. Cassuto, "A Venetian Paroḳet and Its Design Origins," *Jewish Art,* 14 (1988), p. 41.
40. Roth, *Jews in the Renaissance,* pp. 275–276.
41. Simonsohn, *History of the Jews,* p. 661, n. 293; pp. 662, 666.
42. Adler, "Rise of Art Music," esp. pp. 362–364; idem, "La pénétration de la musique savante dans les synagogues italiennes au XVIIe siecle: Le cas particulier de Venise," *Gli ebrei e Venezia, secoli XIV–XVIII: Atti del convegno,* ed. G. Cozzi (Milan, 1987), p. 527ff.
43. Adler, "Rise of Art Music," p. 364.
44. On Rossi's madrigals, see Newman, "Madrigals of Salamon de' Rossi." For a brief overview of his career, see Simonsohn, *History of the Jews,* pp. 671–675.
45. The title page reads in translation "The Songs of Solomon, Psalms and Songs of praise musically arranged for three, four, five, six, seven, eight voices by Solomon de' Rossi dwelling in the holy congregation of Mantua to give thanks to the Lord and to sing for His exalted name in every holy matter, new in the Land" (Simonsohn, *History of the Jews,* p. 673).
46. See Adler, "Rise of Art Music," for an analysis of all known texts related to the performance of art music in Italian synagogues in the late sixteenth and seventeenth centuries, including Modena's introduction to Rossi's *Canto.*
47. Newman, "Madrigals of Salamon de' Rossi," p. 21ff.; Roth, *Jews in the Renaissance,* pp. 301–303.
48. The interior of the Scuola Tedesca in Ferrara is decorated with musical emblems, and musical symbols once adorned the exterior of the Cinque Scuole in Rome and the interior of Il Tempio in the same building. On the Roman synagogues, see J. Pinkerfeld, *The Synagogues of Italy: Their Architectural Development since the Renaissance* (Jerusalem, 1954), pp. 17–19, figs. 19, 20 (Hebrew).
49. *The Jewish Encyclopedia* (New York and London, 1906), vol. 8, p. 424.
50. Cf. F. M. La Cave, "Effigies Antonii Vivaldi," in *Portraits of Composers and Musicians in Prints and Drawings: Collection Music Department Haags Gemeentmuseum* (The Hague, n.d.) (microfiche).
51. Simonsohn, *History of the Jews,* pp. 656–669.
52. According to C. Roth, Hebrew drama was presented in the ghetto of Venice as early as 1531 (*Venice* [Philadelphia, 1930], pp. 199–200).
53. See Mark Cohen, ed. and trans., *The Autobiography of a Seventeenth Century Venetian Rabbi: Leon Modena's "Life of Judah"* (Princeton, 1988), especially pp. 5–6.
54. Gaglia, "Gli argenti," p. 117ff.
55. See the essay by Emily Braun below.
56. See S. Zucotti, *The Italians and the Holocaust* (New York, 1987).
57. R. Calimano, *The Ghetto of Venice* (Venice, 1987), p. 281.

Fig. 48. Joseph de Levis and Angelus de Rubeis, Inkstand with Three Graces, Verona, 1599, Metropolitan Museum of Art, New York (cat. no. 171)

Fig. 62. Spoils from the Temple in Jerusalem, Arch of Titus, Rome, 81 C.E.

RICHARD BRILLIANT

JEWISH ART AND CULTURE IN ANCIENT ITALY

in memoriam matris synagogae

Except perhaps for that of Jerusalem, the Jewish community of Rome has the longest continuous history, reaching back into the second century B.C.E. Roman Jews are Jews and Romans, deeply engaged in the fabric of the Eternal City, an ancient presence amid the remains of classical antiquity, the Middle Ages, the Renaissance, and later eras (fig. 49). But the Roman ghetto, with its formidable enclosure of body and mind, is the creation not of antiquity but of Pope Paul IV in 1555.[1] Jews in antiquity had a better life.

Jews first came to Italy and Rome probably from Alexandria, the intellectual capital of hellenized Judaism, which produced the Septuagint, the Greek translation of the Hebrew Bible, and the philosophical interpretations of Jewish scripture and religion undertaken by Philo. But the ancient Jews of Italy were not intellectuals; they were for the most part the common working people of the Diaspora, speaking Greek, Aramaic, and later Latin, and leaving tombstones inscribed in Greek, Latin, and even Hebrew; they established Jewish communities all over the Italian peninsula and on Sicily and Sardinia, set up synagogues, and buried their dead, often in underground cemeteries, the catacombs. In the flourishing Roman Empire of the first and second centuries C.E. millions of Jews lived and prospered, with perhaps as many as fifty thousand living in Rome alone. Ancient Jews formed part of the empire and also stood apart from it, enjoying both a particular and an all-too-familiar history.[2]

Knowledge of the ancient Jewish communities of Italy—Rome excepted—is fragmentary and largely dependent on chance archaeological finds and inscriptions. The history of the Jews in Rome, however, formed an important part of Roman history itself, often looming large in the minds of Greek and Roman authors curious about these people with their strange customs or superstitions, whose brethren in the eastern Mediterranean were frequently at war with the Romans.[3] By 139 B.C.E. Jews were numerous enough and peculiar enough to be expelled from Rome by a decree of the praetor, Gnaeus Cornelius Hispanus, but they soon returned. When Pompey the Great conquered Judaea in 63 B.C.E. and desecrated the Temple in Jerusalem,[4] many Jews left the country for the west, lamenting the destruction brought upon their land in biblical terms:

Arrogantly the sinner broke down the strong walls
with a battering ram
and you did not interfere.
Gentile foreigners went up to your place of sacrifice;
they arrogantly trampled [it] with their sandals.
Because the sons of Jerusalem defiled the sanctuary of
the Lord,
they were profaning the offerings of God with lawless
acts;

Fig. 49. Ghetto, Rome, 1989

Because of these things he said, "Remove them far from me;
they are not sweet-smelling."
The beauty of his glory was despised before God;
it was completely disgraced.
The sons and daughters [were] in harsh captivity,
their neck in a seal, a spectacle among the gentiles.

Psalms of Solomon 2.1–6[5]

Subsequent Roman involvement in Hasmonean dynastic troubles further encouraged Jewish immigration, and finally Julius Caesar granted the Jews rights to assemble peacefully and to worship publicly in Rome. By the time of Augustus, in the late first century B.C.E., Trastevere had become a very populous Jewish district,[6] a seminary had been established,[7] and various synagogues had begun to appear.[8] By 19 C.E., however, Tiberius expelled the Jews from Rome for proselytizing among Roman citizens; four thousand Jewish youths were sent on military service to Sardinia, but Jews were allowed to return in 31.[9]

For the next thirty years the Jewish community grew and prospered, until the Jewish revolt in Judaea broke out in 66, culminating in Titus's conquest of Jerusalem in 70 and his subsequent Jewish Triumph in Rome, still commemorated by his triumphal arch at the entrance to the Roman Forum (figs. 2, 62, 65).[10] In the 90s an embassy of great rabbis—Rabban Gamliel, Joshua ben Hananiah, Eleazar ben Arzariah, and Akiba—came to Rome and addressed the Jews in their synagogues. At the same time the Roman emperor Domitian converted the traditional tax paid by all Jews to the Temple in Jerusalem to Roman use; this tax, known as the *fiscus Iudaicus,* was rigorously exacted from all identified Jews.[11]

Under Hadrian in the second century it became increasingly difficult to be a Jew in the Roman Empire, especially after the Bar Kochba War of 132–135. Yet Rabbi Simeon ben Yohai and Rabbi Eleazar ben Yose came to Rome from Judaea, and Rabbi Mattithiah ben Hersh founded a new Jewish seminary in the city. By 204 the emperor Septimius Severus, responding to Jewish proselytism, laid down an edict forbidding conversion to Judaism but otherwise did not legislate against the Jews. Keeping pace with the general decline in the state of the Roman Empire in the third century, the Italian-Jewish community also entered a slow decline, which soon led to religious persecution of Jews under Constantine, early in the fourth century, and to a state of repression under Theodosius at the end. But the Jewish communities, reduced in numbers and in circumstance, survived in many of the Italian towns into the Middle Ages.

The ancient Roman view of the Jew was more complicated than this brief history would reveal. Respect and aversion for Jews seemed joined together, perhaps because the Jews remained strangers to some degree, were usually of an inferior social status,[12]—a sensitive issue in a class-conscious society—and were stubbornly and peculiarly religious. The ambivalence of the Roman attitude is well conveyed by an anecdote told in the Palestinian Talmud:

> Rabbi Abba bar Zemina used to work as a tailor for a Gentile in Rome. The latter wished to compel him to eat the flesh of *nevelah* [an animal not slaughtered according to Jewish ritual law] and threatened to kill him, if he did not do so. Said R. Abba to him: "If you wish to kill, kill, for I shall not eat of the flesh of *nevelah*." Subsequently the Gentile said to him: "Now I can tell you that if you had eaten, I should have killed you. If one is a Jew, let one be a Jew."[13]

Observance of the dietary laws, especially abstinence from pork, was a familiar feature of Jewish practice, long noted by classical authors either as a mark of primitive superstition or with admiration for the exercise of self-control.[14] The ancients took circumcision, with its distinguishing physical feature, as a peculiarly Jewish sign of identification, especially visible in a society where undressing in public places, such as the baths or latrines, was commonplace.[15]

Honoring the Sabbath, although often noticed and even legally supported by the Roman government, was not well understood either with respect to its frequency or its reasons; some would attribute Sabbath observance to superstition or to laziness.[16] Varro, the great Roman erudite of the late Republic, appears to have grasped a more abstract but essential aspect of Judaism when he praised the Jewish worship of God without an image.[17] Three hundred years later Alexander Severus, an emperor of the third century, respected the privileges of the Jews in the exercise of their religion and even went so far as to include an image of Abraham as one of the holy souls (*animas sanctiores*) in the sanctuary of his Lares.[18] In a similar vein Numerius of Apamea, a Pythagorean philosopher of the second century who followed the Alexandrian tradition, thought Plato to be Moses "speaking in Attic [Greek]."[19]

A more hostile and more common attitude toward Jewish religious practice was expressed by Juvenal, the bitter commentator on Roman customs and manners, in the early second century; he satirized the Roman Jews as those who prayed to the clouds and a spirit in heaven, followed the laws of Moses and despised Roman law, abstained from pork, and observed the Sabbath "to keep it lazy."[20] Much of this outsider's knowledge is summed up in the fifth book of the *Historiae* of Tacitus, written around 100 C.E., which describes for a Roman audience the origins of the Jewish people, their religious customs, and their history:

> To establish his influence over the people for all time, Moses introduced new religious practices, quite opposed to those of all other religions. The Jews regard as profane all that we hold sacred; on the other hand, they permit all we abhor. . . . They abstain from pork, in recollection of a plague. . . . By frequent fasts even now they bear witness to the long hunger with which they were once distressed, and the unleavened Jewish bread is still employed in memory of the haste with which they seized the grain. They say that they first chose to rest on the seventh day because that day ended their toils; but after a time they were led by the charms of indolence to give over the seventh year as well to inactivity. Others say that this is done in honor of Saturn.
>
> Whatever their origin, these rites are maintained by their antiquity: the other customs of the Jews are base and abominable. . . . Again, the Jews are extremely loyal toward one another, and always ready to show compassion, but toward every other people they feel only hate and enmity. . . . They adopted circumcision to distinguish themselves from other peoples by this difference. Those who are converted to their ways follow the same practice, and the earliest lesson they receive is to despise the gods. . . . They bury the body rather than burn it. . . . The Jews conceive of one god only, and that with the mind only: they regard as impious those who make from perishable materials representations of gods in man's image; that supreme and eternal being is to them incapable of representation and without end. Therefore they set up no statues in their cities, still less in their temples; this flattery is not paid to their kings, nor is this honor given to the Caesars.[21]

The passage illustrates very well an intelligent, well-informed Roman's view of contemporary Jewish religious practice and behavior, a mixture of knowledge and ignorance, of hostility and grudging respect. But it does more. Tacitus points out that the Jews do not make images of their God, that they do not set up statues in their temples, and that they bury the bodies

of their dead. Greek and Roman artists had created an enormous repertory of images of their gods and filled their temples, shrines, altars, and public places with statues; the Jews did not. Their mental image of God had no plastic representation in art, in man's image or otherwise, and thus left no body of divine images in works of art to look at or to study. Nor did the Jews of ancient Italy leave figural representations of their most sacred and particular religious practices: observation of the Sabbath, refraining from eating pork, and circumcision. What they did leave were representations of their allegiance to the Temple in Jerusalem and to their Torah (cat. nos. 68, 69; figs. 66–69), symbolic expression of their religious and ethnic identity (cat. no. 13; figs. 59, 72), the remains of synagogues (figs. 55–57), numerous inscriptions (cat. nos. 8, 6; figs. 54, 61, 60, 74–75), and the Jewish catacombs (cat. nos. 14, 9; figs. 50, 52–53, 66, 73), in which, as Tacitus had observed, the Jews buried the bodies of their dead.

The so-called Palm-Tree Room of the Vigna Randanini catacomb (fig. 50) typifies the condition of the Jewish catacombs in Rome, hollowed out underground and filled with thousands of burials like their many Christian counterparts around the city[22] (fig. 51). Cut out of the soft volcanic rock, roomlike chambers have been formed with narrow passages between one burial chamber and another; the walls and often the ceiling (fig. 73) were decoratively painted, and the bodies were placed in caskets of various materials, including marble (cat. no. 13; fig. 72), in the large, horizontal openings cut into the walls. Frequently, as in the Vigna Randanini catacomb, later burials—not necessarily Jewish—made abrupt intrusions into the preexisting painted decorative schemes, obliterating their imagery. Although some of the Jewish catacombs were elaborately painted, emphasizing a symbolic (figs. 59, 66) rather than a figural repertory (fig. 73) and subject to contentious interpretation, most of our knowledge of the persons interred comes from the hundreds of inscriptions that have been recovered, collected, and published (cat. nos. 14, 9, 6; figs. 52–54, 60, 75).[23]

These sepulchral inscriptions, painted or incised on stone slabs, were usually placed on or beside the burial site within the community of the Jewish dead congregated in the catacomb. Most of the inscriptions are limited to a standardized recitation of the names of the deceased and sometimes of the dedicants or living family members as well.[24] Official titles, such as *archon* (a position of leadership in the Jewish community) or *archisynagogus* (head of the synagogue or, less likely, the

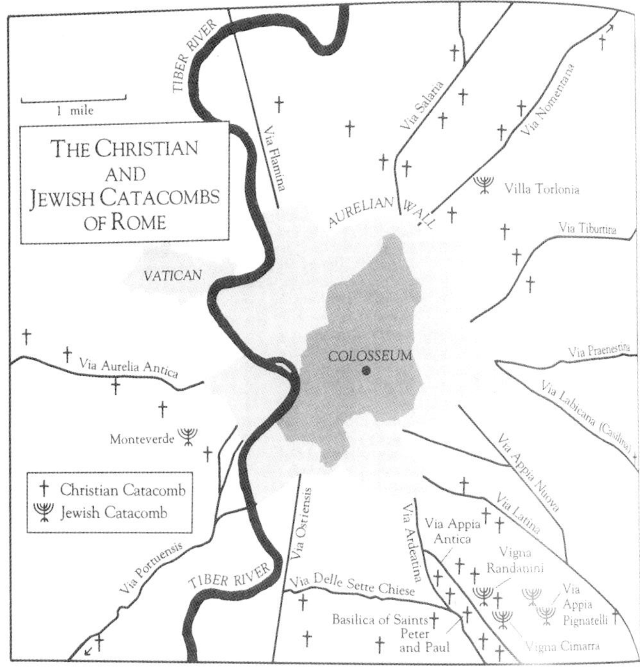

Fig. 50. (opposite) Vigna Randanini catacomb, Rome, second to third century C.E.

Fig. 51. (left) Map of the catacombs, Rome

rabbi) or *mater synagogae* (the leading woman or benefactress), were added proudly in the "Roman fashion" as marks of distinction and honor[25] (thus, Hilaros, the archon of the community of the Volumnenses at Rome [cat. no. 9; fig. 53], and Coelia Paterna, *mater synagogae* of the Brescians [fig. 54]).[26] Typical, if somewhat longer than usual, is the inscription for Alfius Iuda, now in the Vatican Museum and said to be from Capua: "Alfius Iuda, archon, archisynagogue, who lived 70 years, 7 months, 10 days, lies here. Alfa Soteris, with whom he lived 48 years, made this monument for her incomparable worthy husband."[27]

Many of these inscriptions are written in Latin (e.g., that of Alfius Iuda), others in Greek (see fig. 53), indicating the linguistic mix among the Jewish population of Italy. The sepulchral inscription of Tubias Barzaarona from Rome (cat. no. 14; fig. 52) offers the same brief recitation of names in Greek and Latin and adds the word *shalom* (peace) four times in Hebrew at the bottom.[28] Usually at the beginning or at the end of an inscription—sometimes both—invocations of a "peaceful sleep" can be read, the conventional ancient Jewish metaphor of a potentially impermanent death (cat. nos. 14, 9; figs. 52, 53).

A large number of tombstones also bear crudely incised representations of ceremonial objects or objects of cult traditionally associated with Jewish religious practice and Jewish identity. This persistent but limited symbolic repertory includes representations of the seven-branched candelabrum, or menorah (figs. 52, 60); the *lulav* and *etrog* of the Feast of Tabernacles; the Torah shrine, or ark; flasks or bottles (of wine?); the shofar; and even round cakes of matzah for Passover (fig. 53). Similar symbols, especially the menorah, appear on paintings in the Jewish catacombs (figs. 59, 66); even frequently in the Jewish catacomb in the Villa Torlonia in Rome;[29] in the Jewish catacombs at Beth She'arim in Israel;[30] in Jewish synagogues in Ostia (fig. 55), Sardis (fig. 57), and Beth Shean (fig. 67); on sarcophagi (fig. 72); and even on clay lamps (cat. no. 29; fig. 58).[31] That the prevalence of these symbolic representations in acknowledged Jewish contexts bespeaks their significance to the users cannot be denied. Yet this does not settle the complex question of their meaning, especially marked by the controversies between E. R. Goodenough, the great collector of Jewish symbols, and his critics over their meanings: as identifying signs of and for Jews; as images eliciting positive emotional responses from their users; as representations incorporating meanings rooted in Jewish mysticism, recondite theology, and rabbinic tradition; or as "mere decoration."[32]

The ancient Jewish community of Italy apparently was not deeply infused with Philonic (Alexandrian) mysticism, however, and despite occasional references to the Roman community in the Talmud,[33] rabbinic Judaism in Rome probably did not have either the intensity or the profundity of the theological discourse found in Jerusalem or Babylonia. As Morton Smith has pointed out in his sensitive criticism of Goodenough,[34] the practices of Judaism—rabbinic or otherwise—were very varied in the Roman Empire, especially after the fall of Jerusalem in 70 C.E. Thus the employment of a Jewish symbolic language probably diverged according to local custom, itself influenced by contemporary Hellenistic or Roman religious and eschatological beliefs, and did not conform to some supposedly normative iconographic program.

Fig. 52. (opposite) Burial Plaque, Rome, fourth century C.E., Museo Nazionale Romano, Rome (cat. no. 17)

Fig. 53. (left) Burial Plaque, third century C.E., Museo Nazionale Romano, Rome (cat. no. 12)

Fig. 54. (above) Burial Plaque, Brescia, second to third century C.E., Museo Civico, Brescia

The repertory of "Jewish" signs was, however, widely diffused and remained relatively consistent for centuries, suggesting that in effect there was a common denominator of belief, some recognized kernels of meaning in the symbols themselves. In this light scholars, in the exercise of reasonable interpretation, have found these symbols to be making the following allusions: principally, the menorah refers to the original candelabra in the Temple in Jerusalem (see figs. 14, 15), to the everlasting light of God, and possibly to the presence of sanctity; the Torah shrine, to the Temple and to the scrolls of the Law, housed in a specially constructed Ark of the Covenant in the Diaspora synagogue, thus connecting the present place of communal worship with the past and future Temple; the lulav and etrog, to Tabernacles (Sukkoth) and to the coming of the Messiah, traditionally associated with that feast; and the shofar, immediately associated with the New Year and the Day of Atonement, to the reaffirmation of faith, the heralding of the Day of Judgment (most appropriate in the catacombs), and ultimately to the acknowledgment of the sovereignty of God.

Signs of identity, symbols of connection, repositories of faith and hope, these few significant images constituted the bulk of the figural repertory of the Jewish catacombs, inscriptions, and synagogal architecture in Roman Italy. Unfortunately there is little known topographical correlation between the Jewish catacombs of Rome (text figure) and the Roman synagogues,[35] although the Monteverde catacomb is not far from Trastevere and the Vigna Randanini catacomb is close to the Via Appia Antica and Porta Capena, both Jewish districts.

In the absence of other than fragmentary remains detached from their archaeological contexts,[36] the synagogue at Ostia, accidentally discovered in 1961, assumes major importance (figs. 55–56; text figure, plan).[37] Ostia, the ancient port of Rome, had a Jewish community drawn to the bustling town on the Tiber River by its extensive commercial activity. Although the building blends easily into the local Roman architectural environment, the layout (fig. 55) and the presence of Jewish symbols on the architectural elements (cat. no. 10; fig. 56) and on clay lamps found in the excavations (cat. nos. 25–28) and detailed inscriptions (cat. no. 8; fig. 61) support its identification as a synagogue.

Diaspora synagogues have no standard design and range widely in size and in the splendor of their appointments from the fairly unpretentious (Ostia) to the luxurious and grand synagogue of Hellenistic-Roman Sardis in western Asia Minor (fig. 57).[38] The excavator of the Ostia synagogue, Maria Floriani Squarciapino, believed that beneath the present fourth-century building (fig. 55) she found evidence of an earlier syna-

Fig. 55. (opposite, top) Synagogue, Ostia, first to fourth century C.E.

Fig. 56. (opposite, bottom) Architrave of the Torah Shrine from the Synagogue at Ostia, third century(?) C.E., Soprintendenza Archeologia, Ostia (cat. no. 10)

Fig. 57. (above) Synagogue, Sardis, second to third century C.E.

Fig. 58. (left) Oil Lamp, Rome, mid-fourth to fifth century, Museo Nazionale Romano, Rome (cat. no. 29)

gogue of the first century, remodeled in the late second or third century, and then extensively rebuilt or redesigned at least once in the fourth. Unfortunately the various stages of the synagogue's building history are difficult to disentangle. The plan of the last, surviving phase of the synagogue shows that the building was entered from the street into an anteroom, then one turned at a right angle into a long room, running east and west, passing through two pairs of tall columns along the central axis toward the *bemah,* placed in the center of the curving west wall; the Torah shrine was attached to the south wall and to one of the tall columns; one approached the Torah shrine up a short flight of stairs set between two small columns, while facing eastward toward Jerusalem.

The location of the bemah and the Torah shrine changed from one building period to another, but there is general agreement that the third-century remodeling included the Torah shrine (*keibotos*) of Mindis Faustos, whose dedicatory inscription still survives (fig. 61). The inscription begins with the diplomatic and traditional Latin invocation for the well-being of the emperor(s) and then proceeds, in good Greek lettering of the second century, to proclaim the setting up of the Torah shrine according to the sacred Law.[39] The last two lines of the inscription were recut in a later epigraphic style, however, and it is only in the last complete line that the names of Mindis Faustos appears, suggesting perhaps that he repaired or usurped someone else's dedication. The slab itself was used to repair the floor of the present building in the fourth century, so perhaps even Mindis Faustos had been forgotten, or the building converted to other uses, in late antiquity.

The mixture of Greek and Latin in the Mindis Faustos inscription, the presence of pagan Roman and Jewish formulae—for the health of the emperors and in accordance with Jewish law—and the changing epigraphical styles all demonstrate the close relationship between the Ostian Jewish community and contemporary Roman life in the empire. The menorah that served as a Jewish symbol in the Ostia synagogue (cat. no. 10; fig. 56), in the Jewish catacomb at Venosa in southern Italy (fig. 59),[40] and on a Jewish burial plaque from the Vigna Randanini catacomb in Rome (fig. 60)[41] was familiar not only to Jews but also to the

Fig. 59. (opposite, top) Arcosolium in the catacomb, Venosa, fourth to fifth century

Fig. 60. (opposite, bottom) Burial Plaque, Vigna Randanini catacomb, first to third century C.E., The Jewish Museum, New York, JM 5–50

Fig. 61. (above) Inscription of Mindis Faustos, from the synagogue at Ostia, second to third century C.E., Soprintendenza Archeologia, Ostia (cat. no. 8)

Fig. 63. Judaea Capta Coin: Emperor Titus, Rome, 79 C.E., The Jewish Museum, New York (cat. no. 22)

Fig. 64. Judaea Capta Coin: Emperor Titus, Caesarea, 71–81 C.E., The Jewish Museum, New York (cat. no. 21)

Romans. Otherwise it is difficult to account for the prominence of the menorah in the famous relief representing the procession of the spoils of the Temple (figs. 62–65) on the Arch of Titus (fig. 2).[42] The Flavian emperors Vespasian and Titus had advertised their victory in the Jewish War and the pacification of the province of Judaea in a series of coins, beginning in 71. These coins represent *Judaea capta* on the reverse, the captured province personified as a female barbarian seated submissively beneath a palm tree in the presence of the emperor or of a male barbarian (fig. 63), or they depict Victory writing the glorious record of the Roman conquest on a shield (fig. 64). But the Arch of Titus, erected posthumously by his brother and successor Domitian and placed in the most public of places in the center of Rome, commemorates the triumphal procession with the most explicit representation of the menorah, the key item of the spoils, as described by Josephus in *The Jewish War* (V.5.5):

> The most prominent of the spoils were those captured in the Temple at Jerusalem—a golden table and a lampstand made of gold. The central shaft was fixed to a base, and from it slender branches extended like the prongs of a trident with the ends forged into lamps; these numbered seven.

Roman triumphal art is very specific because in propagandistic monuments ostensible fact appeared to confirm the asserted reality of imperial victory. Therefore it is most likely that the menorah on Titus' arch actually depicts the original object from the Holy Temple in Jerusalem, especially when the sculptor would have had access to it among the spoils of war permanently stored in the Temple of Jupiter Optimus Capitolinus in Rome. Given the Hellenistic style of the metalwork, including the mythical monsters in the panels on the base (fig. 65), the Flavian relief should be taken as a faithful copy, possibly the only faithful copy,[43] of the candelabrum from Herod's Temple in Jerusalem, a symbol par excellence of the Roman victory over the Jews in Judaea that all who saw the monument would readily comprehend.

Fig. 65. Detail, Arch of Titus, Rome, 81 C.E.

Fig. 66. (top) Arcosolium, catacomb of Villa Torlonia, Rome, first to fourth century C.E.

Fig. 67. (above) Mosaic pavement from the synagogue at Beth Shean, Beth Shean, second half of the fifth to early sixth century C.E., Israel Museum, Jerusalem

How poignant, then, is the frequent appearance of the menorah as a triumphant symbol in conjunction with the Torah shrine: in the third-century painting in the Jewish catacomb in the Villa Torlonia in Rome (fig. 66),[44] three hundred years later in the mosaic pavement of a synagogue in Beth Shean, Israel (fig. 67),[45] and in several gold glass fragments of the fourth century from the Roman catacombs (cat. nos. 34–35; figs. 68–69).[46] In all these instances the menorah, an image of everlasting light, appears together with a representation of the Torah shrine—ambivalently symbolizing the synagogal ark and the Temple ark in Jerusalem—and other familiar symbols of Jewish ritual. The Beth Shean mosaic (fig. 17), a representation for all seasons, displays the shofar and incense shovels, but not the lulav and etrog found in the catacomb paintings (figs. 55, 66), on the Roman gold glasses (cat. nos. 34–36; figs. 68–69), and on sepulchral inscriptions (fig. 53).[47] Recently Archer St. Clair suggested that the combination of the Torah shrine, or Ark of the Covenant, with menorot and the etrog and lulav refers specifically to the Feast of Tabernacles, and through it conveys to the viewer the perennial hope for the coming of the Messiah and the restoration of the Temple in Jerusalem in a time of peace.[48] His argument is very convincing, particularly in the context of Jewish funerary art. That was surely the natural environment for expressing a great longing for the messianic advent and everlasting peace, traditional aspirations of the individual Jew and even more so of the community in which the Jew lived, died, and was buried.

That Jewish community existed, however, within the much larger community of the Roman Empire, with its rich secular and religious traditions and with its varied artistic culture. Jews drew heavily on this culture for so much of their art:[49] techniques of painting, mosaic, engraving (figs. 52–54, 61, 74), and sculpture (fig. 72); style, methods of composition, the placement of artworks in architecture (fig. 57); and even the choice of the catacombs for burial. What Jews had for their very own, at least at the beginning of the empire, were the repertories of Jewish symbols and the Hebrew Bible.

Even the Hebrew Bible might have been more accessible to Diaspora Jews in the West through the Septuagint,[50] which brought knowledge of the Bible to a wide audience in the language of classical intellectual culture. Surely the biblical account itself—stories of the patriarchs, of Moses and the Exodus, of Saul and David

Fig. 68. (above) Fragments of a Cup Bottom with Jewish Symbols, Rome, 300–350 C.E., Metropolitan Museum of Art, New York (cat. no. 34)

Fig. 69. (below) Fragment of a Cup Bottom, Rome, fourth century C.E., Israel Museum, Jerusalem (cat. no. 35)

and the Philistines, of the prophets, of Mordecai and Esther, of Jonah and of Daniel, of the many instances of divine revelation and rescue—formed a vital part of the Jewish heritage in antiquity and stocked the minds of Jews with vivid mental images, often enriched and shaped by midrashic interpretation.[51] These images of biblical stories and characters were not restricted to the immaterial imagery of the mind but were in fact turned into visual narratives and explicit pictorial representations of divine intervention in human affairs. The extensive cycles of paintings in the mid-third-century C.E. synagogue at Dura Europos in eastern Syria (fig. 71), discovered in 1932, demonstrate beyond any reasonable doubt that the rabbinic law of idolatry did not forbid figural representation when the figures themselves were not the objects of veneration and the likeness of God was unrepresented.[52]

The wall paintings of the Dura synagogue, painted in tempera on dry plaster, were completed about 244–245; they served the inspirational and confirmational needs of this Jewish community on the eastern frontier of the Roman Empire.[53] Appearing at the interface between classical and Near Eastern cultures, the Dura paintings drew on the artistic repertories and pictorial styles of both to express these Jewish themes of rescue and revelation in the past and potentially in the future. In the excerpt shown here (fig. 71), taken from the north side of the west wall of the main meeting room of the synagogue, the two registers represent, from left to right: Moses and the Burning Bush, Exodus and Crossing the Red Sea, Ezra and the Law, the Temple, and the Ark of the Covenant in the Land of the Philistines. Moses and Ezra are dressed like Greek philosophers, the architectural representations look Greco-Roman, yet the stiff, frontal poses of the principal figures, the massed groups, and the perspective have an oriental character. The images themselves, clearly set in well-defined frames, are readily comprehended even now, as is the linear flow of the narrative of the Exodus, bespeaking both a tradition of biblical repre-

sentation and a well-prepared audience. The Jews of Dura congregated for worship in the synagogue, looked at the paintings that originally covered all four walls of the rectangular room, and faced the west wall and the Torah niche in the center of that wall in which the scrolls of the Law were kept, and beyond that wall toward Jerusalem in the west.

Nothing like the Dura synagogue paintings survives in exclusively Jewish contexts in Italy, but in the early Christian monuments of Rome, especially in the catacombs (fig. 70), Judeo-Christians and Christians alike drew on the Hebrew Bible for similar inspiration, similar confirmation of the continuing act of faith.[54] The pictorial models may have passed through intermediaries, such as cartoons or, more likely, illustrated Bibles, even Jewish Bibles, before their illustration was preempted by Christian use and rejected by Jews as a sign of the growing differentiation between the two religious communities. Whatever the medium of transmission, many Christian catacombs of the late third and

Fig. 70. (opposite) *Crossing of the Red Sea,* Via Latina catacomb, Rome, first to fourth century C.E.

Fig. 71. (above) West wall, synagogue of Dura-Europos, before 256 C.E., Museum, Damascus

Fig. 73. Cubiculum 1, Vigna Randanini catacomb, Rome, first to fourth century C.E.

fourth centuries in Rome have extensive pictorial representations of Old Testament material. None of them, perhaps, is as richly decorated as the Via Latina catacomb, discovered in 1955, where in cubiculum C (fig. 70) the Crossing of the Red Sea is depicted, an image of salvation, both pictorially and functionally close to the Dura Synagogue painting (fig. 71).[55]

In the third and fourth centuries late antique religious practices were synthetic, witness the Via Latina catacomb that incorporates, or assimilates, pagan, Jewish, and Christian subjects and themes into its extensive repertory of wall and ceiling paintings. This process was not unique. Goodenough in his multivolume *Jewish Symbols in the Greco-Roman Period* stressed—some would say overstressed—the conversion of pagan, especially Dionysiac, material into Jewish themes and monuments. An examination of the interior of cubiculum I in the Jewish catacomb in Vigna Randanini (fig. 73)[56] reveals that there was very little "Jewish" about its decoration, even if there is no doubt about its religious affiliation. Indeed the medallion in the center of the vault shows Victory crowning an athlete with immortality, a thoroughly secular subject and not "Jewish" in any way. Similarly, the famous Season sarcophagus in the Terme Museum (fig. 72) falls completely within the repertory of Roman art with one signal exception, especially when the old attribution to the Vigna Randanini catacomb has been rejected.[57] But for the symbolic menorah in the tondo held by the Seasons—instead of the usual portrait bust(s) of the deceased or Victory—nothing about this sarcophagus is Jewish: not the style of sculpture, typical of the Diocletianic period of about 300, nor the seasonal imagery, a well-established sepulchral and eschatological motif in Roman art, nor the young satyrs beneath the tondo trampling grapes, symbolic of Dionysiac cult. What then is Jewish about this sarcophagus? The menorah, an unlikely symbol for a non-Jew; the fact that there is no certain pagan findspot; and possibly the original occupant, whose body is now and forever lost.

Perhaps the study of the Jewish presence in ancient Italy should focus not on art per se, but rather on the material remains of Jewish culture. The burial plaque of Aurelia Protogenia from the Vigna Randanini cata-

Fig. 72. Front of Sarcophagus with Menorah, Rome, end of the third century, C.E., Museo Nazionale Romano, Rome (cat. no. 16)

comb (cat. no. 6; fig. 75)[58] exemplifies the important conjunction of faith (the lulav and etrog, symbols of Tabernacles) and family (a daughter in memory of her mother). Soon the repression of Jews in late antiquity would limit their numbers and reduce their circumstances but would not extinguish their piety, their allegiance to the faith of their ancestors.[59]

In 363 a marble tombstone was set up in Catania, Sicily, with the following inscription in Latin, with some Hebrew:[60]

> Peace on Israel, Amen, Amen, Peace on Samuel. I, Aurelius Samuel, have acquired a tomb for myself and for my wife Lasiferina, who died on the twelfth day of the kalends of November, on Friday, the eighth day of the lunar month, when Merobaudes was consul for the second time with Saturninus. She lived twenty-two years in peace. I implore you by the respect owed the patriarchs, I implore you by the Law the Lord has given to the Jews not to open this tomb, not to place other bodies with our bones. If someone does open it, he must pay a fine of ten pieces of silver.

Although many Jewish monuments, tombs, and synagogues of ancient Italy have been lost, this stone was undisturbed, a physical remnant of the Jewish community of Catania in the late Roman Empire. Would that the barbarians of the modern world had been so respectful of a well-cut Roman tombstone on the Via Appia (fig. 74)! The Semitic names of the freedmen Baricha, Zabda, and Achiba are not necessarily Jewish, but only a scholarly vandal could have known that one or more of them might be.[61]

Notes

1. See L. Finelli, I. Insolera, and A. F. Marciano, *Il Ghetto* (Rome, 1986).
2. J. Juster, *Les juifs dans l'empire romain,* 2 vols. (Paris, 1914); M. Radin, *The Jews among the Greeks and Romans* (Philadelphia, 1915); M. Grant, *The Jews in the Roman*

World (London, 1973); E. M. Smallwood, *The Jews under Roman Rule from Pompey to Diocletian* (Leiden, 1977); H. J. Leon, *The Jews of Ancient Rome* (Philadelphia, 1960); G. La Piana, "Foreign Groups in Rome during the First Centuries of the Empire," *Harvard Theological Review* 20 (1927): 183–403; C. Giordano and I. Kahn, *The Jews in Pompei, Herculaneum, and in the Cities of Campania Felix* (Naples, 1971); A. Milano, *Storia degli ebrei in Italia* (Turin, 1963); J.-B. Frey, *Corpus Inscriptionum Iudaicarum,* vol. 1, *Europe* (Rome, 1936) (abbreviated as Frey).

3. T. Reinach, *Textes d'auteurs grecs et romains relatifs au judaïsme* (Paris, 1895); M. Stern, *Greek and Latin Authors on Jews and Judaism,* 3 vols. (Jerusalem, 1976–1984) (abbreviated as Stern).
4. According to Josephus, *Jewish War* I.8; idem, *Antiquities of the Jews* XIV.3.4. See N. Bentwich, *Josephus* (Philadelphia, 1914); L. H. Feldman and G. Hata, *Josephus, Judaism, and Christianity* (Detroit, 1987), esp. p. 71ff., M. Stern, "Josephus and the Roman Empire as Reflected in *The Jewish War*"; the complete works of Josephus have been published in the Loeb Library edition (Cambridge, Mass., 1926–1965).

Fig. 74. (above) Burial Inscription of a Jewish Freedman, Via Appia, Rome, early second century C.E.

Fig. 75. (opposite) Burial Plaque, Vigna Randanini catacomb, Rome, second to third century, The Jewish Museum, New York (cat. no. 6)

5. H. Charlesworth, ed., *The Old Testament Pseudepigrapha,* vol. 2 (New York, 1985), pp. 651, 652 (trans. R. B. Wright); S. Holm-Nielsen, "Religiöse Poesie des Spätjudentums," *Aufstieg und Niedergang der römischen Welt* II.19.1 (1979): 152 ff., 180ff.
6. S. Collon, "Remarques sur les quartiers juifs de la Rome antique," *Mélanges d'Ecole Française de Rome* 57 (1940): 72–94; R. MacMullen, *Roman Social Relations 50 B.C. to A.D. 284* (New Haven, 1974), p. 83, no. 72; p. 180.
7. Philo, *Legatio ad Gaium,* ed. E. M. Smallwood, 2d ed. (Leiden, 1970).
8. E.g., the synagogues of the Augustesii, Agrippesi, Erodi, Volumnesii, Calcaresii, Campesi, of the Hebrews, the Seceni, the Suburesii, the Tripolitani, the Vernacoli, of Elea, and of the Arca of Lebanon or of Severus. See Leon, *Jews of Ancient Rome,* pp. 135–166; A. Momigliano, "I nomi delle prime 'synagoghe' romane e la condizione giuridica delle comunità in Roma sotto Augusto," *Rassegna mensile di Israel,* 2d ser., 6, no. 7 (1931): 283–292; M. Avi-Yonah, "Places of Worship in the Roman and Byzantine Periods," *Antiquity and Survival* 2 (1957): 260–275.
9. Tacitus, *Annals* II.85.4; Dio Cassius *Roman History* LVII.18.5a.
10. Josephus, *Jewish War,* bks. II–VII; Tacitus, *History* I, II; for the triumph of Titus, see Josephus, *Jewish War* VII.5.3–6.
11. See Suetonius, *Life of Domitian* 12.1.
12. So Cicero, in *Pro Flacco* 28.66–29, comments on their mob behavior and avarice; Martial, in *Epigram* XII.57.13, 14, that a Jew taught his mother to beg; Juvenal, in *Satire* VI.542–547, on Jews as beggars and fortune-tellers, and in *Carmen* III.5–20, on Jews as hay sellers near the Porta Capena at the Via Appia, a well-known Jewish district in the first and second centuries.
13. From Palestinian Talmud Sevi'it IV.2.2 (Venice, 1525), p. 35b, quoted in E. E. Urbach, *The Sages,* trans. I. Abrahams (Cambridge, Mass., 1986), p. 359.
14. E.g., Juvenal, *Satire* XIV.96–106; Plutarch, *Quaestiones convivales* IV.4–62, Stern no. 258; Porphyry, *De abstentia* IV.11–44, Stern no. 445.
15. E.g., Horace, *Sermones* I.9.70; Martial, *Epigram* VII.30; Juvenal, *Satire* XIV.86–106; *Scriptores Historiae Augustae,* "Hadrian," 14.1–2, which blames the Bar Kochba uprising on Hadrian's ban on circumcision; see also Juster, *Les juifs,* vol. 1, pp. 263–271.
16. E.g., Horace, *Sermones* I.9.69; Seneca, *De superstitione,* in Augustine, *City of God* VI. 11, Stern no. 186; Martial, *Epigram* IV.4; Plutarch, *Quaestiones convivales* IV.6.2. See also J. Mann, "Le sabbat juif et les poètes latins," *Revue d'histoire et de littérature religieuses* 8, nos. 3–5 (1903): 335; R. Goldenberg, "The Jewish Sabbath in The Roman World up to the Time of Constantine the Great," *Aufstieg und Niedergang der römischen Welt* II.19.1 (1979): 414–447.
17. In Augustus, *City of God* IV.31, Stern no. 72a.
18. *Scriptores Historiae Augustae,* "Severus Alexander," XXII.4, XXIX.2, 3; see A. Momigliano, "Severo Alessandro archisynagogus, una conferma alla Historia Augusta," *Athenaeum,* n.s., 12, no. 2 (1934): 151–153; S. Settis, "Severo Alessandro e i suoi Lari," *Athenaeum* n.s., 50 (1972): 237–251.
19. In Clement of Alexandria, *Stromata* I.22.150.4, Stern no. 363a; but Apuleius, in *Apologia* 90, took Moses as a sorcerer.
20. Juvenal, *Satire* XIV.96–106; see R. Humphries, *The Satires of Juvenal* (Bloomington, Ind., 1958), p. 164.
21. Tacitus, *History* V.4.1–5.4, trans. J. Jackson, Loeb Library edition (Cambridge, Mass., 1969), pp. 181–183; see B. Wardy, "Jewish Religion in Pagan Literature during the Late Republic and Early Empire," *Aufstieg und Niedergang der römischen Welt* II.19.1 (1979): 592–644; and in the same volume, Goldenberg, "The Jewish Sabbath," pp. 414–447.
22. See R. Garrucci, *Cimitero degli antichi ebrei scoperto recentemente in Vigna Randanini* (Rome, 1862); N. Müller, *Die judische Katakombe am Monteverdi zu Rom* (Leipzig, 1912); D. Mazzoleni, "Le catacombe ebraiche di Roma," *Studi romani* 23, no. 3 (1975): 289–302; H. W. Beyer and H. Leitzmann, *Die judische Katakombe der Villa Torlonia in Rom* (Berlin and Leipzig, 1930); V. M. Fasola, "Le due catacombe ebraiche di Villa Torlonia," *Revista di archeologia cristiana* 52 (1976): 7–62; E. R. Goodenough, *Jewish Symbols in the Greco-Roman Period,* vols. 2, 3 (Princeton, 1953).
23. The principal publication of these inscriptions was made by Frey (1936), revised by B. Lifshitz, *Corpus of Jewish Inscriptions* (New York, 1975); see also L. H. Kant, "Jewish Inscriptions in Greek and Latin," *Aufstieg und Niedergang der römischen Welt* II.20.2 (1987): 671–713.
24. See Leon, *Jews of Ancient Rome,* pp. 93–121, for the names.
25. For an old but still useful discussion of these titles and the organization of local Jewish communities, see Juster, *Les juifs,* vol. 1, pp. 409–496, esp. pp. 443ff., 450ff.; ibid., p. 167ff.
26. Fig. 3b, Frey no. 343; fig. 3c, Frey no. 639; and A. Garzetti, ed., *Inscriptiones italiae* Vol. X. Regio X, Fasciculus V, *Brixia,* Pars I (Rome, 1984), no. 204.
27. Some inscriptions include both the titles *archon* and *archisynagogus,* e.g., Vatican Museum no. 30876, Frey no. 553.
28. Frey no. 497.
29. Beyer and Leitzmann, *Die judische Katakombe,* pls. 4, 6, 7.

30. B. Mazar, *Beth She'arim: Report on the Excavations 1936–1940,* vol. 1, *Catacombs 1–4* (New Brunswick, N.J., 1973), p. 228, pls. III, X, XVIII, XIX, etc.
31. See Goodenough, *Jewish Symbols,* vols. 2, 3.
32. Ibid., vol. 4, *The Problem of Method: Symbols from Jewish Cult* (1954), esp. pp. 43ff., 71ff. (the menorah), 99ff. (Torah shrine), 145ff. (lulav and etrog), 167ff. (shofar); see also M. Smith, "The Image of God," *John Rylands Library Bulletin* 40 (1957–1958): 473–512.
33. Babylonian Talmud, Megillah 26b; and see the story of Rabbi Abba bar Zemina above.
34. M. Smith, "Goodenough's *Jewish Symbols* in Retrospect," *Journal of Biblical Literature* 86 (1967), pp. 53–68; M. Avi-Yonah, *Israel Exploration Journal* 6 (1956): 194ff.; E. Bickerman, *L'antiquité classique* 25 (1956): 246ff.; 26 (1957): 532f.; 28 (1959): 517f.; *Harvard Theological Review* 58 (1965): 127ff.; J. Neusner, *Conservative Judaism* 17 (1963): 77ff.
35. See note 8 above.
36. See L. I. Levine, *Ancient Synagogues Revealed* (Jerusalem and Detroit, 1982), p. 164ff.; J. Gutmann, ed., *The Synagogue: Studies in Origins, Archaeology, and Architecture* (New York, 1975); R. Wischnitzer, *The Architecture of the European Synagogue* (Philadelphia, 1964), pp. 3–13; A. T. Kraabel, "The Diaspora Synagogue: Archaeological and Epigraphic Evidence since Sukenik," *Aufstieg und Niedergang der römischen Welt* II.19.1 (1979): 477–510.
37. M. Floriani Squarciapino, *La Synagoga di Ostia* (Rome, 1964); idem, "The Synagogue at Ostia," *Archaeology* 16 (1963), 194–203; A. M. Rabello, "Ostia," *Encyclopedia Judaica,* vol. 12 (1971), pp. 1506–1509; F. Zevi, "La Sinagoga di Ostia," *Rassegna mensile di Israel* 38 (1972): 131–145; Kraabel, "The Diaspora Synagogue," p. 497ff.; R. Meiggs, *Roman Ostia,* 2d ed. (Oxford, 1973), p. 587f.
38. G. M. A. Hanfmann, *Letters from Sardis* (Cambridge, Mass., 1972), esp. fig. 168; A. R. Seager, "The Building History of the Sardis Synagogue," *American Journal of Archaeology* 76 (1972): 425–435; idem, *Archaeology at the Ancient Synagogue of Sardis, Turkey: Judaism in a Major Roman City* (Muncie, Ind., 1974).
39. Cf. the Latin inscription of Plotius Fortunatus, archisynagogus, also from the Ostia synagogue (cat. no. 9); see M. Floriani Squarciapino, "Plotius Fortunatus archisynagogus," *Rassegna mensile di Israel* 36 (1970): 183–191.
40. See C. Colafemmina, "Nuove scoperte nella catacomba ebraica di Venosa," *Vetera Christianum* 15, no. 2 (1978): 369–382, pl. VI; idem, "Archeologia ed epigrafia ebraica nell'Italia meridionale," in *Italia Judaica: Atti del I convegno internazionale* (Rome, 1983), pp. 199–210, figs. 1–13; H. J. Leon, "The Jews of Venusia," *Jewish Quarterly Review* 44 (1953–1954), pp. 267–284.
41. Frey, no. 200.
42. See M. Pfanner, *Der Titusbogen* (Mainz, 1983); for the procession of the spoils, see p. 50ff., pls. 54–67.
43. See B. Narkiss, in K. Weitzmann, ed., *Age of Spirituality* (New York and Princeton, 1979), pp. 370, 371, who states that according to Mishnaic rule it was forbidden to portray an exact image of the Temple menorah; see M. Kon, "The Menorah of the Arch of Titus," *Palestine Exploration Quarterly* (1950): 25ff.; J. H. Herzog, "The Menorah on the Arch of Titus," in *Essays in Honor of S. M. Mayer* (Jerusalem, 1960), pp. 95–98; A. Negev, "The History of the Seven-Branched Candelabrum," *Eretz Yisrael* 8 (1967): 123–210 (in Hebrew).
44. Beyer and Lietzmann, *Die judische Katakombe,* p. 24ff., pls. 12, 13; Goodenough, *Jewish Symbols,* vol. 2, p. 39ff.
45. N. Tsori, "The Ancient Synagogue at Bet Shean," *Eretz Yisrael* 8 (1967): 149–168; A. Cohen-Mushlin, in Weitzmann, *Age of Spirituality,* no. 343.
46. A. Cohen-Mushlin, in Weitzmann, *Age of Spirituality,* pp. 347, 348; Goodenough, *Jewish Symbols,* vol. 2, p. 108ff.; I. Schüler, "A Note on Jewish Gold Glass," *Journal of Glass Studies* 8 (1966): 59–60; Archer St. Clair, "God's House of Peace in Paradise: The Feast of Tabernacles on a Jewish Gold Glass," *Journal of Jewish Art* I (1985): 6–15.
47. Note, however, that the mosaic floor of the synagogue at Hammat Tiberias, Israel, dated about 300, similar in other respects to the much later Beth Shean mosaic, does represent the etrog and lulav (Weitzmann, *Age of Spirituality,* no. 342).
48. St. Clair, "God's House of Peace in Paradise," pp. 5–15; see also W. Wirgen, "The Menorah as a Symbol of Afterlife," *Israel Exploration Journal* 14 (1964): 102ff.; V. A. Klagsbald, "The Menorah as Symbol: Its Meaning and Origin in Early Jewish Art," *Jewish Art* 12–13 (1986–1987): 126–134; H. C. Cavallin, "Leben nach dem Tode im Spätjudentum und im frühen Christentum," *Aufstieg und Niedergang der römischen Welt* II.19.1 (1979): 242–345.
45. See R. Brilliant, "Remembering and Jewish Art," *Jewish Art* 12–13 (1986–1987): 257–260.
50. See E. Bickerman, "The Septuaginta as a Translation," *Proceedings of the American Academy for Jewish Research* 38 (1959): 1–39.
51. See V. A. Klagsbald, "La symbolique dans l'art juif," *Revue des études juives* 144, no. 4 (1985): 408–438, on Jewish art and its midrashic background.
52. See E. Urbach, "The Rabbinical Laws of Idolatry in the Second and Third Centuries in the Light of Archaeological and Historical Facts," *Israel Exploration Journal* 9 (1959): 149ff., 229ff.; E. R. Goodenough, "The Rabbis and Jewish Art in the Greco-Roman Period," *Hebrew Union College Annual* 32 (1961): 269ff.

53. The literature on the Dura synagogue paintings is extensive; see C. H. Kraeling, *The Synagogue: The Excavations at Dura Europus: Final Report,* vol. 8, pt. 1 (New Haven, 1956); Goodenough, *Jewish Symbols,* vols. 9–11 (1958–1964); J. Gutmann, ed., *The Dura-Europos Synagogue: A Re-evaluation (1932–1972),* (Missoula, Mont., 1973); Weitzmann, *Age of Spirituality,* no. 341 (B. Narkiss).
54. See J. Gutmann, "Early Synagogue and Jewish Catacomb Art and Its Relation to Christian Art," *Aufstieg und Niedergang der römischen Welt* II.21.2 (1984): 1313–1342; idem, "The Dura Europos Synagogue Paintings and Their Influence on Later Christian and Jewish Art," *Artibus et Historiae* 17 (1988): 25–30; E. Testa, *Il simbolismo dei giudeo-christiani* (Jerusalem, 1962); Weitzmann, *Age of Spirituality,* pp. 420ff. (E. Dinkler), 449ff. (H. L. Kessler); K. Weitzmann, "The Question of the Influence of Jewish Pictorial Sources in Old Testament Illustration," in J. Gutmann, ed., *No Graven Images: Studies in Art and the Hebrew Bible* (New York, 1971), pp. 79–95.
55. A. Ferrua, *Le pitture della nuova catacomba di Via Latina* (Vatican City, 1960); L. Kötzsche-Breitenbach, *Die neue Katakombe an der Via Latina in Rom* (Münster, 1976), pp. 17ff., 79ff.; W. N. Schumacher, "*Reparatio vitae.* Zum Programm der neuen Katakombe an der Via Latina zu Rom," *Römische Quartalschrift* 66, nos. 3–4 (1971): 125–173; W. Tronzo, *The Via Latina Catacomb* (University Park and London, 1986), esp. pp. 1ff., 24ff., 51ff.; U. Schubert, *Studia Judaica Austriaca,* vol. 2, *Spätantikes Judentum und frühchristliche Kunst* (Vienna, 1974), who discusses in great detail the relationship between the Via Latina catacomb paintings and the Dura synagogue.
56. Goodenough, *Jewish Symbols,* vol. 2, pp. 14–33; vol. 3, figs. 734ff.
57. Goodenough, *Jewish Symbols,* vol. 2, p. 26f.; A. Konikoff, *Sarcophagi from the Jewish Catacombs of Ancient Rome,* (Stuttgart, 1986), no. 14; G. M. A. Hanfmann, *The Season Sarcophagus in Dumbarton Oaks,* vol. 2 (Cambridge, Mass., 1951), no. 493; A. Giuliano, ed., *Museo Nazionale Romano: Le Sculture,* vol. 1 (Rome, 1985), no. III.10, pp. 151–153 (M. E. Micheli).
58. Frey (1975 ed.), no. 217.
59. See L. Cracco Ruggini, "Jews and Romans in the Last Decades of the Empire," in *Italia Judaica,* pp. 38–65; B. Blumenkranz, *Juifs et chrétiens dans le monde occidental 430–1096* (Paris, 1960).
60. Frey no. 650; G. Libertini, "Epigrafe giudaico-latina rinvenuta a Catania," *Atti della Reale Accademia delle Scienze di Torino, Classe di Sc.-Morali, Stor. Filologiche* 64 (1929): 185–195.
61. Frey no. 70; *Corpus Inscriptionum Latinarum* VI.4.27959; R. Brilliant, "Remembering and Jewish Art," pp. 259, 260, fig. 1.

Fig. 76. *Seal of Theodora with Jewish Symbols,* Rome, third to fifth century, Museo Nazionale Romano, Rome (cat. no. 23)

Fig. 77. Leon (Yehudah) bar Yehoshua (de Rossi) and Joel ben Simeon, *Mah Nishtanah, Maḥzor* (Prayer Book for Festivals), northern Italy, second half of the fifteenth century, Jewish National and University Library, Jerusalem (cat. no. 46)

EVELYN M. COHEN

HEBREW MANUSCRIPT ILLUMINATION IN ITALY[1]

Illuminated Hebrew manuscripts from Italy, more than those of any other region inhabited by Jews in the Middle Ages and the Renaissance, convey a sense of everyday life and customs. Although Sephardic and Ashkenazic books are often richly illustrated, they do not contain the profuse details and range of subjects found in manuscripts from Italy. This is due in part to the breadth of material chosen to be illustrated; in addition to prayer books, Haggadot, and Bibles, rabbinical texts and scientific works were also adorned with contemporary scenes.

The earliest illuminated manuscripts from Italy are believed to have been written in Rome toward the end of the thirteenth century.[2] Most of these are Bibles embellished with ornamental initial word panels and decorative marginal designs but not illustrated. Perhaps the earliest extant manuscript with depictions of scenes relating to the text is a psalter that does not contain a colophon but is generally accepted as being from thirteenth-century Emilia.[3] The initial words of various psalms are appropriately adorned with little scenes depicting King David, choral groups singing God's praises, and for Psalm 137, the mourners by the river of Babylon (fol. 198).

By the fourteenth century manuscripts containing references to Jewish customs appear. The most notable example is a copy of the halakhic rulings of the Italian rabbi, Isaiah di Trani the younger (thirteenth century), dated 1374.[4] Some text illustrations portray everyday life in Italy, including carpenters at work and the sale of a ship between two men. Others represent specifically Jewish practices in scenes depicting a man lighting a Ḥanukkah menorah, the making of an *eruv,* the stoning of a man, a sukkah and a half-length figure of a man holding the Four Species, and a scene of men at court (the Sanhedrin).[5]

At the turn of the century another rabbinic text, the *Mishneh Torah* by Maimonides, was also illustrated, providing us with a valuable record of some Jewish practices.[6] Included among the depictions are scenes of punishment by stoning; a man holding a Torah scroll and a man seated by his bed, ready to recite the Shema; a man washing another's hands before the recitation of the Shema; a synagogue scene with a man standing near the Torah ark; and a depiction of a *kohen* (priest) with his hands raised for the priestly benediction.[7]

It was in the fifteenth century that Italian manuscript illumination depicting scenes of Jewish life reached its zenith. For example, the opening pages of each of the four sections of the Vatican Library's copy of Jacob ben Asher's legal treatise, the *Arba'ah Turim,* depict, respectively, a synagogue scene, animals being slaughtered according to Jewish ritual, a wedding, and a courtroom scene.[8] The manuscript, copied in Mantua

in 1435, is illuminated in the contemporary International Style and reflects the influence of works by other painters from Lombardy.[9]

Although an indigenous Italian style already existed, immigrant Jewish illuminators brought with them their native artistic practices. The most famous scribe and artist to come from Germany was Joel ben Simeon. Eleven manuscripts bearing his name are known, and several others have been linked to his workshop.[10] The colophons of Joel's manuscripts indicate that he resided in Cologne and Bonn. He was active in both Italy and Germany, however, and his art was influenced by that of both regions.

Among Joel ben Simeon's earliest known works is a Haggadah that was executed in 1454, often referred to as the Second New York Haggadah of the Library of The Jewish Theological Seminary of America, New York (cat. no. 37). The manuscript displays Joel's mastery of the scribal arts. Many of his words visually take on a life of their own, being formed from overlapping letters that create an almost sculptural effect; the ascenders and descenders of various letters frequently terminate in extremely ornamental forms. Most striking is Joel's use of zoomorphic and anthropomorphic letters (see fols. 34v, 54v; fig. 78). There is a long tradition of this kind of artwork, both in Hebrew and Latin manuscripts,[11] but Joel's combinations of animal and human forms are original and engrossing. The scribe also employed inventive motifs to decorate initial words, as evidenced by *Ki lo na'eh,* the last liturgical poem in this manuscript. The word *Ki* is framed by unusual designs such as rabbits (fol. 57v) and dancing figures (fol. 58), which are placed at right angles around the square spaces.[12]

The Seminary Haggadah, written according to the Italian rite, contains a colophon on the last leaf (fol. 59), in which the copyist states, "I the scrivener Joel the son of Simeon (of blessed memory), who is known as Feibush the Ashkenazi, from the city of Cologne on the river Rhine, wrote, vocalized, and decorated this Haggadah and finished it in the month of Elul, in the year [5]214." It is noteworthy that Joel, presumably working in Italy, emphasizes his German roots. In fact, the word *Ashkenazi* is highlighted with pen work above it.

In an undated Haggadah, today housed in Geneva,[13] Joel once again includes his nickname, Feibush, and the fact that he was an Ashkenazi. These two manuscripts share some decorative features as well, notably the placement of an initial word on a curtain suspended from a wooden bar and held by hands at either end,[14]

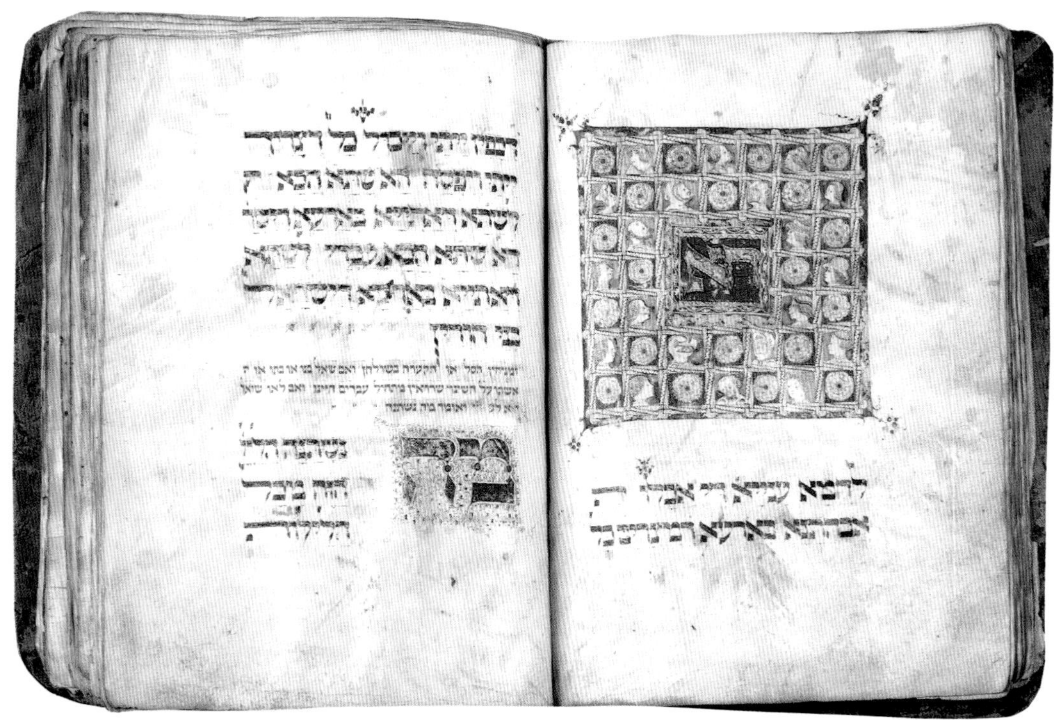

the use of atlas figures to support architectural elements,[15] and most strikingly, the use of a large gridlike space filled with heads of people from different strata of society.[16] In the Seminary Haggadah (see fig. 79) this area is composed of forty squares in which faces and rosettes are alternately placed, forming a large square that functions as the initial word panel for the word *Ha* in the middle. The text begins with the words "This bread of affliction" and continues with an invitation to all to join in the seder. Although the meaning of the decoration is vague, it is striking that the faces represent a cross section of medieval society, including knights, jesters, and peasants. The source of this image is unclear as well but may be related to painters' pattern books found in southern Germany. An example of this type of work is the *Wiener Musterbuch,* from the first half of the fifteenth century.[17] It consists of fifty-six drawings highlighted with red and white on paper and backed with wooden panels.

Joel, working in Germany and northern Italy, was inspired by art from both centers. His work in turn influenced that of other Italian illuminators of Hebrew manuscripts. A fifteenth-century *maḥzor,* or prayer book, the first volume of which is in the Jewish National and University Library, Jerusalem (cat. no. 46),[18] is a noteworthy example. Although the first scene and

Fig. 78. (opposite) Joel ben Simeon, *Ometz,* Haggadah, Italy, 1454, The Library of The Jewish Theological Seminary of America, New York (cat. no. 37)

Fig. 79. (above) Joel ben Simeon, *Ha laḥmah anyah,* Haggadah, Italy, 1454, The Library of The Jewish Theological Seminary of America, New York (cat. no. 37)

the richly illuminated floral borders are executed in a typically Italian manner, the subsequent illustrations have the flavor of Joel's style, in which forms are defined primarily by outlines and modeling is minimal. The text begins with the daily prayers, and appropriately, at the bottom of the page a man is depicted awakening in his bed; he is about to be assisted in bathing by the servant near the fountain in the center of the scene and finally recites his prayers by reading from a book (see fig. 80).

The most striking relationship between this manuscript and the art of Joel ben Simeon is found in the Exodus scene depicted as a double-page spread across the bottom of folios 115v–116. In both style and detail the representation closely resembles that found in the *Ashkenazi Haggadah,* now in London, a work in which Joel identifies himself as the artist.[19] In each, the Israelites are shown between the columns of fire and smoke at the moment when the waters of the Red Sea are beginning to separate. Moses is depicted in both books with a similar profile, including a pointed, jutting beard. Most striking is the portrayal of the Egyptians in pursuit at the right. The soldiers are preceded by a small figure walking in front and holding a staff. Pharaoh, placed close to the picture plane and wearing a crown, is similar in both, as is the depiction of a horse-drawn wagon at the end. The Jerusalem manuscript, however, includes a depiction of a gate and crenellated architecture. Although these elements do not appear in the *Ashkenazi Haggadah,* their representation is reminiscent of architectural renderings in Joel's repertory.[20]

In the Jerusalem maḥzor the pursuit of the Egyptians appears at the bottom of a page that begins with the text *Ha laḥma anya* (The bread of affliction). Above these words is a seder scene in which seven men are standing around a table, holding up a basket containing matzot and leafy vegetables. The depiction of the basket and the placement of the figures are almost identical to those in a maḥzor in London.[21] The floral borders of the pages are embellished with half-length figures and a matza; the man on the extreme left appears to be preparing ḥaroset.

The final illustration in the first volume of the manuscript (fig. 81) depicts Moses receiving the Tablets of the Law in the margin of the text for Shavuot, the festival that commemorates this event. Moses is shown standing on Mount Sinai under the blaring trumpets in the sky, holding the Ten Commandments by staves on

Fig. 80. (opposite) Leon (Yehudah) bar Yehoshua (de Rossi) and Joel ben Simeon, "Awakening and Morning Prayers," *Maḥzor* (Prayer Book for Festivals), northern Italy, second half of the fifteenth century, Jewish National and University Library, Jerusalem (cat. no. 46)

Fig. 81. (above) Leon (Yehudah) bar Yehoshua (de Rossi) and Joel ben Simeon, "The Giving of the Law," *Maḥzor* (Prayer Book for Festivals), northern Italy, second half of the fifteenth century, Jewish National and University Library, Jerusalem (cat. no. 46)

either side. By rendering the Tablets of the Law in this manner, the artist alludes to the display of the Torah itself as it is raised in the synagogue service. In the bottom border of the page, the Israelite men, women, and children are led by the figure of Aaron. The composition of this scene is similar to that found in the *Rothschild Maḥzor* (cat. no. 82),[22] though in the latter work Aaron's place is taken by Joshua, for the scene is used to illustrate the text of *Pirkei Avot* (Sayings of the Fathers), which begins, "Moses received the Torah from Sinai and handed it down to Joshua."

The *Rothschild Maḥzor,* written in Florence in 1492, was decorated by three different workshops; two of them are Florentine, while the third, even at this late date, reflects the art of Joel ben Simeon.[23] This workshop executed most of the text illustrations in the prayer book and consequently conveyed the most information about Jewish life in Italy at this time.

Among these scenes is the depiction of a man wearing a tallit and holding a Torah scroll that is covered with a brocade cloth (fol. 125v). As no Torah mantles are extant from this period, this illustration and related ones appearing in other Italian manuscripts provide us with information about ceremonial art that no longer exists. Also represented, accompanying an elegy for the Ninth of Av on folio 220v (fig. 83), is a depiction of a man reading from a prayer book. In accordance with the customs of this fast day, he is barefoot.

A lengthy colophon on folio 469 of the *Rothschild Maḥzor* specifies that it was written for Elijah ben Joab of Vigevano ben Abraham of the Gallico family. The coat of arms of the Norsa family appears ten times in this manuscript, however, suggesting that the prayer book was intended as a gift commemorating a marriage between members of these two families.[24] It has already been noted that the inscription of the wheel of fortune at the beginning of the manuscript (fig. 84) ap-

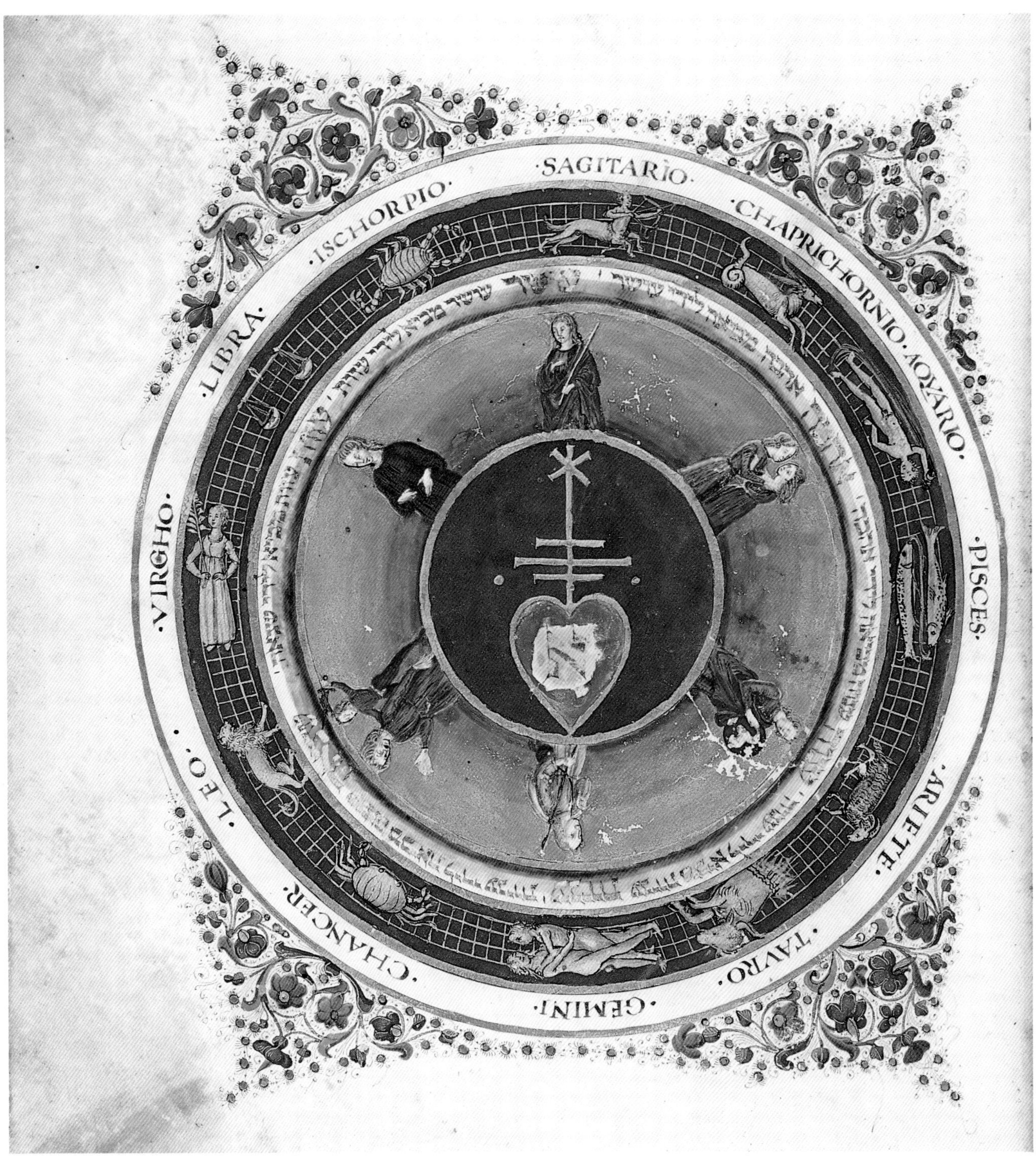

Fig. 82. (opposite, left) "Moses Receiving the Tablets of the Law," *The Rothschild Maḥzor,* Florence, 1492, The Library of The Jewish Theological Seminary of America, New York (cat. no. 43)

Fig. 83. (opposite, right) "Man Praying (Tisha b'Av)," *The Rothschild Maḥzor,* Florence, 1492, The Library of The Jewish Theological Seminary of America, New York (cat. no. 43)

Fig. 84. (above) "Zodiac and Wheel of Fortune," *The Rothschild Maḥzor,* Florence, 1492, The Library of The Jewish Theological Seminary of America, New York (cat. no. 43)

Fig. 85. "Gates of Prayer," *Hanhagot mikol hashanah,* Italy, fifteenth century, Princeton University Library, Princeton (cat. no. 44)

pears in another Hebrew manuscript on a page that contains a kabbalistic formula with astrological references used to predict the success of a marriage.[25] The signs of the zodiac were a popular motif on Italian marriage contracts of the seventeenth and eighteenth centuries, as the parties wanted to be wed at a propitious time to a mate who was born under a compatible constellation.[26] In the center of the concentric circles on this page is an enigmatic design that might be a reference to the manuscript's owner, possibly Elijah himself. The letter aleph is placed within a logo, and although this sign has not yet been found elsewhere, it is reminiscent of an owner's mark that appears on some early sixteenth-century Italian pottery.[27] As the coats of arms employed by Jewish families in Italy were invented to emulate the long-standing tradition of their Christian neighbors, the unusual insignia found here might reflect a similar adaptation from the surrounding culture.

Coats of arms were frequently incorporated into the borders of both Hebrew and Latin manuscripts in the fifteenth century. Manuscripts commissioned by Jews were often illuminated by Christian workshops, and consequently, although the details of the subject matter might be specifically Jewish, the format of the pages and the design elements were frequently similar to those of Christian books. The *Hanhagot mikol hashanah* (Prayer Book for Various Jewish Rituals; cat. no. 44) in the Princeton University Library is a striking example of a manuscript depicting Jewish ceremonies that was undoubtedly illuminated by a Christian workshop.[28] The book contains twenty-six text illustrations dealing with the life-cycle events of circumcision, redemption of the firstborn son, betrothal and nuptials, and finally death; scenes of charity and prayer are depicted as well. Some of these events appear in many Italian Hebrew manuscripts, while others are rare. Several works portray circumcision, but the Princeton codex begins with depictions of the birth and inspection of the child, which are followed by two scenes relating to circumcision. Both this manuscript and a prayer book from Pesaro dated 1481 depict the redemption of the firstborn, and in both the mother plays an active part in the ceremony.[29] Marriage is represented in many Italian manuscripts, but the Princeton prayer book contains several scenes, including depictions of the candle bearers, the betrothal, and the nuptial ceremonies.[30]

The ritual for the bettering of dreams appears in many prayer books; in the Princeton manuscript and the *Rothschild Miscellany*[31] the event is illustrated as well. In both, the dreamer, accompanied by two witnesses, is shown standing before an elderly bearded man.

Seven scenes in the Princeton manuscript are devoted to prayer, some individual, others communal. An interesting representation appears on folio 33 (fig. 85), where the gates of prayer are depicted in the outer border. Another interesting scene (fol. 44) portrays a woman engaged in individual prayer. Although this is not the only example of a praying woman,[32] the image is rare. In addition an unusual number of scenes are devoted to death. In both this manuscript and the *Rothschild Miscellany,* which contains two scenes concerning this subject, the mourners are depicted wearing black garments.[33] The Princeton prayer book, however, includes six scenes dealing with death (fig. 86). Perhaps the most striking is to be found on folio 56, where in a very Christian-looking representation, a figure of Death gives the soul of the deceased, portrayed as a nude child, to a winged angel.

The Princeton manuscript contains a full-page miniature of Job (fol. 150v) placed within a lavishly illuminated border. Related images appear in two other Hebrew manuscripts from Italy, one at Yale University and the other in Jerusalem, both of which are devoted to the books of Psalms, Job, and Proverbs.[34] These manuscripts, which are sometimes referred to by the Hebrew acronym *Sifrei emet,* both begin with a miniature of David standing on the slain body of Goliath depicted in accordance with a tradition that goes back to medieval Christian representations of Virtue triumphant over Vice. In both the undated work in Jerusalem and the Yale University manuscript of 1467 (cat. no. 40), the scene is framed by a lush foliate border. The same is true for the miniature at the opening of the Book of Job, where a seated Job is accompanied by three figures at the left, and the whole is placed within lavish borders. The adornment of the beginning of Proverbs differs in the two works. Whereas the Jeru-

Fig. 86. "Mourning," *Hanhagot mikol hashanah,* Italy, fifteenth century, Princeton University Library, Princeton (cat. no. 44)

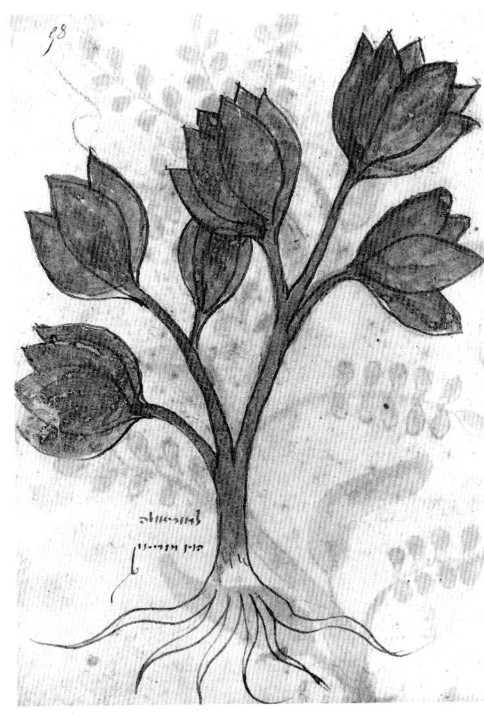

Fig. 88. Page, Medical Herbal, Italy, second half of the fifteenth century, Bibliothèque Nationale, Paris (cat. no. 45)

salem manuscript once again begins with a full-page miniature, this time depicting the Judgment of Solomon (fol. 186v), the scene is relegated to the bottom margin of a magnificently illuminated floral border on folio 153 of the Yale manuscript (fig. 87). The colophon at the end of this manuscript does not mention the artist's name. Although his identity is still subject to debate, the painter undoubtedly produced one of the finest examples of illumination found in a Hebrew manuscript.

Aside from biblical scenes and depictions of events relating to Jewish life and customs found in prayer books and rabbinical treatises,[35] Hebrew manuscripts also contain images of secular life in Renaissance Italy. These depictions are found in scientific and medical treatises,[36] the most noteworthy of which is a copy of Avicenna's *Canon of Medicine* in Bologna, which includes many scenes of physicians attending patients and various medical treatments.[37] The medical herbal, in use since antiquity, also belongs in this general category. Herbals depicted various plant forms, and their texts explained their medicinal uses. An herbal from the Bibliothèque Nationale, Paris (cat. no. 88), exemplifies this type of text. In this manuscript 130 different plants are represented; they are identified by inscriptions in Hebrew and sometimes Latin. In the depiction of laurel on folio 58 (fig. 88), the herb's name appears in Hebrew and in Latin written in Hebrew characters. Some of the inscriptions tell which conditions the plants could cure.

By the close of the fifteenth century, with the rise in the production of printed books, manuscript production began to wane. Some notable examples continued to be written and decorated, however, as exemplified by the Haggadah written by the noted author and scribe Abraham Farissol for his friend Joseph Norsa in Ferrara in 1515 (cat. no. 48).[38] With the exception of one recently rediscovered scene on folio 5, the rest of the illustrations (e.g., fig. 90) were executed by a later, presumably Christian artist who had little understanding of the events he was asked to depict.

In contrast, another Haggadah from this period (cat. no. 52) displays many links with the iconographic programs found in fifteenth-century manuscripts, specifically with those of Joel ben Simeon. The motif of the faces of various members of society placed within a rectangular field divided into squares appears on folio 7v before the text of *Ha laḥma anya,* as it did in the manuscript by Joel ben Simeon of 1454 men-

Fig. 87. "Proverbs," *Sifrei Emet,* Italy, 1467, Beinecke Library, Yale University, New Haven (cat. no. 40)

Fig. 90. (above) Abraham Farissol and an unknown artist, "The Exodus," Haggadah, Ferrara, 1515, The Library of The Jewish Theological Seminary of America, New York (cat. no. 48)

Fig. 89. (opposite) Haggadah, Italy, late sixteenth century, Private Collection (cat. no. 52)

tioned above. The style is clearly later, however, and reflects an interest in caricature and grotesque faces similar to those in the works of Leonardo da Vinci. The double-page scene depicting the flight of the Israelites from Egypt on folios 19v–20 is even more strikingly similar to the representation in the *Ashkenazi Haggadah* than that found in the Jerusalem manuscript discussed above (cat. no. 46). Specific and minute details, such as the inclusion of broken wheels on the Egyptian wagon, echo the depiction in the London manuscript. A relationship to other sixteenth-century Haggadot may be found as well, and the delicately rendered seder scene on folio 21, with its inclusion of a dog under the table, is reminiscent of a similar scene on folio 14v of the Ferrarese Haggadah by Farissol.

Although the production of illuminated manuscripts in codex form declined drastically in the following centuries, the decoration of Esther scrolls, marriage contracts, and historical documents flourished in Italy in the seventeenth and eighteenth centuries.[39] Biblical subjects were depicted on *megillot* and *ketubbot* alike, as evidenced by an eighteenth-century Esther scroll decorated with scenes of Jonah and Jacob (cat. no. 55; fig. 91) and the *ketubbah* from Livorno dated 1751 that depicts the Binding of Isaac (cat. no. 110). Similar techniques, such as the use of cutout designs, are found in both types of manuscripts. Motifs that were prevalent in Christian works, such as personified representations of virtues, seasons, senses, and elements, also appear in the decorative programs of scrolls (see cat. no. 57; fig. 29) and marriage contracts, (see cat. no. 111). These are the inheritors of the rich tradition of manuscript illumination in which Christian and Jewish motifs were combined to form an expressive reflection of the Jewish experience in Italy.

Notes

1. I would like to thank Michel Garel, Sharon Liberman Mintz, Shalom Sabar, and Menahem Schmelzer for their assistance in the preparation of this essay.
2. For a description of these manuscripts, see L. M. Ottolenghi, "Un gruppo di manoscritti ebraici romani del sec. XIII e XIV e la loro decorazione," in *Studi sull'ebraismo italiano* (Rome, 1974), pp. 141–158. For a general discussion of the illumination of Hebrew manuscripts in Italy, see B. Narkiss, *Hebrew Illuminated Manuscripts* (Jerusalem, 1969), pp. 36–39; J. Gutmann, *Hebrew Manuscript Painting* (New York, 1978), pp. 27–31; L. M. Ottolenghi, "Alcuni manoscritti ebraici miniati in Italia Settentrionale nel secolo XV," *Arte Lombarda* 60 (1981): 41–48; idem, "Miniature ebraiche italiane," in *Italia Judaica: Atti del I convegno internazionale* (Rome, 1983), pp. 211–227; and most recently, idem "Manoscritti ebraici miniati nelle biblioteche dell'Emilia-Romagna," *Arte e cultura ebraiche in Emilia-Romagna* (Ferrara, 1988), pp. 172–173.
3. For a thorough study of this manuscript, see T. Metzger, "Les illustrations d'un psautier hébreu italien de la fin du XIIIe-siècle. Le Ms. Parm. 1870–de Rossi 510 de la Bibliothèque Palatina de Parme," *Cahiers archéologiques* 26 (1977): 145–162.
4. London, British Library Ms. Or. 5024.
5. These scenes appear on fols. 184v, 225v, 19, 40v, 64v, 70v, and 241, respectively. Some of these illustrations are reproduced in T. and M. Metzger's *Jewish Life in the Middle Ages* (New York, 1982), figs. 235, 239, 353, 369, 371.
6. Jerusalem, Jewish National and University Library Ms. Heb. 4° 1193. The manuscript was actually copied in Spain in the fourteenth century and later decorated in Italy. Although illuminated copies of the *Mishneh Torah* were produced in Sephardic and Ashkenazic regions, only in Italy did the illustrations clearly relate to the text. For a brief discussion of the Jerusalem manuscript, see Narkiss, *Hebrew Illuminated Manuscripts,* p. 134.
7. These illustrations appear on fols. 22v, 32, 33, 33v, and 40v, respectively.
8. Vatican City, Biblioteca Apostolica Vaticana Cod. Ross 555; the illustrations appear on fol. 12v, between fols. 127v and 128, fol. 220, and between fols. 292v and 293.
9. This stylistic relationship has already been noted in Gutmann, *Hebrew Manuscript Painting,* p. 104.
10. Joel ben Simeon has been written about extensively. For important information and further bibliography, see Narkiss, *Hebrew Illuminated Manuscripts,* pp. 171–172, no. 42: J. Gutmann, "Thirteen Manuscripts in Search of an Author: Joel ben Simeon, Fifteenth-Century Scribe-Artist," *Studies in Bibliography and Booklore* 9 (1969–1971): 76–95; M. Metzger, *La Haggada enluminée: Étude iconographique et stylistique des manuscrits enluminés et decorés de la Haggada du XIIIe au XVIe siècle* (Leiden, 1973), pp. 376–379, 388–390, 403–405; M. Beit-Arié, "Joel Ben Simeon's Manuscripts: A Codicologer's View," *Journal of Jewish Art* 3–4 (1977): 25–39; S. Edmunds, "The Place of the London Haggadah in the Work of Joel ben Simeon, *Journal of Jewish Art* 7 (1980): 25–34; D. Goldstein, *The Ashkenazi Haggadah* (New York, 1985), pp. 9–10; and the facsimile edition of the *Washington Haggadah* (forthcoming).
11. Earlier examples in Hebrew manuscripts can be found predominantly in works from Spain, for example, in the fourteenth-century *Golden Haggadah* (London, British Library Add. Ms. 27210) and *Cervera Bible* (Lisbon, Biblioteca Nacional Ms. 72) and in the *Kennicott Bible* of 1476 (Oxford, Bodleian Library Ms. Kennicott I), whose decoration was based upon the preceding work. In Latin texts these forms already appear in Merovingian manuscripts from the seventh century. A notable later example is found in an Italian sketchbook from the end of the fourteenth century attributed to Giovannino dei Grassi, which was copied by the German artist Master E. S. in the 1460s. See J. J. G. Alexander, *The Decorated Letter* (New York, 1978), p. 111.

Fig. 91. "Jonah and the Whale," Scroll of Esther, Italy, seventeenth–eighteenth century, Private Collection (cat. no. 55)

12. Another depiction of dancing portrayed toward the end of the text of the Haggadah is found in the Ashkenazic manuscript known as the *Ḥilek and Bilek Haggadah* (Paris, Bibliotheque Nationale Ms. hébr. 1933), fol. 38. This Haggadah dates to the fifteenth century as well; the scene might allude to a contemporary practice of celebration that took place at the end of the seder.
13. Geneva, Martin Bodmer Collection Cod. 81, formerly Dyson-Perrins Ms. 124.
14. This motif does not decorate the same initial words in these two works. The curtains differ stylistically as well, with the Seminary example displaying a more sophisticated spatial illusion.
15. These elements appear at different points in the Haggadot. In the Geneva manuscript the initial word, *Lefikhakh,* is placed alone within the architectural form, while in the New York manuscript the motif spans a double page containing a rather lengthy text describing the procedures at the seder meal. Although the motif of arches supported by columns with caryatid figures at the base appears in many fourteenth-century Ashkenazic *maḥzorim,* Joel ben Simeon might have been inspired by Romanesque portals on cathedrals in northern Italy. Similar atlas figures appear, for example, on the cathedrals of Ferrara and Cremona.
16. The heads form a full-page miniature on fol. 4v of the Geneva manuscript. The design is incorporated into an initial word panel on fol. 15v of the New York Haggadah.
17. See *Meisterwerke: Führer durch das Kunsthistorisches Museum,* no. 1 (Vienna, 1968), pl. 59; M. Leithe-Jasper and R. Distelberger, *Kunsthistorisches Museum Wien: Schatzkammer und Sammlung für Plastik und Kunstgewerbe* (Munich, 1982), p. 60.
18. For an extensive study of this manuscript, see M. Metzger, "Un *maḥzor* italien enluminé du XVe siècle," *Mitteilungen des Kunsthistorischen Institutes in Florenz* 20 (1976): 159–196.
19. For further information concerning the manuscript, see Goldstein, *Ashkenazi Haggadah,* pp. 9–15.
20. In addition the connection between this scene and that found in a maḥzor in London (British Library Ms. Harley 5686, fol. 60v) has already been noted in Metzger, "Un *maḥzor* italien," p. 184.
21. This is the manuscript cited in note 20 above. See ibid., fig. 18.
22. For a detailed study of this work, see *The Rothschild Maḥzor: Florence 1492,* intro. by E. M. Cohen and M. Schmelzer (New York, 1983).
23. Another example of an Italian manuscript illuminated primarily in an advanced fifteenth-century style, yet inexplicably containing illustrations in the retardataire style of Joel ben Simeon is found in a halakhic miscellany containing the texts of *Sha'arei Dura* and *Hilkhot Niddah* (Hamburg, Staats- und Universitätsbibliothek Cod. Heb. 337). On folio 75v, depicted in a contemporary Renaissance style, a bridegroom is shown placing a ring on his bride's finger. Both are elegantly attired, but on the left side of his mantle, the man wears a circular badge that identifies him as a Jew.
24. The Norsa family coat of arms was usually depicted with Moors' heads, but the *stemma* appears with Caucasian faces as well, in both the *De Bry Psalter* (Switzerland, Carl Alexander Floersheim Art and Judaica Collection) and later, in a marriage contract from Verona, 1695 (Venice, Museo Correr M. 37198).
25. See *The Rothschild Maḥzor,* p. 55, n. 50.
26. See S. Sabar, "The Beginnings and Flourishing of *Ketubbah* Illustration in Italy: A Study in Popular Imagery and Jewish Patronage during the Seventeenth and Eighteenth Centuries," (Ph.D. diss., University of California, Los Angeles, 1987), p. 206ff.
27. Examples may be found in T. Wilson, *Ceramic Art of the Italian Renaissance* (Austin, 1987), nos. 164, 168.
28. For a comprehensive study of the various miniatures in this manuscript, see E. Panofsky, "Giotto and Maimonides in Avignon: The Story of an Illustrated Hebrew Manuscript," *Journal of the Walters Art Gallery* 4 (1941): 27–44; idem, "Giotto and Maimonides in Avignon: A Postscript," *Journal of the Walters Art Gallery* 5 (1942): 124–127.
29. Budapest, Hungarian Academy of Sciences Ms. Kaufmann A 380 II, fol. 228v. See B. Narkiss and G. Sed-Rajna, *Index of Jewish Art: Iconographical Index of Hebrew Illuminated Manuscripts,* vol. 4 (Jerusalem and Paris, 1988).
30. Other notable wedding scenes are found in the *Rothschild Miscellany,* Jerusalem, Israel Museum Ms. 180/51, fol. 120v; the Pesaro manuscript mentioned in note 29 above, fol. 230; Parma, Biblioteca Palatina Ms. Parm. 3596, fol. 275; and the Vatican *Arba'ah Turim,* mentioned above. The Pesaro manuscript also includes an unusual scene of the presentation of the *ketubbah,* fol. 231v.
31. *Rothschild Miscellany,* fol. 118.
32. A praying woman is depicted, for example, in the *Maraviglia Siddur,* an Italian manuscript executed by Joel ben Simeon in 1469 (London, British Library Add. 26957).
33. *Rothschild Miscellany,* fols. 121v, 122v.

34. The *Rothschild Miscellany* begins with these three texts, but the illustrations differ from those in the Jerusalem (Israel Museum Ms. 180/55) and New Haven (Yale University, Beinecke Library Ms. 409) manuscripts.
35. A most striking example of the later is found in a richly illuminated copy of the *Mishneh Torah* that is bound in two volumes (Vatican City, Biblioteca Apostolica Vaticana Cod. Ross. 498, and private collection, New York).
36. For example, *Sefer ha-Keritot* (Greater Book of Surgery) by Bruno da Lungoburgo (Vatican City, Biblioteca Apostolica Vaticana Cod. Vat. ebr. 462) and the medical miscellanies in Paris (Bibliothèque Nationale Ms. hébr. 1181) and Cambridge (University Library Ms. Dd. 10.68).
37. Bologna, Biblioteca Universitaria Ms. 2197. For the most recent and thorough study of this and related manuscripts, see G. Tamani, ed., *Il Canon medicinae di Avicenna nella tradizione ebraica* (Padua, 1988).
38. For a more complete discussion of this work, see E. M. Cohen, "The Illustrations in Abraham Farissol's Haggadah of 1515," *Jewish Art* 12–13 (1986–1987): 89–95.
39. For more information and further bibliography for decorated scrolls, see M. Metzger, "The John Rylands Megillah and Some Other Illustrated Megilloth of the Fifteenth to Seventeenth Centuries," *Bulletin of the John Rylands Library* 45 (1962): 148–184; idem, "A Study of Some Unknown Hand-Painted Megilloth of the Seventeenth and Eighteenth Centuries," *Bulletin of the John Rylands Library* 46 (1963): 84–126. For studies of decorated marriage contracts, see Liliana Grassi, ed., *Ketubbot italiane: Antichi contratti nuziali ebraici miniati* (Milan, 1984); and especially the writings of S. Sabar: "The Use of Christian Motifs in Illustrations of Jewish Marriage Contracts in Italy and Its Meaning," *Journal of Jewish Art* 10 (1984): 47–63; "The Beginnings of Ketubbah Decoration in Italy: Venice in the Late Sixteenth to the Early Seventeenth Centuries," *Jewish Art* 12–13 (1986–1987): 96–110; "Beginnings and Flourishing of *Ketubbah* Illustration."

Fig. 92. Torah Mantle, southern Italy, seventeenth century, Comunità Israelitica, Rome (cat. no. 132)

DORA LISCIA BEMPORAD

JEWISH CEREMONIAL ART IN THE ERA OF THE GHETTOS

The birth of the ghetto as a place of enforced habitation, one of the aberrations of the modern era, paradoxically was also a catalyst for the development of Jewish ceremonial art in Italy. In practice the ghettos, while serving as prison-neighborhoods in which Jews were forced to reside, also offered security. Until the mid-sixteenth century the threat of expulsion had been ever-present for Jews on the Italian peninsula, but only as a result of extraordinarily grave political events brought about by the Counter-Reformation was this threat carried out. The delineation of a neighborhood inhabited exclusively by Jews created a separate world with architectural and cultural needs completely different from those of the population beyond the ghetto walls. It is highly probable that the certainty of being able to remain in one place indefinitely, albeit under conditions of humiliating segregation, favored the growth, if not the birth, of ceremonial art that enriched and embellished places of worship to a degree that went beyond ritual needs.

It is significant that practically no artifacts remain from the preghetto period. Ignoring the illuminated codices, the incunabula, and later printed books, which represent a completely separate and distinct expressive form, there are only a few extant synagogue objects dating from before the sixteenth century that can be attributed to Italy. Among them are an ark from Modena, dated 1472 (fig. 93),[1] a pair of Sicilian Torah finials, generally attributed to the fifteenth century,[2] and a Torah pointer from Ferrara dated 1488.[3]

The ark from Modena exemplifies the Gothic style that characterized ceremonial art in Italy, in both Christian and Jewish circles, at a time when the Renaissance was in full flower in other cultural spheres. Its small dimensions indicate that the ark was part of a commensurately small environment, and its wooden material allowed it to be transported whenever the Jewish community found it necessary to move unexpectedly following one of the recurrent expulsion edicts.

The Torah finials from Sicily, generally dated to the mid-fifteenth century, are a unique case. Their vivid Moorish style links them to a culture outside Italy, although their tower form represents a prototype upon which most Italian Torah finials were patterned in later centuries.

There is also scant iconographic evidence for the reconstruction of Jewish ceremonial art in Italy before the birth of the ghettos. The few images that remain are for the most part contained in illuminated codices, and they often fail to fill substantially the vast lacunae in our knowledge of this early period. For example, the celebrated miniature of a man with a Torah that decorates a page in the *Rothschild Maḥzor,* (cat. no. 43; fig. 94) shows the scrolls covered, probably with vel-

Fig. 93. Torah Ark, Modena, 1472, Musée de Cluny, Paris (Cl. 12237)

vet (the design seems to reproduce the popular pomegranate motif), but without any other ornamentation.[4]

But these few examples cannot provide a full picture of Jewish ceremonial art before the sixteenth and seventeenth centuries. Although architecturally significant synagogues came into being at the same time as, or immediately following, the establishment of the ghettos, the passage of the centuries has left a dearth of material for the construction of a valid history of Judaica. The Italian-Jewish patrimony must be reconstructed city by city, since each community and each ghetto had its own development due to both their individual histories and their varying relationships with the governments under whose jurisdiction they fell.

In the sixteenth century Jews in certain cities experienced stable living conditions for decades, allowing them to establish religious centers of some importance. Elsewhere, however, a lack of security and a reduced Jewish population prevented the development of synagogue architecture. We can glean some information about synagogues that were transformed or destroyed over the centuries from arks, which, thanks to their sacred nature, were often the only elements to be preserved. The ark from Urbino, created in 1500 but modified in 1624, was clearly designed and realized in an extremely pure Renaissance style by artists who frequented the Montefeltro court (cat. no. 114; fig. 30). In this piece the perfect assimilation of Jewish content within that refined culture can be seen.[5] Fragments of the ark of the Catalan synagogue in Rome, dated around 1519, were recently identified in the storerooms of the temple in Rome.[6] The use of marble in place of wood responded to the needs of a population uprooted from its place of origin but seeking a permanent settlement in a new, if inhospitable, country.

The erection of synagogues in Venice at the dawn of the sixteenth century had a different background. The Venetian ghetto, established in 1516, was the first in Italy. Immediately following that date, the various ethnic groups making up the Jewish population began to build their own synagogues. The first, the great German synagogue, was built between 1528 and 1529; the Canton synagogue was built between 1531 and 1532 (fig. 95); the Italian synagogue in 1572; the Levantine and Spanish synagogues were built at almost the same time.

The desire to make places of worship the center of ghetto life is attested to by the Jewish communities' turning to well-known architects. Baldassare Longhena or a follower was engaged for the first rebuilding of the Spanish synagogue in Venice around the mid-sixteenth century, and Girolamo Rainaldi was hired to expand the Catalan synagogue in Rome between 1622 and 1628. The renovation of the Italian synagogue in Florence can be attributed to Bernardo Buontalenti, who also designed the marble ark immediately after the establishment of the Florentine ghetto in 1570.[7] Whether these structures were modest or elaborate, great attention was given to their interiors. Yet not until the following century did sufficient material survive to allow us to trace a history of ceremonial objects and Torah ornaments.

There are innumerable reasons for this gap: some are connected to the history of Italian Jewry; others are similar to the turns of fate that plagued the survival of precious ornaments from churches and palaces throughout the peninsula. Both silver objects and textiles have always fallen victim to their own intrinsic value. Every threat of war, every falling out of favor with the governing bodies, every compelling financial necessity, could be the occasion to borrow both public and private wealth. For example, during Charles V's siege of Florence in 1529, the governors of the republic may have requested that Jews donate the same amount of silver that was being demanded from the city's churches. Nearly three centuries later the Jews of Livorno had to hand over lamps to provide for the military expenses of French troops.[8] The story of a laver and basin preserved in the Florence synagogue, reconstructed through archival evidence, might be an anomaly, or it might reflect a typical situation. The two objects were donated to the Levantine synagogue by Samuel Anselmo di Leone Gallico in 1808. When the Napoleonic invasion was imminent, the Gallico family decided to melt down its silver. Once the danger had passed, part of the metal was used to make the laver and basin.[9] This is perhaps an isolated case, yet it is likely that Jews in Italy were subjected to increasingly pressing requests for money and sacrificed their own wealth when serious threat of expulsion loomed.

Textiles suffered a similar fate. It has been documented, although not in Jewish circles, that rich fifteenth- and sixteenth-century textiles, woven entirely of the purest gold and silver, were often burned to recover the precious metals. This must have befallen synagogue decorations as well, which helps explain the total absence of objects and hangings from before the second half of the sixteenth century.

Fig. 94. Ornamental page, *Ein Kamokha, The Rothschild Maḥzor,* Florence, 1492, The Library of The Jewish Theological Seminary of America, New York (cat. no. 43)

Fig. 95. (above) Interior of the Canton Synagogue

Fig. 96. (opposite, left) Torah Crown, Florence, 1836, Comunità Israelitica, Florence (cat. no. 211)

Fig. 97. (opposite, right) Giuseppe Bartalotti, Pair of Torah Finials from the Scuola Catalana, Rome, c. 1750, Comunità Israelitica, Rome (cat. no. 196)

It is also possible that in certain cases silver objects were melted down to create new pieces. This is a less acceptable hypothesis, although there is one rare piece of evidence of such an occurrence. The inscription on a Florentine Torah crown dated 1836 (cat. no. 211; fig. 96) explains in some detail that the new ornaments (crown and finials) were made from old silver pieces too worn out to be of further use and that the new pieces were made in a completely different style. It was more common for damaged objects to be sparingly integrated with other objects. Sometimes they were reworked centuries after their original creation; in other instances, only decades later. In either case the original style was generally ignored, and instead elements were replaced according to criteria quite at odds with modern theories of restoration. One of the most interesting and skillful examples of this practice is the reworking or completion by the Roman silversmith Giuseppe Bartolotti of a pair of Venetian Torah finials (cat. no. 196; fig. 97). Only the dome and upper level of the tower, embellished with large acanthus leaves, remained from the original pieces. Without deviating from contemporary fashions of Roman goldsmithery, the artist created an extraordinarily homogeneous object. Because of the rather top-heavy structure of Torah finials, particularly those from Venice, their shafts often broke, necessitating repeated restorations. The pair of finials embellished with coral from the Florence synagogue was repaired innumerable times, specifically in that more fragile area (cat. no. 197).[10]

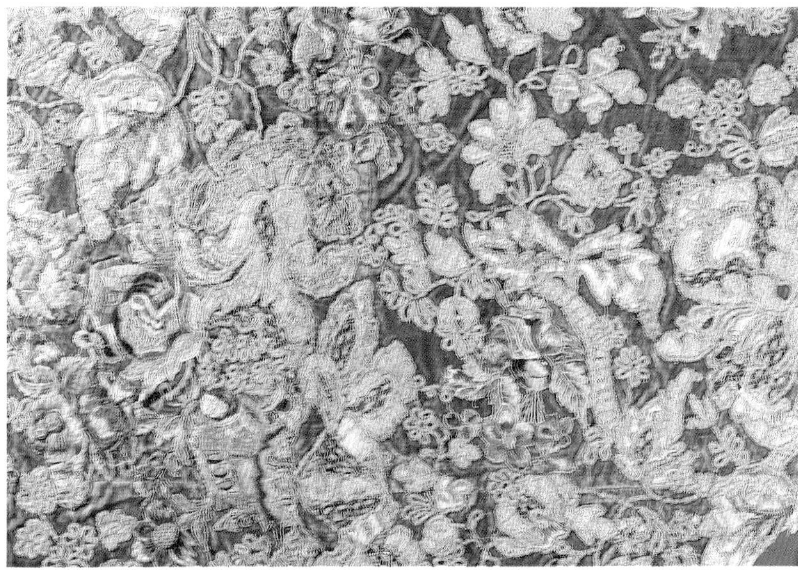

Fig. 98. Curtain for the Torah Ark (detail), Venice, nineteenth century, Comunità Israelitica, Rome (cat. no. 149)

With textiles the problem of wear is even more apparent. Most of the ornaments are made of silk, an extremely weak and perishable material. In cases where fabrics were in such poor condition that they could no longer be used, they were integrated into other pieces in such a rough fashion that their destruction was often accelerated. A truly masterful piece of handiwork can be seen in a seventeenth-century Roman Torah mantle (cat. no. 137). The structural weave of the fabric had been completely loosened, but this deterioration was stopped through the use of regularly spaced vertical stitches, simulating a complicated "Arabian point" embroidery.

Indeed embroideries, particularly seventeenth-century examples that were made mostly of gold and silver and padded with tow or leather to give them greater body, were often too heavy for the delicate fabric, resulting in extremely damaging stress. To preserve them, the embroideries were transferred to new fabrics that were often dissimilar to the original ones in both composition and color, irremediably distorting the original tactile and chromatic relationships. An obvious case is the Torah curtain now in Rome, whose original ivory background was replaced by a bright blue velvet (cat. no. 149; fig. 98).[11]

Textiles originally destined for lay use were also reworked. Dresses (for example, bridal gowns) were often donated to the synagogue, and these would be turned into Torah furnishings (mantles, reader's desk covers, binders). Thus one sees the smallest pieces arranged along the seams in order to re-create the original design.[12] The blue Torah mantle embroidered with silver now in Rome (cat. no. 132; fig. 92) is evidently the result of this sort of operation. The piece was made with great skill, and only the design that is not perpendicular to the border and the decorative motif simulating a chevron, both cut out of the underlying fabric, give away its provenance.

There are also examples of strange reworkings of silver objects originally destined for other ends. For example, amulets often underwent radical transformation, as in the case of a nineteenth-century Torah shield (cat. no. 214; fig. 99) that the donor, Meir Morpurgo, had adopted from an eighteenth-century amulet. This piece was divided lengthwise and mounted at the center of a shield as if it were a jewel. We can compare this to similar but less complex examples in Bologna or Genoa, where the silversmiths transformed such pieces into Torah shields, adding chains and supports in order to hang them from the staves of the Torah scroll.

In still other cases lavers and basins made for family and lay use became liturgical objects as soon as they were donated to the synagogue (see cat. no. 232; fig. 100–101). Sometimes this exchange of functions made for a rather subtle distinction between those objects that had a truly Jewish character and those that did not. The fact that through family tradition an object had been used solely for a particular religious occasion was often sufficient reason for it to become a religious object.

Personal donations always had great importance in the Jewish world. It was rare for the community directly to acquire objects destined for synagogue use. Instead they were more often donated by individuals. Every event of family or community life worthy of being solemnized (birth, bar mitzvah, marriage, even death) was an occasion to enrich the public patrimony and to endow the synagogue and the Torah scrolls with new decoration. In a culture whose art was circumscribed by many restrictions, this was a way of satisfying the aesthetic sense. And indeed the dignity of the place of worship demanded (and Jews themselves wanted) such embellishments, without, however, violating religious prohibitions. Within the narrow confines of the ghetto, every manifestation of private wealth was limited by rigid sumptuary laws so that os-

Fig. 99. (top, left) Torah Shield, Venice, eighteenth century, Comunità Israelitica, Venice (cat. no. 214)

Fig. 100. (top, right) Laver and Basin from the Catalan Synagogue, Rome, before 1740, Comunità Israelitica, Rome (cat. no. 232)

Fig. 101. (above) Laver from the Catalan Synagogue (detail), Rome, before 1740, Comunità Israelitica, Rome (cat. no. 232)

tentation would not provide a pretext for civil authorities to impose new taxes. Thus the donation of rich, luxurious ornaments served both to beautify the synagogue and to demonstrate the wealth of the donor.

Many Jewish ornaments, whether silver or textiles, bear dedicatory inscriptions for much the same reason. The inscription doesn't always correspond to the moment of the work's execution; sometimes it refers to a restoration or to a transformation of the object, but just as often it can be linked to a specific commission. The latter cases are obviously the most interesting. From a purely art-historical viewpoint the inscriptions supply precise points of reference allowing us to date objects that, because of their stylistic backwardness, might otherwise be difficult to place.[13] Behind every inscription is a story, an event of particular importance for the individual and for the community: the joys and sorrows of family life, the renovation of a synagogue, the investiture of a new rabbi, the annual choice of the Bridegroom of the Law, or the renewal of community appointments. All were significant events in which private citizens wanted to commemorate their participation.[14]

Three inscriptions separated from one another by several decades convey the history of a pair of lamps in the form of cornucopias (cat. no. 230; fig. 102). The same is true of the Torah crown and finials commissioned by the Rimini brothers and donated to the Levantine synagogue by one of their sons forty years later (cat. nos. 197, 205; figs. 107, 108). In contrast, embroidered inscriptions are rarely contemporaneous with the textiles themselves. Writing was often utilized on these objects also as decoration, exploiting the aesthetic potential of the Hebrew characters. The Torah curtain and reader's desk cover in Venice are examples of this; passages are inserted within the medallions arranged at the center of each side (see cat. no. 142; fig. 103). On a Torah mantle in Florence, the words of the Nineteenth Psalm are intermingled with spirals and blossoms.[15]

Another characteristic decoration of textiles is a coat of arms, which replaces an inscription with the name of the donor.[16] Coats of arms were often richly embroidered and framed and were frequently rendered in relief at the focal point of the composition as we can see this on a Torah cover, now in New York (see cat. no. 152; fig. 104). Sometimes an inscription accompanies the coat of arms, explaining the family's origins. The difficulty of interpreting symbols that weren't cod-

ified by a solid heraldic tradition necessitated clarification of the family's name through text. Indeed it was rare for families with the same surname to have identical crests.

The use of coats of arms on synagogue silver is almost unknown, however, at least in Italy, although they appear frequently on domestic objects, particularly prayer-book bindings and scroll cases. Silver book covers were the traditional gift of a bride to her groom on their wedding day, usually decorated with the coats of arms of the families or perhaps only that of the groom (cat. no. 237; fig. 105). Religious confraternities were likewise accustomed to embellishing ceremonial objects with symbols that expressed their humanitarian goals. For example, the Matir Assurim confraternity, which redeemed Jews held in state prisons for nonpayment of debts, had as its emblem a small bird fleeing from a cage.

Fig. 102. (opposite, top) Synagogue Sconce in the Shape of a Cornucopia, Venice, end of the seventeenth century, Comunità Israelitica, Venice (cat. no. 230)

Fig. 103. (opposite, bottom) Curtain for the Torah Ark (detail), Venice, end of the sixteenth century, with later additions, Comunità Israelitica, Venice (cat. no. 142)

Fig. 104. (above) Cover for the Torah, Italy, c. 1700, The Jewish Museum, New York (cat. no. 152)

Fig. 105. Book Cover (Wedding Present), Rome, eighteenth century, The Jewish Museum, New York (cat. no. 237)

The presence of dedicatory inscriptions, coats of arms, and emblems indicates the closeness of the relationship between patrons and artists. There have always been questions concerning the identity of those who created Judaica: whether they were Jewish artists or craftsmen, whether they were Christians who worked according to designs or instructions from Jewish patrons, or whether the invention and execution were the work of artisans with no connection to the Jewish community.

In this regard it is necessary to make a distinction between artisans who produced silver objects, textiles, and embroideries. Metalwork was most strongly tied to individual creativity and required an intensive artistic education. It was also necessary to join a guild, which one did either by paying an enrollment tax, by apprenticing in the workshop of a master, or by taking advantage of a close relationship with an artist who had already "matriculated." Even if they wanted to comply with these rules, Jews faced opposition from the surrounding populace and the authorities. Because they did not enjoy the same rights as other citizens and always lived with the threat of expulsion, it was difficult for Jews to participate in an artistic life regulated by rigid social laws.

As a result of the Counter-Reformation, Jews were deprived of their most elementary civil rights, including the ability to choose a craft or profession freely. For example, the proclamation of the Roman ghetto in 1555 specified that Jews could practice only *strazzeria seu cenceria,* or trading in used textiles, repressing the practice not only of other trades but of the so-called liberal arts as well. Such conditions did not encourage the development of Jewish artists or goldsmiths.

There were, however, isolated exceptions. At the time of the institution of the Florentine ghetto in 1571, Jews were registered in the guild of silk makers which

Fig. 106. Torah Crown, Italy, 1770–1771, Comunità Israelitica, Livorno (cat. no. 207)

also included goldsmiths. Until 1644 there were some fifty of them known to practice these crafts as registered matriculants, but not as masters. It was only in 1649 that they were prevented from registering in the guilds and from selling precious merchandise (gold, silver, etc.). This interdiction confirms that until that time Jews had been active in that area of commerce.[17] In Mantua the Jewish quarter even had a street of goldsmiths.[18]

Even if there were some Jewish goldsmiths, it is impossible to attribute objects to them with certainty. Stylistically all the silver ornaments used by Italian Jews reflect the artistic culture of their place of origin. Early pieces can rarely be dated, and only at the beginning of the ghetto period is it possible to form typological groupings.

In fact, most of the artists who made synagogue ornaments were Christians. This is verified by the hallmarks, particularly on works from Rome and Florence. But a correct examination of Italian-Jewish ceremonial art, an analysis of its four-century history, requires the use of criteria that vary according to place and time. We already hold some of the pieces to this complicated puzzle. It is clear that during the Renaissance, when Italian nobility demonstrated a certain benevolence toward Jews, some Jewish goldsmiths were able to make names for themselves. For example, Benvenuto Cellini recalled that at the beginning of his career he worked for Graziadio, a Jew from Bologna who earned a rather good living,[19] although unfortunately we know nothing more about him. The figure of Joseph de Levis, a bronzesmith and foundryman who worked in Verona and whose activity from 1585 to 1611/14 has been partially reconstructed, is the predominant figure in the rather sketchy picture that emerges (cat. nos. 170–171, 173–175; fig. 48).[20]

Fig. 107. Torah Finial, 1752, Comunità Israelitica, Florence (cat. no. 197)

The presence of this artist in the Veneto confirms a hypothesis that until now has been undocumented. From the second half of the seventeenth century until the beginning of the eighteenth, Venice held a virtual monopoly on the production of Judaica. Ornaments of Venetian silver were found in practically all Italian synagogues, with most dated to the middle decades of the eighteenth century (e.g. cat. no. 207; fig. 106). Almost all carry one or more hallmarks, which makes it possible to identify the city of origin and to attribute the objects to specific workshops.[21] The forms and decorations of these objects are repetitive, indicating that the Venetian workshops specializing in the production of Judaica possessed repertories of designs upon which the objects were modeled. There were probably Jewish goldsmiths working in these ateliers who were unable to assume the official rank of master and were limited to working under the mark of the workshop.[22] The career of Moise Zoref, a Venetian silversmith, supports this hypothesis,[23] and helps explain the discrepancy between Christian and Jewish ceremonial objects that emerged from the same workshops.

Up to this point, however, we are in the area of pure speculation. But we find ourselves on more solid ground when we turn to archival research, which has brought to light the names of some Jewish goldsmiths. Particularly in the eighteenth century in cities governed by liberal regimes that were open to the ideas of the Enlightenment, we find sporadic mention of Jewish artists. In Florence the decline of the Medicis in 1737 was followed by the accession to power of the house of Lorraine, which brought unexpected freedom to the Jewish population. Jews were again able to enroll in guilds and to choose their professions. We know that Aronne Wolf, a Jew from Brandenburg who lived in Livorno, engraved the first seal for Francis I of Lorraine when he visited Tuscany in 1739. The author of the agreement on the engraved stones described him as a "professor of engraving in all metals."[24] During the second half of the eighteenth century, four Jewish families of jewelers had workshops in neighboring streets outside the Florentine ghetto.[25] From the available documentation it seems that they were only merchants, because they depended on outside workers, but it cannot be ruled out that they too might have contributed to the creation of precious objects. It is certain, however, that a member of the Finzi family was a trusted jeweler of the grand dukes of Lorraine in the 1830s.[26] Of all the regions of Italy, Tuscany had the strongest tradition of Jewish participation in the jewelry trade. In Livorno, where Jews had always enjoyed great freedom, they even held a monopoly over the coral trade; they caught the coral in the seas off Sicily and cut and worked it in Livorno. This is perhaps why so much Italian Judaica is embellished with this material (see cat. nos. 197, 205; figs. 107–108). Yet these activities, more pertinent to the jewelry trade than to silversmithery, had little to do with the creation of ritual ornaments, although it is possible that the jewelers' daily contact with Florentine goldsmiths allowed them to choose the best craftsmen of the time. This seems to be confirmed by the Torah finials and crown commissioned by the Rimini brothers, who were jewelers.

The situation was quite different in Piedmont, where from the second half of the eighteenth century on, Jewish goldsmiths were able to practice their craft. Under the rule of the Savoy family, the Jewish population knew few restrictions. The ghettos were created only in the eighteenth century and in any case were not regulated by the rigorous laws that governed the Jews of many other cities. Until the beginning of the eighteenth century, many Jews were enrolled in the goldsmiths' academy. These Jewish goldsmiths exercised their art on behalf of both Jewish and Christian patrons.[27] Some, such as Pacifico Levi and Benaja Segre, demonstrated not only great technical skill but also an ability to adapt contemporary styles with the same vacillation between rococo and neoclassicism that characterizes church silver of the period (cat. nos. 201–202, 210, 217–218).

In contrast to Piedmont, with its relatively liberal atmosphere, other regions clearly excluded Jews from the practice of silversmithery. Rome and the Papal States offered little to Jews who wanted to venture into this area, and the severity of restrictive measures must have set an example for all Christendom.[28] For example, the edict circulated by Pope Pius VI on April 5, 1775, prohibited any Christian silversmith from making amulets for Jewish children, which until that point had apparently been one type of work they did.[29] In Rome those Jews wanting to become goldsmiths had no other route but conversion. Even the partial data in our possession make it possible to hypothesize that Piedmont and the Veneto were isolated cases, since the presence of the surname Orefice in the list of Jewish names in those regions suggests that there was widespread practice of this craft.

Fig. 108. Torah Crown (detail), Venice, 1752, Comunità Israelitica, Florence (cat. no. 205)

When it came to textiles, the situation was completely different. To produce textiles, it was necessary to possess workshops and looms, or at least rather complicated equipment, and this was generally not possible for Jews. Furthermore the considerable investment necessary for the tools and raw materials of such an operation would have required the assurance of being able to remain in one place. Yet in the textile field there was a tradition more strongly rooted than that in the field of goldsmithery or metalwork. Before their expulsion from southern Italy at the end of the fifteenth century, many Jews practiced the craft of weaving. When barred from this profession, Jews turned to trading in silk products. During the fifty years that they were allowed to enroll in the silk guild, numerous Florentine Jews were registered as silk wholesalers or retailers, as tailors, coat makers, or as merchants in other areas related to textiles. In the years that followed, when the government of the grand dukes became more rigid, proclamations regulating the textile trade always included chapters devoted explicitly to Jewish merchants.[30] The free port of Livorno was an extremely important clearinghouse for goods from the languishing Tuscan economy. The Levantine Jews' possession of commercial bases in North Africa and in the Middle East made it possible for them to trade not only with other Italian-Jewish merchants but also with foreigners. This activity explains why the artistic wealth of Italian synagogues consists primarily of textiles, generally of extraordinarily high quality. The wide availability of silk products in the ghettos is also demonstrated by the presence in synagogues of luxurious and frequently rare textiles, often with designs that are unusual for the area. For example, there was a large quantity of bizarre textiles with exotic and whimsical designs, most of which were widely distributed from Venice, the major center of production.

In Emilia-Romagna Jews not only traded in silk products but also possessed manufacturing facilities of some importance. In Ferrara as early as 1613 there were Jewish chapters of the silk guild, while in 1547 in Reggio Emilia, one of the most important Italian centers of production, Abram di Barochus was authorized to produce fabrics in silk, gold, and silver. In this same city, at the end of the eighteenth century, two weavers, Israel di Leone Forti and Simon Vita Ottolenghi, were summoned during an inquiry conducted by the council of silk guilds to solve a production crisis.[31]

The existence of Jewish weavers has also been documented in Piedmont. In 1742 Moyse da Costa was allowed to exercise the craft of "maker of silk, gold, and silver fabrics." It is probable that he was the first in a series of silk makers who were able to set up their own manufacturing facilities[32] in an atmosphere of greater freedom that also favored Jewish silversmiths.

We don't know the legal position of Jewish silk makers in all cities, however, or the type of textiles they produced. Except in those rare locations where we know that Jewish silk makers were active, we must assume that most textiles were acquired and then fashioned into synagogue ornaments. The problem of embroideries is similar in some respects but very different in others. All Italian synagogues have a wealth of embroidered hangings. Their technical and stylistic characteristics were generally closely linked to their place of production and can often be attributed to professional embroiderers. These embroiderers used every available refinement of the art to create richly detailed, substantial designs. Since the Middle Ages in Italy, embroidery, like all other creative professions, was practiced by males. Only toward the end of the sixteenth century did embroidery become an important part of the education of women. Working at home and without special equipment, they used their skills both for private ends, such as the preparation of trousseaux for themselves and their daughters, and professionally, as a community service. The handiwork of Jewish embroiderers can be identified from dedicatory inscriptions with the name of the craftswoman, confirming that this craft was carried out within the houses of the ghetto (see cat. nos. 000; figs. 00). Many embroiderers wanted their skill to be acknowledged. The "esteemed wife of Samuel Foa," who left her mark along the edge of an embroidery of 1582, demonstrated a precocious adaptation of contemporary textile models (see cat. no. 124; fig. 108). Hannah, daughter of Jehiel Senigallia, left us a splendid piece of lacework dated 1635 (cat. no. 125; fig. 110); Esther Gallico, working around 1740, made at least two pieces now in the Florence synagogue;[33] in 1734 Bella, daughter of Itzhak, made a Torah mantle in an extraordinary orientalizing style. These are only a few of the many examples of such work, but they suffice to demonstrate that throughout the four centuries of Jewish ceremonial art and in all the cities of Italy, the same phenomenon was at work. Yet even when there is no signature, we can presume that the author was a Jewish embroiderer. Indeed, in comparison with in scriptions on silver pieces, embroi-

Fig. 109. Honorata, wife of Samuel Foa, Torah Binder, Italy, 1582–1583, The Jewish Museum, New York (cat. no. 124)

dered inscriptions are reproduced much more faith-fully and without uncertainty, indicating a thorough knowledge of Hebrew writing. The embroideries that have been analyzed seem to be the work of professionals, and it is doubtful that their art was destined for the narrow Jewish market alone. Along with marriage contracts and scrolls, embroideries are the only Jewish figurative expression that was truly autonomous during the period from the era of the city-states to emancipation.

Beyond the decorative and floral motifs derived from contemporary embroideries, there were very interesting scenes and symbolic elements depicted on Torah curtains and reader's desk covers, especially from Rome and Venice. It is very significant that these textiles were chosen for special iconographic treatment since they were hung at the focal points of the synagogue and presented to the faithful a series of symbols that were easily recognizable. They could also conceal a less superficial interpretation, however, tied to relationships between elements of the composition. Most of the Torah curtains with complex iconography come from Venice, leading one to conclude that their content was influenced by the kabbalistic studies that thrived in that city. This was probably not the only factor that led to the use of elaborate imagery. Clearly the surrounding Catholic world also exerted a strong influence, particularly as a result of the Counter-Reformation. Throughout the seventeenth century the church insisted upon the necessity of indoctrinating the faithful through images. It is also significant that the use of symbols and images on Torah curtains is a typically Italian phenomenon. Despite the fact that there are never human or animal figures, these pieces push the limits of ortho- the limits of orthodoxy. Italian Judaism, with its flexible and cosmopolitan mentality, could bring these figurative motifs into its synagogues.[34] The most splendid examples date from the seventeenth century and include the Torah curtain made in 1680 by Simḥah, wife of Menaḥem Levi Meshullami (cat. no. 144; fig. 41), the one embroidered by Leah Ottolenghi in 1698 (cat. no. 145; fig. 42); the most iconographically complex Torah curtain that has come to light, probably made for the rebuilding of the Italian synagogue in Florence in 1672;[35] the one embroidered by "Stella, wife of Isacco Perugia."[36] Symbols of the Temple or the holidays and significant events of the Jewish year are not always represented at the center of the Torah curtains, but in most cases there are embroidered depictions of the Tablets of the Law emerging from fiery clouds, and, less frequently, images of the walled city of Jerusalem atop hills (see fig. 41). The same symbols sometimes appear on other objects, for example, on numerous Torah mantles from Rome (see cat. nos. 135, 137; fig. 111).

The wealth of symbols on these textiles contrasts sharply with the poverty of the symbols reproduced on silver objects, with the exception of those made in Venice. Torah finials in particular followed a rather repetitive decorative scheme of temple ornaments, vestments of the high priest, and liturgical and musical instruments. From a formal viewpoint these were among the more complex objects, although it would be a mistake

Fig. 110. Torah Binder (detail), Padua, c. 1630, Comunità Israelitica, Padua (cat. no. 125)

to consider them separately from other silver pieces that decorate the Torah. In many cases Torah finials and crowns, and more rarely Torah shields, were designed according to a unified iconographic program that addressed both structure and decoration. Due to the large gaps that exist in the history of Italian Judaica, we cannot reconstruct the development of these formal and decorative solutions, especially since most Jewish ceremonial objects are difficult to date prior to the eighteenth century, by which time the typological development of Torah ornaments was completed.

In his *Riti ebraici,* Leone Modena supplies us with brief, but extremely precious insights into the form of ceremonial objects:

> If the Owner of the Book be able, he has the ends of the Staves which come out beyond the Parchment, which they call *Hez Hayyim* covered with Silver in the shape of Pomegranats [*sic*] (which for that reason they still call *Rimmonim*) Bells, or some such thing; at the Top is a Coronet of Silver, which either goes round about them, or else half way and hangs before them. This Crown they call *Hatara* or *Cheder Toza* [*sic*] and all this work varies according to the Customs of the Place or of the particular Family of the Owners.[37]

Fig. 111. Torah Mantle, Rome, early eighteenth century, Comunità Israelitica, Rome (cat. no. 135)

As we can see from these descriptions, in practice the ornaments can be reduced to two categories: Torah finials and Torah crowns. Among Sephardim, the Torah shield was identified with the crown and lost the functional character it had in the Ashkenazic world. In Venice, according to Rabbi Modena, Torah finials were shaped like pomegranates. (The Hebrew word *rimmonim* literally means pomegranates.)

The tower-shaped finials found in so many communal collections imitated local architectural structures, most often church campaniles. For example, in Florence Brunelleschi's dome of Santa Maria del Fiore was used as a point of reference for the design of Torah finials (see cat. no. 192; fig. 112). In time the tower form came to be reinterpreted freely until it lost all architectural connotations (see cat. no. 197; fig. 107). In the nineteenth century there was a return to forms that were clearly inspired by buildings, although in many cases these referred explicitly to the Orient, in keeping with contemporary eclectic tendencies. The forms continually oscillated between the tower and the pomegranate, and in the nineteenth century the pomegranate form evolved into other fruits with similar

meanings, such as the pinecone and the thistle flower, or into rounded forms without any naturalistic reference (cat. no. 204). In both cases there is one constant iconographic element: a small vase at the top of the finial containing a bunch of flowers, probably symbolizing life, which echo the blossom forms that wrapped in long spirals around the shaft of the finial.

The close symbolic connection between various Torah ornaments and the deliberateness of the relationship between object and ornamentation can be verified by an analysis of domestic Hanukkah lamps. Wall lamps began to appear at the end of the sixteenth century and were generally cast in bronze. The artists who made them drew freely upon contemporary bronzework, not only figures of animals but also biblical figures, putti, or even mythological scenes (cat. no. 180; fig. 113). Some of these Hanukkah lamps can be attributed to Jospeh de Levis or to craftsmen in his circle (see cat. no. 177; fig. 38). We don't know whether his reputation as a bronze caster and his fame in Verona and Venice during the second half of the sixteenth century allowed him to develop a new way of thinking about these objects or whether he was adhering to an established artistic tradition. From the beginning of the sixteenth century until the late eighteenth century, however, Hanukkah lamps characterized by exuberant decoration were widespread throughout northern Italy. On many more recent examples worn-out molds are used, and there is a somewhat superficial refinishing, but we can still recognize, albeit indistinctly, a sixteenth-century prototype.

In comparison with Hanukkah lamps, cradle amulets, typically Italian and conceptually derived from the Catholic world, present a much more common iconography: the symbols of the high priest and the Temple, sometimes the Star of David, generally rather rare in other ornaments until the second half of the nineteenth century (cat. nos. 223–227; fig. 114).[38]

In the last century new images were introduced, some of which would have been unthinkable at an earlier time. In a group of Torah shields and crowns in Parma, the silversmith went so far as to introduce human figures inspired by the Bible. In Rome, probably coinciding with the new climate of emancipation, some Torah crowns were decorated with panoplies of arms. Throughout Italy rigid orthodoxy

Fig. 112. (opposite, left) Torah Finial, Tuscany, late sixteenth century, Comunità Israelitica, Florence (cat. no. 192)

Fig. 113. (opposite, right) Ḥanukkah Lamp, Italy, sixteenth to seventeenth century, The Jewish Museum, New York (cat. no. 180)

Fig. 114. (above) Amulets, Italy, seventeenth to nineteenth century, The Jewish Museum, New York (cat. nos. 186, 223–227)

was abandoned, perhaps in an attempt to adapt to the surrounding world. It seems as if the significance codified by a millennial tradition was lost in the search for originality.

In defining the origin and the character of Italian ceremonial art, it is necessary to remember a common denominator: the strong Sephardic and Levantine substratum. Before the expulsion from Spain, the Jewish population of Italy did not constitute a numerically significant group, although it had undergone a continual, if slow, growth after the arrival of French and German Jews beginning in the thirteenth century.[39] In certain communities the unexpected increase in population after the Iberian expulsion and the concomitant introduction of decidedly different usages and customs had a very strong impact. In other cases there was less pressure for change. In any event we cannot address the study of Italian-Jewish art without considering the massive arrival of Jews with their own customs and religious traditions. Initially the new arrivals and the original inhabitants kept to themselves; later there was a tendency toward assimilation and acceptance. Yet, even after centuries, different ethnic groups sometimes continued to prefer certain types of objects or particular decorative schemes; although after Italian Jewry settled into ghettos in the sixteenth and seventeenth centuries, it is nearly impossible to distinguish ceremonial objects destined for different synagogues on the basis of form and style.[40]

As for silver, both ceremonial and domestic, if it is impossible to trace its artistic history before the establishment of the ghettos, it is not much easier for the period immediately following. In every community, except Rome, there are no more than three or four seventeenth-century objects, a number insufficient to allow us to draw a picture of the local patrimony. Yet during the seventeenth century various ethnic groups (Italian, Sephardic, Levantine, Ashkenazic) became fully assimilated, resulting in a homogeneity that is reflected in Torah ornaments. Rather than embodying the style of any ethnic group, these objects took on forms and decorations that were fully characteristic of local artistic culture: the subtly pictorial use of metal in Piedmont, the decorative and structural exuberance of Venice and Padua, the Renaissance dignity of Florence, the baroque quality of Rome.

All these communities with their distinctive cultural characteristics, evidence a common element toward the end of the seventeenth century: the preponderance of Torah ornaments from Venice (cat. nos. 197–198, 204–205, 209, 212, 214, 219; figs. 107–108). Practically everywhere, in the smaller communities as well as the most populous ghettos, there were objects bearing the mark of the lion of Saint Mark, the official emblem of Venice, and those of the workshops where Jewish goldsmiths were employed or where the various Jewish communities commissioned ceremonial objects.

The earliest Venetian examples were clearly produced at the end of the seventeenth century. Both crowns and finials are characterized by extreme heaviness, by the symmetrical arrangement of decorations, by the preference for volutes and rather swollen acanthus leaves, by the choice of flowers, by the contrast between the shininess of concave parts of the glazing of protruding areas, and by the superposition of symbols and decorative elements executed separately and applied later. All these characteristics demonstrate a preference for various levels of decoration related to the illusionistic tendencies of the late baroque. Perhaps it was the unusual nature of these objects or the fact that they were composed of a satisfying mix of forms, decorations, and symbols that ensured their success.

As repressive measures against Jews were relaxed in the eighteenth century, there was an increased demand for ceremonial objects, corresponding to the growing desire for luxury. Every workshop possessed basic models that could be modified. Infinite series of combinations could be created by interchanging the various parts, allowing the patron to choose the variation that best suited his needs. Since it was common for Torah finials and crowns to be commissioned and donated to synagogues together, the dedicatory inscriptions were often engraved on the base of the crowns, which were designed for that very purpose. Silver prayer-book covers were also based on prototypes that had been in use for centuries. Jewish objects from the end of the eighteenth century are not very different from those dated several decades earlier. Only their rigid structure and more schematic decoration betray a late date. The dominance of Venetian workshops did not halt local production of Jewish silver. This tradition had been well established when goldsmithery took root in each of the Italian cities, or at least the most important ones. Since non-Jewish artists created most Jewish silver ceremonial objects, when the Italian tradition of goldsmithery began to decline, these works reflected the lack of originality and innovation that generally characterized the craft.

More than any other city, Rome maintained a strong tradition of goldsmithery and was a major center at the end of the eighteenth century. The cosmopolitan nature of the city, due principally to the presence of the Holy See, drew great artists, foreigners as well as Italians. The exchange of experience and teaching renewed the local tradition, as can be seen in Jewish ceremonial objects. Unlike works from other Italian cities, Roman pieces depart notably from Jewish artistic tradition, with both decoration and compositions modeled on objects produced for churches and palaces. For example, some of the Torah finials show an undeniable similarity to ceremonial maces; the only difference lies in the replacement of putti with rampant lions, roosters, or other animals, often symbolizing the name of the donor (cat. no. 193).[41] After achieving an extraordinary richness and exuberance that set their work apart from that of other cities, these Roman artists later adapted neoclassical aesthetics. Those who received commissions for Jewish ceremonial objects lost no time in applying the new style, giving Rome a reputation for turning out some of the highest-quality work in the entire peninsula.

The work produced in Piedmont followed another path and is unfortunately all of a relatively late date, the oldest pieces coming from the mid-eighteenth century. It is important to consider the different functional requirements and consequently the formal differences that characterize this body of work. This region was more exposed to foreign influences, and its Jewish population was formed not only of the usual Spanish and German immigrants but also of French-Provençal groups. Throughout the region we find a completely different style of Torah ornaments, reflecting French influence. For example, there is a distinct relationship between certain Piedmontese Torah finials and great French buildings of the region. Instead of being used simultaneously with finials, individual Torah crowns were placed in each of the staves. Thus they are smaller, more elongated, and are generally decorated with symbols of the Temple, embossed or cut into the silver (see cat. nos. 201–203; fig. 46). The closed crowns, clearly of Ashkenazic origin, are also typically Piedmontese: four strips rise up, join at the top, and are surmounted by either a crown or an orb.

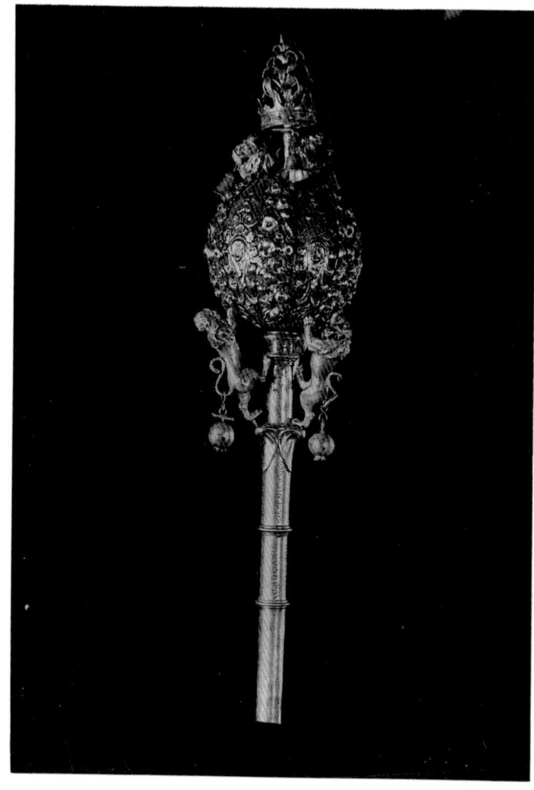

Fig. 115. Torah Finial, 1651, Comunità Israelitica, Rome (cat. no. 193)

Piedmontese Torah shields also display local characteristics, specifically a predilection for a heraldic shield form flanked by rampant lions and framed by curtains (see cat. nos. 217–218). As for domestic production, in addition to large seder plates decorated with biblical scenes, it is important to mention the large kiddush goblets. The Piedmontese goblet is characterized by its large size, by the elongation of the stem and the joint, and especially by its cover, often crowned by fanciful finials (see cat. no. 234; fig. 117).

The work from Genoa, while rather rare, is also very individualized. Genoese Torah crowns are all rather late, but there are some finials that date to the early eighteenth century. Their form is always round, with rather agitated contours. Bells hang halfway down the main element, with musical symbols engraved into the thin plate.[42] Curiously, most nineteenth-century Torah finials are of the tower type, based on the Venetian models that were available in Genoa. Torah shields are rare, and two of the extant examples are really amulets that were modified.

In the eighteenth century the proximity of Emilia-Romagna to Venice impeded the development of an autonomous ceremonial art. Most Torah ornaments bear the mark of the lion of Saint Mark, and even some of those that were definitely made locally imitate Venetian models. In this region and in cities such as Mantua,[43] however, there are some pieces that exhibit local characteristics. In Ferrara there are plaques bordered by volutes and vegetal motifs with dedicatory inscriptions. From the lower edge hang bells (see cat. nos. 215–216), an element that had not previously appeared on these objects, except in Piedmont.

While eighteenth-century synagogue silver was comparable in quality to work created for the church, something very interesting happened in the following century. Competition from foreign producers, especially in France, led to a decline in Italian silversmithery. At the same time, however, Jewish silver, with its particular formal and decorative requirements, allowed artists to move away from habitual schemes. In the first half of the nineteenth century they began to intro-

Fig. 116. (opposite) Giuseppe Fontana, Torah Finials, Turin, 1816–1817, The Jewish Museum, New York (cat. no. 200)

Fig. 117. (left) Bartolomeo Bernardi, Kiddush Goblet, Turin, 1778–1816, Collection of a Jewish family from Turin, New York (cat. no. 234)

duce Moorish elements characteristic of the temples of Florence, Turin, Trieste, and Vercelli. Torah finials often imitated contemporary buildings, while Torah shields abandoned heraldic or crown forms, assuming the shape of an ornamental cartouche. And Torah pointers, which in the past were only superficially inspired by the human limbs from which they take their name, were now shaped like arms, with bracelets and garments embellishing the form. As in all Italian goldsmithery after the mid-nineteenth century, the Jewish ornaments are characterized by eclecticism, reflecting the influence of the Near East in the introduction of subtle arabesques and the use of colored materials such as coral, ivory, and turquoise, which transformed the objects into veritable jewels. While synagogue art of the last century is qualitatively superior to contemporary work, it was still not outstanding, even though the best artists of the time were given commissions.

Unfortunately the work produced in our century has no history. The demographic decline, the persecutions under fascism, the war, and perhaps a certain disaffection on the part of Jews for their own synagogues, have resulted in a cessation of noteworthy donations. But in Italy as well as in the rest of the world, there is renewed interest in this ceremonial patrimony, which has always been overlooked despite its extraordinary artistic value. Perhaps this new attention will allow posterity to experience the same emotions and the same desire to bear witness to their faith through the ornaments of the temple.

Notes

1. Paris, Musée de Cluny; see V. Klagsbald, *Catalogue raisonné de la collection juive du Musée de Cluny* (Paris, 1931), pp. 94–96. The same collection also contains an officiant's pulpit, contemporary to the Modena ark, but of unknown provenance.
2. Palma de Mallorca, Cathedral Treasury; see J. Gutmann, *Jewish Ceremonial Art* (New York and London, 1964), fig. 1.
3. Jerusalem, Nahon Museum; see U. Nahon, *Ornamenti del Sefer Tora* (Jerusalem, 1966), fig. 23. Rabbi Ferdinando Belgrado, who donated the Torah pointer to the Italian synagogue in Jerusalem, didn't know the pointer's origin, as it had belonged previously to Rabbi Sorani.
4. The miniature is on fol. 125v. See *The Rothschild Maḥzor: Florence 1492,* intro. by E. M. Cohen and M. Schmelzer (New York, 1983), fig. V.
5. V. B. Mann, "The Recovery of a Known Work," *Jewish Art* 12–13 (1986–1987), pp. 269–278.
6. The marmoreal fragments of the ark were recognized by Bice Migliau on the basis of descriptive reports compiled by the Hebrew University and by reports presented by the municipality of Rome in 1885–1886, before the demolition of the ghetto. Currently this ark is the subject of in-depth scholarly analysis, the results of which have not yet been published. A brief sample of this research can be gleaned from "Il risanamento del ghetto: Le vicende dell'edificio delle Cinque Scole," in *Roma capitale 1870–1911: Architettura e urbanistica,* exh. cat. (Rome, 1984), p. 444.
7. D. Liscia Bemporad, "La Scuola italiana e la Scuola levantina nel Ghetto di Firenze: Prima ricostruzione," *Revista d'arte* 38, no. 2 (1964): 14–18.
8. A. S. Toaff, "Cenni storici sulla Comunità Ebraica e sulla Sinagoga di Livorno," *Rassegna mensile di Israel* 21 (1955): 423–424.
9. D. Liscia Bemporad, "Atarot Fiorentine," *MCM,* no. 3 (1985): 46.
10. The latest restoration, carried out in the Opificio delle Pietri Dure in Florence, also attempted to make the objects stable and solid so that they might still be used without having to replace the shaft, weakened by innumerable and rough solderings in the past.
11. Only in recent times have textiles been given their historical and artistic due. Previously whenever alterations were necessary, even important ones, the textiles were put in the eager hands of ill-prepared embroiderers.
12. See Israel Museum, *From the Secular to the Sacred,* exh. cat., ed. I. Fishof (Jerusalem, 1985); C. Mossetti, "La schedatura dei manufatti tessili in alcune considerazioni di carattere metodologico," in *Ebrei a Torino,* exh. cat. (Turin, 1984), pp. 163–164.
13. This is particularly true in certain cities. In others, such as Rome, there was a complete adaptation to the artistic fashion of the moment.
14. Research indicates that an increase in ceremonial objects was closely connected to events that involved the synagogue and the community.
15. D. Liscia Bemporad, "I ricami datati della Sinagoga di Firenze," in *I tessili antichi e il loro uso* (Turin, 1986), pp. 73–74.
16. For more information on Jewish heraldry and related bibliography, see F. Pisa, "Parnassim: Le grandi famiglie ebraiche italiane dal secolo XI al XIX," *Annuario di studi ebraici* 10 (1984): 291–491.
17. Bemporad, "Atarot fiorentine," p. 42.
18. C. Roth, *History of the Jews of Italy* (Philadelphia, 1946), p. 376.
19. B. Cellini, *La Vita,* ed. P. Scarpellini (Rome, 1967), pp. 13–14.
20. For further information, see C. Avery, "Giuseppe de Levis of Verona, a Bronze Founder and Sculptor of the Late Sixteenth Century: Bells and Mortar, Figure Style," *The Connoisseur* 181 (1972): 179–188; 182 (1973): 87–97; see Vivian B. Mann, "The Arts of Jewish Italy," above, and cat. nos. 170–171, 173–175, below.
21. The most common workshop hallmarks are *ZC* with the insignia of a tower; *AC* with the insignia of a tower; *PL G* with the insignia of a lily; *ZP* with the insignia of a water bird; *RC* with the insignia of three moons. For more on these marks, see G. Mariacher, *Oreficeria sacra nel Friuli occidentale,* exh. cat. (Pordenone, 1976). For information about Venetian hallmarks on Jewish objects, see H. Lazar, "Jonah, the Tower and the Lions: An Eighteenth-Century Italian Silver Book Binding," *Journal of Jewish Art* 3–4 (1977): 58–73.
22. This hypothesis was verified verbally by Professor Giovanni Mariacher, who thinks it is possible to confirm situations of this type, although one has to take into account that there is still a scarcity of in-depth analysis of Venetian goldsmithery and hallmarks.
23. F. Landsberger, "Jewish Artists before the Period of Emancipation," *Hebrew Union College Annual* 16 (1941): 374.
24. The text is "Memorie degli intagliatori moderni di pietre dure, camei e gioie del secolo XV fino al XVIII" (A. S. Toaff, "Vita artistico-letteraria degli ebrei a Livorno nel '700," *Rassegna mensile di Israel* 8 (1933): 371.
25. Bemporad, "Atarot fiorentine," p. 44.
26. State Archives of Florence, Imperial and Royal Courts, n. 4796. These families of Florentine jewelers will be the subject of a forthcoming publication.
27. B. Terracini, "L'emancipazione degli ebrei piemontesi," *Rassegna mensile di Israel* 15 (1949): 65; P. Gaglia, "L'arredo in argento," in *Ebrei a Torino,* pp. 142–147.

28. For more information on the Roman situation and for an inventory of art objects owned by Jews, see G. L. Masetti Zannini, "Ebrei, artisti, oggetti d'arte (documenti romani dei secoli, XVI e XVII)," *Commentari* 25 (1974): 281–301.
29. A. Milano, "L'editto sopra gli ebrei," *Rassegna mensile di Israel* 19 (1953): 120.
30. Bemporad, "I ricami datati," pp. 69–70.
31. M. Bondini and G. Busi, eds., *Cultura ebraica in Emilia Romagna* (Rimini, 1987), pp. 585–586.
32. P. Gaglia, "L'arredo in argento," p. 146.
33. Bemporad, "I recami datati," pp. 69–70.
34. Jewish Museum, *Treasures of the Jewish Museum,* ed. N. L. Kleeblatt and V. B. Mann (New York, 1986), p. 70.
35. This Torah curtain is in the possession of the Florence synagogue.
36. This Torah curtain is in the collection of the Jewish Museum, Venice.
37. This treatise was written by Modena in 1619 (L. Modena, "Historia de' Riti Ebraici," [trans. as *The History of the Present Jews Throughout the World* (London, 1707), p. 33]).
38. For further information, see Klagsbald, *Catalogue raisonné,* pp. 25–26.
39. For further information, see A. Milano, *Storia degli Ebrei in Italia* (Turin, 1963).
40. D. Liscia Bemporad, "Arte ceremoniale ebraica in Italia," *Commentari* 25 (1974): 261–262.
41. S. Fornari, *Gli argenti romani* (Rome, 1968), p. 132; *Tesori d'arte sacra a Roma,* exh. cat. (Rome, 1975), p. 179.
42. Bemporad, "Arte ceremoniale," figs. 7, 8.
43. S. Cusin, *Arte nella tradizione ebraica* (Milan, 1963), pp. 36–37.

Fig. 118. Antonietta Raphaël Mafai, *Autoritratto con violino* (Self-Portrait with Violin), 1928, Private Collection, Rome (cat. no. 310)

EMILY BRAUN

FROM THE RISORGIMENTO TO THE RESISTANCE: ONE HUNDRED YEARS OF JEWISH ARTISTS IN ITALY

He wondered if there were any Jews in Italy. If so, they must be strange Jews: how can you imagine a Jew in a gondola or at the top of Vesuvius?" Such were the musings of the Russian Jew Mendel, the protagonist of Primo Levi's novel *Se non ora, quando?* (If Not Now, When?). When Mendel and his partisan comrades finally arrive at the other side of the Brenner Pass after a long and harrowing journey through eastern Europe and Germany, they discover an odd country where Christians know the Ten Commandments by heart, "but at most they observe two or three." Although the presence of Italian Jews was far less incongruous than imagined by Mendel, their position was clearly unique in Europe: "Italian Jews are as odd as the Catholics. They don't speak Yiddish, in fact, they don't even know what Yiddish is. They only speak Italian; or rather, the Jews of Rome speak Roman, the Jews of Venice speak Venetian, and so on. They dress like everybody else, they have the same face as everybody else."[1]

A shared history of cultural diversity and tenacious longevity bonded Italian Jews to their Christian compatriots in a country beset by centuries of regional factionalism and foreign domination. When unification was finally achieved during the Risorgimento, between 1848 and 1870, the Jews found themselves to be separate among equals, sharing a new national identity as "Italians." Jews were extended full participation in a still-malleable nation with the potential to forge the political ideology and economic interests of the ruling elite. The process of social assimilation was so rapid over the following decades that religious practice became the only external factor that distinguished Jews from other Italians. Emancipation had dramatically altered the ingrained experience of interaction with the culture of the majority outside the ghetto walls. If a creative dialectic of opposition continued, it evolved out of subtle tensions wrought by unanimous acceptance and exceptional achievement in modern Italian secular life.

These factors had specific implications for the visual arts and for the first generation of modern Jewish artists, who turned to their vocation with the same ambition and in the same abundant numbers as their coreligionists in other professions.[2] Italian-Jewish artists were notably absent from the ranks of aesthetic radicals and seem overall rather conservative in style (although the traditional Francophile model of the avant-garde is of limited usefulness for an understanding of late nineteenth- and early twentieth-century Italian art). No Jews number among the original Futurists or members of the Metaphysical painting movement, and the two most advanced modernists, Amedeo Modigliani and Mario Cavaglieri, chose to live as ex-

patriots in France. Yet many Jewish artists and critics played salient roles in the story of modern Italian art. Serafino De Tivoli and Ulvi Liegi have come down in history as the "first" and the "last" of the Macchiaioli, respectively, while Modigliani is perhaps Italy's best-known and most popularly cherished modern master abroad. A high percentage of Italian-Jewish artists devoted themselves to portraiture, and some, such as Mario Nunes Vais, shaped the historical image of the famous people of their time. A Jewish critic, Margherita Sarfatti, initiated the Novecento movement, influencing the aesthetics and cultural politics of fascism for a decade and beyond. Roberto Melli was a founding member of the Valori Plastici group, while Antonietta Raphaël Mafai and Carlo Levi were leading protagonists of the Scuola romana and the Sei di Torino, respectively.

The question of a Jewish identity among these artists is difficult to discern and a precarious matter. (One must also keep in mind that the documentation being considered pertains to the middle and upper classes and intellectual elite.) With few exceptions, their religion is rarely mentioned in their critical biographies as an influential factor. Nor did they constitute a highly visible or ethnically distinct group, like the eastern European Jews who migrated to Paris in the early twentieth century and formed the "Circle of Montparnasse." The issue had already been addressed by the art historian Paolo D'Ancona (the son of the literary critic Alessandro and nephew of the painter Vito) (cat. no. 271e; fig. 119) in his article "Four Jewish Masters."[3] Referring to De Tivoli, D'Ancona, Liegi, and Modigliani, he argued that one could talk of Jewish artists but not of a modern Jewish art per se, due to the strong ties of these artists to their Italian roots. D'Ancona concluded that a characteristically Jewish art would arise only from a similar attachment to the soil of Israel.

Although it is difficult to characterize elements of a Jewish style in Italian painting and sculpture, the presence of an ethnic identity in these works should not be so easily dismissed. It emerges most obviously in rare instances of religious subject matter and also in the context of political ideology and class interests and in the microhistory of familial and personal relationships. The emergent class of Italian Jewry nurtured a self-perception that constantly mediated between public and private life, between religious and national identity.

In a hundred-year period marked by overt patriotism, a dual identity was taken for granted or as a matter of pride. But as the twentieth century progressed the notion of *italianità* changed as much as that of *ebraicità*. The rise of Zionism in the 1920s and the cultural chauvinism of the Fascist regime in the 1930s brought new pressures to bear. Some Jewish artists conceived of an art that was inherently Latin and Mediterranean and that extolled myths of national greatness. Others consciously looked beyond the borders of Italy to the European avant-garde to reassert the tenet of creative freedom inherent in Italian liberalism. But here again their choices depended on political and nationalistic sentiments, rather than on an innate sense of Jewishness.

Despite the hints of impending crises, decades of varying levels of assimilation and integration and unquestioning patriotic devotion made the enactment of the Racial Laws in 1938 seem all the more incredible to Italian Jews. As Dan Vittorio Segre wrote in his *Memoirs of a Fortunate Jew,* his parents had grown up in "a climate of obsolete Judaism and of vigorous nationalism" and "shared all the virtues and prejudices typical of a generation of Jewish bourgeois sure of themselves, affluent and respected, and totally unconscious of the dangers that lay waiting for them in the future."[4]

The Risorgimento, 1848–1870

It is fitting that the first Jewish artists of modern Italy—Serafino De Tivoli and Vito D'Ancona—were associated with the Macchiaioli, the artistic movement intimately linked to the Risorgimento in image and deed, and the one dedicated to the development of an innately Italian style. The Macchiaioli consisted of some eleven artists who gathered to debate painting and politics at the Caffè Michelangiolo in Florence.[5] They are best known for their depictions of everyday life and the particular characteristics of the Tuscan landscape based on a style of painting *all'aperto* (plein-air) developed around 1860. The word *macchia* means patch or stain and refers to the broad brushwork and bold tonal contrasts captured in sketches such as D'Ancona's *Signora in giardino* (Lady in the Garden, 1861–1862; cat. no. 255; fig. 120).[6] The Macchiaioli incorporated this heightened effect, or "violent chiaroscuro," into their finished works, in contrast to the tonal nuance and descriptive detail of more traditional painting procedures. The artists' identification with the regional landscape of Tuscany was an expres-

Fig. 119. (opposite) Mario Nunes Vais, *Alessandro D'Ancona with His Son Paolo,* 1908, Istituto Centrale per il Catalogo e la Documentazione, Gabinetto Fotografico Nazionale, Collection Nunes Vais, Rome (cat. no. 271 e)

Fig. 120. (above) Vito D'Ancona, *Signora in giardino* (Lady in the Garden), c. 1861–1862, Private Collection, Montecatini (cat. no. 255)

sion of patriotism, as was their rebellion against the foreign-dominated academies in favor of a more sincere and truthful way of seeing aligned with the progressive ideology of liberalism. The aesthetic of the Macchiaioli came to fruition during the chief events of unification, and many of the artists, including De Tivoli and D'Ancona, fought as volunteers in the campaigns against Austria in northern Italy and with Giuseppe Garibaldi in the liberation of Rome and the south.[7]

De Tivoli is known as the "father of the macchia" for his key role in inspiring the younger Tuscan painters to pursue the new tonal effects rendered all'aperto. Born to a merchant family in Livorno, De Tivoli trained in Florence under the Hungarian-born Carlo Markò (1791–1860), a landscape painter in the tradition of Claude Lorrain. Around 1854 De Tivoli and a small group of artists began to paint in the countryside around the village of Staggia near Siena. The experience of the "Staggia school" was a prelude to De Tivoli's trip to the Universal Exhibition of 1855 in Paris. There he viewed the works of the Barbizon painters and was influenced by the landscapes of Alexandre-Gabriel Decamps, Constant Troyon, and Rosa Bonheur. According to Telemaco Signorini, the chronicler of the Caffè Michelangiolo, when De Tivoli returned from Paris, he became the leading exponent of "the most progressive ideas of that time" and the initiator of the "violent chiaroscuro" that characterized the macchia technique.[8]

La questua (Begging for Alms; cat. no. 254; fig. 121), painted in 1856, shortly after his return to Florence, stands halfway between more traditional landscape practices and the innovative means of preserving the vibrancy of the sunlit impression in the finished painting. A mendicant knocks at the gate of a country estate, while compositional elements such as the winding path and dark masses of foliage, gleaned from seventeenth-century Dutch examples or indirectly through the Barbizon school, lead the eye to a distant view of Florence. More precocious is the rapid notation of tonal contrasts in the foreground plane and the rendering of the portal with areas of sunlit masonry and cast shadow, a motif favored by the Macchiaioli a few years later. De Tivoli's fame rests as a forerunner rather than an innovator; by 1861 his picturesque compositions were soon surpassed by the bolder techniques of the younger artists. In 1864 he departed for London to join his brother Felice, also a painter, and then traveled to Paris, where he remained until 1890, painting some works in the full plein-air style of the Impressionists.

De Tivoli's most influential period was undoubtedly between 1856 and 1864, when he and D'Ancona were the leading personalities and polemicists of the Caffè Michelangiolo. D'Ancona, who was affectionately known as the *riccone* (very rich one) of the group, was also instrumental in introducing the painters Signorini, Vincenzo Cabianca, and Odoardo Borrani, to the Caffè circle.[9] The close bond between the two Jewish artists of the Macchiaioli was fondly recorded by their contemporary Adriano Cecioni, who noted that De Tivoli 'became all the more endearing when he argued with D'Ancona':

> To see these two facing each other at the same little table, both of the same race, similar in stature, voice, in their way of talking and laughing, and above all in their intelligence; to see these two men telling each other off without swearing or ever losing their tempers, rather, smiling all the while, even as they exchanged witty and cutting remarks, was among the best entertainment at the Caffè Michelangiolo.[10]

D'Ancona was the fourth of nine children in one of the most illustrious families in nineteenth-century Florence, whose political affiliations and professional successes serve as a paradigm of the Jewish experience in the period of the Risorgimento. In writing the family memoirs some two generations later, Flora Aghib Levi D'Ancona affirmed that a "grand ideal united the young D'Ancona brothers: they had learned in the family that one suffered and died for Italy and the obligation to love *la patria*."[11] Their uncle, the banker Laudadio Della Ripa, was a friend of Baron Bettino Ricasoli (who led Tuscany into the Risorgimento), the literary scholar Gianpietro Vieusseaux, and the composer Gioacchino Rossini, connections that helped his nephews in their highly successful careers in politics, science, and the humanities.[12] Such rapid rise to prominence was bound to cause some negative reactions; for example, the appointment of the youngest son, Alessandro, as professor of literature at the University of Pisa in 1861 caused a few detractors to query, "how will an Israelite be able to comment on the Canticle of Paradise?"[13]

The numerous portraits and precious domestic scenes painted by D'Ancona during his career attest to

Fig. 121. Serafino De Tivoli, *La questua* (Begging for Alms), 1856, Private Collection, Bologna (cat. no. 254)

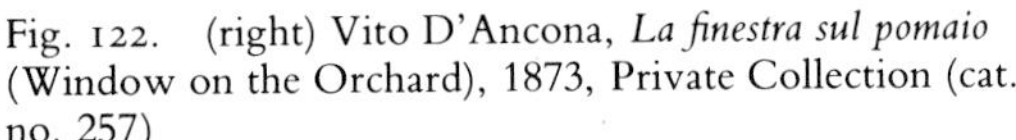

Fig. 122. (right) Vito D'Ancona, *La finestra sul pomaio* (Window on the Orchard), 1873, Private Collection (cat. no. 257)

Fig. 123. (opposite) Vito D'Ancona, *Nudo* (Nude), 1873, Civica Galleria d'Arte Moderna, Milan (cat. no. 258)

the family's closeness and their material comforts. From the mid-1860s to 1874 he lived in Paris, where he was a regular visitor at the Villa Madrid, the home of his brother Giacomo and his wife, Henriette Oulman. They had married in 1862 at the temple on the Rue de la Victoire, where, to the dismay of certain friends, the choir sang the prayer "Dal tuo stellato soglio" (From your starry threshold) from Rossini's opera *Moïse.*[14] *La finestra sul pomaio* (Window on the Orchard; cat. no. 257; fig. 122) depicts the delicate figure of Henriette's sister Blanche Oulman, looking out onto the dense foliage of the Villa Madrid. As in his other paintings of the period, passages of loose brushwork combine with finely wrought details and areas of an enamel-like finish, endowing the atmosphere of D'Ancona's work with a characteristic preciosity.

Signora in giardino is one of the few essays by D'Ancona painted in a pure Macchiaioli style; he is best known for his intimate interiors and sensuous nudes. *Signora in conversazione* (Woman in Conversation, c. 1875; cat. 259) revels in the jewel-like tints and tactile stuffs of the Dutch genre painters—Gabriel Metsu, Gerard Terborch, and Pieter de Hooch—whose works D'Ancona studied in the Louvre and knew earlier from the collection of Prince Anatole Demidoff housed in the Villa San Donato outside Florence. The hushed atmosphere is transformed into a more erotic reverie in *Nudo* (Nude, 1873; cat. no. 258; fig. 123), with the artist's preferred motifs of curtains, lush carpets, and ornate backdrops. Signorini compared D'Ancona's nudes with those of Titian (particularly *Sleeping Woman*; cat. no. 261, fig. 47), but their un-

abashed immediacy had more in common with paintings by Gustave Courbet, whom D'Ancona knew in Paris. Half a century later Emilio Cecchi attributed the brooding languidness to D'Ancona's Jewish blood: "one could say that ethnic reasons accentuated the carnal pleasure in an artist so utterly taken by female beauty that he hardly ever painted anything but women," adding that "the life of Vito, favored by material comfort, developed under the sign of Venus to the point of illness and decadence."[15] Cecchi was undoubtedly alluding to the chronic syphilis that plagued the artist. Like many of the female figures of his work, their faces hidden or seen from behind, D'Ancona was secretive and withdrawn, a tendency that increased along with his physical disability. Although he remained a bachelor all his life, he fathered a child, Giulietta, whose portrait he painted on several occasions; her mother, Giulia, is most likely the subject of *Portrait of a Woman in a Shawl* (cat. no. 260) in the collection of the Israel Museum.

Upon his return to Florence in 1874, D'Ancona frequently convalesced and painted at Volognano, the estate of his uncle Laudadio Della Ripa in the village of Pontassieve. One of his last images (cat. no. 256; fig. 124) depicts the family retreat and its fertile slopes, which yielded wheat, vines, and olive trees. Emancipation finally ended the restrictions forbidding Jews to own property; they reacted swiftly to the centuries of cramped and communal quarters, investing in villas in the city and country.[16] In addition to reflecting the relatively new phenomenon of Italian Jews as landed gentry, Della Ripa's cultivation of Volognano followed the most progressive ideas of the Tuscan sharecropping sys-

Fig. 124. Vito D'Ancona, *Veduta di Volognano* (View of Volognano), 1878, Private Collection (cat. no. 256)

tem known as the *mezzadria*. These agrarian reforms and advances were led by Baron Ricasoli and the Accademia Georgofili, which also counted Della Ripa, Cesare D'Ancona, and their coreligionist the geologist Gustavo Uzielli (1839–1911) among its members. Uzielli later wrote a book on Leonardo da Vinci's scientific projects, with illustrations by Signorini. It is also significant, as Albert Boime has noted, that both Cesare D'Ancona and Uzielli were active leaders of the Società Geografica, founded in 1867 to further "exact knowledge of the Italian soil."[17]

D'Ancona's images of the well-favored milieu to which he belonged contrast with the poverty and communal life of the ghetto, from which Jews had only recently been liberated, in the case of Rome, as recently as 1870. Surprisingly, the social conditions of these segregated quarters were not a subject for the Jewish artists of this or the following generation. Many of them, like De Tivoli, hailed from Livorno, which never had a ghetto, or like D'Ancona, had enjoyed a life not only of freedom but also of privilege. The early emancipation of Jews in Piedmont and Tuscany partially accounts for this situation, but in general there is a pronounced avoidance of ghetto imagery by Jewish artists, as if they never looked back. And later images by fellow Italians, such as Signorini's *Il ghetto a Firenze* (The Ghetto in Florence, 1882; cat. no. 262; fig. 125) or the photographs of the Roman community of the late 1880s, by Count Giuseppe Primoli emphasize the picturesque quality of a vanishing way of life rather than the ill effects of a sequestered environment.[18] So rapid was the process of assimilation that Jewish artists looked to the comforts of the present rather than to the past to affirm their new status. The nature of emancipation as a form of "social contract" did much to encourage an alliance with bourgeois interests. As Andrew Canepa has shown, Italian Jews were expected to overcome the negative and stereotypical image associated with the poor and mendicants of the ghetto and embark on a course of "social betterment," and the notables of the community responded in kind.[19] Indeed the paintings of this and the subsequent generation reveal that the identity of Italian Jews was divided along class rather than ethnic lines.

Fig. 125. Telemaco Signorini, *Il Ghetto a Firenze* (The Ghetto in Florence), 1882, Galleria Nazionale d'Arte Moderna, Rome (cat. no. 262)

Fig. 126. Vittorio Corcos, *Sogni* (Dreams), 1896, Galleria Nazionale d'Arte Moderna, Rome (cat. no. 268)

The person and portraits of Vittorio Matteo Corcos best illustrate the ease of integration of Italian Jews into the artistic and literary circles of the belle époque. Born in Livorno in modest circumstances, Corcos enjoyed a quick rise to success with the help of the Parisian dealer Goupil and found himself a favorite of European royalty and high society. Although Corcos pleased his patrons with a conservative style and richly honed palette akin to those of Léon Bonnat, he was equally adept with plein-air landscapes, for example, the street scene painted in the early 1880s (cat. no. 269). The painting is inscribed at lower left to his dear friend "Signor Tivoli," probably Serafino De Tivoli, and is a testament to the circle of Italian artists (including Vito D'Ancona) who gathered around the expatriot Giuseppe de Nittis in Paris. De Nittis was often taken to be Jewish, a misperception that may have arisen from his association with De Tivoli and Corcos. In his memoirs he clarified the matter, noting that the Jewish issue seemed of peculiar importance to the French.[20]

Corcos returned in 1886 to Florence, where he painted the prominent and the fashionable of the Umbertian and Giolittian eras. His most notorious portrait, however, was that of his mistress, Elena Vecchi (cat. no. 268; fig. 126), the daughter of a naval officer who earned his fame as Jack La Bolina, the author of popular adventure stories. *Sogni* (Dreams) belongs to a long line of impressionist images of women reading, but the model is not interrupted with book in hand or disturbed in a moment of reverie. Instead the yellow Flammarion novels lie closed on the bench, while Vecchi gazes provocatively at the viewer. Her crossed legs and indecorous pose were considered scandalous for the period, causing quite a stir when the painting was exhibited in Florence in 1896.

Corcos admitted that he catered to female vanity, painting his sitters as they wanted to be seen, ennobling the features of a marchesa, even though her mother was obviously a fish vendor.[21] Though he was renowned as a painter of beautiful women, Corcos's facility with the brush often gave his works a wistful sweetness that could become formulaic. Many critics have pointed to his male portraits as evidence of his mastery of human character. Certainly there is little flattery in his depiction of his close friend Pietro Ferragni (1836–1895), better known by the pen name Yorik (cat. no. 127; fig. 267). Ferrigni was best known

Fig. 127. Vittorio Corcos, *Ritratto di Yorik* (Portrait of Yorik), 1889, Museo Civico "G. Fattori," Livorno (cat. no. 267)

Fig. 128. Vittorio Corcos, *Ritratto di Emilio Treves* (Portrait of Emilio Treves), 1907, Studio Paul Nicholls, Milan (cat. no. 270)

as the drama critic for *La Nazione,* but his art reviews remain a fundamental source of information on the period. Corcos mocks the physical bulk of Yorik at the expense of the writer's own sarcastic wit. The text scribbled on the wall to the right reads: "If the likeness of the man painted here isn't young, graceful, tall, and slender, you can blame the paintbrush! For heaven's sake, you can't find fault with the original!" Corcos portrayed the less than perfect physique of the Jewish publisher Emilio Treves (1834–1916) with equal honesty (cat. no. 270; fig. 128). Treves fought as a volunteer with Garibaldi in Naples before establishing his publishing house in Florence in 1861. The Treves name was associated with the literary giants of the period, such as Gabriele D'Annunzio, Edmondo De Amicis, Grazia Deledda, and Ada Negri. It was the most important publishing company in Italy at the end of the century and one of several prominent firms in Jewish hands.[22]

Corcos also painted portraits of his close friends Ulvi Liegi and Adolfo Belimbau, who along with Alberto Pisa formed a circle of Jewish artists in Livorno and Florence.[23] Liegi was the first to supersede the impressionist and naturalist tendencies that dominated late nineteenth-century Tuscan painting. Born to a well-to-do family in Livorno, he trained at the Accademia di Belle Arti in Florence under Giuseppe Ciaranfi but soon left for informal tutelage in plein-air painting with Signorini. He was also a frequent visitor at the studio of the older master Giovanni Fattori, and he became a patron of the Macchiaioli. Perhaps Liegi's independent means inspired the aesthetic confidence that led him to experiment with a looser handling and coloristic vibrancy, already apparent in his *Lo studio del pittore* (The Studio of the Painter; cat. no. 263) of 1885, dedicated to a Jewish friend, "A. Gonnelli Gilda Levi Naim" in the lower right. *La modellina* (The Young Model; cat. no. 265; fig. 129) painted in 1889, reflects the artist's direct contact with postimpressionist currents in Paris. The influence of the Pont-Aven school was evident in his paintings of the following decades, which were characterized by an increasingly antinaturalistic use of color, applied in broad, unmodulated areas and often outlined in the cloisonné style. Liegi was first and foremost a landscape painter, devoted to views of his native Tuscany. Yet toward the end of his life, in the mid-1930s, possibly affected by the rise of anti-Semitism, he turned to his Jewish heritage, painting the interior of the Li-

Fig. 129. Ulvi Liegi, *La modellina* (The Young Model), 1889, Galleria d'Arte Moderna, Palazzo Pitti, Florence (cat. no. 265)

vorno synagogue (cat. no. 266; fig. 130) and organizing a museum of Judaica there.[24]

Like Liegi, the photographer Mario Nunes Vais was favored by independent wealth. He began taking photographs in 1885 and always considered himself a dilettante, never working for commission or livelihood. His success, like that of Corcos, rested on his talent for portraiture, which similarly brought him far-reaching contacts and friendships among the Italian cultural elite. Nunes Vais, however, evolved a style of photography that was almost without style in a period that wallowed in aesthetic affectation; his lens captured a sincerity of character and assured elegance that seemed to exude naturally from the sitter, a combination of forthrightness and formality well suited to the privileged class in the age of positivism.

Nunes Vais shaped the public image of the leading personalities of his time, including D'Annunzio (cat. no. 271e; fig. 131), Filippo Tomasso Marinetti and the Futurists, and later the youthful leader of the recently formed Fascist government, Benito Mussolini (see cat. no. 271k). Eleonora Duse would not be photographed by anyone else. His pastime became an official project in 1908, when he was asked by Guido Biagi, who headed the Laurentian Library in Florence, to collaborate on the creation of a "photographic pantheon" of illustrious men and women. Needless to say, a cross section of Nunes Vais's photographs is a veritable who's who of prominent Jewish Italians: the politicians Luigi Luzzatti (cat. no. 271c), Sidney Sonnino (cat. no. 271j), Claudio Treves (cat. no. 271f), and Anna Kuliscioff; the musicians Alberto Franchetti (see fig. 131), Giorgio Polacco, and Felice Boghen (cat. no. 271g); the actor Ugo Piperno (cat. no. 271d) and playwright Sabatino Lopez (cat. no. 271a); the writers Amelia Rosselli (cat. no. 271h; fig. 132), Margherita Sarfatti (cat. no. 271l; fig. 149), Alessandro and Paolo D'Ancona (see fig. 119); the publisher Emilio Treves; and the Orvieto brothers, Angiolo (cat. no. 271b; fig. 135) and Adolfo.

Nunes Vais conceived of his pantheon of great Italians as a public legacy, but he also took more informal reportage: records of immigrants embarking at the port

of Genoa, the leisure activities at the Pancaldi baths in Livorno, Florence street scenes, horse racing at the Cascine, and even Buffalo Bill at the Campo di Marte. Particularly revealing are the images of his country residence in the outskirts of Florence, a fifteenth-century villa in the hands of the family since 1868. While Nunes Vais made his portrait studies in a borrowed studio in Florence and maintained a house in the city, the focus of family life was his villa at Pian dei Giullari. There he spent weekends and holidays with his wife, Sofia Uzielli, whom he married in 1881; their only child, Laura, born in 1894; family; in-laws; and their intimate circle of friends. He documented the working farm and the life of the peasants, including their religious celebrations (see cat. no. 271s), and made a similar series of photographs of the landholdings of the Uzielli in Sensone, near Siena. Images of domestic life on the farm, such as Sofia posing with the livestock (cat. no. 271n; fig. 133), or his brother-in-law Giuseppe Uzielli on his way to hunt (see cat. no. 271q), underline the status of gentleman farmer and benefits of country life that the

Fig. 130. (opposite) Ulvi Liegi, *Interno della sinagoga* (Interior of the Synagogue at Livorno), c. 1935, Museo Civico "G. Fattori," Livorno (cat. no. 266)

Fig. 131. (above, left) Mario Nunes Vais, *Gabriele D'Annunzio with Alberto Franchetti,* 1906, Istituto Centrale per il Catalogo e la Documentazione, Gabinetto Fotografico Nazionale, Collection Nunes Vais, Rome (cat. no. 271 i)

Fig. 132. (above, right) Mario Nunes Vais, *Amelia Rosselli,* c. 1929, Istituto Centrale per il Catalogo e la Documentazione, Gabinetto Fotografico Nazionale, Collection Nunes Vais, Rome (cat. no. 271 h)

Fig. 133. (above) Mario Nunes Vais, *Sofia Nunes Vais Feeding the Chickens,* c. 1895, Istituto Centrale per il Catalogo e la Documentazione, Gabinetto Fotografico Nazionale, Collection Nunes Vais, Rome (cat. no. 271 n)

Fig. 134. (opposite, left) Mario Nunes Vais, *The Families of Mario Nunes Vais and Alberto Issel,* Istituto Centrale per il Catalogo e la Documentazione, Gabinetto Fotografico Nazionale, Collection Nunes Vais, Rome (cat. no. 271 m)

Fig. 135. (opposite, right) Mario Nunes Vais, *Angiolo Orvieto,* Istituto Centrale per il Catalogo e la Documentazione, Gabinetto Fotografico Nazionale, Collection Nunes Vais, Rome (cat. no. 271 b)

Italian Jews of Piedmont, Emilia-Romagna, and the Veneto had been enjoying for half a century (and which would also contribute to the political conservatism of many Jews in agrarian areas and later to their support of fascism[25]).

In an age when religion was the only factor distinguishing Jews from their fellow Italians, Nunes Vais's images provide a valuable microhistory of a continued Jewish identity on the level of personal relationships. Although they easily gained acceptance in the professional sphere, Italian Jews tended to socialize with their coreligionists, and there were few mixed marriages well into the twentieth century.[26] The Nunes Vais archive contains images that testify to the close ties between Nunes Vais, Liegi, and Corcos (see cat. no. 271p). There are individual portraits of Liegi's parents, Adolfo and Clery Levi, as well as a gathering including Liegi; his wife, Paola; and the Nunes Vais clan (cat no. 2710; fig. 134). Liegi left his own impressions of his friend's estate, painting the vineyards in the 1890s, as well as an exquisite plein-air study of a woman seated on the terrace of the villa (cat. no. 264).[27]

Another group portrait includes the Jewish artist Alberto Issel (1848–1926); his wife, Giulia; and their children (cat. no. 271m). Born in Genoa, Issel was part

of a group of landscape artists who painted in Liguria and Piedmont before turning to ceramics and furniture design in the 1880s. By the turn of the century his decorative arts factory was one of the most successful in Italy. Issel's designs, such as his desk of 1902, appealed to wealthy collectors and shipbuilders, who could afford the elaborate detailing and profuse floral ornament of his Liberty style furniture.[28] Finally, among the visual archives of the Pian dei Giullari is an image of the Viterbo family of Florence, pictured at the entrance to the estate; the young child is none other than the sculptor Dario Viterbo (1890–1961) (cat. no. 271u), who was active in Italy and France between the world wars.[29]

In many ways Nunes Vais's photographs parallel certain written memoirs that describe turn-of-the-century upper-class Jewish life, where celebrations of major religious holidays provided a fragile continuity in the face of a beckoning secular culture, as readings of Jewish texts on the Sabbath alternated with classics from the library of Vieusseux.[30] This was the generation that felt heir to two cultural legacies and allegiance to one homeland: Italy. Years later the rise of Zionism (which initially had a limited reception in Italy) and nascent political anti-Semitism brought new conflicts to the surface and a crises of identity best expressed by Angiolo Orvieto (see fig. 135) in his poem *Il vento di Sion* (The Wind of Zion):

The beckoning mirage of Zion
is small comfort to a Florentine Jew
even if I too dream happily of palm trees
and of Temple's columns arisen again
Too much lively Latin wind
has stirred my Eastern blood
lulled by age old indolence
Palm trees, yes, but the cypresses of Florence?
The Temple, yes, but what of this cathedral
with its marble flowering in the sky?
I am not like him, the one who calls for me
like a human bell, for I would not be able
to turn my back on my Tuscan people
even though at times they cry "Down with the Jews"

Here are my roots, too painful
to sever . . . and then, for what dream?
The Messiah will come, but perhaps not quite yet
Leave me be with this air, these bronzes
and Verrochio's marbles, the smiling images of Ghirland
with the octaves of my beloved Poliziano![31]

Bourgeoisie and Bohemia

The avant-garde emerged in Italy toward the end of the first decade of the new century as overlapping currents of neoimpressionism and symbolism from Paris and Munich were absorbed and reinterpreted by artists in Rome, Milan, Turin, and Venice. The careers of Cavaglieri and Modigliani reflect the synthesis of these various influences into original and highly personal styles. Isolated masters in the modernist mainstream, both chose to live in France, yet neither gave up his citizenship. Within their works and biographies one can still detect the accentuated refinement and background of privilege and culture that made Jews of their class seem the most Italian of Italians.

Cavaglieri's sumptuous images and lushly painted canvases celebrate the finer things of life—interiors brimming with antique furniture, exotic stuffs, and collectibles—and the aristocratic ambience to which he was born (cat. no. 272; fig. 136). His father and grandfather never worked for a living but accrued income from landholdings in Polesine in the Veneto, which was part of the rich agricultural region of the Po. From 1900 until 1917 Cavaglieri lived mainly in Padua and participated in the lively artistic developments around the Ca' Pesaro in Venice. The secessionist exhibitions housed in this palazzo on the Grand Canal were begun in 1908 as an alternative to the conservative Venice Biennale, with its unfavorable disposition toward younger artists, and were an important vehicle for the introduction of modernism in Italy.[32] Arturo Martini, Gino Rossi, and Felice Casorati began their careers here, while in 1910, as Marinetti launched his manifesto *Contro Venezia passatista* in the Piazza San Marco, Ca' Pesaro hosted the first individual exhibition by the Futurist Umberto Boccioni.

Cavaglieri's early work belongs to the symbolist and postimpressionist milieu of Ca' Pesaro, specifically the

Fig. 136. (opposite) Mario Cavaglieri, *Piccola russa* (The Little Russian), 1913, Private Collection, Bassano del Grappa (cat. no. 272)

Fig. 137. (left) Mario Cavaglieri, *Il baule e i vasi cinesi* (The Trunk and the Chinese Vases), 1915, Collection Ermes Drago, Marostica (cat. no. 273)

intimist style of Pierre Bonnard and Edouard Vuillard. In 1911 he visited Paris, where he was influenced by the bold colorism and rapid brushwork of the Fauves. His mannered worldliness and painterly virtuosity also bore much in common with two other well-known painters from Ferrara: Giovanni Boldini and the younger Filippo de Pisis. Although Cavaglieri exhibited at Ca' Pesaro from 1909 until 1913, the elegance of his female sitters proved just as palatable to the juries of the Biennale, where he debuted in 1914 with *Piccola russa* (The Little Russian; see fig. 136). The model wrapped in fur is Giulietta Catellini, who met Cavaglieri in 1912 and soon became ensconced among the finery of his home and studio. Giulietta became the artist's lifelong model and companion, but not without struggle. Her parents were opposed to the mixed marriage, and in 1915 she married Count Marazzani Visconti; as fate would have it, the countess was widowed young, and she married Cavaglieri in 1921.

Il baule e i vasi cinesi (The Trunk and the Chinese Vases; cat. no. 273; fig. 137) of 1915 typifies Cavaglieri's iconography of precious objects, from oriental vases to majolica, furniture inlaid with wood and ivory, statuettes, and silver candelabra, united in an almost abstract composition of swirling arabesques of color. As in this still life, he often squeezed the paint out of the tube directly onto the canvas, building up the surface in high relief and carrying the patterned environments of the Nabis to a painterly extreme. *Elena e Cecilia* (Elena and Cecilia; cat. no. 274; fig. 138) literally and figuratively reflects the ornate and luminous decor of Venetian interiors with their Murano glass and gilded mirrors. The exotic flavor that permeates his work has as much to do with contemporary Liberty taste as with the Byzantine heritage of Venice and his own Jewish roots. There is little in these canvases that reveals the break with bourgeois society so aggres-

Fig. 138. (above) Mario Cavaglieri, *Elena e Cecilia* (Elena and Cecilia), 1917, Collection Ermes Drago, Marostica (cat. no. 274)

Fig. 140. (opposite) Amedeo Modigliani, *Tête* (Head), 1911–1912, The Philadelphia Museum of Art. Gift of Mrs. Maurice J. Speiser in memory of her husband (cat. no. 278)

sively proclaimed by his Futurist contemporaries or the subsequent disruptions of World War I.

Cavaglieri's sensuous handling of paint has often been compared with the agitated surfaces of Chaim Soutine or Marc Chagall and attributed to a common ethnic background.[33] But the expressionism of the eastern European Jews who belonged to the School of Paris derived from a different cultural context. There is little inquietude in these works of padded comfort; Cavaglieri's gestural brushwork is not at odds with the world, but completely absorbed in it, weaving a luscious fabric like the oriental carpets and shawls contained within. Style and subject evoke a protected surrounding that muffles and obliterates any intrusion from outside.

It is no coincidence that Cavaglieri's interiors prompted Giorgio Bassani, in his essay on the artist, to recall the old residences of the agrarian upper class in Ferrara.[34] The objects accumulated between laden walls attest to old family wealth, unquestionable taste, and an assured sense of stability. They recall the cultivated, secluded, and falsely secure existence of the Jewish family described in Bassani's *Il giardino dei Finzi-Contini* (The Garden of the Finzi-Contini), who would later perish in a concentration camp. Born to this rarified world, Cavaglieri chose never to abandon it; in 1925 he escaped its imminent decline by moving to an estate in Peyloubère-par-Pavie in France. There he continued to paint Giulietta and splendid interiors, and he also sketched the surrounding countryside, often in the company of Filippo de Pisis. Cavaglieri returned to Italy temporarily during World War II; he survived those years hiding in Piacenza, but twenty-three relatives in the Venetò perished after being deported in 1943.

The tendency to see a disposition toward sensuality or anxiety in the style of modern Jewish masters has also often been applied to Modigliani. Here too such an interpretation seems forced if one considers the very lack of overt expressionism in Modigliani's work (cat. no 275; fig. 139) and the rarified elegance that permeates it. Although his art matured within the Jewish circle of Montparnasse, there is no trace of the ethnic motifs of Chagall, the dissipating line of Jules Pascin, or the "smeary painting" said to reflect the ghetto origins of Soutine. So argued Paolo D'Ancona in his article on the four artists, which refuted the notion of a common ethnic element and emphasized their diversity within the larger context of a modern expressionism.[35]

Fig. 139. (opposite) Amedeo Modigliani, *L'amazzone* (The Amazon), 1909, Mrs. Alexander Lewyt, New York (cat. no. 275)

Modigliani's stylistic refinement is most evident in his sculptures (see cat. no. 278; fig. 140) and their related studies. The roughly hewn and bulbous limbs of Modigliani's *Cariatide* (Caryatid; cat. no. 280) typify his efforts at direct stone carving, inspired by the example of Constantin Brancusi. But technical ability must not be confused with conceptual intent: in the series of studies for the figure, mass and volume are consistently reduced to a play of ovoids and cylinders, and the primitive urge gives way to a graceful, flowing line. Modigliani conceived his stone heads as part of a "temple to beauty" and exhibited seven in the Salon d'Automne of 1912, entitling them "Têtes ensemble décoratif." The critic Lamberto Vitali (who is also Jewish) characterized Modigliani's art as "refined to the extreme," noting that in the context of the "new primitives" of twentieth-century art, Modigliani was to Picasso what Botticelli was to Masaccio.[36]

The biography of Modigliani is well known, if not legend: his impoverished conditions in Paris, the excesses of drugs and alcohol, the ignored genius, his early death followed by the suicide of his mistress, Jeanne Hébuterne. The details of his more auspicious origins tend to get lost within this tale of deprivation and excess. He was born in Livorno to a well-off and prestigious Mediterranean Jewish family (his mother's family claimed Spinoza among its ancestors). Shortly after Modigliani's birth, his father was involved in a business failure, and the household was reduced to more modest circumstances. (One wonders if this change in fortune didn't also precipitate the artist's antibourgeois rebellion; his brother Giuseppe Emanuele went on to become a prestigious figure in the Italian Socialist party). Nonetheless he was raised in a highly cultured environment, reading D'Annunzio and Nietzsche in his early adolescence. His degree of sophistication and aestheticism, so far removed from the realism of the Macchiaioli followers under whom he first trained, are further revealed in his letters to the companion of his student days, the painter Oscar Ghiglia (which were first published by Paolo D'Ancona in 1930). Modigliani eventually made his way to Paris, via Venice, in 1906. Ghiglia continued his career in Florence under the enlightened patronage of Gustavo Sforni, a Jewish collector and possibly the first in Italy to buy works by Vincent van Gogh and Paul Cézanne.[37]

Fig. 142. Amedeo Modigliani, *Portrait de Manuello* (Portrait of Manuello) [Manuel Humbert], 1916, Los Angeles County Museum of Art. Gift of Mr. William Wyler (cat. no. 281)

Fig. 141. Amedeo Modigliani, *Portrait de Joseph Levi* (Portrait of Joseph Levi), 1910, Private Collection (cat. no. 276)

Modigliani moved from Montmartre to Montparnasse in 1909. His connections with the Jewish personalities of Paris (including the part-time dealer Joseph Levi [see cat. no. 276; fig. 141]) has been vividly recounted by Kenneth Silver, who has also stressed Modigliani's singular position in this milieu.[38] Both Jewish and Italian, Modigliani was equally at ease sketching the Star of David or the Crucifixion and could praise the aesthetics of Raphael in Hebrew script. He was heir to a double Mediterranean tradition and endowed with a breadth of cultural reference. In addition to the circles of the French and eastern European artists, he frequented the Iberian colony in Paris, including the Portuguese Jew Amadeo de Souza Cardoso and the Catalan sculptor Manuel Humbert (see cat. no. 281; fig. 142).[39]

It is tempting to think that this cosmopolitanism reveals his identity as an Italian Jew, specifically an Italian Jew from Livorno. The city had benefited from its status as an international port under the auspices of the grand dukes of Tuscany, who granted religious freedom and commercial advantages to the Jews and Marranos in the second half of the sixteenth century. Livorno attracted Jews from the Levant and Spain, whose rich culture was imported and mixed with that of "indigenous" Italian Jews, although the Sephardic element remained dominant. Indeed Modigliani's art, with its multiple references to ethnic and Near Eastern art as well as Greek, Etruscan, and Renaissance sources, finds an analogy in the linguistic pluralism and flexibility of his native tongue. The local Livornese dialect, with its blend of Catalan, Spanish, Portuguese, Italian vernacular, and Roman-Jewish vocabulary, was unique in Italy. As Guido Bedarida has noted, waves of immigration from the Iberian peninsula, North Africa, and the Levant made Livorno "not only the famous 'little Jerusalem' but also, with its ancient dialect, the center of a lively Mediterranean synthesis."[40]

Despite the speculative nature of discerning racial and national qualities in the art of Modigliani, his dual identity had special resonance for Italian artistic life after his death. He was not well known in his native country until his first small retrospective, an exhibition of twelve paintings at the Venice Biennale of 1922, which made a negative impression if any at all. The critic Enrico Thovez, for one, declared his indignation at seeing "twelve ugly and unformed heads that a child of five might have drawn."[43] The rather academic painter Cipriano Efisio Oppo (later head of the Fascist artists' syndicates) saw in Modigliani's painting a supremely refined and elegant superficiality that smacked of "class."[42]

Far more important and successful was the exhibition organized at the Biennale of 1930 by the art historian Lionello Venturi, which included some thirty-nine paintings and dozens of drawings. Critics were quick to claim Modigliani as a native son (understandable given his posthumous international fame) regardless of his religion. One review pointedly compared him with the "pagan" Antonio Mancini, proclaiming the "Israelite" Modigliani to be "the most Christian, to wit, the most spiritual and merciful painter" of the time. Sarfatti, writing in Mussolini's flagship paper *Il Popolo d'Italia,* lauded him as one of the guiding spirits of modern art, while emphasizing his role in reasserting the particularly Tuscan element of the Italian heritage. Modigliani's true champion, however, was Venturi, who believed that great artists had to absorb the culture of their own time, which in the twentieth century, had its center in Paris and the heritage of Cézanne. For this reason he considered Modigliani to be more Italian than Antonio Canova (who was, in his opinion, a slave to the aesthetic of German neoclassicism) because he reconciled "antithetical cosmopolitan" influences in an innately Italian equilibrium.[43] The issue took on a darker accent later in the decade. As the Fascist regime grew more repressive, Modigliani the "bohemian" became a special symbol of creative freedom for younger artists in an epoch increasingly characterized by cultural chauvinism. Conversely, around 1937 Modigliani the "Jew" became the focus of an antimodernist, anti-Semitic attack led by a vocal, if small, group of Fascists, who supported the cultural policies of German National Socialism.[44]

Trieste

Like Livorno, the port of Trieste boasted an especially rich Jewish tradition. Both cities enjoyed the fruits of emancipation long before other parts of Italy (Trieste due to the Patent of Tolerance enacted by Emperor Joseph II in 1782), and paradoxically such freedom seems only to have encouraged the retention of a strong cultural and regional identity. The community was composed largely of Venetian Jews (hence its support of the irredentist movement), who were joined by Jews from Germany, the eastern Mediterranean, and the Papal States. By the late nineteenth century Italian remained the language of trade, but the central European influence gave Trieste a special character. The triple identity of the city's Jews was exemplified in the person and novels of Ettore Schmitz, who wrote under the name Italo Svevo, meaning the "Italian Swabian."[45]

Fig. 143. Isidoro Grünhut, *Ritratto del pittore Umberto Veruda* (Portrait of the Painter Umberto Veruda), 1886, Museo Civico Revoltella–Galleria d'Arte Moderna, Trieste (cat. no. 285)

In the mid-nineteenth century artists from Trieste looked to the Venice Academy for their training; this orientation changed to Munich in the second half of the century and to Paris early in the twentieth.[46] Among the first to import the realism of Franz von Lenbach and William Liebl to Trieste was the Jewish artist Isidoro Grünhut, who studied at the Munich Academy in the mid-eighties. Nicknamed "Gobbo" (hunchback) because of his crooked posture, Grünhut was primarily a portraitist and caricaturist. His image of Umberto Veruda (1868–1904) dates from 1886 (cat.

Fig. 144. Arturo Rietti, *Ritratto del Maestro Barbasetti* (Portrait of Maestro Barbasetti), c. 1907, Museo Civico Revoltella–Galleria d'Arte Moderna, Trieste (cat. no. 288)

no. 285; fig. 143), and their days together at the Munich Academy, before Grünhut turned to a looser impressionist-naturalist style. Along with Carlo Wostry (1865–1943), Grünhut and Veruda formed part of the original group of artists and writers who gathered at the Circolo Artistico.[47] Grünhut left his native city in 1887 for Rome and later Florence, while Veruda remained in Trieste, where he met Svevo at the Circolo Artistico in 1890. The two became close friends, and the artist served as a model for the character of the sculptor Stefano Balli in Svevo's *Senilità* (As a Man Grows Older).[48]

The works of two other Jewish artists, Arturo Rietti and Gino Parin, show the influx of symbolist and secessionist trends into the great port city of the Austro-Hungarian empire. Their concentration on portraiture also reflects a growing interest in psychological realism, paralleled by the narratives of Svevo.[49] Though Rietti trained at the Munich Academy from 1884 to 1886, he was later influenced by the work of Eugène Carrière, with its enveloping atmosphere and tonal nuances (cat. no. 288; fig. 144). His ability to capture an elusive elegance in the medium of pastel made him popular among society and literary figures in Trieste,

Fig. 145. Gino Parin, *Armonia in bianco e rosso* (*Harmony in Red and White*), 1914, Museo Civico Revoltella–Galleria d'Arte Moderna, Trieste (cat. no. 283)

such as the Countess Sordina (cat. no. 287; fig. 194) and Svevo's wife, Livia Veneziani Svevo. Rietti later developed a large clientele in Milan, where he settled in 1904. Parin also trained in Munich, where he remained until the outbreak of World War I, working as a graphic illustrator in the secession style. After his return to Trieste, Parin painted *Armonia in bianco e rosso* (Harmony in Red and White; cat. no. 283; fig. 145), reminiscent of the mannered poses and sumptuous backgrounds of portraits by Franz von Stuck, and continued to paint symbolist images of women in tenebrous interiors into the 1920s (see cat. no. 284; fig. 195).

While it is difficult to detect nuances of an ethnic identity in the styles of these late nineteenth-century intimists, the probing of psychological depths led to a growing sense of detachment rather than unquestioned assimilation among the Jewish artists and writers of Trieste. After World War I Trieste became the first Italian city to embrace the writings of Freud, with immediate effect, most notably in Svevo's novel *La coscienza di Zeno* (Confessions of Zeno, 1923). As Giorgio Voghera has shown, all of the figures involved in the study of psychoanalysis in Trieste were Jewish or half Jewish: Edoardo Weiss, the first Freudian disciple in

Fig. 146. (above) Arturo Nathan, *Autoritratto* (Self-Portrait), 1927, Museo Civico Revoltella–Galleria d'Arte Moderna, Trieste (cat. no. 292).

Fig. 147. (opposite) Arturo Nathan, *Statua naufragata* (Shipwrecked Statue), 1930, Museo Civico Revoltella–Galleria d'Arte Moderna, Trieste (cat. no. 289)

Italy; Svevo; the poet Umberto Saba; the critic Roberto (Boby) Bazlen; Voghera's father, Guido; and the painter Arturo Nathan.[50]

Another Jewish artist, Vittorio Bolaffio, is largely remembered for his close friendship with Saba, and his life and painting have been interpreted as reflecting a quiet desperation.[51] Born to a wealthy family, Bolaffio lived by choice in squalor and solitude, tormented by a lack of confidence in his own work. Most comfortable as a draftsman, he constantly sketched shipyards and sailors, which culminated in his cycle of paintings of the port. Despite the bustling activity of the scenes, these allegories are beset with a melancholy expressed in a twilight palette, which presages Trieste's imminent economic decline. Bolaffio's most famous work, however, is the image of Saba against the blue of the Adriatic sea (cat. no. 286; fig. 177). Saba, in turn, dedicated one of his best-known poems, *La brama* (1930), to Bolaffio:

> Devotedly he extends his hand
> that trembles from anxiety, to color his canvases.
> Above he paints sails
> in the sun, emblazened encounters
> of figures, sunsets on the shores
> of the sea and starboard
> and on every thing a light
> of sanctity, that comes from his heart
> and reflects on those of others.[52]

Arturo Nathan's art specifically reflects his history as a psychoanalytic patient and the melancholy, self-critical disposition that characterized the circle of Jewish intellectuals around Weiss. Nathan began to draw as a means of self-exploration, with the encouragement of Weiss. Among his first works, dating from the mid-1920s, are a series of self-portraits with his eyes closed or locked in a meditative rapture (see cat. no. 292; fig. 146) and his body sheathed in a pristine white cloth. By the end of the decade he was painting the stormy seas and desolate shores of the Adriatic coast as allegories of alienation and destruction (see cat. no. 289; fig. 147). *Scoglio incantato* (Enchanted Rock; cat. no. 290) has been compared with the closing scene of apocalypse in Svevo's *Confessions of Zeno*.[53] Nathan expressed the workings of his subconscious with a highly personal iconography of shipwrecks, volcanoes, naval materiel, and fragments of antique architecture and statuary. His

juxtapositions of idiosyncratic objects and the unnaturally still atmosphere were directly influenced by the work of Giorgio de Chirico, however, whom he first met in 1925; Nathan was subsequently grouped with the school of Metaphysical painting.[54]

Ferrara

The subject of Nathan and de Chirico permits a small diversion to Ferrara and the years 1916–1919, when the city became home to the painters and poets of the metaphysical school and traditional Jewish culture exerted a notable influence on one of the most important movements of the twentieth-century avant-garde. De Chirico and his brother Alberto Savinio arrived in Ferrara from Paris on military duty in 1916 and were joined by the poet Filippo de Pisis and the former futurist painter Carlo Carrà. Although none of the protagonists was Jewish, they were enamored of the Ferrara ghetto and the mystical tradition of the kabbalah.

The Jewish community of Ferrara prospered during the Renaissance under the protection of the Este family until the famous walled city came under papal rule at the end of the sixteenth century. Though liberated in

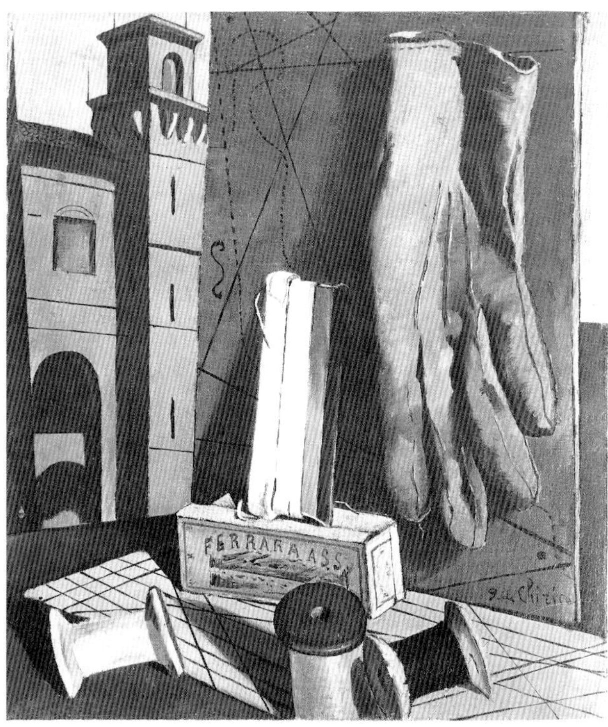

Fig. 148. Giorgio de Chirico, *The Amusements of a Young Girl,* 1916(?), Collection, The Museum of Modern Art, New York. James Thrall Soby Bequest

1860, the ghetto maintained its distinctive flavor into the twentieth century and provided a sense of mystery and metaphysical surprise evoked by de Pisis in his book *La città dalle cento meraviglie* (City of a Hundred Marvels, 1922) and by Savinio in *Hermaphrodito* (Hermaphrodite, 1918). Carrà described their artistic camaraderie and inspiration in the "shadow of a Jewish café," while "mannequins beheaded in the ghetto play at idylls with the paper stars of the Verdian night."[55] The strange biscuits that dominate the still lifes and enchanted rooms of de Chirico's Ferrara period were a type of bread associated with the ghetto bakeries, and they also figure as key iconographical elements, their origins duly noted, in the poetry of de Pisis and Savinio. *The Amusements of a Young Girl* (fig. 148) contains the spools of thread and matchboxes found in the windows of ghetto shops, as described by de Pisis in the narrative of the "Asilo Infantile Israelitico," which he dedicated to de Chirico. Finally the painting *Jewish Angel,* with its large single eye, may refer to the *maggid,* or divine power, that visited the kabbalists; de Chirico undoubtedly found the kabbalistic theme of redemption through mystic revelation sympathetic to his own theory of metaphysical art, which was based on the premise of prophecy and initiation.[56]

Jews and Fascist Culture, 1919–1945

After Mussolini's rise to power in 1922, Italian artists and intellectuals began the task of defining a new culture that would embody the spirit of fascism. The debate over style and ideology continued for two decades; yet as fascism changed from a revolutionary movement to a dictatorship in 1925 and an increasingly repressive regime in the 1930s, Mussolini never declared an official style and continued to patronize both avant-garde and conservative groups. The professional activity of Jewish artists during this period sheds a clear light on an otherwise ambiguous relationship between the avant-garde and the regime: a relationship of commitment, collusion, and subsequent betrayal.

Like other Italians, Jews chose to support or resist Fascism on the basis of political and nationalistic beliefs, regardless of their identity as Jews: anti-Semitism did not enter into Fascist ideology until the invasion of Ethiopia and the alliance with Nazi Germany in 1936.[57]

Hence some Jewish artists pursued styles that dovetailed with the regime's propagandistic imperatives for an inherently Italian art, while others consciously looked to European sources. It was only with the Racial Laws of 1938 that equivocation became impossible and art bore witness to a resurgence of Jewish identity.

The first and most influential theorist of a Fascist art was Jewish: the writer and art critic Margherita Sarfatti (1880–1962; see fig. 149), whose unquestionable intellectual contribution and prodigious output has been unduly, if understandably, neglected because of the more sensational aspects of her biography and the postwar sensitivity to her political beliefs.[58] She was born to Amedeo Grassini and Emma Levi in Venice; her cousin Giuseppe Levi was a noted biologist and anti-Fascist in Turin (and father of the writer Natalia Ginzburg). Sarfatti was first tutored in art history by Antonio Fradeletto, later the director of the Biennale, who introduced her to the theories of John Ruskin at a time when French postimpressionism was making inroads into Venice; the dual notions of the social utilitarianism and modernist autonomy of art would remain basic to Sarfatti's aesthetics throughout her career.

In 1902 Sarfatti moved to Milan with her husband, the lawyer Cesare Sarfatti (1866–1924), whom she had married four years earlier. He was also from a prominent, though less wealthy, Jewish family. Whereas Sarfatti had abandoned her Jewish heritage, Cesare joined the Milanese Zionist group in 1902 and remained a zealous supporter of that movement. Both were active in the Socialist party; Sarfatti became associated with the circle of Anna Kuliscioff and in 1909 assumed the position of art critic for the Socialist paper *Avanti*. In 1911 an ambitious and more radical socialist, Benito Mussolini, took over the editorship of the paper. They began an intimate relationship around World War I, which lasted for some two decades. In 1918 she became the art critic for Mussolini's Fascist daily *Il Popolo d'Italia* and its related publications, and beginning in 1922 she also directed *Gerarchia,* the regime's journal of political theory (edited by Eloisa Foà, one of Sarfatti's Jewish friends from Milan).[59] In 1925 she wrote the first biography of Mussolini, which became a best-seller published in many languages. Above and beyond her relationship with the future Duce, however, Sarfatti's political allegiance typified the belief of many strident nationalists (Jews and gentiles alike) who were disillusioned with the failed promise of the Risorgimento and

Fig. 149. Mario Nunes Vais, *Margherita Sarfatti,* c. 1915, Istituto Centrale per il Catalogo e la Documentazione, Gabinetto Fotografico Nazionale, Collection Nunes Vais, Rome (cat. no. 271 l)

saw in fascism a means of regenerating Italian society.[60] Indeed it remains to be determined to what extent Sarfatti influenced Mussolini in matters of politics as well as art.

Around 1910 Sarfatti began to hold her salon, which attracted the preeminent talents of pen and paintbrush, including members of the newly formed futurist movement. She was an early champion of the then-unknown Boccioni, who rendered her portrait on several occasions (see cat. no. 293; fig. 21), and in 1910 Cesare successfully defended Marinetti against charges of obscenity resulting from his book *Mafarka la futurista* (Mafarka the Futurist).[61] But after the war Sarfatti and Marinetti found themselves in opposite aesthetic camps and rivals for recognition as the leader of an official Fascist art. Sarfatti was the moving force behind the Novecento Italiano, and her art theory and criticism underline some of the more salient contradictions of the "return to order" movement in Italy, which she championed.

The Novecento began as a group of seven artists who exhibited for the first time together at the Galleria Pesaro in Milan in March 1923.[62] Mussolini officiated at this occasion, as he would at the first national exhibition of the Novecento four years later. Sarfatti promoted her aesthetics not only in the Fascist flagship press but also in numerous other journals and exhibition catalogues in Italy and abroad, and she published two books on the history of modern art.[63] In the immediate postwar years Sarfatti emphasized the return to solidity and "plastic construction" in the general context of an Italian tradition and in reaction against the "eccentric, obscure, and arbitrary" in art. In the early 1920s her emphasis on accentuated mass and volume reflected the contemporary style of magic realism, which retained the slightly disquieting and dreamlike atmosphere of metaphysical painting. There was little rhetoric of "vigor" and "discipline" in her art criticism until later in the decade, parallel with the conservative evolution of fascism. By 1930 Sarfatti explicitly paired the Novecento with the "rhythm of fighting passion and fervent renewal that emerged with the redeeming toil of fascism." Though nationalistic in matters of art, Sarfatti was far from being provincial; throughout her writings is a basic support of modernist developments, especially the postimpressionists and Cézanne (whom she once claimed as Italian in origin).[64]

In 1926 the Novecento became a national movement with an exhibition of works by more than one hundred painters in Milan. The enlargement of Sarfatti's domain also led to her fall from power, since the label expanded to include too many diverse artists, dissolving any theoretical coherency. The modern edge of the Novecento's magic realist style gave way to increasingly naturalistic and less original revisitations of figurative art. Internal rivalries and envy of Sarfatti's personal power signaled the end of the Novecento by the early 1930s. In the meantime the modernist elements of the group made them ripe for attack by a group within the Fascist party, which accused the Novecento of "masonic conspiracy" and included veiled references to Sarfatti as "Shylock."[65] Yet Sarfatti continued to support more progressive aspects of art as critic for the Turin paper *La Stampa* from 1932; she also commissioned the rationalist architect Giuseppe Terragni to design the tomb of her beloved youngest son, Roberto, who died in action in World War I (he was decorated posthumously).

Sarfatti converted to Catholicism in 1928, four years after the death of her husband. That same year she could claim to Alma Mahler that there was no "Jewish question" in Italy and that Mussolini would never follow Hitler's anti-Semitic policies.[66] She fled a decade later, just before her books were removed from Italian libraries and bookstores. Despite her fall from favor with Mussolini and her life in exile in Latin America from 1939 to 1947, one is hardpressed to find a resurgence of Jewish identity in Sarfatti's memoirs, *Acqua passata* (nor does she negate her Fascist past).[67] Nevertheless a passage in her book reveals an awareness of the irony of her situation: she alludes to the fact that the British writer Israel Zangwill based his story of a family Passover dinner, "Chad Gadya" (in *Dreamers of the Ghetto,* 1898), on his visit to the Sarfatti family palazzo in Venice in the 1890s, when she was an adolescent: the story points moralistically to the tragedy that befalls a young Jew (inspired by Sarfatti's brother) who abandons his faith.[68]

Sarfatti's notion of an art that reflected the formal properties of an inherently Italian tradition was not that far removed from the theories of the Roman journal *Valori Plastici* (Plastic Values, 1918–1922), which was cofounded by the Jewish artist Roberto Melli and the critic Mario Broglio.[69] Melli's art exemplifies the reaction of the Italian avant-garde in its incorporation of the modernist experiments of the prewar period into a new syntax of order and harmony. He was born in Ferrara to a stationery wholesaler who wanted his son to become an accountant, but Melli was inspired to follow a different vocation after he began to visit the studios of local artists. In 1911 he settled in Rome and developed his sculpture in the milieu of the Ro-

Fig. 150. Roberto Melli, *Interno* (Interior), 1919, Private Collection, Rome (cat. no. 299)

Fig. 151. (above) Roberto Melli, *Scenografia* (Scenography), 1936, Private Collection (cat. no. 301)

Fig. 152. (opposite) Corrado Cagli, *Guerrieri* (Warriors), 1933, Private Collection, Rome (cat. no. 304)

man Secession. A work such as *Signora dal cappello nero* (Woman with a Black Hat, 1913; cat. no. 297), while indebted to analytical cubism, already shows Melli's independent path toward synthetic composition and the emphatic use of void and cast shadow to define volume and space. By 1918 Melli had given up sculpture, announcing in his first article in *Valori Plastici* that the inviolability of form had been "tragically dissolved" once and for all by Michelangelo. He turned to painting and the structural value of pure, unmodulated color as the means to establish a new "plastic" sense.[70]

Melli's initial efforts reflect the influence of de Chirico and Carrà, who were also part of the Valori Plastici circle. *Composizione con oggetti* (Composition with Objects, 1918; cat. no. 298) includes the mannequin head common to metaphysical painting, but here the faceless form is replaced by the features of his wife, Anna Meotti. Anna modeled again for *Interno* (Interior, 1919; cat. no. 299; fig. 150), in which the disconcerting juxtapositions of the earlier composition give way to a more subtle tension created by luminous vibrations of tonal harmonies restricted to a monochrome palette. Like Giorgio Morandi, with whom he shared a magic realist style in the early 1920s, Melli created a highly cerebral art; both were "hermits of pure painting," living in isolation, restricting their subject matter to the immediate world around them, focusing on the infinite nuances of tonal harmonies in defining the intangible qualities of space.

In the early 1930s Melli became a leading exponent of *pittura tonale* (tonal painting) (cat. no. 301; fig. 151) and a point of reference for a group of younger artists: Corrado Cagli, also Jewish; Giuseppe Capogrossi; and Emanuele Cavalli (who in 1935 married Vera Haberfeld, the niece of Edoardo Weiss). The latter three exhibited together in Paris in December 1933, where the French-Jewish critic Waldemar George christened them the "Ecole de Rome," commenting on the inherent humanism and Latin qualities of their style (after beginning his catalogue text with a lengthy quotation from Mussolini on Fascist doctrine). George had earlier championed the "clarity and abstraction" of the Italian magic realists against the "Jewish-romantic style of Soutine and the surrealists."[71] Melli and the *tonalisti* articulated their theories in the journals *Quadrante* and *Il Tevere* (ironically, later the vehicle of the anti-Semitic, antimodernist campaign). The purism of Melli's canvases could likewise be attributed to the "classical" and "Mediterranean" qualities increasingly promoted by the

regime. Nevertheless, in the *Manifesto del primordialismo plastico* (Manifesto of Plastic Primordialism) of 1933, Melli made it clear that the Italian principle of "plasticity" excluded anything extraneous to the autonomous values of color and volume, which constituted the only means of representing the primordial elements of light and space.[72]

On the whole Melli's art had no overt political content or allegory, with the rare exception of a commissioned portrait of Mussolini.[73] Quite different was the intention of Cagli, who combined the technique of tonal painting with historical subject matter and didactic purpose. For Cagli the "primordial" referred to both the fundamental building blocks of pure composition and the primeval origins of myth and race. *I neofiti* (The Neophytes, 1934; cat. no. 305) and *Guerrieri* (Warriors, 1933; cat. no. 304; fig. 152) reflect this interest in biblical and heroic themes, rendered in his preferred medium of tempera and encaustic (in emulation of historical techniques). *I neofiti* also contains a direct citation from Piero della Francesca, who was the preferred quattrocento master of the tonalisti because of the heightened reality of his static, monumental forms. Some of Cagli's images, such as *Il cavallo di Mussolini* (Mussolini's Horse) or *La spedizione punitiva* (The Punitive Expedition), bordered on propaganda, but his style remained curiously unrhetorical, mediated in its immediacy by the degree of abstraction, deliberate archaism, and the dreamlike atmosphere inherent in the tonal painting.[74]

Fig. 153. Antonietta Raphaël Mafai, *Veduta dalla terrazza di via Cavour* (View from the Terrace of via Cavour), 1930, N. M. de' Angelis, Rome (cat. no. 311)

Cagli realized his ideas on a grand scale with a series of public commissions that have for the most part not survived, due to their temporary nature as well as stylistic controversy and, later, censorship. His theory of a public art had much in common with that of Mario Sironi, the Novecento painter who led the mural painting movement in the 1930s.[75] Under Sironi's auspices, Cagli was commissioned to paint a mural, *Preparativi per la guerra* (Preparations for War) for the V Milan Triennale in 1933, which was destroyed along with the some thirty other public artworks in the ensuing critical controversy over the project. For the VI Triennale of 1936 he painted *Battaglia di San Martino* (The Battle of San Martino), depicting the Risorgimento event, and which along with its stylistic inspiration, Paolo Uccello's *Battle of San Romano,* is today permanently installed in the Galleria degli Uffizi in Florence.[76] Cagli's propensity for the monumental set him apart from the intimism of the other tonalisti, and their artistic brotherhood soon dissipated. He nonetheless remained one of the most forceful personalities in Rome in those years, writing polemical articles on mural painting, organizing exhibitions, and conceiving the program for the Galleria della Cometa, which became a focal point for the artists of the Scuola romana.

The tonalisti formed one main component of the Scuola romana; the other was a trio of artists—Antonietta Raphaël Mafai, Mario Mafai, and Scipione (Gino Bonichi)—whose work eschewed nationalistic sentiments and was deliberately untraditional and unprogrammatic.[77] While the tonal paintings of Melli and Cagli exhibit few Jewish nuances and in fact reflect complete integration into an indigenous Italian tradition, the art of Raphaël reflects an absolute pride in "difference."

Fig. 154. Antonietta Raphaël Mafai, *Yom Kippur nella sinagoga* (Yom Kippur at the Synagogue), 1931, Private Collection, Rome (cat. no. 312)

Of all the twentieth-century Italian-Jewish artists, Raphaël is the only one whose art can truly be termed "Jewish," and it is no coincidence that she was foreign-born, the daughter of a rabbi in Kovno, Lithuania. After her father's death Raphaël went to London and eventually made her way to Rome. There in 1925 she met Mario Mafai, who had been recently expelled from the Academy, who encouraged her to take up the paintbrush. "I am Nordic, Lithuanian," Raphaël later wrote. "Reaching the Mediterranean coast was like a revelation for me. It seemed that I could feel the colors vibrating around me, I would say, even more than someone who had always lived in the south."[78]

Mafai and Raphaël were soon living together in a studio on the via Cavour and, in the constant company of Scipione, began to paint the cityscape and the venerable monuments of Rome in a decidedly eccentric light (see cat. no. 311; fig. 153). In a review of 1929 the critic Roberto Longhi described their style as "that obscure area where a decrepit impressionism changes into a hallucinatory expressionism, in kabbalah and magic" and noted the novelty of the "school of the via Cavour," as he called them, in the context of the classicizing tendencies of contemporary Roman painting.[79] Although it is difficult to determine the exact degree and order of influences among the three painters, Raphaël's autodidactic manner mixed with the exoticism of the School of Paris was crucial in determining the group's expressionistic direction.

In the same review of the First Fascist Syndicate Exhibition, Longhi also referred to Raphaël as the "little foster sister of Chagall."[80] Her work abounds with folkloric and ethnic motifs, including portraits of her parents drawn from memory and the mystical impression of the crowds in a synagogue on Yom Kippur (cat. no. 312; fig. 154).[81] A self-portrait of 1928 (cat.

Fig. 155. Antonietta Raphaël Mafai, *La Fuga da Sodoma* (Flight from Sodom), 1935–1936 (bronze cast, 1968), Private Collection, Rome (cat. no. 313)

no. 310; fig. 118) shows the influences of Moïse Kisling and Raphaël's first love—music—which she had studied and taught in London. Raphaël painted her immediate surroundings, capturing the bohemian flavor of a household filled with musical instruments, oriental shawls, and her family's Judaica, which inspired her as much for its religious significance as its theatrical effect.[82]

Raphaël turned to sculpture in the mid-1930s, and it eventually became the primary medium for her preferred subjects, family portraits and biblical themes. Her early efforts were influenced by Aristide Maillol and the dramatic tenor of Auguste Rodin's *Balzac,* especially in the case of the over life-size *La fuga da Sodoma* (The Flight from Sodom; cat. no. 313; fig. 155), begun in 1935. After many years out of the public eye, Raphaël began to show again, placing her sculptures in the syndicate exhibitions of 1937 and 1938. The Racial Laws intervened, however, and the Mafai family sought safety in Genoa in the autumn of 1939.[83] It was there, in relative isolation, that she was able to concentrate more on her sculpture, endowing it with an ever-greater psychological realism enhanced by agitated surfaces akin to those of Jacob Epstein. Raphaël later focused on the sensuality of the female form and the themes of fertility and genesis expressed through the use of fragments and distortion, a direction that had no parallel in contemporary Italian sculpture, with its emphasis on an ancient, indigenous past.

The idiosyncratic style of Raphaël and the school of via Cavour, with its utter indifference to the regime and its cultural policies, was subtly, but politically charged. With the figure of Carlo Levi, however, art and resistance took on a more concrete relationship and commitment to the anti-Fascist cause. Though he trained in medicine, Levi was a writer, a political activist, and by profession, a painter. He was born in Turin to an assimilated, nonpracticing Jewish family; his father had a working-class background, while his mother was from a more affluent milieu; she was the sister of the Socialist leader Claudio Treves (see cat. no. 271f). Levi's first mentor, the liberal activist Piero Gobetti (1901–1926) introduced him to the painter Felice Casorati, whose magic realist style influenced Levi's early portraits of his family (cat. no. 321; fig. 156). Casorati's school was a center of liberal thinking, open to French modernism and strongly influenced by the ideals of Venturi.[84] Casorati included among his young pupils another Jewish artist, Paola

Fig. 156. Carlo Levi, *Il fratello e la sorella* (Brother and Sister), 1925, Fondazione Carlo Levi, Rome (cat. no. 321)

Levi Montalcini, whose twin sister, Rita, later won a Nobel Prize in Medicine and whose brother Gino became a noted rationalist architect.[85] Though little of Levi Montalcini's early work survives, the languid forms of *Estate* (Summer) (cat. no. 320) reflect the lyrical expressionism of the generation of Casorati's pupils, which had little to do with the nationalistic rhetoric of the regime.

Beginning in 1925 Levi traveled frequently to Paris, and his style became more relaxed under the influence of the impressionists and the fauves. This orientation toward French modernism was the basic premise of the Sei di Torino (Turin Six), which Levi founded in 1929 with the painters Francesco Menzio, Jesse Boswell, Gigi Chessa, Enrico Paulucci, and Nicola Galante. It was the first artists' group of the Fascist period consciously to oppose the monumentality and mythmaking inherent in the aesthetics of Sarfatti's Novecento. Though the Sei di Torino disavowed any ideological connotations in painting in favor of "pure poetry," the programmatic nature of the group was plainly stated by their critical champion, Venturi, who

Fig. 157. (opposite) Carlo Levi, *Ritratto di Leone Ginzburg* (Portrait of Leone Ginzburg), 1933, Fondazione Carlo Levi, Rome (cat. no. 327)

Fig. 158. (above) Corrado Cagli, *I fratelli Rosselli* (The Rosselli Brothers), 1937, Eredi Cagli, Rome (cat. no. 308)

argued for their cosmopolitan quality and success in "evading the danger of national prejudice in their painting."[86]

In 1931 Levi joined the clandestine anti-Fascist movement Giustizia e Libertà, led by the Jewish brothers Carlo and Nello Rosselli (see cat. nos. 323, 326), the sons of the writer Amelia Rosselli (see fig. 132). The group also included the family of Giuseppe Levi (the cousin of Sarfatti) and the charismatic Russian Jew Leone Ginzburg, whom Levi depicted with his famous "red hands" (cat. no. 327; fig. 157) in 1933. This was the close-knit circle of family and friends, the "secret complicity" fondly recalled in the stories of Natalia Ginzburg, who married Leone in 1938.[87] A disproportionately large number of Jews made up the ranks of anti-Fascists, yet the movement was not inherently Jewish, nor were the Jews involved particularly religious. Their allegiance to social freedom has nonetheless been interpreted as the expression of a Jewish consciousness, one that Nello Rosselli himself voiced at the 1924 Livorno Convention. This opinion was seconded by their colleague the writer and histo-

Fig. 159. Carlo Levi, *Il figlio della Parroccola* (The Son of the Parroccola), 1936, Fondazione Carlo Levi, Rome (cat. no. 329)

Fig. 160. Carlo Levi, *Nudo piccolo* (Small Nude), 1935, Fondazione Carlo Levi, Rome (cat. no. 328)

rian Norberto Bobbio, who, while not Jewish, recorded that his intimate Jewish friends were all anti-Fascists because of their innate "critical spirit" and lack of "traditional prejudices and provincialism."[88] The Rosselli brothers later died martyrs, assassinated by the Fascists while in exile in France in June 1937. This event was recorded by Levi in his *Self-Portrait with Bloodied Shirt* (Florence, Galleria degli Uffizi) and in a drawing by Cagli (cat. no. 308; fig. 158).

The Fascists arrested Levi for his political activities in 1934 and again the following year.[89] (On the second occasion Levi was working on a painting when the police came to his door; they let him finish the work before they took him away.)[90] He was subsequently sentenced to political confinement in the province of Lucania, in southern Italy. There he became enchanted with the peasants of a remote and barren land and a way of life entirely removed from contemporary society (cat. no. 329; fig. 159). His experiences there—the superstitions of the peasants, their awe of his "magical" abilities as a doctor—formed the basis of his book *Cristo si è fermato a Eboli* (Christ Stopped at Eboli, 1945). The period of exile also proved fertile for his painting, as can be seen in the *Nudo piccolo* (Small Nude; cat. no. 328; fig. 160), in which figure and landscape are united in a swelling, organic whole.[91] A luscious and expansive brushwork endowed his depictions of the peasants and their land with a vitalism and a larger significance. Although Levi never dwelt on his Jewishness, it was this very ability to capture the "absolute" character of ordinary things, giving them a universal, "biblical" quality, that he saw as a fundamental and profoundly Jewish characteristic of his close friend Saba.[92]

ARTE NOSTRA E DEFORMAZIONE EBRAICA

"...l'internazionalismo d'Israele"

IL GRAN CONSIGLIO

Il giudeo Epstein ammira il suo "capolavoro": la "Genesi".

La separazione del popolo italiano dagli ebrei avrà le sue conseguenze nell'arte.

L'influenza d'Israele vi si è fatta sentire fin da quando il movimento europeista, incanalato per la prima volta ne «La Voce», distrusse ciò che ancora rimaneva presso di noi d'una coscienza nazionale in questo campo.

Prima vi era una nostra parziale dipendenza dalla Francia; poi neppure questa è bastata. Si è raggiunto così il maggiore disorientamento mai avuto.

E' stato il contrapposto della situazione di quattro secoli prima. Allora la preminenza durava perchè il nostro popolo, più dotato come razza, aveva saputo tenere questa attività rigorosamente distinta.

* * *

Ecco quanto poteva dire Michelangelo, nei dialoghi di Francesco d'Olanda:

«Le opere che si fanno in Italia sono quasi le sole che possiamo chiamare pitture. E' per questo che chiamiamo italiana la buona pittura; e se in un'altra terra si facesse l'uguale, le daremmo il nome di quella terra o provincia. Non v'ha nulla di più nobile e di più devoto della buona pittura perchè nulla evoca e sussiste in egual modo la devozione negli spiriti elevati come la difficoltà della perfezione, e l'unisce a Dio; perchè una buona pittura non è altra cosa se non una copia della perfezione di Dio, ed una rimembranza della pittura divina; una musica ed una melodia che solo l'intelletto può percepire non senza difficoltà. E questa pittura è così vera, che pochissimi giungono ad eseguirla e a raggiungerla».

«E dico di più (e chi ciò noterà lo terrà in gran conto) che di tutti i paesi che il sole e la terra illuminano, non si può dipingere bene che in Italia. Ed è cosa quasi impossibile far bene se non qui, ci fossero pure nelle altre contrade migliori ingegni che dei nostri, se ve ne possono esistere; e questo per le ragioni che vi dirò».

«Prendete un grande pittore di un'altra nazione, ditegli di dipingere quello che gli aggrada o delle cose di cui non si possa parlar male, come Santi e Profeti. Ciò che più gli piace e che sa far meglio, lo faccia; prendete poi un cattivo scolaro italiano e chiedetegli di tracciare uno schizzo, o di dipingere ciò che volete, e lo faccia. Troverete, se ve ne intenderete, che lo schizzo di quell'allievo ha più sostanza in quanto ad arte che il dipinto del maestro, e quel ch'ei avrà cercato di fare varrà più di quel che l'altro avrà fatto».

«Domandate poi ad un grande maestro che non sia italiano, che per ingannare me o Francesco d'Olanda cerchi di contraffare o d'imitare un'opera, che sembri italiana, e se non può essere delle migliori, sia mediocre o cattiva: ed io vi certifico che sull'istante si riconoscerà che quell'opera non fu fatta in Italia, nè da mano italiana».

«Così affermo che nessuna nazione nè gente potrà appropriarsi od imitare il modo di dipingere italiano, che sùbito non sia riconosciuto per straniero, qualunque sforzo e lavoro abbia fatto».

«E se per miracolo alcun d'essi riuscisse a dipingere bene, tutto ciò che si potrebbe dire, anche se non imitasse l'Italia, sarebbe soltanto che dipinge come un Italiano».

«Così che non si chiama italiana qualunque pittura fatta in Italia, ma qualunque pittura buona e artistica; e giacchè in Italia si fanno le buone opere di pittura più rispettosamente e maestrevolmente che in qualunque altro paese, noi chiamiamo italiana la buona pittura; la quale, pur se si facesse in Fiandra od in Ispagna (che più a noi s'accosta) a condizioni che sia buona, sarà pittura italiana; perchè questa nobilissima scienza non è di nessuna terra, ma venne dal cielo; e però fin dalle antiche età si mantenne nella nostra Italia più che in qualunque altro regno del mondo, e penso che vi si manterrà per sempre».

* * *

Una nobilissima scienza, una copia della perfezione di Dio: ecco il modo nostro di intendere la pittura. La quale è interamente oggettiva. Ma il suo oggetto non è una verità accidentale: ma una realtà sostanziale vista nella natura».

Perciò la pittura italiana, a cominciare da quella di Pompei, fino a quella di Piero e Masaccio, eccelle nel costruire e nello spaziare. Dopo l'antichità, Piero fu il primo ad ottenere, dal reciproco rapporto dei toni, il volume, la profondità, e la lontananza. Masaccio si servì pure del chiaroscuro: l'uno e l'altro raggiungendo il massimo dell'oggettività plastica.

La pittura straniera, al contrario, essendo superficialmente ed accidentalmente veristica, è rimasta lungi da questa oggettività. Ecco ciò che ne dice Michelangelo:

«Si dipingono in Fiandra, propriamente per ingannare la vista esteriore, delle cose gradevoli o delle cose di cui non si possa parlar male, come Santi e Profeti. Questa pittura si compone di drappi, di casupole, di verdure campestri, di ombre d'alberi, di fonti e ruscelli, ed essi chiamano ciò paesaggio con qualche figurina qua e là.

E tutto questo, che passa per buono per certi occhi è in realtà senza ragione; un'arte senza simmetria nè proporzione, senza discernimento, nè scelta, nè disegno, in una parola senza sostanza e senza nerbo».

* * *

In tutti i tempi, questo verismo è stato l'arte di alcune nazioni europee. Ultima, la Francia. Ove, per reagirvi, gli è succeduta una forma che deriva pure da una psiche a noi estranea: la pittura soggettiva.

E' chiara la incoerenza di questa espressione. Una pittura, se davvero soggettiva, non è pittura. Potrebbe diventare, al più, ornamento. Ma giammai rappresentazione. In questa, infatti, il soggetto deve sparire, interamente annullato dall'oggetto.

In realtà il post-impressionismo, per la sua pretesa di esprimere solo «il sentimento» indipendentemente da ogni dato esterno, è finito per divenire una pittura, dove il colore, perduta ogni funzione plastica, vale solo per i suoi accostamenti armonici. Nè più nè meno come in un tappeto: è il caso di Matisse e di tanti altri.

Un'altra forma di pittura soggettiva è l'espressionismo. In questo «il sentimento» si sfoga nella deformazione. Uno dei primi esempi sono stati i ritratti di Van Gogh: seguiti, a distanza, da un vasto movimento, germanico: Hofer, Bruckner, Kokoscka, la «Compagnia del Ponte» e molti altri.

La partecipazione degli Ebrei alla pittura, intensificatasi un trentennio or sono, ha esasperato, e modificato queste due correnti. Tanto il deformazionismo che la pittura di accostamenti hanno preso nelle loro mani un aspetto magico. A Kokoscka sono succeduti Chagall e Segall e al colorismo, piatto, sfatto, e quasi ornamentale di Matisse, si è affiancata la pittura astratta, anche più affine al temperamento degli ebrei: Picasso ha concentrate tutte queste correnti. Anche il cubismo di cui è stato il padre era una forma di pittura soggettiva: anzi per la sua astrazione geometrica e, quindi, per il suo totale distacco dalla natura, raggiungeva lo stadio più acuto cui quella pervenisse.

La guerra mondiale e la propaganda comunista hanno dato il massimo sviluppo alla pittura ebraica. Prima i cenacoli dadaisti, poi, in Germania, il «Gruppo di Novembre», legato al movimento spartachista, confessavano apertamente anche scopi antisociali. Dichiaravano di volere affrettare col loro sempre più accentuato infaticismo artistico, lo sfasciamento dell'ordine esistente.

* * *

In Italia, la pittura soggettiva, suddivisa in queste correnti, si è ripercossa nel dopoguerra. Estranea al genio del popolo, in qualunque forma essa si presentasse, ha profondamente nociuto. Nel tronco derivato da Matisse ha fatto strage a Torino e a Milano, dove il gusto degli accostamenti superficiali e piatti, soppianta la vera pittura. Nel suo tronco deformazionista, ha fatto strage, si può dire dappertutto, ed ha trovato il suo maggiore esponente in Carrà. Questi si è assimilato del tutto la mentalità soggettiva: diffondendola tra i giovani; e comunicando soprattutto ad essi l'illusione che la pittura, non essendo legata ad alcuna realtà esterna, possa essere affrontata senza studio.

Ne è stato conseguenza il diffondersi della mentalità polemica. Come fatto arbitrario ed interamente soggettivo, l'arte non si risolve più in opere, ma solo in tendenze. Nel loro giocare e nel loro succedersi (cioè, come si dice, nella loro «dialettica») consiste il lavoro degli artisti. Il successivo affermarsi di elementi interamente ebraici («Cometa», «Grup-

Un'interpretazione ebraica dell'eroismo: un gruppo di mutilati ritratto dal giudeo Otto Dix.

54

55

Fig. 161. *La Difesa della Razza,* I, no. 6 (20 October 1938), Library of The Jewish Theological Seminary of America, New York (cat. no. 331 c)

The Racial Laws and the Holocaust

Carlo Levi and Raphaël Mafai made a point of painting whatever and however they wished, but their artistic individuality was also tolerated by the regime, which never persecuted the avant-garde or promoted the concept of "degenerate art," as the Nazis did. As of July 1938, however, Jewish artists were excluded from exhibitions and censored on the grounds of their race.

The confluence of antimodernist and anti-Semitic sentiments had in fact begun slightly earlier, supported "unofficially" by Mussolini.[93] With the invasion of Ethiopia in 1936 a more insidious cultural policy promoted the idea of empire and the superiority of the Italian "race." The attacks against modern art under the rubric of an "international Bolshevik and Jewish conspiracy" was restricted to a small but vocal group led primarily by Giuseppe Pensabene and Telesio Interlandi in the journals *Il Tevere, Quadrivio,* and *La Difesa della Razza* (cat. no. 331c; fig. 161). Interlandi and Pensabene attempted to organize a "degenerate art" campaign modeled on the Nazi cultural policy and the famous Munich exhibition of 1937. Their efforts were short-lived and of limited success, due to the lack of anti-Semitism among the intelligensia (they provoked Marinetti to lead a counterattack in the press), the long-term understanding between the Fascist regime and the Italian avant-garde, and the hardly credible fanaticism of the articles.[94]

Ironically it was Cagli, the painter of "modern myths," who became the most visible victim of the anti-Semitic laws in the realm of the visual arts. It is paradigmatic of the ambiguity of Fascist policy concerning both culture and the Jews, that as late as 1937 Cagli was chosen to decorate the Italian pavilion at the Universal Exhibition in Paris with a grand cycle on Italian history

(cat. no. 306; fig. 24). The panels were ordered destroyed by Galeazzo Ciano, minister of foreign affairs, in the middle of the project ostensibly because of their unconvincing style. (Pensabene had accused them of being "defeatist.") Less veiled excuses were needed for the removal of Cagli's fresco *Orfeo* (Orpheus), painted for the Venice Biennale of 1938, after the enactment of the Racial Laws.[95]

Cagli also had a high profile in Roman art circles as one of the principals of the Galleria della Cometa, which was opened by the collector and dealer Countess Mimi Pecci-Blunt in April 1935. The gallery and its press became a lively center for the *tonalisti* and other young Roman artists and intellectuals, including the half-Jewish writer Alberto Moravia (cat. no. 325; fig. 176). In the space of three years, the Cometa exhibited works by Cagli, Levi, Melli, and Moravia's sister, the painter Adriana Pincherle (see cat. no. 330). The prominence of Jewish artists led Pensabene to attack the gallery in a series of anti-Semitic reviews in *Quadrivio* and *Il Tevere,* which contributed to its closing in the summer of 1938.[96]

Another notable episode occurred in June 1937 at the reopening of the Galleria di Roma, a state-sponsored exhibition space, of which the young Jewish critic Dario Sabatello (b. 1911) was the newly appointed director. Sabatello was surprised at the time that Alessandro Pavolini, president of the Confederation of Professionals and Artists, had appointed him, a Jew, to such a visible position, given the growing anti-Semitic tendencies of the regime. From 1932 to 1934 Sabatello had his own gallery on the Via Babiuno, where he mounted exhibitions of the younger artists of the Scuola romana. He had also served as the art critic of *Il Tevere* before it became an anti-Semitic journal under Interlandi.[97] The first exhibition at the Galleria di Roma included works by modern Italian masters: Modigliani, Casorati, Sironi, and others. As Sabatello was giving the inaugural speech, Pensabene interrupted the proceedings with anti-Semitic remarks directed at Modigliani's *Nudo rosso* (The Red Nude, 1917–1918, Milan, Mattioli Collection). In the ensuing scuffle Sabatello punched Pensabene; he was taken to court and removed from his position as gallery director, though without further reprisals.

Above and beyond the ideological repercussions of the Racial Laws, Jewish artists suddenly found their personal relationships and professional routines disrupted and, with the German occupation (beginning in September 1943), found themselves hiding for their lives. Liegi, Corcos, and Nunes Vais died in the mid-1930s, just before the onset of what was simply unimaginable to their generation of Italian Jews. Angiolo Orvieto lived to see his Florentine villa occupied by the Gestapo. In the wake of persecutions, Cagli left in 1938 for Paris and New York. He enlisted in the United States army in 1941 and was among the forces that liberated the camp at Buchenwald in 1945, an event that he recorded in a series of drawings.[98]

Melli hid in a convent in Rome; a self-portrait of 1944 (cat. no. 303; fig. 162) is uncharacteristic for its psychological content, with Melli glancing out from under his hat in a guarded fashion, cloaked by layers of outer garments. The Mafai left their shelter in Genoa, returning to precarious conditions in Rome in September 1943. Sometime during the racial persecutions Raphaël executed the small terra-cotta *Mosè* (Moses with Ritual Shawl; cat. no. 315) as a gesture of defiance and faith.[99] (A postwar work, *La fuga* [The Flight, 1958; cat. no. 318; fig. 163], with the fragments

Fig. 162. Roberto Melli, *Autoritratto con guanto bianco* (Self-Portrait with White Glove), 1944, Private Collection (cat. no. 303)

Fig. 163. (opposite) Antonietta Raphaël Mafai, *La fuga* (The Flight), 1958, Private Collection, Rome (cat. no. 318)

Fig. 164. (above) Aldo Carpi, *Il dottor Toni Goscinski mentre suona il violino,* 1945, Collection Carpi Family, Milan (cat. no. 335)

Fig. 165. Aldo Carpi, *Cadaveri davanti al crematorio* (Cadavers in Front of the Crematorium), 1945, Collection Carpi Family, Milan (cat. no. 337)

of three children attached to the fleeing mother, is also an allegorical recollection of these years.) Pincherle and Levi Montalcini were forced to adopt a clandestine existence, while Levi hid in occupied Florence (with Saba), participating in the Resistance.[100]

A more tragic journey awaited the artist Aldo Carpi, chair of painting at the Brera Academy, who was betrayed by a jealous professional colleague and arrested by the Fascists outside Milan. Though he was ostensibly rounded up as a Jew (Carpi is a common Jewish surname), his father had converted a generation before, and his mother's family was Catholic.[101] He was sent to Mauthausen for his anti-Fascist activities and then to Gusen. Originally sentenced to hard labor, the injured Carpi was fortunate to have fallen into the care of a Polish deportee, Dr. Goscinski (cat. no. 335; fig. 164). It was there, against all odds, that Carpi kept a diary and sketches on paper—"a friable paper, the worst imaginable"—that he found in the infirmary. Carpi's profession proved to be his salvation: he was released from further hard labor and began to paint pictures for the SS (although he would certainly have been killed had his writings and private drawings been found). He began a diary on Christmas of 1944 in the form of letters to his wife, Maria, and their six children.[102] The drawings consist of sketches rendered on the same pages with the written diary, others done on separate sheets immediately before and after the liberation of the camp by the Americans, and another series drawn later from memory (cat. no. 336; fig. 165). The diary letters describe the indescribable in a tone of moderation and empathy like that of his fellow Italian Primo Levi, who later recorded his ten months in Auschwitz in *Se questo è un uomo* (Survival in Auschwitz).[103] And like Levi, who quoted Dante to keep his sanity in the midst of the hell around him, Carpi drew images of Petrarch, Don Quixote, even Beethoven, to remind himself of the existence of a humanity.

Aldo Carpi and Primo Levi survived the camps, but others were not as fortunate. Gino Parin was deported and died in Bergen-Belsen on his way to Dachau. Arturo Nathan sustained injuries in hard labor at Belsen; with the approach of the allies he was sent to Biberach and was found dying when the camp was liberated. A foreign Jew, the German artist Rudolf Levy (1875–1944) was arrested by the Gestapo in Florence in 1943 and died the following year before reaching Auschwitz.[104]

And After

Eighty-five percent of Italy's Jews survived the Holocaust, more than in any other European nation save Denmark.[105] But the lives of Italian Jews were disrupted, in many cases irreparably. Italy lost part of its Jewish population to immigration to America and Palestine, and those who remained began a slow and painful reconstruction.[106]

The artists of the previous and highly assimilated generation resumed their careers: Melli began teaching painting at the Accademia di Belle Arti in Rome and in 1948 established the Istituto di Solidarietà Artistica for the improvement of the living and working conditions of artists. Raphaël exhibited again after years of interruption, concentrating for the most part on sculpture and continuing to explore Jewish and feminist themes (cat. no. 316; fig. 166). Toward the end of his life Carlo Levi painted a cycle of pantheistic landscapes of enormous tree trunks, gnarled, splayed in sexual metaphor, and bursting with life. Cagli turned to abstraction, inspired by the themes of growth and metamorphosis. Levi Montalcini is active in Rome, and since the 1970s has concentrated on the formal properties of linguistics and mathematics in her abstract painting, sculptures, and reliefs. Pincherle lives and paints in Florence.

Though the fervent nationalism that marked the period from the Risorgimento to the Resistance was a thing of the past, the dual identity of Jewish Italians persisted. To discern the nuances of a specifically Jewish identity in the postwar years, one must turn to the precise literary form of the narrative recollection, as Stuart Hughes has done in his study *Prisoners of Hope: The Silver Age of Italian Jews, 1924–1974.*[107] It is in the stories of Natalia Ginzburg, Giorgio Bassani, and Primo Levi, the memoirs of Dan Vittorio Segre, Rita Levi Montalcini, or the less famous who have recorded their familial experiences before the war that Italian Jewry today finds its fullest expression. Like elegies, these recollections mourn the loss of a more innocent age while also celebrating the lives of the survivors.

Fig. 166. Antonietta Raphaël Mafai, *La sognatrice* (The Dreamer), 1946, Private Collection, Rome (cat. no. 316)

Acknowledgments

The modern section of the exhibition and catalogue research would not have been possible without the generous assistance of many colleagues and friends. I would like to thank those people who so generously provided of their time and hospitality for personal interviews: Miriam, Giulia, and Simona Mafai, Guido and Gigliola Lopez, Mr. and Mrs. Ermes Drago, Dr. and Mrs. Piero Foà, Fiammetta Sarfatti, Pierangela Sarfatti, Oriana Calabi, Paola Sacerdoti, and Guido Sacerdoti, Paola Levi Montalcini, Daisy Margadonna Nathan, Annalena Limantani, Dario Sabatello, and Renata Sabatello, Adriana Pincherle, Cioni Carpi, Giorgio and Liliane Sacerdoti.

I am also grateful to Geraldo Baligioni, Maria Rosselli, Sava Levi D'Ancona, Miriam Coen, Lara Vinca Masini, Diane di Cabaldo, Carlo Levi Foundation, Pietro Castelpietra, Amedeo Porro, Philip Cannistraro, Gigliola De Donato, Anne Rossi-Doria, Giuseppe Gentile, Adachiara Zevi, Ninetta Ferrazzi, Domenico Fago, Mario Toscano, Fabio Benzi, Maria Teresa Contini, Viviane Vareilles, Noemi Bonazzi, Cora Rosavear, Emily Bilski, Elisabeth Castelfranco-Tedesco, and most particularly, my research assistant, Francesca Morelli.

Notes

1. P. Levi, *If Not Now, When?* trans. W. Weaver (New York, 1985), pp. 67, 324–325.
2. Among the artists not included in the exhibition are Adolfo Belimbau (Cairo 1845–1938 Florence), Moses Levy (Tunis 1885–1968 Viareggio), Adolfo Levier (Trieste 1873–1953), Arrigo Minerbi (Ferrara 1881–1960 Padua), Italo Nunes-Vais (Tunis 1860–1932 Florence), Gabriella Oreffice (Padua 1893–1984 Venice), Alberto Pisa (Ferrara 1864–1930 Florence), Clemente Pugliese-Levi (Vercelli 1855–1936), Giorgio Settala (Trieste 1895–1960 Florence), and Dario Viterbo (Florence 1890–1961 New York). Further names are found in G. Bedarida, *Ebrei d'Italia* (Livorno, 1950), pp. 137–142. A more extensive list of Italian-Jewish artists is being compiled by Mr. Samuel Sondak of Livorno, and I thank him for sharing his research with me.
3. P. D'Ancona, "Quattro maestri ebrei della pittura moderna italiana," in *Scritti in memoria di Sally Mayer (1875–1953)* (Milan, 1956).
4. D. V. Segre, *Memoirs of a Fortunate Jew: An Italian Story* (Bethesda, Md., 1987), p. 23.
5. The following discussion on the Jewish artists of the Macchiaioli and their relationship to the Risorgimento is indebted to A. Boime and his excellent study "The Macchiaioli and the Risorgimento," in Frederick S. Wight Art Gallery, University of California, *The Macchiaioli: Painters of Italian Life 1850–1900,* exh. cat., ed. E. Tonelli and K. Hart (Los Angeles, 1986), pp. 33–71.
6. The aesthetics of the macchia are discussed in detail by N. Broude, *The Macchiaioli: Italian Painters of the Nineteenth Century* (New Haven and London, 1987), esp. pp. 3–12, who also examines their innovations in the context of traditional academic sketching practices.
7. See Boime, "The Macchiaioli," pp. 41–43, and in the same catalogue, D. M. Smith, "Tuscany and the Italian Risorgimento," pp. 28–32. D'Ancona and De Tivoli both participated in the skirmishes with the Austrians in the villages of Curtatone and Montanara. De Tivoli also fought in 1848 with Garibaldi in the defense of the Roman republic and in the following years. On the participation of Jews in the military campaigns of the Risorgimento, see S. Foa, *Gli ebrei nel Risorgimento italiano* (Rome, 1978). Another Jewish volunteer and patron of the Macchiaioli, Gustavo Uzielli, received a medal for his bravery at the battle of Porta Capua and commissioned Giovanni Fattori to paint the event. This information will be published in a forthcoming article by Ellen Kaplan of the University of California, Los Angeles. I thank her for the information.
8. T. Signorini, *Caricaturisti e caricaturati al Caffè Michelangiolo* (Florence, 1952), p. 88.
9. Broude, *The Macchiaioli,* pp. 256–259. D'Ancona's role as cultural mentor to Signorini and his generosity toward the younger artist are discussed by U. Ojetti in *Ritratti d'artisti italiani* (Milan, 1911), p. 51–52.
10. A. Cecioni, *Opere e scritti* (Milan, 1932), pp. 151–155.
11. F. Aghib Levi D'Ancona, *La giovinezza dei fratelli D'Ancona* (Rome, 1982), p. 49. The parents of the D'Ancona brothers, Giuseppe and Ester Della Ripa, left their native Pesaro when the regime of Pope Leo XII (1813–1929) grew more repressive, eventually settling in Florence in 1848, where Ester's brother, Laudadio Della Ripa, had successfully established his banking business a decade earlier.
12. Sansone (1814–1894) followed his uncle into finance, was a key member of Ricasoli's provisional government in 1859, and later one of the three Jews in the first Italian parliament. Giacomo, the fifth-born (1828–1892), was physician to the court of Egypt and moved to Paris in the 1860s to become Rossini's personal physician. A leading agriculturist and geologist, Cesare, the third-youngest (1832–1908), cofounded the Italian Botanical Society. The daughters, Alessandrina and Adele, both married Jews, as did their brothers. Adele and her husband, Emanuele Padoa, helped a young, impoverished Pietro Mascagni through school. His opera *L'amico Fritz,* whose protagonist is a young Alsatian Jew, is dedicated to them. The most famous of the siblings was the youngest, Alessandro (1835–1914). A literary scholar and journalist, he served as a mediator between Cavour and Tuscan liberals and furthered the cause of the Risorgimento as editor of the Florentine newspaper *La Nazione.* The other D'Ancona siblings

were Prospero (1818–1865) and Salvatore (1823–1907).

13. Aghib Levi D'Ancona, *La giovinezza,* p. 120. On anti-Semitism in Italy, see the essay by Mario Toscano in this catalogue.
14. Aghib Levi D'Ancona, *La giovenezza,* p. 83.
15. E. Cecchi, "Vito D'Ancona." *Bollettino d'arte* 6 (1927): 291–304.
16. A. Momigliano, "The Jews of Italy," *New York Review of Books,* 24 October 1985, p. 23.
17. Boime, *The Macchiaioli,* p. 58. On Uzielli, see also note 7. Della Ripa's desire to be a gentleman farmer and his relationship with Ricasoli and the Georgofili are recorded by Aghib Levi D'Ancona, *La giovinezza,* pp. 37–38, who adds that he was also inspired early on by Benozzo Gozzoli's fresco of the grape harvest in the Camposanto of Pisa.
18. M. Della Seta, *Vecchie istantanee al Portico d'Ottavia: Fotografie del conte Giuseppe Primoli* (Rome, 1978). The one exception was Signorini's earlier image, *Il Ghetto di Venezia* (The Venice Ghetto) which created a stir at the First National Exhibition of 1861. It depicted the quarter's miserable living conditions and also served as a metaphor for the city's subjugation to Austria. See Boime, "The Macchiaioli," pp. 59–60.
19. A. Canepa, "Emancipation and Jewish Response in Mid-Nineteenth-Century Italy," *European History Quarterly* 16 (1986): 403–439.
20. G. De Nittis, *Taccuini 1870–1884* (Bari, 1964), pp. 26–27. I am grateful to Paul Nicholls for bringing this work to my attention. See also Buzzichini and Piazzi, eds. *Taccuino di Musetta* (Milan, 1945), pp. 71–72; V. Pica, *Giuseppe de Nittis* (Milan, 1914), pp. 52–53.
21. On Corcos, see U. Ojetti (signed Il Conte Ottavio), "Accanto alla Vita," in *L'Illustrazione Italiana* 21 (April 1909), pp. 377, 380; U. Ojetti (signed Tantalo), "Cose viste," *Corriere della sera,* 18 November 1933.
22. Though born the son of a rabbi in Trieste, he later converted; his Jewish heritage is discussed in G. Lopez, "Infanzia e giovinezza di un grande editore: Emilio Treves," *La Rassegna mensile di Israel* 36 (July–September 1970): 213–231. The involvement of Jews in publishing at the turn of the century is noted in A. Boralevi, "Angiolo Orvieto, 'Il Marzocco,' la società colta ebraica" in *Il Marzocco: Atti del seminario di studi,* ed. C. Del Vivo (Florence, 1985), p. 224.
23. On Belimbau, see G. Daddi, *Eugenio Cecconi* (Lecco, 1973), pp. 33–42. Corcos's portrait of Belimbau (1897) belongs to the estate of the Belimbau family, Genoa; Corcos's portrait of Liegi is reproduced in R. Monti and G. Matteucci, eds., *Prima dell'avanguardia da Fattori a Modigliani,* exh. cat. (Florence, 1985), p. 40. The Museo Civico G. Fattori, Livorno, has a small portrait of Liegi by Alberto Pisa (1894–1895).
24. A. Toaff, "Il museo della comunità israelitica," *Liburni Civitas* 4 (1931): 87.
25. Momigliano, "The Jews of Italy," p. 22; S. Hughes, *Prisoners of Hope: The Silver Age of the Italian Jews, 1924–1974* (Cambridge, 1983), pp. 116–118.
26. See the microhistory of the Jews of Piedmont, especially, L. Allegra, "La comunità ebraica di Torino attraverso gli archivi di famiglia," in *Ebrei a Torino: ricerche per il centenario della sinagoga, 1884–1984,* exh. cat. (Turin, 1984), pp. 31–36.
27. The friendship among Nunes Vais, Corcos, and Liegi is noted in G. Matteucci, "Ulvi Liegi e Oscar Ghiglia: due personalità fra tradizione Macchiaiola e tendenze moderne," in R. Monti and G. Matteucci, eds., *Prima dell'avanguardia* (Florence, 1985), p. 44.
28. Issel's work is discussed in the larger context of Italian art nouveau in G. P. Weisberg, *Stile Floreale: The Cult of Nature in Italian Design,* exh. cat. (Miami, 1988), p. 73 and plate 61.
29. Viterbo studied painting at the Accademia di Belle Arti in Florence before turning to sculpture in the years preceding World War I. During the racial persecutions he and his wife moved to New York. Ada Vera Viterbo published her memoirs, *La mia vita con Dario* (Florence, 1981); see also the monograph by Lara-Vinca Masini, *Dario Viterbo* (Florence, 1973).
30. Such were the recollections of Silvia Levi Vidale, who was a descendant of the Treves, Finzi, Orvieto, and Ambron families. (Her grandfather Marco Treves was the main architect of the Florence synagogue; Angiolo and Adolfo Orvieto were second cousins.) Vidale principally describes the family gatherings at the villa La Querciola just outside of Florence ("far enough to be in the country but not too far to violate the law prohibiting travel on the Sabbath"), which was acquired by the Finzi in 1832. La Querciola originally had a chapel on the ground floor, which the Finzi converted to a "scuola"; there was also a prayer room upstairs. Yet the observance of rites had declined, creating an irremediable gap between the elders and her generation: "in that religious atmosphere we learned hardly anything about religion except the sense of something solemn and mysterious that distinguished us from others who went to mass on Sunday." Excerpts from the memoirs are published in G. Lopez, "Quattro grandi famiglie ebree a Firenze (Treves, Finzi, Orvieto, Ambron) nei ricordi inediti di Silvia Levi Vidale," *La Rassegna Mensile di Israel* 51 (January–April 1985): 118–134. The Vieusseux library was founded in 1821 in Florence by Gianpietro Vieusseux and was the intellectual center of Florence at midcentury.
31. A. Orvieto, *Il vento di Sion* (Florence, 1928), reprinted in Boralevi, "Angiolo Orvieto," p. 230. This translation is by Alex Bayer. Orvieto is best known as the founder of the journal *Il Marzocco* (1896–1932), which was the first to publish D'Annunzio, Giovanni Pascoli,

and Luigi Pirandello and was the leading Florentine journal of late nineteenth-century aesthetics. Articles on Jewish subjects were rare, but several of its contributors were Jewish. Boralevi discusses the rise of Orvieto's Jewish identity over the decades from the late nineteenth century through the rise of Zionism.

32. The palazzo of Ca' Pesaro was donated by Felicità Bevilacqua La Masa to the city of Venice in 1898 with the stipulation that the foundation encourage younger artists. The annual exhibitions were begun in 1908 under the directorship of Nino Barbantini and continued uninterrupted until the war. See *Venezia: Gli anni di Ca' Pesaro, 1908–1920* (Milan, 1987) and on Cavaglieri, pp. 131–135.
33. See, for example, the essays by D. Milhau and V. Vareilles in Musée des Augustins, *Hommage à Mario Cavaglieri,* exh. cat. (Toulouse, 1974), pp. 23–80. Cavaglieri painted only one specifically Jewish subject, which is an oil sketch dating from 1905 of an elderly patriarch with a prayer shawl; I am grateful to Dr. Vareilles, who is preparing a catalogue raisonné of the artist's works, for this information.
34. G. Bassani, "Un inedito di Mario Cavaglieri," *Paragone,* no. 39 (March 1953): 51–53.
35. P. D'Ancona, *Modigliani, Chagall, Soutine, Pascin: aspetti dell'espressionismo* (Milan, 1952).
36. L. Vitali, "Modigliani," *Preferenze* (Milan, 1950), pp. 95–102. Vitale (b. 1896) is one of the most influential twentieth-century Italian critics and the foremost scholar of Giorgio Morandi and author of the Morandi catalogue raisonné.
37. Little is known about Sforni (Florence 1888–1939 Bologna). He inherited a substantial fortune upon the death of his father in 1906 and subsequently traveled frequently to Paris, where he purchased works by van Gogh, Cézanne, Utrillo, and Degas. He also owned many works by Fattori and was a patron of Ghiglia and Llewelyn Lloyd (1879–1949). I am very grateful to Geraldo Baligioni, husband of the niece of Sforni, for this information. The correspondence between Ghiglia and Sforni is collected in P. Stefani, *Oscar Ghiglia e il suo tempo* (Florence, 1985).
38. K. Silver, "Jewish Artists in Paris, 1905–1945," in Jewish Museum, *The Circle of Montparnasse,* exh. cat., ed. K. Silver and R. Golan (New York, 1985), pp. 18–20. Levi lived in Montmartre; his son, the restorer Gaston Levi, was a friend of Modigliani and commissioned the portrait. I thank Levi's daughter, Mrs. Richard Lasser, for this information.
39. R. S. Torroella, "Modigliani y nosaltres," in *Modigliani 1884–1920,* exh. cat. (Barcelona, 1983), pp. 13–21.
40. G. Bedarida, *Ebrei di Livorno: Tradizioni e gergo* (Florence, 1956), pp. xi–xxi. See also A. Milano, *Storia degli ebrei in Italia* (Turin, 1963), pp. 322–328. Momigliano has stated that Livorno had a particular Jewish style of its own, "which is preserved in the books of Elia Benamozegh and of which perhaps the paintings of Modigliani show traces" ("The Jews of Italy," p. 22).
41. In L. Venturi, "The Collection of Modern Art of Signor Gualino and the Modigliani Room at the Venice Biennial Exhibition," *Formes* (July 1930): 9–10; see also note 84 below.
42. C. E. Oppo, "Una mostra postuma di Modigliani (1921)," in *Forme e colori nel mondo* (Rome, 1931), pp. 287–295.
43. The cross section of criticism is found in L. Venturi, "Divagazioni sulle mostre di Venezia e di Monza, con la risposta ad Ojetti," *L'arte* (July 1930): 396–405.
44. See for example, the incident described by Dario Sabatello, see note 97 below.
45. The issue of Svevo's Jewishness is addressed in Hughes, *Prisoners of Hope,* pp. 30–46.
46. On the artists of Trieste from the mid-nineteenth century through the first half of the twentieth, see G. Montenero, "Nella città del realismo borghese il fiore della desolazione fantastica," in *Quassù Trieste,* ed. L. Mazzi (Bologna, 1968); Stazione Marittima, *Arte nel Friuli-Venezia Giulia 1900–1950,* exh. cat. (Trieste, 1981). I thank Dr. Montenero and Aldo Castelpietra of the Civico Museo Revoltella for their assistance with my research on the artists of Trieste.
47. C. Wostry, *Storia del Circolo Artistico di Trieste* (Udine, 1934), esp. pp. 34–55. In his chronicle Wostry also mentions Arturo Rietti and Gino Parin.
48. Veruda responded in kind, painting several portraits of the author and his family. Their relationship was the subject of an exhibition and catalogue: Civico Museo Revoltella-Galleria d'Arte Moderna, *Umberto Veruda: pittore di "Senilità,"* (Trieste, 1962). See also Castello di San Giusto, *Artisti triestini dei tempi di Italo Svevo,* exh. cat., eds. S. Molesi and C. Mosca-Riatel (Trieste, 1979).
49. Montenero, "Nella città del realismo," p. 151.
50. G. Voghera, *Gli anni della psicanalisi* (Pordenone, 1980).
51. See the personal remembrances collected in Palazzo Revoltella, *Vittorio Bolaffio, 1883–1931,* exh. cat. (Trieste, 1975).
52. See ibid., p. 123. Translation by Allen Mandelbaum.
53. *Artisti triestini,* pp. 70–71. "There will be a tremendous explosion, but no one will hear it and the earth will return to its nebulous state and go wandering through the sky, free at last from parasites and disease" (I. Svevo, *The Confessions of Zeno,* trans. B. de Zoete [New York, 1958], p. 398).
54. J. Thrall Soby characterized Nathan as a later follower of the metaphysical school in *The Early de Chirico* (New York, 1941), p. 62. De Chirico recalled his meetings with Nathan in "Arturo Nathan, pittore e poeta," *Domenica,* 3 June 1945. See also Palazzo Revoltella, *Arturo Nathan, 1891–1944,* exh. cat. (Trieste, 1976).

55. F. de Pisis, *La città dalle cento meraviglie* (Ferrara, 1922), esp. "Indigeni," pp. 479–480, and "Asilo infantile israelitico," pp. 484–488; A. Savinio, *Hermaphrodito* (Turin, 1974), originally published in *La voce* (1918), esp. "'Frara', città del Worbas," pp. 48–55, and "L'ora ebrea," pp. 56–57; C. Carrà, "Arcobaleno di latta smaltata," *Avanscoperta,* 15 May 1917, reprinted in M. Fagiolo dell'Arco, "Carlo Carrà, 1915–1919: The Wonder of the Primeval," in *Carlo Carrà: The Primitive Period, 1915–1919,* exh. cat., ed. M. Fagiolo dell'Arco (Milan, 1987), p. 21.
56. I thank the de Chirico scholar Maurizio Fagiolo dell'Arco for originally bringing the Jewish origin of the biscuits to my attention. De Chirico may have known the story of the famous Italian Kabbalist Mose Luzzato of Padua (1707–1746), who caused a controversy when he claimed to have enjoyed the special revelations of the maggid, or "Jewish angel." On de Chirico and the theme of revelation, see P. Baldacci, "De Chirico and Savinio: The Theory and Iconography of Metaphysical Painting," in *Italian Art in the Twentieth Century,* ed. E. Braun (London and Munich, 1989), pp. 61–70.
57. Mussolini's response to the "Jewish question" was motivated by political opportunism rather than any belief in a biological theory of racial supremacy. The issue is a complex one and has been considered in depth in M. Michaelis, *Mussolini and the Jews: German-Italian Relations and the Jewish Question in Italy, 1922–1945* (Oxford, 1978); R. De Felice, *Storia degli ebrei italiani sotto il fascismo,* 2 vols. (Turin, 1977). For a critique of Michaelis, see M. Toscano "Gli ebrei in Italia dall'emancipazione alla persecuzione," *Storia contemporanea* 17 (October 1986): pp. 905–954.
58. Philip Cannistraro and Brian Sullivan are the authors of the forthcoming biography of Sarfatti, the first in either English or Italian. The following material, with the exception of the discussion of the Novecento, is based entirely on their research. Sarfatti's daughter Fiammetta Gaetani and daughter-in-law Pierangela Sarfatti have also shared their thoughts, personal remembrances, and hospitality, for which I am very grateful.
59. Dr. Piero Foà of Detroit was particularly kind in sharing information on his family, his Jewish heritage, and his personal experience as a young man in Fascist Italy. Eloisa's husband, Dr. Carlo Foà was head of the Department of Physiology at the University of Milan.
60. Sarfatti was also an active member of the Società Umanitaria di Milano, an organization founded by Prospero Mosé Loria for the education and elevation of the lower classes, with attention to the problems of workers' housing and living conditions. The socialist and anarchic syndicalist roots of early Fascism are detailed in E. Gentile, *Le origini dell'ideologia fascista, 1918–1925* (Bari, 1975).
61. Sarfatti sent a letter of introduction for Boccioni to Fradeletto in December 1909 (M. Mimita Lamberti, "La stagione di Ca' Pesaro e le Biennali," in *Venezia: Gli anni di Ca' Pesaro,* pp. 49–50.
62. On the history of the Novecento, see R. Bossaglia, *Il "Novecento italiano"* (Milan, 1979). The original group exhibited at the Galleria Pesaro, which was owned by Lino Pesaro, one of the most influential dealers in Milan. Bossaglia (p. 8) notes that when they were first discussing names for the group, one of the artists suggested "Il Candelabro," since the group consisted of seven painters; the idea was dropped since the religious symbol had no particular significance for them, even though both Pesaro and Sarfatti were Jewish.
63. Sarfatti contributed to numerous art journals, including *Poligono, Le arti plastiche, Formes,* and *Nuova antologia*; she was also a novelist (*Il palazzone* [1929] is partially autobiographical) and wrote books on her travels to Tunisia and the United States. Her books on art included *Segni colori e luci* (1925) and *Storia della pittura moderna* (1930). She also organized exhibitions of the Novecento throughout Europe.
64. A selection of Sarfatti's criticism is reprinted in Bossaglia, *Il "Novecento italiano."* The comment on Cézanne is found in "L'esposizione futurista a Milano," *Il Popolo d'Italia,* 4 April 1919.
65. Bossaglia, *Il "Novecento italiano,"* pp. 42–45. The attack against the Novecento in the press was led by Roberto Farinacci in his paper *La Regime fascista,* published in Cremona. Farinacci admired the cultural policy of the Third Reich and created the annual exhibition the Premio Cremona in 1938 to encourage a style of academic realism and decidedly propagandistic themes. On the reference to Shylock, see "Fronte, corbezzoli!, unico" *Il Regime fascista.* 20 June 1933, reprinted in Bossaglia, pp. 153–155.
66. A. Mahler Werfel, *Mein Lieben* (Frankfurt, 1960), pp. 191–192, as recounted in her diary of April 1928.
67. In an interview with the author, Fiammetta Sarfatti recounted that her mother said that the pain of the anti-Semitic laws was like that of her son "Roberto dying all over again."
68. M. Sarfatti, *Acqua passata* (Rocca San Casciano, 1955), pp. 41–42.
69. On *Valori Plastici,* see J. Lukach, "De Chirico and Italian Art Theory," in Museum of Modern Art, *De Chirico,* exh. cat., ed. W. Rubin (New York, 1982), pp. 35–54.
70. R. Melli, "Prima rinnegazione della scultura," *Valori Plastici,* 15 November 1918, pp. 13–16.
71. W. George, *Exposition des peintres romains: Capogrossi, Cavalli, Cagli, Scalvi* (Paris, 1933). His essay on the "italiens de Paris" for an exhibition at the Galleria di Milan in 1930 is reprinted in part in M. Fagiolo dell'Arco, *Scuola romana: pittura e scultura a Roma dal*

1919 al 1943 (Rome, 1986), p. 60. On the context of George and anti-Semitic art criticism in France, see R. Golan, "The 'Ecole Francaise' vs. the 'Ecole de Paris': The Debate about the Status of Jewish Artists in Paris between the Wars," in *The Circle of Montparnasse,* pp. 81–87, esp. 86.

72. "Primordialismo plastico," 31 (October 1933), reprinted in F. Benzi, ed., *Emanuele Cavalli* (Rome, 1984), p. 140.
73. F. Callari, "Roberto Melli: pittore," *Corriere padano,* 12 May 1937. The location of the painting is unknown.
74. The works are reproduced in *Il Milione,* no. 9 (February–March 1933).
75. Compare, for example, Cagli's "Muri ai pittori," *Quadrante* (May 1933): 19–20, with M. Sironi, "Pittura murale," *Il Popolo d'Italia,* 1 January 1932, reprinted in E. Camesasca, *Mario Sironi: Scritti editi e inediti* (Milan, 1980), pp. 113–115. Camesasca's book also contains a brief synopsis of the controversy surrounding the decoration of the V Milan Triennale, 1933, and the subsequent destruction of the public artworks, including Cagli's *Preparativi per la guerra* (pp. 443–447).
76. C. L. Ragghianti in his essay on the mural in Palazzo Strozzi, *Cagli: La Battaglia di San Martino per Firenze,* exh. cat. (Florence, 1979), pp. 9–15, discusses Cagli's humanism, uncelebratory style of mural painting, and his particular interpretation of the Risorgimento subject as a subtle protest against Fascist edicts.
77. On the historiography and the postwar ideological connotations of the term *Scuola romana,* see E. Braun, "The Scuola Romana: Fact or Fiction?" *Art in America* 76 (March 1988): 128–136.
78. Excerpt from Raphaël's diary, in F. D'Amico, *Antonietta Raphaël Sculture,* exh. cat. (Rome–Milan, 1985), p. 86.
79. R. Longhi, "La mostra romana degli artisti sindicati: Clima e opere degli irrealisti," *L'Italia Letteraria,* 14 April 1929.
80. It has not been determined exactly when Raphaël came into contact with the Jewish painters of Paris, where she lived for the winter of 1919 and visited again in 1925. During her third Paris sojourn, between 1930 and 1933, she met Chagall, who advised her to wait until her painting matured further before exhibiting (D'Amico, *Raphaël,* p. 89).
81. In letters from London to Mafai dated 28 August 1931 and 1 September 1931, Raphaël wrote: "I've quickly begun a little sketch; an impression of Yom Kippur in the synagogue in the evening; perhaps it's risky on my part having to give the impression of a multitude of Israelites praying. (Reprinted in M. Fagiolo dell'Arco and E. Coen, eds., *Raphaël scultura lingua viva* [Rome, 1978].)
82. Interview with Miriam Mafai by Daniela Fonti in *Il Giornale dell'Arte* 54 (March 1988): 17. I thank the Mafai family for their generosity in assisting with this exhibition, particularly Miriam Mafai, with whom I had many valuable conversations.
83. In Genoa the Mafais were aided by the collectors Alberto della Ragione and Emilio Jesi, a Jew. Jesi (b. 1902) was one of the first and most important collectors of modern art in Italy, see M. Fagiolo dell'Arco and V. Rivosecchi, eds., *Scuola romana: Artisti tra le due guerra,* exh. cat. (Milan, 1988), p. 296. During her stay in Genoa, Raphaël executed a portrait bust of Jesi (1940; in gesso, Russoli collection, Milan, and in onyx, Museo d'Arte Contemporanea, A. Della Ragione collection, Florence).
84. Among other activities, Venturi advised the Turin industrialist Riccardo Gualino on his art collection (they met in 1918) and persuaded him to buy paintings by Modigliani. Gualino was the first Italian collector to acquire work by the Livorno artist, and the paintings he owned formed the basis of the Modigliani retrospective in Venice in 1930, organized by Venturi. See M. Bernardi, *Riccardo Gualino e la cultura torinese* (Turin, 1970), esp. pp. 21–22 and n. 43. In 1931 Venturi refused to sign the Fascist oath required of university professors. He left Italy in 1939 for Paris and then New York, continuing his anti-Fascist activities abroad.
85. On Turin between the wars and the Levi Montalcini family, see R. Levi Montalcini, *Elogio dell'imperfezione* (Milan, 1987). Another Jewish painter, Giorgina Lattes, presently living and working in Rome, was also a student of Casorati. See Granario della Fattoria "le Terrazze," *Giorgina Lattes: Un percorso pittorico dal 1930 al 1980,* exh. cat. (Numana, 1987), which reproduced her 1933 portrait of Leone Ginzburg.
86. L. Venturi, in Bloomsbury Gallery, *Exhibition of New Italian Painting by Carlo Levi, Francesco Menzio, Enrico Paulucci,* exh. cat. (London, 1930). On the Sei di Torino, see I Sei Pittori di Torino (Levi, Menzio, Chessa, Paulucci, Galante, Boswell), "Il quadro storico," *Le arti plastiche,* 15 December 1929, and A. Bovero, ed., *Archivi dei sei pittori di Torino* (Rome, 1965).
87. N. Ginzburg, *Tutti i nostri ieri* (1952) and *Lessico famigliare* (1963). On Ginzburg's writing and its relation to a Jewish sensibility, see Hughes, *Prisoners of Hope,* pp. 96–113 and p. 149.
88. On Rosselli and the Livorno Convention, see D. Felice, *Storia degli ebrei,* pp. 107–110. N. Bobbio, "Ebrei di ieri e ebrei di oggi di fronte al fascismo," in *La Difesa della Razza* (special number of *Il Ponte*) 34 (November–December 1978): 1314–1315. The issue of Carlo Levi and his Jewish identity in the context of anti-Fascism is discussed in Hughes, *Prisoners of Hope,* pp. 65–76, 93–101, as well as in S. Segre-Amar, "Tes-

timonianza," in Archivio dello Stato, *Carlo Levi, Disegni dal carcere 1934: Materiali per una storia,* exh. cat. (Rome, 1983), pp. 43–47, who notes that socialism was the new religion of many assimilated Jews who saw in it a "modern interpretation of their ancient ideals."

89. Levi was arrested in the spring of 1934 for suspected activities with Giustizia e Libertà after the so-called Ponte Tresa affair, when two other members, Sion Segre-Amar and Mario Levi, were caught at the Swiss-Italian border with anti-Fascist material. Of the seventeen subsequently arrested, eleven were Jews (including Ginzburg and members of both Levi families): the event was critical in associating Jews with anti-Fascism and led to some anti-Semitic reaction in the press. Levi's involvement in Giustizia e Libertà and the drawings executed during his stay in prison are the subject of the 1983 exhibition catalogue cited in note 88 above.
90. As recounted to me by Levi's niece and nephew, Paola and Guido Sacerdoti, who added immeasurably to my understanding of the artist and provided invaluable insight into the man. I also thank the Fondazione Carlo Levi, Rome, for facilitating my research.
91. The subject of the painting is Paola Olivetti, born Levi, the sister of Natalia, wife of the Turin industrialist Adriano Levi and the lover of Carlo Levi during the 1930s.
92. C. Levi, "Saba e il mondo ebraico," reprinted in G. De Donato, ed., *Carlo Levi: Coraggio dei miti: Scritti contemporanei, 1922–1974* (Bari, 1975), pp. 226–242. Both Hughes, *Prisoners of Hope,* and Segre-Amar, "Testimonianza," see Levi's interpretation of Saba as the key to his own Jewish identity.
93. Aside from sporadic publications such as Giovanni Preziosi's *I Protocolli dei Savi Anziani di Sion* of 1921, the anti-Semitic press did not begin to gain ground until 1933 and then increasingly after 1936. See Milano, *Storia,* pp. 690–692, and De Felice, *Storia degli ebrei,* pp. 311–331.
94. The antimodernist attacks had begun even earlier under the auspices of Farinacci and against Sarfatti and the Novecento (see note 65). The attempt to organize a "degenerate art" campaign in Italy and the subsequent reaction by artists and intellectuals has been detailed in E. Crispolti's fundamental study, *Il mito della macchina e altri temi del futurismo* (Trapani, 1969), pp. 580–843. For a synopsis of the issues, see F. Tempesti, *Arte dell'Italia fascista* (Milan, 1976), pp. 214–249. What remains to be determined is the existence of a less obvious anti-Semitism in arguments for an "inherently" Italian art in professional journals and major newspapers, for example, the writings of the prominent critic Ugo Ojetti in *In Italia: L'arte ha da essere Italiana?* (Milan, 1942).
95. G. Pensabene "La XXI Biennale di Venezia," *Il Tevere,* no. 183 (May 1938): 3, described Cagli's paintings for both the Paris pavilion and the Biennale as "full of that depressing, ragged, and antiheroic sense of the race which we want to exclude once and for all from our exhibitions" (in the same article Massimo Campigli is also cited as being Jewish). The panels for the Paris pavilion were salvaged and are reproduced along with an account of Pensabene's attacks on Cagli in E. Crispolti, *Il Cagli romano,* exh. cat. (Milan, 1985), pp. 64–70, 173–183.
96. On the milieu of the Galleria della Cometa, see Fagiolo Dell'Arco and Rivosecchi, *Scuola romana,* esp. pp. 288–289.
97. The following was recounted to me personally by Sabatello in an interview in Rome in April 1988. The incident at the inauguration is also described in Fagiolo Dell'Arco and Rivosecchi, *Scuola romana,* p. 305.
98. Cagli's drawings of the period witness a resurgence of biblical themes; there is also a drawing entitled *Il rabbino e l'angelo* (The Rabbi and the Angel, 1938; private Collection). The sketches from Buchenwald are reproduced in H. Wurm and C. Benincasa, *Corrado Cagli: La notte dei cristalli* (Rome, 1975).
99. As recounted by Raphaël to the owner of the work and repeated to the author in a letter of 6 September 1988.
100. Levi Montalcini, *Elogio,* pp. 105–116, and M. Marcucci, "Moravia, di nome Adriana," *La Repubblica,* 11 March 1988.
101. Carpi's story is recounted in P. Carpi, ed., *Aldo Carpi: Diario di Güsen* (Milan, 1971), which contains an introduction with an account of his arrest and deportation and the transcript of the original diary with explanatory notes. See also Sirmione, Castello Scagliero, *Barberi, Belgiojoso, Carpi, Music, Slama: Artisti italiani nei campi di sterminio nazisti,* exh. cat. (Milan, 1985).
102. What Carpi didn't know was that two of his sons, Fiorenzo and Cioni (also involved in the Resistance), were forced to flee to Switzerland. Pinin was imprisoned, and Paolo was captured by the SS, deported, and did not return from the camp of Gross-Rosen. I thank the Carpi family of Milan, especially Cioni Carpi, for its assistance.
103. P. Levi, *Survival in Auschwitz and The Reawakening: Two Memoirs,* trans. S. Woolf (New York, 1986); *Se questo è un uomo* was originally published in 1947.
104. Levy was in Paris in the years before World War I. He returned to Germany in the 1920s and made his way to Italy in 1938 (Silver and Golan, *The Circle of Montparnasse,* p. 106).
105. As detailed in S. Zuccotti, *The Italians and the Holocaust* (New York, 1987).
106. M. Toscano, "Tra identità culturale e partecipazione poltica: Aspetti e momenti di vita ebraica italiana (1956–1976)," *Annuario di studi ebraici 1985–1987,* vol. 11 (Rome, 1988), pp. 293–325.
107. Hughes, *Prisoners of Hope* (see note 25 above).

Fig. 167. "Symbolic Motifs," *The Rothschild Maḥzor,* Florence, 1492, The Library of The Jewish Theological Seminary of America, New York (cat. no. 43)

ALLEN MANDELBAUM

A MILLENNIUM OF HEBREW POETRY IN ITALY

IN MEMORY OF DAN PAGIS

A "renegade" Jew from Judaea living in Rome and writing in Aramaic and then—with help—in Greek, Josephus is at once an emblem of defeat and displacement, of cosmopolitan acculturation and of a dismembered community. Yet somewhat more than eight centuries after his death, the anonymous Hebrew *Sefer Josipphon* (c. 953), (figs. 168, 169) based on Josephus' *Jewish War* as mediated by a Latin version, will begin its life as a popular work, circulating in very communal settings, speaking not as an exiled Jew's address and justification in a pagan arena, but as a text of comfort, consolation, solidarity within Jewish precincts. And the life of the *Sefer Josipphon* will be long.[1]

The *Sefer Josipphon* hardly matches the complexities of Josephus, but it is not subliterature. Jefim Hayyim Schirmann, the most comprehensive scholar-critic of Hebrew poetry in Italy, a man somewhat ill at ease with adornment and elaboration, was not awry in measuring the prose of the *Josipphon* as "lively and fluent" with "a mastery of prose vocabulary seldom encountered even during the Golden Age of Hebrew poetry in Spain."[2] Above all, that tenth-century prose is particularly visible evidence of a southern Italian audience—an audience that was also to welcome and to produce Hebrew *piyyut* over four centuries, the ninth to the twelfth. The centers were Oria, Venosa, Otranto, Bari, Siponto, and Trani. Our ability to chart the protagonists has been somewhat enhanced by Aḥimaaz ben Paltiel in the eleventh-century chronicle of his ancestors, his *Megillat Aḥimaaz*.[3] Amid the mists of his (often appealing) tales of wonder-working, there are precious indications that allow us to see the visage of Jewry in Byzantine Italy. With clues from Aḥimaaz and much work by Schirmann and others we can configure a rich tradition that includes: Shephatiah bar Amittai, Amittai bar Shefatiah, Zebadiah, Silano of Venosa, and Elijah ben Shemaiah, with the latter possibly preceded in Bari by the tenth-century or—at the latest—eleventh-century figure of Abraham ben Isaac with an Aramaic *reshut*.[4] Add to these, for the cohabitation of verse and prose, the rhymed-prose form of Aḥimaaz's own text, punctuated at one piyyut-istic point by a doubled alphabetical acrostic followed by a nominal acrostic.[5] (This is, of course, minor acrostic play. Ezra Fleischer's only exclamation point in his *Hebrew Liturgical Poetry in the Middle Ages* is reserved for a kaph repeated sixteen times at the end of a *rahit* where Amittai follows an acrostic alphabet with "*Amittai cha-zak.*")[6] And then, back to the anonymous author of the prose *Josipphon* for an unrhymed, unmetered poetic *kinah*.[7]

Finally, consider the unique trans-piyyut intrusion into Shabbetai Donnolo's preface to his commentary on the *Sefer Yeẓirah*.[8] There the long monorhymed runs in the two unequally long verse-paragraphs

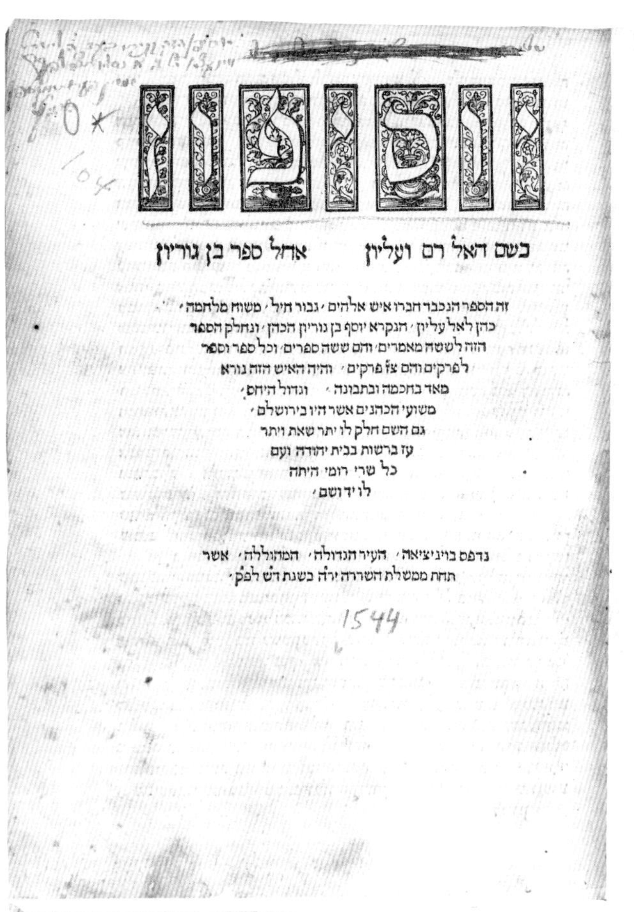

יוסיפון

כשם דאל רם ועליון אחל ספר בן גוריון

זה הספר הנכבר חברו איש אלהים · גבור חיל · משוח מלחמה ·
כהן לאל עליון · הנקרא יוסף בן גוריון הכהן · ונחלק הספר
הזה לששה מאמרים · והם ששה ספרים · וכל ספר וספר
לפרקים והם צז פרקים · והיה האיש הזה נורא
מאד בחכמה ובתבונה · וגדול היחס ·
משועי הכהנים אשר היו בירושלם ·
גם השם חלק לו יתר שאת ויתר
עז ברשות בבית יהודה ועם
כל שרי רומי היתה
לו יד ושם ·

נדפס בויניציאה · העיר הגדולה · המהוללה · אשר
תחת ממשלת השררה יר״ה בשנת דש לפק ·

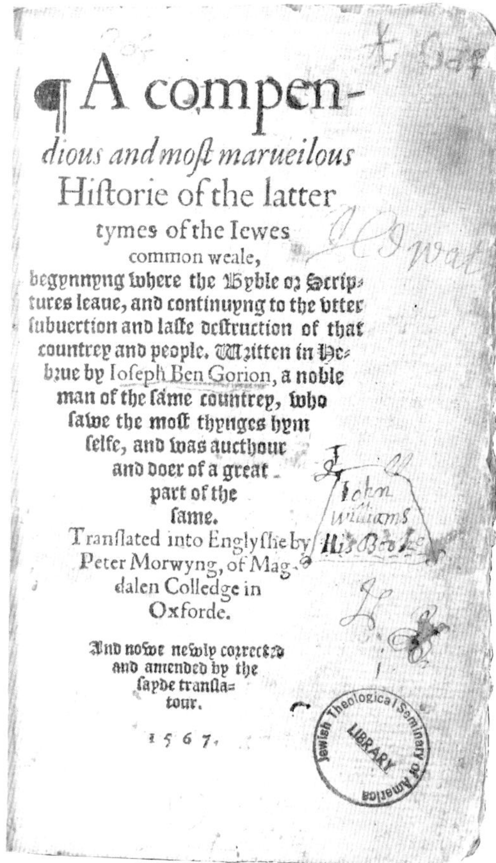

¶ A compendious and most marueilous Historie of the latter tymes of the Iewes common weale, begynnyng where the Byble or Scriptures leaue, and continuyng to the vtter subuersion and laste destruction of that countrey and people. Written in Hebrue by Ioseph Ben Gorion, a noble man of the same countrey, who sawe the most thynges hym selfe, and was aucthour and doer of a great part of the same.

Translated into Englyshe by Peter Morwyng, of Magdalen Colledge in Oxforde.

And nowe newly corrected and amended by the sayde translatour.

1567.

as well as the nominal acrostic are fully piyyut-like. Donnolo not only spells out his name at line beginnings but also writes about himself as author-proprietor *in* the poem, invoking the Lord's "shalom rav": "bountiful peace, blessings, and boundless, splendid consolations . . . to anyone who . . . transcribing this, my book of inquiries . . . transcribes it in the name of Shabbetai, without erasing my name from this, my book of mysteries . . . [for] he will indeed understand the labors I have undergone, expending all my powers." Such reader-transcribers are then encouraged to copy faithfully the very "prefatory rhymes" that they are reading—or better, first encouraged, then threatened with "erasure from the land of the living" if they erase the lines that will allow Donnolo to be remembered. But "with all that," he concluded, "I do trust in the Lord to repay my labors, on which most of my years have been spent . . . explaining mysteries, books secret, closed, and profound—explaining more than my predecessors have done."[9] But that unique intrusion, its very non-piyyut-like I, does link even southern Italy to later secular verse, just as Amittai's epithalamium for the wedding of his sister Cassia is a *yotzer,* foreshadowing in piyyut the long line of occasional poetry in Italy.[10]

We know that "foreshadowing," however tempting as a notion, is tricky indeed when applied to a history as beleaguered by harassment, expulsions, forced conversions, pogroms, slaughter, as is the history of the Jews. And at the end of the thirteenth century, southern Italian Jews underwent a cruel, decimating campaign of forced conversion. What Byzantium (and Saracen invaders) did not accomplish, the Angevins and Dominicans did.

But southern Italy was the first European center of piyyut, and on the peninsula it is the starting point of a continuous line of Hebrew verse that lasted in Italy until the beginning of our century (fig. 170). It is, then, not too amiss, in taking stock of the southern Italian corpus, to see both what it was and what later lines extend from it. Some things are clear: (1) Southern Italy is linked not only to Babylonian piyyut, but also to that earliest stronghold of piyyut, Palestine, where—we now see—Yannai and Kallir formed classical piyyut probably as early as the sixth century. (2) Piyyut went hand in hand with learning; both Oria and Bari had significant yeshivot. (3) The lines of force and transmission sometimes led southern Italian piyyut into the Ashkenazic prayer service. (4) Piyyut is, almost by definition, communal in conception and destination. But this is especially so in Italy—south, center, or north; Italian-Jewish worshipers were very participative.[11] (5) The communal base of piyyut does have some echo in the communal nexus of Italian occasional verse:

Fig. 168. (opposite, left) *Sefer Josipphon,* Venice, 1544, The Library of The Jewish Theological Seminary of America, New York (mic. 80746)

Fig. 169. (opposite, right) *A Compendious and Most Marveilous Historie of the Iewes* . . . (English translation of the *Josipphon*), London, 1567, The Library of The Jewish Theological Seminary of America, New York (mic. 5896)

Fig. 170. (above) Anonymous liturgical poem. Italy c. 1251, Syndics of Cambridge University Library, Cambridge Taylor-Schechter Genizah Research Unit (T-S Ki.83)

Amittai's epithalamium is a point in what will be an enduring line: occasional verse is spawned again and again. Weddings, circumcisions, deaths, synagogue foundings, degree completions: these were staples of Hebrew verse for as long as it survived—through the nineteenth century (fig. 172). Seen after the epithalamium-yotzer of Amittai, much later "occasional" verse often seems lesser. But it is pleasant verse in many of its embodiments, often gracious, often endearing, even occasionally memorable (I am thinking of Isaiah Bassani's epithalamium, the work of a writer almost as itinerant as Immanuel of Rome: he lived in Mantua, Cento, Padua, and died in Reggio in 1739).[12] Not that the I-ness of a poet is a necessary index of a work's noncommunal character: after all, Dante's *Comedy* is replete with himself and is yet a "national" poem; and if the United States has any "national" poem, it is Whitman's extension of his "Song of Myself" in *Leaves of Grass* (no "nation" of antiquity could have opted so). But the communal character of Italian verse at times involves too close a relation between poet and audience: a negation of all distance—a point to which I shall return. (6) There is some tendency in southern Italy—and later elsewhere—to enter what I have seen at times as a "hallucinarium," that place in which techne seems all-absorbing to the poet. Whether or not the units are strophes—couplets, tercets, quatrains, octaves—or solid blocks (often shaped by the acrosticalphabet lengths at line beginning), it is *contiguous* or nonintervaled rhyme (mitigated only by a refrain, if ever) that takes firm hold in Italy, until that grip is loosened by rival forms from Italian verse.

Earlier I mentioned the southern Italian reshut in Aramaic by Abraham ben Isaac: it has a 31-line monorhymed run on khā (which, of course, Schirmann's Hebrew translation does not mime). But even after the later intrusion of Italian noncontiguous rhyme (or in the case of Dante's *Comedy,* a rhyme code that constitutes non-contiguity as a binding, exclusive rule: no two contiguous lines can rhyme), monorhymed long runs resist in Hebrew: Immanuel of Rome, the very one to introduce noncontiguous rhyme, does not at all eschew contiguous rhyme (and I do not mean in his rhymed prose): he has one monorhymed run that lasts for 67 lines, *with a regular syllable count*—and my myopic count may be short[13]—and one particularly surging run of 98 lines in *Maḥberot* 25, a "song of songs" sung on a celebrated drunkard, Ephron. Joseph Barukh ben Yedidyah of Urbino (who lived in Mantua, Modena, and Busseto), writing in 1659, has a monorhymed run of 43 lines;[15] Jacob Frances, in the seventeenth century, has a 59-line monorhymed run in his kinah for the death of his brother's wife;[16] the eighteenth-century Paduan Sabbato Vita Marini has a 32-line monorhymed run;[17] and the Livornese Malachi Cohen, in his lament for the death of Rabbi Ḥayyim Ibn Atar in 1743, a 30-line run.[18] And if we grant Leone Ebreo (Judah Abrabanel) Italian citizenship after his expulsion from Spain in 1492 (the last half of his life is spent in Naples, Genoa, Barletta—then back to Naples), we might add to his enduring *Dialoghi di amore* in Italian, the more fleeting evidence of his 1503 Naples lament on the state of his time, with its 139-line monorhymed run.[19]

These Scrutinistic items, with their numerical tallies, are not only a quirky extrapolation of that ink-beset frame of mind or viscera that, relatively recently, would lead Paul Valéry to say: "Not the least of the pleasures of rhyme is the rage it inspires in those poor people who think they know something more important than a *convention.* They hold the naive belief that a thought *can* be more profound, more organic . . . than any convention."[20] That might do—at points—for Immanuel of Rome and some later Hebrew poet-gymnasts in Italy, but it hardly sheds light on rhyme and liturgical verse. At its origins rhyme is chiefly a percussive—and mnemonic—complement and instigator of prayer. The *non*communal dimension of such rhyme is that rhyme-pressure may encourage elitist, hermetic, exacerbated wordplay, epithet multiplication, etc.; for Schirmann, who prizes "sincerity and conviction," much of this will be "superfluous erudition," "subtle allusions," "intricate and cumbersome," "turgid." And where he does not question the poet's sincerity, Schirmann will, for instance, protest against Elijah ben Shemaiah's "archaic language, even resuscitating rare or obsolete words of Greek origin . . . allusiveness . . . difficult vocabulary . . . complicated style"—and, in what we might call a non-Valéry perspective, will only bless a *seliḥah* that is for him "unique in Elijah ben Shemaiah's poetry," a seliḥah "*all in unrhymed verse* [italics mine] except for two final rhymed lines . . . phrased in simple, noble terms, recalling some of the loftiest passages in the Scriptures . . . even worthy of being compared with them."[21] Schirmann did not mention the *At-Bash* acrostic pressure in the poem, but in any case, he is on target in terms of that seliḥah's quality.

Rhymed or unrhymed, acrostic or not, a poem might well be weighed in another scale used elsewhere by Valéry, a scale somewhat different from the one mentioned above: "The Psalms, for example, are of the nature of both hymn and elegy, a combination that forms a remarkable alliance between collective sentiments lyrically expressed and those which proceed from a person's inner being and faith."[22] Not a bad stab at defining the nature of piyyut at its richest—and with the exemplar of Psalms, which lies both beyond and within the travail of piyyut. Then again, if we see complicated rhyme as resulting in elitist exacerbations, there is another stance that sees a kind of self-effacement of the *paytan* under overformal pressures: self-effacement that can be a central—and for us, possibly not recoupable—poetic good. But there is some justified perplexity and thrashing about in Fleischer's assessment of the perhaps *excessive* weight of conventions accepted by *both* the poet and the Italian praying community, especially when to short line and contiguous rhymes, the Italians later added syllable counts. Or, as he says: "Yes, later *paytanim* freed themselves from many of these constraints, but they did that too late. By then, the stylistic climate of the school had already been set, and that style persisted even when it was no longer compelled to do so [by metric constraints]; both *paytanim* and worshippers had grown used to it, and they did not have the strength to change it."[23]

Yet even where a code has difficulty in crossing easily into our habits of reading silently or aloud, its very limits—its concentrations and constrictions—can invite more-than-scholarly recuperation. (In our own decades Kallirian piyyut has been much more appreciated than in Haskalah times, just as elsewhere, the pre-Renaissance French *grands rhétoriqueurs* have undergone not inconsiderable—and creditable—rehabilitation.)

Despite his sometimes difficult style, Solomon ben Yehudah ha-Bavli (the Babylonian) is not subject to Schirmann's strictures.[24] Indeed, for me the model critical edition of his poems by Fleischer offers us a complex, intriguing, memorable body of work, a point of arrival, though ha-Bavli was the probable point of departure for piyyut as it emerged in the Roman community, beginning in the tenth century and consolidating in the eleventh.[25] A late arrival with respect to the Apulian centers, Rome would vaunt in the eleventh century as paytan Jeḥiel ben Abraham, the father of Nathan, the author-compiler of the *Arukh*;[26] later, in the thirteenth century, the family of Anav-im produced five paytanim: two physician-poets, Benjamin ben Abraham (also known as Benjamin del Mansi) and Ẓedakiah ben Benjamin; Abraham ben Yoav; Moses ben Abraham; and Jeḥiel ben Jekuthiel. These Roman familial links are paralleled by the role of the Kalonymus family in Lucca and then in Germany. And just as the *Arukh* signals *piyyut* and learning as complementary in Rome, so does the scholarly achievement of Kalonymus ben Moses stand beside his poetic work. His son, Meshullam, though he emigrated to Germany and was buried in Mainz, was reputed to be a follower of Solomon ha-Bavli, and may well have spent time in Rome. Before these two, probably in the late tenth century in Lucca, stands Moses ben Kalonymus, who figures often as fountainhead for German piyyut. But, as Fleischer (who can hardly be accused of *campanilismo*) notes, both Meshullam and Moses, the Kalonymides, who were the first to author arduous *kedushtaot* in Germany, were sons of Italy. And behind them lay the earliest *kedushtah* produced in Europe—by the southern Italian Amittai.[27]

We have had to cite a number of *kinot* and *seliḥot* up to this point, a point where Judeo-Italian offers us a significant text.[28] The anonymous (*no* nominal acrostic here) "Judeo-Italian elegy" was discovered by E. S. Artom in a fifteenth-century Ferrarese *maḥzor* (where it was transliterated into Hebrew) and splendidly commented on by Umberto Cassuto in 1929.[29] Cassuto dates the elegy as early as the end of the twelfth century, and no responsible philologist would date it later than the thirteenth. Its provenance may be the southern Marches, but in any case is surely central Italian, to be linked with the Roman school. Composed in monorhymed tercets (*canto-quanto-santo,* etc.) with an assonantal intrusion in one tercet (*osti-forti-porti*), its Hebrewness is blatant: as Gianfranco Contini notes, "the meter is absolutely outside the norm of Italian usage." It is not contiguous rhyme as such that marks it as unusual in Italian (there is some propensity to monorhymed "batches" in the earlier Italian *Ritmo Cassinese* and the *Ritmo su Sant' Alessio* and, still earlier, in the *Ritmo Laurenziano*), but monorhymes within equal strophes—in this case, tercets (commonplace in Hebrew). Its second "abnormal" characteristic with respect to its Italian context is its four-stress-per-line metric with a variable number of syllables, descended with a difference, we might say, from the long tradition of word count as central to line formation in much of previous piyyut. We have piyyut, Judeo-Italian, and then, with Immanuel of Rome, the greatest poet of medieval (or early Renaissance) Italy, an exuberant explosion of secular verse.

Fig. 171. *Cofanetto* (Small Casket or Box), Ferrara(?), second half of the fifteenth century, The Israel Museum, Jerusalem (cat. no. 236)

Immanuel was born in Rome about 1260 and died after 1328.[30] Way stations in the six decades of his life were Perugia, Fermo, Fabriano, Camerino, Ancona, and Verona. His restlessness may have been abetted by the displeasure of Italian *baale batim* with the eroticism of his verse (see below for Moses da Rieti's displeasure a century later and, for a fuller list of the displeased, see Jarden).[31] Way stations for his scholarship were a Hebrew grammar and commentaries on many books of the Bible.[32] But scholarship and restlessness alike found an enduring place in Immanuel's masterpiece, his poetic work the *Maḥberot* (Compositions), in twenty-eight sections.

At his back Immanuel heard and absorbed the poetry of the golden age in Spain and its quantitative meters. At his side he heard Dante; the lyrics of the *dolce stil nuovo*; the realistic, provocative, burlesque line exemplified by Cecco Angiolieri (a line that Dante also absorbed); and what Contini differentiates as a "popular"-*giullaresca* (minstrel) line. He did not hear the deeper intellectual strain of Cavalcanti or the probing mental music—and images—of Dante, nor did he see-feel-possess Dante's lust for structure. From his Hebrew predecessors in Arab-inspired Spain, he took many lyric conventions, the native Hebrew arsenal of images and snatches from the Song of Songs, and as form for the separate sections of the *Maḥberot,* the *makama,* rhymed prose interrupted and enhanced by metric interludes as the journeying poet recounts encounters, meditations, verbal duels and exchanges.[33] From Italian poetry he borrowed intervaled rhyme in one of its most enduring forms, the sonnet (for which the Hebrew term *shir zahav,* "the golden song," plays on the numerical: *z-h-v* in Hebrew adds up to fourteen),[34] the first European borrowing of that form from Italian; and specifically from Dante, the impetus for the last section of the *Maḥberot,* a journey through hell and heaven in somewhat stumbling imitation of the *Comedy*.

But the leaped-into dream-narrative of that twenty-eighth section—with its tedious catalogues, lame connections in its tellings ("and when from there . . . and when from there . . ."), and resolute refusal to intercalate rhymed prose, Immanuel's dominant mode in the *Maḥberot,* with any other form—reminds us precisely in its loose attachment to the first twenty-seven sections that Immanuel is the master of non sequiturs, the great digressor. No Dantesque structural energy—but vitality, yes, and often boisterous or obsessed. For every vagrant impulse Immanuel has fashioned sonnet, quatrain, epigram, or winning prose harangue that weaves through escapades of love, word duels, songs of insult, random pieties and desperations. He has invention in conceits and the cunning of an ironsmith in shaping Hebrew. Thus, when he is adapting from Italian Ruggieri Apuliesi's *Serventese* on the endless trades and skills the speaker has mastered, Immanuel outdoes his model in percussive fervor and the anaphoric delirium of his line-beginning *anis*, I-I-I.[35] These are not confessional I's: they are the I of the swaggering minstrel, the I of "look what I can do-invent-sing," the I that assumes an immediately appreciative public, a public warm, benevolent, delighted.

Not that judgment is important in reading him. There is little time for it. The line of his verse is serpentine; before one coil, recoil is done, another has begun. And there is—so often—generous *copia* in him. (To abet his abundance, Immanuel—following Jarden's intrepid count—uses about seventeen thousand expressions drawn from the language of the Bible, seven hundred from Talmudic sources and six hundred from medieval Hebrew.)[36] And Immanuel's fare is various—whether, hungry, he is praising what might feed him ("for heart's redeemer is the leek, / and garlic, onion—they're my peace," as "garlic" becomes "earth's stag and blossom: // Grace did bear him, Glory robed him, / over him—the Great Bear and her sons. // And wheel in wheel, like heaven's spheres, / the onion's skin; the leek, Elisha's / wand, in wondrous miracles"), or assessing a shrew ("so shall a man assay his soul / enduring evil womankind— / for as the howling desert wolf— / her hair may change, but not her mind"), or wryly recording love's disillusions:

Be not dismayed
if one whose ardor,
but today,
was fragrant
as mandragora

should find his splendor
all has fled
when he's a-bed
with his beloved,
Ophra;

for the sun
is not eclipsed
and not undone
until the moon
and he are one—

Fig. 172. Marriage Contract, Mantua, 1689, The Library of The Jewish Theological Seminary of America, New York (cat. no. 107)

or contemplating the joys of Camerino, where the conjured bodies of its welcoming women offered "two cakes of purest manna as our fare," women who, on his departure, cried out, "Alas, the wanderer, / who rends our hearts' enclosure."[37]

And it is as wanderer that Immanuel echoes most, even down to our century. We have five poems by Immanuel in Italian; four are sonnets.[38] The second and third of these are cadenzas on the adaptability of the wanderer, who wears whatever coat most suits: "I'm an errant Jew, yet not a Muslim, / and I don't set my ship toward Christians,"—one, in sum, who wants the best "of every law . . . / the Christian's gobbling, guzzling, // good Moses' seldom fasting, / and the wantonness of Macón [Islam], / which keeps no faith from the waist down" and "Guelf or Ghibelline, black or white— / just pick your color, whichever you like . . . // O, Treachery, dear comrade, you / can count on me—I'm turncoat-true: / I shan't be wanting, when it comes / to backing up the one who's won." The last of these five poems is *Bisbidis* (the word plays on *bisbiglio,* "whisper, murmur"): fifty-three quatrains, each with its three first lines rhyming together and the fourth lines all ending with the same rhyme, a refrain-family of sounds—not words— linking the fifty-three quatrains (*aaar, bbbr, cccr,* etc.). Here the wanderer conjures, in burlesque mode, the court of Can Grande in Verona: "I've searched, the earth / in length, in breadth; / on land and sea— / diligently. // I've been to Syria, / seen Herminia / and—it seems to me— / most of Romany. // I've seen the Sultan / on hill and plain; / now I'll explain / Can Grande's fame."

The wanderer wanders down to our century (and on the way surely encounters John Skelton) in the Yiddish of Yankev Glatshteyn's "Reizeman" (The Traveling Man):[39]

> A traveling man came from afar.
> He'd seen the Rhine, Frankfurt-am-Main and Palestine,
> everywhere gone, everything seen—
> the aging, saging traveling man . . .
> . . . .
> And so refrains the traveling man:
> "Rode all over, even under the clover,
> over the Don and Sambatyon,
> in Russia, in Prussia,
> in Japan, Hunan and Shushan,
> everywhere known, everywhere been,
> everything shown, everything seen."

And in the background of those echoes, there is the unforgettable scattering-array of onomatopoeic syllables in Immanuel's *Bisbidis*: "*giach giach giach / . . . duduf duduf / . . . muz muz / . . . usu usu / . . . stututu ifiu ifiu ifiu / . . . cui cui / . . . gu gu / . . . guuu uu,*" the trumpets' "*bobobò bobobò / bottombò bobobò / Bobobottombò bobobottombò*" and—in what is only a partial list—the "*Bis bis bis / Bisbidis bisbidis /Bisbidisis*" of a whisper.

Immanuel did not whisper in his time and after. There are many manuscripts of his work; the first complete printed edition of any Hebrew poet, the Brescia edition of 1492 under the Soncino imprint; four other editions before Jarden's, and six partial editions. Among others the Frances brothers heard him well, as did Tchernichowsky later.

But, as noted above, Moses da Rieti (c. 1388–1460), in miming Dante's *Comedy*—or more particularly, his *Paradiso*—in *Mikdash Me'at* (The Little Sanctuary), completed about a century after Immanuel's death, took special care to exclude Immanuel from his paradise. In the readers' aids Moses himself appended to his work in part 2, discourse 6, Moses notes that he has not listed Immanuel among the array of glories because of "his language and his matter in his love poems."[40] There has been an established tendency to downgrade Moses' work, some of this perhaps in response to Goldenthal's hyperbolic labeling of Moses as the "Italian Dante" in his 1851 edition. But Pagis, admitting many weaknesses, calls attention to the fluency of Moses and to "impressive dramatic passages that have no equal in all the annals of the Haskalah."[41] The former virtue is related not simply to Moses' introducing terza rima into Hebrew, but to the way in which his syntax is able to move in supple fashion, bonding tercet to tercet—his *not* overfrequent use of tercet end as sentence end. The second virtue is noted by Pagis in the scene that opens part 2, discourse 4, where the speaker encounters a patriarchal figure who then reveals himself as Moses' father. The passage appears in T. Carmi's *Penguin Book of Hebrew Verse* with a fine prose translation;[42] for me, it is one passage where Moses, speaking of his biological father, can vie with Dante's image of the patriarchal Cato at the beginning of *Purgatory* and the fatherly Virgil at many points in the *Comedy*. And one cannot question Moses' reach for the sublime in a register so different from any native to Immanuel—a reach that sometimes touches its object.

The sequence of post-Dante Hebrew otherworlds is completed by two works that ended as a diptych in one volume. The first, *Tofteh Arukh* (Hell Arrayed), was written by Moses ben Mordecai Zacuto, who was born in Amsterdam about 1620, was educated there and in Posen; then lived in Verona, Padua, Venice (1645), and in Mantua, where he served as rabbi from 1663 until his death in 1697. A Cordoverean kabbalist—and somewhat sympathetic to Shabbateanism at first, though he turned against the apostate—his kabbalism does spill into the 125 five-line stanzas (*abbaa*—an interesting collocation) of his *Tofteh Arukh.*[43] While he spent himself on a work that waited for posthumous publication in Venice in 1715, a lesser poet, Jacob Daniel Olmo, adopted Zacuto's meter and applied it to paradise in his *Eden Arukh* (Paradise Arrayed), then published his 277-stanza sequel together with the *Tofteh* in 1743.

These two works move us three centuries past the *Mikdash Me-at,* into the century of Ramḥal (Rabbi Moses Luzzatto), whom the Haskalah saw as a principal predecessor-figure in the emergence of modern Hebrew poetry. But those three centuries, too often,

Fig. 173. Scroll of Esther (detail), northern Italy, late eighteenth century, Collection of Michael and Judy Steinhardt, New York (cat. no. 57)

as Pagis says, seen as a time of decline, have their own riches; and as early as 1934 Schirmann's anthology had much available evidence therefor. This is the area, I should say, where Giuliano Tamani is most justified in his recent laments over the lack of critical editions needed for a truly sufficient history of the literature of Italian Jewry. Tamani's complaint appeared in an essay of his on Mordecai Dato (1525–1591/1601), and though Tamani is belligerently anxious to see literature *as* literature, his own attention, in treating Dato, to Dato's kabbalism also invites us to wish for *someone's* full story of kabbalah in its Italian *poetic* context.[44]

In addition to Dato himself, those three centuries include the principal figures, Yoseph Zarfati and the Frances brothers, Immanuel and Jacob; and flanking them, Raphael of Faenza, Leone Modena, and Moses Zacuto, as author not only of the *Tofteh Arukh* but also of the *Yesod Olam,* long thought to be the first drama in Hebrew.[45]

Raphael of Faenza, who lived in Florence around 1450, is the earliest in this line; not atypical is his poem of beseeching (shortened here in this knitted adaptation):

Beloved, hear my plea,
O Galantina.

Your lips are honey sweetly strong;
feast, comely kind, your tongue
upon my palate, un-
ashamedly, night long
shall we loud sing renewal's song
while love's own congregations,
as vast as bannered legions,

hymns of love resound,
O Galantina.

Alone upon my bed,
I dreamt your wanton dress,
your grace; my lovely, let
me tell your excellence
in bright terrazzo halls and rest
my head between your breasts,
that tower built of turrets.

Beloved, summon me,
O Galantina.

Zarfati has a double soul. It is he who, with much grace, introduced ottava rima into Hebrew (the origins of ottava rima are obscure, but it is surely Boccaccio who, as poet, elevated it to elect status) and he who, in the wake of a controversy in 1519, could pound out monorhymed malediction with a cudgel.

But the widest and most effective versatility, drawing on the modes of Immanuel of Rome with the freedom of parity across the centuries, belongs to the brothers Frances. Witness Immanuel Frances conjuring Pappus the lovesick innkeeper in search of his gazelle:

. . . . his heart, a roast
upon the spit of longing, turns—he burns:
O gaze, gazelle, down from your window where
with passion and *tendresse* your gallant yearns.

But see his fallen face and form, his paunch
that pines—and eyes that have spilled endless tears;
his bald-spot's chill, his stray gray locks hang damp
with dew, and like the tom-cat he appears,

who stalks the rooftops, howling bitterly—
alone, because the fog withholds his she.

Or some of Immanuel's chiseled grave-notes:

THE DRUNKARD
Lifelong, no water touched my lips;
it's wine that quenched me all my years;
therefore, o reader, I beseech
you—water not my grave with tears.

THE HOTHEAD
Here lies one sense-less, prone to fury;
as from an archer's arrows, flee,
o passerby, lest in his wrath,
he hurl this tombstone straight at thee.

THE FAIR ONE
A girl more fair than any other
rests below, yet none is found
among her swains who now would lie
beside his lovely on this ground.

THE PHYSICIANS
Give gracious thanks, o reader, to your Lord
that he who lies here was not your physician,
for had he been, his epitaph you'd never
read now—but rest instead in his position.

Beyond the compact cleverness, both Frances brothers are capable of more spacious modes, sufficiently vital to let one see the following poem by Mordecai Dato not as an icon of decline of Italian Hebrew verse in these centuries, but, with the emphasis on "glow" rather than "ashes," as an icon of Pagis's position:

O mock me not, if I still carol
songs of lust, though I am old;
beneath the ashes *glow* the coals—
within me wakes my heart, though I
may sleep; and if my hair be pale
as moons, not so my quality.

Baroque antecedents then for modern Hebrew, though it will hardly inherit the bilingual play of Leone Modena in 1584, with the sounds of a meaningful Hebrew line transcribed into, and paired with, Italian, resulting in different but still meaningful words. This is an expansion of echo rhymes to the whole line, but in *two* languages; an expansion that Ephraim Luzzatto (see below) also tries—after Moses Ḥayyim Catalano had done it in 1642. Hallucinarium? Yes—but persistent, and not less so when Judah Italki published in 1740 a poem with all its words beginning with the Hebrew letter shin.[46] Baroque? Yes, but also well suited to the early rhétoriqueurs I mentioned above and not unrelated to Raimbautz de Vaqueiras's twelfth-century plurilingual poem (though without interlanguage homophony) in Provençal, Italian, French, Gascon, and Hispano-Portuguese.

The pleasures of such play can be many, but it is something other that northern Haskalah will seek from Italy: new matter, freer themes, prosodic impetus, and linguistic clarity—a *kind* of classicism—and for that they will turn to a most complex protagonist of eighteenth-century Italy.

The figure of Ramḥal (acronym for Rabbi Moses Hayyim Luzzatto) later evoked Bialik's moving encomium—and one of the finest evocations in Schirmann's scholarly prose. It begins:

On the first day of Sivan (May 21, 1727), a strange thing happened within the walls of the Ghetto of Padua. The young Moses Ḥayyim Luzzatto, scion of a distinguished, well-to-do Jewish family (fig. 174), a young man learned in things worldly and Judaic, a poet who had given rise to many hopes with his skills, felt that he had come into touch with extra-natural forces. He had been preparing himself for such an experience for a long time: he had strived to have his spirit enter a state of ecstasy; he had centered his thoughts and professed the unity of God each quarter-hour, until on that day he had awakened from sleep and suddenly seemed

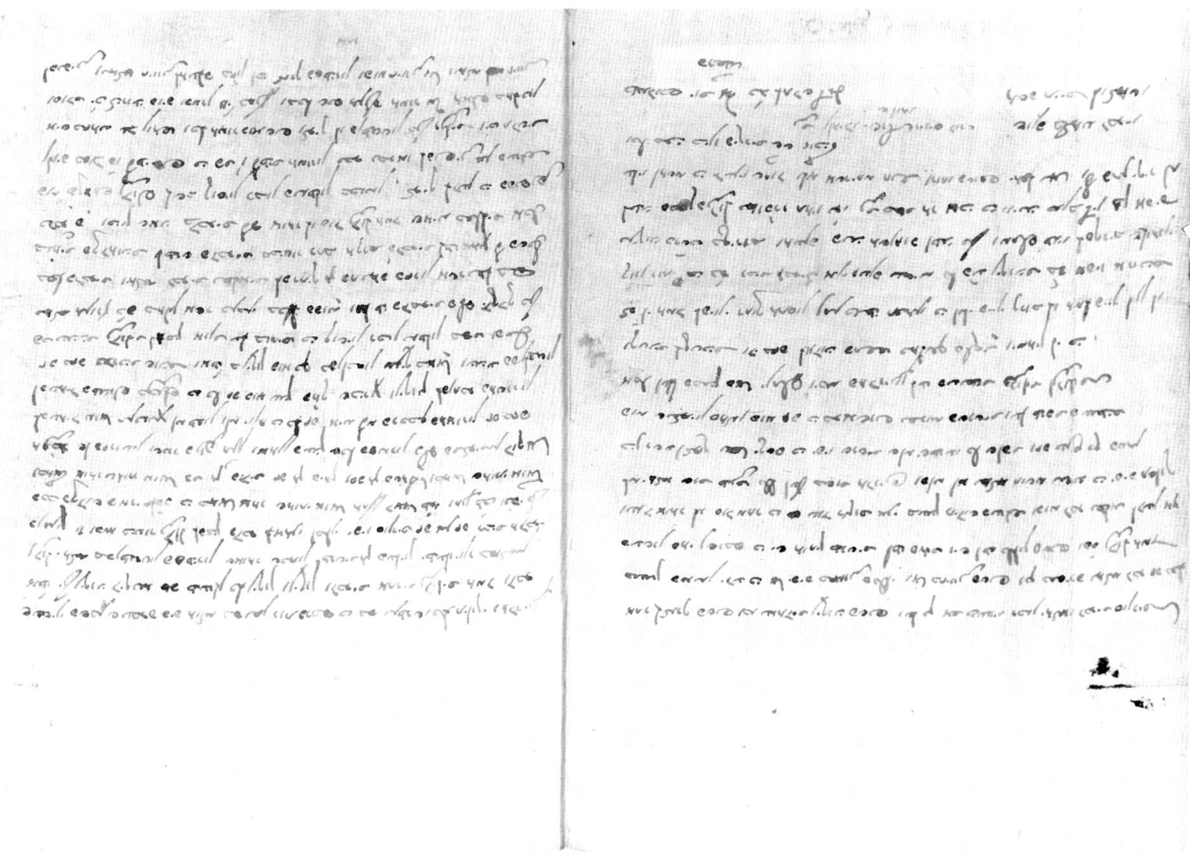

Fig. 174. Letter from Moses Ḥayyim Luzzatto, 30 August 1729, The Library of The Jewish Theological Seminary of America, New York (mic. 8520 a)

to hear a mysterious voice speaking to him—but speaking through the mouth of Luzzatto himself. This was the first revelation to him of the mysterious "*maggid*" ("speaker"); from then on, he heard him often. . . . He deepened more and more his study of secret wisdom; together with a group of close friends he formed a separate group in Padua for the constant study of the *Zohar*; finally, he reached the awareness that his visions were announcing to him his destiny—to bring closer to his people the hour of redemption. The topics and daring contents of his writings on things secret roused the suspicions of his contemporaries. They had not forgotten the bitter experiences of the Jews after the preceding messianic movements [Shabbatai Zvi and what followed in his wake]. And so, they began to persecute without mercy the dreamer of dreams, one who had frightened them. On the first of Sivan, Luzzatto's tragedy began; it reached its end, on a dateless day, in 1746.[47]

A dateless day—and an unknown tomb—some twenty years later, in Safed; Ramḥal was then forty years old. After conditions in Padua—the warnings, admonitions, controversies, Venetian urgings that his writings be burned—made life in Italy intolerable for him, Ramḥal had gone to Amsterdam in 1735. There he had lived, not in silence, but not as a teacher of messianic kabbalism.

When Amsterdam too became too "difficult" for him, he had moved to Safed. Kabbalist in many of his writings, ethical teacher in his famous *Mesillat Yesharim* (The Path of the Upright), Luzzatto was also a truly gifted poet. His occasional verse is still readable; but above all it is his three verse dramas in Hebrew that led to the Haskalah's esteem for him—and Bialik's seeing in him "the father of modern Hebrew poetry."[48]

Some find spillover from Luzzatto's kabbalism to his poetry—and some see none.[49] In terms of the aesthetic "attention" of Luzzatto, one thing is clear: he is a scrupulous craftsman, an extremely conscious practitioner of poetry and writer on poetics. And in the milieu to which he was close there were no rigid boundaries in the way time and sentiment were allotted. Luzzatto's friend, kabbalistic teacher, and defender was Isaiah Bassani. But Bassani himself is not only the author of a lovely epithalamium in terza rima; he had begun a translation into Hebrew of Ovid's *Metamorphoses,* using Anguillara's Italian Renaissance version as his base. With one hundred octaves done, Bassani handed over the continuation of his work to Vita Marini (one of whose monorhymed runs I mentioned above). Schirmann has seven of Marini's octaves in his anthology; they are from the Creation portion of book 1 of the *Metamorphoses*—and very appealingly executed. End of tale: Bassani was one of Luzzatto's close group of friends, those immediately inspired by him. In effect, what one has in Italy is not a sudden Haskalah eruption, but a long tradition of wordly knowledge and Hebraic learning and wisdom dwelling side by side—with kabbalah as a frequent ingredient in that range of concerns and commitments. And those concerns did include a feel for the grace and force of the verse-line as it is made and as it is heard; there was delight in other languages—and utmost love for Hebrew. In that sense the string of works on grammar and prosody that Italy offers are not only works of *cucina* but of *officina*—not simply recipe books but necessary instruments in forging meaning and verse-music: the labors of reconciling Spanish quantitative meters and Italian syllabic meters (yet with certain stress constraints), the realities of Hebrew pronunciation in Italy and the "correct" status of *shva* and *patach, piano* rhyme (feminine, with stress on the penultimate syllable) *and* final-syllable rhyme. And amid his messianic longings, Ramḥal did devote himself to those questions too.

There is indeed a brightness, a freedom, even a sweetness, in the lyrical passages of Ramḥal's later two plays. But whether or not they reflect kabbalah, they do reflect Arcadia, rather stiff allegorical articulations, and—of course—the *Pastor Fido* of Guarini. Couple this with the role of Metastasio for Ephraim Luzzatto, and of Metastasio and Pope for Samuel Romanelli,[50] and one can see a somewhat starched entry of Hebrew into the end of the eighteenth and beginning of the nineteenth century—and into the origins of northern Haskalah.

Yet the other—and very different—just-mentioned Luzzatto, Ephraim (Angelo), in the same century (1729–1792), can join Ramḥal as an Italian Hebrew poet who bridges the way to modern Hebrew poetry and reinforces Pagis's objections—noted above—to overrapid conclusions about the decline of Hebrew poetry. This Luzzatto from San Daniele in Friuli, graduated in medicine from Padua, was an elegant, worldly physician for much of his life, and one aware that the physician himself may be stricken, in need of remedies, when the patient is especially lovely. A small conceit, but the poet was liberating in his influence on the range of Hebrew verse—as was his brother, Isaac (1730–1803), also a physician graduated from Padua, who practiced in San Daniele. His sonnets join those of Joseph Almansi (1801–1860) as a penultimate chapter in the Hebrew sonnet in Italy; even as his second wife made him a brother-in-law of Samuel David Luzzatto.

Samuel David Luzzatto (acronym, Shadal; 1800–1865), the major figure in Italian Jewry of the nineteenth century, is best known as scholar, thinker, vital human center of Judaic studies in Padua, editor of Judah ha-Levi, significant in-gatherer of medieval Hebrew poetry. Essentially traditional, even Mosaic if you like, rather than Maimonidean—but too complex to be quickly characterized—Shadal was also a man of broad poetic culture and at home in his emancipating century, even to the point of sloganizing progress, in wishful images: "Religious hate is done, forever forgotten . . . / An age of freedom, liberty, and learning . . . peace in the land."

It is the spirit of Shadal that fostered and that animates the last chapter in the history of Hebrew poetry in Italy and the Hebrew sonnet. The protagonist is Vittorio Castiglioni (1840–1911), born in Trieste in 1840, and teacher there until he became chief rabbi of Rome in 1903. He was a disciple of Shadal, and the Triestine poet, Rachel Morpurgo (1790–1871) was both cousin and protégée of Shadal. And it is Castiglioni who prefaces Morpurgo's verse volume *Ugav Raḥel* (Rachel's Lute) in 1890. Geography has its weight in Italian—and Hebrew Italian—writing. Castiglioni's and Morpurgo's volumes are hardly major. But they serve as mirrors, lenses. Also, end points can be as significant and, in the case of these two poets, I

Fig. 175. Solomon Alexander Hart, *The Feast of the Rejoicing of the Law at the Synagogue in Leghorn, Italy,* 1850, The Jewish Museum, New York (cat. no. 252)

should say, as moving as beginnings—and surely more synoptic. If with the emancipation, Italian Jewry acquired more daily ease, it was also often given to more indistinct and complacent modes. But there is a solidity in Castiglioni and Morpurgo: one touches sentiments beyond post-Risorgimento rhetoric. Yes, among Castiglioni's 126 sonnets in his *Nizmei Zahav* (Golden Rings, 1906), there is one for Victor Emmanuel III's visit to the new Roman synagogue, but there are also sonnets to Metastasio, Shadal (three), for Rashi's eight hundredth *jahrzeit,* on the defeat of Russia in its war with Japan, and on the death of Herzl. Beyond these, the gamut of the occasional verse is a synoptic run through the themes of occasional verse in close to a millennium. And there is even a glimpse into the hallucinarium with the nominal acrostic of Niccolò Tommaseo (fourteen letters) beginning each line of the sonnet to him.

Morpurgo has more arduous excursions into the hallucinarium, with two squared-off eight-words-by-eight-words-poems; eight columns of the same baseline eight words, identical in order on the top horizontal axis and the first right-hand vertical axis, then, in shifting order in the remaining seven horizontal axes and, as a result, in the seven vertical axes—making poetic sense, however, in all permutations, and with internal rhyme pairings in the baseline. All this, with four children and no steady maidservants, as we learn from the biographical preface of Castiglioni. Castiglioni is sensitive, too, in the prefatory essay on the role of women in Israel, a defense against those who judge "without knowledge and without justice, enemies and persecutors of the laws and practices of Israel." And, with less apologetic fervor, and still-useful analytics, Castiglioni adds, to that essay on women and the biography of Morpurgo, a rather comprehensive essay on Hebrew prosody in Italy. Sum these with Morpurgo's own poem on those who doubt the understanding and poetic skill of women and her charming early (1816) reply to a sonnet by Shadal that queried her unmarried state, her "disdaining every fine young man"—a reply that, mirroring identically Shadal's rhyme words, tells him that she found the right man, but her parents objected to him, to which her response can only be, "Then I'll never marry—not even the Messiah." (That tale does have a happy end: she finally married the man she wanted, Jacob Morpurgo.) That same sonnet starts off with a quatrain that depends on a *Zohar* text, which in that context is an index of the long, domesticated connubium between Italy and varied forms of kabbalah. (Ramḥal was a casualty not so much of kabbalah as of its Shabbatean extension-deformation.)

The Triestine end of the "communal" Hebrew-Jewish line in Castiglioni gives way, in Italian, to Umberto Saba (fig. 177) of Trieste (1883–1957). In the generation after Pascoli and D'Annunzio, after the canonical duo, Ungaretti and Montale, stands Saba—and remember that in Italy the elect code of literature is still poetry rather than prose. Saba was son of a father (Ugo Eduardo Poli) who converted to Judaism (taking the name Abramo) in order to marry Saba's mother, Felicità Rachele Coen, from the family line of Shadal. Abramo—a convert, but restless—soon abandoned his family. It is Saba who—after so many generations of communal poetry in Hebrew—gives us, in Italian, an I-with-a-vengeance.

Saba's elder by about a score of years was Italo Svevo (1861–1928); and his junior by four years was the early suicide, Carlo Michelstaedter (1887–1910). The voices of those three protagonists of the Triestine enclave—the poet, the novelist, the philosopher—are much alive today, but Svevo and Michelstaedter speak things different to different exegetes. Which may be as it should be.[52]

Fig. 176. (above) Carlo Levi, *Ritratto di Alberto Moravia* (Portrait of Alberto Moravia), 1932, Fondazione Carlo Levi, Rome (cat. no. 325)

Fig. 177. (below) Vittorio Bolaffio, *Il poeta Umberto Saba* (The Poet Umberto Saba), c. 1924, R.A.I., Radiotelevisione Italiana, Sede Regionale, Friuli-Venezia Giulia, Trieste (cat. no. 286)

Notes

In the following notes, where the reference is listed as Schirmann without title, that means: J. H. Schirmann, *Anthology of Hebrew Poems in Italy* (in Hebrew), (Berlin, 1934), the basic and still-invaluable anthology. Fleischer without further title means: E. Fleischer, *Hebrew Liturgical Poetry in the Middle Ages* (in Hebrew) (Jerusalem, 1975), with matters Italian concentrated on in pt. 3, pp. 423–484. Pagis without further title means: D. Pagis, *Change and Tradition in the Secular Poetry* (in Hebrew) (Jerusalem, 1976); the third part, pp. 245–355, is devoted to Italy.

1. See the essay by David B. Ruderman above.
2. The quote from Schirmann is on pp. 256–257 of the English version of his essay cited in note 21 below.
3. See note 1 above.
4. For southern Italian texts, see B. Klar's edition of the *Megillat Aḥimaaz* (Jerusalem, 1946), with a new edition in 1973; one seliḥah of Aḥimaaz himself published later by Klar in his *Language Studies and Topics in Poetry and Literature* (in Hebrew) (Tel Aviv, 1954); of course, Schirmann; Abraham ben Isaac of Bari's Aramaic reshut, with Schirmann's translation into Hebrew, in *Leshoneynu*, 21 (1957): 212–219, "An Aramaic *Piyyut* by an Early Italian" (in Hebrew); Y. David's edition of Amittai's poems (Jerusalem, 1975), of Zebadiah (Jerusalem, 1972), and of Elijah ben Shemaiah (Jerusalem, 1977); and Silano of Venosa in Klar's *Aḥimaaz*, pp. 67–70. For further figures, see Schirmann's essay.
5. Schirmann, p. 55.
6. Fleischer, p. 445. For the acrostic aspects of the hallucinarium, see first, A. M. Haberman, *A History of Hebrew Liturgical and Secular Poetry in the Middle Ages* (in Hebrew) (Ramat Gan, 1970), pp. 253–258; then see Fleischer, pp. 85–88, and throughout the book. Finally, follow carefully Fleischer's prosodic and acrostic details in the headnotes to the twenty-nine poems in his edition of Solomon ha-Bavli (in Hebrew) (Jerusalem, 1973).
7. This *Josipphon* kinah also has no acrostic. It is the only poem before 1707 in Schirmann's anthology to lack all three: meter, rhyme, acrostic.
8. See note 1 above.
9. Schirmann, pp. 15–16.
10. Ibid., pp. 5–8.
11. Fleischer, pp. 428–429.
12. Schirmann, pp. 429–435.
13. Ibid., p. 164.
14. D. Jarden, ed., *The Cantos of Immanuel of Rome* (in Hebrew), 2 vols. (Jerusalem, 1957), vol. 2, pp. 455–459.
15. Schirmann, p. 274.
16. Ibid., pp. 292–294.
17. Ibid., pp. 389–390.
18. Ibid., pp. 399–400.
19. Ibid., pp. 217–222. For the modes of Hebrew rhyme, see B. Hrushovski, "Prosody, Hebrew," *Encyclopedia Judaica*, vol. 13 (1971), pp. 1195–1240.
20. P. Valéry, *The Art of Poetry*, tr. D. Folliot (New York, 1958), p. 179.
21. Schirmann's critique is in his "The Beginning of Hebrew Poetry in Italy and Northern Europe, 1: Italy," in *World History of the Jewish People—The Dark Ages*, ed. C. Roth (Tel Aviv, 1966), pp. 249–266; a fuller version with more quotations and up-to-date bibliography is in Hebrew in idem, *Studies in the History of Hebrew Poetry and Drama*, vol. 2 (Jerusalem, 1979), pp. 9–30. The poem of ben Shemaiah is in Schirmann, pp. 46–47.
22. Valéry, *Art of Poetry*, pp. 284–285.
23. Fleischer, p. 476.
24. Schirmann, "The Beginning."
25. E. Fleischer, ed., *The Piyyutim of Solomon ha-Bavli* (in Hebrew) (Jerusalem, 1973).
26. See note 1 above for Nathan and for the Anav-im [Anau] family.
27. Fleischer, pp. 445–446.
28. For a notably lucid state-of-the-art comment on Judeo-Italian at large, see G. Sermoneta, "Considerazioni frammentarie sul giudeo-italiano," *Italia* 1, no. 1 (1976): 1–29, and its sequel in *Italia* 1, no. 2 (1978): 62–106, and L. Cuomo, "In margine al giudeo-italiano: note fonetiche morfologiche e lessicali," *Italia* 1, no. 1 (1976): 30–53.
29. For Cassuto, see his "Un' antichissima elegia in dialetto giudeo-italiano," in *Silloge linguistica dedicata alla memoria di G. I. Ascoli nel primo centenario della nascita* (Turin, 1929), pp. 349–408; and for Artom's discovery, his "Un' antica poesia italiana di autore ebreo" in *Rivista Israelitica* 10 (1913–1915), p. 90ff. For a more recent edition of the elegy, see G. Contini, ed., *Poeti del duecento*, 2 vols. (Milan, 1960), with Contini's preface and the poem in vol. 1, pp. 35–42, and note in vol. 2, pp. 796–797; but still useful is G. Lazzeri, *Antologia dei primi secoli della letteratura italiana* (Milan, 1940), then (Milan, 1954), where the elegy is on pp. 177–193.
30. The critical edition of Immanuel is D. Jarden, ed., *The Cantos of Immanuel of Rome* (in Hebrew), 2 vols. (Jerusalem, 1957).
31. Ibid., vol. 1, p. 40.
32. See ibid., pp. 18–19.
33. Immanuel is indebted to Judah Al-Ḥarizi, who a century before had first translated the great Arabic *makamist* Al-Ḥariri, and then fashioned his own Hebrew makama masterwork, the *Taḥkemoni*. For the fundamental differences between them, see Pagis, pp. 260–263.
34. Immanuel Frances, in *Metak Sefatayim* (Gracious Speech), his treatise on rhetoric and *ars poetica*, proposes

a name for the sonnet drawn from a place name in Lev. 1:1—*Di-zahav,* where not only *z-h-v* add up to 14, but *d-i,* too, does.

35. Jarden, *Cantos,* vol. 1, pp. 174–177: *Maḥberot* 10, ll. 163–224. It was Cassuto who tracked Immanuel's source (see note 29 above).
36. Jarden, *Cantos,* vol. 1, p. 37.
37. Here and elsewhere in this scanning, the translations from Hebrew are mine—and *at times* indebted to two out of the three sheaves I did for *Commentary* in 1951.
38. Jarden, *Cantos,* vol. 2, pp. 559–569.
39. *Selected Poems of Yankev Glatshteyn,* trans. R. Fein (Philadelphia, 1987), pp. 85–87.
40. Moses da Rieti, *Sefer Mikdash Me'at,* ed. J. Goldenthal (Vienna, 1851), p. 106.
41. Pagis, p. 251.
42. T. Carmi, ed., *Penguin Book of Hebrew Verse* (New York, 1981), pp. 434–435.
43. For Zacuto's kabbalism and his "moderation," see G. S. Scholem, *Sabbati Sevi* (Princeton, 1973) (revised and augmented translation of the original Hebrew [Tel Aviv, 1957]), esp. pp. 501–503, 768–770.
44. G. Tamani, "Parafrasi e componenti poetici in volgare e in caratteri ebraici di Mordekhay Dato," in *Italia Judaica: Atti del I convegno internazionale* (Rome, 1986), pp. 233–242.
45. For Zarfati (who died in 1527), see Schirmann, pp. 223–235. For Jacob Frances (born in Mantua in 1615 and died in Florence in 1667), see the *Complete Poems of Jacob Frances* (in Hebrew), ed. P. Naveh (Jerusalem, 1969). For Immanuel Frances, (born in Livorno in 1618, he died in Livorno after 1710), see *The Divan of Immanuel Frances* (in Hebrew), ed. S. Bernstein (Tel Aviv, 1932). For data on Dato, see ibid., and for Leone Modena (1571–1648) see *The Divan of Leon Modena* (in Hebrew), ed. S. Bernstein (Philadelphia, 1932). For Zacuto's incomplete *Yesod Olam* (The Foundation of the World), see A. Berliner's edition (Berlin, 1874) and S. Sierra's essay (in Italian) in *Italia Judaica,* pp. 278–293. For the play attributed by Schirmann to Judah Sommo (1527–1592), see *The First Hebrew Play, Ẓaḥut Bedḥuta de-Kiddushin,* ed. J. Schirmann (Jerusalem and Tel Aviv, 1965), which Schirmann calls "a heavy and difficult title," which is meant to mean "a marriage comedy." Schirmann's study of the play first appeared in 1946 and is now in his *Studies in the History of Hebrew Poetry and Drama,* 2 vols. (Jerusalem, 1979), pp. 115–138. (For the loss of so many of Sommo's works in the Turin library fire, see pp. 117–118.) To this haversack note, one should now add Pagis's study, "Baroque Trends in Hebrew Poetry," in *Italia Judaica,* pp. 263–277, dealing with a minor but obviously popular subgenre, which "appeared around 1645 in Italy (probably Venice) and shortly afterwards in Spanish-Jewish circles in Amsterdam": riddles involving an "enigmatic picture and . . . a long and intricate Hebrew poem." Finally, A. Rathaus has dealt more fully than Schirmann, *Anthology,* pp. 342–346, would have led us to expect, with Yehoshua Josef Levi (birth and death dates unknown), a Venetian of the late seventeenth and early eighteenth century; see Rathaus, "The Philosophical Poetry of Joshua Joseph Levi," (in Hebrew) *Italia* 4, no. 1 (1985): 7–26 (in the Hebrew-numbered portion of that journal).
46. Schirmann, *Studies,* vol. 2, pp. 232–233.
47. Ibid., p. 139, the opening of a chapter on the plays, which concludes on p. 175.
48. Cited by A. M. Haberman, in *Topics in Poetry and Piyyut of the Middle Ages* (in Hebrew) (Jerusalem, 1972), at the beginning of his essay, "A New Poem by Moses Ḥayyim Luzzatto," pp. 222–225.
49. For Luzzatto's texts, see *The Poems of Moses Ḥayyim Luzzatto* (in Hebrew), ed. S. Ginzburg, with his headnotes and comments, completed and prefaced by B. Klar (Jerusalem, 1948), and *The Plays of Moses Hayyim Luzzatto* (in Hebrew), ed. S. Ginzburg (Tel Aviv, 1927). Schirmann's essay on the plays is especially rich (see note 47 above); and Klar's preface is very useful on the issue of kabbalistic spillover. The three plays are the early Samson play, *Maaseh Shimshon* (The Doings of Samson), *Migdal Oz* (The Tower of Strength), and *Layesharim Tehillah* (Praise to the Just).
50. Romanelli (1757–1814) joins the line of wanderers that runs from Immanuel down: born in Mantua, he lived in Berlin, Vienna, London, and died in Casale Monferrato in 1814. One way station, Morocco, occasioned his rather well-known account of that stretch in *Masa Be-Arav* ("Travels in Morocco" will do). Romanelli touches base at vital places of the Enlightenment, feels Napoléonism deeply, and is an interesting nomad in the framework of social history. As poet and verse dramatist, he can be read today in Schirmann's edition of Romanelli's *Selected Writings* (in Hebrew) (Jerusalem, 1968). But the truly enticing piece of writing is Schirmann's biography of Romanelli in *Studies,* vol. 2, pp. 239–293. For Ephraim Luzzatto's work, see *Ayleh Bnai Ha-Neurim* (Youthful Work), ed. J. Fichman (Tel Aviv, 1942), and Schirmann's essay in *Studies,* vol. 2, pp. 217–238.
51. For Shadal, see *Kinor Naim* (The Pleasing Lyre) (Warsaw, 1913).
52. My own choice for wisest exegete of Svevo is N. Lebowitz, in her *Italo Svevo* (New Brunswick, N.J., 1978). For an especially lucid reading of Michelstaedter's *La persuasione e la rettoricha* (Persuasion and Rhetoric), T. Harrison's forthcoming essay in *Modern Language Notes* is worth waiting for.

Fig. 186. *Reader's Desk Cover,* Italy, 1685–1686, The Jewish Museum, New York (cat. no. 151)

The Ancient Period

WORKS IN STONE

1. **Cast of the Arch of Titus**

Original: Rome, 81 C.E.

Plaster

81½ × 123 × 30 in. (207 × 312.4 × 76.2 cm)

New York, The Metropolitan Museum of Art

2. **Capital with Menorah**

Porto or Rome, fourth century C.E.

Stone, carved

7⅛ × 9¼ × 9¹⁄₁₆ in. (18 × 23.5 × 23 cm)

Vatican City, Monumenti, Musei e Gallerie Pontifici (30893)

This capital, as well as others discovered with it, was found in the ruins of a hostelry in Porto, the ancient Portus Traiani, eleven miles from Rome. The hostelry was built around 398 and fell into disuse some three to four hundred years later. For some researchers these finds together with the tombstones in a local Porto collection testified to the existence of a Jewish community there.[1] Harry J. Leon, however, suggested that the capitals and the inscriptions were Roman material that was later taken to Porto.[2]

A crudely engraved menorah appears on each face of this example, suggesting some ceremonial usage, perhaps to support a canopy over a grave.[3]

VBM

Bibliography: Goodenough, *Jewish Symbols,* vol. 2, pp. 51–52; vol. 3, fig. 793.

1. Frey, *Corpus Inscriptionum Iudaicarum,* pp. 396–407; Goodenough, *Jewish Symbols,* vol. 2, p. 51ff.
2. H. J. Leon, "The Jewish Community of Ancient Porto," *Harvard Theological Review* 45 (1952): 165–175.
3. Goodenough, *Jewish Symbols,* vol. 2, p. 52.

3. **Capital**

Rome or Porto, fourth century C.E.

Stone, carved

11¹³⁄₁₆ × 12¾ × 13⅜ in. (30 × 32.5 × 34 cm)

Vatican City, Monumenti, Musei e Gallerie Pontifici (30896)

For discussion and bibliography, see cat. no. 2.

4. **Capital**

Rome or Porto, fourth century C.E.

Stone, carved

6½ × 8⅞ × 8⅝ in. (16.5 × 22.5 × 22 cm)

Vatican City, Monumenti, Musei e Gallerie Pontifici (30899)

For discussion and bibliography, see cat. no. 2.

5. **Capital**

Rome or Porto, fourth century C.E.

Stone, carved

11¾ × 12³⁄₁₆ × 12³⁄₁₆ in. (30 × 31 × 31 cm)

Vatican City, Monumenti, Musei e Gallerie Pontifici (30894)

For discussion and bibliography, see cat. no. 2.

6. **Burial Plaque**

Rome, Vigna Randanini Catacomb, second to third century

Marble, incised

11⁵⁄₁₆ × 11¹⁵⁄₁₆ × 1 in. (28.2 × 28.8 × 2.5 cm)

New York, The Jewish Museum, Gift of Dr. Harry G. Friedman (F 4715)

The Latin inscription on this stone reads: *AVRELIA. PROTOGE/NIA.AVR[ELIAE].QVINTILLE/ MATRI KARISSIM[A]E/QV[A]E.VIXIT ANNIS. LX/M[ENSIBUS]V.B[ENE].M[ERENTI].POSVIT* (Aurelia Protogenia set up [this stone] to Aur[elia] Quintilla, her dearest mother, who lived sixty years, five m[onths], in grateful memory).

Although the symbol depicted at left, an *etrog,* or citron, emblematic of the feast of Tabernacles, is often found on works of Jewish art of the Roman period, the symbol at the right is ambiguous, combining features of the pomegranate with those of the *lulav,* or palm frond.

VBM

Bibliography: R. Garrucci, *Dissertazioni archeologiche di vario argomento* (Rome, 1865), no. 5; H. Vogelstein and P. Reiger, *Geschichte der Juden in Rom* (Leipzig, 1896), no. 148; E. Diehl, *Inscriptiones Latinae Christianae Veteres II* (Berlin, 1927), no. 4964; J.-B. Frey, *Corpus of Jewish Inscriptions* (Rome, 1936; reprint, New York, 1975), no. 217; Goodenough, *Jewish Symbols,* vol. 3, fig. 777; H. J. Leon, *The Jews of Ancient Rome* (Philadelphia, 1960), no. 217; Jewish Museum, *Israel in Antiquity,* exh. cat., by A. S. Ackerman and S. L. Braunstein (New York, 1982), no. 129.

7. **Burial Plaque**

Rome, Vigna Randanini Catacomb, second to third century

Marble, incised

7¼ × 12³⁄₁₆ in. (18.5 × 31 cm)

New York, Collection of Gloria Abrams

The Greek inscription reads: **CΑΛΠΙΝΓΙ ΟΥC ΝΗΠΙ ΟΥC** (Salpingius, a child). Flanking it are two ram's horns (*shofrot*) and two vine leaves. Both the Midrash and Saint Gregory the Great refer to Salpingius as a Jewish name.[1]

VBM

Bibliography: R. Garrucci, *Dissertazioni archeologiche di vario argomento,* p. 172; H. Vogelstein and P. Reiger, *Geschichte der Juden in Rom* (Berlin, 1895–1896), p. 472, n. 99; E. Diehl, *Inscriptiones Latinae Christianae Veteres II* (Berlin, 1927), p. 502, no. 4961; J.-B. Frey, *Corpus of Jewish Inscriptions* (Rome, 1936; reprint, New York, 1975), no. 162; H. J. Leon, *The Jews of Ancient Rome,* p. 289, no. 162, fig. 55.

1. Frey, *Corpus of Jewish Inscriptions,* no. 162.

8. **Inscription of Mindis Faustos** (fig. 61)

Ostia, second to third century C.E.

Marble, incised

14⅛ × 21⅜ × 1 to 1⅜ in. (36 × 54.3 × 2.5 to 3.5 cm)

Ostia, Soprintendenza Archeologica (Magazzino epigrafico inv. no. 8978)

This inscription written in both Latin and Greek reads (in translation): "For the well-being of the emperor! Mindis Faustos established and built [the synagogue] with his own funds and set up the Ark (*keiboton*) of the Sacred Law."[1] Mindis Faustos's inscription, which dates to the late second or early third century, is important for the dating of the earlier phases of the synagogue building, prior to the remodeling in the fourth century. It is uncertain, however, whether Mindis Faustos was the original donor, since there is an obvious break in the stone just above the penultimate line in which the name appears and the last line is written in different characters than the remainder of the inscription.[2]

The inscription is also significant in indicating the presence of a fixed ark prior to the later remodeling.[3] Not all early synagogues had this feature; the synagogue at Dura Europos, which is contemporaneous with this earlier building phase at Ostia, also had an ark that was part of the building structure.

VBM

Selected Bibliography: M. F. Squarciapino, "The Synagogue at Ostia," *Archaeology* 16 (1963): 203; idem, "Plotius Fortunatus Archisynagogus," *Rassegna mensile di Israel* 36 (1970): 184–185; G. Foerster, "A Survey of Ancient Diaspora Synagogues," in *Ancient Synagogues Revealed,* ed. L. Levine (Jerusalem and Detroit, 1982), p. 170.

1. I want to thank Richard Brilliant for this translation and for that of cat. no. 19, the inscription of Plotius Fortunatus.
2. M. F. Squarciapino, "Plotius Fortunatus Archisynagogus," p. 185.
3. Ibid.

9. **Inscription of Plotius Fortunatus** (fig. 179)

Ostia, second to third century

Marble, incised

8⅞ × 17⅛ × 1³⁄₁₆–1½ in. (22.5 × 43.7 × 3.5 to 4 cm)

Ostia, Soprintendenza Archeologica (Maggazzino epigrafico Ostia inv. no. 11694)

The inscription reads: *Plotio Fortunato/archisyn. fec. Plotius/Ampliatus Secundinus/ Secunda. P.T. N. et Ofilia Basilia co[n]iugi. B. M.* (Plotius Ampliatus, Plotius Secundinus, and Secunda, his children, and Ofilia Basilia, his wife, have done [this in honor of] Plotius Fortunatus, archisynagogus).

This stone was found in 1969 in the course of excavations in the southern part of Ostia. It is significant in establishing the existence of the office of the archisynagogus in that city.[1] The holder of that title was the most important official of Jewish community, the spiritual leader who ordered the services.[2] He was also responsible for the construction and maintenance of synagogue buildings and represented the Jewish community before the government and people of Rome.

VBM

Bibliography: M. F. Squarciapino, "Plotius Fortunatus Archisynagogus," *Rassegna mensile di Israel* 36 (1970): 183–191.

1. M. F. Squarciapino, "Plotius Fortunatus Archisynagogus," p. 188.
2. On the office, see Leon, *Jews of Ancient Rome,* p. 171ff.

10. **Architrave from the Torah Ark of the Ostia Synagogue** (fig. 56)

Ostia, third century(?)

Marble, carved and painted

12⅝ × 18⅞ × 72⅜ in. (32 × 48 × 184 cm)

Ostia, Soprintendenza Archeologica, Scavi di Ostia (inv. no. 1883)

This architrave is one of a pair that rested on the columns of an aedicula housing the Torah ark of the Ostia synagogue.

The short side of each architrave is decorated in low relief with Jewish symbols of the messianic age which are also found at other Jewish sites of the period: the menorah, shofar, *etrog* and *lulav*; there are traces of paint on the menorah.

MFS

Selected Bibliography: M. F. Squarciapino, "La Sinagoga di Ostia," *Bolletino d'arte,* 4th ser., 40 (1961): 329–330; idem, "The Synagogue at Ostia," *Archaeology* 16 (1963): 197; G. Foerster, "A Survey of Ancient Diaspora Synagogues," in *Ancient Synagogues Revealed,* ed. L. I. Levine (Jerusalem and Detroit, 1982), p. 170.

11. **Lid of a Child's Sarcophagus**

Rome (Monteverde catacomb), third century C.E.

Marble, carved

14 × 30 in. (35.6 × 76.2 cm)

Vatican City, Monumenti, Musei e Gallerie Pontificie (30776)

A child is shown reclining on the lid, a bunch of grapes in his left hand. Other grapes are depicted at his head and feet, pecked at by birds. With his right hand the child caresses a dog. This lid was found in the rubble

Fig. 179. *Inscription of Plotius Fortunatos,* Ostia, second to third century, C.E., Soprintendenza Archeologia, Ostia (cat. no. 9)

of the Monteverde catacomb when it was excavated in the nineteenth century; the head was severed from the body.

Scholarly debate has centered on whether the lid was made to be placed in the Monteverde catacomb, which was used by Jews, or whether it represents an intrusion from another burial site. If an intrusion, then the lid depicts a child at a symposium, without any significance for Jewish iconography. Erwin R. Goodenough held that the lid represented a stock figure posed to "symbolize the happiness of heaven in terms of what was originally the Dionysiac eschatological banquet, one which was carried over . . . into both Judaism and Christianity to represent immortality."[1] Thus, for Goodenough the lid is yet another example of the Jewish appropriation of originally pagan symbolism.

VBM

Selected Bibliography: E. Munkacsi, *Romai Naplo* (Budapest, [1930]), ill. facing p. 20; Frey, *Corpus Inscriptionum Iudaicarum,* pp. cxxv–cxxvi; Goodenough, *Jewish Symbols,* vol. 2, pp. 11–13; vol. 3, fig. 736; Leon, *Jews of Ancient Rome,* pp. 210–211.

1. Goodenough, *Jewish Symbols,* vol. 2, p. 11. For the opposite view, that the sarcophagus lid is an intrusion, see Frey, *Corpus Inscriptionum Iudaicarum,* vol. 1, pp. cxxv–cxxvi.

12. **Burial Plaque** (fig. 53)

Rome (Monteverde catacomb), third century C.E.

Marble slab; corroded on the right side and broken on the lower corner of the same side

$11\frac{13}{16} \times 9\frac{1}{16} \times \frac{3}{4}$ in. (30 × 23 × 2 cm); letters: $\frac{9}{16} \times \frac{3}{4}$ in. (1.4 × 2 cm)

Rome, Museo Nazionale Romano (epigraphic storeroom, I, II, 6; inv. no. 77645)

Ἐνθάδε κῖτε Ἱλαρὸς,
ἄρχων ἀπὸ συναγωγ-
ῆς Βολυμνησίων,
ζήσας ἔτη λε'· Ἐν (ε)ἰ-
ρήνῃ ἡ κοίμησις
αὐτοῦ· Μνία ⟨α⟩ὐτοῦ.[1]

(Here lies Hilaros, Archon to the Volumnesian community, who lived thirty-five years. May he rest in peace; [praised be] his memory!).

The text commemorating the archon wishes for him a serene repose and exalts his memory with the formula μνία αὐτοῦ (εἰς εὐλογίαν). Hilaros was a common name in Rome.[2] The Volumnesian community he served[3] is mentioned four times in the commemorative slabs of the Monteverde catacomb.[4] It is probable that the community was located in Trastevere and took its name from a personage whom many scholars are inclined to identify with a certain Volumnius, procurator of Syria during the Augustan age, who was concerned with Jewish affairs during the late years of the first century B.C.E.[5]

The paleography of the inscription, rather careless in certain respects, presents a particular type of *H*.[6] This letter, the overall quality of the inscription, and the chronology of the catacomb's use support a date around the third century C.E.

The guidelines for the writing are clearly visible on the surface of the slab. The following symbols also appear: A Torah ark, *lulav*, shofar, matzot, and a flask.[7]

CR

Bibliography: Frey, *Corpus Inscriptionum Iudaicarum*, no. 343.

1. The word μνεὶα usually written μνία appears in various combinations: in two cases (Frey, *Corpus Inscriptionum Iudaicarum* nos. 148, 343) the word is followed by a genitive and nothing else, intended perhaps as εἰς εὐλογίαν (Leon, *Jews of Ancient Rome*, p. 126).
2. This was an extremely common name in Rome, particularly in Latin (see J. Kajanto, *The Latin Cognomina*, [Helsinki, 1965], pp. 11, 13, 29, 67–69, 96, 134, 260). There are innumerable examples in pagan inscriptions (see *Corpus Inscriptionum Latinarum*, vol. 4, *Indices*); nine examples in *Inscriptiones Christianae Urbis Romae VII saec. antiquiores*, n.s., vol. 1, nos. 695, 3439; vol. 4, nos. 10650; 12473; vol. 5, no. 14336; vol. 7, nos. 19806–19807, 20571 bis, 20577. It is less frequent in Greek: five examples in *Incriptiones Graecae Urbis Romae*, nos. 435, 448, 610, 667, 919; there is one example in Frey, *Corpus Inscriptionum Iudaicarum*, no. 342 (in addition to the present example).
3. For Archon, see entry for cat. no. 13.
4. Frey, *Corpus Inscriptionum Iudaicarum*, nos. 345, 402, 417, 523.
5. Ibid., pp. LXXII–LXXIII; Leon, *Jews of Ancient Rome*, pp. 157–159.
6. Analogous examples (dated between the second and third centuries) are noted and presented with photographs in N. Müller and N. A. Bees, *Die Inschriften der jüdischen Katakombe am Monteverde zu Rom* (Leipzig, 1919), pp. 11–12, nos. 3, 6, 87, 121, 129.
7. For these symbols, among the most common in Jewish iconography, see Goodenough, *Jewish Symbols*, in general and, in particular, volume 12 for a summary and volume 13 for the figurative apparatus. Also see Leon, *Jews of Ancient Rome*, pp. 198–201. At the back of his collection, Frey lists the overall number of examples (*Corpus Inscriptionum Iudaicarum*, p. 663). When the slab was found, the objects formed by two concentric circles recalling unleavened bread were interpreted as simple small plates.

13. **Burial Plaque**

Rome (Monteverde catacomb), third century C.E.

Marble, carved, cut off along the lower left corner and along the right edge

8¼ × 1415/16 × 1 3/16 in. (21 × 38 × 3 cm)

Rome, Museo Nazionale Romano (epigraphic storeroom, I, 2, 6; inv. no. 77643)

This plaque was found in 1919 during the quarrying of tufa stone in the Monteverde catacomb.[1] It reads:

'Εν͡κθάδε κεῖθαιν
Πομπώνις ὁ δὶς
ἄρχων τῆς συνα=
γωγῆς καλκαρήσις; ἔ
ζησεν ἐτῶν ξ', ἐν ἰρ=
ήνη κύμη=
σις αὐτοῦ

(Here lies Pomponius, twice Archon of the Calcarense community. He lived sixty years. May his sleep be peaceful).

The presence of the menorah is noteworthy. It is represented often on Jewish inscriptions from Rome. Indeed, in a total of 534 texts it appears some 144 times, usually alone. Through the variants that we know, we can guess that its form was inspired by the candelabra used in the synagogues of the diaspora rather than by the one in the Temple of Jerusalem. Endowed with both decorative and religious value as a symbol of Judaism, the menorah must also have possessed a higher symbolic significance, but it is difficult to establish precisely what that was.[2]

The inscription is a rather meager one and serves to recall a Πομπώνις (Pomponius).[3] The συναγωγῆ καλκαρήσις, stating that he was twice archon,[4] opens up numerous problems. First of all, the origin of his name is uncertain. Some scholars think that it is derived from a professional corporation formed by Jews working with lime;[5] others think that it is a topographical designation.[6] By analogy, if one considers the names of other Roman synagogues (*Suberensis, Campensis*), this latter hypothesis would seem more convincing. But at this point another problem arises, that is, the area of the city where this community lived. In general, every community tended to bury its own dead in the nearest catacomb. Consequently, since *s. Calcarensis* appears in six Roman-Jewish inscriptions, all coming from the Monteverde cemetery,[7] it is likely that this community was nearby, even if we cannot be sure exactly where.[8] Finally, we still need to clarify the relationship between *s. Calcarensis* in Rome and a community using the same name, documented in an inscription from Porto.[9]

The archaeological context and the paleography support a date around the third century C.E.

MLC

Bibliography: Frey, *Corpus Inscriptionum Iudaicarum,* no. 384.

1. R. Paribeni, in *Notizie degli scavi di antichità* (1919): 60ff.
2. Goodenough, *Jewish Symbols,* vol. 12, pp. 79–83; Leon, *Jews of Ancient Rome,* pp. 196–198.
3. Πομπώνις, an extremely frequent variant for Πομπώνιος, is a Greek transliteration of a widely used Latin *nomen,* both masculine and feminine, in pagan and Christian inscriptions in Rome: Jory-Moore, *Index Vocabulorum,* XVI, pp. 4643–4647; Moretti, *Inscriptiones Graecae Urbis Romae,* 4 cases; *Inscriptiones Christianae Urbis Romae VIII saec. antiquiores,* 22 cases. Also see Leon, *Jews of Ancient Rome,* p. 84.
4. For Archon, see entry for cat. no. 12.
5. G. La Piana, in *Harvard Theological Review* 20 (1927): 357, compares a *corpus naviculorum Iudaeorum,* attested to in the third century C.E. Yet he is forced to admit that such a corporation never assumed the form of συναγωγή. See also S. Collon, in *Mélanges d'archéologie et d'histoire de l'Ecole Française de Rome* 57 (1940): 77ff., joins the professional solution with a topographical one, since the place of habitation and the work place of some workers often coincided.
6. Leon, *Jews of Ancient Rome,* pp. 142–144; Frey, *Corpus Inscriptionum Iudaicarum,* pp. lxxv–lxxvi.
7. In addition to the inscription under discussion, see Frey, *Corpus Inscriptionum Iudaicarum,* nos. 304, 316, 433, 504, 537. Of these, the first three certainly come from the Monteverde cemetery; the fourth, urban in origin, probably has the same provenance; the fifth, found in Porto, could possibly also have the same origin.
8. None of the solutions proposed thus far is convincing, however. Collon, in *Mélanges,* pp. 77ff., thought the answer lay in the region northeast of the city, near Porta Collina, based on the site where *Corpus Inscriptionum Latinarum,* vol. 6, nos. 9223, 9224, was found, mentioning a "schola Calcarensium"; Frey, *Corpus Inscriptionum Iudaicarum,* p. lxxvi, thought of the area near the Circus Flaminius, which was called Calceria as early as the mid-eleventh century C.E.; J. Derenbourg, in *Mélanges Renier* (1887): 440, on the basis of *Corpus Inscriptionum Iudaicarum,* no. 537, where the inscription καρκαρησιων is found, thought of the area around the *carcer* of the Circus Maximus.
9. Three hypotheses can be formulated regarding the Porto text (Frey, *Corpus Inscriptionum Iudaicarum,* no. 537): (1) There was just one community, in Rome, and the dead buried in Porto had come from there; (2) there were two distinct and independent communities; (3) there were two distinct but dependent communities. I find the third hypothesis most probable and would reject the other two: the first because it seems difficult to believe that an individual in an urban community, who died a few kilometers from Rome, would not be buried in Rome in the cemetery of his own community; the second because it seems absurd that there would be two nearby centers like Rome and Porto with two independent communities with the same name. See J.-B. Frey, in *Rivista di archeologia cristiana* 8 (1931): 86ff. On Porto, see G. Sacco, *Iscrizioni greche d'Italia* (Rome, 1984), p. 101; H. J. Leon, in *Transactions of the American Philological Association* (1953): 67, 84.

14. **Sarcophagus Cover of Faustina, with Theatrical Masks and Funerary Inscription** (fig. 3)

Rome (area around the Via Appia, outside Porta S. Sebastiano), second half of the third century C.E.

Marble; fragment broken on two sides and in back; chips in the upper ends of the acroteria

5 15/16 × 35 × 2 3/8 in. (15.1 × 89 × 6 cm)

Rome, Museo Nazionale Romano (inv. no. 67613; formerly in the Museo Kircheriano)

This fragment is from the front section of a sarcophagus cover that must have belonged to a lenōs sarcophagus because of the curve at the left. At right is a rectangular tablet bordered by a small, smooth cornice filled with the funerary inscription of a deceased Jew. Flanking the tablet are two acroteria covered with female theatrical masks; both have pierced mouths and eyes. The mask on the right has simplified curly hair, and a conical two-tiered hat. The one at left has fat curls. Toward the left end of the cover is a similar acroterium with another female comedy mask that has curly hair. A drill was used sparingly in the hair of the masks, in particular, in the acroterium on the right.

The use of double sloping covers with acroteria, of which this fragment forms one part, is based on east Greek models from the second and early third centuries C.E. In Roman urban context this form seems to have been used above all in the last third of the third century. The acroteria are generally decorated with leonine heads and palm motifs as well as the motif of the theatrical mask seen on this example; these are also well documented as corner acroteria for Roman city sarcophagus covers until the fourth century.[1]

One should also keep in mind that Dionysian masks appear on another sarcophagus fragment found in a Jewish catacomb of Rome.[2] Certain scholars (Schultze, Frey, Vogelstein) have suggested that the fragment comes from the tomb of an actress, based on the presence of the theatrical masks, but this is completely conjectural, as Leon has already pointed out. Indeed the theatrical masks, linked in origin with the Dionysiac world and consequently a symbol of hope in immortality,[3] constitute a motif that was so widespread in the figurative repertory of Roman urban funerary art that they could be considered stereotypical elements.[4]

On the basis of the typological and stylistic characters, it seems that the fragment can be assigned to the second half of the third century C.E.

MS

The inscription is in Greek[5] and Hebrew.

ἐνθάδε κεῖ-
ται Φαυστῖνα
שלום

Here lies Faustina.[6] *In peace.*

The deceased's Jewish identity is expressed by the unequivocal symbols painted beneath the inscription—the shofar, the menorah, and the *lulav*—and by the proclamation of peace in Hebrew.

MB

Bibliography: *Corpus Inscriptionum Graecarum,* vol. 4 (Berlin, 1859), no. 9920; Frey, *Corpus Inscriptionum Iudaicarum,* vol. 1, no. 283; H. J. Leon, in *Hebrew Union College Annual* 5 (1928): 301ff., 306; M. Simon, in *Bibliothèque des Écoles Françaises d'Athènes et de Rome* 166 (1948), p. 73; Leon, *Jews of Ancient Rome,* pp. 217ff., 234, n. 1, 306, fig. 46.

Bibliography: F. Ficoroni, *Le maschere sceniche e le figure comiche d'antichi romani* (Rome, 1735), p. 209ff; idem, *Dissertatio de larvis scenicis et figuris comicis antiquorum Romanorum* (Rome, 1750), p. 99, pl. LXXI; idem, *Gemmae antiquae litteratae aliaeque rariores* (Rome, 1758), p. 70; E. Herzog, in *Bollettino dell'Istituto di Corrispondenza archeologica* (1861): 99; R. Garrucci, *Cimitero degli antichi ebrei scoperto recentimente in Vigna Randanini* (Rome, 1862), p. 63; idem, in *Dissertazioni archeologiche di vario argomento,* vol. 2 (Rome, 1865), p. 155ff; idem, *Storia dell'arte cristiana nei primi otto secoli della chiesa,* vol. 6 (Prato, 1880), p. 166, pl. 491, fig. 17; V. Schultze, *Archäologische Studien über altchristliche Monumente* (Vienna 1880), p. 271, no. 21; idem, *Die Katakomben* (Leipzig, 1882), pp. 182, 248; A. Berliner, *Geschichte der Juden in Rom,* vol. 1 (Frankfurt am Main, 1893), p. 78, no. 45; H. Vogelstein and P. Rieger, *Geschichte der Juden in Rom,* vol. 1 (Berlin, 1896), p. 52ff., nn. 9, 61, 63, 463, p. 60, n. 33; N. Müller, *Die jüdische Katacombe am Monteverde zu Rom* (Leipzig, 1912), p. 99, no. 6; N. Müller, in *Dissertazioni della Pontificia Accademia Romana di Archeologia,* 2, no. 12 (1915): 284, no. 3; J. Juster, *Les juifs dans l'empire romain,* vol. 2 (Paris, 1914), pp. 223, 309, n. 3, 317, n. 10; R. Paribeni, in *Nuovo Bollettino di Archeologia Cristiana* 12 (1915): 95; H. Leclercq, *Dictionnaire d'archéologie chrétienne,* vol. 8, pt. 1 (Paris, 1928), col. 780s, no. 21, vol. 10, pt. 2 (Paris, 1932), col. 2649, fig. 7809; J.-B. Frey, in *Biblica* 15 (1934): 289; H. Vogelstein, *History of the Jews in Rome* (Philadelphia, 1940), p. 43; A. Ferrua, in *Epigraphica* 3 (1941): 35; F. Cumont, *Recherches sur le symbolisme funéraire des romains* (Paris, 1942), app. 2, p. 494, n. 1; Goodenough, *Jewish Symbols,* vol. 2, p. 25, vol. 3, fig. 787, vol. 12, p. 35; B. Kanael, *Die Kunst der antiken Synagogue* (Munich and Frankfurt am Main, 1961), p. 70, fig. 56; A. Milano, *Storia degli ebrei in Italia* (Turin, 1963), fig. 6; M. Simon, *Verus Israel* (Paris, 1964), p. 73; H.-A.-R. L. Geller, *Roma Ebraica: Jewish Rome* (Rome, 1983), p. 154, pl. 28–29; A. Konikoff, *Sarcophagi from the Jewish Catacombs of Ancient Rome: A catalogue raisonné* (Stuttgart, 1986), p. 46ff., no. 15, pl. 12.

1. See T. Brennecke, *Kopf und Maske: Untersuchungen zu den Akroteren an Sarkophagdeckeln* (Berlin, 1970), p. 171ff. For the analogous use of theatrical masks as end points for double sloping covers, see, for example, a cover in the Pretestato Museum (M. Guetschow, "Das Museum der Praetextat-Katakombe," *Atti della Pontificia Accademia Romana di Archeologia, Memorie* 4 [1938]: 141ff., pl. XXIII, 2). See also a fragment in the Louvre (F. Baratte, *Catalogue des sarcophages en pierre d'époques romaine et paléochrétienne: Musée du Louvre* [Paris, 1985], p. 232, n. 141), as well as another one in the Museo Nazionale Romano (M. E. Micheli, "Le Sculture," in *Museo Nazionale Romano,* vol. 1, pt. 2 [Rome, 1981], wing II, n. 13).
2. H. W. Beyer and H. Lietzmann, *Jüdische Denkmäler,* vol. 1, *Die jüdische Katacombe der Villa Torlonia in Rom* (Berlin and Leipzig, 1930), p. 32, pl. 23a.
3. See Cumont, *Recherches sur le symbolisme,* p. 162.
4. For general information on the motif, see A. K. H. Simon, *Comicae Tabellae* (Ensdetten, 1938); G. Krien, in *Maske und Kothurn* 1 (1955): 79ff.; T. B. L. Webster, in *Bulletin of the Institute of Classical Studies,* suppl. 24 (1969).
5. For a discussion of the frequent use of Greek in inscriptions in Jewish circles in Rome, and for the percentual distribution in the major catacomb complexes of the city, see C. Vismara, in *Dialoghi di archeologia,* 3d ser., 5, no. 1 (1987): 119, with bibliography.
6. For the notable circulation of Latin names in the Roman Jewish community, which essentially used the Greek language, see H. Solin, in *Aufstieg und Niedergang der Römischen Welt,* vol. 29, pt. 2 (Berlin and New York, 1983), pp. 655–666; see also Vismara, p. 119ff., with bibliography; for this name in particular, see Frey, *Corpus Inscriptionum Iudaicarum,* vol. 1, pp. 617, 621; and J. Kajanto, *The Latin Cognomina,* 36, 2 (Helsinki, 1965), p. 272.

Fig. 178. Cover of Sarcophagus of Artemidora, with Putti's Games and Inscribed Tablet, Rome, courtyard of the Palazzo Randanini, last quarter of the third century, C.E., Kircheriano Museum, Rome (cat. no. 15)

15. **Cover of Sarcophagus of Artemidora, with Putti's Games and an Inscribed Tablet** (fig. 178)

Rome (courtyard of the Palazzo Randanini), last quarter of the third century C.E.

Fine grained marble, carved; made up of two fragments (the right forearm of the penultimate putto on the right is broken); some chipping along the borders; surface worn away in many points; traces of red color within the letters

10¼ × 42½ in. (26 × 108 cm)

Rome, Museo Nazionale Romano (inv. no. 67612; formerly in the Museo Kircheriano)

The cover, of which the upper portion remains, belongs to a child's sarcophagus and is decorated with putti playing children's games. A narrow *tabula* set within a simple frame at center contains a Greek funerary inscription. In the panel at the left are three putti: the first putto, next to the tabula, is winged and moves a stick and wheel to the right, turning his head to the left, toward the other putti, who are wingless. One of these approaches the first putto, offering him an object in his extended right hand; the other, at the extreme left, stands frontally watching the other two with his chin in his left hand and his right hand lowered to hold another wheel which overlaps the side border of the panel. In the panel at the right stand four frontal putti, all winged, two of whom have a short mantle hanging from their shoulders. The first putto to the right uses his left hand to roll a small wheel, pierced from the center down by an inclined plane formed by two beams placed at an angle to each other. The other three putti watch him. The first putto to the left holds another small wheel in his right hand and a branch (probably a palm) in his left hand; the second putto participates in the game, lifting his right arm upward and his left arm to his face. The third putto stretches out his right arm and holds another small wheel to his chest with his left hand, while three other wheels rest on the ground.

The relief is not very high. The bodies are powerful but well proportioned; the faces almost swollen, with roundish cheeks; flat, broad noses; large, oblong eyes with heavy eyelids; and eyebrows rendered as grooves. A drill was used for small holes in the eyes, noses, mouths, umbilici, and genitals; it was also used abundantly for the putti's puffy, curly masses of hair. Only the putto at the center on the left has longer locks, marked by short furrows of the drill.

This composition conforms to the practice (rather frequent, at least after the mid second century C.E.) of decorating sarcophagi with infantile figures, more or less clearly identifiable by their wings as putti, involved in play.[1] Representations of the games of the circus and palestra are very common in Roman sepulchral art, where the presence of children is used metaphorically, but there are also examples of children's games represented in a realistic fashion.[2] This lid confirms that the image of the winged spirit, the putto, which could refer both to the erotic realm and to the soul of the deceased, could be interchangeable at a conceptual level with the realistic representation of the deceased child. There are several examples of analogous compositions.[3]

Thematic and stylistic elements support a dating in the last quarter of the third century C.E., when the funerary repertory, used indiscriminately by pagan and Christian patrons or, as in this case, by Jews, was drawing upon new, expressive stylistic modes, as well as upon subjects from everyday life, employed in symbolic fashion.[4] In this context the comparison indicated by Gerke is particularly telling. He mentions the sarcophagus of S. Callisto with a lion hunt, to which one could add the already cited sarcophagus in the Museo Nazionale Romano, which is particularly close to this example in the treatment of the puttis' anatomy and especially in the rendering of the faces and hair.

MS

ἐνθάδε
κοιμᾶται
Αρτεμιδώ–
ρα ἐν εἰρήνῃ

(Here lies Artemidora. In peace.)

The funerary dedication to Artemidora, a baby girl, was initially thought to be Christian and later hypothesized as Jewish,[5] and as such was inserted by Lifshitz in his introductory remarks to Frey's *Corpus Inscriptionum Iudaicarum.*[6] It should be noted, however, as Leon has already mentioned, that the initial formula of this text is quite rare among catacomb inscriptions. The verb κοιμῶμαι occurs only four times,[7] and I would add that, unlike the example here, it appears in a secondary position with respect to the text, never linked to the adverb ἐνθάδε. Furthermore, the formula ἐν εἰρήνῃ, widely diffused among Christian inscriptions, is present only occasionally in Jewish inscriptions, and the name Artemidora doesn't appear at all in the collection of names of Jews in Rome. It does appear to have had a certain currency, especially in its masculine form, in pagan circles, however; it also appears once, in Greek, in a Christian text.[8]

MB

Bibliography: G. A. Guattani, *Monumenti antichi inediti ovvero sulle antichità e belle arti di Roma per l'anno 1786* (Rome, 1786), p. 40, pl. 3; A. Kirchhoff, *Corpus Inscriptionum Graecarum,* vol. 4 (Berolini, 1856), p. 564, no. 9805; L. Becq De Fouquières, *Les jeux des anciens, leur description, leur origine, leur rapports avec la religion, l'histoire, les arts et les moeurs* (Paris, 1869), p. 123; R. Garrucci, *Storia dell'arte cristiana nei primi otto secoli della Chiesa,* vol. 5 (Prato, 1879), app., p. 151, pl. 401, 8; V. Schultze, *Archäologische Studien über altchristliche Monumente* (Vienna, 1880), p. 260ff., no. 6; idem, *Die Katakomben* (Leipzig, 1882), p. 182; R. Grousset, *Etude sur l'histoire des sarcophages chrétiens* (Paris, 1885), p. 52, no. 12 bis; *Inscriptiones Christianae Urbis Romae septimo saeculo antiquiores,* vol. 1 (Rome, 1922), p. 262, no. 2048; F. J. Dölger, *Die Fischdenkmäler in der frühchristlichen Plastik, Malerei und Kleinkunst* (Munster, 1927), vol. 4, pl. 257, 1; H. Leclerq, *Dictionnaire d'archéologie chrétienne,* vol. 7, sec. 2 (Paris, 1927), col. 2525ff., fig. 6255; vol. 8, sec. 1 (Paris, 1928), col. 779, n. 6; R. Paribeni, *Le Terme di Diocleziano e il Museo Nazionale Romano* (Rome, 1932), p. 332, no. 1213; F. Gerke, *Die christlichen Sarkophage der vorkonstantinischen Zeit* (Berlin, 1940), pp. 21, n. 5; 47, n. 5; 54, n. 1; 59, n. 1; 69, n. 5; 98, nn. 1, 2; 103, n. 1; 111, n. 4; 127, n. 15; 208, n. 2; 209, n. 4; 360, BI, I 5, pl. 40, 3; Leon, *Jews of Ancient Rome,* p. 344ff., no. 733c; F. W. Deichmann et al., *Repertorium der christlich-antiken Sarkophage,* vol. 1, *Rom und Ostia* (Wiesbaden, 1967), p. 314, no. 766, pl. 121; H. Sichtermann, in *Deutsches Archäologisches Institut Mitteilungen Römische Abteilung* 76 (1969): 293, pl. 94, 1; B. Lifshitz, Prolegomenon to reprint of Frey, *Corpus Inscriptionum Iudaicarum,* vol. 1 (New York, 1975), p. 42, no. 733c; *Museo Nazionale Romano: Le Sculture,* vol. 1 (Rome, 1979), p. 328; G. Koch and H. Sichtermann, *Handbuch der Archäologie,* vol. 3, *Römische Sarkophage* (Munich, 1982), p. 212, nn. 58, 62; A. Konikoff, *Sarcophagi from the Jewish Catacombs of Ancient Rome: A Catalogue Raisonné* (Stuttgart, 1986), p. 49ff., III, 16, pl. 13.

1. For this particular motif, see F. Matz, *Röm. Meisterwerk* (1958), p. 45ff.; K. Schauenburg, in *Antike Welt* 7 (1976): 30ff.; Koch and Sichtermann, *Römische Sarkophage,* p. 206ff.
2. For infantile games in the Greek and Roman world, see C. Daremberg and E. Saglio, *Dictionnaire des antiquités grecques et romaines,* vol. 3, sec. 2 (Paris, 1904), p. 1356ff.; Spiele: Hug; H. Van Hoorn, *De vita atque cultu puerorum monumentis antiquis explanatis* (Amsterdam, 1909).
3. Compare a cover in the Chiaramonti Museum with putti playing with wheels to the left of the tablet and youths with tunics to the right (Dölger, *Die Fischdenkmäler,* pl. 256, 1). See also the cover of a sarcophagus (nonurban) in Bellocq, P. Kranz, *Jahreszeitn-Sarkophage: Entwicklung und Ikonographie des Motivs der vier Jahreszeiten auf Kaiserzeitlichen Sarkophagen und Sarkophagdeckeln* (Berlin, 1984), p. 284, n. 577, pl. 120, 1. For comparisons with the left-hand scene, see the other sarcophagus covers in the Museo Nazionale Romano (*Museo Nazionale Romano: Le Sculture,* vol. 1, no. 193). See others from S. Cecilia (neg. DAI 1938.125), from Isola Sacra (neg. DAI 69.1091), from Cesano (neg. DAI 70. 1041; this one also depicts a putto holding a palm branch). For comparisons with the right-hand scene, see a sarcophagus in the Vatican Museum (neg. DAI 1942, 107).
4. See F. Gerke, in *Forschungen und Fortschritte* 13, no. 2 (1937): 17ff.
5. Leon, *Jews of Ancient Rome,* p. 218.
6. Lifshitz, Prolegomenon to reprint of Frey, *Corpus Inscriptionum Iudaicarum,* p. 42, no. 733c.
7. Frey, *Corpus Inscriptionum Iudaicarum,* nos. 150, 281, 365, 390.
8. See H. Solin, *Die griechischen Personennamen in Rom* (Berlin and New York, 1982) (*Corpus Inscriptionum Latinarum, Auctarium*), pp. 27, 29. For similarities to other names rather widely circulated in the Jewish world, see Leon, *Jews of Ancient Rome,* p. 390.

V.B.

16. **Sarcophagus Front with Victories with Shields, Seasons, and a Menorah** (fig. 72)

Rome, end of the third century C.E.

Fine-grained marble, broken along the two short sides; chipped lower listel; coffered sarcophagus, from which the central and right half of the front has been preserved; the front portion is framed by a smooth, protruding listel that decorates the upper and lower borders

27⅛ × 49⅝ × ¼ in. (69 × 126 × .06 cm)

Rome, Museo Nazionale Romano (inv. no. 67611; room III; formerly in the Museo Kircheriano)

At the center of the relief is a shield held by two winged Victories with their bodies frontal, their faces in profile. Each Victory is shown in contrapposto pose, with one leg covered by a chiton, while the other rests behind, covered by thick folds of a long gown. The arms are extended, and the hands support the shield in a relaxed manner. The broad faces with incised eyes; flattened noses; and small, swollen lips are framed by coiffures in a Hellenistic style: puffy, with long locks and one tuft of hair arranged above the head and another on the shoulders. The bodies are heavy and not well proportioned; the drapery of the gowns is rendered with rigid furrows, made with a drill. Facial features are poorly defined, and the rendering of the hair indicates an excessive use of the drill. The only elements carved in a refined manner are the wings, with their finely drawn upper elements. On the shield is the representation of a menorah whose curved arms are formed of small spheres and are topped by oil lamps placed as mirror images of each other. The body of the menorah rests directly upon a tripod base. A smooth, protruding fillet with angular profile serves as the border of the shield.

Below the shield is a carved *lenōs* (a basin with rounded ends) with two leonine heads within which three small satyrs are crushing grapes; the central one is depicted from the back, the other two frontally. Their slender bodies are gracefully rendered, their eyes are rendered with a drill, and their short, curly hair with a drill point. Near the *lenōs* is a wicker basket overflowing with bunches of grapes, some of which have fallen to the ground.[1]

At the side of the right-hand Victory is a naked genius representing a season with a cloak buttoned over his right shoulder, covering his entire back, standing in contrapposto pose, holding a wicker basket full of fruits with his right arm, and with his left, two geese. His face, characterized by a broad jaw, full lips, large and elongated eyes, and slightly flattened nose, is framed by a hairdo of short ringlets that form a puff below the ears and are rendered with deep drill furrows. Next to him another Season was depicted, but only fragmentary traces remain: the lower part of the right leg, the right hand holding a hare by the paws, an edge of the cloak. Two putti play at the feet of the Victory and Seasons; one holds a hare while the other rides astride a dog. They have slender, crudely rendered bodies and short hair made with deep drillings. The missing left half must have contained carvings of the other two Seasons, following a well-defined and serial figurative plan, present on numerous other sarcophagi.[2]

The theme of Victories holding shields dates back to honorific monuments and was repeated in the funerary art of the imperial age.[3] On numerous monuments putti take the place of Victories with shields, but in the case of official art, the "borrowed iconography" remains intact, as can be seen in a relief from the Hadrianic era, where two putti support a shield with a painted commemorative inscription.[4] The subject goes back to the heroizing of the deceased, represented in Greek art with the erection of a trophy by a *nike* (Victory), a theme adopted by the Romans.[5] The motif originally alludes to personal apotheosis, manifested in official art by the *clipeus virtutis* (the shield of the victorious) but in its derivative form loses its celebratory functional significance, assuming a purely ornamental value.[6] But the insertion of a portrait in the shield gives the theme eschatological significance,[7] with allusions to a private apotheosis to another realm of being, while earlier its accepted meaning was secular, having to do with the commemoration of the virtues and accomplishments of the deceased.[8] The group of standing Victories with shields, perhaps of eastern origin,[9] is documented in an honorific monument from the time of Sulla, where two Victories standing in a heraldic position are arranged along the sides of a shield embellished with a laurel festoon.[10] The motif of the shield held by Victories appears on oil lamps during the early imperial age,[11] then on coins,[12] and finally on funerary monuments. It is only in the late second century C.E. that the shield, which supports the passage of the deceased to the other world,[13] begins to contain a portrait; this phenomenon probably stems from a desire to commemorate the appearance of the deceased.[14] There are many different opinions as to the origins of the shield portrait image (*imago clipeata*), but many maintain that it is Greek.[15]

The iconography of the four *Horai,* or seasonal spirits, with their attributes, dates to the Hellenistic period, when the year was divided into four parts; earlier representations included three figures at most. In the Hellenistic era the garments and the attributes became specific to each Season who bears characteristic fruits.[16] In Roman times, beginning in the second century C.E., the Horai become male personages depicted as putti, and later, beginning in the third century, they resemble young men. One of the first monuments with seasonal putti is an altar dating from the Hadrianic period, now dismantled, but formerly in the Gardens of Sallust in Rome. The representation of the Seasons became a preferred motif for sarcophagus decoration and mosaics in the late imperial age, although the Seasons appear on funerary monuments as early as the first century C.E.

The four Seasons have a rich and complex symbolism, bearing witness both to the beauty of life on earth and to the generosity of nature, as well as to the various ages of man and his transitory condition.[17] The Seasons depicted on Christian sarcophagi allude to the dogma of the Resurrection.[18] The area beneath is usually reserved for motifs that evoke the survival or blessed rebirth of the deceased.[19] Cumont maintained that in both examples the allusion to Dionysian mysteries is obvious; the seasonal spirits on this sarcophagus might also refer to the mystery cults of Attis and of Mithra.[20]

Around the second to third century C.E. a Jewish figurative art began to take shape. The use of pagan motifs became common, and their theological meaning was preserved without falling into purely decorative applications.[21] The vine motif, taken from the Dionysian cult, passed to the monotheistic religions without losing its symbolic significance, connected to astral immortality; the vine became a widely diffused motif in both Jewish and Christian art.[22]

This sarcophagus comes from a pagan workshop. It was purchased by a Jew whose religious sensibilities were not offended by the figurative carvings. Cumont's research loses its incisiveness only when the author maintains that the purchaser was a Jew disposed to pagan theology; yet the conclusions of this learned scholar are still plausible because there is little evidence of Jewish monuments displaying human and animal images. The exceptional mosaic floor decorations of the Hammath-Tiberias synagogue, dated to the fourth century C.E., make up for that lack[23] with their representation of Helios in a chariot, the twelve zodiac signs, and the four Seasons. Thus it is not necessary to think of a "Judeo-pagan" sarcophagus, but rather of a sarcophagus from the pagan repertory, used by a Jew. The motif of the Seasons is a recurrent one and does not point to a specific commission, intended either as a reference to the resurrection or to Dionysian influence.[24] Thus Cumont's and Goodenough's thesis seems doubtful, that is, that there is symbolic significance to the decoration as a whole, with the juice of the vine becoming the drink of immortality, and the cycle of the Seasons connected to the passage from death to life or to resurrection. This interpretation is possible, but not certain, in already existing pagan art and is also probable for Jewish art. It isn't necessary to posit religious syncretism to justify these representations, for they become allegorical.[25] Simon's statements clarify how the Jews, who moved away from traditional prohibitions against the use of imagery and wanted to translate into images the idea of victory of life over death and the principle of anthropomorphism, had to resort to a common iconographic repertory.[26]

Attention should, however, be given to the observance of Mosaic law on the part of the Jew who purchased the sarcophagus; he requested that the shield be carved, not with his own portrait, but rather with an image peculiar to Judaism: the menorah.[27] The menorah is the symbol of the seven planets according to Philo[28] and Josephus.[29] The seven planets are the eyes of Jehovah (Zech. 4:1–13), and the candelabrum represented in funerary art reflects the celestial menorah and, placed near the ark, becomes a symbol of the light of the Law, which will be the salvation of the faithful.[30] One should also remember the fourth book of the Maccabees, which promises martyrs that they will be transformed into heavenly bodies.[31] The menorah carved into the shield bears witness to the fact that the deceased was a Jew and that he was recalled to eternal life in the celestial constellations.[32] The candelabrum is represented in 144 inscriptions found in the Roman catacombs, in Roman paintings in Venosa and Sulcis, on capitals in Porto, and on three other Roman sarcophagi.[33] A sarcophagus that was preserved in the garden of the Villa Torlonia, now lost, bore carvings of a candelabrum and other Judaic symbols.[34]

In conclusion, the sarcophagus from the Museo Nazionale Romano belongs to the large class of sarcophagi with Victories and Seasons.[35] It was purchased from an ordinary workshop by a Jew who commissioned the carving of the candelabrum.

The presence of drill work in the gowns and in the modeling of the bodies helps support a dating at the end of the third century C.E. The coiffure, rendered in small furrows, and the stereometric form of the skullcaps are typical elements of the Tetrarchic period.[36]

SAD

Bibliography: P. Kranz, *Die Antiken Sarkophagreliefs* V. 4, *Jahreszeitensarkophage. Entwiklung und Ikonographie des Matris des vier Jahreszeiten auf kaiserzeitliche Sarkophagen und Sarkophagdeckeln* (Berlin, 1984); A. Konikoff, *Sarcophagi from the Jewish Catacombs of Ancient Rome: A Catalogue Raisonné* (Stuttgart, 1986), pp. 43–46.

1. For more on the *lenōs* decorated with leonine heads, see V. Saladino, in *Atti a memorie dell'Accademia Toscana di Scienze e Lettere la Colombaria* 48, n.s., 34 (1983): 3ff., and bibliography cited there.
2. The sarcophagi in the Musée du Louvre, Paris (G. A. Hanfmann, *The Season Sarcophagus in Dumbarton Oaks,* vol. 2 [Cambridge, 1951], no. 468, fig. 44); in the Villa Doria Pamphili in Rome (ibid., no. 496, fig. 68), in Porto (ibid., no. 471, fig. 47), and the two examples from Cagliari (ibid., nos. 492a, 495, figs. 66, 67) illustrate the same sequence, with a central shield held by Victories and with the four Seasons.
3. T. Hoelscher, *Victoria Romana* (Mainz, 1967), p. 130ff., pl. 13.
4. G. A. Mansuelli, *Le sculture della Galleria degli Uffizi,* vol. 1, pt. 2 (Rome, 1958), p. 170ff., n. 149, fig. 146; Hoelscher, *Victoria Romana,* p. 117ff., pl. 15, 3. There are numerous contributions that attempt to define the chronological development of the motif of putti holding shields (see Hanfmann, *The Season Sarcophagus,* vol. 2, p. 12, n. 71; K. Schauenburg, "Ganymed und Hahnenkämpfe auf römischen Sarcophagen," *Archäologischer Anzeiger* [1972]: 501ff.; idem, "Die Sphinx unter dem Clipeus," *Archäologischer Anzeiger* (1975): 280ff.; H. Sichtermann, "Göttlicher Enthusiasmus Dionysisches und Apollinisches auf römischen Sarkophagen des 3. nachchristlichen Jahrhunderts," *Deutsches Archäologisches Institut Mitteilungen: Römische Abteilung* 86 [1979]: 362, n. 86; K. Schauenburg, in *Eikones Festschrift Hans Jucker* [Bern, 1980], p. 153ff.).
5. H. Brandenburg, "Meerwesensarkophage und Clipeusmotiv: Beiträge zur Interpretation römischer Sarkophreliefs," *Jahrbuch des Deutschen Archaeologischen Instituts* 82 (1967): 226.
6. Ibid., pp. 227, 232.
7. H. Jucker, *Das Bildnis im Blätterkelch,* Bibliothece Helvetice Romana, no. 3 (Alten-Lausanne and Freiburg, 1961), esp. p. 139.
8. F. Matz, "Stufen der Sepulkralsymbolik in der Kaiserzeit," *Archaeologischer Anzeiger* (1971): 103–104, 108ff.
9. F. Cumont, "Un fragment de sarcophage judeo-paien," *Revue Archéologique* 4 (1916): 4.
10. Hoelscher, *Victoria Romana,* pl. 12; W. Helbig, *Führer durch das öffentliche Sammlungen klassischer Altertümer,* 4th ed., vol. 2 (Tübingen, 1966), no. 1650.
11. Hoelscher, *Victoria Romana,* p. 130, pl. 13, fig. 3.
12. Ibid., p. 131.
13. J. Engemann, *Untersuchungen zur Sepulkralsymbolik der Spätrömischen Kaiserzeit* (Munster, 1975), p. 35ff.
14. R. Turcan, *Les sarcophages romain à représentations dionysiaques: Essai de chronologie et d'histoire religieuse* (Paris, 1966), pp. 94, 507.
15. J. Bolten, *Die Imago Clipeata: Ein Beitrag zur Porträt und Typengeschichte* (Paderborn, 1937), p. iiff.; R. Bianchi Bandinelli, *Roma: L'arte romana nel centro del potere* (Milan, 1976), p. 87ff.; for an up-to-date bibliography, see V. Galliazzo, *Sculture greche e romane del Museo Civico di Treviso* (Rome, 1982), p. 196ff., n. 71; G. Rosada, "Una stele romana con medaglione dai restauri di S. Donato a Murano," *Aquileia Nostra,* 51 (1980): 206ff., n. 56. The symbolism tied to the inclusion of the portrait in the shield is complex (Jucker, *Blätterkelch,* p. 139; Matz, "Stufen der Sepulkralsymbolik," pp. 104, 108ff.).
16. Athenaeus, 5, 198b. (For an English translation, see C. B. Gulick, *Athenaeus, The Deipnosophists* 2 [London, 1928], p. 396.)
17. F. Cumont, *Recherches sur le symbolisme funéraire des Romains* (Paris, 1942), p. 490ff.
18. Minitius Felix, 34; see F. Piper, *Mythologie der christliche Kunst,* vol. 2 (1851), p. 321, n. 4. The Barberini sarcophagus, now in the Musée du Louvre, Paris, depicts two putti with shields and four male Seasons, with the busts of two spouses in the shield and the area below it occupied by putti gathering grapes. In the Terme fragment the space beneath the shield is occupied by a scene of the crushing of the grapes (for the frequent use of this subject beneath the shield, see L. De Vita, in *Studi Miscellanei* 20 [1972]: 55; see also M. Bonanno, in *Prospettiva* 13 [1978]: 49, n. 25).
19. Turcan, *Les sarcophages,* p. 563.
20. Cumont, "Un fragment," p. 6.
21. See the important contribution of R. Turcan, "Les sarcophages romains et le problème du symbolisme funéraire," *Aufstieg und Niedergang der römischen Welt,* vol. 2, pt. 16 (Berlin and New York, 1978), pp. 1700–1735.
22. See the entry for *vigne* in *Dictionnaire d'archéologie chrétienne,* vol. 15, pt. 1, col. 3113ff.; Goodenough, *Jewish Symbols,* vol. 3, pp. 311–327.
23. L. I. Levine, ed., *Ancient Synagogues Revealed* (Jerusalem, 1981), pp. 63–69; M. Dothan, *Hammath Tiberias: Early Synagogues and the Hellenistic and Roman Remains* (Jerusalem, 1983).
24. Hanfmann, *The Season Sarcophagus,* vol. 1, p. 195; vol. 2, p. 88.
25. M. Simon, "Symboles soteriologiques chez les juifs de la Diaspora," in *La soteriologia dei culti orientali nell'impero romano: Atti del Colloquio Internazionale* (Leiden, 1982).
26. For more on this issue, see J.-B. Frey, "La question des images chez les juifs à la lumière des recentes découvertes," *Biblica* 15 (1934): 265–300; E. Urbach, "The Rabbinical Laws of Idolatry in the Second and Third Centuries in the Light of Archaeological and Historical Facts," in *Israel Exploration Journal Reader* (1981), pp. 162–195; M. Simon, "Symboles soteriologiques," p. 796; for the transformation of the nike into an angel in Christian, and perhaps Jewish, iconography, see Goodenough, *Jewish Symbols,* vol. 7, p. 143ff., with earlier bibliography.
27. E. Ehrlich, *Die Kultsymbolik im Alten Testament und im nachbiblischen Judentum* (Stuttgart, 1959), pp. 94–95, 128 ff.
28. *Quis rer. divin. her.* 221; *Vita Mosis* 2:102; esp. *Quaest.,* in Exod. 2:73ff.
29. *Antiquities of the Jews* 3.145; *Jewish War* 5.217; see the study of J. H. Charlesworth, "Jewish Interest in Astrology during the Hellenistic and Roman Period," in *Aufstieg und Niedergang der römischen Welt,* vol. 2, pt. 20 (Berlin and New York, 1987).
30. For a funerary interpretation of the menorah, see K. H. Rengstorf, "Zu den Fresken in der jüdischen Katakombe der Villa Torlonia," *Rom: Zeitschrift für die Neutestamentliche Wissenschaft* 31 (1932): 33–60; the theme is taken up again by Goodenough, *Jewish Symbols,* vol. 4, p. 78; also see Leon, *Jews of Ancient Rome,* p. 227.
31. A. Dupont-Sommer, *Le quatrième livre des Machabees* (Paris, 1939).
32. Simon, "Symboles soteriologiques," p. 795. Wirgin makes a puzzling comparison, grouping the figure of the menorah carved into the shield with the birth of Venus on the Ludovisi throne, because both are symbols of eternal life (W. Wirgin, "The Menorah as Symbol of After-Life," *Israel Exploration Journal Reader* [1981]: 965–968; see also idem, "The Menorah as Symbol of Judaism," ibid., pp. 961–964; for the menorah in general, see L. Yarden, *The Tree of Light: A Study of the Menorah* [London, 1971]).
33. The material has been classified by Goodenough, *Jewish Symbols,* vol. 2.

34. In *Notizie degli scavi di antichità* (1920): 155, fig. 2.
35. For critical discussion, see Hanfmann, *The Season Sarcophagus;* and F. Matz, "Ein römisches Meisterwerk: Der Jahreszeitensarkophag Badminton-New York," *Jahrbuch des Deutschen Archaeologischen Instituts* 73 (1958).
36. The historical motivations of Micheli, who dates the sarcophagus to the first decade of the fourth century, are rather moving (M. E. Micheli, "Le sculture," in *Museo Nazionale Romano,* vol. 1, sec. 8, pt. 1 [Rome, 1985], pp. 151–153). He states that the representation of the shield finds justification "at a moment when declarations of religious faith different from that of the State would have corresponded to edicts of tolerance." All scholars of Jewish history agree that the repression of the Jews was marked by proclamations of tolerance (M. Simon, *Verus Israel: Etude sur les relations entre chrétiens et juifs dans l'empire romain 135–425,* Bibliothèque des Ecoles françaises d'Athenes et de Rome, no. 166 [Paris, 1964]; the title of the book by E. M. Smallwood, *From Pagan Protection to Christian Oppression* [1979], is laconic).

17. **Burial Plaque** (fig. 52)

Rome (Vigna Randanini catacomb), fourth century C.E.

Marble, engraved; broken along the lower left corner and corroded along the upper right edge

9⅝ × 18⁵⁄₁₆ × 2⅜ in. (24.5 × 46.5 × 6 cm)

Rome, Museo Nazionale Romano (epigraphic storeroom, I, II, 1; inv. no. 67679)

> 'Ενϑάδε κεῖται Τουβιας Βαρζααρω-
> να ϰαὶ Παρηιοριος υἱὸς Τουβια
> Βαρζααρωνα.
>
> *Hic est positus Tubias Barzaha-*
> *rona et Perecorius filius*
> *Tubiae Barzaharona.*
> (*duae* menorah[1]).
>
> שלם [כך!]

(Here lie Tobias Barzaharon and Paregorius, son of Tobias Barzaharon.)

The inscription, which memorializes two deceased, Tobias Barzaharon and his son Paregorius,[2] is interesting because of its three languages: Greek, the language most commonly spoken and consequently most commonly written by Jews in Rome; Latin, the official language, also rather widespread, although less common than Greek in Jewish inscriptions; Hebrew, by far the rarest language among Roman Jews, who used it almost exclusively for formal rituals and acclamations.[3]

The formula ἐνϑάδε κεῖται . . . , very common in Greek inscriptions, is correctly translated here with the corresponding Latin phrase, *hic est positus,* which is much rarer in Jewish epigraphy in Rome.[4]

The paleographic characters and the span of time when the catacomb remained in use support a date around the fourth century C.E.[5]

CR

Bibliography: Frey, *Corpus Inscriptionum Iudaicarum,* no. 497.

1. For the significance and breadth of use of the menorah, by far the most prevalent symbol in Jewish art and epigraphy, both ancient and more recent, see entry for cat. no. 13.
2. *Tubias Barzaharona* (and the corresponding Greek, which always appears in binomial form), clearly Semitic in origin, seems to be unique in the Roman epigraphic repertory. *Paregorius,* however (with variations in spelling and with the corresponding female form *Paragore/-ria*), appears relatively often in *Inscriptiones Christianae Urbis Romae septimo saeculo antiquiores,* n.s., vol. 2, no. 4205; vol. 3, nos. 8136, 9061; vol. 5, no. 14528; vol. 6, no. 15630; vol. 7, nos. 17541a(?), 18508, 19152–19153; and in *Corpus Inscriptionum Latinarum,* vol. 6 (four examples): nos. 13175, 13379, 15531, 29339. It is noteworthy that the present example is the only case in which this name, Greek in origin (Leon, *Jews of Ancient Rome,* p. 103), also appears written in this language.
3. For more about the alternate or integrated use of the three languages—Latin, Greek, and Hebrew—in Jewish inscriptions in Rome, see Leon, *Jews of Ancient Rome,* pp. 75–78, 240–241; I. Kajanto, in *Die Sprachen im Römischen Reich der Kaiserzeit* (Cologne and Bonn, 1980), esp. pp. 84–85, 92.
4. Frey mentions only two other examples in addition to our own (*Corpus Inscriptionum Iudaicarum,* nos. 228 [from Rome], 570 [from Venosa]).
5. H. Solin, *Die griechischen Personennamen in Rom* (Berlin and New York, 1982), p. 1248, without bearing in mind the dating of the catacomb, raises the limit to between the fourth and fifth centuries C.E.

18. **Burial Plaque**

Rome, Monteverde Catacomb, fourth century C.E.

Marble, slightly broken along the upper edge

16¹⁵⁄₁₆ × 9⁷⁄₁₆ × 1³⁄₁₆ in. (43 × 24 × 3 cm)

Rome, Museo Nazionale Romano (epigraphic storeroom, I, 2, 2; inv. no. 67699)

> ῏Ωδε κεῖ-
> τ⌜αι⌝ Σαλώ(μη),
> θυγάτηρ Γα-
> δία, πατρὸς
> συναγωγῆς
> ⌜Ε⌝βρ⌜αί⌝ων.ἐβί-
> ωσεν (ἔτη) μα'.
> ἐν εἰρήνῃ
> ἡ κοιμή-
> σ{ε}ις αὐτῆς.

(Here lies Salo, daughter of Gadias, father of the Synagogue of the Jews. She lived forty-one years. May her sleep be peaceful.)

This funerary inscription is in remembrance of a certain Σαλώ,[1] daughter of Γάδιας,[2] who has been identified with the homonymous personage mentioned on another plaque.[3] In this latter inscription, found in Porto, two other daughters of Γάδιας, Σάρρα and Κάρα, are mentioned, if the new reading of the text is precise.[4]

This Γάδιας (Gadias) is identified in the inscription under examination as πατὴρ συναγῆς(Ἁἰβρέων) (father of the Jewish synagogue). This is a highly honorific title conferred upon greatly esteemed personages, but it doesn't seem to imply any clear communal responsibility other than good deeds.[5] In Rome this title is mentioned in nine inscriptions, sometimes specifying the community where the individual was πατήρ,[6] sometimes with the generic indication of πατὴρ συναγωγῆς or συναγωγιῶν, given that he could also be *pater* of more than one community at a time.[7]

There has been much discussion on the origins of the name of this Jewish community in Rome. Some scholars think it was derived from the language spoken by the people, i.e., Hebrew, in which the rituals were probably carried out;[8] others think it came from the place of origin of the people in question.[9] But perhaps the explanation that makes the most sense is the one that links this name to the first Jews who lived in the territory of Rome, who could have adopted the name to distinguish themselves from other ethnic or religious communities.[10] This hypothesis could find confirmation in the fact that this community probably lived in Trastevere, the location of the first Roman-Jewish settlements,[11] if it is true that they buried their dead in the Monteverde catacomb,[12] from which the only four examples of σ. Ἑβραίων known to us have come.[13]

The archaeological context and paleography support a dating around the fourth century C.E.

MLC

Bibliography: A. Kirchhoff, *Corpus Inscriptionum Graecarum,* vol. 4 (Berlin, 1859), no. 9909; Frey, *Corpus Inscriptionum Iudaicarum,* no. 510.

1. This name, Semitic in origin, like many others that are particularly common in the Monteverde catacomb, was mistakenly completed as Σαλώ[μη] in *Corpus Inscriptionum Graecarum,* no. 9099. It seems that what we really have here is the abbreviated form, Σαλώ[μη]. Outside Jewish circles, but still in Rome, the name is mentioned in Moretti, *Inscriptiones Graecae Urbis Romae,* no. 1323; *Inscriptiones Christianae Urbis Romae VIII saec. antiquiores,* vol. 9, no. 25495. See also Leon, *Jews of Ancient Rome,* p. 110.
2. Γάδιας is also a name with Semitic origins: see Leon, *Jews of Ancient Rome,* p. 104. In the transliteration, *Gadius* is mentioned in *ICUR,* vol. 2, no. 4483.
3. Frey, *Corpus Inscriptionum Iudaicarum,* no. 535.
4. Frey, *Corpus Inscriptionum Iudaicarum,* no. 535, is a fragment of a marble slab (50 × 51 × 5.5 cm; letters 1.8 × 2.8 cm), now in the Vatican Museum (Lap. Ebraico ex Laberanense, inv. no. 30873). The text, engraved on a reused support, was made over two periods. Our discussion is concerned with the interpretation of the later text. This is the way J.-B. Frey interprets lines 4–6 in *Rivista di archeologia cristiana* 8 (1931): 86–88, then addressed again in *Corpus Inscriptionum Iudaicarum:* Γά / δια τοσκα / οα. H. J. Leon interprets the text as Γαδίατος. Κά / ρα in *Transactions of the American Philological Association* 84 (1953): 67–72, and in *Jews of Ancient Rome,* no. 535, followed by G. Sacco, *Iscrizioni greche d'Italia: Porto* (Rome, 1984), p. 110ff., n. 91.
5. Leon, *Jews of Ancient Rome,* p. 186; Frey, *Corpus Inscriptionum Iudaicarum,* pp. xcv–xcvi.
6. See Frey, *Corpus Inscriptionum Iudaicarum,* nos. 88 (π. σ. Καμπησίων, from the Via Appia), 494 (π. υ. Βερνάκλων), of unknown provenance; 509 (π. σ. Ἐλαίας), perhaps from the Monteverde catacomb; 510 (π. σ. Αἰβρέων), from the Monteverde catacomb; 535 (π. τῶν Ἑβρέων), from Porto; 537 (π. σ. τῶν Καρκαρησίων), from Porto.
7. See ibid., nos. 93 (π. σ.), from the Via Appia; 271 (π.), from the Via Appia; 508 (π. συναγωγίων), perhaps from the Monteverde catacomb.
8. For Hebrew, see E. Schürer, *Geschichte des jüdisches Volkes,* III, 1909, p. 83; N. Müller and N. A. Bees, *Die Inschriften der jüdischen Katakombe am Monteverde zu Rom* (Leipzig, 1919), p. 32, n. 14; for Aramaic, see A. Momigliano, "I nomi delle prime sinagoghe romane e la condizione giuridica delle comunità in Roma sotto Augusto," in *Rassegna Mensile di Israel* 6 (1931–1932): 290.
9. From Samaria; see J. Derenbourg, in *Mélanges Renier* (Paris, 1887), pp. 439ff.; from Giudea, see Frey, *Corpus Inscriptionum Iudaicarum,* pp. lxxvi–vii and H. Vogelstein and P. Rieger, *Geschichte der Juden in Rom,* vol. I (Berlin, 1896), no. 40; from Egypt, see A. Kirchoff, in *Corpus Inscriptionum Graecarum,* (Berlin, 1859), no. 9909.
10. Leon, *Jews of Ancient Rome,* p. 149; E. La Piana, in *Harvard Theological Review* 20 (1927): 356, n. 26.
11. E. La Piana, in *Harvard Theological Review* 20 (1927): 346; Leon, *Jews of Ancient Rome,* p. 136; S. Collon, in *Mélanges d'archéologie et d'histoire de l'Ecole Française de Rome* 57 (1940): 77ff.
12. For more on the issue of the location of Roman-Jewish communities, see entry for cat. no. 13.
13. See Frey, *Corpus Inscriptionum Iudaicarum,* nos. 291, 317, 510, 535 (the latter, found in Porto, perhaps comes from the Monteverde catacomb; for this problem, see entry for cat. no. 13.

19. **Burial Plaque**

Roman Empire, fourth to fifth century

Marble, incised

9½ × 11 × 1⅛ in. (24.1 × 28.2 × 2.9 cm)

New York, The Jewish Museum, Gift of Samuel Friedenberg (JM 3–50)

Most of the burial inscriptions uncovered from the Jewish catacombs of Rome and Venosa were written in Greek or Latin. A small number bear an additional

Hebrew word or phrase, in this case a defective spelling of *peace,* { Hebrew }. The main inscription in Latin reads *HIC POSITVS/ EST FLAES EBR/EVS* (Here lies Flaes the Jew). Above are three incised symbols of the Temple—a shofar, a menorah, and a *lulav* (a ram's horn, a seven-branched candelabrum, and a palm frond)—which signify belief in its restoration.

VBM

Bibliography: Goodenough, *Jewish Symbols,* vol. 3, no. 893; Jewish Museum, *Israel in Antiquity,* exh. cat., by Ackerman and Braunstein, no. 130; Kleeblatt and Mann, *Treasures,* pp. 26–27.

METALWORK

20. ***Judaea Capta* Coin: Emperor Vespasian**

Rome, 71 C.E.

Gold, 7.1 gm

New York, The Jewish Museum (X1983–88)

In order to commemorate their victories, the Romans struck coins such as the *Aegypto Capta, Germania Capta,* and *Dacia Capta.* The *Judaea Capta* coins, the most impressive and largest series, were struck in gold, silver, and bronze in Rome, at other European mints, and in Caesarea. The interest in so dramatically commemorating the Roman triumph in Judaea is significant. Jewish and Christian beliefs were rapidly spreading among the once-pagan upper classes in Rome. The victory in Jerusalem signified the triumph of paganism over monotheism and the superiority of the traditional Roman way of life.

The obverse of this coin features a portrait of the emperor Vespasian surrounded by his name and title in Latin. A mourning Jewess sitting beneath a trophy is depicted on the reverse.

GMG

Obverse: *IVDAEA* (Judaea)

Bibliography: Jewish Museum, *Coins Reveal,* exh. cat., by Y. Meshorer (New York, 1983), no. 70.

21. ***Judaea Capta* Coin: Emperor Titus**

Caesarea, 71–81 C.E.

Bronze, 12.5 gm

New York, The Jewish Museum, Gift of the Samuel and Daniel M. Friedenberg Collection (FBS 28)

On the obverse of this coin is a portrait of Titus surrounded by his name and title in Greek. The reverse of the coin features imagery commemorating the Roman victory in Jerusalem. A captive Jewess, her hands tied behind her back, is portrayed seated beneath a trophy, a celebratory monument made of armor. A shield, possibly representing the spoils of war, is placed to her side.

The *Judaea Capta* coins (see also cat. nos. 20, 22) minted at Caesarea use Greek text, since Latin was not generally known in the eastern Mediterranean.

GMG

Obverse: ΙΟΥΔΑΙΑΣ ΕΑΛΩΚVΙΑΣ (captured Judaea)

Bibliography: Jewish Museum, *Coins Reveal,* exh. cat., by Y. Meshorer (New York, 1983), no. 84.

22. ***Judaea Capta* Coin: Emperor Titus**

Rome, 79 C.E.

Bronze, 11.65 gm

New York, The Jewish Museum, Gift of the Samuel and Daniel M. Friedenberg Collection (FBS 39)

Titus, the son of Vespasian, was emperor of Rome from 79 to 81 C.E. Titus commanded the forces that besieged and captured Jerusalem, destroying the Second Temple in 70 C.E.

This coin (see also cat. no. 21) features a portrait of Titus surrounded by his name and title in Latin. On the reverse is a depiction of a mourning Jewess sitting beneath a palm tree, a symbol of Judaea, with a pile of weapons to the left.

GMG

Obverse: *IVDAEA CAPTA / SC* (captured Judaea / S[enatorial] D[ecree]

Bibliography: Jewish Museum, *Coins Reveal,* exh. cat., by Y. Meshorer (New York, 1983), no. 82.

23. **Seal of Theodora with Jewish Symbols** (fig. 76)

Rome, third to fifth century C.E.

Bronze, cast

Seal: 2$\frac{5}{16}$ × 1 in. (5.9 × 2.5 cm); ring: 1⅛ dm in. (2.9 cm)

Rome, Museo Nazionale Romano, Antiquarium (case 9; inv. no. 54350)

The rectangular seal is framed by a thin fillet. At the center, in a square field, is the representation of a menorah flanked by a *lulav* at right and a shofar at left. This in turn is surrounded by letters in relief, arranged in two rows, forming the woman's name *THEODORA*. In the back is a cast ring. The provenance of this piece is not known, but it was probably found in a Jewish catacomb, given that such objects were often used to mark the bottom of tombs.

A relevant comparison can be made with a seal from Sardinia.[1] Both seals have the same Jewish symbols: the menorah, the lulav, and the shofar, and both contain proper names that link them to a specific person. Comparisons can also be made to two similar seals published by Garrucci, the first with the word *oiec,* the second with the abbreviation *Cela,*[2] which Frey interpreted as the name *Celadus.*[3] A bronze stamp from Antioch in the Reifenberg collection bears the same three symbols.[4] Another seal in the British Museum, London, bears the name *Leontios* and depicts a bunch of grapes, a lulav, and the menorah.[5]

The symbols on these seals are found in a funerary context on tombstones in Palestine[6] and in the Jewish catacombs of Vigna Randanini in Rome.[7] They also appear on oil lamps, for example, a lamp from Syria whose handle is made up of a large menorah flanked by a palm branch and a shofar.[8]

As for the name *Theodora,* it appears on the seal in its Greek form, although it is written in Latin characters. The Greek form suggests an eastern background for the owner or Hellenized Jewish circles within the Roman community. The same name recurs twice in its Greek form on Roman sepulchral inscriptions:[9] a painted inscription from the Jewish catacomb on the Via Nomentana and a marble plate from the Jewish catacomb on the Via Appia.[10] In Rome the name appears perhaps once in its Latin form,[11] and on a gold glass in the British Museum where a family group is represented.[12] In its Greek form the name also appears on a wedding ring.[13]

LM

Bibliography: R. Paribeni, *Le Terme di Diocleziano e il Museo Nazionale Romano,* vol. 1 (Rome, 1928), p. 333, no. 1205; R. Paribeni, *Le Terme di Diocleziano e il Museo Nazionale Romano,* vol. 2 (Rome, 1932), no. 1233; E. Munkacsi, *Romai Naplo* (Budapest, [1930]), facing p. 16; A. Reifenberg, *Ancient Hebrew Arts* (New York, 1950), p. 145, no. 1; E. R. Goodenough, *Jewish Symbols,* vol. 2; *The Archaeological Evidence from the Diaspora,* vol. 2 (New York, 1953), p. 218, fig. 1015.

1. Bull, *Arch. Sardo, Anno VII* (November 1861), p. 91: R. Garrucci, "Sculture non cimiteriali," in *Storia dell'arte cristiana,* vol. 6 (Prato, 1880), p. 164, pl. 491.
2. Frey, *Corpus Inscriptionum Iudaicarum,* nos. 647, 648; Garrucci, "Sculture non cimiteriali," nos. 6, 7, pl. 491; Goodenough, *Jewish Symbols,* vol. 2, p. 217, figs. 1010, 1011.
3. Without any reliable evidence, Goodenough interprets this as the beginning of a magical formula. For him, the same view holds for a seal with the abbreviation *IANU,* which Frey interprets as Ianurius (Goodenough, *Jewish Symbols,* vol. 2, p. 217, fig. 1012).
4. Reifenberg, in *Palestine Exploration Quarterly* (1939): pl. 33, 2, p. 198; see p. 194, 2 and idem, *Ancient Hebrew Arts,* p. 142, no. 1.
5. Goodenough, *Jewish Symbols,* p. 218, fig. 1015; Reifenberg, in *Palestine Exploration Quarterly,* n. 3, idem, *Ancient Hebrew Arts,* p. 142, p. 2; O. M. Dalton, *Catalogue of Early Christian Antiquities* (1901), n. 487.
6. Goodenough, *Jewish Symbols,* vol. 1, p. 88, vol. 2, fig. 99.
7. Goodenough, *Jewish Symbols,* vol. 1, fig. 767, vol. 2, figs. 22, 768.
8. Reifenberg, *Ancient Hebrew Arts,* p. 147, no. 4. On architectural elements, see Goodenough, *Jewish Symbols* (for the capitals from the synagogue of Cafarnau, vol. 2, fig. 477; for those from the synagogue of Ascalona, vol. 2, figs. 575–576). For mosaics, such as those from the synagogue of Jericho, see ibid., vol. 2, fig. 666, vol. 1, p. 261.
9. Frey, *Corpus Inscriptionum Iudaicarum,* no. 30.
10. Frey, *Corpus Inscriptionum Iudaicarum,* p. 57, n. 83.
11. Ibid., no. 487.
12. O. M. Dalton, *Catalogue of Early Christian Antiquities and Objects from the Christian East* (London, 1901), p. 120, no. 609.
13. Ibid., p. 21, no. 127.

24. **Amulet** (fig. 26)

Near East, sixth to eighth century

Silver: engraved

1⅞ × 1½ in. (3.9 × 4.6 cm)

Rome, Museo Nazionale Romano (inv. no. 5366)

This fragmentary piece which was found in the Tiber, is engraved on both sides. On the recto is a Hebrew inscription* set within a field framed by two rude pilasters with molded bases that rest on a podium consisting of a series of bands of various motifs, one of which includes a further inscription. Since the lateral profiles of the amulet follow the curvature of the podium and the outlines of the pilasters, the plaque must have terminated in a triangular pediment, a logical crowning of the space defined by the pilasters. It was probably furnished with a suspension ring. On the recto is an urn from which emerges a symmetrical arrangement of floral elements; the urn rests on a decorated pedestal.

The particular text and its placement within an aedicula in the form of a tempietto is certainly not ornamental and emphasizes the wish to identify the text as something sacred and exalted. The motifs found on this amulet are typical of engraved gems of the Roman imperial period that bear representations of a divinity within a temple,[1] iconography which was then used on coins.[2]

The rude depiction of the pilasters, found frequently in the late antique is an inheritance of classical, architecture, has parallels, on a larger scale, on other late antique monuments, for example the apse of the Basilica of Qal Laozeh. The motif of the urn from which emerge symmetrical vegetal elements can be found on antique funerary reliefs of the imperial period.[3] Perhaps not by accident, the short sides of a Byzantine sarcophagus in S. Apollinare in Classe in Ravenna is decorated with an urn within an aedicula supported by rude pilasters.

An interesting comparison can be made with a Hebrew amulet in silver which was acquired by W. R. Rylands in Palestine at the beginning of this century.[4] It consists of a smooth rectangle with a hook whose sides are formed as a tempietto on a podium that is inscribed on both sides. The comparison with this amulet is close and Gaster's conclusion that the Palestinian amulet is modern raises the question why the maker used this particular form. One must suppose that he based it on a preexisting model. This supposition is confirmed by the existence of other modern Hebrew amulets stemming from Peria and Kurdistan which, although simpler and under Islamic influence, are formed as rectangles surmounted by a triangle.

On the basis of all these comparisons, we suggest that this piece is a Hebrew amulet of antique origin, a distant precursor of those commonly known. Most of the modern silver examples are of varying forms. An examination of the technical and artistic qualities of the incised decoration on this piece recalls the late antique, with a probable provenance in the eastern Mediterranean, and does not suggest a copy made in the last several centuries based on antique models.

LV

Unpublished

*Editor's Note: The inscription in the main field is a mix of biblical quotations and names of angels:[5]

ישא ה׳ פניו אליך
פספסים
וישם לך שלום

דיוניסים [כך!]
סנוי סנסנוי סמנגלף
יהי שלום בחילך שלוה
בארמנותיך ה ישמרם

("The Lord lift up his countenance to you") [Num. 6:26]/Paspasim[6] / "and grant you peace" (Num. 6:26)/ Deyonisim [*sic*]/Sanvai, Sansanvai, Semanglof/ "May there be well-being within your ramparts, peace in your citadels" (Ps. 122:7)/ May the Lord keep you (var. on Num. 6:24). Below in the stylobate is the name of the owner:

יוסף ב [ב]רוך יהודה יצ״ו

"Joseph the son of [B]arukh Yehudah . . . "

VBM

1. For example, Aphrodite (London, British Museum, inv. no. G 139/56139); Asclepius (London, British Museum, inv. no. G. 72.6–4.1196); Serapis (Paris, Cabinet des Medailles); Zeus (Oxford, Ashmolean Museum, inv. no. 1892.1550).
2. For example, on the coins of second Jewish Revolt (132–135 C.E.) which bear depictions of the Ark of the Covenant within the Jerusalem Temple (e.g., NYJM, *Coins Reveal*), nos. 102 and 104.
3. Dresden, Staatlichi Kunstsammlungen, Inv. no. 2. V. 2750. Similar texts are found on later Italian amulets (cat. nos. 186 and 226).
4. E. J. Pilcher, *A Hebrew Amulet,* in "Proceedings of the Society of Biblical Archaeology," 32 (1910), pp. 125–126; M. Gaster, *A note on "A Hebrew Amulet,"* in "Proceedings of the Society of Biblical Archaeology," 32 (1910), pp. 156–158; British Museum: G. F. Hill, *Catalogue of the Greek coins of Palestine* (*Galilee, Samarie, and Judaea*) (London 1914), pp. 284–287, 32–33; E.A.T.W. Budge, *Amulets and superstitions* (Oxford 1930), pp. 212–238; J. Marques-Riviere, *Amulettes, talismans et pantacles ans les traditions orientale et occidentale* (Paris 1938), pp. 15–65.
5. *Paspasim* and *Deyonisin* are portions of the twenty-two letter name of God, commonly found on amulets. According to Schrire, the origin of the name is obscure and is said to be the equivalent of the beginning of the Priestly Blessing, parts of which are inscribed on this example. (T. Schrire, *Hebrew Amulets* [London, 1966], p. 97.) The writer of this amulet alternated phrases of the biblical text with their amuletic equivalent, the twenty-two letter name of God.
6. These are names of angels.

CLAY

25. **Oil Lamp**

Ostia, second to third century

Clay

H: 3½ in. (9 cm); Diam: 2⅞ in. (7.3 cm)

Ostia, Soprintendenza Archeologica, Ostia magazzini (inv. no. 5931)

A bird, perhaps a dove, perched on a small branch is the main decoration of this single-wick lamp. A wreath motif frames the center field. All of the forms are flat and stylized.

MFS

Unpublished

26. **Oil Lamp**

Ostia, second to third century

Clay

H: 4⅛ in. (10.6 cm); Diam: 3⅜ in. (8.7 cm)

Ostia, Soprintendenza Archeologica, Ostia magazzini (inv. no. 5935)

This lamp was found in the area behind the Torah ark of the synagogue. Its decoration has become so indistinct that it is impossible to identify a specific motif.

MFS

Unpublished

27. **Oil Lamp**

Ostia, second to third century

Clay

H: 3⅝ in. (9.2 cm); Diam: 2¹¹⁄₁₆ in. (6.9 cm)

Ostia, Soprintendenza Archeologica, Ostia magazzini (inv. no. 12501)

This single-wick lamp was found in the anteroom of the synagogue, which was furnished with an oven. It bears the representation of the most significant furnishing of any synagogue, the Torah ark in which the scrolls of the Law are stored, and which serves as a focus of prayer. The doors of the ark are shown open; the row of three circles at the bottom may represent a row of scrolls laid on a shelf. Similar images are found on gold glass (see cat. nos. 34–36; figs. 68, 69). A bead and reel molding frames the image.

MFS

Unpublished

28. **Oil Lamp**

Ostia, second to third century

Clay

H: 3¼ in. (8.2 cm); Diam: 2¾ in. (7 cm)

Ostia, Soprintendenza Archeologica, Ostia magazzini (inv. no. 13351)

This lamp was found during an early excavation of Ostia and was formerly in the fortress of Julius II. It is decorated with a ritual image found on a similar lamp discovered in a synagogue anteroom (see cat. no. 27). The main image is an open Torah ark whose triangular pediment is decorated with a circle.

MFS

Unpublished

29. **Closed-Channel "African" Oil Lamp with Menorah**[1]

Rome (Tiber), mid-fourth to fifth century

Red-orange clay (Munsell 10R 4/8), well cleaned and compact; red-orange paint (Munsell 10R 4/6), brilliant, lightly cleaned; some lime encrustations; traces of blackening on the lip

5 × 3⅜ × 1½ in. (12.7 × 8.7 × 3.9 cm) (with handle)

Rome, Museo Nazionale Romano (inv. no. 51151)

This oil lamp has a fully vertical grooved handle. Only the upper half of the body remains, and the end of the lip is incomplete. The back is slightly convex and is decorated with a double palm motif in relief within a band outlined by grooving. A seven-branched menorah on a tall tripod base decorates the central circular disk. A herringbone border surrounds the disk.

This lamp can be compared with a somewhat similar one in the Ostia Museum.[2] The same type of menorah can also be seen on other examples.[3]

MS

Unpublished

1. See N. Lamboglia, "Tipologia e cronologia delle lucerne romane, classificazione Dressel, Apuntes sobre cronologia ceramica," in *Publicaciones del Seminario de Argueologia y Numismatica Aragonesa* (1952), p. 31; G. Pohl, "Die frühchristliche Lampen vom Lorenzberg bei Epfach, Landkreis Schongau: Versuch einer Gliederung der Lampen vom Mediterranen Typus," in *Schriftenreihen zur Bayerischen Landgeschichte,* vol. 62 (Munich, 1962), pp. 219–228, 3c; A. Provoost, "Les lampes antiques en terre cuite: Introduction et essai de typologie general avec des details concernant les lampes trouvées en Italie," *Antiquite Classique* 45 (1976): 7, var. 2; *Enciclopedia dell'arte antica classica e orièntale: Atlante delle forme cerameche,* vol. 1, *Terra sigillata: lucerne,* ed. L. Anselmino and C. Pavolini (Rome 1981), forme VIII C 2a, fig. 1 (this type is most often mentioned in Tunisia and in Italy, see p. 192ff.).
2. Frey, *Scriptionum Iudaicarum,* p. 465, fig. a.
3. Goodenough, *Jewish Symbols,* vol. 3, pl. II, no. 927 (lamp type Pohl 2a); P. Cintas, *Céramique punique* (Paris, 1950), pl. XXXVI, no. 589 (lamp type Pohl 2h).

30. **Ovoid Oil Lamp with Menorah**

Rome (Palatine), late fourth to first half of the fifth century

Clay; beige clay (Munsell 7.5YR7/8); a beige layer (Munsell 7.5YR6/4); worn-away surface with some cracks; traces of blackening on the lip

⅞ × 3⁹⁄₁₆ × 4⅝ in. (2.3 × 9.1 × 11.8 cm)

Rome, Museo Nazionale Romano (inv. no. 53693/1)

This ovoid lamp without a handle is incomplete in the lower half of the body except at the end of the lip. There is a relief decoration of a seven-branched menorah with ring-shaped base in the broad and slightly hollowed-out disk. The menorah is decorated by short, parallel lines. The lip barely projects and is entirely filled by the wick hole.

This lamp is comparable to others on exhibition (see cat. nos. 29, 31, 32, 33). The type of menorah appears on a round-lipped oil lamp from Alexandria[1] and on an imitation "African" oil lamp from the upper catacomb of Villa Torlonia (where, however, the menorah has a half-moon-shaped base).[2]

MS

Bibliography: G. Ghirardini, *Catalogo del Museo Palatino* (Rome, 1881), no. 686.

1. E. R. Goodenough, *Jewish Symbols,* vol. 3, pl. 1, no. 925.
2. U. M. Fasola, "Le due catacombe ebraiche di Villa Torlonia," in *Revista di archeologia cristiana* 52 (1976): 59, fig. 27.

31. **Ovoid Oil Lamp with Menorah**

Rome, late fourth to first half of the fifth century C.E.

Rosy clay (Munsell 5YR7/8); a beige layer (Munsell 7.5YR6/4); slightly encrusted surface; traces of blackening on the lip; good matrix

1¼ × 3¼ × 4¼ in. (3.2 × 8.2 × 10.8 cm)

Rome, Museo Nazionale Romano (inv. no. 189381; previously in the Museo Kircheriano)

This lamp lacks a handle. Its lip has been composed of two fragments and partially completed in plaster. Its high border slopes toward the outside. A menorah with seven slender branches on a tall, circular base is the relief decoration. The short lip is entirely filled by the wick hole. The body has a lenticular outline and a raised circular bottom.

MS

Unpublished

32. **Ovoid Oil Lamp with Menorah**

Rome (Vallicelliana), late fourth to first half of the fifth century

Rosy beige clay (Munsell 5YR7/6); slight traces of a rosy layer (Munsell 7.5Y36/4); worn-away surface with encrustations; traces of blackening on the lip

1⅛ × 3⅜ × 4¼ in. (2.9 × 8.5 × 10.9 cm)

Rome, Museo Nazionale Romano (inv. no. 55264)

This ovoid oil lamp lacks a handle. It has a narrow, rounded border, and a relief of a seven-branched menorah on a high tripod base in the lower disk, between the two oil holes. The lip is very short and entirely filled by the wick hole. The body is in lenticular sections; the bottom has a broad, flat foot. The matrix is worn.

This example seems clearly to be an oil lamp produced in Italy in the area of Rome, inspired by the forms of the so-called African lamps[1] and compares typologically with other examples discovered in Rome.[2]

MS

1. It can be considered a variation of the type Provoost 8k.
2. Goodenough, *Jewish Symbols,* vol. 3, pl. II, no. 935 (with identical decoration); A. Ferrua, "Scoperta di una nuova regione della catacomba di Commodilla," *Rivista di archeologia cristiana* 33 (1957): 66, fig. 4.51; U. M. Fasola, "Le due catacombe ebraiche di Villa Torlonia," ibid. 52 (1976): 60, fig. 28a (second row, first example to the left, decorated with the figure of a bird).

33. ***Henchir-es-srira* Type "African" Oil Lamp with Menorah**[1]

Rome, early fifth to sixth century C.E.

Red-orange clay (Munsell 10R5/8), with micaceous elements; red-orange paint (Munsell 10R5/6), very worn away, chipping along the edges; worn-away surface with some scratches; traces of blackening on the lip

1⅛ × 2½ × 3½ in. (2.9 × 6.3 × 8.8 cm) (with handle)

Rome, Museo Nazionale Romano (inv. no. 69641; previously in the Museo Kircheriano)

This oil lamp has a grooved vertical handle and two vertical notches at the base. Only the upper half of the body remains. The back is narrow, slightly convex, and decorated with a border of oblique parallel lines. A relief of a nine-branched menorah on a low tripod decorates the central disk. The lip is almost completely filled by the large hole for the wick. The matrix is worn.[2]

MS

Unpublished

1. Type Dressel-Lamboglia 31; Pohl 2 h; *Atlante* form VIII A 2a, fig. 2.
2. For identical example in typology and decoration, see L. Hautecoeur, *Catalogue du Musée Alaoui,* vol. 1 (Paris, 1910), no. 589, pl. XXXVI.

GLASS

34. **Fragments of a Cup Bottom with Jewish Symbols**

Rome, 300–350 C.E.
Gold glass

(a) 3½ × 1½ in. (8.9 × 3.8 cm); (b) 1½ × 1¼ in. (3.8 × 3.2 cm)

New York, The Metropolitan Museum of Art, Rogers Fund, 1918 (18.145.1 a, b)

The decorative field of this cup is divided into two registers surrounded by a now-fragmentary Latin inscription: *CI BIBAS CVM EVLOGIA CONP[arare]* (Drink with blessing in preparation. . . .) The partial remains of a banqueting dais and a fish on a platter suggest that the bottom register was occupied by the scene of a meal held in honor of the dead, a motif also found on pagan and Christian examples. The top register is filled with symbols of the synagogue and the ancient Temple in Jerusalem. Among them are a pair of menorot, an open Torah ark showing rolled scrolls arranged on shelves, a shofar, and an *etrog* (citron). The same symbols appear on a variety of objects from this period, for example, tombstones, oil lamps, and architectural decorations (see cat. nos. 6, 27, 10; figs. 75, 56).

VBM

Bibliography: R. Garrucci, *Vetri ornati di figure in oro,* 2d ed. (Rome, 1864), pl. V, no. 3; J.-B. Frey, *Corpus Inscriptionum Iudaicarum,* vol. 1, *Europe* (Rome, 1936), no. 518; A. Reifenberg, *Ancient Hebrew Arts* (New York, 1950), p. 151; Goodenough, *Jewish Symbols,* vol. 2, pp. 111–112, and vol. 3, fig. 973; I. Schuler, "A Note on Jewish Gold Glass," *Journal of Glass Studies* 8 (1966): 56, 60, no. 7; D. Barag, "Glass," in *Encyclopaedia Judaica,* vol. 7, cols. 604–612; A. Cohen-Mushlin, "Fragments of Cup Bottom with Torah Ark and Temple Implements," in Metropolitan Museum of Art, *Age of Spirituality,* exh. cat., ed. K. Weitzmann, (New York, 1979), no. 348.

35. **Fragment of a Cup Bottom** (fig. 69)

Rome, fourth century C.E.

Gold glass

Diam: 4½ in. (11.4 cm)

Jerusalem, Israel Museum (66.36.14)

The decoration of this gold glass is an expanded version of the symbolism represented on the upper register of the fragments from the Metropolitan Museum of Art, New York (cat. no. 34; fig. 68). An open Torah ark with three shelves, each holding three scrolls housed in separate compartments, occupies the top register. The ark is flanked by two birds perched on orbs, who hold in their beaks ribbons that may represent the cords of a curtain veiling the ark.[1] In the bottom register is a single menorah flanked by addorsed lions whose heads turn backward and upward towards the flaming lamps atop the branches. The remaining space is filled with a *lulav* and an *etrog,* a shofar, an amphora (possibly for oil), and two perforated disks, representing unleavened bread.

Addorsed lions appear on another gold glass fragment, now in Wurzburg; the remaining symbols on the lower register appear on a fragment in the British Museum, London.[2]

VBM

Bibliography; *Encyclopaedia Judaica,* vol. 7, no. 2; A. Eitan, "The Menorah as a Symbol," *Israel Museum News* 3 (1968): 47; E. Revel-Neher, *L'arche d'alliance dans l'art juif et chrétien du second au dixième siècles* (Paris, 1984), pp. 105–106, fig. 25; idem, "L'alliance et la promesse: Le symbolisme d'Eretz-Israel dans l'iconographie juive du moyen age," *Jewish Art* 12–13 (1987): 139, fig. 5.

1. Revel-Neher, *L'arche d'alliance,* p. 106.
2. *Encyclopaedia Judaica,* vol. 7, pl. 1, nos. 5, 6.

36. **Fragment of a Cup Bottom**

Rome, fourth century C.E.

Gold glass

2½ × 2¼ in. (6.3 × 5.8 cm)

Vatican City, Museo Sacro of the Vatican Library (no. 479)

The decoration of this gold glass is unique among all those extant. At center is a temple set within a courtyard framed by a colonnade. The objects depicted between temple and colonnade (two bronze-colored columns, a flaming menorah, a *lulav* and *etrog,* two golden canthari, and two jars) indicate that the building represented is the Temple in Jerusalem. Further, the canthari, jars, and the booths depicted outside the colonnade specifically refer to the Feast of Tabernacles and to the ceremony of the Drawing of the Water, which was held on each of the seven days of the festival.

Tabernacles was the most important and joyous holiday celebrated in the ancient Temple. Following its destruction, items used on the festival, such as the *lulav* and *etrog,* the booths, and the canthari filled with water and wine, became symbolic of belief in the rebuilding of the Temple and the coming of the messianic age. Thus the Greek inscription on this cup, OIKOC IPH[νη]C (house of peace), together with the palm trees that signify victory and eternal life, refer to the future. The second inscription, "take the blessing with all who are thine," is similar to those found on Christian and Jewish cups used on ceremonial occasions and often implanted in the walls of tombs.

VBM

Bibliography: A. St. Clair, "God's House of Peace in Paradise: The Feast of Tabernacles on a Jewish Gold Glass," *Journal of Jewish Art* 11 (1985): 6–15 (the earlier literature is cited there).

The City States and Ghetto Periods

MANUSCRIPTS

37. **Haggadah** (figs. 78–79)

Scribe and artist: Joel ben Simeon

Italy, 1454 (completed in the month of Elul [5]214)

Ink and gouache on vellum; 59 leaves

10¹³⁄₁₆ × 8⅛ in. (27.5 × 20.6 cm)

New York, Library of The Jewish Theological Seminary of America, from the collection of Mortimer L. Schiff (Mic. 8279)

This haggadah is decorated with inventive initial word panels, and zoomorphic and anthropomorphic letters. The iconographic program differs from the other haggadot executed by Joel in that an outstretched arm on folio 26 is the only obvious text illustration in the work. None of the traditional figures, such as the Four Sons, the Exodus from Egypt, or the matzah and *maror,* is depicted. In the colophon on folio 59, the scribe states that he "wrote, vocalized, and decorated the haggadah." The text was censored by Fr[a] Hipp[olitu]s Ferr[arens]es in 1601. The manuscript is in its original binding of tooled brown leather over wooden boards.

EMC

Bibliography: B. Italiener et al., *Die Darmstadter Pessach-Haggadah* (Leipzig, 1927), p. 281; M. Fooner, "Joel ben Simeon, Illuminator of Hebrew Manuscripts in the Fifteenth Century," *Jewish Quarterly Review,* n.s., 27 (1937): 217–232; A. Marx, "The Darmstadt Haggadah," *Studies in Jewish History and Booklore* (New York, 1944), p. 269; The Jewish Museum, *Illuminated Hebrew Manuscripts from the Library of The Jewish Theological Seminary of America,* exh. cat., by T. L. Freudenheim (New York, 1965), no. 33; B. Narkiss, *Hebrew Illuminated Manuscripts* (Jerusalem, 1969), pp. 124, 171; J. Gutmann, "Thirteen Manuscripts in Search of an Author: Joel ben Simeon, Fifteenth-Century Scribe-Artist," *Studies in Bibliography and Booklore* 9 (1970): 76–95; M. Metzger, *La Haggada enluminée: Étude iconographique et stylistique des manuscrits enluminés et décorés de la Haggada du XIIIe au XVIe siècle,* vol. 1 (Leiden, 1973), pp. 435–436, figs. 400, 409–411, 417, 474; M. Beit-Arié, "Joel ben Simeon's Manuscripts: A Codicologer's View," *Journal of Jewish Art* 3–4, (1977): 25–39; S. Edmunds, "The Place of the London Haggadah in the Work of Joel ben Simeon," *Journal of Jewish Art* 7 (1980): 25–34; D. Goldstein, *The Ashkenazi Haggadah* (New York, 1985), p. 9; NYPL, *A Sign,* no. 37; *Index of Jewish Art* (forthcoming).

38. **Prayer Book** (fig. 27)

Italy, fifteenth century

Ink, gouache, and gold leaf on vellum, edges gilt and gauffered; I + 354 + I leaves

5 9/16 × 4 in. (14.2 × 10.2 cm)

New York, Library of The Jewish Theological Seminary of America, Gift of Max Schloessinger (Mic. 8224)

The opening page of the manuscript is decorated with an illuminated border that contains a coat of arms, possibly of the Gallico family, held by two putti at the bottom. In addition to four text illustrations, there are many floral borders in the outer margins. The text begins with gold letters on a painted initial word panel; initial words are decorated with pen designs in blue, purple, and red ink throughout the manuscript. The decorative borders in this prayer book are similar to those found in Christian manuscripts from this period.

EMC

Bibliography: The Jewish Museum, *Illuminated Hebrew Manuscripts from the Library of The Jewish Theological Seminary of America,* exh. cat., by T. L. Freudenheim (New York, 1965), no. 15; T. and M. Metzger, *Jewish Life in the Middle Ages* (New York, 1982), no. 142; *Index of Jewish Art* (forthcoming).

39. ***De pratica seu arte tripudii vulgare opusculum***

Guglielmo Ebreo da Pesaro (active 1437–1481)

Italy, 1463

Ink on parchment

11½ × 9 in. (29.2 × 22.8 cm)

New York, Public Library (MGZMB-RES.72-254)

Of the ten surviving Renaissance treatises on the dance, seven were written by Guglielmo Ebreo da Pesaro. In his *De pratica seu arte tripudii vulgare opusculum* of 1463, Guglielmo attempted to do for dance what Alberti had done for architecture, that is, to establish the theoretical basis of the art form. His work differs from that of Christian writers in that Guglielmo included biblical references to justify dance as a spiritual activity that brings one closer to God.[1] Only one illuminated example of the treatise is extant (Paris, Bibliothèque Nationale f. ital. 476). It contains a miniature of a man dancing with two ladies (fig. 39), which is thought to be a portrait of the author and an illustration of dancing as an activity motivated by urbane decorum.[2] Guglielmo is mentioned in court records from 1437 through 1481 describing festivals that were held as far south as Naples and as far north as Venice, Padua, and Milan. At some point in his career, probably in 1468, the year he was knighted, Guglielmo converted to Catholicism and became known as Ambrogio *ballerino* (the dancer).[3]

VBM

Unpublished

1. P. Castelli, "Il moto aristotelico e la 'licita scientia': Guglielmo Ebreo e la speculazione sulla danza nel XV secolo," in Palazzo Lazzarini, *Mesura et arte del danzare: Guglielmo Ebreo da Pesaro e la danza nelle corti italiane del XV secolo,* exh. cat. (Pesaro, 1987), p. 37.
2. Ibid., p. 43.
3. P. Castelli, "La kermesse degli Sforza pesaresi," in ibid., p. 22.

40. **Book of Psalms, Job, and Proverbs (*Sifrei emet*)** (fig. 87)

Florence, 1467 (5 July)

Ink, gouache, and golf leaf on vellum, edges gilt and gauffered; 187 leaves

4 5/16 × 3 in. (11 × 7.6 cm)

New Haven, Yale University, Beinecke Library (Ms. 409)

This manuscript contains many initial words that are decorated with red and purple pen work and a few that are illuminated. Full-page miniatures precede Psalms and Job, and illuminated borders decorate five folios and the opening pages of each of the three books. The colophon on folio 187v states that this manuscript, written for Signor Jacob Jacomo, the son of Rabbi Benjamin, was completed on July 5 in the year [5]227 (1467). The scribe's name has been erased. The illumination has been attributed by Mirella Levi D'Ancona to Antonio di Niccolo di Lorenzo, though Francesco d'Antonio del Cherico and Filippo di Matteo Torelli have also been suggested. Although different in style, the illustrations are similar in subject to those in the Book of Psalms, Job, and Proverbs in Jerusalem (Israel Museum Ms. 180/55).

EMC

Bibliography: *Catalogue of Western Manuscripts and Miniatures,* sale cat. Sotheby's, London, 9 July 1969, lot 63; B. Narkiss, *Hebrew Illuminated Manuscripts* (Jerusalem, 1969), p. 39; A. de la Mare, "The Library of Francesco Sassetti (1421–90)," in *Cultural Aspects of the Italian Renaissance: Essays in Honour of Paul Oskar Kristeller* (Manchester and New York, 1976), p. 197, n. 81; W. Cahn and J. Marrow, "Medieval and Renaissance Manuscripts at Yale: A Selection," *Yale University Library Gazette* 52 (1978): 232–233, no. 57.

41. *La nozze di Costanzo Sforza e Camilla d'Aragona*

Naples, after 1475

Ink and gouache on parchment

8⅛ × 5⅜ in. (20.6 × 13.7 cm)

Vatican City, Biblioteca Apostolica Vaticana (urb. 899)

In 1475 Costanzo Sforza, ruler of Pesaro (1447–1483), married Camilla d'Aragona in a wedding described as "one of the most splendid of the Italian Renaissance."[1] The numerous celebrations were recorded in contemporary chronicles and in illuminated manuscripts such as this one. The contribution of the Jewish community to the festivities is recorded on two pages of *La nozze*. On folio 88r is an illustration of "La regina di Saba, regina ebrea," riding on an elephant, a symbol of the loyalty of the community to the married couple, and on folio 91r, "Boaz e la montagna," which uses the scene of Boaz emerging from the mountain to symbolize the ascent of the Sforza dynasty.

VBM

Bibliography: Palazzo Lazzarini, *Mesura et arte del danzare: Guglielmo Ebreo da Pesaro e la danza nelle corti italiane del XV secolo,* exh. cat. (Pesaro, 1987), p. 24, no. 85 (where the earlier literature is cited).

1. P. Castelli, "La kermesse degli Sforza pesaresi," in *Mesura et arte del danzare,* p. 22.

42. **Holiday Prayer Book**

Italy, c. 1480

Ink, gouache and gold leaf on vellum; III + 326 + II leaves

5 × 3⅜ in. (12.7 × 8.5 cm)

New York, Library of The Jewish Theological Seminary of America (Mic. 4106)

This small Holiday Prayer Book contains prayers for Rosh ha-Shanah, Yom Kippur, and Sukkot. Seven of its pages are decorated with initial word panels in blue and gold and illuminated floral borders on the right-hand margin. The name *Ephraim,* which is emphasized by designs in the borders of folios 36 and 100v, might identify the scribe. The text was censored by Dominico Irosolimitano in 1600.

EMC

Unpublished

43. *Rothschild Maḥzor* **(Prayer Book)**

(figs. 7, 82–84)

Scribe: Abraham Judah ben Yeḥiel of Camerino

Patron: Elijah ben Joab of Vigevano ben Abraham of the Gallico family

Florence, 1492 (completed 24 Adar [5]252)

Ink, gouache, and gold leaf on vellum; edges gilt and gauffered; I + 477 + I leaves

11 5⁄16 × 8 1⁄16 in. (28.7 × 20.5 cm)

New York, Library of The Jewish Theological Seminary of America, Gift of Baron Edmond de Rothschild (Mic. 8892)

This *maḥzor,* containing prayers and special readings for the entire liturgical year, was illuminated by three different workshops. There are approximately thirty text illustrations, and more than two-thirds of the folios are embellished with floral borders and decorative initial word panels. As the Norsa family emblem appears ten times in this work, even though it was written for Elijah ben Joab of the Gallico family, it is possible that the manuscript was made to commemorate a wedding between these two illustrious families. The text was censored by Fra Luigi da Bologna in 1599 and by Giovanni Domenico Vistorini in 1609. The book cover of wooden board covered with red velvet and embellished with metal bosses is probably original.

EMC

Bibliography: B. Narkiss, *Hebrew Illuminated Manuscripts* (Jerusalem, 1969), p. 39, pl. 52; M. Metzger, "L'aide et les risques qu'offrent le décor et l'illustration pour dater et localiser les manuscrits hébreux médiévaux," in *La paléographie hébraïque médiévale* (Paris, 1974), p. 122; T. and M. Metzger, *Jewish Life in the Middle Ages* (New York, 1982), no. 140, pls. 197, 381; *The Rothschild Maḥzor: Florence 1492,* intro. by E. M. Cohen and M. Schmelzer (New York, 1983); NYPL, *A Sign,* no. 61; *Index of Jewish Art* (forthcoming).

44. ***Hanhagot mi-Kol ha-Shanah* (Prayer Book for Various Jewish Rituals)** (figs. 85–86)

Italy, fifteenth century

Ink, gouache, and gold leaf on vellum; 150 leaves

4 5/16 × 3 1/8 in. (11 × 8 cm)

Princeton, Princeton University Library (Garrett Ms. 26)

This manuscript with texts dealing with birth, marriage, death, and rituals of daily life is decorated with twenty-six text illustrations and two full-page miniatures. Some of the pages are framed with elaborate inhabited gold-leaf borders. Many of the initial words and section headings are written in gold and embellished with painted panels, and many of the margins are decorated with illuminated floral designs. An unexecuted illustration on folio 65 has its gold-leaf border in place. Because of an eighteenth-century forgery at the end of the manuscript (which was misunderstood by its writer to be the beginning, as he did not know that Hebrew books are read right to left), the work was mistakenly believed to have been a text by Maimonides, decorated by Giotto in Avignon. The intarsia book cover with the forged arms of Cardinal Battaglia was added as part of the deception.

EMC

Bibliography: E. Panofsky, "Giotto and Maimonides in Avignon: The Story of an Illustrated Hebrew Manuscript," *Journal of the Walters Art Gallery* 4 (1941): 27–44; idem, "Giotto and Maimonides in Avignon: A Postscript," *Journal of the Walters Art Gallery* 5 (1942): 124–127; J. Bloch, *The People and the Book,* exh. cat. (New York, 1954), pp. 42–44; D. Diringer, *The Illuminated Book: Its History and Production* (London, 1967), fig. III, 18 b; T. and M. Metzger, *Jewish Life in the Middle Ages* (New York, 1982), no. 230, pls. 109, 341; NYPL *A Sign,* no. 45.

45. **Medical Herbal** (figs. 8, 88)

Italy, c. 1500

Ink and watercolor on paper, gilt edges; XXXI + 74 + VII leaves

8 1/4 × 6 1/8 in. (21 × 15.5 cm)

Paris, Bibliothèque Nationale (Ms. hébr. 1199)

The manuscript contains full-page illustrations of 130 plants. Each page includes a caption in Hebrew and sometimes in Latin or in Latin written in Hebrew characters, identifying the image. Supplementary notes are included on folios 67–74v. The illustration on folio 45 includes the figure of a devil, as the plant Saint-John's-wort was believed to drive him away. The binding, which is not original, bears the coat of arms of Cardinal de Richelieu, the prime minister under Louis XIII, who died in 1642.

EMC

Bibliography: G. Bonnier, *Flore complète* (Paris, 1927), vol. 2, p. 91, no. 549, pl. 105, vol. 5, p. 68, no. 1379, pl. 276; T. and M. Metzger, *Jewish Life in the Middle Ages* (New York, 1982), no. 195, pls. 244–246.

46. ***Maḥzor* (Prayer Book)** (figs. 77, 80–81)

Scribe: Leon (Yehudah) bar Yehoshua (de Rossi) of Cesena

Northern Italy, second half of the fifteenth century

Ink, gouache, and gold leaf on vellum; 319 leaves

10 1/8 × 7 1/4 in. (25.7 × 18.5 cm)

Jerusalem, Jewish National and University Library (Ms. Heb. 8° 4450)

This is the first half of a *maḥzor* containing prayers for the entire liturgical year. The manuscript begins with a scene of the morning ritual of a man awakening, washing, and saying his prayers. The later illustrations for Passover and Shavuot are executed in the style of Joel ben Simeon (see cat. no. 37; figs. 78, 79). The relationship is most striking in the double-page depiction of the Exodus, where the rendering of Moses parting the Red Sea before the Israelites is similar not only in general conception but also in unusual minor details to the depiction of this episode in the *Ashkenazi Haggadah* (London, British Library Ms. Add. 14762). Four pages are illuminated with floral borders, and initial words are decorated with pen flourishes throughout. The scribe's colophon appears on folio 197; he calls attention to himself by placing dots above the name Yehudah on folio 148. The second volume of the maḥzor, which contains the liturgy for Rosh ha-Shanah, Yom Kippur, and Sukkot, is in the collection of George Weill, Jerusalem.

EMC

Bibliography: M. Metzger, *La Haggada enluminée: Étude iconographique et stylistique des manuscrits enluminés et décorés de la Haggada du XIIIe au XVIe siècle,* vol. 1 (Leiden, 1973), figs. 357, 358; idem, "Un mahzor italien enluminé du XVe siècle," *Mitteilungen des Kunsthistorischen Institutes in Florenz* 20 (1976): 159–196; T. and M. Metzger, *Jewish Life in the Middle Ages* (New York, 1982), no. 68, pl. 294; D. Goldstein, *The Ashkenazi Haggadah* (New York, 1985), fig. 6; M. Nadav and R. Weiser, eds., *Selected Manuscripts and Prints from the Treasures of the Jewish National and University Library,* exh. cat. (Jerusalem, 1985), p. 23, no. 37; M. Beit-Arié, "Codicological Description and Analysis of the Washington Haggadah," facsimile edition of the Washington Haggadah (forthcoming).

47. ***Maḥzor*** **(Prayer Book)**

Italy, c. 1500

Ink, gouache, and gold leaf on vellum; gilt edges; 457 leaves

5¾ × 4³⁄₁₆ in. (14.7 × 10.6 cm)

New York, Private collection

This manuscript begins with a beautiful architectural rendering festooned with illusionistically depicted sapphires, rubies, and pearls. The gold crown placed under the pediment alludes to the words "crown of kingship" in the text of the daily prayer. The border of the verso of this folio is illuminated with a wide ornamental border. Throughout the manuscript, initial words, written in gold leaf, are set against painted panels; the only other text illustration is the depiction of the *maror* (bitter herbs) in the Passover Haggadah. The text was censored by Dominico Irosolimitano and by Fra Hipp[olitus] Ferr[arens]is in 1601.

EMC

Bibliography: E. Sarnow, *Katalog der ständigen Ausstellung der Stadtbibliothek, Frankfurt a. M.,* exh. cat. (Frankfurt, 1920), no. 10; G. Swarzenski and R. Schilling, *Die illuminierten Handschriften und Einzelminiaturen des Mittelalters und der Renaissance in Frankfurter Besitz* (Frankfurt, 1929), p. 256, no. 232.

48. **Haggadah** (fig. 90)

Scribe: Abraham Farissol

Patron: Joseph Norsa, son of Mordecai Yehudah

Ferrara, 1515 (21 Ḥeshvan [5]276)

Ink and watercolor on vellum; II + 23 + II leaves

11¼ × 7⅝ in. (28.6 × 19.4 cm)

New York, Library of The Jewish Theological Seminary of America, from the Collection of Elkan N. Adler (Mic. 4817)

This manuscript, written by Abraham Farissol, contains thirteen text illustrations, the last of which was left unfinished. These scenes were probably executed by a later artist. A recent restoration has uncovered a partially drawn seder scene on folio 5; it is similar in style to the elaborate initial word panel on that page and might be by Farissol's own hand. The abundance of wine stains in this Haggadah testify to its frequent use. The text was censored by Dominico Irosolimitano in 1601 and by Gio[vanni] Domi[ni]co Carretto in 1618.

EMC

Bibliography: E. N. Adler, *Catalogue of Hebrew Manuscripts in the Collection of Elkan Nathan Adler* (Cambridge, 1921), p. 34; E. N. Adler, "Jewish Art," in *Occident and Orient: Gaster Anniversary Volume* (London, 1936), pp. 40, 43; A. Marx, "The Darmstadt Haggadah," in *Studies in Jewish History and Booklore* (New York, 1944), p. 269; F. Landsberger, "The Illumination of Hebrew Manuscripts in the Middle Ages and the Renaissance," in *Jewish Art,* ed. C. Roth (Jerusalem, 1961), p. 420, fig. 211; The Jewish Museum, *Illuminated Hebrew Manuscripts from the Library of The Jewish Theological Seminary of America,* exh. cat., by T. L. Freudenheim (New York, 1965), no. 36; Marx, *Bibliographical Studies,* p. 279; D. B. Ruderman, *The World of a Renaissance Jew* (Cincinnati, 1981), p. 160; E. M. Cohen, "The Illustrations in Abraham Farissol's Haggadah of 1515," *Jewish Art* 12–13 (1986–1987): 89–95; NYPL, *A Sign,* no. 42; *Index of Jewish Art* (forthcoming).

49. ***Siddur Roma***

Scribe: Abraham Farissol

Ferrara, 1528 (10 Nisan [5]288)

Ink, gouache, and gold foil on vellum; 137 + II leaves

4⅞ × 6¾ in. (12.4 × 17.2 cm)

New York, Library of The Jewish Theological Seminary of America, from the collection of Mayer Sulzberger (Mic. 8257)

In the colophon on folio 137v, Farissol stated that this was his work, done in Ferrara on the tenth of Nisan in the year [5]288 (1528). He also employed pen flourishes to draw attention to his name, Abraham, on folios 58v and 84, and he playfully sketched a little head on folio 67. The lavish gold letters, painted initial word panel, and decorative border on the opening page are the only illumination in the manuscript and are the work of an unidentified artist. In the center of the bottom border a blank space was left for an owner to add his coat of arms. The text was censored by Fra Luigi da Bologna in 1601.

EMC

Bibliography: D. B. Ruderman, *The World of a Renaissance Jew* (Cincinnati, 1981), p. 160.

50. *Pinkas* (Expense Register of the Italian Congregation of Venice)

Venice, 1574–1734

Ink on paper; 189 leaves

8¹⁄₁₆ × 6⅛ in. (20.4 × 15.5 cm)

New York, Library of The Jewish Theological Seminary of America (Mic. 8593)

This text, the record book of the expenditures of the Italian synagogue in Venice, provides a record of daily communal life during the ghetto period. Payments to the many employees of the synagogue (the *ḥazzan* [cantor], the scribe, and the teacher) are all recorded. An entry of 1626 by Leone Modena (see cat. no. 79) is on folio 21b. Modena received payment for six months of service as the cantor, teacher, and secretary of the congregation. The register also provides a record of the charitable activities of the community, both for the needs of the local community and for the support of Jews residing in the Holy Land, most notably for the Italian settlement in Safed.

Two other registers from this congregation are extant. One is the record book and regulations of a committee of the community covering the period from 1643 to 1684 (New York, Library of The Jewish Theological Seminary of America Mic. 8594). The third *pinkas* is the annual register of the congregation's debits and credits for the years 1663 to 1731 (Jerusalem, Central Archives of the Jewish People IT1098).

GMG

Provenance: Venice, Talmud Torah.

Bibliography: D. Carpi, *Peulat 'K' K' Italiani' she-be-Venezia le-ma'an a'niyei Eretz Yisrael* (Tel-Aviv, 1978–1979), pp. 14–16; M. R. Cohen, ed. and trans., *The Autobiography of a Seventeenth-Century Venetian Rabbi: Leon Modena's Life of Judah* (Princeton, 1988), p. 241; R. Pacifici, "I regolamenti della scuola italiana a Venezia," *Rassegna Mensile di Israel* 5 (1930): 401.

51. *Peleḥ Rimmonim* (Slice of Pomegranates)

Menaḥem Azariah da Fano (1548–1620)

Asti, 1580–1581

Scribe: Judah Aryeh son of Joshua

Ink on paper; 175 leaves

7⅜ × 5½ in. (18.8 × 14 cm)

New York, Library of The Jewish Theological Seminary of America (Mic. 1586)

Italy was a major center of kabbalism in the sixteenth and seventeenth centuries. Italian kabbalists developed a unique synthesis of mystical traditions imported from other centers and philosophic approaches typical of northern Italian Renaissance humanism.

Menaḥem Azariah da Fano was the leading Italian kabbalist of the late sixteenth century. He was a student of Rabbi Israel Sarug (active 1590–1610), a kabbalist from Safed who moved to Italy and spread the teachings of the legendary Rabbi Isaac Luria (1534–1572). This manuscript is an abridgment of and commentary on *Pardes Rimmonim* by Rabbi Moses Cordovero (1522–1570). Cordovero's work provides a traditional Spanish kabbalistic concentration on the Zohar, while simultaneously exploring magical and philosophical kabbalah. Da Fano's commentary reveals the influence of philosophic thought on Italian kabbalism as a result of the influences of Renaissance Neoplatonism. Christian kabbalists such as Pico della Mirandola and Johannes Reuchlin were intrigued by this speculative approach.

Menaḥem Azariah da Fano served as the *mohel,* or circumciser, of Leone Modena (see cat. no. 79). Ironically Modena was a fierce opponent of kabbalism and vehemently attacked kabbalah in his work *Ari nohem.*

This manuscript bears the signatures of two church censors from Asti, dated 1582. There are no expurgations of the text, indicating contemporary Christian interest in and approval of kabbalistic thought.

GMG

Unpublished

52. **Haggadah** (fig. 89)

Italy, sixteenth century

Ink and gouache on vellum; 39 leaves

10 13/16 × 7¾ in. (27.5 × 19.8 cm)

New York, Private collection

This manuscript, which was decorated by three different hands, has an elaborate iconographic program that includes almost thirty-five text illustrations. Many of the depictions are striking in their similarity to haggadot executed by Joel ben Simeon, especially the *Ashkenazi Haggadah,* and to manuscripts related to Joel's workshop, for example, the fifteenth-century *maḥzor* now in Jerusalem (see cat. no. 46). Unfortunately, perhaps because some of the pigments were fading, a later hand painted over the outlines of many of the original illustrations. Some floral designs were added by yet another artist. The text was censored by Dominico Irosolimitano in 1599 and by Gio[vanni] Dom[inico] Carretto in 1618.

EMC

Bibliography: E. Sarnow, *Katalog der ständigen Ausstellung der Stadtbibliothek, Frankfurt a. M.,* exh. cat. (Frankfurt, 1920), no. 9; B. Italiener et al., *Die Darmstadter Pessach-Haggadah* (Leipzig, 1927), pp. 254–261, pls. 10–13; G. Swarzenski and R. Schilling, *Die illuminierten Handschriften und Einzelminiaturen des Mittelalters und der Renaissance in Frankfurter Besitz* (Frankfurt, 1929), pp. 258–259, no. 234; D. Diringer, *The Illuminated Book: Its History and Production* (London, 1967), figs. III, 27 b and III, 29 b; M. Metzger, *La Haggada enluminée: Étude iconographique et stylistique des manuscrits enluminés et décorés de la Haggada du XIIIe au XVIe siècle,* vol. I (Leiden, 1973), figs. 6, 57, 99, 119, 166, 188, 202, 293, 384, 385, 402.

53. **Medical Diploma of Emanuel Colli**

Aloysius Foppa

Padua, 18 September 1682

Ink and gouache on vellum, 4 leaves

9⅝ × 6¾ in. (24.4 × 17 cm)

Berkeley, California, Judah L. Magnes Museum (73–8)

In the period between 1517 and 1721 approximately 250 Jews from central and eastern Europe graduated from the University of Padua's medical school. Padua's medical school curriculum included liberal arts, Latin, and classical scientific texts as well as the latest advances in anatomy, botany, chemistry, and clinical medicine. Jewish students gained scientific knowledge and also explored a novel social milieu. After graduation they were able to participate in an international brotherhood of fellow graduates, a community of educated, intellectually sophisticated, and inquisitive Jews.

Like other non-Catholics, Jews received their diplomas from a secularly appointed procurator, rather than from the local bishop, who served as chancellor of the university. Jewish diplomas were secularized. Standard Paduan diplomas began "*In Christi Nomine Aeterni*" and dates are listed as "*Anno a Christi Nativitate,*" whereas the diplomas for Jews incorporated the phrases "*In Nomei Dei Aeterni*" and "*currente anno.*"

It was customary in northern Italian universities to commission diplomas in the form of small illuminated books, a tradition that was probably modeled on the form of official Venetian documents called *ducali,* which contained oaths of office for the doge or for the governors of the republic. This diploma by Aloysius Foppa features elaborate floral borders. On the verso of the first leaf is a portrait of the diploma's recipient in an oval shield. A small circular shield containing representations of two bearded men, possibly a rabbi and a doctor, is placed above the portrait. Below the portrait is the Colli family coat of arms in an oval shield.

The floral borders with insects and the arrangement and character of the portraits are very similar to those found on a second diploma by Foppa in the collection of the New York Academy of Medicine. This diploma for Jacobus de Curnis, dated December 16, 1670, features portraits of a saint and of the Virgin and Child. The absence of Christian iconography on Colli's diploma indicates that just as the diploma text was secularized for Jewish graduates, so too was the decoration.

Emanuel di Isaaco Colli, known in Hebrew as Menaḥem Yeḥiel, was originally from Ancona. He is known to have written Hebrew poetry and was the author of an introduction to the prayer book *Sha'ar Bat Rabim* (Venice, 1712–1713), entitled "Hadrat Kodesh." Colli also wrote a brief preface to the Hebrew medical encyclopedia *Ma'aseh Tuviyyah,* written by a fellow graduate of the University of Padua, Tobias Cohn (1652–1729). In 1714 Emanuel's son Isaaco graduated from the University of Padua's medical school.

GMG

Bibliography: Jewish Community Museum, *Fifty Treasures: Judaica and Hebraica from Bay Area Collections,* exh. cat. by J. R. Goldyne (San Francisco, 1984), no. 13.

54. **Scroll of Esther**

Italy, seventeenth century

Ink and gouache on parchment; cutwork

118 × 5⅞ in. (299.7 × 14.9 cm)

New York, The Jewish Museum,
Gift of Dr. Harry G. Friedman (F 2003)

The text of this scroll is framed by borders of brightly colored flowers and vegetal scrollwork. An eagle with outstretched wings, holding a swag of ribbon in its beak, is placed at the top of each panel. The eagle and the floral patterns are cut out, thereby lightening the overall heaviness of the profuse and vividly colored decoration.

A very similarly decorated cutout *megillah* is in the collection of the Museo Nahon, Jerusalem (ON495).

GMG

Unpublished

55. **Scroll of Esther** (fig. 91)

Italy, eighteenth century

Ink, gouache, and gold paint on parchment

7$^{13}/_{16}$ × 131½ in. (19.9 cm × 333.9 cm) (The introductory benedictions are on a separate piece of parchment, with two text columns, 12¼ × 7$^{11}/_{16}$ in. [31.2 cm × 19.5 cm])

New York, Private collection

The scroll begins with a scene of Jonah in the mouth of a great fish, depicted in a cartouche inside the scalloped edge of the parchment. This is followed by the text, which is written in sixteen columns and framed by borders decorated with flowers, birds, and animals. The text columns are separated by gold borders, each containing a bird. The scroll concludes with a delicately rendered miniature of Jacob's Dream.

EMC

Bibliography: J. Bloch, *The People and the Book,* exh. cat. (New York, 1954), p. 40, no. 10.

56. **Book of Emblematic Vignettes Presented to Pope Clement XIV** (fig. 28)

Rome, 1769

Ink and gouache and gold leaf on vellum; folio, 62 leaves

10⅞ × 7⅞ in. (27.6 × 20 cm)

New Haven, Yale University, Beinecke Library (Hebrew 90)

This volume was presented to Cardinal Lorenzo Ganganelli (Clement XIV) by the Jewish community on the occasion of his arrival in Rome in 1769 to assume the papal throne. The text is written in Latin and Hebrew. After a series of prefatory folios with dedicatory verses and the papal coat of arms, the pages are each decorated with a biblical motto written first in Hebrew and then in Latin, accompanied by an appropriate vignette.

Because of its proximity to the papal see, the Jewish community of Rome often interceded on behalf of Jews elsewhere in Italy. The community was also subject to special taxes in conjunction with papal investitures and utilized these occasions to curry favor with the new pope.

VBM

Unpublished

57. **Scroll of Esther and Sheet of Blessings** (fig. 29)

Northern Italy, mid-eighteenth century

Ink, gouache, gold and silver paint on parchment

Scroll: 21½ × 202⅝ in. (54.6 × 514.7 cm)

Sheet of Blessings: 21⅜ × 21¼ in. (54.3 × 54 cm)

Collection of Judy and Michael Steinhardt

This illuminated scroll belongs to a group of six *megillot.*[1] All are large and decorated according to an elaborate program. The text is written within an arcade supported by paired twisted columns wound with vine leaves. Atop each arch is an allegorical figure, such as Justice or Music, flanked by animals, vases of flowers, and scenes from the story of Esther. Additional scenes appear in the cartouches below the text. The detached sheet with the blessings recited before and after the reading of the scroll on the holiday of Purim is similarly decorated.

It is generally agreed that all these scrolls were created in Italy during the eighteenth century and that differences in the execution of the figures and decorative motifs suggest that more than one artist was responsible for their production. A more specific localization and dating is provided by comparison with an illuminated marriage contract written in Mantua in 1751, formerly in the Zagayski collection.[2] On the *ketubbah* the text is framed within a single elaborate arch whose column shafts are partially formed of atlantes. Putti similar to those on an Esther scroll in Padua sit on the volutes of the entablature flanking a figure of Moses holding the Tablets of the Law. The dress and treatment of this figure are close to those of Mordecai on the sheet of blessings belonging to the scroll in Padua. Therefore, based on the provenance of the marriage contract and of the Padua scroll, the only example still in an Italian collection, these scrolls should probably be dated to the mid-eighteenth century and attributed to northern Italy.

VBM

Bibliography: *Catalogue of Western Manuscripts and Miniatures,* sale cat. Sotheby Parke Bernet, London, 1976, lot. 71.

1. The others are: Budapest, National Academy of Sciences; London, Jewish Museum no. 291; Padua, Comunità Israelitica; Paris, Musée de Cluny Cl. 18305; Strasbourg, University Library.
2. *The Michael M. Zagayski Collection of Rare Judaica,* sale cat. Parke-Bernet Galleries, New York, 1964, lot 336.

58. **Omer Book** (fig. 181)

Italy, c. 1800–1810

Ink and gouache on paper; silver binding; cast and engraved; I + 56 + I leaves

3⅛ × 2⅛ in. (8 × 5.5 cm)

New York, Collection of Dr. and Mrs. Solomon Feffer

The period between Passover and Shavuot is marked by the counting of the omer, a span of seven weeks beginning on the sixteenth of Nisan, the day on which the offering of the new grain harvest, or omer, was brought to the Temple in Jerusalem. This book contains the blessing for counting the days of the omer, Ps. 67 (traditionally recited upon counting because it contains seven seven-word verses, thus alluding to the seven weeks), and a calendar of the forty-nine days. The formula for counting each day is recorded, and a full-page miniature depicting a biblical scene is placed on the opposite page. The arrangement of the biblical scenes is unusual. It generally follows a chronological order but is not consistent and includes glaring juxtapositions such as the Binding of Isaac adjacent to Daniel in the Lion's Den.[1]

This manuscript forms a group with five other Italian miniature omer books in public collections. Two examples are in the collection of the Library of The Jewish Theological Seminary of America, New York (Mic. 4105, Mic. 4243); a third is in the collection of the Israel Museum, Jerusalem (180/28); the fourth is in the collection of the Jewish Museum, London,[2] and a fifth recently sold at auction.[3] The Feffer manuscript features delicate, painterly miniatures not found in the other examples, which are more naive. The handling of figures and space in the first miniatures of this manuscript is quite fine, featuring gentle brush strokes and careful modeling. The miniatures toward the end of the manuscript are inferior in quality, however, and it is probable that they are by a different hand than the more accomplished examples. There is no colophon; this manuscript can, however, be dated by comparison with others in the group. The London manuscript includes a colophon dated 1802–1804, and the New York manuscript (Mic. 4243), by the same hand as the London omer book, is dated 1803.

The binding of the omer book dates from the nineteenth century and is ornamented with an engraved border of leaves and rushes. A cast trefoil-shaped clasp closes the book. The front of the binding features a cryptic monogram; on the back is a gooselike bird holding a stalk of wheat, possibly a variation on one of the many Jewish family shields featuring birds holding branches in their beaks, as well as a reference to the grain of the omer offering.

GMG

Unpublished

Fig. 181. Omer Book, Italy, c. 1800–1810, Dr. and Mrs. Solomon Feffer, New York (cat. no. 58)

1. I am indebted to Esther Goldman for her advice regarding this manuscript.
2. See R. D. Barnett, *Catalogue of the Permanent and Loan Collections of the Jewish Museum, London* (London, 1974), no. 633.
3. *Jewellery and Judaica,* sales cat., Sotheby's, Tel-Aviv, April 1989, lot 435.

59. *Sefer Pizmonim shel Milah* (Book of Hymns for Circumcision)

Senigallia(?), 1808–1809

Ink and gouache on paper, tooled leather binding; 50 leaves

8⅜ × 5¼ in. (21.3 × 13.4 cm)

New York, The Moldovan Family Collection

This *mohel* (circumciser's) book contains prayers and hymns for the circumcision ceremony and a record of the infants circumcised by Ḥayyim Abraham, son of Jacob Samson Shabbetai, of Senigallia.

The manuscript includes two decorated pages. The frontispiece features an ornamented rectangular frame enclosing two columns surmounted by an arch. The artist devoted particular attention to the rendering of the polychromatic marble of the columns. On the second page of the manuscript is a miniature of the Binding of Isaac, a biblical event associated with circumcision, enclosed within an ovoid frame surrounded by a decorated rectangular border. The painterly miniature depicts Abraham wielding a knife above his kneeling son as an angel stays Abraham's hand. A ram is seated beneath a bush in the background. Sketchy outlines are filled with washes conveying a soft, atmospheric setting, heightened by the cloud-filled sky and billowing drapery of Abraham's costume.

GMG

Unpublished

60. *Versetti Postuinmus da Vari Professori Dedicati al Sig. A. Crocolo*

Michele Bolaffi (1768–1842)

Livorno, 1825

Ink and gouache on parchment; leather binding with gold tooling

9⅝ × 7⅛ in. (24.5 × 18 cm), 79 leaves

Cincinatti, Library of the Hebrew Union College—Jewish Institute of Religion (HUC Ms. 1825)

Michele Bolaffi was well known as a composer, performer, and poet. At the age of fifteen he composed the music for Daniel Terni's religious drama *Simḥat Mitzvah,* written for the inauguration of the Florence synagogue. Bolaffi composed primarily for the Livorno synagogue, but his works were performed in various Italian communities, including Florence and Casale Monferrato. He also had a successful career as a secular musician in England, Germany, and France. He served as the musical director to the duke of Cambridge in 1809, briefly as the royal Kappelmeister at Hanover, and at the court of Louis XVIII of France between 1815 and 1818. Bolaffi wrote an Italian adaptation of Solomon ibn Gabirol's poetry and translated Voltaire and Jacques de Lille into Italian.

This manuscript includes various liturgical compositions by Bolaffi, including hymns, psalms, and a prayer for the sovereign. Many pages are decorated with painted borders. An arcuated portal with putti and musical instruments frames the frontispiece. It is topped by the Hebrew inscription "Sing to the Lord a new song" (Ps. 33:3, Isa. 42:10). A dedicatory page is surrounded by a rectangular frame filled with scrolling branches, grapevines, and floral motifs. The book is bound in green leather with a gilt Hebrew inscription:

נדבת לבית הכנסת של דוד ויצחק למנוחת נפש אביהם אהרן קרוקולו

(A donation to the synagogue by David and Isaac for the rest of the soul of their father Aaron Crocolo).

GMG

Bibliography: I. Adler, *La Pratique Musicale Savante Dans Quelque Communautés Juives En Europe Aux XVIIe et XVIIIe Siècles,* Paris, 1966, p. 127, no. 7.

PRINTED BOOKS

61. ***Arukh***

Nathan ben Jeḥiel of Rome (1035–c. 1110)

Printer: Obadiah, Menasheh, and Benjamin de Roma

Rome, c. 1469–1472

Ink on paper, folio, 308 leaves

14 15/16 × 10⅝ in. (38 × 27 cm)

New York, Library of The Jewish Theological Seminary of America (Heb. 90)

This text is the first systematic dictionary of midrashic and Talmudic language and was based primarily on gaonic scholarship and on the author's knowledge of the etymology of Aramaic, Latin, Greek, Arabic, and Persian words. Nathan ben Jeḥiel's work acted as a bridge between the once-powerful rabbinical academies of Babylonia and the increasingly prominent European centers of Jewish culture, transferring tools of scholarship to new centers of learning.

This volume is one of four known works believed to be the earliest publications of the first Hebrew printing press. Its products all employ Hebrew type of a Germanic character, suggesting that the very first Hebrew printers were German immigrants.

GMG

Bibliography: M. Marx, "On the Date of Appearance of the First Printed Hebrew Books," in *Alexander Marx Jubilee Volume* (New York, 1950), pp. 481–501; NYPL, *A Sign,* no. 167; Steinschneider, *Bodleiana,* no. 6632, 1; Zedner, *British Museum,* p. 608.

62. **Commentary on the Pentateuch**

Rashi (Rabbi Solomon ben Isaac, 1040–1105)

Printer: Abraham ben Garton

Reggio di Calabria, 1475

Ink on paper, 116 leaves

6 × 7⅛ in. (15.2 × 18.1 cm)

New York, Library of The Jewish Theological Seminary of America (no. 10682)

This is a fragment of the earliest known Hebrew printed book with a complete colophon. Rashi's commentary on the Pentateuch was traditionally used as a basic study text, and it was thus a natural choice for publication at this very early date in the history of Hebrew printing.

GMG

Bibliography: M. Marx, "On the Date of Appearance of the First Printed Hebrew Books," *Alexander Marx Jubilee Volume* (New York, 1950), p. 484; Steinschneider, *Bodleiana,* no. 6927, 1.

63. ***Pentateuch with Rashi's Commentary***

Printer: the sons of Israel Nathan Soncino

Naples, 1490–1491

Ink on vellum

10½ × 7½ in. (26.7 × 19 cm)

New York, Library of The Jewish Theological Seminary of America (Heb. 21)

The Pentateuch was first printed in Italy as early as 1480. This edition included Rashi's popular commentary (see cat. no. 62) and additional texts read in the synagogue service, haftarot and *megillot.* In Italy the Scroll of Antiochus was publicly read on Ḥanukkah, and in order to address the needs of the local market, this text was also included in this edition. The haftarot, *megillot,* and Scroll of Antiochus are not found in this volume and may have been bound separately. This text does not include chapter and verse divisions. These divisions of the biblical text were a Christian development, which only became popular in Jewish circles in sixteenth-century printed editions.

This text features an elaborately decorated border on the first page of Genesis (fol. 1r) composed of cherubim hunting. They chase rabbits, deer, and a peacock against a background of interwoven spiraling branches. A blank shield is placed on the lower portion of the border so that the owner of the book could record his family coat of arms. In this edition the border is correctly aligned for a Hebrew publication, with the widest border at left, so that the larger margin is on the outer edge of the page. This border is found in other books published in Naples in 1491–1492, for example, *L'aquila volante,* published by Aiolfi de' Cantoni. An early Hebrew Bible without a colophon has been identified as a publication of the Neapolitan Soncino press of around 1491–1492 because of its use of this border. The carving of this border has been tentatively attributed to Moses ben Isaac, the brother-in-law of the printer Azriel Gunzenhauser.

Initial word blocks decorated with a border of scrolling floral branches mark the opening pages of four of the five books of the Pentateuch; the opening word of Genesis is flanked by cherubim. The first word of Numbers is less elaborately handled; it is composed of poorly matched individual letter blocks.

GMG

Bibliography: D. Sandler Berkowitz, *In Remembrance of Creation* (Waltham, Mass., 1968), no. 141; J. Bloch, "Hebrew Printing in Naples," in *Hebrew Printing and Bibliography,* p. 127; C. Roth, "The Border of the Naples Bible of 1491–2," *Studies in Books and Booklore* (Farnborough, England, 1972), pp. 71–80; Steinschneider, *Bodleiana,* no. 11; Zedner, *British Museum,* p. 96.

64. ***Meshal ha-Kadmoni* (The Fable of the Ancient)**

Isaac ben Solomon ibn Sahula (b. 1244)

Printer: Gershom Soncino

Brescia, 1491

Ink on paper, quarto, 86 leaves

7⁹⁄₁₆ × 11½ in. (19.2 × 29.2 cm)

New York, Library of The Jewish Theological Seminary of America (Heb. 45)

Ibn Sahula wrote this collection of fables and allegories in rhymed prose in order to provide Jewish readers with an original Hebrew work in place of translations of popular literature such as *The Voyages of Sinbad the Sailor,* widely read by Jews in the Middle Ages.

This was the first illustrated Hebrew printed book; seventy-seven woodcuts from sixty-five different blocks depict various scenes from the fables. Human and animal characters are portrayed with simple, expressive lines. Ibn Sahula illustrated his own manuscript, and many illuminated medieval copies of *Meshal ha-Kadmoni* are known. The woodcuts in this edition thus continued traditions established in manuscripts within the new, technologically advanced medium of printing.

GMG

Bibliography: British Library, *Illustration,* no. 8; Habermann, "Jewish Art," pp. 169–170; Steinschneider, *Bodleiana,* no. 5415, 1; Zedner, *British Museum,* p. 380.

65. ***Maḥberot***

Immanuel ben Solomon of Rome (c. 1261–after 1328)

Printer: Gershom Soncino

Brescia, 1491

Ink on paper, quarto, 160 leaves

8⅝ × 6¼ in. (22 × 16 cm)

New York, Library of The Jewish Theological Seminary of America (Heb. 43)

This collection of poems and *melitzot* (rhymed prose) was the first book of Hebrew secular poetry to be printed. Most of the poems are witty discussions of such subjects as wine, love, and riddles, but the work also includes elegies and religious poetry. Immanuel harmoniously blended the meters, figurative imagery, and narrative style of the Spanish Judeo-Arabic *maqama* form with elements modeled on contemporary Italian Renaissance writings. This collection also includes the first Hebrew Petrarchan sonnet. The last composition in the *Maḥberot,* a description of a journey through hell and paradise, was clearly modeled on Dante's *Divina commedia.* The collection was controversial because of its erotic themes; Joseph Caro (1488–1574) stated in the *Shulḥan Arukh* that it was forbidden to read it.[1] Gershom Soncino edited portions of the text to remove elements that were perceived as heretical.

GMG

Provenance: Mayer Sulzberger.

Bibliography: British Library, *Illustration,* no. 46; Carmilly-Weinberger, *Censorship,* pp. 215–216; Habermann, *Ha-Madpisim,* p. 44, no. 5; Hill, *Lowy,* no. 113; NYPL, *A Sign,* no. 136; Steinschneider, *Bodleiana* no. 5269, 1; Zedner, *British Museum,* p. 324.

1. Oraḥ Ḥayyim, Hilkhot Shabbat 307:16.

66. ***Annuli per eum composti super astrologiam utilitates*** **(The Astronomical Ring)**

Bonet de Lattes

Printer: Andreas Freitag

Rome, 1493

Ink on paper
8¼ × 5½ in. (20.1 × 14.0 cm)

New York, Library of The Jewish Theological Seminary of America (L 71)

Bonet de Lattes, who was also known by his Hebrew name, Ya'akov ben Immanuel Provinciale, served as the papal court physician for Alexander VI and Leo X. As is indicated by his Latin and Hebrew names, Bonet originally lived in Provence; his family came from the town of Lattes, near Montpellier. In the last decades of the fifteenth century many Provenzale Jews emigrated to Italy because of anti-Semitic disturbances and sporadic local orders of expulsion, culminating in Louis XII's general expulsion order against the Jews of Provence in 1498.

After leaving Provence, Bonet initially settled in Carpentras, where he wrote this work, and then moved to Rome, where the book was published. This Latin treatise, which is dedicated to Pope Alexander VI, describes an astronomical instrument invented by de Lattes. De Lattes's ring-dial allowed one to measure solar and stellar altitudes and to determine the precise time of day, even after sunset. De Lattes is well known due to an unusual Hebrew letter addressed to him by Johannes Reuchlin, the Christian Talmudist (see cat. no. 68). Reuchlin appealed to de Lattes to use his influence at the papal court to protect Reuchlin's book *Augenspiegel* from proscription by the Dominicans of Cologne. It is probable that de Lattes was successful in protecting Reuchlin, who was tried in his own diocese as he had requested in his letter.

GMG

Bibliography: *JE,* vol. 3, pp. 305–306; Marcus, *The Jew,* pp. 159–163; Zinberg, *Jewish Literature,* vol. 4, pp. 56, 86.

67. ***Poema di Serafino***

Serafino Aquilano dei Ciminelli (1464–1500)

Printer: Hieronymous Soncinum

Fano, 1505

Ink on paper

6 × 3¾ in. (15.2 × 9.5 cm)

New York, Library of The Jewish Theological Seminary of America (*R)

Gershom Soncino, using his Latin name, Hieronymus, published many Italian and Latin works, including this collection of Italian poetry by Serafino dei Ciminelli. Serafino's poetry was based on Petrarchan models and enjoyed wide public appeal, as Soncino noted in his publisher's foreword to this edition. He stated that Serafino's sonnets were everywhere sung and imitated by "lords, knights, doctors, counts, gentlemen, priests, friars, scholars, soldiers, plebeians, Hebrews, and other races."[1] Soncino's inclusion of "Hebrews" in this list indicates that he wanted this publication to appeal to his coreligionists, who were already familiar with the books of his family's Hebrew press (see cat. nos. 63–65), as well as to the general Italian readership.

GMG

Bibliography: Marx, *Bibliographical Studies,* p. 134.

1. For a discussion of Serafino's popularity and Soncino's statement, see T. L. Huguelet, "Sarafino Aquilano: Musician and Poet of the Late Quattrocento," in *Renaissance Papers, 1968,* ed. G. Walton Williams (Durham, N.C., 1969), pp. 1–3.

68. **Babylonian Talmud, Tractate *Mo'ed Katan***

Printer: Daniel Bomberg

Venice, 1521

Ink on paper

13⅜ × 9⅞ in. (34 × 25 cm)

New York, Library of The Jewish Theological Seminary of America (Talmud 39)

The first complete edition of the Babylonian Talmud was published in Venice by Bomberg, a Christian printer from Antwerp, between 1519 and 1523. Previously only individual tractates had been printed. In a letter to Johannes Reuchlin, the Christian defender of the Talmud, Bomberg wrote that Pope Leo X, son of Lorenzo de' Medici, specifically requested publication of the Talmud. Bomberg employed Rabbi Ḥiyya Meir ben David to act as editor and members of the Adelkind family to serve as printers in order to ensure the quality of the Aramaic and Hebrew texts. The foliation and arrangement of the commentaries established in this edition became the standard on which all later editions were modeled. Tractate *Mo'ed Katan* discusses primarily laws relating to *ḥol ha-mo'ed,* the intermediary days of festivals.

GMG

Bibliography: Amram, *Makers,* pp. 160–188; Bloch, *People and the Book,* p. 122; Bloch, "Venetian Printers," pp. 69–78; NYPL, *A Sign,* no. 183; NYPL, *Treasures,* 9:13; Rabinowitch, *Ha-dfasat ha-Talmud,* pp. 30–38; Rosenthal, "Daniel Bomberg"; Steinschneider, *Bodleiana,* no. 1778 (II).

69. **Biblia** (fig. 182)

Printer: Duarte Pinel (Abraham ibn Usque) for Jeronimo de Vargas (Yom-Tov ben Levi Athias)

Ferrara, 1553

Ink on paper, folio

11½ × 7¾ in. (29.2 × 19.7 cm)

New York, Library of The Jewish Theological Seminary of America (RAD cop. 1)

This text is the earliest printed Spanish translation of the Hebrew Bible. It was printed in two distinct editions. One, intended for Spanish Jews, was dedicated to Dona Gracia Nasi (see cat. no. 169) and featured a colophon with a Hebrew date and the printers' Hebrew names. It also included a schedule of weekly readings from the prophets, *haftarot.* The edition intended for a Christian audience was dedicated to Duke Ercole d'Este of Ferrara and bore a colophon dated March 1, 1553, which lists Pinel and Vargas as printer and publisher. In the Christian edition the translation of Isa. 7:14 allowed for a Christological interpretation of the text by using the term *virgen.* The Jewish edition used the Spanish term for young woman, *moca,* or, for fear of the Inquisition's censure, a transliteration of the Hebrew *almah.*

Some surviving copies of this Bible are composed of elements drawn from the different editions. For example, this copy is dedicated to Ercole d'Este but otherwise contains the elements of the edition intended for a Jewish audience. It is probable that a hasty binding led to confusion.

The dual nature of this publication reflects the double identities of the printer and publisher. Duarte Pinel and Jeronimo de Vargas lived as Christians in their respective homelands, Portugal and Spain. After their emigration to Ferrara they reverted to their families' original Jewish faith and began to use the names Abraham ibn Usque and Yom-Tov ben Levi Athias. Athias recognized the need for the publication of Jewish texts in the vernacular in order to facilitate the return of *conversos* to Judaism.

The galleon with one shattered mast sailing in a storm-tossed sea depicted on the frontispiece is symbolic of the steadfastness of sixteenth-century Spanish Jewry despite the hardships of the expulsion and Inquisition.

GMG

Bibliography: Amram, *Makers,* pp. 280–283; Berkowitz, *In Remembrance,* no. 194; *Encyclopaedia Judaica* vol. 16, col. 21; Marx, *Bibliographical Studies,* pp. 7, 32; Roth, "Jewish Printers," pp. 52–54.

70. **Responsa**

Judah ben Eliezer Ha-Levi Minz (c. 1408–1506)

Printer: Alvise Bragadini

Venice, 1553

Ink on paper, 136 leaves

7⅞ × 5$^{15}/_{16}$ in. (20 × 15 cm)

New York, Library of The Jewish Theological Seminary of America (IBA)

Rabbi Judah Minz is believed to have arrived in Padua from his native Mainz following the expulsion of the

Jews from that city in 1462. In Padua he studied with Rabbi Asher Enschechin, a German Talmudist. Minz later became the rabbi of Padua and head of the renowned yeshivah in that city, thereby establishing a dynasty of Ashkenazic rabbinical leadership in Italy.

The decisions in this volume relate primarily to questions of Jewish family law but also address issues specific to the social and religious needs of fifteenth-century Italian Jewry, such as the legal status of apostate Jews or the ruling permitting men to wear women's clothes, or vice versa, for Purim masquerades. Included in this edition are the responsa of Minz's grandson-in-law Rabbi Meir Katzenellenbogen, known as the Maharam of Padua. The frontispiece bears the printer's mark of the house of Bragadini, three crowns symbolizing the "crown of Torah, the crown of priesthood, and the crown of royalty" (Ethics of the Fathers 4:17). Portions of this text were expurgated by church censors in Mantua around 1595–1597 and in 1618 in order to remove elements seen as a challenge or an affront to Christian doctrine.

GMG

Provenance: Mayer Sulzberger.

Bibliography: Steinschneider, *Bodleiana,* no. 5744, 1; Zedner, *British Museum,* p. 395.

71. *Ateret Zekenim* (Crown of the Elders)

Don Isaac Abrabanel (1437–1508)

Printer: Tobia Foa

Sabbioneta, 1557

Ink on paper, quarto, 44 leaves

8⅛ × 6 in. (20.6 × 15.2 cm)

New York, Library of The Jewish Theological Seminary of America (NA)

Don Isaac Abrabanel was born in Lisbon and served as treasurer to King Alfonso V of Portugal. Forced to flee Portugal following Alfonso's death, he moved to Castille, where he entered the service of King Ferdinand and Queen Isabella. Following the expulsion of the Jews from Spain in 1492, Abrabanel was one of the many Spanish Jews who settled in Italy. Don Isaac was subsequently employed in the service of the king of Naples, Ferrante I, and his heir, Alfonso II, and followed the royal family to Messina after the French sack of Naples in 1494. Don Isaac subsequently moved to Corfu and then to Monopoli, eventually settling in Venice in 1503.

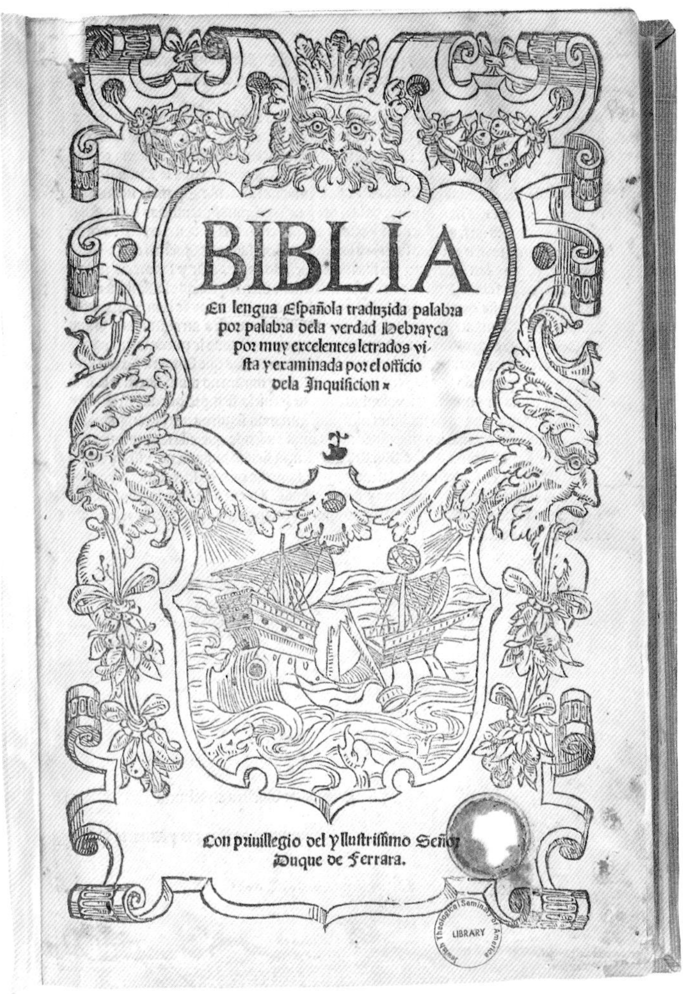

BIBLIA

En lengua Española traduzida palabra por palabra dela verdad Hebrayca por muy excelentes letrados vista y examinada por el officio dela Inquisicion

Con priuillegio del yllustrissimo Señor Duque de Ferrara.

Fig. 182. *Biblia,* Printed by Duarte Pinel (Abraham ibn Usque), Ferrara, 1553, The Library of The Jewish Theological Seminary of America, New York (cat. no. 69)

Abrabanel was an extremely prolific writer throughout his many travels and despite his numerous responsibilities as a statesman. He is renowned as a biblical exegete and philosopher. In this work Abrabanel examines the concept of God and the meaning of prophecy. He criticizes Aristotelian and Averroist philosophies and declares his admiration for kabbalistic thought.

The Foa press at Sabbioneta was active for a short period following the papal ban on Hebrew printing in 1553 and the subsequent burning of the Talmud (see cat. no. 83). With the end of Hebrew printing in

Venice, small presses in more tolerant city-states flourished. Foa was able to attract leading unemployed Venetian craftsmen, such as Cornelio Adelkind, to his press (see also cat. no. 68). After the printing of Hebrew books was once again permitted in Venice in 1563, the press at Sabbioneta, like most of the smaller presses, ceased activity. The Foa family remained active as printers in Venice, Pisa, and Amsterdam until the eighteenth century. The printer's mark of the Foa press, based on the Foa coat of arms, is found on the frontispiece of this volume (see also cat. no. 116).

GMG

Bibliography: Steinschneider, *Bodleiana,* no. 5302, 40; Yaari, "Ha-Madpisim B'nei Foa," *Kiryat Sefer,* 17 (1940): 408, no. 18.

72. **Haggadah**

Printer: Giacomo Rufinelli

Mantua, 1560

Ink on paper, folio

10¾ × 7¾ in. (27.3 × 19.7 cm)

New York, Library of The Jewish Theological Seminary of America (*LC)

This is the only known Hebrew book whose text was printed from woodblocks rather than movable type. Rufinelli was a Christian, and the production of the haggadah was supervised by Isaac ben Samuel Bassan, the sexton of a Mantua synagogue. The text is typographically identical to that of the famed Prague Haggadah of 1526 and employs varying sizes of Ashkenazic letters. The marginal woodcuts of the Mantua Haggadah also show the influence of the Prague Haggadah but simultaneously reveal the impact of contemporary Italian Renaissance art. In the Prague Haggadah the verse "But I took your father Abraham from beyond the Euphrates and led him through the whole land of Canaan and multiplied his offspring" (Josh. 24:3) is illustrated with a depiction of Abraham and an oarsman in a rowboat; in the corresponding Mantua woodcut, Abraham is seated in a gondola, while a gondolier in a plumed hat stands in the prow. The Mantua Haggadah also features a depiction of a seated, bearded Wise Son wearing a pointed, knobbed Jewish hat. The arrangement of the figure and drapery closely resembles that of Michelangelo's Jeremiah of the Sistine ceiling, revealing a willingness to adapt elements of Italian art for Jewish usage. Italian Renaissance borders featuring playful putti and floral festoons were adapted from other publications for use in the Mantua Haggadah and were often mutilated when cut to fit the text layout.

GMG

Provenance: Elkan Nathan Adler.

Bibliography: British Library, *Illustration,* no. 29; Marx, *Bibliographical Studies,* p. 48; Roth, "Illustrated Haggadah," p. 172; *Sha'arei Sefarim,* p. 7; Steinschneider, *Bodleiana,* no. 2679; Wischnitzer, "Passover in Art," pp. 315–316; Yaari, *Haggadot,* no. 18; Yerushalmi, *Haggadah and History,* pp. 37–39, pls. 22–26; Zedner, *British Museum,* p. 440.

73. ***D'rashot HaTorah*** (fig. 31)

Shem Tov ben Joseph ben Shem Tov ibn Shem Tov (active 1461–1489)

Printer: Lorenzo Pasquato

Padua, 1567

Ink on paper; 81 leaves

11 × 7⅝ in. (27.9 × 19.4 cm)

New York, Library of The Jewish Theological Seminary of America

The frontispiece of this book consists of an ornate arcuated portal, lavishly decorated with putti, portrait medallions, and foliage. A depiction of the Binding of Isaac is placed in an oval cartouche in the pediment and is surmounted by a majestic eagle. This same frontispiece was also used in books printed in Venice (1565) and in Cracow (1575).

Provenance: Mayer Sulzberger.

GMG

Bibliography: Amram, *Makers,* p. 338; B. Yaniv, *Sixteenth-Eighteenth Century Bohemian and Moravian Parochot with an Architectural Motif* [Hebrew] Ph.D. Dissertation, Hebrew University, Jerusalem, 1987, vol. I, p. 96.

74. ***Me'or Einayim* (Enlightenment to the Eyes)**

Azariah de' Rossi (c. 1511–c. 1578)

Mantua, 1573–1575

Ink on parchment, 198 leaves

8⅞ × 6½ in. (22.5 × 16.5 cm)

New York, Library of The Jewish Theological Seminary of America (*O cop.1)

This work consists of three sections: (1) *Kol Elohim,* a description of the earthquake in Ferrara of 1571 and a discourse comparing classical and medieval non-Jewish sources with biblical, Talmudic, and medieval Jewish literature regarding the cause and significance of earthquakes; (2) *Hadrat Zekenim,* a Hebrew translation of the Greek pseudepigraphic *Letter of Aristeas,* which describes the preparation of the Septuagint, the Greek translation of the Hebrew Bible; (3) and *Imrei Binah,* the largest component, a sixty-chapter study of Jewish history. In this third section Rossi compared traditional Hebrew texts, especially the Talmud (but not the Bible), with classical, Hellenistic, and patristic sources. His writings are clearly indebted to the works of contemporary Italian Renaissance scholars. Dante and Petrarch are frequently cited, and Rossi's critical historical method was greatly influenced by the works of Pico della Mirandola.

Rossi rejected many traditional historical accounts. For example, he disclosed that *Sefer Josipphon,* regarded by medieval scholars as an authoritative source of the Second Temple period, was actually an unreliable medieval compilation, containing falsified historical facts and based only partially on Josephus' writings. The most important and revolutionary element of Rossi's work was his rejection of the antiquity of the Jewish calendar, revealing that a calendar beginning at creation was not used in the biblical, Talmudic, and gaonic periods and that the Bible and other ancient sources provided insufficient evidence for the construction of a chronology from creation.

Because of its radical departure from traditional methods and conclusions, Rossi's work provoked great controversy. In 1573 the rabbis of Venice, headed by Samuel Katzenellenbogen, the son of the Maharam of Padua (see cat. no. 70), banned the book; a ban was then declared in many other Italian cities. In Ferrara, Venice, and Mantua only Jews over the age of twenty-five were allowed to read the book without special rabbinic permission. In Safed in 1575 a text of excommunication was prepared for the signature of Joseph Caro, the author of the *Shulḥan Arukh,* but Caro died before he signed the edict. This copy contains a handwritten edict requiring any Jew in possession of the book to destroy it. A printed broadside of this ban, issued by Caro's students, including Moshe Alshekh (d. after 1593), is also found in this volume.

Rossi later wrote an apology in response to his critics' attacks, *Mazref la-Kesef,* which discusses the issues of the calendar and chronology.

Provenance: David Cassel.

Bibliography: British Library, *Illustration,* no. 3; Carmilly-Weinberger, *Censorship,* p. 212; Steinschneider, *Bodleiana,* no. 4448, 1; Zedner, *British Museum,* p. 66.

75. *Cremona Fidelissima Citta*

Antonio Campi

Printer: Casa Dell'Auttore per Hippolito Tromba & Hercoliano Bartoli

Cremona, 1582

Ink on paper

16⅟16 × 10¼ in. (41.1 × 26 cm)

New York, Metropolitan Museum, 24.50.1

This book, containing a history of the city, portraits of celebrities and a series of portraits and short biographies of Milanese rulers and their consorts, includes maps that are the earliest Italian prints known by a Jewish engraver. A large foldout map of Cremona engraved by David de Laude is found on page 81. A second map by this engraver, a two page spread of the region surrounding Cremona, is found on pages 130–131. Both maps are signed "David de Laude Hebreus Cremone Incid . . . "

David de Laude's skill as an engraver is evident in these maps. They are highly detailed and cartographically sophisticated. The foldout map is bordered by four cartouches decorated with well-modeled *putti* and scrollwork. Fine crosshatching defines the various decorative elements, and undulating lines convey the swirling waters of the moat surrounding the city. The regional map includes a title enclosed in a ribbon and small depictions of architectural highlights, primarily churches, in the various city centers.

Jewish involvement in cartography was long established in pre-expulsion Spain, including such well-known makers as Abraham Cresques (d. 1387). It is thus probable that the tradition of Jewish involvement in mapmaking led to Campi's use of a Jewish engraver for his work. No examples of purely artistic or decorative engravings by Jews are known from this period.

GMG

Bibliography: Cecil Roth, *The Jews in the Renaissance* (New York, 1959), p. 193; E. Tietze-Conrat, "Notes on Portraits From Campi's *Cremona Fidelissima*" *Raccolta Vinciana,* 17 (1954), pp. 251–260.

76. ***Sefer ha-Minhagim* (Book of Customs)**

Edited and translated by Simeon Levi Guenzberg

Printer: Giovanni di Gara

Venice, 1593

Ink on paper, quarto

7½ × 5¼ in. (19 × 13.3 cm)

New York, Library of The Jewish Theological Seminary of America (BM 700 I818 1593)

In the late fifteenth and sixteenth century, Ashkenazic immigrants created a thriving center of Yiddish literature and printing in northern Italy. This work is a Yiddish translation of Isaac Tyrnau's fourteenth-century Hebrew text detailing the customs and ritual practices of the Jewish year. Simeon Levi Guenzburg, who escaped to Venice in 1592 following the raid of his printing press in Tannhausen, edited and translated the original Hebrew text. The first edition of this work appeared in 1590. In 1593 a second edition with a calendar for seventy years and woodcuts depicting various annual ceremonies was issued. These woodcuts were acquired or copied by Amsterdam printers and were often reproduced in later editions of the seventeenth and eighteenth centuries.

This volume is bound with wooden covers bearing a carved and dated inscription identifying the probable original owner of this book:

עקיבה בר משה חיים זל שנת שנז

(Akiva son [of] Moshe Ḥayyim [of] b[lessed] m[emory] [the] year [5]357 [1596/1597]).

GMG

Provenance: Judah A. Joffe.

Bibliography: Edelmann, *Denmark,* no. 20; Epstein, "Illustrated Customal"; NYJM, *Kings and Citizens,* no. 28; Schmeruk, "D'fusei Yiddish," p. 153, no. 19; Steinschneider, *Bodleiana,* no. 3820.

77. **Haggadah (Judeo-Italian issue)** (fig. 15)

Printer: Giovanni da Gara

Venice, 1609

Ink on vellum, folio, 24 leaves

11⅛ × 7⅝ in. (28.3 × 19.4 cm)

New York, Library of The Jewish Theological Seminary of America (Yaari, no. 35)

This Haggadah was published in three issues (Judeo-Italian, Judeo-Spanish, and Judeo-German), each with a different translation, in order to answer to the varying linguistic needs of the Italian, Sephardic, and Ashkenazic members of the Venetian-Jewish community. Israel Zifroni, an Italian-Jewish printer who had participated in the printing of the Talmud in Basel from 1578 to 1580, planned the printing of this edition. Its illustrations were highly innovative and served as models for many later editions. They include the first composite compositions of the ten plagues and of thirteen scenes depicting various stages of the seder. The narrative illustrations, which were prepared especially for this edition, are arranged in a thematic order, paralleling the seder service. The first part of the haggadah is illustrated with scenes of the liberation from Egypt, while other biblical and messianic themes are featured in the latter part. Throughout the volume the Italianate lettering of the text is surrounded by borders composed of classical architectural elements, and large woodcut initials containing tiny representations of highlights of the seder mark the beginning of pages.

GMG

Bibliography: Roth, "Illustrated Haggadah," pp. 173–174; Steinschneider, *Bodleiana,* no. 2688; Wischnitzer, "Passover in Art," pp. 316–318; Yaari, *Haggadot,* no. 35; Yerushalmi, *Haggadah and History,* pp. 40–41, 61–62, pls. 44–45; JNUL, *Selected,* no. 44.

78. ***Canti Ha-Shirim Asher li-Shelomo*** (fig. 14)

Salomon de' Rossi (c. 1570–c. 1630)

Printer: Pietro and Lorenzo Bragadini

Venice, 1624

Ink on paper, quarto

10 × 7¼ in. (25.4 × 18.4 cm)

New York, Library of The Jewish Theological Seminary of America (*L 1624)

Salomon de' Rossi was a prominent viol player and composer at the court of Mantua and was highly praised for his madrigals and intermezzi. In 1606 Duke Vincenzo Gonzaga exempted Rossi from wearing the Jewish badge, thereby recognizing the composer's elevated status. Thirteen volumes of Rossi's musical works were published during his lifetime.

This collection of synagogal choral compositions was the first Hebrew book to be printed with musical notation, and it established the standard for the insertion of the Hebrew text in reverse to correspond to the left-to-right direction of the score. The innovative character of this publication is announced on the title page, where the works are described as "something new on earth" (Jer. 31:22).

Although Rossi's synagogal compositions are devoid of instrumentals, the influences of contemporary church music and Venetian monodic song style are apparent. The compositions for various psalms and other liturgical works are arranged for three to eight voices. Leone Modena (see cat. no. 79) was the editor of this publication, and his responsum declaring the worthiness and halakhic propriety of synagogal choral music is included in the preface to this edition.

GMG

Bibliography: Adler, "Hebrew Writings," pp. 285–288, no. 590; JNUL, *Manuscripts and Rare Books,* no. 235; JNUL, *Selected,* no. 57b; Marx, *Bibliographical Studies,* p. 72; Newman, *Madrigals*; Newman and Rikko, *Thematic Index*; NYJM, *Jewish Patrons,* no. 19; Rikko, ed., *Ha Shirim.*

79. ***Historia de Riti Hebraici*** (fig. 11)

Leone Modena (1571–1648)

Printer: Giovanni Calleoni

Venice, 1638

Ink on paper

5¾ × 3⅝ in. (14.6 × 9.2 cm)

New York, Library of The Jewish Theological Seminary of America

Leone Modena was a prominent Venetian rabbi, scholar, and writer. He wrote in his autobiography that he pursued twenty-six occupations at various points in his lifetime, including translator, broker, matchmaker, and writer. Modena was famed as a versifier in Hebrew, Italian, and Latin and was an instructor and leading authority for the Christian Hebraists of his period.

Modena wrote this book in 1614–1615 at the suggestion of an English nobleman in order to provide King James I with a source outlining the basic practices of Judaism. An apologetic appeal for the social toleration of Jews underlies this work. Since the *Riti* was initially written as a private work addressed to a Protestant audience, Modena was not fearful of church censorship. In 1637 Modena's friend the French Catholic theologian Jacques Gafarel arranged for publication of the first edition in Paris. Modena, fearful of the church's censure, appealed to the Inquisition, saying that he was not responsible for the work's redaction. In fact Gafarel had censored the work prior to publication. Modena further censored this second edition, published in Venice in 1638.

A portrait of the bald, bearded author appears in the bottom shield of the frontispiece. He is depicted bareheaded, reflecting Modena's statement in his responsum on head covering that he uncovered his head when speaking to noblemen.[1] Since this book addressed a king, Modena has shown respect by baring his head.

GMG

Bibliography: *Encyclopaedia Judaica,* vol. 7, cols. 253–254, vol. 12, cols. 202–204; Marcus, *The Jew,* pp. 405–408; NYJM, *Jewish Patrons,* no. 17; *The Autobiography of a Seventeenth-Century Venetian Rabbi: Leon Modena's Life of Judah,* trans. and ed. M. R. Cohen, (Princeton, 1988). Zinberg, *Jewish Literature,* vol. 4, pp. 146–147.

1. See Y. Rivkind, "Tshuvat ha-Rav Yehuda Aryeh Modena al Giluei ha-Rosh," in *Louis Ginzberg Jubilee Volume* (New York, 1945), pp. 401–424.

80. ***Sefer Mesilat Ha-limud* (The Book of the Path of Study)**

Judah Leib, son of Zev

Printer: Antonio Schmid

Vienna, 1825

Ink on paper, leather binding; 122 pages

8$\frac{1}{16}$ × 5¼ in. (20.5 × 13.3 cm)

Private collection

This primer for teaching children to read Hebrew was presented to Simone Toscano in 1845 by the Talmud

Torah (religious school) of the Comunità Israelitica in Rome. Although printed in Vienna, the book was designed for export and includes an Italian translation. The dedicatory inscription includes the stamp of the community bearing the Hebrew text "Let not this Book of the Teaching cease from your lips" (Josh. 1:8).

GMG

Unpublished

81. **Books from the Library of a Jewish Family**

Petrarca Con Doi Com Menti Sopra Li 50 Netti et Can Zone

1522 (?)

Title page missing

6⅞ × 4⅜ in. (17.5 × 11.1 cm), 258 leaves

Secundi Historiae Mundi, Libri XXXVII
C. Plini

1539

14¼ × 9½ in. (36.2 × 24.1 cm)

Hist . . . Esternes de Romani di . . .

Appiano

Printer: Aldi Fisii

Venice

1551

5¾ × 3¾ in. (14.5 × 9.6 cm), 216 pages

Sentencias Y Dichos de divers Sabios Y Antiguous Auctiones, Ass Griegos Como Latinos

M. Nicolas, ed.

Printer: Gabriel Giolito de Ferrariis Y Sus Hermanos Ehel

Venice

1553

5⅞ × 3¾ in. (14.9 × 9.5 cm), 72 pages

Descrittione Di Tutta Italia Di F. Leandro Alberti

Leandro Alberti

Printer: Ludovico de gli Ananzi

Venice

1567

8 × 5⅝ in. (20.3 × 14.3 cm), 504 pages

Ex Libris Bonna Olivetti Levi

Delle Guerre Ciorli

Appiano Alissadrino

Printer: Camillo Franceschini

Venice

1575

5¾ × 1⅜ in. (14.5 × 3.4 cm), 279 pages

Ex Libris Bonna Olivetti Levi

Valerii Maximi Dictorum Factorum Q

Printer: Apud Joan Gryphium

Venice

1575

5¾ × 3⅝ in. (14.6 × 9.2 cm), 238 leaves

Libro di Marco Aurelio Con L'horologia de' Prencipi

Printer: Fabio & Agostino Zoppini Fratelli

Venice

1581

7¾ × 5¾ in. (19.7 × 14.6 cm), 355 leaves

Ex Libris Bonna Olivetti Levi

Descrittione di Tutta Italia

Fra Leandro Alberti

Printer: Gio. Battista Porta

Venice

1581

8⅞ × 6½ in. (22.4 × 16.5 cm), 631 pages

Historia Naturale Di G Plino Secondo

M. Ludovicho Domenichi, trans.

Printer: Gio. Battista Uscio

Venice

1589

7⅞ × 5¾ in. (19.9 × 14.6 cm), 1242 pages

Paragraphi in divi Iustiniani Institione Compraehensi

Printer: Apud Iuntas

Venice

1593

6⅝ × 4⅜ in. (16.8 × 11.1 cm), 391 pages

Dialoghi del Sig. Speron Speroni Nobile Padovano

Printer: Roberto Meietti

Venice

1596

8 × 5½ in. (20.3 × 14 cm), 597 leaves

Opere di G Cornellio Tacito Annali, Historiae, Costumi de Germain e Vita di Agricola

Venice

1618

5⅜ × 6⅜ in. (13.6 × 16 cm)

Ex Libris Moise Arone Levi

Opera Chirurgico—Anatomico

Pauli Barbetti

Printer: Petri Masiae Fraribosti

Patavii

1679

5¼ × 2⅞ in. (13.3 × 7.2 cm), 450 pages

Teatro Italiano o sia scetta di tragedie per uso della scene, vols. I, II

Printer: Jacopo Vallaisi

Venice

1723

I: 6⅛ × 4⅛ in. (15.5 × 10.5 cm), 403 pages;
II: 6⅛ × 4 in. (15.5 × 10.2 cm), 424 pages

Oeuvres Diverses de Mr Pierre Bayle, Tome IV

Pierre Bayle

Printer: Compagnie des Libraires

La Haye

1738

15½ × 9¾ in. (39.3 × 24.8 cm), 916 pages

Storia de' Giudei e de Polpoli Vicini, Dalla decadenza dei Reami d'Israele, e di Giua fino alla Morte di Gesu Cristo, vol. I, II, V, VI

Printer: Giambatista Pasqual

Venice

1738

6⅝ × 4¼ in. (16.8 × 10.8 cm), I: 293 pages; II: 375 pages; V: 368 pages; VI: 241 pages

Amusements des dames ou recueil d'histoires galantes tirées des meilleurs auteurs de ce siècle, vol. II, III

The Hague

1763

5³⁄₁₆ × 3 in. (13.2 × 7.6 cm), II: 435 pages;
III: 442 pages

Histoire des Revolutions Arrivées dans le Gouvernment de la République Romaine, Tome III

Abbe de Vertot

Printer: Babuty Fils

Paris

1767

6½ × 3⅝ in. (16.5 × 9.2 cm), 448 pages

Les oeuvres galantes et amoureuses d'Ovide, Tome I

Printer: Luccia Vitalevi Rocca

Amsterdam

1771

5⅜ × 3⅛ in. (13.5 × 8.0 cm), 232 pages

O Horatii Flacci Carmina Expurgata

Josepho Juvencio

Printer: Franciscum ex Nicolao Pezzana

Venice

1771

6 × 3⅜ in. (15.2 × 8.6 cm), 559 pages

Ex Libris Levi M.

Descriptions des Beautés de Gènes et de ses Environs

Printer: Yves Gravier

Genes

1788

6⅝ × 4 in. (16.8 × 10.2 cm), 368 pages

Manuel des Autorités Constituées de la République Française

Printer: Dufart & Dessene

Paris

An 5 (1797)

5⁷⁄₁₆ × 3⅜ in. (13.8 × 8.6 cm), 408 pages

Histoire de Francois Premier, Tome V

Gaillard

Printer: Saillam & Nyon

Paris

1799

6½ × 3⅝ in. (16.5 × 9.2 cm), 511 pages

English Grammar Adapted to the Different Classes of Learners with an Appendix Containing Rules and Observations for Assisting the More Advanced Students

Lindley Murray

Printer: Josiah B. Baldwin

Bridgeport

1826

6⅝ × 4 in. (16.8 × 10.2 cm), 312 pages

Ex. Libris Anne D. Steele

La Secchia Rapita

Alessandro Tassoni

Title page missing

6⅝ × 4⅛ in. (16.8 × 10.5 cm), 495 pages

Introduzione al calcolo differenziale e integrale

Elia Cassin (1835–1910)

Turin, 1854–1855

Ink on parchment; leather binding: stamped and gilt

11⅜ × 16³⁄₁₆ in. (28.9 × 41.2 cm) open dimensions

This manuscript contains the notes written by Elia Cassin for a course in Differential and Integral Calculus given by Professor Erba at the University of Turin in 1854–1855. Cassin studied engineering at the University soon after it opened its door to Jewish students. He was later involved in the building of railroads in Sardinia and Turkey.

Recompense al valor militaire, Parte II

(n.p.: n.d.)

Ink on paper, printed; 314 pages

9¾ × 6³⁄₁₆ in. (24.7 × 15.8 cm)

Private collection

This book, printed by the Jewish communities of Italy, lists all those Jews who were honored for service during World War I.

WORKS ON PAPER

82. **Decree Expelling the Jews from Naples**

Naples, 1504

Ink on paper

11½ × 8⅜ in. (29.2 × 21.3 cm)

New York, Library of The Jewish Theological Seminary of America (H11a)

Following the expulsion of the Jews from Spain in 1492, many Iberian Jews, including Don Isaac Abrabanel (see cat. no. 71) fled to Naples. This refuge was short-lived, however. In 1495 the kingdom of Naples was conquered by the Spanish, and an order for the expulsion of Jews from Naples was issued in the following year. The expulsion orders continued until 1510, when a definitive edict was issued. Neapolitan Jews were forced to move to other, more liberal Italian city-states, including, ironically, those under papal rule. Two hundred wealthy Jews were granted special permission to remain in Naples; this number eventually swelled to six hundred. The Jews of Naples were expelled again in 1533, readmitted in 1535, and expelled again in 1541. In 1735 the kingdom of Naples came under Bourbon rule, and Jews were readmitted in 1740.

GMG

Unpublished

83. **Edict for the Confiscation and Burning of the Talmud**

Venice, 21 October 1553

Ink on paper, printed

12¼ × 8 in. (31.1 × 20.3 cm)

New York, Library of The Jewish Theological Seminary of America (no. 04501)

The confiscation and burning of the Talmud in sixteenth-century Italy were prompted by the rivalry between two Christian printers of Hebrew books in Venice and by the religious fervor of the Counter-Reformation. An edition of Maimonides' *Mishneh Torah* with a commentary by Rabbi Meir Katzenellenbogen, the Maharam of Padua (see cat. no. 70), was published by the Bragadini press in 1550. A second edition of Maimonides' text issued by Giustiniani in the same year sparked a feud, with Bragadini claiming that Giustiniani was maliciously attempting to destroy his press. Katzenellenbogan appealed to the renowned legal authority Rabbi Moses Isserles of Cracow (1525/30–1572) to protect his efforts and investment. Rabbi Isserles issued an edict of excommunication against any Jew who purchased Giustiniani's books. Giustiniani attempted to counter the rabbinical edict by encouraging apostate Jews to denounce Rabbi Katzenellenbogen's commentary as objectionable to the church. Bragadini also became embroiled, encouraging papal edicts against Giustiniani and thereby provoking the denunciation of other Hebrew works.

The denunciation of specific works developed into a wholesale attack on Hebrew literature, encouraged by the fanaticism of the Dominicans and the Inquisition. Following an examination of the issues by a council of cardinals, Pope Julius III issued a bull ordering the public burning of the Talmud. The first burning took place in Rome on September 9, 1553, the first day of Rosh Hashanah. Cardinal Caraffa, the grand inquisitor, encouraged the spread of the decree throughout Italy. The edict on exhibition, dated October 21, 1553, is for the confiscation and burning of the Talmud and related works in Venice. The destruction was very thorough. The sixteenth-century Italian scholar of Spanish origin Rabbi Judah di Lerma describes in the second edition of his *Leḥem Yedudah* how the entire first edition of fifteen hundred books had been burned in Venice.[1]

The repercussions of the destruction of Hebrew books in Venice were very great. Venice lost its position as the center of Hebrew printing, and presses were forced to move to other locations (see cat. no. 71). Hebrew printing was reestablished in Venice in the following decades, but the rabbis of Venice required official approval of all texts, practicing self-censorship in order to prevent further confiscations and destruction.

GMG

Bibliography: NYPL, *A Sign,* no. 172.

1. See Amram, *Makers,* p. 269.

84. **Decree Expelling the Jews from Bologna**

Bologna, 1590

Ink on paper, printed

16¼ × 11½ in. (41 × 29.2 cm)

New York, Library of The Jewish Theological Seminary of America (H9)

In the fifteenth and throughout most of the sixteenth centuries Bologna was a center of Jewish culture under the leadership of such noted scholars as Obadiah Sforno and Azariah de' Rossi (see cat. no. 74). In 1513 Bologna reverted to direct papal rule, however, and the religious fervor of the Counter-Reformation resulted in anti-Semitic policies that put an end to Bolognese-Jewish life. The Talmud was burned in Bologna in 1553, and Jews were confined to a ghetto in 1556. In 1569 Pius V expelled the Jews of Bologna. They were readmitted by Sixtus V in 1586, only to be expelled again in 1590, as documented by this edict. After the expulsion order of 1593, issued by Clement VIII, the Jews of Bologna disinterred their dead and reburied them in Pieve di Cento. The Bolognese-Jewish community was not reestablished until 1796, after the French conquest of Italy. The Jews were again expelled in 1836, following the return to papal rule. In 1859 the city of Bologna was annexed to Piedmont, and Jews were granted equal rights.

GMG

Unpublished

85. ***Vue d'un des quatre angles de la maison des juifs illuminées. Veduta d'uno de quatro angoli del ghetto illuminato***

Cojetanus Blancus after Joseph Maria Piovanus after Bernardus Vitonus

Turin, 1737

Engraving on paper, hand-colored

11¾ × 16¼ in. (30 × 41.5 cm)

New York, The Moldovan Family Collection

This engraving portrays the ghetto of Turin, a single building that had formerly been used as a hospital for beggars. It was originally published in the book *La Sontuosa Illuminazione della Città di Torino,* printed in Turin by Giovanni Battista Chais in honor of the marriage of Charles Emmanuel I, king of Sardinia, and Elizabeth Theresa, princess of Lorraine; hence the print letter in Italian and French. It is the eleventh of fourteen views of scenic and architectural highlights of Turin by various architects, draftsmen, and engravers. Since this engraving is dated 1737, it is probable that it was commissioned especially for this publication.

GMG

Bibliography: A. Rubens, *A Jewish Iconography* (London, 1981), no. 1695.

86. ***Piazza Giudia***

Giuseppe Vasi (1710–1782)

Rome, mid-eighteenth century

Engraving on paper

8¼ × 11¹³⁄₁₆ in. (21 × 30 cm)

New York, The Moldovan Family Collection

Vasi engraved a suite of four scenes of the Rome ghetto (see also cat. no. 87). In this work the entrance to the ghetto can be seen on the right. The *sbirri* (police) occupied the small house at left center, where they detained latecomers. A man is seen urinating against the wall of this building, indicating disdain either for the police or for the ghetto's Jewish residents.

Vasi was the engraver to the court of Naples and was knighted.

GMG

Bibliography: S. Fornari, *La Roma del ghetto* (Rome, 1984), p. 14; A. Rubens, *A Jewish Iconography* (London, 1981), no. 1688.

87. ***Isola Tiberina verso occidente***

Giuseppe Vasi (1710–1782)

Rome, mid-eighteenth century

Engraving on paper

8¼ × 12⅝ in. (21 × 32 cm)

New York, The Moldovan Family Collection

This is one of a suite of four scenes of the Rome ghetto engraved by Vasi (see cat. no. 86). The Isola Tiberina is an island in the Tiber adjacent to the ghetto. The same scene was engraved by Vasi's student Giovanni Battista Piranesi.

GMG

Unpublished

88. ***Pars canalis magni ultra pontem Hebreorum Venetus (Partie du grand canal plus outre du Pont de Juif à Venise)***

Anonymous

Venice(?), c. 1750

Engraving on paper, hand-colored

12½ × 16¾ in. (31.75 × 42.5 cm)

New York, The Moldovan Family Collection

This engraving portrays a typical Venetian view of palazzi, canals, gondolas, gondoliers, and well-dressed ladies and gentlemen. The inclusion of any Jewish element in the iconography appears to be happenstance, in that the *pontem Hebreorum* was part of an overall scenic vista well suited to the souvenir trade for which such prints were intended.

GMG

Unpublished

89. ***Scene of a Jewish Funeral: Transport of the Body to the Cemetery*** (fig. 13)

Giovanni del Pian (1764–1800)

Venice, c. 1784

Engraving on paper

17 × 20¹⁵⁄₁₆ in. (43.2 × 53.2 cm)

New York, Library of The Jewish Theological Seminary of America (C.3.1.30)

This print is one of a suite of four engravings of Venetian-Jewish scenes executed by Giovanni del Pian. Eighteenth-century travelers frequently purchased prints illustrating local or exotic customs, and the suite addressed this souvenir market.

Del Pian portrayed a uniquely Venetian-Jewish funeral in great detail. The coffin with sloped top, indicating that the deceased was a man of note, is lowered by the pallbearers, possibly members of the Ḥevrah Kaddisha, the burial society, into a gondola for transport to the Jewish cemetery on the island of San Nicolò di Lido. A dwarf carries an alms box, collecting funds from the mourners.[1] In the gondola sit tearful mourners. Overlooking the canal are a group of men observing the funeral. In this group del Pian has included standard Venetian types: a monk and a man masked for a masquerade.

The print letter bears a description of contemporary Venetian-Jewish funeral customs. The Hebrew inscription on the front of the coffin is cryptic, probably as a result of a non-Jewish artist's unfamiliarity with the Hebrew language.

GMG

Bibliography: NYJM, *Jewish Patrons,* no. 52; A. Rubens, *A Jewish Iconography* (London, 1981), no. 621.

Fig. 184. Ferdinando Fambrini after Omabano Rosselli, *Interior of the Livorno Synagogue,* Livorno, 1793, Comunità Israelitica, Livorno (cat. no. 90)

1. A dwarf is also depicted in the burial scene *La sepoltura,* engraved by Francesco Novelli in Venice in 1789, and based on Bernard Picart's composition (Amsterdam, 1723). Picart did not include a dwarf in his scene. It is possible that del Pian and Novelli were documenting historical reality, that there was a dwarf who belonged to the Venetian Ḥevrah Kaddisha in the late eighteenth century.

90. ***Interior of the Livorno Synagogue*** (fig. 184)

Ferdinando Fambrini after Omabano Rosselli

Livorno, 1793

Hand-colored engraving on paper

22⅞ × 34¼ in. (58 × 87 cm)

Livorno, Comunità Israelitica

In 1593 Grand Duke Ferdinand I granted the Jews of Livorno the privilege of having a synagogue. This first synagogue was later expanded and remodeled to create one of the grandest synagogues in Europe. Earthquakes in the eighteenth century caused the Livorno community to fear for the building's stability and prompted structural and decorative improvements in 1787, under the direction of the architect Ignazio Fazzi. This detailed print portrays the interior of the synagogue in the late eighteenth century. The unusually angled and foreshortened view accentuates the grandeur of the space. The lavishly decorated marble ark, composed of four columns supporting a scrolled pediment, was situated on the southern wall. The other walls were divided into three levels of arched galleries. The upper two levels formed the women's galleries and were covered with gracefully curved grilles. The synagogue was lavishly furnished and decorated with a polygonal marble *bemah* surrounded by a balustrade, gold-lettered inscriptions, wooden wall revetments, and abundant foliate ornament.

Ferdinando Fambrini was active as an engraver in Venice in the eighteenth century. Omabano Rosselli may have been a member of the well-known Jewish Rosselli family.

GMG

Selected Bibliography: A. Rubens, *A Jewish Iconography* (London, 1981), no. 1676; A. Toaff, "Il Museo della Comunità Israelitica," *Liburni Civitas* IV (1931): 91–92.

91. **Design for a Torah Curtain and a Reader's Desk Cover**

Livorno, 1815

Watercolor and ink on paper

18¾ × 14½ in. (47.6 × 36.9 cm)

New York, The Jewish Museum,
Gift of Dr. Harry G. Friedman (F 4102)

At the center of the Torah Curtain are crowned Tablets of the Law surrounded by a border of vine scrolls, a composition that appeared on many Italian curtains of the eighteenth century.[1] What is unusual about this design is the inclusion of musical instruments (two harps), and symbols of royalty and priesthood (a crown, a mitre, and lavers). The drawing for the matching Reader's Desk Cover gives details of the works' commission:

נדבת / בני חברת מהרה בתולת / שנת / כי באמ׳ו׳נה׳
ע׳ש׳י׳ם׳ / לפג

(The donation of members of the Confraternity . . . of the Maidens [in] the year 'for they dealt honestly' [5575 = 1814–1815]).

An Italian inscription in the lower border reads:

Prospettive della Gran Tenda e della Coperta del Pulpito, esistente nel Tempio degl'Israeliti / di Livorno Dono offerto dalla Pia Confraternita di Maritar Donzelle di Detta Città, presentate . . . 5 Maggio 1815 . . . art Livorno . . . David Vita e Rosa Bonfil . . .

(View of the large curtain and of the cover of the pulpit extant in the Temple of the Israelites of Livorno offered by the holy Confraternity of those who give Maidens in Marriage of That City, presented . . . the fifth of May, 1815 . . .
David Vita and Rosa Bonfil).

The significance of the names is uncertain due to the loss of portions of the inscription. In the middle of the inscription is a coat of arms, a tower from which emerges a lion facing left. Although similar coats of arms appear on Livornese marriage contracts, they are not identical to this one.[2]

VBM

Bibliography: *Rare Judaica from the Collection of Tullio Castelbolognesi, Rome,* sale cat., Parke-Bernet Galleries, New York, 1956, lot. 84; NYJM, *Fabric of Jewish Life,* no. 9.

1. See V. Klagsbald, *Catalogue raisonné de la collection juive du Musée de Cluny* (Paris, 1981), no. 133.
2. U. Nahon, *Holy Arks and Ritual Appurtenances from Italy in Israel* (Tel-Aviv, 1970), p. 200; L. Grassi, ed., *Ketubbot italiane* (Milan, 1984), no. 28.

92. ***Die Bekehrung der Juden in Roma***

Von Guise after Hieronymus Hess (Swiss, 1799–1850)

Rome, 1823

Hand-colored lithograph on paper

16¼ × 20¾ in. (41.3 × 52.7 cm)

New York, Library of The Jewish Theological Seminary of America (H9)

This print after Hess's watercolor *Judenpredigt* depicts a conversionist sermon that Jews were forced to attend. *Judenpredigt* has been regarded as Hess's most fully developed work. Its depiction of numerous Jews under the scrutiny of monks is rendered with precise detail, and Hess has portrayed the varying reactions of Jews attending the service, ranging from boredom to fear. Although some of Hess's depictions of Jews can be regarded as satirical, his portrayal of the extreme ferocity of the preaching monk conveys the artist's criticism of the proceedings and his sympathy for those who were forced to attend such events.

A second state of this print contains a print letter stating that the original was in the collection of the architect J. Heimlicher of Basel and that von Guise worked under the supervision of Hess.

GMG

Bibliography: J. J. Imhof, *Der Historienmaler Hieronymus Hess von Basel* (Basel, 1887), pp. 10–11.

93. ***Das Innere einer Sinagoge in Rom***

Von Guise after Hieronymus Hess (Swiss, 1799–1850)

Rome, c. 1823

Hand-colored lithograph on paper, with graphite

12 × 18 in. (30.5 × 45.7 cm)

New York, The Jewish Museum (F 4427C)

Hess's composition portrays the frenetic activity occurring during services at the Tempio Italiano in the Cinque Scole of Rome. Very few of the men are actually listening to the reading of the Torah; the vast majority are talking and arguing with their neighbors. Hess appears to be satirizing the lack of decorum at synagogue services.

Hess may be presenting this scene as a variant of the New Testament account of the money changers in the Temple (Matt. 21:12).[1] The Tempio Italiano was often called *il tempio,* so that the correlation between the synagogue and the Temple in Jerusalem would have been especially clear. In Hess's depiction the Decalogue follows the Christian model, with the letters *aleph* through *yud* arranged so that four commandments are on the first tablet and six on the next.[2] This further supports a reading of the scene in a Christian allegorical context. In actuality the tablets atop the ark in the Tempio Italiano were inscribed with two-word abbreviations of the Ten Commandments in the traditional Jewish arrangement of five commandments on each tablet.

Hess has carefully observed details of dress. Most of the men attending the services are clean-shaven Europeans, dressed in stylish frock coats and top hats. The remainder are bearded eastern European Jews dressed in caftans and tall fur hats and North African or Ottoman Jews dressed in turbans and robes.

Many of the details of the interior of the Tempio have also been accurately portrayed. The friezes depicting symbols of the twelve tribes, the Temple implements, and various scenes from the Bible are all clearly shown, as are many of the Hebrew inscriptions. The artist has taken some liberties with the spatial arrangement of the synagogue, however, compressing the longitudinal axis to fit the picture frame. Hess placed the *bemah,* traditionally at one end of Italian synagogues, at the center, making it the focal point of his composition.

A second state of this lithograph includes a letter stating that the work was published in Karlsruhe by J. Velten after an original in Rome in the possession of Albert Bertel Thorvaldsen, the noted Danish sculptor and collector, and that Hess supervised Von Guise's work.

GMG

Bibliography: J. J. Imhof, *Der Historienmaler Hieronymus Hess von Basel* (Basel, 1887), pp, 10–11.

1. I am indebted to Norman Kleeblatt for this insight.
2. I would like to thank Evelyn Cohen for pointing out this feature to me.

94. ***Rue de la Synagogue***

Anonymous

Rome, 1837

Watercolor on paper

17½ × 14⅜ in. (44.5 × 36.5 cm)

Rome, Comunità Israelitica

In 1555 Pope Paul IV issued a bull that restricted the Jews of Rome to a single synagogue. Pius V later agreed to allow one building to contain five synagogues. This arrangement satisfied the legal restriction and allowed Jews of various rites and origins to maintain their distinct traditions. In one wing of the complex were the Catalan, Sicilian, and New (Italian) rite synagogues, while the Castilian synagogue was on the ground floor of the other wing and the Tempio Italiano was on the level above. The Cinque Scole (five synagogues) complex also included a library, school, cloakroom, and home for the poor. This work portrays the Piazza delle Scole, the square surrounding the Cinque Scole. It predates the later addition of a columned porch that provided external access to the New synagogue.

The artist has depicted the modest exterior of the synagogue complex. Only the interiors, which could not be seen by the average Italian, were lavishly ornamented, so that their splendor would not incite anti-Semitism.

GMG

Unpublished

95. **Plans for the Tempio Maggiore Israelitico in Reggio Emilia** (fig. 192)

Reggio Emilia, 1859

Ink on paper

7 × 7$^{13}/_{16}$ in. (18 × 20 cm)

Reggio Emilia, Archivio di Stato (Marchelli 2001–5)

First built in 1672, the year following the institution of the ghetto, Reggio Emilia's synagogue remained essentially unaltered until 1755, when an elaborate ark was commissioned from the sculptor Agostino Canciani. In the mid-nineteenth century the decision was made to completely restructure the building because of its deteriorating state.

A local architect, Pietro Marchelli, designed a simple neoclassical building covered by a large flattened and coffered dome with a projecting lantern over a nearly square room. The space was arranged so that the congregation was separated from the sanctuary. Despite a nearly central domical plan, there was no central placement of a *bemah,* as at Livorno.

The synagogue was preceded by a shallow vestibule, which stretched across the width of the building. Above this were the women's galleries, connected to the main hall through openings in the west wall. The north, south, and west walls were decorated with columns on the ground level and pilasters above. Large windows set between pilasters filled the north and south walls.

Along the east wall, steps led to a raised choir, in the center of which was the eighteenth-century ark set in an apsidial extension beyond the east wall. The extension was large enough to house the ark, set against the furthest wall, as well as built-in wooden seats flanking the ark and a reader's table in front of it. The extension was screened by four freestanding Ionic columns and a marble balustrade, which appears to have relegated the congregation to being spectators rather than participants in the service.

Light came into the room from above, so that immediately upon entering the synagogue the viewer's eyes were led to the tabernacle, and further up to the cupola, searching, in Andrea Balletti's words, "for the source of the light." Collaborating with Marchelli on the work were Pasquale Zambini, who painted the cupola; Alessandro and Gaetano Tosi, who did the gilding; and Pietro Landini, who was responsible for the silver. Despite the date on this drawing, the new synagogue was inaugurated on January 15, 1858.

SG

Bibliography: A. Balletti, *Il Tempio Maggiore Israelitico di Reggio nell'Emilia* (Reggio Emilia, 1908).

96. **Plan of the Livorno Synagogue**

Livorno, 1860

Gray and black watercolor on paper

24 × 17⅝ in. (61 × 45 cm)

Livorno, Museo Civico Giovanni Fattori

The Jewish community of Livorno was one of the most prosperous in the world between 1600 and 1800. Its main synagogue was expanded and remodeled many times over the centuries in response to the growing numbers and wealth of Livorno's Jews. The synagogue was in existence before 1640, when it was expanded into adjacent houses, and it was enlarged again in 1693, when it was joined with another building and the interior was surrounded on three sides by arcades. Donors had their names inscribed on the gallery parapets.

In 1740 the marble ark, composed of four columns that supported a heavy scrolled and garlanded pediment, was designed by the sculptor Giovanni di Isidoro Baratta of Carrara. It was installed in 1742. Baratta was also commissioned to design a matching bemah, but a design by David Nunes was the one that was executed in 1743. This was a polygonal marble platform surrounded by a balustrade. In their colorful, curvilinear designs, both ark and bemah recalled contemporary baroque furnishings.

In the eighteenth century, when earthquakes threatened the synagogue's stability, Ignazio Azzi was employed to remedy the situation and to add an extra women's gallery above the existing one. Work was completed by 1789. The hall measured 25.8 by 28.2 meters, with three tiers of arches surrounding the central space, which contained ark and bemah. The arcades consisted of wide bays, articulated with Tuscan columns on the ground level and Ionic pilasters above. Elaborate grilles further separated the women's galleries from the central space; the interior was richly decorated, with gold-lettered inscriptions on walls and ceiling (see cat. no. 252).

The synagogue was remodeled again in 1846–48. Jewish symbols were substituted for some earlier decorations, and chandeliers and red curtains were added. The bemah was enlarged to accommodate a choir, and the ark was raised. Subsequent changes included new doors for the ark in 1875 and the installation of an organ in 1903.

SG

Unpublished

97. **Project for the New Facade of the Jewish Temple**

Luigi Bosi

Livorno, 14 April 1875

Pencil on paper

21¼ × 14⅛ in. (54 × 35.9 cm)

Livorno, Museo Civico Giovanni Fattori

The rear exterior of the Livorno synagogue was redesigned in 1875, when it became the more visible part of the synagogue due to demolitions that created the small Piazza Nuova. Luigi Bosi, a local architect, was responsible for the new, restrained, classically inspired facade. Colored glass was added in 1915. The synagogue, one of the most impressive in all of Europe, was totally destroyed in World War II.

SG

Unpublished

98. ***The Ghetto, Rome***

William Luson Thomas after Louis Haghe (1806–1885)

London (?), second half of the nineteenth century

Colored engraving on paper

13 × 9¹⁵⁄₁₆ in. (33 × 25.3 cm)

New York, The Moldovan Family Collection

This scene captures the cramped space of the Roman ghetto. It is portrayed in a decidedly Italianate manner with romantic shadowing and an emphasis on architectural elements such as arches and timber roof supports, yet the stiffness of the figures reflects a Victorian sense of formality typical of English popular prints. The depiction of the Virgin and Child hanging at the right of the composition indicates that Christians and Jews lived in close contact.

Louis Haghe was the royal draftsman during the reign of Queen Victoria. He is most renowned for his engravings, including his works after David Roberts published in *Holy Land, Egypt, and Nubia*. After 1850 Haghe abandoned engraving and concentrated on watercolors. He was a founder and later president of the New Society of Painters in Water Colours. As is stated on the print letter of this engraving, the watercolor on which this print is based was included in one of the society's exhibitions. Thomas was a lesser-known engraver who often carved woodcuts for publication in popular periodicals.

GMG

Unpublished

99. **Miniature of Consolinas Valobra Cassin (1852–1922)**

G. Gennaro

Turin, 1897

Oil on paper; gold

Diam: 1⅜ in. (3.5 cm)

Private collection

VBM

Unpublished

100. **Miniature of Marco (Mose) Sonnino (b. 1865)**

Rome, c. 1900

Oil on paper; ribbon

Diam: 1⅛ in. (2.9 cm)

New York, Collection of Mark A. Sonnino

VBM

Unpublished

101. **Plans for the Tempio Israelitico in Bologna**

Attilio Muggia

Bologna, 1918

Ink on paper

Bologna, Comunità Israelitica

Though Jews have resided in Bologna off and on since the third or fourth century, the modern community dates from the emancipation of 1859, when Jews were given civil rights. The community was officially founded in 1911, and a large synagogue designed by Attilio Muggia was inaugurated in 1928.

Muggia's design shows a large, square room covered by a cross vault with a skylight in the center. The ark wall and the wall opposite are divided into two levels with pilasters and Liberty-style (art nouveau) decoration. On the other two walls are the women's galleries, supported by columns. The effect is similar to contemporary theater balconies. The ark is flanked by columns attached to the wall, surmounted by Tablets of the Law and surrounded by a balustrade. Though the reader's desk and the ark are set behind the balustrade on a slightly raised platform, the activities before the ark would have been clearly visible to the congregation.

Muggia's design provides the space and light required for the service, achieving a certain monumentality of scale that is neither overdone nor ostentatious. He mixed classical elements with more modern Liberty designs.

SG

Bibliography: S. M. Bondoni and G. Busi, eds., *Cultura ebraica in Emilia-Romagna* (Rimini, 1987), pp. 70–71.

WORKS ON PARCHMENT, VELLUM OR LEATHER

102. **Decorated Leather Panels for the Synagogue**

Venice, sixteenth century

Leather, tooled, punched, painted, and gilt

CI 31: 48¼ × 17¾ in. (123 × 45 cm);
CI 40: 24⅜ × 17¾ in. (61.5 × 45 cm);
CI 51: 29½ × 36¼ in. (75 × 92 cm)

Venice, Comunità Israelitica (nos. CI 31, 40, 51)

Decorated leather wall hangings were introduced into Italy from Spain in the fifteenth century, and their use became widespread during the next hundred years.[1] Venice was the leading Italian center for the manufacture of these luxurious hangings made to grace the walls of palaces. In the collection of the Comunità Israelitica, Venice, are three sets of leather hangings, one from the sixteenth century (to which the three pieces discussed here belong), a second seventeenth-century series, and a later series of indeterminate date.

The decoration of the first group is the most elaborate and well executed. Three different types of motifs appear: Doric columns that undoubtedly framed the fields of the hanging,[2] floral motifs, and inscriptions. All are stamped, painted, and gilt, so that the original effect of the composition would have been sumptuous. The floral motif appears on a leather fragment in the Bardini Museum, Florence, reused to repair a chair back (inv. 1151). According to the records of the Comunità, these pieces came from the Spanish Synagogue, a provenance that accords well with the history of the form and with the inscriptions:

אדם אל אל הבין תפלתך
במכון שבתו ירום הפלך
ראשית חכמה יראת אל מלך
היד תפארתו תציץ באור שכלם
מקירות לב תק[ר]א נקי כפים
שלום על ישראל רחב ידים

(Man, unto the Lord who understands your prayer
In His dwelling place [variation on Ps. 33:14], He raises the staff
"The beginning of wisdom is the fear" [Ps. 111:10] of the Lord King
Majesty of his glory blossoms [variation on 1 Chron. 29:11 and Isa. 28:1] in the light of your intellect
From the recesses of the heart call [variation on Prov. 16:21] "He who has clean hands" [Ps. 24:4]
"May it be well with Israel" [Ps. 125:5 or 128:6], "Wide Hands"[3] [Isa. 33:21]).

VBM

Unpublished

1. F. Scalia, "Leather Panel," in Port of History Museum, *Florence for Philadelphia: Art from Florentine Collections,* exh. cat. (Florence, 1982), p. 117.
2. Cf. *Palazzo Vecchio: Committenza e collezionismo medicei* (Florence, 1980), p. 158, no. 295.
3. The expression is used here as an allusion to God.

103. **Marriage Contract**

Venice, 1614

Ink and gouache on parchment

34½ × 24½ in. (87.6 × 62.3 cm)

New York, The Jewish Museum, Gift of Jakob Michael (JM 68–60)

Groom: Abraham, son of Solomon Abrabanel

Bride: Dona Gracia, daughter of Aaron de Paz

This is one of the earliest extant decorated Venetian *ketubbot,* or marriage contracts. It was written for members of two prominent Sephardic families: Abraham, son of Solomon Abrabanel, and Dona Gracia, daughter of Aaron de Paz, who were married in Venice on 13 Sivan 5374 (May 21, 1614).[1] The custom of utilizing elaborately decorated marriage contracts was brought to Italy by emigrants from Spain.[2] Parallels for the composition—paired horseshoe arches set beneath a word panel, the whole framed by borders of varying sizes—can be found in Spanish Hebrew manuscripts.[3]

The right arch contains the main text, the contract of marriage, while the articles of engagement are inscribed at left. They list a dowry of 5,500 ducats, to which the groom added 2,750 ducats, for a total obligation of 8,250 ducats, an unusually large sum for a Jewish dowry and one that approaches the scale of those offered by affluent Venetian merchant families.[4]

The quotation in square Hebrew letters that forms one of the borders is drawn from the Book of Ruth (4:11–12), and refers to the house of Perez, whose descendant was King David. The Abrabanels claimed Davidic ancestry.

VBM

Bibliography: S. Sabar, "The Beginnings and Flourishing of Ketubbah Ilustration in Italy: A Study in Popular Imagery and Jewish Patronage during the Seventeenth and Eighteenth Centuries" (Ph.D. diss., University of California, Los Angeles, 1987), p. 116, n. 93, and pp. 136–137, n. 140; idem, "The Beginnings of *Ketu'bbah* Decoration in Italy: Venice in the Late Sixteenth to the Early Seventeenth Centuries," *Jewish Art* 12–13 (1987): 106, fig. 10.

1. Abraham died a few years after his marriage, on 26 Adar 5378 (1618). For his epitaph, see A. Berliner, *Luhot Avanim: Hebraische Grabinschriften in Italien,* pt. 1, *Venedig,* (Frankfurt, 1881), no. 178.
2. Sabar, "Beginnings and Flourishing of Ketubbah Illustration," p. 102ff.
3. Compare, for example, Narkiss, *Hebrew Illuminated Manuscripts in the British Isles,* vol. 1, *The Spanish and Portuguese Manuscripts* (Jerusalem and London, 1982), figs. 447–450.
4. Sabar, "Beginnings and Flourishing of Ketubbah Illustration," p. 136, n. 140.

Fig. 190. Marriage Contract, Venice, 1614, The Jewish Museum, New York (cat. no. 103)

104. **Marriage Contract**

Rivarolo, 1660 (Friday, 8 Adar 5420)

Ink and gouache on parchment

27³⁄₁₆ × 19¹⁄₁₆ in. (69.1 × 48.4 cm)

Groom: Yitzḥak Natan Guastalla

Bride: Sarah, daughter of David bar Elyakim Levi Monpireno

New York, Collection of Yosef Goldman

This *ketubbah* is perhaps the earliest and finest extant example among the many marriage contracts embellished with this elaborate program. The richly decorated border that frames the text contains symbols of the twelve tribes paired with and surmounted by the signs of the zodiac. Along the top these representations are flanked by personifications of the four seasons, and at the bottom by scenes alluding to the four elements; in the side borders they alternate with vignettes depicting the senses of sight, hearing, taste, and smell. In the center of the semicircular area above, a depiction of Jerusalem is surrounded by six scenes from Ps. 128. The rest of the space is filled in with vines, birds, and two fountains. The cartouches in the upper corner were left blank for the inclusion of coats of arms.

EMC

Unpublished

105. **Marriage Contract**

Rome, 1680 (Wednesday, 8 Sivan 5440)

Ink and gouache on parchment

37¼ × 23⅝ in. (94.6 × 60 cm)

Groom: David, son of Yitzḥak Masini

Bride: Consola, daughter of Moshe Sepili

New York, Library of The Jewish Theological Seminary of America (No. 48)

This rectangular *ketubbah* with a scalloped bottom edge is decorated with a floral border flanked by wedding benedictions and verses from Ruth. The text of the marriage contract is placed within two columns surmounted by a triangular pediment containing an inscription from Prov. 5:18. The couple's combined coat of arms appears at the bottom.

EMC

Bibliography: S. Sabar, "The Beginnings and Flourishing of *Ketubbah* Illustration in Italy: A Study in Popular Imagery and Jewish Patronage during the Seventeenth and Eighteenth Centuries" (Ph.D. diss., University of California, Los Angeles, 1987), p. 158.

106. **Privilege for the Ambron Family**

Rome, 1687

Ink and gouache on parchment

12½ × 16 in. (31.8 × 40.6 cm)

New York, Library of The Jewish Theological Seminary of America (L2)

This document granted the Ambron family the right to reside outside the ghetto in Rome. It is the earliest of a series of such privileges for this family in the Library of The Jewish Theological Seminary. The Ambrons emigrated to Italy from Spain following the expulsion of 1492 and were very prominent in Jewish communal life in Rome in the eighteenth and nineteenth centuries (see cat. no. 196).

Following the Italian custom of decorating private documents, this privilege has a border of softly painted flowers.

GMG

Unpublished

107. **Marriage Contract**

Mantua, 1689 (Friday, 12 Av 5449)

Ink on parchment

27⁹⁄₁₆ × 22¼ in. (70 × 56.5 cm)

Groom: Avraham, son of Rafael Trabuto

Bride: Pesla, daughter of Naaman Naaman

New York, Library of The Jewish Theological Seminary of America (No. 126)

The text of this engraved *ketubbah* is written in a rectangular space framed by an elaborate double border containing several biblical scenes. Most of the events depicted are from Genesis, but surprisingly, a scene of Susannah and the Elders is placed in the bottom border. The inclusion of this representation coupled with the appearance of a personified God in some of the scenes has led scholars to believe the artist was Christian. The decorative borders are surmounted by a representation of Adam and Eve, nude, reclining on either side of the Tree of Knowledge. Two blank cartouches held under crowns by winged putti were left blank for the inclusion of coats of arms.

EMC

Bibliography: F. Landsberger, "'Illuminated Marriage Contracts with Special Reference to the Cincinnati Ketubahs," *Hebrew Union College Annual* 26 (1955): 518–520; C. Roth, "Representations of God in Jewish Art," *Proceedings Papers: Fourth World Jewish Congress of Jewish Studies,* vol. 2 (Jerusalem, 1967), p. 140; E. S. Saltman, "The 'Forbidden Image' in Jewish Art," *Journal of Jewish Art* 8 (1981): 42–53.

Editor's Note: On Rafael Trabuto, see Gerald Green, "Texts and Studies in Italian Jewish History during the Sixteenth and Seventeenth Centuries," Ph.D. dissertation, The Jewish Theological Seminary of America, 1974, p. 7.

108. **Sukkah Decoration with Micrography**

Italy, seventeenth century

Ink and gouache on vellum on board; paper border

22¹⁵⁄₁₆ × 23⅝ in. (58.2 × 60 cm)

New York, The Jewish Museum (S 1443)

This plaque was used as a wall decoration in a *sukkah,* a booth built for the festival of Tabernacles in commemoration of the booths that sheltered the Israelites after the Exodus from Egypt. Inscribed in the center of this panel is the biblical commandment for dwelling in *sukkot*—"You shall live in booths seven days" (Lev. 23:42)—surrounded by other verses relating to the festival (Lev. 23:40–44; Deut. 16:13). This panel also includes the entire Book of Ruth written in micrographic geometric and vegetal patterns that encircle the central inscription and fill the upper-left corner. The decoration of the other three corners is composed of chapters

8 through 11 of Proverbs. The entire panel is surrounded by a border inscription in large letters from Prov. 11:24–30.

The choice of the text used on this panel is unusual. The Book of Ruth is read on the festival of Shavuot; Ecclesiastes is read on Sukkot and is more common on sukkah decorations (see cat. no. 109). Several eighteenth-century suites of Italian sukkah decorations are known.[1] A similar panel in the collection of the National Museum of American History, Washington, D.C. (217680), contains the same text in its central inscription and concentric circles as found on this panel, but the floral and geometric patterns and corner tendrils contain the micrographic text of Song of Songs. It thus appears that these two panels were part of a set of five wall decorations, in which each panel contained the complete text of one of the five *megillot* (scrolls): Esther, Ruth, Ecclesiastes, Song of Songs, and Lamentations.

GMG

Unpublished

1. See S. Makover, "The Iconographic Program of a Series of Italian Sukkah Decorations," in *The Proceedings of the Ninth World Congress of Jewish Studies* (Jerusalem, 1985), pp. 37–43.

109. **Sukkah Decoration with Micrography**

Italy, seventeenth century

Ink and gouache on vellum on board, paper border

29½ × 22⅝ in. (75 × 58 cm)

Washington, D.C., National Museum of American History (RSN 82632Z00)

This panel was used as a decoration for a *sukkah*. The central motif is the abbreviated text of the Ten Commandments placed within an arcade whose outline evokes the Tablets of the Law. Each tablet encloses a crown, and above the arches is a larger crown. Together they represent "the crown of Torah, the crown of priesthood, and the crown of royalty" (Ethics of the Fathers 4:17). Birds, flower-filled vases, interlacing geometric patterns, and scrolling floral and leaf motifs complete the decoration.

All the ornamental motifs on this panel are composed of micrographic writing including the complete text of Ecclesiastes, which is read on the intermediary Sabbath of Sukkot. The combination of the Decalogue and Ecclesiastes is also found on a series of paper sukkah decorations in the collection of the Jewish Museum, New York (F 4662–4774), and was probably based on the verse "Fear God and keep his commandments" (Eccles. 12:13).

This panel resembles a sukkah decoration in the collection of the Jewish Museum, New York (F 5851), with Ps. 76, a liturgical selection for Sukkot. It is decorated with a border of large letters and micrographic verses from Samuel I. The architectural framework, capital forms, vases, and floral and leaf motifs of the New York panel are almost identical to those found on this example from Washington, suggesting that they were created by the same hand. As the dimensions of the two panels are nearly identical, they may have been part of the same suite. The Washington example may have been the central panel, as it is visually and textually more impressive. Other panels similar to the New York panel would have completed the set, creating an aesthetically and textually sophisticated program of sukkah decorations.

The ornamental motifs and lettering style found on this panel and the corresponding New York panel closely resemble those of a second sukkah decoration in the collection of the Jewish Museum, New York (S1443), and a matching panel in the National Museum of American History (217680; see cat. no. 108). It is probable that all were made by the same artist-scribe. A fifth panel, also in the Washington collection (RSN 82631Z01), can also be attributed to the same hand.

GMG

Bibliography: C. Adler and I. M. Casonowicz, "The Collection of Jewish Ceremonial Objects in the Collection of the United States National Museum," *Proceedings of the U.S. National Museum* 34, no. 1630 (1908): no. 107.

110. **Marriage Contract**

Livorno, 1751

Pen and ink, gouache, and gold paint on parchment

21 × 13½ in. (53.5 × 34.3 cm)

New York, The Jewish Museum, Gift of an anonymous donor (U 8440)

Groom: Eliahu, son of Solomon Judah Hayyim Teglio al-Fierino

Bride: Duna Rachel, daughter of Isaac Yeshurun

This marriage contract was created in the Hebrew year 5511 (1751). Its decoration was modeled on the work of Giovanni di Isidoro Baratta of Cararra (1670–1747), who designed the altar of the Livorno cathedral, the sculptural decoration of other Livornese churches, as well as the Torah ark of that city's synagogue. This *ketubbah* and the ark share common stylistic elements: the columns set at an angle to the plane of the entablature, the cartouches above and below the central field, and variously colored "marble" inlays.[1] The putti that hold up the largest cartouche are close in style to similar figures in the Chiesa di San Ferdinando, Livorno, sculpted by Baratta around 1740.[2] That these mythological figures appear on a work of ceremonial art is a measure of Jewish acculturation to Italian life and is paralleled in the imagery of Hebrew poetry written in Italy from the seventeenth century on.[3]

VBM

Bibliography: Kleeblatt and Mann, *Treasures,* pp. 92–93.

1. The Livorno synagogue was destroyed by the Nazis and is today known only from engravings and photographs. For the ark, see J. Pinkerfeld, *The Synagogues of Italy: Their Architectural Development since the Renaissance* (Jerusalem, 1954), figs. 57–58 (Hebrew); E. Munkacsi, *Livornoi Regisegek: Antiquitates Liburnenses* (n.p., n.d.), fig. 5.
2. For the church of S. Ferdinando, see Kleeblatt and Mann, *Treasures,* p. 92.
3. D. Pagis, *Change and Tradition in the Secular Poetry: Spain and Italy* (Jerusalem, 1976), p. 277 (Hebrew).

111. **Marriage Contract**

Modena, 1756 (Friday, 5 Ḥeshvan 5517)

Ink and gouache on parchment, cutout

29¾ × 19⅞ in. (75.5 × 50.5 cm)

Groom: Isaac Ḥayyim, son of Shlomo Ḥayyim Sanguine

Bride: Rosa, daughter of Joseph Ḥai Naḥman

New York, Library of The Jewish Theological Seminary of America (No. 269)

This *ketubbah* is decorated with a series of intricately cut out borders. The outer one is decorated with floral motifs, while the wider inner border contains the signs of the zodiac, which are depicted counterclockwise, beginning at the top right. Personifications of the four seasons are represented in the corners. The letters of the Aramaic inscription "with a good sign and good fortune" are also formed by cutouts of floral designs. The whole is surmounted by a floral border that contains the combined coat of arms of the two families placed under a crown.

EMC

Unpublished

112. ***Sheḥitah* (Ritual Slaughter) and *Bedikah* (Inspection) Certificate for Samuel, Son of Isaac Luzatto**

Venice, 1768–1774

Ink and gouache on parchment

18⅛ × 11¹⁵⁄₁₆ in. (46.0 × 30.3 cm)

New York, Library of The Jewish Theological Seminary of America (62034)

In Italy personal certificates were frequently decorated. This custom was also followed by Italian Jews, who commissioned the decoration of secular documents, such as privileges (see cat. no. 106) and university diplomas (see cat. no. 53), and of religious certificates, most frequently *ketubbot,* or marriage contracts (see cat. nos. 103–105, 107, 110–111), and *sheḥitah* certificates such as this one.

This text is a *kabbalah,* a signed document attesting to the bearer's fitness as a ritual slaughterer and as an inspector of meat to ensure kashrut, observance of the dietary laws. Its decoration is related to contemporary *ketubbah* decoration. The parchment is cut to create a pediment form at top, a common feature of Italian ketubbot. Two separate texts—one certifying Luzatto as a shoḥet (slaughterer), the second certifying him as a *bodek* (inspector)—are surrounded by an elaborately decorated frame composed of cartouches, floral motifs, and putti. At the top of the certificate is a cartouche containing the Luzatto family coat of arms flanked by two putti, one of whom holds a *ḥalef,* or slaughtering knife. The frame consists of twelve scrollwork cartouches, a parallel to the twelve cartouches containing the signs of the zodiac on late eighteenth-century Venetian ketubbot. Here the cartouches contain pen and ink drawings of animals, with precise renderings of the texture of fur and feathers and of details such as severed throats and spurts of blood. A biblical quote or citation from the halakhic literature relating to sheḥitah is inscribed below each miniature. The animals on the right are all quadrupeds, and those on the left are birds. One cartouche contains an arrangement of six slaughtering knives, each bearing an inscription. The bottom of the frame is decorated with two rectangular cartouches containing drawings of a goat and a deer, which flank additional texts related to the laws of slaughtering. The similarities between sheḥitah certificates, as seen in this example, and contemporary ketubbot suggest that the same makers produced both types of certificates.[1]

The text of the *bedikah* certificate includes a warning that Luzatto should review the laws relating to slaughtering and inspection. This certificate may therefore have served a didactic purpose. Both texts on this certificate were signed by Rabbi Simḥah Calimani.

A decorated sheḥitah certificate from Mantua dated 1773 is also in the collection of The Jewish Theological Seminary Library. Other examples of decorated certificates for *shoḥetim* are found in the Salvatore Fornari collection, Rome; the Museo Nahon, Jerusalem; and in the Central Archives for the History of the Jewish People, Jerusalem.

GMG

Bibliography: J. J. Berman, *Shehitah: A Study in the Cultural and Social Life of the Jewish People* (New York, 1941), p. 94.

1. For a discussion of Italian *ketubbot* and their relationship to contemporary decorated *sheḥitah* certificates and other decorated objects, see S. Sabar, "The Beginnings and Flourishing of Ketubbah Illustration in Italy: A Study in Popular Imagery and Jewish Patronage during the Seventeenth and Eighteenth Centuries," (Ph.D. diss., University of California, Los Angeles, 1987), pp. 147–150.

113. Plaque of the *Ba'alei Brit* (Masters of the Covenant) Confraternity

Mordecai Shalom Gallici

Venice, 1792–1793

Ink and gouache on parchment; frame: wood, carved and gilt

34⅛ × 18½ in. (86.5 × 47 cm)

Venice, Comunità Israelitica (235)

This plaque features a detailed painting of a circumcision above a poem describing the activities of the *Ba'alei Brit* (Masters of the Covenant) Confraternity, which was dedicated to providing funds for the poor to circumcise their sons. Confraternity members acted as *sandekim* (also known as *ba'alei brit,* the honorees who hold infants during circumcisions) and payed for the circumciser's fee and the celebratory meal. The rhymed text declares that the members are "mentioned in this book," and thus it is probable that the painting includes specific portraits.

Details of the circumcision ceremony are accurately portrayed in the painting, such as the support for the feet of the *sandek* and the implements used by the *mohel* (circumciser). The various participants and the crowd of onlookers are dressed in stylish western European costume, except for one man in eastern European costume and another in a turban, who are included to suggest the diverse geographic backgrounds of the confraternity's members. The large crowd and elegantly appointed hall indicate the festivities customary at eighteenth-century Venetian circumcisions, thereby explaining the need for the confraternity to finance such events for the poor. The plaque is set in a carved, gilt frame decorated with a combination of subtle rococo shellwork and neoclassical motifs, such as laurel branches and an urn.

Gallici's signature appears at the bottom of the plaque, where he is listed as the *sofer* (scribe) of the confraternity. It is unclear whether Gallici painted the circumcision scene or only wrote the text on the plaque.

Above the circumcision scene:

נדבת / הבחור כמר גבריאל בן / המנוח כמר אבטליון / מאלטא

(Donation of the youth . . . Gabriel son of the deceased . . . Abtalion Malta).

Below the scene:

(B[less] G[od])

הן אמת מה שאמרו חכמים
זריזים למצות הנם מקדימים
הנה זאת חקרנוה כל הימים
כן היא חבר האנשים שלמים
אשר נקבו בספר זה ימים
ונקראת בעלי ברית אב תמים
כלם פה ובלב אחד מקדימים
לעסוק במצות אל רם על רמים
לתת ידים למול בשמנה ימים
בני עניים דלים וערומים
שאין לאל ידם להוציא דמים
ופורעים אותה ביקרים דמים
מתמיד שנותכם כל הימים
יבלו ימים בטוב ובנעימים
יראו זרע ויאריכו ימים
יזכר לראות בבנין בית עולמים

(It is true what the sages say:

The zealous go early to observe commandments[1]
That this we have examined all the days
So this the confraternity of the complete men
That are mentioned in this book of days
And are called "Masters of the Covenant"
(Gen. 14:13), Righteous Father
All are here and with one heart come early
To participate in the commandment
of the Lord of the height of heights
To give the funds[2] to circumcise at eight days
The sons of the poor, impoverished, and unclothed
That have not in their hands the funds
And uncover it [the expense][3] with cherished funds
For consistently they give every day
May they celebrate days with delights and pleasantries
May they see offspring and have long lives[4]
May they be privileged to see the building of an
everlasting House).

Below the central text:

הצעיר שבצעירים מרדכי שלום גאליקו
סופר החברה... במרר ובן שמנת
ימים ימול לכם כל זכר

(The youth among youths Mordecai Shalom Gallici, scribe of the confraternity . . . "Every male among you shall be circumcised at the age of eight days" Gen. 17:12; = [5]553 = 1792–1793]).

GMG

Bibliography: *Jewish Art Treasures in Venice* (New York, 1973), pp. 39, 94.

1. Variation on BT Pesaḥim 4a.
2. Play on word for "blood."
3. Play on circumcision terminology.
4. Variation on Isa. 53:10.

WOOD AND IVORY

114. **Torah Ark**

Urbino, c. 1500 (refurbished 1624)

Wood, carved and painted

94 × 110 × 34 in. (239 × 279 × 86.4 cm)

New York, The Jewish Museum (S 1431)

In its original form a two-story cabinet carved with fluted pilasters and other classicizing architectural details, this ark resembled the wooden decoration of the *studioli* in the Gubbio and Urbino palaces of the dukes of Urbino.[1] The wood was stained a warm red-brown, and a gilt inscription was painted in the frieze that read in part: "You shall be established through righteousness" (Isa. 54:14).

The ark was refurbished in 1624. Most of the exterior was painted a teal blue. The outer doors were gilded, their inner surfaces were covered with a Decalogue set in a floral field, and a new inscription replaced the old.[2] Another inscription was added on the panels of the second story: six verses of a poem in rhymed couplets based on biblical phrases that include or rhyme with the Hebrew word for ark, *aron*. The poem extols God and asks for the deliverance of the people of Urbino, a reference either to its Jewish community or to the general populace. In addition the ark was furnished with a domed superstructure, now lost, whose appearance is recorded in a manuscript of 1704, the *Sefer Ha-Maftir di Urbino* (Jerusalem, Nahon Museum of Italian Jewish Art).[3]

The refurbishing of the ark coincided with the pronouncement of decrees favorable to the Jewish community by Duke Francesco Maria II della Rovere, and may have been intended to celebrate them.[4]

VBM

Bibliography: *Art Treasures and Antiquities from the Davanzati Palace*, sale cat., American Art Galleries, New York, 1916, lot 322; Kayser and Schoenberger, *Jewish Ceremonial Art*, no. 1; idem, *Jewish Ceremonial Art*, 2d ed. (Philadelphia, 1959), no. 1; Kleeblatt and Mann, *Treasures*, pp. 52–53.

1. For illustrations of the *studioli*, or studies, of the dukes see V. B. Mann, "The Recovery of a Known Work," *Jewish Art* 12/13 (1986–1987): 272, fig. 5; Metropolitan Museum of Art, *Masterpieces of Fifty Centuries*, exh. cat. (New York: 1979), no. 194; F. Windisch-Graetz, *Möbel Europas: Renaissance und Manierismus* (Munich, 1983), p. 201; S. Colombo, *L'arte del legno e del mobile in Italia* (Busto Arsizio, 1981), pls. 31–38, 41–43.
2. For the complete text and translation of the inscriptions, see Mann, "Recovery of a Known Work," pp. 275–276.
3. U. Nahon and G. Sarfatti, eds., *Sefer Ha-Maftir di Urbino: Manoscritto ebraico del 1704* (Jerusalem, 1964), p. 21 (of manuscript facsimile). For an illustration of the relevant page, see ibid., p. 277, fig. 10.
4. For the texts of these edicts, see G. Luzzatto, *I banchieri ebrei in Urbino nell'età ducale* (Verona and Padua, 1903), pp. 54–55.

115. **Torah Staves of Nathanael Trabot** (fig. 180)

Italy, second half of the fifteenth century

Wood, carved and stained

11¹³⁄₁₆ × 6⁵⁄₁₆ dm in. (30 × 16 cm)

Ramat Aviv, Gross Family Collection

Nathanael Trabot worked as a punctuator of Hebrew manuscripts in the last quarter of the fifteenth century and into the sixteenth century. He also wrote manuscripts, for example, a copy of the legal compendium the *Mordecai* bearing a colophon dated 1539. His father had emigrated to Italy from France and later settled in Jerusalem.[1] Nathanael's son, Peretz Yeḥiel, is known to have written liturgical poetry.

On stylistic grounds the staves should be dated to the late fifteenth century. The leaf motif along the bottom and the multiple-lancet windows appear on a Gothic chalice dated to that period.[2]

VBM

Unpublished

1. On the Trabuto family, see G. Green, "Texts and Studies in Italian Jewish History during the Sixteenth Century" (Ph.D. diss., Jewish Theological Seminary of America, 1974).
2. Braunschweigisches Landesmuseum, Herzog Anton Ulrich-Museum and Dom am Burgplatz, *Stadt im Wandel,* exh. cat. vol. 2 (Braunschweig, 1985), no. 1130.

Fig. 180. Staves for the Torah Scroll of Nathaniel Trabuto, Italy, c. 1525, Gross Family Collection, Tel Aviv (cat. no. 115)

116. **Foa Coat of Arms**

Italy, seventeenth to eighteenth century

Wood, carved and stained

14 × 9¼ in. (35.5 × 23.5 cm)

New York, Collection of Daniel M. Friedenberg

In Italy heraldic devices were not the exclusive right of the nobility and were used by the bourgeoisie. Jews could therefore adopt them in emulation of their Christian neighbors. The use of coats of arms by Jews in Italy may date to as early as the eleventh century and was prevalent by the seventeenth century.

The Foa coat of arms consists of a palm tree topped by a six-pointed star, a Magen David, flanked by rampant lions. It was used as a printer's mark on books produced by the Foa press (see cat. no. 71) and is found on a Hanukkah lamp by Pietro Zappati (1759–1781) in the collection of the Museo della Comunità, Rome (284/461), and on a snuffbox in the collection of the Jewish Museum, New York (F 4925).

GMG

Unpublished

117. **Violin with Hebrew Inscription** (fig. 40)

Sanctus Seraphin (1699–after 1758)

Venice, c. 1725–1744

Wood

14 × 8 in. (35.6 × 20.3 cm)

New York, The Jewish Museum, Given in memory of Yosef and Gittel Hilman

Sanctus Seraphin was a renowned maker of violins and other stringed instruments whose products are famed for their superb woods and finishes and for the beauty of their tone. He was greatly influenced by the instruments of the Cremonese Amati family, the teachers of Antonio Stradivari and most of the other great Italian violin makers of the seventeenth and eighteenth centuries.

It has been suggested that Seraphin may have been a Jew who subsequently converted because Jews were barred from the craft guilds in seventeenth- and eighteenth-century Venice. On the back of this violin is a Hebrew inscription in eastern European cursive identifying a previous owner of the instrument as

Fig. 189. Chair of Elijah, northern Italy, eighteenth century, Jacobo and Asea Furman Collection, Santiago (cat. no. 118)

"Alfred." This violin has been adapted for modern play and features an elongated, angled neck and metal strings in place of the original short, straight neck and gut strings.

GMG

Unpublished

118. **Chair of Elijah**

Northern Italy, eighteenth century

Wood, carved, painted, gessoed, appliquéd with gold and silver leaf; silk brocade

60 × 30 × 27 in. (154.9 × 76.2 × 68.6 cm)

Santiago, Collection of Jacobo and Asea Furman (JF 121)

During a circumcision a "godfather" holding the infant sat in this chair, his legs supported by the high footrest. Two similar examples are known: one in the Comunità Israelitica, Ferrara,[1] and the other in the collection of the Sir Isaac and Lady Edith Wolfson Museum, Hechal Shlomo, Jerusalem.[2] The chair in Ferrara came from the Jewish community in Lugo; the one in Jerusalem came from Mantua, suggesting a northern Italian attribution for this example.

VBM

Bibliography: Jewish Museum, *Personal Vision: The Jacobo and Asea Furman Collection of Jewish Ceremonial Art,* exh. cat., by S. L. Braunstein (New York, 1985), no. 14.

1. Palazzo dei Diamanti and Palazzo Paradiso, *Meraviglie dal ghetto: Arte e cultura ebraiche in Emilia-Romagna,* exh. cat. (Ferrara, 1988), no. 108.
2. Y. L. Bialer and E. Fink, *Jewish Life in Art and Tradition* (New York, 1976), pp. 74–75.

119. **Lion Finial for a Chair of Elijah**

Italy, eighteenth to nineteenth century

Wood, carved, gessoed, and gilt

7½ × 3 × 3½ in. (19.1 × 7.6 × 8.9 cm)

Washington, D.C., National Museum of American History (no. 315219)

When this piece entered the Smithsonian Institution from the collection of Ephraim Deinard, it formed part of an Elijah chair, the ceremonial seat used during circumcisions (see cat. no. 118).

VBM

Unpublished

120. **Mantle Clock**

Maker: Nigra

Vercelli, 1804

Carved, lacquered, and gilt wood; glass; ormolu

22½ × 11½ × 7½ in. (56.9 × 29.7 × 19 cm)

New York, Private Collection of a Jewish Family from Turin

This clock is decorated with a combination of neoclassical elements, such as the columns supporting a pediment, and heavy rococo relief ornament.

GMG

Unpublished

121. **Torah Encased in a *Tik***

Northern Italy, 1831–1832

Ink on parchment; wood, carved, gessoed, painted, and gilt

27¾ × 15¾ in. (70.5 × 40 cm)

New York, The Jewish Museum, Gift of Joseph E. Adler (JM 24–49)

The custom of placing the Torah scroll in a *tik,* or cylindrical case, can be traced back to fourteenth-century Spain and may have come to Italy directly with Sephardic émigrés or indirectly via the Levant. This example is very similar to one of comparable dimensions now in the Musée de Cluny, Paris (Cl. 12331).[1] Both are twelve-sided, with each face bearing neoclassical appliqués. Series of moldings form the bases, and inverted moldings form the entablatures. From the top rise elements of an openwork crown of the Torah. The friezes of both bases and entablatures are inscribed with poems referring to their dedications.[2] Unfortunately there are gaps in the inscription on the Jewish Museum tik, and some portions are illegible. The remaining sections indicate a rhymed poem, a date of 1831–1832 and that the tik was dedicated by a woman together with a cover and another object:

(top frieze)

. . . society . . .	... חברה ...
. . . crown . . .	... כתר ...
in a very pleasant case	בתוך נרתיק מאד נאה
and beautiful, bound	ויפה צרורה
With a cover . . .	עם מפה ...
. . . were clearly made	... ברורה עשה
for the rest of her soul	למנוחת נפשה ...
her name was Ḥayyah.	... חיה שמה

(bottom frieze)

Her soul was bound up	נצררה נפשה
with ten righteous women	עם עשרת נשים צדקניות
in the bond of life . . .	בצרור החיים ...
. . . . ten	
to the house of Tuvia	ולבית טובייא ...
who is called Menaḥem	הכי נקרא לו ... מנחם
the year 55[00] and ninety	שנת ה׳ת׳ק׳ ותשעים
and seven since the Creation	ושבע ליצירה
his work was finished.	מלאכתו נגמרה

VBM

Bibliography: NYJM, *Jewish Patrons,* no. 16.

1. V. Klagsbald, *Catalogue raisonné de la collection juive du Musée de Cluny* (Paris, 1981), no. 122.
2. The practice of composing poems for the dedication of arks can be dated to 1623, the date of the inscription on an ark from Urbino (cat. no. 114).

122. ***Menorot* for the Synagogue** (fig. 187)

Italy, nineteenth century

Wood, carved and gilt; metal, gilt

19 × 14 in. (48.2 × 35.5 cm)

New York, The Jewish Museum, Gift of Dr. Harry G. Friedman (F 2829 a, b)

Gilt and painted candlesticks are commonly found in synagogues in the Veneto.

VBM

Unpublished

123. **Fan of Clotilde Castelnuovo**

China, late eighteenth to early nineteenth century

Ivory, carved

7½ × 11¼ in. (19.1 × 28.6 cm)

Collection of the grandchild of Clotilde Castelnuovo

VBM

Unpublished

Fans such as this were made in China for the trade with the West. Three similar examples are in the collection of the Metropolitan Museum of Art, New York (33.82.19, 33.82.20, 42.150.8).

TEXTILES

Torah Binders

124. **Torah Binder** (fig. 109)

Italy, 1582–83

Honorata, wife of Samuel Foa

Linen embroidered with silk threads

7½ × 112³⁄₁₆ in. (19 × 285 cm)

New York, The Jewish Museum, Gift of Dr. Harry G. Friedman (F 4927)

Two characteristics of this binder are typical of Sephardic examples: the floral motifs and its dedication by a woman. The inscription reads:

לכבוד התורה התמימה הרימה ידי תרומה אנכי
אונוראטה ת״מא אשת כמ״הר שמואל פואה יצ״ו הלא
מצער היא שנת השמ״ג לפק

In honor of the pure Torah, my hand raised an offering, I Honorata . . . wife of . . . Samuel Foa . . . "it is such a little one" (Gen. 19:20), the year 5343 [1582–83]. The repeating pattern of branches, oak leaves, and grape clusters is derived from printed pattern books and is found on various types of sixteenth-century domestic textiles.

VBM

Bibliography: Jewish Museum, *Fabric of Jewish Life* (New York, 1977), no. 16; C. Grossman, "Womanly Arts: A Study of Italian Torah Binders in the New York Jewish Museum Collection," *Journal of Jewish Art* 7 (1980): 38, fig. 6; Kleeblatt and Mann, *Treasures,* pp. 56–57.

125. **Torah Binder** (fig. 110)

Hannah Senigallia Camerina

Venice, 1630

Linen, embroidered, cutwork, and chain stitch; cutwork fringe; net ground; silk satin background; linen lining

5⅞ × 142½ in. (15 × 362 cm)

Padua, Comunità Israelitica (176a)

The inscription reads:

משם ה׳ מבורך חנה מנשים תבוריך הובילה שי לתורה
מפה לעז תפארה עם אבה יחיאל סניגאליה ירא האל גם
תעל גם תסלח בעלה יהודה עלה צור יאריך ימיהם כן
לחמיה הכהן אברהם קאמרינה ניסן ש״ין צד״י השנה ל:א׳

(From the name of God blessed, Hannah . . . brought a gift to the Torah, a binder[1] to the strength of the splendor [variation on Jer. 48:17] with her father Yeḥiel Senigallia, also may he rise, also may he be forgiven, her husband Judah . . . also her father-in-law, the *kohen,* Abraham Camerina, Nisan [5]390 [1630] A[men]).

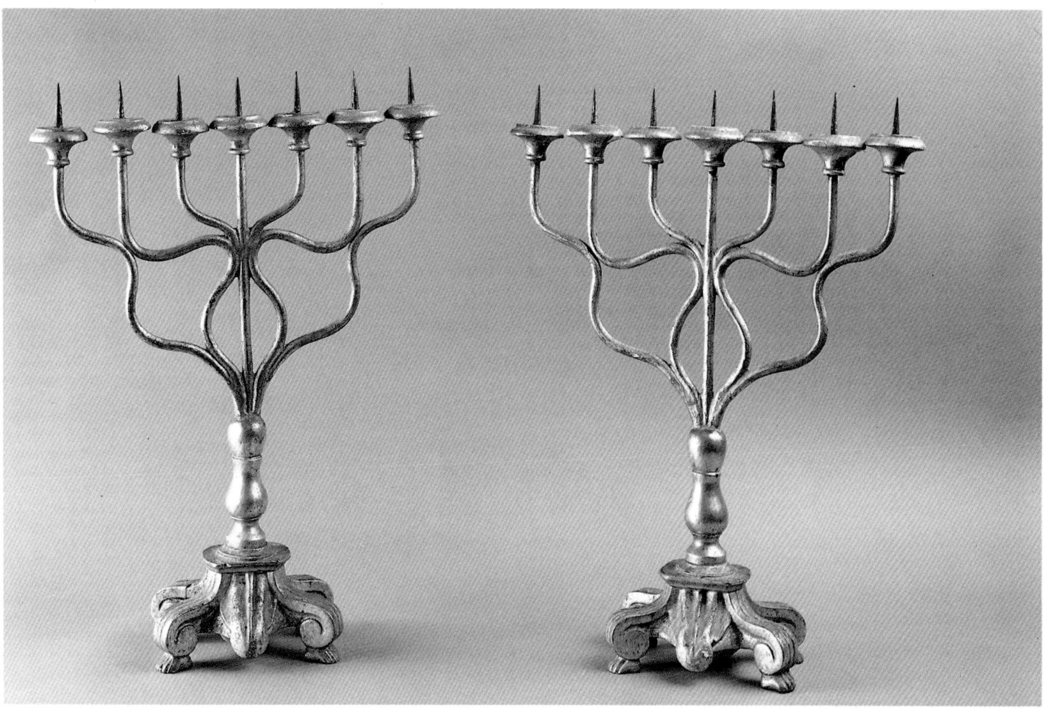

Fig. 187. Menorot for the Synagogue, Italy, nineteenth century, The Jewish Museum, New York (cat. no. 122)

The date indicated by the inscription is of great importance not only to the history of Jewish art but also to the history of Italian lace. By the second half of the sixteenth century, this craft began to flourish, stimulated by the diffusion of pattern books. Those produced by Vinciolo and earlier by Vecellio were particularly responsible for the codification of forms and decorations in lacework and continued to be utilized up to the second half of the following century. Designs similar to that of this binder, geometric forms inserted within squares, are typically Venetian. The net ground undoubtedly added during a later restoration (as was the satin lining), is very unusual. Another unique element is the motif "clubs" or staffs, used to break up the inscription which is characteristic of Italian velvet from the beginning of the second half of the sixteenth century.

DLB

Unpublished

1. The word *mappah* is used here in the sense of "binder" for the rhyme scheme.

126. **Torah Binder**

Rome, 1638

Silk satin, embroidered with silver threads and ribbon in couching stitch and quilted with linen threads; braid and fringe with rings of silk and spun silver; taffeta lining

10¼ × 133½ in. (26 × 339 cm)

Rome, Comunità Israelitica (inv. no. 464 C)

The inscription reads

זאת המטפחת של כמ״ר רפאל יצ״ו בכמר מרדכי מלירושי ז׳ל שנת שצח לפק

(This is the binding of Signor Rafael . . . Son Mordecai De Rossi in the year [5]398 [=1637–38])

חדשוה משה אפרים מלירושי יצ״ו למ״נ אביו בג״ע שנת הת״קז ליצירה

(It was restored by Moshe Efraim De Rossi . . . for the r[epose of the] s[oul] of his father in the G[arden] of E[den] in the year 5507 [=1746–47] of the creation)

The double inscription indicates that the piece was restored about a century after the binder was first embroidered. Probably it was necessary to consolidate the embroidery threads, executed in couching stitches, with the new stitches. The stitches that now pass through the red taffeta lining probably belong to an additional adjustment, relatively recent in date, which is also true of the braided section. The checkered motif arranged in horizontal rows alternates bunches of wheat, feathers, and ribbons, which are interlaced according to a scheme of small ogives. This design is characteristic of contemporary textiles used for clothing, which, after the late sixteenth century, favored rather simple modules.

DLB

Unpublished

Torah Mantles

127. **Torah Mantle and Binder** (fig. 92)
132.

Rome, 1643–1644 (fragment with inscription); first half of the seventeenth century (rest of binder and Torah mantle)

Mantle: silk satin embroidered with silk threads in brown, beige, and pink, and with spun gold around a core of silk; gold tinsel and ribbon in satin and couched stitches and raised couched stitch attached with scattered stitches; satin appliqués; braid of mantle: spun gold; fringe in white and silver silk; coarse linen and synthetic taffeta lining

Binder: silk satin transferred to gros de Tours embroidered with spun gold around a core of silk and spun silver around a core of white silk in chain stitch, herringbone, and satin stitch; braid of binder: spun silver around a core of white silk, executed in a Genoese stitch with a festoon motif

Mantle: 35⁷⁄₁₆ × 103⅛ in. (90 × 262 cm); Binder 9⁹⁄₁₆ × 111⅜ in. (24.3 × 283 cm)

Rome, Comunità Israelitica (486, 486c)

This mantle, which comes from the Sicilian Synagogue in the Roman ghetto, is the result of the recomposition of a suit, the parts of which were skillfully put together to form the mantle and binder. Indeed, on the Torah mantle the embroidery design is not perpendicular to the hem, indicating that the mantle was recut from a preexisting piece. Furthermore the border, formed of a motif that imitates braid, was clipped off along with the underlying satin and later resewn. This rather common practice, seen on many other examples in Roman synagogues, allowed the preservation of textiles that had been intended for profane use that otherwise would have been lost. Also typically Roman is embroidery that is not arranged freely along the surface of the textile, but that forms a repeat pattern in imitation of woven brocade. In fact, this embroidery simulates a type of design featuring small ogives arranged in horizontal rows in a checkerboard arrangement, a composition that was very popular during the first half of the seventeenth century. The rectangle sewn onto one end of the binder comes from another textile. Its inscription and the crest have been badly recut along with the underlying satin fabric and added to a new background of gros de Tours. Its inscription reads:

כב מר שלמה / יצ״ו כ׳מ׳ר׳ / מקמפנייאנו / י׳צ״ו׳ שנת / בק׳דו׳ש׳ ישראל / תתהלל / כבד את ה׳

(Salomone Campagnano, . . . "And glory in the Holy One of Israel" [Isa. 41:16] . . . the year 5424 [1643–1644] "Honor the Lord" [Prov. 3:9]).

The original embroidery seems to correspond chronologically to the date of donation, as can be seen from an analysis of the small vine shoot motif forming a border, which is typical of the period. We don't know

Fig. 185. Rikah Polacco, Torah Binder, Florence(?), 1662–1663, The Jewish Museum, New York (cat. no. 128)

when the two textiles were sewn together, but the quality of the new fabric and the type of lining used (starched linen) suggest that this occurred in the eighteenth century.

DLB

Unpublished

128. **Torah Binder** (fig. 185)

Rikah Polacco

Florence(?), 1662–1663

Linen embroidered with silk and metallic threads; modern lining

110¾ × 6½ in. (281.4 × 16.5 cm)

New York, The Jewish Museum,
Gift of Cora Ginsburg (1988–21)

This exquisite needlepoint binder is divided into two bands of decoration: on top, a series of naturalistically rendered flowers (tulips, roses, etc.), and below, an inscription that reads

לכבוד האל ותורתו מעשה ידי מרת ריקה מב״ת אשת המפואר כמר חיים בר יוסף פולאקו ס״גל י״צ׳ו בשנת ה׳ת׳כ׳ג׳ לפ״ה

(In honor of God and his Torah, the work of Signora Rikah . . . wife of . . . Ḥayyim, the son of Joseph Polacco, the Levite . . . in the year 5423 a[ccording to the] l[arge counting]).

In 1702–1703 Joseph, son of Ḥayyim Polacco, rededicated a needlepoint Torah curtain that was originally fabricated in 1675–1676 and is now in the Victoria and Albert Museum, London (511–1877).[1] It is closely related stylistically and iconographically to an unpublished and undated curtain in the Jewish Museum in Florence, which may have been made contemporaneously with the London curtain or shortly thereafter. The inclusion of numerous flowers on the Victoria and Albert curtain, the style of rendering, and the date of the curtain suggest that it may have been made by Rikah Polacco, wife of Ḥayyim and presumably Joseph's mother, and the maker of this binder.

VBM

Unpublished

1. S. Cohen, "A 17th-Century Parochet," *The Jewish Chronicle,* 10 July 1953. See cat. no. 145 for a related curtain in the collection of The Jewish Museum, New York.

129. **Torah Binder with *Shofrot* and Trumpets**

Leonora Colorni

Italy, 1692–1693

Linen: embroidered with silk threads

127 × 15 in. (322.6 × 8.2 cm)

Washington, National Museum of American History, 315209

For most of its length, this binder is embroidered with a repeat pattern of flowers. Both ends, however, are decorated with embroidered trumpets,[1] *shofrot* (ram's horns), Tablets of the Law, and the following inscriptions:

above the musical instruments, "Raise a shout before the Lord, the king," Ps. 98:6; above the Tablets of the Law, "The teaching of the Lord is perfect, renewing life," Ps. 19:8; below the Tablets

לכבוד הא[־]ל הכבודה מרת / ליאנורה אשת כ״מ
חנניה . . . קולורני יצ״ו שנת חמשת / אלפים תנ״ג לפק
ליא

"For the honor of the Lord, Leonora wife of Ḥananiah Colorni . . . the year 5453" (=1692–93)

(above the Tablets of the Law) "The teaching of the Lord is perfect, renewing life," Ps. 19:8

VBM

Unpublished

1. The curved form of the trumpets is typical of seventeenth-century examples. (Cf. Jeremy Montagu, *The World of Baroque and Classical Musical Instruments* [Woodstock, 1979], figs. 46 and 47.)

130. **Torah Binder**

Rome, mid-seventeenth century

Silk satin embroidered with polychrome silk and metallic threads in couched, satin, and chain stitches; spangles; gros de Tours lining

6¾ × 114 in. (17 × 291 cm)

Rome, Comunità Israelitica (inv. no. 570/317)

The binder was donated by the Efrati family to the Castilian Synagogue, although the crest is that of the Tedeschi family. The coat of arms is inserted within an oval shield, flanked by two curled volute motifs of a mid-seventeenth-century type. The composition of the embroidery belongs to the same period, for example, the framing of the central motifs (exotic birds alternating with flowers within volutes and cornices) by two bands of vine shoots joined by small flowers. The scalloped form of one of the borders is completely original, however, and can be attributed to Rome on the basis of comparison with other embroideries.

DLB

Bibliography: F. Pitigliani, *Permanent Exhibition of the Jewish Community of Rome* (Rome, [1962]), p. 24.

131. **Torah Binder**

Florence, late seventeenth century

Red brocatelle on white ground

6¹¹⁄₁₆ × 128⅜ in. (17 × 346 cm)

Florence, Comunità Israelitica (1241)

Even though this brocatelle appears to be an impressive fabric, it is actually a fairly poor material. In fact, it utilizes linen or silk waste wefts for the ground to give its structure greater solidity, while the silk weft and warp threads are rather sparse. Tuscany produced a large number of such fabrics, employing, with little variation, large ogives with a pomegranate at their center. It is rare to find these in Jewish use, since more valuable cloths were generally preferred. There are other binders similar to this one in design and technique, however, in the synagogue of Florence.

DLB

Unpublished

133. **Torah Mantle**

Italy, late seventeenth century

Silk velvet; silk, embroidered with silk and metallic threads; metallic fringe

31⅛ × 10¼ in. (79 × 26 cm) (width at top)

New York, The Jewish Museum, H. Ephraim and Mordecai Benguiat Family Collection (S 255)

This mantle is decorated with a series of three embroidered arches; each is flanked by spiral columns entwined with flowers, fronted by a balustrade and topped by a crown. Pieces of seventeenth-century cut velvet fill the space beneath each arch.[1] A series of converging parallel stripes along the hem lends an illusion of receding space and reinforces the spacial relationships suggested by the architectural elements. The only published parallel is a nineteenth-century mantle in

Turin that features a more elaborate treatment of a vista seen through an arcade.[2]

This mantle entered the Jewish Museum's collection along with a matching Torah curtain and valance (S 303, S 303a).[3]

VBM

Bibliography: NYJM, *Fabric of Jewish Life,* no. 8.

1. See R. Bonito Fanelli, *Five Centuries of Italian Textiles, 1300–1800: A Selection from the Museo del Tessuto, Prato,* exh. cat. (1981), nos. 48, 74.
2. *Ebrei a Torino,* exh. cat. (Turin, 1984), pp. 215–217.
3. NYJM, *Fabric of Jewish Life,* no. 7.

134. **Torah Mantle**

Italy, seventeenth to eighteenth century

Silk, embroidered with silk and metallic threads

34⅝ × 13¾ in. (88 × 35 cm)

New York, The Jewish Museum (1988–32)

The fine quality of the needlepoint suggests an early date, close to that of the binder by Rikah Polacco (cat. no. 128; fig. 185). A three-dimensional effect is achieved through the raised metallic threads at the center of each serrated quatrefoil. Abstract motifs like those on this mantle also appear on needlepoint Torah curtains, mantles, and binders in various communal collections.[1]

VBM

Unpublished

1. For example, a Torah binder and a mantle (Florence, Museum of Jewish Art nos. 79, 1423) and a Torah curtain (Venice, Comunità Israelitica no. II–8–11).

135. **Torah Mantle** (fig. 111)

Rome, late seventeenth century

Silk velvet embroidered with silk threads twisted with spun gold and gold threads around a core of silk in couched and satin stitches; fringe and tassels of spun gold; taffeta lining

33⅞ × 60¼ in. (86 × 153 cm)

Rome, Comunità Israelitica (inv. no. 413)

Like many other textiles preserved in the Rome synagogue, this piece is characterized by the heaviness of the embroidery, executed entirely with metallic threads. The symbols represented—the ark, the menorah, the laver, the fountain, and the three altars (one flaming, one perfumed, and one for making bread)—are arranged along the sides and center of the mantle, while long vine shoots of gold tie them together, running across the entire surface. This way of organizing the design and the ability to obtain the greatest number of effects with different stitches are typical of late seventeenth-century Roman embroidery, as are the wide fringe of the mantle and the strongly scalloped cape. Fruit trees (olive, pomegranate, pear), vines, and wheat are embroidered within every bend of the scallops. The rich border with small tassels is also original, while the original lining was recently replaced by purple silk taffeta.

DLB

Bibliography: F. Pitigliano, *Permanent Exhibition of the Jewish Community of Rome* (Rome, [1962]), fig. 4, no. 163.

136. **Torah Mantle**

Franco-Italian production, 1750 or later

Diapered silk fabric, damask with several silk brocade wefts and one of golden wire wound around a silk core; silk and gold lamé braid; cotton lining

30¹¹⁄₁₆ × 47 in. (78 × 120 cm)

Florence, Comunità Israelitica (1017)

The *point rentré* technique, invented by the Frenchman Jean Revel around 1730, is used here to create a motif of a highly naturalistic character. The technique dates the textile to after 1730 but before the middle of the century, when it had already gone out of fashion. The production of this mantle probably coincided with the renovation of the furnishings of the ghetto's two synagogues beginning in 1750. The fact that many Jews traded in silks accounts for the richness of this piece as well as its non-Florentine provenance.

DLB

Unpublished

137. **Torah Mantle**

Rome, second half of the seventeenth century

Mantle: silk gros de Tours (with the effect of a false background, due to the loosening of one of the two weaves of pink silk and silver thread) embroidered with silk threads, and beige twisted with gold thread, gold thread spun around silk, gold tinsel, and ribbon, in couched and satin stitches; fringe and small tassels of gold (around the lower hem); taffeta lining

Cape: antique silk satin woven with spun silver around a core of silk; fringe and braid of spun silver and silk

39 × $77\frac{3}{16}$ in. (99 × 196 cm)

Rome, Comunità Israelitica (inv. no. 416/19)

Like many other synagogue textiles, this piece, donated by the Lattes family to the Catalan Synagogue, was extensively reworked. The mantle is the original fabric; the cape probably comes from another textile. The embroidery, executed almost entirely in gold threads worked in different widths and forms to obtain pictorial effects, completely ruined the supporting textile. Instead of transferring it to a new support, the restorer stopped the disintegration of the background fabric, which had become completely unraveled, by adding perpendicular running stitches to simulate a complicated "Arabian" stitch. The original design was a tight interweaving of oak leaves and flowers, visible only underneath the lower part of the cape, where it escaped the wear and tear of time.

This motif is typical of Italian production from the second half of the seventeenth century. The embroidery with various symbols on the surface of the mantle, together with vine shoots mixed with fruits, leaves, and wheat, belong to this same period. The fringe is also original. But the fragment that comes from another textile can be dated immediately after the mid-seventeenth century, when the vogue for tulips influenced European textile production.

DLB

Unpublished

138. **Torah Mantle from the Scuola Siciliana**

Rome, first half of the seventeenth century

Satin, embroidered with silver threads wound around a core of white silk in couching stitch and french knot; silk velvet; braid of metallic threads spun around a core of white silk; gold and silver braid and fringe; satin lining

$33\frac{7}{8}$ × $60\frac{1}{4}$ in. (86 × 153 cm)

Rome, Comunità Israelitica (inv. no. 491a,b/215)

The mantle, a gift from the Mazarino family to the Sicilian Synagogue, is characterized by a very particular technique and design. The mantle is decorated with small circles of velvet appliqued in horizontal rows that are surrounded by an embroidered braid. The circles alternate red and blue. Any empty spaces are covered in silver threads. The result is very fanciful, but also a bit rough in execution, resembling embroideries made in small geometrical modules during the late sixteenth and early seventeenth century. As in other Roman pieces, we can see a tendency to reproduce through embroidery repeated motifs that imitate woven textiles.

DLB

Unpublished

139. **Torah Mantle**

Venice(?), late eighteenth century

Silk velvet embroidered with frisé gilt wire wound around a silk core; gold lamé, frisé silver wire, wound around silk core; silver lamé; sequins; fringe of gold plied yarn; leather tassels wound with gilt wire and lamella; cotton lining

$41\frac{1}{87}$ × 65 in. (104.5 × 165 cm)

Florence, Comunità Israelitica (1476)

The piece has evidently undergone some alterations and may have been made from a small Torah curtain. The usual cape is missing, and the gathering has been achieved by means of a simple ribbon. The embroidery, which covers a large part of the surface, appears very heavy as a result of stuffing in some parts, as well as the extensive use of gold and silver. The central vase overflowing with flowers, fruit, grape leaves, and spikes, is in *rocaille* taste, as are other decorations. Nevertheless the stiffness of the border embroidery and of the other elements reflects neoclassical taste and places the date of its execution at the end of the eighteenth century. It was probably produced in the Veneto, where such tastes were more persistent.

DLB

Unpublished

140. **Torah Mantle**

Venice, late eighteenth century

Silk velvet embroidered with silk floating stitches and metallic threads; metallic ribbon in underside and couching stitch; taffeta trim; spangles; synthetic diamonds; silver foil; wool and leather padding

29⅛ × 37¾ in. (74 × 96 cm)

Venice, Comunità Israelitica

This Torah mantle was donated to the Levantine synagogue by the Artom family, originally from the city of Asti. The use of so many different materials combined to achieve plastic and luminous effects shows the French influence in Piedmont. The abundance of braid of different types and the dimensions are also typical of this area. The overall richness lends extraordinary impact to the central shield, to the crown surmounting it, and to the emblem of the Levites inserted within it. A certain stiffness of the contours of the ornamental motifs supports a late eighteenth-century date. The inscription reads

לכבוד התורה

(in honor of the Torah).

DLB

Unpublished

Curtains for the Torah Ark

141. **Curtain for the Torah Ark** (fig. 25)

Italy or Ottoman Empire, mid sixteenth century

Wool, knotted

54½ × 44¼ in. (139 × 112.5 cm)

Padua, Comunità Israelitica

This synagogue textile from Padua is extraordinary for several reasons. It is, first of all, one of the earliest Torah curtains in existence. It is also a rare example of a rug that is transitional in style between the Mamluk and Ottoman periods of Islamic art, including typical Mamluk border designs and knotting techniques along with motifs such as tulips, which are characteristic of Ottoman art. But the most unusual aspect of this curtain is its incorporation of iconographic elements drawn from the frontispieces of Hebrew books printed in Italy during the sixteenth century: the illusionistic rendering of an arched portal seen in perspective, which is similar to the first page of *D'rashot haTorah* printed in Padua in 1520–1527 (cat. no. 73); the menorah, symbol of the ancient Temple in Jerusalem;[1] and the sentence from Ps. 118:20: "This is the gateway to the Lord, the righteous shall enter through it." The result is a work that shows both the impact of printing on the creation of ceremonial art and its role in transmitting stylistic and iconographic elements from one culture to another. Either the weaver was a foreigner working in Italy, or he had access to Italian printed books in his native land. Previously rugs such as this one were thought to have been made in Cairo, the Mamluk capital until 1517, when the city was conquered by the Ottoman Turks. Recent scholarship has revealed that there was an atelier of rug weavers associated with the sultan's court in Istanbul early in the sixteenth century, however. The quality of this work suggests that it stems from this court atelier, while the very prominent role of Jews in trade between the Ottoman Empire and Italy during the sixteenth century accounts for the commission and the rug's presence in an Italian synagogue.

VBM

Bibliography: *Mitteilungen . . . Jüdischer Kunstdenkmäler I,* fig. 15; A. G. Grimwade et al., *Treasures of a London Temple* (London, 1951), p. 53, n. 66; F. Landsberger, "Old-Time Torah-Curtains," in *Beauty in Holiness: Studies on Jewish Customs and Ceremonial Art,* ed., J. Gutmann (New York, 1970), p. 144, fig. 4; A. Boralevi, "Un tappeto ebraico italo-egiziano," *Critica d'arte* 49, no. 2 (1984): 34–47; idem, "Three Egyptian Carpets in Italy," in *Oriental Carpet and Textile Studies,* vol. 2, *Carpets of the Mediterranean Countries* (London, 1986), pp. 211–220; W. B. Denny, "The Origin and Development of Ottoman Court Carpets," in ibid., p. 255; B. Yaniv, "Sixteenth- to Eighteenth-Century Bohemian and Moravian Parochot with an Architectural Motif," (Ph.D. diss., Hebrew University, 1987), vol. 1, p. 96 (Hebrew).

1. For a comparable menorah on a frontispiece, see Amram, *Makers,* p. 369.

142. **Curtain for the Torah Ark**

Venice, end of the sixteenth century (with later additions)

Silk velvet embroidered with silk appliqués, silk, and metallic threads

93¾ × 59 in. (238 × 150 cm)

Venice, Comunità Israelitica (21 T)

The large ogival compartments forming the design of the central panel reflect the patterns of sixteenth-century woven textiles.[1] A similar date is indicated by the embroidery technique, silk appliqué, which appears on dated Torah curtains of the period.[2] The choice of inscription, the priestly blessing (Num. 6:24–

26; cf. cat. no. 24), and the coat of arms with laver and basin embroidered in the top cartouche indicate that the donor was a *kohen,* that is, a member of a priestly family, or a Levite. The panel below the coat of arms appears to be a later replacement.

VBM

Bibliography: G. R. Sullam, "Catalogo delle opere," in *Oggetti del culto ebraico,* ed. F. Faranda (Bertinoro, 1988), pp. 32–33.

1. See R. B. Fanelli, *Five Centuries of Italian Textiles, 1300–1800: A Selection from the Museo del Tessuto, Prato* (Florence, 1981), pp. 96–105; E. Casalini et al., *Tesori d'arte dell'annunziata di Firenze* (Florence, 1987), no. 181.
2. See cat. no. 143, n. 1, above.

143. **Curtain for the Torah Ark**

Italy, 1643–1644

Silk and silk damask, appliquéd and embroidered with metallic threads

65 × 45½ in. (165 × 115 cm)

New York, The Jewish Museum, Gift of Dr. Harry G. Friedman (F 3580)

Despite the mid-seventeenth-century date of this curtain, both its technique and its composition are derived from Renaissance artistic traditions. Embroidery by means of silk appliqué is commonly found on sixteenth-century textiles, including two Torah curtains: an Italian example in a private collection dated 1582, and the famous curtain created by Salomon Perlsticker in Prague in 1547, based on Italian models.[1] On this example the appliqués form vine scrolls in the rectilinear compartments of the border, and a crown, a coat of arms, and cartouches in the center field. The additive, symmetrical nature of the composition and the planar character of the work resulting from the appliqués are characteristic of Renaissance art.

There are two inscriptions. One, in the cartouches of the border, is commonly found on Torah curtains of the late sixteenth century: *May He cause His face to shine toward us; Selah* (Ps. 67:2).[2] The second, in the center field, is specific to this curtain and includes a chronogram for the date:

כתר תורה / שנת / שבת קדש / ל־״־ / ה״שי

Crown of Torah/ the year "a holy sabbath of the Lord" [Ex. 16:23]/ *The L[ord] b[lessed be He].* The word *holy* is marked to indicate the year [5]404 (1643–44).

VBM

Bibliography: Kayser and Schoenberger, *Jewish Ceremonial Art,* no. 7; Jewish Museum, *Fabric of Jewish Life* (New York, 1977), no. 2; Kleeblatt and Mann, *Treasures,* pp. 60–61.

1. See H. Volavkova, *A Story of the Jewish Museum in Prague* (Prague, 1968), fig. 81, for an illustration of the Perlsticker curtain. See also, Kleeblatt and Mann, *Treasures,* fig. 17.
2. E.g., F. Faranda, ed., *Oggetti del culto ebraico* (Bertinoro, 1988), p. 32, fig. 13, where the curtain is dated to the late seventeenth century. It should be dated to the late sixteenth century (see cat. no. 142).

144. **Curtain for the Torah Ark** (fig. 41)

Venice, 1680–1681

Simḥah, wife of Menahem Levi Meshullami

Silk embroidered with silk and metallic threads, metallic fringe

85¹⁄₁₆ × 55⅛ in. (216.1 × 140 cm)

New York, The Jewish Museum, Gift of Professor Neppi Modona, through Dr. Harry G. Friedman (F 2944)

Works with representational decoration are rare in the corpus of Italian Torah curtains. This curtain is further distinguished by its close relationship to another, slightly earlier Venetian curtain with an expanded version of the same iconography: a depiction of Jerusalem below and the Giving of the Law above.[1] The latter subject is indicated by the hands of God holding tablets that emerge from the heavenly clouds.

The mountain flanked by flowering vines has a dual significance. It is Sinai, which flowered at the moment of the Giving of the Law,[2] and it is also Moriah, according to the inscription surrounding its peak ("The mountain which God has desired for His abode," Ps. 68:17). According to Jewish legend, one of the reasons Sinai was chosen as the site of revelation was that it was originally part of Mount Moriah, and in the messianic age Sinai will return to its place of origin.[3]

The appearance of Jerusalem on these two Venetian curtains suggests a link to illuminated marriage contracts. Northern Italian examples were often decorated with representations of the holy city accompanied by the quotation "I prefer Jerusalem above my chief joy" (Ps. 137:6), which appears on this curtain above the walls.

The use of this imagery on the two curtains may have been inspired by the contracts and by Jewish mystical ideas that emphasized attachment to the land of Israel.[4]

The Giving of the Law is commonly found on curtains used on the holiday of Shavuot, which commemorates that event (see cat. no. 145; fig. 42).[5]

VBM

Bibliography: Kayser and Schoenberger, *Jewish Ceremonial Art,* no. 5; Jewish Museum, *Fabric of Jewish Life,* no. 3; Jewish Museum, *The Jewish Patrons of Venice,* no. 3; Z. Vilnay, *The Holy Land in Old Prints and Maps,* trans. E. Vilnay and M. Nurock (Jerusalem, 1963), p. 32; Kleeblatt and Mann, *Treasures,* pp. 70–71.

1. See Vivian B. Mann, "The Arts of Jewish Italy," above. For a recent reproduction of the curtain see D. Cassuto, "A Venetian Paroḳet and Its Design Origins," *Jewish Art* 14 (1988): 42, fig. 1.
2. M. Jaffe, *Levush ha-Tekhelet: Orakh Ḥayyim* (Berdichev, 1818), no. 494. I would like to thank Rabbi Reuven Fink for this reference.
3. L. Ginzburg, *Legends of the Bible* (Philadelphia, 1956), p. 378.
4. Cassuto, "A Venetian Paroḳet," p. 43.
5. For example, see C. Mossetti, "La schedatura dei manufatti tessili in alcune considerazioni di carattere metodologico," in *Ebrei a Torino* (Turin, 1984), pp. 172–173.

145. **Curtain for the Torah Ark** (fig. 42)

Venice(?), 1698–1699

Leah Ottolenghi

Linen embroidered with silk and metallic threads

70 × 48 in. (177.8 × 122 cm)

New York, The Jewish Museum, Gift of Dr. Harry G. Friedman (F 3432)

This curtain belongs to a group of three needlework examples distinguished by their complex iconographic scheme; the others are in the Victoria and Albert Museum, London, and the Jewish Museum of Florence.[1] All three curtains share the same basic composition: a central portal, enclosing symbolic references to the Giving of the Law at Sinai, which is surrounded by cartouches framing symbols of holy days and holy sites.

The same symbols appear on all three curtains and in the same positions relative to the central field. When these symbols are read as a group or in pairs, three themes are apparent: the reading of the Torah on Sabbaths and holy days, with an emphasis on special Sabbaths or on occasions that commemorate the Giving of the Law; personal and national redemption (e.g., in the second row of cartouches, reading from top to bottom, are depictions of the tombs of the patriarchs and matriarchs in Hebron opposite the Mount of Olives, site of the resurrection of the dead in messianic times); finally, the symbols and quotations also present an itinerarium of holy sites. All three themes are combined in the central field, beneath the arch. The *lulav* and *etrog* (citron) flanking the Tablets represent both a place, the flowering Mount Sinai, and a festival—Sukkot, or Tabernacles—when these plants are used in ritual and special portions of the Torah are read. Since ancient times they have also been a symbol of the messianic age or redemption (see cat. nos. 10, 19; fig. 56).

VBM

Bibliography: Kayser and Schoenberger, *Jewish Ceremonial Art,* no. 5; Jewish Museum, *Fabric of Jewish Life,* no. 3; Roth, *Jewish Art,* rev. ed., p. 121, fig. 114; Kleeblatt and Mann, *Treasures,* pp. 72–73.

1. The Florence curtain is unpublished; the London example was published by Sol Cohen ("A 17th-Century Parochet," *The Jewish Chronicle,* 10 July 1953, p. 15ff.

146. **Curtain for the Torah Ark**

Italy, late seventeenth century

Silk velvet, silk and metallic brocade embroidered with silk and metallic threads

72⅘ × 41 in. (184 × 104 cm)

New York, The Jewish Museum, H. Ephraim and Mordecai Benguiat Family Collection, S 303

This portal composition derives from the frontispieces of Hebrew books printed in Italy from the sixteenth century on.[1] The enclosed cut velvet dates to the seventeenth century,[2] while the Decalogue within a glory at the top of the arch is commonly found on Italian Torah Curtains and other synagogue textiles beginning in the seventeenth century.[3] The flames, clouds, and horns surrounding the Tablets are based on the biblical descriptions of Moses Receiving the Law (Ex. 19:16, 18–19).

This curtain entered The Jewish Museum with a matching mantle (cat. no. 133), and a matching valance (S 303a).

VBM

Bibliography: NYJM, *Fabric of Jewish Life,* no. 7.

1. For example, see fig. 33. For another curtain based on printed models, see cat. no. 141.
2. See above cat. no. 133, n. 1.
3. For example, see *Ebrei a Torino,* p. 173. A later curtain with this iconographic motif is cat. no. 148. For a *mappah* with the same symbolism see U. Nahon, *Holy Arks and Ritual Appurtenances from Italy in Israel* (Tel Aviv, 1970), p. 149.

147. **Curtain for the Torah Ark**

Ancona, 1754–1755

Simhah Viterbo

Silk embroidered with silk and metallic threads; metallic fringe

85 × 68⅛ in. (216 × 173 cm)

New York, Collection of Peter Ehrenthal

Floral motifs are the most common decoration found on seventeenth- and eighteenth-century Italian Torah curtains. Frequently the flowers emerge from a centrally placed vase, as on this example. The embroidery describes carnations, roses, grapes, and pomegranates as well as more stylized floral forms. According to documentary photographs, this curtain originally hung in the Ancona synagogue.

VBM

Bibliography: *Judaica: Books, Manuscripts, and Works of Art,* sale cat., Sotheby's, Jerusalem, May 1985, lot 242.

148. **Torah Curtain for Shavuot**

Raḥel Modigliani and three other women

Pitigliano, 1833–1834

Net embroidered with silk threads; silk

97⅛ × 74½ in. (248 × 189.5 cm)

New York, The Jewish Museum, Gift of Professor and Mrs. E. G. Machlin and Mrs. Meyer S. Siegel in honor of their father, Signor Azeglio Massimo Servi (JM 61–61)

According to Erna Servi Machlin, who, together with her sister and husband, donated this work to the Jewish Museum, four young virgins, one of them Raḥel Modigliani (of the painter Amedeo's family), created this curtain. In order to accomplish their task in an atmosphere of holiness, the four women embroidered each morning while fasting. An inscription records the completion of their work:

ש״ התק״צ״ד

(t[he year] 5594 [1833–1834]). Their curtain was hung in the synagogue of Pitigliano on Shavuot, the holiday that commemorates the Giving of the Law at Sinai. That event is symbolized by the Tablets of the Law framed by an aureole at center. The remainder of the embroidery consists of naturalistically rendered flowers and birds, including peacocks. Some of the flowers emerge from amphorae set in the four corners of the central field. This motif is common on northern Italian Torah curtains from the seventeenth century on.

VBM

Unpublished

149. **Curtain for the Torah Ark** (fig. 98)

Venice(?), early eighteenth century

Silk embroidered in various shades of silk; spun and gilt copper threads; spiral and curly metallic tinsel; in *punti pieno e raso* and couched stitches; silk velvet; painted cotton; fringe and tassels of silk and spun gold; taffeta lining

66¼ × 49³⁄₁₆ in. (168 × 125 cm)

Rome, Comunità Israelitica (inv. no. 673/418)

This Torah curtain was donated to the new Italian synagogue by the Della Rocca family. It is not known when the embroidery was transferred to the new fabric, but this probably occurred in the nineteenth century, since the red taffeta lining is typical of that era. The fringe, made up of many small tassels formed by winding metallic thread around thin strips of leather, is comtemporary with the embroidery. The background was originally cream-colored cotton or satin, so that the renovation completely changed the chromatic relationship between the background and the embroidery. Probably the Torah curtain resembled the *ganzi* textiles produced in Venice, on which the background could barely be glimpsed from behind the gold brocade motifs. A Venetian attribution seems probable, which is further supported by the imitation of the *dentelle* lace produced at the end of the seventeenth century in imitation of Lyons production. Yet the naturalism of the large flowers and the insertion of small houses and other landscape elements point to a date in the first quarter of the eighteenth century.

DLB

Unpublished

Covers for the Torah and the Reader's Desk

150. **Reader's Desk Cover**

Venice, early nineteenth century

Silk velvet with two brocade weaves in silver around a core of white silk; gros de Tours lining

36⅜ × 71⅞ × 32⅝ in. (92.3 × 182.6 × 83 cm)

Venice, Comunità Israelitica (49T)

The brocade design of this cover imitates embroidery; the decorative motif, which runs along only the lower portion, is a series of pinecones flanked by long leaves that are joined together at the bottom and arranged horizontally. Similar, but smaller, motifs run above and below these; others, still smaller, form the side borders. The design and the brocade effect that imitates embroidery relate to work produced in Lyons at the beginning of the nineteenth century. The coarseness of the velvet and the heaviness of the brocade, however, characterize local production.

DLB

Unpublished

151. **Reader's Desk Cover** (fig. 186)

Italy, 1685–1686

Silk, embroidered with silk and metallic threads; linen embroidered with silk threads; metallic braid; silk and metallic fringe

76¾ × 57½ in. (195 × 146 cm)

New York, The Jewish Museum, The Eva and Morris Feld Judaica Acquisitions Fund (1981–319)

The inscription embroidered in the center field indicates that this reader's desk cover was donated by a widow in memory of her husband:

לכבוד ה׳ / נדבת / הכבודה מרת שרה / אשת כמה׳ה׳הר
יוסף יהושע / יונח שנת תמ״ו לפק / תורת ה׳ תמימה
משיבת נפש / עדות ה׳ ליא

(In honor of the Lord / the donation of / Signora Sarah / the wife of . . . Joseph Joshua / laid to rest [in] the year [5]446 (1685–1686) . . . / "The teaching of the Lord is perfect, renewing life; the decrees of the Lord" [Ps. 19:8] w[ill be for a] b[lessing] A[men]). The remainder of the embroidered decoration is floral.

VBM

Unpublished

152. **Cover for the Torah**

Italy, c. 1700

Silk embroidered with silk and metallic threads

20 × 25½ in. (49 × 65 cm)

New York, The Jewish Museum, Gift of Dr. Harry G. Friedman (F 4126)

The size of this textile suggests that it was used to cover the Torah between readings. At center is a rampant lion with jutting tongue facing left set within a heraldic shield, the coat of arms of the donor. This device was used by several Italian-Jewish families, making a more precise identification of the donor difficult (for example, see cat. no. 183).

VBM

Bibliography: NYJM, *Fabric of Jewish Life,* no. 11.

153. **Torah Cover**

Florence, first half of the nineteenth century

Satin embroidered with gold wire and lamella wound around a silk core; frisé, tinsel in the satin stitch, couching, stem stitch technique; braid trimmed with gold lamella wound around a silk core, waved and file

33⅞ × 15¾ in. (86 × 40 cm)

Florence, Comunità Israelitica (1027)

The cover is embroidered on both sides. The golden threads therefore pass through the fine fabrics, now lacerated in various areas, keeping them together. Despite the great richness of the piece's surface design, its execution is stiff. This is especially evident in the corner panels and in the central motif, which seem to date to the neoclassical period. Yet the profusion of scattered flowers and their delicacy push the date of execution to around the 1830s, when there was a predilection for floral elements. Surrounding the central motif, a crowned Tablets of the Law, is an inscription:

נדבה ל״ה כבוד לשמו להדרת תורה לפאר בית תפארתו

(Donated to God to honor, to guard the glory of his Torah, and to adorn the house of its splendor).

DLB

Unpublished

Miscellaneous Textiles

154. **Circumcision Ensemble**

Venice, last quarter of the eighteenth century (shirt, gown, cushion cover, bonnet, stockings, shoe), c. 1848 (sheet, handkerchief, binder, *tallit katan*)

Cotton fringe, executed in needlework; satin lining; taffeta tapes edged in pink velvet; cotton muslin, embroidered in satin, back and shadow stitches

Shirt: 9⅞ × 7½ in. (25 × 19 cm); gown: 33½ × 10¼ in. (85 × 26 cm); cushion cover: 26⅜ × 13¾ in. (67 × 35 cm); bonnet: 7⅞ in. (20 cm); stockings: 8 1/16 × 2¾ in. (20.5 × 7 cm); shoe: 4 5/16 × 2 in. (11 × 5 cm); sheet: 32⅝ × 32¼ in. (83 × 82 cm); handkerchief: 11 × 11 7/16 in. (28 × 29 cm); binder: 34⅝ × 5½ in. (88 × 14 cm); *tallit katan*: 23¼ × 24¼ in. (59 × 61.5 cm)

Venice, Comunità Israelitica

This circumcision ensemble, donated to the Venetian community by Amedeo Sarfatti, was made in two different eras. We know that the older group, made up of the shirt, gown, cushion cover, bonnet, stockings, and shoes, was made for the father of Marco Mordecai (1816–1885), who was presumably born at the end of the eighteenth century. The other pieces belonged to Amedeo Grassini (1848–1908), son of Marco Mordecai and Colomba Gentilomo, whose initials, *AG*, were embroidered on the *tallit katan*. The neoclassical style of the fringe, with its regular succession of small and rigid oblong motifs, confirms the oral history. The later pieces, much simpler both in concept and execution, carry through certain themes, such as the small symmetrical vine shoots with a rose at the center that ornament the upper vamp of the only remaining shoe, thus making the entire ensemble homogeneous.

DLB

Unpublished

155. **Baby's Binder of Gabriele Sonnino (1900–1985)**

Rome, 1900

Lace, machine made

8 × 94 in. (20.3 × 238.8 cm)

Collection of the grandchildren of Gabriele Sonnino

VBM

Unpublished

156. **Tefillin Bag of Jacob de Joseph Barukh Caravalho**

Venice, c. 1696

Silk, velvet embroidered with metallic threads

11¼ × 7 7/16 in. (28.6 × 18.9 cm)

New York, Collection of Mrs. Irene Roth

The coat of arms of the Caravalho family, a crowned shield with five stars, is embroidered on both sides of the bag. According to the owner, this tefillin bag was given to Jacob de Joseph Barukh Caravalho by his bride, Anna. (See cat. no. 240 for the portrait of Joseph Barukh Caravalho.)

VBM

Bibliography: NYJM, *Jewish Patrons,* no. 31.

157. **Tefillin Bag from the Vitali Family**

Conegliano, nineteenth century

Silk velvet embroidered with silk, metallic threads, and sequins; metallic fringe

6½ × 5½ in. (16.6 × 14 cm)

Venice, Comunità Israelitica

VBM

Unpublished

158. **Panel for a Prayer Shawl Bag**

Italy, eighteenth century

Silk, embroidered with silk threads

21⅞ × 20⅝ in. (55.5 × 52.5 cm)

New York, The Jewish Museum, Gift of Dr. Harry G. Friedman (F 691)

The decorative motifs and composition of this panel are similar to Torah curtains of the eighteenth century. The inscription in the arch reads:

הזהיר במצות ציצ[י]ת זוכה לטלית נאה

("He who is diligent about [the commandment] of fringes merits a beautiful prayer shawl" [Babylonian Talmud, Sabbath, 23b]). Below is an embroidered laver and basin accompanied by the rubric

עבודת הלוים

(the service of the Levites), which suggests that the panel was made for a Levite.

VBM

Bibliography: NYJM, *Fabric of Jewish Life,* no. 72.

159. **Bag for a Prayer Shawl and Prayerbooks**

Asti, beginning of the nineteenth century

Red silk velvet, gold braid; red and white silk braid and tassel; red taffeta lining

16¾ × 15¾ in. (42.5 × 40 cm)

Venice, Comunità Israelitica (no. 210)

This bag was owned by the Artom family, originally from Asti, in Piedmont. It was a local custom in Asti to carry prayerbooks, *tefillin,* and prayer shawls in such large bags.[1] Both examples in the Venice Museum are larger at the bottom and closed by a braid that passes through holes in the top. The decoration is limited to braid, which is very sumptuous and of two sizes. The larger ones form a central square and intersect the smaller ones with a series of loops. The flower and leaf motif was common from the late eighteenth century until the mid nineteenth century; the largeness of the bag, however, suggests a date at the end of the eighteenth century.

DLB

Unpublished

1. Another bag from Asti is also in Venice; see G. Reinisch Sullam, *Il Ghetto di Venezia: Le sinagoghe e il museo* (Rome, 1985), no. 7, pl. 7.

160. **Prayer Shawl**

Italy, nineteenth century

Silk embroidered with silk threads

65¾ × 47¼ in. (167 × 120 cm)

Venice, Comunità Israelitica

Prayer shawls embroidered with flowers, such as this one, are unique to Italian Judaica, and examples from the seventeenth century on can be found in various public and private collections. This example came from the Alberto de Benedetti family in Padua.

VBM

Unpublished

161a. **Embroidered Folder for an Epithalamium**

Italy, eighteenth century

Silk embroidered with silk and metallic threads and tinsel; paper, painted; metal, punched

10⅜ × 8½ in. (16.5 × 21 cm)

Washington, D.C., B'nai Brith Klutznick Museum (inv. no. 168)

Riddles in the form of poems written in a mixture of Hebrew and Judeo-Italian became popular among Italian Jews in the mid-seventeenth century and remained an important literary genre through the mid-nineteenth century (see cat. no. 161b).[1] This folder was made to enclose such a poem composed by Asher Viterbo for the wedding of Fellice and Giudicca Coen and bears an inscription in two languages, Italian and Hebrew, one on each side of the folder:

Presente di Primirie / Da Presentarsi ai Mag. Coanim / Fellice Coen. con / Giudicca Coena Vivano.

מנחת בכורים / להקריב לוי זוג מעלת הכהנים / פנחס כהן / עם גיודיקא כהנת יחיו

(An offering of first fruits [Lev. 2:14] to Pinchas Coen, with Giudicca Coen Vivano). The inscriptions fill a border surrounding the central field, which is embroidered with the coat of arms of the Coen family (two blessing hands on a crowned shield) held by four putti.

VBM

Unpublished

1. For a general discussion of literary Hebrew riddles, see D. Pagis, "Baroque Trends in Italian Hebrew Poetry as Reflected in an Unknown Genre," in *Italia Judaica. Atti del II convegno internazionale* (Rome, 1986), pp. 263–277.

161*b*. **Wedding Riddle Broadside**

Israel Gedaliah, son of Moses Cois, the doctor

Italy, seventeenth to eighteenth century

Ink on paper; woodblock and metal type

20¹⁵⁄₁₆ × 16¼ in. (52.2 × 43 cm)

New York, Library of The Jewish Theological Seminary of America (44)

The festivities at Italian-Jewish celebrations frequently included riddle contests. Riddles were most frequently composed for weddings in an effort to amuse the bride and groom and were given to guests a week or more before the wedding so that they could prepare solutions (see cat. no. 161*a*). This riddle poem was written for the celebration of the wedding of Moses Ḥayyim the Cohen, son of Neḥemiah, and Neḥama, daughter of Samuel Menaḥem. At the wedding celebration the guests would present their solutions to the riddle, and a winning answer would be rewarded with a prize, such as silver spoons or an elegant hat. The riddles often played on humorous similarities between Italian and Hebrew words.[1]

This broadside is topped by a woodcut of a large cherub holding a trumpet and laurel wreath. A depiction of a well, part of the riddle, is placed above a rhymed sextet describing a man falling into a well. In order to solve such a riddle, the wedding guest had to be proficient in Hebrew and Italian and have the ability to decipher an enigmatic image. This poetic genre reflects the literary and artistic sophistication of the Italian-Jewish community during the seventeenth and eighteenth centuries.

GMG

Unpublished

1. For a general discussion of riddle poems and their usage, see D. Pagis, "Baroque Trends in Italian Hebrew Poetry as Reflected in an Unknown Genre," *Italia Judaica* 6 (1986): 263–278.

162. **Sheet and Matching Pillowcases from the Trousseau of Clotilde Castelnuovo Sonnino**

Italy, c. 1896

Linen; lace

Sheet: 127½ × 102 in. (323.9 × 259.1 cm); Pillowcases (each); 23⅜ × 32¼ in. (59.4 × 81.9 cm)

Collection of the Great-grandchildren of Marco and Clotilde Sonnino

VBM

Unpublished

163. **Wedding Fan of Clotilde Castelnuovo**

Giovanni Gilardini

Turin or Rome, 1896

Lace; mother-of-pearl; silk tassel; gold handle

13½ × 24¼ in. (34.3 × 61.6 cm)

Private collection

VBM

Unpublished

164. **Miniature Wedding Dress**

Ditta E. Porati

Milan, 1920s

Silk embroidered with beads; linen; lace

Dress: 33⅝ × 28 13/16 in. (85.4 × 73.2 cm); Jacket: 13 11/16 × 33 in. (34.8 × 83.9 cm)

Private collection

This miniature gown, modeled on the wedding dress of Onorina De Benedetti Treves, was made for the celebration of the fiftieth anniversary of her marriage to Beniamino Colombo. It was worn by their granddaughter Renata Colombo Treves (b. 1918). A label sewn inside the collar of the jacket identifies the maker: *Ditta E. Porati / Milano / Forniture Teatrali.*

VBM

Unpublished

165. **Tablecloth Used on Passover**

Venice, seventeenth century

Lace

64½ × 227 in. (163.9 × 576.6 cm)

Collection of the grandchildren of Emma and Gabriele Sonnino of Rome

VBM

Unpublished

166. **Cover for the *Afikomen***

Italy, eighteenth to nineteenth century

Linen embroidered with linen

Diam: 18 in. (45.5 cm)

New York, The Jewish Museum, Gift of Rose S. Goldberg in memory of her brother, Edward J. Sovatkin (JM 150–75)

This delicate embroidery was used to cover the *afikomen,* the portion of the middle of the three matzot set aside to be eaten at the conclusion of the seder meal. It bears the inscription צפון (hidden), alluding to the practice of hiding this portion of matzah until the end of the seder. The name of the owners is embroidered in the outer border: משפחת לוצאטו (the Luzzatto family).

VBM

Bibliography: NYJM, *Fabric of Jewish Life,* no. 205.

167. **Medal Commemorating Benjamin, Son of Elijah Beer, the Physician**

Venice(?), 1497–1503

Bronze, cast

Diam: 6⅞ in. (17.5 cm)

Paris, Bibliothèque Nationale

This cast medal was discovered in Lyons, France, in 1656 and has been the center of scholarly debate for approximately three centuries. The obverse features an elegant head crowned by a laurel wreath, surrounded by a lengthy, cryptic inscription in Hebrew, Latin, and Greek. On the reverse is a Latin inscription encircling a blank area. The medal is dated with a strange formulation, *D-III-M,* which can be interpreted as either 1497 or as 1503. Various scholars have attempted to ascertain the meaning and date of the inscriptions and the identity of the subject.

In 1696 the Jesuit priest C. F. Menestrier published the medal and identified the subject as King Louis I (778–840) of France. This theory was not questioned until the early nineteenth century, when Gerson Levy remarked that there are no known portrait medals of French kings prior to Charles VII (1403–1461). In 1876 Leopold Zunz discovered the acrostic in the Hebrew inscription, thereby linking Beer to the medal.

Benjamin Beer was the son of Elijah Fonte di Sabato, a fifteenth-century papal court physician who also treated King Henry IV of England. Whether the portrait depicts Benjamin is unclear, however. Zunz believed that the inscription indicated Beer's prediction of the date of the coming of the Messiah. Louis Loewe believed that Beer was an adherent of the false Messiah Asher Lemlein and that the medal declared Lemlein's prediction of the Messiah's arrival in 1503. Abraham Geiger later suggested that the portrait depicted Beer and was issued to commemorate his death in 1503. More recently Daniel Friedenberg has stressed that despite the cryptic inscriptions and enigmatic portrait, the medal is symbolic of the inner spiritual quest of sixteenth-century Jewry plagued by the Inquisition. The latest study, by Samuel Kottek, suggests that the medal was cast around 1470 from a preexisting example and that an inscription discussing immortality and the importance of humility was added by Benjamin Beer at the end of his life, in 1497 or 1503. Kottek has attributed the original struck medal to Giovanni Boldu (d. c. 1477) or one of his students. Boldu was the maker of a medal with a Hebrew and Latin inscription dated 1458.

Obverse: (translation based on Kottek)

בגזרת נוהג ית׳ מרצון נצחי בתם כל משפט העדר
הצורהִ ראיתי אורך לזמן ישיגהו הקץ ואתבונן בהשגחת
אלי רומי השאיר רשומם ואעלוז פדותך אוחיל יוי שדי
רב וסלח וי גח וע עי.
מי בת תע שא תל חו בן ימין בן כרש

τα Ωροσις. umilitas

By the decree of the Guide b[lessed be He] through the will of the Eternal while all judgment ceases and the image disappears, I will see Your light at the time when redemption will take place. And I reflect on the providence of my Lord, my Highest. May a trace be guarded. And I rejoice, praying for the mercy of your redemption. Oh Lord, great and forgiving. B[ut I] k[now that my] V]indicator] l[ives]; I[n the end He will] t[estify on] e[arth] [Job 19:25]. O [that You] w[ould] h[ide me] i[n Sheol], C[onceal me] u[ntil] Y[our anger] p[asses], S[et] m[e a] f[ixed time] t[o attend to me] [Job 14:13]. Humility, Humility!

Diacritical marks indicate an acrostic: "Benjamin s[on of] . . . Elijah Be'er the physician, M[ay he live] m[any] g[ood] y[ears]."

בנימין בכמההר׳ר
אליהו באר הרופא י׳ש׳ר׳ו.

GMG

Selected Bibliography: C. F. Menestrier, *Histoire civile ou consulaire de la ville de Lyon,* vol. 3 (1696), pp. 219–220; G. Levy, in *Mémoires de l'Académie de Metz,* 28 August 1836; L. Loewe, "Memoir on the Lemlein Medal," *Numismatic Chronicle* 19 (April 1856–January 1857): 237–270; A. Geiger, "Eine mittelalterliche jüdische Medaille," *Zeitschrift der Deutschen morgenländischen Gesellschaft* 12 (1858): 680–693, 12 (1859): 272–275; L. Zunz, "Eine merkwürdige Medaille," in *Gesammelte Schriften,* vol. 3 (1876), pp. 87–97; D. M. Friedenberg, *Jewish Medals from the Renaissance to the Fall of Napoleon (1503–1815)* (New York, 1970), pp. 72–77, 138–139; S. S. Kottek, "Humilitas: On a Controversial Medal of Benjamin Son of Elijah Beer the Physician (1497?–1503?)," *Journal of Jewish Art* 11 (1985): 41–46.

168. **Medal of Elijah de Latas and His Mother, Rica** (figs. 35–36)

Rome, 1552

Bronze, cast

Diam: 1½ in. (3.8 cm)

New York, The Jewish Museum, Gift of the Samuel and Daniel M. Friedenberg Collection (FBG 66)

Medals were frequently commissioned by the sixteenth-century Italian nobility and bourgeoisie. The depictions of Elijah de Latas and his mother, Rica, on this medal resemble the idealized portraits found on many Italian medals of this period. On the obverse is the profile portrait of Elijah, grandson of Bonet de Lattes, who was an astronomer and a physician to the papal court (see cat. no. 66). The soft curls of Elijah's hair and beard are delicately modeled. Rica de Lattas is portrayed on the reverse as an elegant woman. The maker was particularly concerned with depicting her stylish coiffure and decorated cap and with modeling the gentle folds of drapery around her throat. Italian inscriptions surround both portraits. Elijah is described as *ebreo* on the medal which combines a declaration of Jewish identity with the adoption of a style prevalent in the larger society.

Obverse: *ELIA DE LATAS EBREO MD52*

Reverse: *SUA GIENTRICE RICA.*

GMG

Bibliography: D. M. Friedenberg, *Jewish Medals from the Renaissance to the Fall of Napoleon (1503–1815)* (New York, 1970) pp. 42, 128.

169. **Medal of Gracia Nasi the Younger**

Ferrara, 1558

Pastorino di Giovan Michele de' Pastorini (c. 1508–1592)

Bronze, cast

Diam: 2⅝ in. (6.6 cm)

New York, The Jewish Museum, Gift of the Samuel and Daniel M. Friedenberg Collection (FB 77)

Medals of Jewish subjects such as Gracia Nasi the younger illustrate the Jewish community's awareness of contemporary Renaissance art. In this period medals developed as an art form, modeled after antique coins commemorating the deeds of Roman emperors. The medal of Gracia Nasi is the earliest of a Jewish subject to incorporate a Hebrew inscription, the sitter's name (גרציאה נשיא). Its accompanying Latin inscription records her age: *A[nno] AE[tas] XVIII* (in the year of her age eighteen).

The inscriptions on this medal and the use of Hebrew are particularly significant, indicating the subject's attainment of financial independence and her return to Judaism. Gracia Nasi the younger inherited the fortune of the Marrano Mendes family on her eighteenth birthday.[1] Earlier her mother, Brianda Mendes, and her aunt, Beatrice De Luna Mendes, had left Portugal, eventually settling in Venice in 1546. They arrived as Christians, but Beatrice reverted to Judaism, taking the name Gracia Nasi, thereby coming into conflict with her still-Catholic sister. One January night in 1553 their nephew Joseph Nasi and several accomplices abducted Gracia the younger from her mother's palazzo and fled with her to Ferrara. Subsequently Joseph and Gracia reached Ravenna and married; they eventually settled in Constantinople, where Joseph rose within the sultan's government and was named duke of Naxos. For his part in the abduction, Joseph was banished from Venice by the Council of Ten; a price was put on his head and on those of his accomplices. Only through the intervention of the Ottoman government was the banishment lifted, some fourteen years after it was first imposed.

VBM

Bibliography: A. Armand, *Les médailleurs italiens des quinzième et seizième siècles,* vol. 1 (Bologna, 1966), pp. 36, 202; D. M. Friedenberg, *Jewish Medals from the Renaissance to the Fall of Napoleon (1503–1815)* (New York, 1970), pp. 44–46, 128; Jewish Museum, *A Tale of Two Cities* (New York, 1982), no. 144; Kleeblatt and Mann, *Treasures,* pp. 54–55.

1. This account is based on Benjamin Ravid's "Money, Love and Power Politics in Sixteenth-Century Venice: The Perpetual Banishment and Subsequent Pardon of Joseph Nasi," in *Italia Judaica: Atti del I convegno internazionale* (Rome, 1983), pp. 159–181.

170. **Bell with Gagiona Family Coat of Arms**

Joseph de Levis (1552–1611/14)

Verona, 1590s

Bronze, cast

H: approx. 7⅞ in. (20 cm)

London, Victoria and Albert Museum (A.16–1973)

This is a classic example of a bell by Joseph de Levis, whose monogram *I.D.L.* (from the Latin form of his first name, *Ioseph*) is cast in relief on the inside, with traces of a date (159 . . .) above. The coat of arms with a stylized pineapple and a star is that of a Veronese family, the Gagiona.[1]

The bell is one of several artifacts from the de Levis workshop belonging to families identified by coats of arms or inscriptions, either from Verona or further afield, for example, Genoa, Mantua, and Milan. They may have been commissioned specially from those centers or more likely belonged to members of the families who lived or had business or other contacts in Verona. Joseph and his colleagues had only to model the coat of arms afresh in wax, possibly from a seal or signet ring, and attach it to a standard model for a bell in order to be able to take the molds necessary for casting.[2]

The missing handle was probably cast separately and screwed into the crown of the bell: it may have been a figurine, which could have been sold separately by a later owner.

A similar bell, complete with an ornamental handle displaying motifs found on the body of the bell and bearing the identical coat of arms of the Gagiona family, is in the Virginia Museum, Richmond.[3] It is dated 1587 inside and initialed in a trademark *LCFV*, with the *C* possibly standing for "compagni," as in "Levis and Company."

CA

Provenance: Private collection, Hanover.

1. G. B. Crollalanza, *Dizionario Storico-Blasonico*, vol. 1 (Bologna, 1886), p. 104: *D'azzuro, all'ananasso d'oro gambuto e fogliato verde, le code in basso, sormontata da una stella di otto raggi d'oro.*
2. For the method of manufacture, see C. Avery, "Giuseppe de Levis of Verona, Bronze Founder and Sculptor," *Connoisseur,* 181 (November 1972): 179–188.
3. Inv. no. 37–11–24, gift of Mrs. John Kerr Branch in memory of her husband. I am grateful to Joseph Bliss for his assistance and enthusiasm in studying this and other bells in the museum.

171. **Inkstand with Three Graces** (fig. 48)

Joseph de Levis (1552–1611/14) and Angelo de' Rossi

Verona, 1599

Bronze

H: approx. 7$\frac{1}{16}$ in. (18 cm)

New York, Metropolitan Museum of Art, Gift of George Blumenthal, 1941 (41.100.84)

The inkstand, which seems to be unique, consists of a shallow bowl with everted rim, supported by three winged dragons whose forepaws rest on volutes rising from a scrolling foot with shells below. Between the dragons are three harpies with legs and arms terminating in foliate ornaments, a favorite motif of Joseph de Levis (see also cat. nos. 170, 173–175).[1]

On the lid, which is decorated with grimacing masks and three-dimensional volutes, sit three elegantly posed nude women, presumably the three Graces. They are fluently modeled, and their faces and hair are carefully rendered, considering the small scale. The surface texture of Joseph's original wax model is retained through the lost-wax technique of casting, and there is little trace of afterworking in the cold metal. There is a hole with bayonet fitting in the center of the lid, presumably to attach a finial.

Inside the bowl Joseph's normal signature, *IOSEPH DE LEVIS VER. F.*, is cast in relief within a wreath, together with a date *MDIC* (1599) and the barely legible name *RUBEIS*. This is the Latinized form of the name of Joseph's collaborator, Angelo de' Rossi, a sculptor who helped him model one of this best pairs of statuettes, *Saint George* and *Saint John the Baptist,* on the holy water stoups in the church of San Giorgio in Braida, Verona.[2]

De' Rossi is probably responsible for the suave composition of the group of female figures as well as for the sculptural compactness of the work, which is one of the finest decorative objects to have issued from the de Levis foundry, or indeed any other northern Italian foundry, at the turn of the century.

CA

Provenance: George and Florence Blumenthal.

Bibliography: S. Rubinstein-Bloch, *Catalogue of the Collection of George and Florence Blumenthal,* vol. 2 (Paris, 1926), pl. LVII; W. Gramberg, "Der Veroneser Bildhauer Giuseppe de Levis und Guglielmo della Porta," in *Jahrbuch der Kunsthistorischen Sammlungen in Wien,* n.s., vol. 11 (1937), p. 188; C. Avery, "Giuseppe de Levis of Verona, Bronze Founder and Sculptor: Figurestyle," *Connoisseur* 182 (February 1973): 93–95, figs. 11, 12.

1. See C. Avery, "Giuseppe de Levis of Verona, Bronze Founder and Sculptor," *Connoisseur* 181 (November 1972), figs. 2, 9, 14, 15.
2. See Avery, "Giuseppe de Levis of Verona, Bronze Founder and Sculptor: Figurestyle," figs. 6, 7.

172. **Ḥanukkah Lamp** (fig. 34)

Italy, sixteenth century

Bronze, cast

6⅜ × 6⅞ in. (16.2 × 17.4 cm)

Jerusalem, Israel Museum (118/675)

The putti that are the dominant motif on this lamp often appear on inkwells, candlesticks, and like objects created in Italy during the sixteenth and seventeenth centuries. The stylistic features of these figures—the beautifully modeled bodies arranged in graceful contrapposto poses, the use of sashes and belts to emphasize the volume of the chest, the explicit genitalia, cropped wings, and the curly coiffeur that forms a point on the forehead—suggest that the lamp is related to pieces that have been tentatively attributed to the workshop of Niccolò Roccatagliata, active in Venice during the late sixteenth and early seventeenth centuries.[1]

Roccatagliata was a contemporary of Joseph de Levis, and similar motifs can be found in the work of both artists, making definitive attributions difficult.[2] A more complete example of this type is in the Ticho collection, Jerusalem; the right hand of the uppermost putto still remains.[3]

VBM

Bibliography: I. Fishof, "Renaissance Hanukah Lamps from Italy," *Israel Museum News* 8 (1970): 65–67.

1. See Kunstgewerbemuseum Berlin, *Bronzen und Plaketten vom ausgehenden 15. Jahrhundert bis zur Mitte des 17. Jahrhunderts,* vol. 3, ed. K. Pechstein (Berlin, 1968), no. 108; C. Avery, "Giuseppe de Levis of Verona: Decorative Utensils and Domestic Ornaments," *Studies in European Sculpture* (London, 1981), p. 64, fig. 3.
2. See Avery, "Giuseppe de Levis," p. 65; and cat. nos. 170, 171, 173–175.
3. Bezalel Museum, *Ḥanukkah Lamps from the Ticho Collection,* exh. brochure, by H. F[euchtwanger] (Jerusalem, 1960–1961), no. 6.

173. **Bucket or Basin** (fig. 183)

Joseph de Levis (1552–1611/14)

Verona, late sixteenth century

Bronze

5⅛ × 8¹⁄₁₆ dm in. (13 × 20.5 cm)

Jerusalem, Israel Museum (133/281)

This bucket or basin with a swing handle bears the usual signature of Joseph de Levis in cartouches beneath the terminal figures of harpies that serve as mountings for the handle: *JOSEPH DE LEVIS VER. F.* The type of harpy recalls that featured on the Inkstand with Three Graces (cat. no. 171) and on the vaselike zone of the Firedog with Figure of Juno (cat. no. 175). The frieze of harpies round the neck is a standard motif, almost a trademark of the foundry. The blank cartouches supported by draped female figures were probably meant to be engraved with the arms or initials of an owner. This suggests that some objects were manufactured "off the peg" and could be customized to a client's taste. One other similar vessel is known. Formerly in the Lanna collection, Prague, and later in an English private collection, it is more upright in shape, standing on a waisted foot, which is signed underneath.[1] Its lip bears the same ornament as the present example.

The most interesting feature of this bucket, unique in the oeuvre of Joseph, is a circular medallion cast within the basin, which would have been visible through any water contained in it. It is based on Albrecht Dürer's famous engraving *The Sea Monster* (Bartsch 71), perhaps cast from a German medallion or plaquette.

CA

Provenance: Joseph Stieglitz collection.

Bibliography: Israel Museum, *The Joseph Stieglitz Collection: Masterpieces of Jewish Art,* exh. cat., by C. Benjamin (Jerusalem, 1987), no. 280.

1. C. Avery, "Giuseppe de Levis, Bronze Founder and Sculptor: Decorative Utensils and Domestic Ornament," *Connoisseur* 185 (February 1974): 126–127, figs. 10, 11.

174. **Bell with Sun Motif**

Joseph de Levis (1552–1611/14)

Verona, late sixteenth century

Bronze

H: approx. 7⅞ in. (20 cm)

London, Victoria and Albert Museum (A.7–1987)

This bell, only recently discovered on the London art market, bears Joseph de Levis's usual signature in a shield: *JOSEPH DE LEVIS VER. F.* Inside are the numerals *83,* presumably an abbreviation of the year of manufacture, 1583. In another shield is cast a radiant sun with a human face, a device whose meaning remains to be elucidated.

This sun motif was an *impresa* (personal device) of Marchese Ludovico Gonzaga.[1] If the mark is not a family coat of arms, it may refer to the name of an inn (e.g., Albergo del Sole, a common one in Italy) or other establishment. The device was used in the following century by Queen Christina of Sweden, after her abdication and exile in Rome, on the reverse of portrait medals, and also by King Louis XIV of France, the *Roi Soleil* (Sun King). It was adopted later in England by fire insurance companies, surviving in the symbols of such firms as Sun Life.

CA

Unpublished

1. See A. F. Radcliffe, in Victoria and Albert Museum, *Splendours of the Gonzaga,* exh. cat. (London, 1982), no. 51.

175. **Firedog with Figure of Juno**

Joseph de Levis (1552–1611/14)

Verona, late sixteenth century

Bronze

H: approx. 16 in. (40.6 cm)

London, Victoria and Albert Museum (3011/12–1857)

The firedog is one of a pair (both signed behind the blank cartouche below); the other is crowned with a figure of Jupiter (king of the gods and husband of Juno in ancient Roman mythology and religion). They conform to the roughly pyramidal design that was standard in the Veneto during the late sixteenth century: zone upon zone of interlocking figures, classical monsters, grotesques, and foliate ornaments converging by degrees toward a finial, normally a single standing human figure with a symbolic or mythological subject, as in this example.[1]

The figures of Juno and Jupiter are in general reminiscent of statuettes by the doyen of the Venetian school of bronze sculptors, Alessandro Vittoria, but are less convincingly articulated and characterized. Other examples are known, for example, in the Liechtenstein collection.[2]

The female herm figures on the central vase resemble those forming the lugs for the handles on a bucket (cat. no. 173) and a inkstand (cat. no. 171) from the de Levis foundry, while the various sphinxes, hippocampi, dragons, and the scrolling strapwork and swags that link everything together are characteristic of the Venetian school.

CA

Fig. 183. Joseph de Levis, Bucket, Verona, late sixteenth century, Israel Museum, Jerusalem (cat. no. 173)

Bibliography: *Inventory of Objects in the Art Division of the Museum at South Kensington,* vol. 1, *Objects Acquired in the Year 1857* (London, 1868), p. 19; C. D. E. Fortnum, *A Descriptive Catalogue of the Bronzes of European Origin in the South Kensington Museum* (London, 1876), p. 126; L. Planiscig, *Venezianische Bildhauer der Renaissance* (Vienna, 1924), p. 634, figs. 706–707; W. Gramberg, "Der Veroneser Bildhauer Giuseppe de Levis und Guglielmo della Porta," in *Jahrbuch der Kunsthistorischen Sammlungen in Wien,* n.s., vol. 11 (1937), pp. 184–186, figs. 200, 201; C. Avery, "Giuseppe de Levis of Verona, Bronze Founder and Sculptor: 3–Decorative Utensils and Domestic Ornaments," *Connoisseur* 185 (February 1974): 123–125, figs. 1–6.

1. See Planiscig, *Venezianische Bildhauer,* pp. 490–492; A. Pettorelli, *Il bronzo e il rame nell'arte decorativa italiana* (Milan, 1926), figs. 163–168, 171.
2. Planiscig, *Venezianische Bildhauer,* figs. 708–709; a figure of Jupiter is in the Israel Museum, Jerusalem.

176. **Mortar with Hebrew Inscription** (fig. 37)

Servo de Levis (1570–1616/27)

Verona, early seventeenth century

Bronze

H: approx. 4¾ in. (12 cm); Diam: approx. 6¼ in. (16 cm)

Jerusalem, Israel Museum (192/26)

The mortar is signed within a wreath *SERVIVS DE LEVIS VERONA F.* The name is that of Servo (or Servio) de Levis.[1] He was one of Joseph's three nephews; the others were Giovanni Battista and Ottavio. They were the children of Joseph's elder brother Santo, who predeceased him prematurely, around 1580–1582. The nephews worked alongside Joseph's own sons Paolo and Francesco (see cat. no. 182) in the family bronze foundry. The joint signature of the nephews, *SERVO DE LEVIS E FRATELLI* (Servo and his brothers), appeared on bells in and around Verona as early as 1590 (Sirmione, Town Hall), and as late as 1597 (Isola della Scala, Bastia; Verona, City Tower, called Pa Marangona, now destroyed)[2] as well as on a splendid door knocker in the State Hermitage, Leningrad.[3] Servo's name appears on its own after the demise of his brother Ottavio in 1613–1614, on a church bell of 1615 or 1616 now in the Museo di Castelvecchio, Verona.[4] This suggests a possible date of 1615 or later for the present mortar.

The most notable feature of the mortar's decoration is a stylized seven-branched candelabrum flanked by the Hebrew letters *mem* and *resh* crowned with dots. מ'ר' These cannot designate a date, as has been supposed,[5] but should instead be interpreted as initials, either of a name or perhaps of an expression, such as *melekhet rofim,* which may be roughly translated as "physician's craft."[6] There is in a private collection another mortar from the de Levis foundry, this one signed by Paolo, which displays a stylized menorah and an inscription of a pair of Hebrew letters (*lamed* and *daled*). Their meaning is also enigmatic.

The discovery of these two mortars, both probably dating from after about 1610, with their Jewish symbolism, again raises the question of whether the de Levis were Jewish, albeit converts to Christianity (for their dates of birth, except in the case of Joseph, are derived from baptismal records in Verona). This has been assumed to be the case by scholars such as Cecil Roth[7] but denied by others such as the late Professor Ulrich Middeldorf. Roth did not know about the baptismal records, which were published only as recently as 1979 (after the present author's early research on the foundry), and neither scholar knew about the mortars with Hebrew inscriptions, so vital evidence was lacking. So far no work by Joseph himself with Jewish connotations has come to light. This may be purely by chance, or it may be that even though Jewish, he did not dare produce such goods. One wonders whether a more relaxed regime in Verona in the early seventeenth century encouraged the younger members of the family to produce the mortars without fears of reprisals.

CA

Provenance: Joseph Stieglitz collection.

Bibliography: Israel Museum, *The Joseph Stieglitz Collection: Masterpieces of Jewish Art,* by C. Benjamin (Jerusalem, 1987), no. 279.

1. L. Rognini, "I Levi," in *Fonditori di campane a Verona dal XI al XX secolo* (Verona, 1979), p. 74.
2. Ibid., p. 72.
3. State Hermitage, *Catalogue of Italian Renaissance Bronzes,* by S. Androssov and L. Faenson (Leningrad, 1977), no. 74 (in Russian); idem, *Italienische Bronzen der Renaissance aus der Sammlung der Staatlichen Ermitage in Leningrad* (Berlin, 1978), no. 58.
4. Rognini, "I Levi," fig. 36.
5. *The Joseph Stieglitz Collection,* no. 279.
6. Tentative suggestion of Professor Meir Benayahu of Hebrew University, Jerusalem, cited in a letter to the author from Chaya Benjamin, 19 May 1988.
7. C. Roth, *Jewish Art: An Illustrated History,* rev. ed., ed. B. Narkiss (Greenwich, Conn., 1971), p. 178; idem, *The Jews in the Renaissance* (Philadelphia, 1959), p. 198.

177. **Ḥanukkah Lamp with Judith Beheading Holofernes** (fig. 38)

Workshop of Joseph de Levis(?)

Italy, late sixteenth to early seventeenth century

Bronze, cast

10½ × 10⅜ × 2½ in. (27 × 26.5 × 6.5 cm)

Jerusalem, The Sir Isaac and Lady Wolfson Museum, Hechal Shlomo

Iconographically and sculpturally this lamp and a very similar example in the collection of Congregation Emanu-el, New York, are the richest Ḥannukah lamps extant from the late sixteenth to early seventeenth century. The lower portion of the backplate is composed of a relief of Judith Beheading Holofernes. Two three-dimensional putti in complementary contrapposto poses frame the relief and at the same time anchor the pyramidal arrangement of figures in the round that rises from the tray of oil lamps. Above the putti are two reclining elders whose poses likewise complement each other, and above them is a crowning figure, probably Matityahu the Hasmonean, dressed as the High Priest. A mask framed by scrolls completes the repertory of human forms. These are the only known early Italian Ḥanukkah lamps to incorporate the climactic scene of the Judith story; most display the single figure of the triumphant heroine (see cat. no. 180). Furthermore the reclining male figures that may represent sages or biblical heroes suggest an attempt to invest most of the figurative decoration with Jewish meaning. The association of Judith with the Hasmoneans and the institution of Ḥanukkah dates back to the Middle Ages and was mentioned by Leone Modena, whose *Historia degli riti hebraici* (cat. no. 79) was written at the time this lamp was created. An attribution to the de Levis workshop is suggested by the inclusion of decorative motifs such as the mask surrounded by ribbon scrolls that are found on signed works (for example, cat. no. 171), by the complementary poses of the paired figures, which are typical of de Levis's compositions, and by the incorporation of a narrative relief, as many are extant from Joseph's oeuvre. The putti on the Wolfson lamp resemble those on objects recently attributed to the de Levis workshop.[1]

VBM

Bibliography: N. Feuchtwanger, "The Coronation of the Virgin and of the Bride," *Jewish Art* 12–13 (1986–1987): 230, fig. 8; C. Roth, *Jewish Art* (New York, 1961), p. 338, fig. 153.

1. Kunstgewerbemuseum Berlin, *Bronzen und Plaketten von ausgehenden 15. Jahrhundert bis zur Mitte des 17. Jahrhunderts*, vol. 3, ed. K. Pechstein (Berlin, 1968), nos. 89–92.

178. **Ḥanukkah Lamp with Lions**

Italy, sixteenth to seventeenth century

Bronze, cast

7¼ × 8¹¹⁄₁₆ × 2⁹⁄₁₆ in. (18.4 × 22.1 × 6.5 cm)

New York, The Jewish Museum,
Gift of Dr. Harry G. Friedman (F 3110)

The central decoration of the backplate—a mask bearing a basket of fruit from which emerges an urn, cornucopia, winged herms, and animal and human masks—appears on two different lamps: one with confronted lions, as here, and another, more elaborate backplate framed by addorsed sphinxes. Examples of both types can be found in various collections.[1]

VBM

Unpublished

1. The confronted lion backplate appears on two lamps in the Israel Museum (I. Fishof, "Renaissance Ḥanukah Lamps from Italy," *Israel Museum News* 8 [1970]: no. 3; Israel Museum, *The Stieglitz Collection: Masterpieces of Jewish Art*, exh. cat., by C. Benjamin [Jerusalem, 1987] no. 121), on a lamp in the Wolfson Museum, Jerusalem, and on a lamp in the Jacobo and Asea Furman collection, Santiago (no. 18). The backplate with sphinxes appears on a lamp in the Musée de Cluny, Paris (Cl. 12245; V. Klagsbald, *Catalogue raisonné de la collection juive du Musée de Cluny* [Paris, 1981], no. 22), on a lamp in the Israel Museum (*The Stieglitz Collection*, no. 121), and the backplate alone is in the collection of the Museo Bardini, Florence (no. 1078).

179. **Ḥanukkah Lamp**

Italy, sixteenth to seventeenth century

Bronze, cast and engraved

6⅛ × 8⅝ × 2⅜ in. (15.5 × 22.1 × 5.5 cm)

New York, The Jewish Museum,
Gift of Dr. Harry G. Friedman (F 5048)

Two published examples of this lamp are known, both in the collection of the Israel Museum, Jerusalem.[1] The cherub's head that forms the central motif of this type also appears on other domestic objects of the period (see cat. no. 175).

VBM

Unpublished

1. Israel Museum, *Jewish Tradition in Art: The Feuchtwanger Collection of Judaica*, by I. Schachar, trans. R. Grafman (Jerusalem, 1981), no. 344; Bezalel Museum, *Ḥanukkah Lamps from the Ticho Collection*, exh. brochure, by H. F[euchtwanger], (Jerusalem, 1960–1961), no. 5.

180. **Ḥanukkah Lamp with Armed Judith** (fig. 113)

Italy, sixteenth to seventeenth century

Bronze, cast and engraved

8¹⁄₁₆ × 8¹¹⁄₁₆ × 2¹⁄₁₆ in. (20.4 × 22.1 × 5.2 cm)

New York, The Jewish Museum,
Gift of Dr. Harry G. Friedman (F 91)

The appearance of Judith on Ḥanukkah lamps of the sixteenth and seventeenth centuries represents a confluence of two traditions: the Italian artistic tradition, according to which Judith was a symbol of civic and other virtues, and a Jewish literary tradition dating to the Middle Ages that anachronistically linked her story to the Hasmonean revolt. The closest parallels to this lamp are an example in the Victoria and Albert Museum, London (M28–1965), another in the Wolfson Museum, Jerusalem, and a third in the Jewish Museum, New York (F 1318). Later lamps bearing similar Judith figures usually include decorative motifs other than the tritons and masks seen here. The blade of Judith's sword is missing.

VBM

Unpublished

181. **Mortar**

Joseph de Levis (1552–1611/14)

Verona, 1605

Bronze

H: 5½ in. (14 cm)

New York, Collection of Benjamin Zucker

Domestic mortars for grinding herbs or other medicaments in pharmacies or foodstuffs in the kitchen are rarer than bells in the output of Joseph de Levis's foundry. This may be due simply to a lower rate of survival in view of the heavy wear through pounding with the pestle that such functional utensils suffer. A heavier weight of metal is necessary, and this too would tend to encourage melting down as scrap. Other mortars by Joseph are to be found in the Kunstmuseum, Düsseldorf, and in a Florentine private collection.[1]

In addition to the standard signature in an oval cartouche on the side is a large ribbon-like label bearing in the Roman numerals MDCV the date of 1605, making it the last surviving work by Joseph himself. Aftercasts taken from Roman imperial coinage (for example, a *sestertius* of Galba) are applied as decoration to the body of the mortar, indicating a humanist interest in the past, perhaps to suit the refined taste of a scholarly patron or buyer. Such casts of coins appear on other objects from the foundry, for example, a bell in the Virginia Museum, Richmond (inv. 37–11–13) and a bronze *Calvary* in New York, Metropolitan Museum of Art (1981.76).[2]

CA

Bibliography: C. Avery, "A bronze founder and sculptor of the late sixteenth century, Giuseppe de Levis of Verona: new discoveries," *Connoisseur,* 194 (February 1977): 115–117, figs. 4–5.

1. C. Avery, "Giuseppe de Levis of Verona, Bronze Founder and Sculptor," *Connoisseur,* 181 (November 1972): 182–184, figs. 6–8.
2. The bell is unpublished and unsigned but bears the normal de Levis frieze of harpies. For the *Calvary,* see C. Avery, "A bronze founder and sculptor of the late sixteenth century, Giuseppe de Levis of Verona: new discoveries," *Connoisseur,* 194 (February 1977), figs. 4–5.

182. **Crucible**

Paolo and Francesco de Levis (active 1611–1630)

Verona, early seventeenth century

Bronze

H: approx. 4¾ in. (12 cm); Diam: 6¼ in. (16 cm)

London, Victoria and Albert Museum, Alfred William Hearns Gift (M. 26–1923)

This bronze crucible with a projecting handle is unique. It bears in an oval cartouche the inscription *PAVLO FRANC: LEVI VER. F.* and, flanking the handle, the initials, *N.M.,* possibly indicating the owner. When the object was first published, the names were regarded as those of a single member of the de Levis family,[1] but it has since been established that they are in fact the names of Joseph de Levis's two sons, Paolo (1572–1635) and Francesco (1573–1630).[2]

Paolo and Francesco probably entered the family workshop when they reached fourteen, the normal age for apprenticeship. Their names are not recorded separately during Joseph's lifetime, but only in 1611, 1615, 1622, and 1624. This indicates a date for the crucible during the first third of the seventeenth century.

None of the ornaments reflects Joseph's particular repertory, and but for the signature, the piece would have been hard to assign to the de Levis foundry. The hemispherical bowl is decorated with a frieze of acanthus rinceaux around the rim. The feet are extraordinary: they are decorated with inverted masks of the "Green Man" variety; these were presumably adapted from molds used right side up in some other context. The thick wall of the basin would tolerate and retain great heat as well as grinding with a pestle, and the vessel may have had a technical or scientific, rather than a domestic, application.

CA

Bibliography: C. Avery, "Giuseppe de Levis, Bronze Founder and Sculptor: Decorative Utensils and Domestic Ornament," *Connoisseur,* 185 (February 1974), p. 128.

1. C. Avery, "Giuseppe de Levis," p. 128, fig. 15.
2. L. Rognini, "I Levi," in *Fonditori di campane a Verona* (1979), pp. 73–74.

183. **Ḥanukkah Lamp**

Italy, early seventeenth century

Bronze, cast and engraved

8⅜ × 5¾ × 2¹³⁄₁₆ in. (21.3 × 14.6 × 7.3 cm)

Washington, D.C., National Museum of American History (no. 376 672)

The decorative motifs on the backplate of this Ḥanukkah lamp—putti, vine scrolls, and dragons' heads—are drawn largely from the repertory used on Renaissance bronzes for secular use. Only the crown and coat of arms can be associated with Jews and Jewish culture. A rampant lion with bifurcated tongue facing left was the coat of arms of the Malta family of Venice,[1] while the crown may be interpreted as a reference to Torah (learning), priesthood, royalty, or to the crown of a good name. Since the lamp was an item for personal use, it may have been the last meaning that was intended by the inclusion of the crown motif.

VBM

Unpublished

1. The same coat of arms appears on a Venetian marriage contract dated 1796 as the symbol of the Malta family (New York, The Library of The Jewish Theological Seminary of America no. 264a; see NYJM, *Jewish Patrons,* no. 41).

184. **Ḥanukkah Lamp with Centaurs**

Italy, seventeenth century

Bronze, cast

6½ × 10¼ × 2⅞ in. (16.5 × 26.0 × 7.2 cm)

New York, The Jewish Museum, Gift of Dr. Harry G. Friedman (F 93)

The composition of this lamp, a central vertical element (a herm emerging from the snouts of two dolphins topped by an urn and vines) set between two addorsed centaurs blowing horns shaped like cornucopias, appears as part of a larger composition on two other lamps. One is in Turin,[1] and the other is an unpublished piece in the Nauheim collection, now part of the Frankfurt Jewish Museum. All of the decorative elements appearing on these lamps are drawn from the iconographic repertory of Renaissance bronzes for domestic use.

VBM

Bibliography: F. Landsberger, *A History of Jewish Art* (Cincinatti, 1946), pp. 221–223.

1. H. Frauberger, "Über alte Kultusgegenstande in Synagoge und Haus," *Mitteilungen der Gesellschaft zur Erforschung jüdischer Kunstdenkmaler,* 3–4 (1903): 45.

185. **Hanukkah Lamp**

Italy, sixteenth to seventeenth century

Bronze, cast

12¾ × 15½ in. (32.4 × 39.3 cm)

New York, The Jewish Museum, Gift of Dr. Harry G. Friedman (F 2125)

In the thirteenth century a new type of Hanukkah lamp appeared, furnished with a backplate and a suspension ring that enabled the user to hang the lamp on a wall. The earliest examples from northern Spain or southern France are decorated in the same manner as this one: the backplate is formed as a building facade. This decorative scheme probably arose from the custom of displaying Hanukkah lamps near the front of homes in order to publicize the miracle of the holiday.

The facade on this lamp, a triple arcade preceded by a balustrade, is characteristic of Italian *palazzi* of the sixteenth century, suggesting that the lamp can be dated to the sixteenth or seventeenth century. On later Italian examples whose backplates are arcuated, the arch is used as a frame for symbols and no longer has the architectural form seen here.

VBM

Bibliography: Kayser and Schoenberger, *Jewish Ceremonial Art,* no. 123; Kleeblatt and Mann, *Treasures,* pp. 66–67.

186. **Amulet** (fig. 114)

Rome?, c. 1750

Brass, cast, hammered, and engraved

4⅛ × 2⅞ in. (10.5 × 7.3 cm)

New York, The Jewish Museum, Gift of Dr. Harry G. Friedman (F 4527)

This elegant amulet features a seven-branched menorah surrounded by scrollwork and rocaille set in an oval cartouche containing an engraved inscription of the priestly blessing (Num. 6:24–27). These verses have magical significance as they can be read as an acrostic of the twenty-two-letter name of God and also as an inscription invoking a blessing. On the reverse of the amulet are four engraved cartouches containing the text of Jacob's blessing for Joseph (Gen. 49:22). The upper cartouche is topped by a crown. The lowest cartouche contains an engraved coat of arms, a rampant lion flanking a column beneath a crescent moon and a sun, possibly the shield of the Zevi or Bemporad family. The identification with the Bemporad family is likely, as the text of Gen. 49:22 labels Joseph a *ben porat,* the Hebrew derivation of the family's name.

GMG

Bibliography: Maurice Spertus Museum of Judaica, *Magic and Superstition in the Jewish Tradition* (Chicago, 1975), no. 11.

187. **Torah Pointer**

Italy, eighteenth to nineteenth century

Brass, cast, engraved, and gilt

5 7/16 × ⅜ in. (13.8 × 1.0 cm)

New York, The Jewish Museum, Gift of Dr. Harry G. Friedman (F 4078)

The shaft of this elegant pointer is composed of a rope-twist column embellished with scrolling floral motifs. Twisted columns frequently appear on Italian *ketubbot,* ceremonial silver, printed books, and synagogue architecture and may have been regarded as a symbol of Solomon's Temple because of the popular belief that the twisted columns in the Capella della Pietà of St. Peter's, Rome, originally came from the Temple in Jerusalem.[1]

GMG

Unpublished

1. For a discussion of the Italian-Jewish community's awareness of the symbolism of twisted columns, see S. Sabar, "The Beginnings and Flourishing of Ketubbah Illustration in Italy: A Study in Popular Imagery and Jewish Patronage during the Seventeenth and Eighteenth Centuries," (Ph.D. diss., University of California, Los Angeles, 1987), pp. 170–174.

188. **Torah Pointer**

Italy, ca. 1830–1890

Brass: cast, chased, silver-plated

4⅞ × 7/16 in. (12.4 × 1.1 cm)

New York, The Jewish Museum, Gift of Dr. Harry G. Friedman, F2389

The use of paisley motifs and a pumpkin-shaped knop on this pointer indicates that it was crafted during the Rococo Revival.

GMG

Unpublished

189. ***Sheḥitah*** **(Ritual Slaughter) Token**

Papal States, c. 1849 or earlier

Bronze, struck

Diam: 1¼ in. (3.3 cm)

New York, The Jewish Museum, Gift of Samuel and Daniel M. Friedenberg Collection (FB 732)

The *gabela* was a tax imposed by the Jewish community on the slaughter of animals in order to raise funds to pay the *shoḥet,* or ritual slaughterer, and to support communal institutions such as the Talmud Torah, the religious school. Individuals purchased tokens such as this, which were then given to the shoḥet for his services. Its monetary value is three *baiocchi,* a denomination used in the Papal States through 1849.

Obverse: *3 B[aiocchi] / POLLO GRANDE /*
לשחיטת עוף גדול
(3 B[aiocchi] / large chicken / for the slaughter of a large chicken)

Reverse: ת"ת
(R[eligious] S[chool])

GMG

Bibliography: J. J. Berman, *Sheḥitah: A Study in the Cultural and Social Life of the Jewish People* (New York, 1941), pp. 180–181; Jewish Museum, *Coins Reveal,* exh. cat., by Y. Meshorer (New York, 1983), no. 132.

SILVER AND GOLD

Hanukkah Lamps

190. **Hanukkah Lamp**

Francesco Teoli (1658–1728) and Filippo Piccardi (1752–1832)

Rome, 1748 and 1795(?)

Silver, repoussé, chiseled, engraved

Hallmarks: Bulgari, vol. 1, no. 1016, and state stamp; Bulgari, vol. 1, no. 836, and state stamp with a star

26¾ × 18$\frac{5}{16}$ in. (68 × 46.5 cm)

Rome, Comunità Israelitica (inv. no. 211/70)

This example is one of the most beautiful hanging lamps made in Rome. The exuberance of the decoration is typically Roman; it is still markedly baroque, without those asymmetries that characterize the rococo period. During his long life Francesco Teoli was a very active goldsmith, endowed with great technical skill, as can be seen from the richness of the acanthus leaves mixed with pomegranates, grapes, and olive branches, which completely cover the border surrounding the central cartouche. The placement of a menorah in the center, surmounted by a lion facing left and by a large crown, is also typically Roman (and is perhaps the crest of the donor family). The thinness of the plate must have led all too quickly to the wearing away of certain parts, necessitating, as early as the end of the century, the substitution of neoclassical candle holders made by the silversmith Filippo Piccardi. The history of the lamp's donation to the Catalan Synagogue is recorded in the inscription on the border:

נדבת הזקן הנכבד המעולה הנכבד המעולה והמפואר
כ״מר מרדכי מנשי יצ״ו לחיי מסעוד בנו ולחיי אביו
ואשתו בג״ע סדר הבקר אור שנת ה׳ אלקי אבותיכם
יוסף עליכם כנס אלף פעמ״ים ויברך אתכם

(Donation of . . . Mordekhai Menashe . . . Massoud, his son, May his father live, and his wife in [the] G[arden] o[f] E[den], the order of the morning is light, the year "May the Lord, the God of you fathers, increase your numbers a thousand fold, and bless you" [Deut. 1:1] [5]508 [1747–1748]).

DLB

Bibliography: F. Pitigliani, *Permanent Exhibition of the Jewish Community of Rome* (Rome, 1962), no. 124.

191. **Ḥanukkah Lamp for the Synagogue** (fig. 188)

Florence, last quarter of the eighteenth century

Silver, embossed, chiseled, and engraved

Hallmark: *RC* within rectangle

15 × 14$\frac{9}{16}$ in. (38 × 37 cm)

Florence, Comunità Israelitica (no. 238406/301)

Aside from what we know from the object and its inscription—

חברת מתיר אסורים

(Confraternity of *Matir Asurim* [Those Who Free Captives])—we have no documentary information concerning this lamp. The oratory of the Matir Asurim Confraternity was located in a room adjoining the Scuola Italiana, to which it had been moved after the middle of the eighteenth century. In fact, most of the Florentine objects that are known through inscriptions belonged to that oratory and are dated to the late eighteenth century. The date of the piece is also confirmed by its composition and decorations. The rococo shells, the festoons of leaves and flowers, the protruding borders, and the oval medallion are all elements typical of the Florentine ornamental repertory of the last quarter of the eighteenth century. The absence of a mint hallmark and the presence of only the silversmith's initials (as yet unidentified) indicate that the lamp was made after 1781. In that year it was ordered that Florentine products were not to be stamped in cases where the ratio of silver to the alloy failed to conform to that required.

DLB

Unpublished

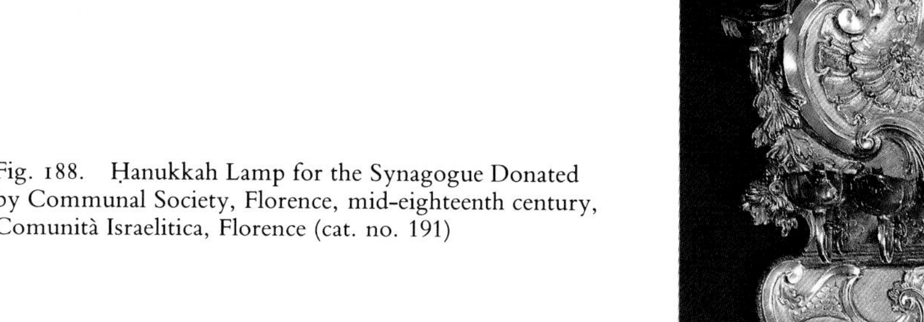

Fig. 188. Ḥanukkah Lamp for the Synagogue Donated by Communal Society, Florence, mid-eighteenth century, Comunità Israelitica, Florence (cat. no. 191)

Finials

192. **Torah Finial** (fig. 112)

Florence, end of the sixteenth century

Silver, embossed, chiseled and engraved; cast and reworked by chisel (pinnacle, columns, balusters, escutcheons)

Hallmarks: striding lion facing right; horse

15¾ × 4⅜ in. (40 × 11 cm)

Florence, Comunità Israelitica (inv. no. 73)

As the dedicatory inscription is completely worn away and therefore illegible, a precise date cannot be assigned to this object. It is, however, one of the earliest Torah finials still extant in Italy. The form of striding lion, the mark of the Florentine mint, was utilized during the last quarter of the sixteenth century. A late sixteenth-century date is also suggested by the extremely classical style of the *tempietto,* which is modeled on Brunelleschi's cupola, and by the decorative motifs. It was probably created, along with its companion, lost during World War II,[1] when the ghetto's synagogues (those of the Italian rite and of the Spanish or Levantine rite) were founded. The other hallmark probably belongs to the workshop that produced the *rimmon.* Research efforts have not yet succeeded in linking any silversmith to this shop. The quality of the object nonetheless suggests that the artist involved was abreast of the latest Florentine stylistic trends.

DLB

Bibliography: D. Liscia Bemporad, "Atarot fiorentine," *MCM,* no. 3 (1985): 43.

1. One of the *rimmonim* was lost during World War II, when the synagogue was robbed of all its treasures. When partisans regained them at the Swiss frontier, some of the *rimmonim* were without their companions.

193. **Torah Finials** (fig. 115)

Rome, 1651

Silver, repoussé, chiseled, cast, chased, and parcel-gilt

Hallmark: Bulgari, vol. 1, no. 140

22 × 5 5/16 dm in. (56 × 13.5 cm)

Rome, Comunità Israelitica (inv. no. 13/75)

The goldsmith executed the traditional pomegranate form of the finials in a sumptuous manner, marking the segments with long fruited vines arranged longitudinally and covering the interstices with symmetrically arranged vegetal and leaf motifs, typical of silver work of the mid-seventeenth century. The same fruit appears in the small bells that hang from the tails of three rampant lions and from the paws of the three half lions supporting the crown at top. It is possible that the presence of this last motif excluded the simultaneous use of a Torah crown. The original shaft was replaced at the end of the eighteenth century. It is curious that the silversmith repeated the writing that was evidently present on the original shaft:

אלו הרמונים נעשו שנת התיא מהוצאת מרת אורה מבת
אשת כמר חיים נטורנאי ז'צ'ל'

(These finials were made in 5411 through the donation of Orah, wife of Ḥayyim Natronai). The replacement of some of the small bells, which had gotten lost, with others that are more open in form can also be dated to 1797.

DLB

Bibliography: F. Pitigliani, *Permanent Exhibition of the Jewish Community of Rome* (Rome, [1962]), p. 15.

194. **Pair of Finials for the Synagogue**

Mantua, seventeenth century

Silver, cast, repoussé, and engraved

24 × 5 dm in. (61 × 12.7 cm)

Hallmarks: *R3 7391*; *SIC*; an illegible mark

New York, The Jewish Museum,
Gift of Samuel and Lucille Lemberg (JM 20–64 a, b)

The large size and heavy weight of these finials suggest that they were used to ornament the reader's desk in a synagogue, a usage known in Spain and brought to Italy after the expulsion of 1492. Their tower form may also be traced to the Spanish dominions, since the earliest pair of tower-form Torah finials was made in fifteenth-century Sicily, which was then ruled by Spain. These examples are three-storied hexagonal towers overlaid with ornament that nearly obscures the architectural forms. The blurred outlines and the richness of the ornamentation are characteristic of baroque metalwork.

VBM

Bibliography: The Jewish Museum, *Loan Exhibit of Antique Ceremonial Objects and Paintings from the Collection of Mr. M. Zagayski,* exh. brochure (New York, 1951), no. 1; idem, *The Silver and Judaica Collection of Mr. and Mrs. Michael M. Zagayski,* exh. cat., by G. Schoenburger and T. Freudenheim (New York, 1963), no. 3, fig. 3; *The Michael M. Zagayski Collection of Rare Judaica,* sale cat., Parke-Bernet Galleries, New York, 1964, lot 293; NYJM, *Jewish Patrons,* no. 9; Kleeblatt and Mann, *Treasures,* pp. 88–89.

195. **Torah Finial from the Scuola Italiana**
(fig. 115)

Francesco Caglieri

Florence, 1730–1732

Silver, embossed, chiseled and engraved; cast and reworked by chisel; parcel-gilt

Hallmarks: striding lion facing left; anchor; *FC* (on the lower part of the stem)

16 15/16 × 5 1/8 in. (43 × 13 cm)

Florence, Comunità Israelitica (450)

This finial was made in Florence, as is indicated by the striding lion, symbol of the Florentine mint. The name of the assayer, whose symbol is the anchor, cannot be identified, but the initials *FC* can be traced to the goldsmith Francesco Caglieri. Although few objects created by Caglieri can be identified, he was very active as a goldsmith in Florence beginning in 1723 and created another pair of *rimmonim* in the collection of the Comunità. In both cases he exhibits the skills of an able and well-prepared artist capable of creating objects that are highly classical and far from Venetian models in both structure and decoration. The inscription indicates that it was donated in 1731 by the Jews of Florence to the Scuola Italiana, the ghetto's most important and oldest synagogue, which was demolished at the end of the nineteenth century. The type of decoration employed, particularly the acanthus leaves, and the molded shape of the finial, confirm that the date of its execution corresponds to that of its donation, as indicated in the inscription:

נדבת יהודי ק״ק איטאליאני פירינצא שנת הצ״א לפ״ק

(A donation of the Jews of the Italian congregation, Florence, the year [5]591 [1730–1731]).

This *rimmon* also lacks its companion (see cat. no. 192).

DLB

Unpublished

196. **Torah Finials** (fig. 97)

Venice, c. 1730; Rome, c. 1767

Unknown silversmith; Giuseppe Bartolotti (1709–1775)

Silver, repoussé, chiseled, engraved, cast, and chased

Hallmarks: Bulgari, vol. 1, no. 234; lion of San Marco; *AG* with the insignia of a tower; *SR* in a rectangular field (stamped onto the cupola and the lower part of the tower)

26¾ × 16⅛ in. (68 × 41 cm)

Rome, Comunità Israelitica (inv. no. 1/65)

These Torah finials present rather complicated problems. The base, the shaft, the center of the tower, and the niches with small vases of flowers must be attributed to Giuseppe Bartolotti.[1] Indeed the structure seems typically Roman and makes clear reference to Bernini's baldacchino in Saint Peter's. The supports for the towers, covered with broad acanthus leaves made from thin silver sheets; the second level flanked by buttresses in the form of broad volutes; the cupola; and the small crowning vases must, however, be assigned to Venice. They are stamped with characteristic Venetian marks whose date accords with the style of the pieces: the lion of San Marco, utilized until the end of the eighteenth century; the initials *AG* and a tower, the marks of a workshop active during the first half of the century;[2] and the initials *SR*, probably the name of a silversmith. Indeed these elements are very similar to the reliquary of San Pietro Orseolo, executed in 1730 by the goldsmith Gerolamo Pilotto after the design of the sculptor-silversmith Antonio Gai, in the workshop with the mark *ZC* and a tower.[3]

We do not know why this complicated assemblage was completed over a span of thirty years, but it is probable that the Venetian workshop commission remained unfinished due to the death of the master and that the project was brought to Rome for completion, where Bartolotti adapted a new structure and decorations to the existing parts. At this later stage an inscription was engraved:

קדש ל״ה לכנסת האטלאני יעא הרמונים עם הפעמונים
כולם כסף צרוף נקנו ממעות שנותרו בגזברות הגביר
הנעלה הזקן ה״וה כ׳ חזקיה עמברון ה׳ יחייהו אשר
בארץ

(Dedicated to the Lord, to the Catalan Synagogue, Amen. These Torah finials with small bells all of worked silver were acquired with money remaining in the coffers of the honorable and aged Ezekiel Ambron, endowed by the Lord with life and wealth on earth).

DLB

Unpublished

1. Bartoletti also created a pair of finials and a crown for another Roman synagogue, Il Tempio.
2. G. Mariacher, *Oreficeria sacra nel Friuli occidentale* (Pordenone, 1976), p. 57; idem, "L'oreficeria sacra veneziana dal XVII al XIX secolo," in *Il tesoro di San Marco* (Florence, 1971), p. 222.
3. Mariacher, "L'oreficeria sacra veneziana," p. 57.

197. **Torah Crown and Finials** (figs. 107–108) 205.

Venice, 1750–1751, restored 1789–1790

Silver: embossed, chiseled, engraved, and incised, cast and gilt; red-orange coral

Hallmarks: lion of San Marco; *PZ G* within lily emblem; *CL*

Crown: 8¼ × 10⅝ in. (21 × 27 cm); finials: 17¾ × 3⅛ in. (45 × 8 cm)

Florence, Comunità Israelitica (441, 458)

Information regarding this set is provided by the inscriptions on the crown:

אחים הכנבדים יעקב חיים רימיני ואחיו שנת ב׳רך׳ י׳קוק
ח׳ילו׳ ופעלי י׳ד׳י׳ו׳ ת׳רצ״ה לפ״ג

(Brothers, descendants of Jacob Isaac Rimini and his brothers, the year "Bless, O Lord his substance, And favor his undertakings" [Deut. 33:11] . . . [5512=1751–1752]).

ע״י הצעיר דוד חיים יצ״ו בכמר יהושע רימיני ז״ל בהגיע
אתה ה לחלקו לי״א קדש לאל ביום ושנת ש׳מ׳חת
ה׳תור׳ה׳ לפ״ק

(By the youth David Ḥayyim . . . son of Joshua Rimini of blessed memory / On the day and year *Simḥat ha-Torah* (Rejoicing of the Law) [[5]550=1789]).

Jacob Ḥayyim Rimini, along with three of his four brothers, matriculated in the Arte della Seta as jewelers in 1765.[1] Perhaps because of their profession, Jacob Ḥayyim, Ephraim, Joseph, and Amedeo were in a position to enrich these objects, which in other respects were very common, with coral drops and buds.

These additions rendered the pieces far richer and more original. In fact, both the finials and crown were made at one of Venice's most prolific workshops, which marked its products with *PZ G* within a lily and which was active by the middle of the eighteenth century. The date 1750–1751 in one of the inscriptions therefore indicates that these objects are among the earliest to bear this mark, in both Jewish and Christian circles. The date certainly corresponds to the time of execution, since the band, which contains the inscription, was created deliberately to house it.

The crown and finials were probably initially loaned to the Florentine ghetto's Scuola Italiana and, later in 1789, donated by David Ḥayyim. The latter was the son of Joshua, head of another branch of the Rimini family. Shortly after their donation, repairs were required: the first, in 1839, was concerned with the shafts;[2] the second, a year later, was performed by Luigi Coppini. Besides further reinforcing parts that had already been weakened through wear, Coppini set out to restore the coral that had been lost.[3] Both pieces were recently conserved at the Opifice delle Pietre Dure of Florence, where both shafts and the corals, which in the past had required many repairs, were once again restored.

DLB

Bibliography: A. Milano, *Storia degli ebrei in Italia* (Turin, 1963), figs. 22–23; D. Liscia Bemporad, "Atarot di Firenze," *MCM,* no. 3 (1985): 46.

1. See Bemporad, "Atarot di Firenze," p. 46.
2. Archives of the Jewish Community of Florence (x, 7, ex file 56, 97/13).
3. Ibid.

198. **Torah Finials**

Ferrara, after 1786

Silver, repoussé, chiseled, engraved, cast, and turned

Hallmarks: Bulgari 4, no. 2660; a rose (?)

12⅝ × 3⅛ in. (32 × 8 cm)

Ferrara, Comunità Israelitica

In their structure and decoration these finials are similar to tower-shaped *rimmonim* from Venice, but they represent local imitations, since one of the hallmarks was used in Ferrara after 1786.

DLB

Unpublished

199. **Torah Finials** (fig. 20)

Maker: H.A.

Turin, 1814–1850

Silver, cast, cut out, chased, engraved, parcel-gilt, and appliquéd; glass stones

Hallmarks: Bargoni, Pl. V, 13

(a) 26½ × 4¹⁵⁄16 dm in. (67.3 × 12.6 cm)
(b) 27 × 5 dm in. (68.6 × 12.7 cm)

New York, The Jewish Museum,
Gift of Dr. Harry G. Friedman (F 2826 a, b)

These large finials, undoubtedly used to decorate the *tevah* (*bemah*) or reader's desk, in a synagogue, were created by an as yet unidentified silversmith who used the Hebrew initials ה"א as his mark. The pair bears two other hallmarks, one for Turin silver after 1814, and the other, the assay mark of Luigi Vernoni (active 1814–1850). In 1864–1865 the finials were dedicated by Giuseppe Ottolenghi (1838–1904):

נדבת הקצין ר' / יוסף יהושע / אוטולינגי / שנת / התקעז

(The donation of Yoseph Yehoshua Ottolenghi [in] the year 5577 [1866]).

Giuseppe Ottolenghi was the first Italian Jew to serve on the general staff of his country; he won both the silver medal for valor and the Cross of Savoy. In 1902–1903 he served as Minister of War. Throughout his life General Ottolenghi was a loyal member of the Jewish community of Italy.[1]

VBM

Bibliography: Kayser and Schoenberger, *Jewish Ceremonial Art,* no. 24; NYJM, *Jewish Patrons,* no. 6.

1. *Encyclopaedia Judaica,* vol. 12, col. 1525.

200. **Torah Finials**

Giuseppe Fontana (active after 1787)

Turin, 1816–1817

Silver, cut out, engraved, parcel-gilt, cast, and punched

Hallmarks: Bargoni, Pl. IV, 3; Pl. X

(a) 11¾ × 7⅜ dm in. (29.9 × 18.7 cm)
(b) 12³⁄16 × 7⁹⁄16 dm in. (31 × 19.1 cm)

New York, The Jewish Museum,
Gift of Dr. Harry G. Friedman (F 5638 a, b)

The form of these crown finials combines features of several published examples, all dated to the period of its manufacture. The cutout leaves and swags of the lower section appear on a pair of crowns by Bernardo Forneri, who was active until 1796, while the staves of the upper portion are similar to a slightly later crown by Pacifico Levi, a Jewish silversmith from Turin who became a master in 1818.[1] On these pieces there is a nice play between the gilt emblems of the Temple and the silver form of the crowns. Along the base of each crown is the inscription:

לכבוד התורה אלול שנת נ׳ת׳ן ע׳ז לפק

(In honor of the Torah. Elul in the year 'He gives strength' [(5)577 = 1816–1817]).

VBM

Bibliography: The Jewish Museum, *Loan Exhibit of Antique Ceremonial Objects and Paintings from the Collection of Mr. M. Zagayski,* exh. brochure (New York, 1951), no. 9 (where the Hebrew date has been misread as 1717, as is also the case in the following publications); idem, *The Silver and Judaica Collection of Mr. and Mrs. Michael M. Zagayski,* exh. cat. by G. Schoenberger and T. Freudenheim (New York, 1963), no. 13; *The Michael M. Zagayski Collection of Rare Judaica,* sale cat., Parke-Bernet Galleries, New York, 1964, lot 298.

1. See P. Gaglia, "L'arredo in argento," in *Ebrei a Torino,* exh. cat. (Turin, 1984), pp. 123, 144.

201. **Pair of Crown-Form Torah Finials**

Pacifico Levi (active after 1818)

Turin, 1822

Silver, repoussé and engraved

Hallmark: Bargoni: L62; Pl. V, 13 (assay mark of Luigi Vernoni); indistinct Turin city mark

8⅜ × 7⅛ dm in. (21.3 × 18 cm)

Turin, Comunità Israelitica (inv. no. 30 a–b ex 16 ex 8 CI 172)

Finials in the shape of crowns are unique to Italian Judaica and may derive from the Sephardic custom of placing both a crown and finials on the staves of the Torah (see also cat. nos. 201–202). This pair was donated by a confraternity:

נדבת • חברת • זריזים • י״ע״א • ביום • ר״ח • התק״פב.

(a donation of the Society of the Eager . . . on the New Moon of Nisan in the year 5582 [1822]). The Society of the Eager was unique to Piedmontese Jewry; the earliest such group was formed in Asti in the early seventeenth century.[1]

VBM

Bibliography: P. Gaglia, *Gli argenti,* in *Ebrei a Torino* exh. cat. (Turin, 1984), pp. 142–146.

1. Elliot Horowitz, "A Jewish Youth Confraternity in Seventeenth-Century Italy," *Italia,* 5 (1985), p. 36ff.

202. **Pair of Crown-Form Torah Finials**

Benaja Segre (active after 1827)

Turin, 1827–1828

Silver, repoussé and engraved

Hallmarks: Bargoni S53; Pl. 12, 1 and 4

8¼ × 7⅝ dm in. (21 × 19.5 cm)

Turin, Comunità Israelitica (inv. no. C 33 a–b ex 7)

This pair is very similar to an earlier set by Pacifico Levi (cat. no. 201) and illustrates the traditionalism inherent in Jewish ceremonial art. The symbols of the Temple on each of the crowns complement one another. According to the inscription, the crowns were

נדבת • אברהם • ברוך • חי • יצו • בשנת • התקפח • למ״בי

(the donation of Abramo Vita de Benedetti . . . in the year 5588 [1827–1828]).

VBM

Bibliography: P. Gaglia, *Gli argenti,* in *Ebrei a Torino,* exh. cat. (Turin, 1984), pp. 152–153.

203. **Pair of Crown-Form Torah Finials** (fig. 46)

Moise Segre (active after 1824)

Turin, 1828

Silver, repoussé and engraved

Hallmark: Bargoni S47(?)

9 × 4⅛ dm in. (23 × 10.5 cm)

Turin, Comunità Israelitica (inv. no. C 19 a–b ex 4 ex 12)

In contrast to the crowns of Pacifico Levi (see cat. no. 210), those of Moise Segre are decorated only with vegetal and pearl motifs and lack the usual cartouches with symbols of the Temple. The inscription, crudely engraved in comparison with the finely executed repoussé inscriptions found on other Turin Judaica, records the donation of the crowns in Fossano, south of Turin:

נדבת כמר יונה חי קולמבו יצו בעיר פוסאנו יג לחודש
רחמים שנת התקפה לפ"ק

(the donation of . . . Jonah Vita Colombo . . . here in the city of Fossano, the thirteenth of the month of compassion [Elul] the year 5588 [1828]). Fossano was one of three Italian cities, along with Asti and Moncalvo, that preserved a special liturgy known as the Afam rite, brought to Italy after the expulsion of the Jews from France in the fourteenth century.

VBM

Bibliography: P. Gaglia, *Gli argenti,* in *Ebrei a Torino,* exh. cat. (Turin, 1984), pp. 148–149.

204. **Torah Finials**

Venice, first half of the nineteenth century

Silver, repoussé, chiseled, cast, chased, and parcel-gilt

Hallmarks: comet; globe with stars; LF (beneath the base)

H: 17½ in. (44.5 cm)

Venice, Comunità Israelitica (170, 170 *bis*)

The form of this pair of Torah finials is unusual. The upper part consists of three large floral clusters joined together, from the center of which a small bouquet emerges, completely cast in silver and partly gilt. Unfortunately the small bells that hung from each of the three buds are missing; they would have served to lighten the overall effect. Flowers were traditionally used as an iconographic motif for Torah finials but were either relegated to the niches of the towers or placed as finials (see cat. nos. 194, 197). In the early nineteenth century, as new forms for ceremonial objects were sought, other cities, such as Parma, developed this form of finials.

The marks are from the Venice mint and date the piece after 1811, an attribution confirmed by decorative motifs such as the vertically linked egg shapes with a rosette at the center on the staff, which derive from French neoclassical models.

DLB

Bibliography: International Fund for Monuments, New York, *Jewish Art Treasures in Venice* (Venice, [1973 ?]), p. 38.

Torah Crowns

206. **Torah Crown**

Giovanni Maria Ronchi (active 1764–1801)

Ferrara, 1764–1777

Hallmarks: Bulgari, part 4, 2658, 2717

Silver, repoussé, engraved, cast, punched, and parcel-gilt

$7\frac{1}{8} \times 7\frac{5}{8}$ dm in. (18.3 × 19.5 cm)

New York, The Jewish Museum, Gift of Dr. Harry G. Friedman (F 3688)

This crown is based on a Venetian type of the seventeenth century.[1] According to the inscription, it was dedicated by

עזיראל חי / ב"כ"ר / ידידיד [כך!] הלוי / יליד צנטו

(Azriel Ḥai, son of Yedidi[ah] Ḥai Halevi, a native of Cento).

VBM

Bibliography: S. Kayser and Schoenberger, *Jewish Ceremonial Art,* no. 36 (where the piece is erroneously dated to the seventeenth century); NYJM, *Jewish Patrons,* no. 8.

1. For example, see *Ebrei a Torino,* exh. cat. (Turin, 1984), p. 121.

207. **Torah Crown** (fig. 106)

Venice, 1771–1772

Silver, embossed, chiseled, engraved, grained, and openwork, cast and gilt

Hallmark: *GM*

$8\frac{13}{16} \times 9\frac{3}{8}$ dm in. (22.5 × 24 cm)

Livorno, Comunità Israelitica (no. 2)

Although it is not possible to identify the silversmith who impressed his initials on the base of this crown, it is possible to trace it to the Veneto, since it is very similar to many other crowns that have been attributed to that city. The shape, and above all the decoration formed by wide and exaggerated vegetal elements, by convex cartouches on the base and concave ones on the upper part, and by flowers along the upper band, were utilized with few variations as early as the first quarter of the eighteenth century. The considerable stiffness of certain elements, the tendency to create a slimmer form by diminishing the diameter in proportion to height, and the mediocre execution of the groups of musical instruments (of which two are lost) inserted in the niches show that the date of the donation is very close to that of production. The donor, whose surname is typically Livornese-Jewish, probably acquired the object in Venice to donate it to his city's synagogue. He did not, however, omit marking its weight, seventy-one ounces, to underscore the extent of his expenditure.

The inscription reads:

נדבה של יצחק ח' לופיס פינירו קדש ל"ה שנת התק"לא

(The donation of Isaac Vita Lopes Piniero. Dedicated to the Lord. The year 5531 [1770–1771]).

DLB

Unpublished

208. **Torah Crown and Finials**

Padua, eighteenth century

Silver, repoussé, engraved, and gilt; colored stones

Hallmarks: *ZP*; *CI*

Crown: 8½ × 9¼ dm in. (21.7 × 23.5 cm);
Finials: 19 × 7½ dm in. (48.3 × 19 cm)

New York, Collection of Peter Ehrenthal (nos. 7422, 7423)

This set of crown and finials is lavishly decorated with scrolling floral motifs, palmettes, cartouches, and Temple implements. The high relief of the repoussé work on the crown creates a monumental, sculptural quality. A similar Paduan crown is in the collection of the Israel Museum, Jerusalem (146/63), as are similar examples of Italian two-storied domed finials surmounted by floral motifs (147/79).[1]

Dedicatory inscriptions state that the crown and finials were donated by a confraternity:

חברת נוח שלום שנת התרלא לפג

(The confraternity of Peaceful Rest the year 5631 [1870–1871]).

GMG

Unpublished

1. Israel Museum, *The Stieglitz Collection: Masterpieces of Jewish Art,* by C. Benjamin (Jerusalem, 1987), nos. 8, 8.1.

209. **Torah Crown**

Venice, mid eighteenth century

Silver, repoussé, chiseled, engraved, openwork

Hallmarks: lion of San Marco; *ZP* with the insignia of a swan

8¹⁄₁₆ × 8⅝ in. (20.5 × 22 cm)

Venice, Comunità Israelitica (no. 34)

The decorative motifs of this crown, formed of shells in volutes and symmetrically arranged garlands of fruits and flowers, appear on many objects produced during the eighteenth century. The workshop that made the crown continued to use these same motifs, with few variations, throughout the century.[1] Comparisons with other Torah crowns found in practically all Italian-Jewish communities[2] and with other objects[3] confirm a dating around midcentury, since there is still no trace of that hardening of decoration and structure that unequivocally illustrates the influence of neoclassical taste.

DLB

Unpublished

1. G. Mariacher, *Arte a Venezia dal medioevo al settecento* (Venice, 1971), p. 209.
2. *Tesori d'arte delle comunità religiose de Trieste* (Udine, 1978), p. 70; *Cultura ebraica in Emilia Romagna* (Rimini, 1987), pp. 153, 158.
3. *Tesori d'arte,* p. 75.

210. **Torah Crown**

Pacifico Levi (active after 1818)

Turin, after 1818

Silver, repoussé and engraved

Hallmarks: Bargoni: L62; Pl. XII, 4; and an illegible mark

16⅛ × 9⅝ dm in. (24.5 × 41 cm)

Turin, Comunità Israelitica (inv. no. C 42 ex 19)

According to the inscription, this crown was

נדבת כמר אברקם יעקב לוי יצו

(donated by . . . Abraham Jacob Levi). It is similar to another in the collection of the Jewish museum in Casale Monferrato (inv. no. 116). On Pacifico Levi, see cat. no. 218.

VBM

Bibliography: P. Gaglia, *Gli argenti,* in *Ebrei a Torino* exh. cat. (Turin, 1984), pp. 142–146.

211. **Torah Crown**

Gaetano Coppini

Florence, 1835–1836

Silver, embossed, chiseled, and engraved

Hallmarks: *marzocco* on the letter *F*; *Coppini* within the lozenge

7¾ × 9⁹⁄₁₆ in. (19.8 × 23 cm)

Florence, Comunità Israelitica (415)

Hebrew phrases from Psalms fill the cartouches: "The decrees of the Lord are enduring (Ps. 19:8); The fear of the Lord is pure (Ps. 19:10); The teaching of the Lord is perfect (Ps. 19:8); The instruction of the Lord is lucid (Ps. 19:9)." The unusual history of this crown is indicated by the inscription in the lower border:

ישלם ה׳ פעלם
לזכרון שכמ״ר אפרים פנצי יצ״ו נדב לבו ליתן שני
רמונים של כסף לחברת מתיר אסורים קדש ל״ה וכאשר
נבלו ונשברו בני החברה הוסיפו על העיקר ועשו העטרה
הזאת ושני רימונים הכל מחדש בשנת ה״ת״קצו לפ״ק

(The Lord will requite them according to their acts. In memory of Ephraim Finzi. He wished to donate two silver finials to the Confraternity *Matir Asurim* [Those Who Free Captives], dedicated to God, and when they were damaged and broken, the members of the Confraternity added to the principal and made this crown and two finials. The whole was renewed in the year 5596 [1835–1836]).

In addition to this crown, Ephraim Finzi donated a pair of *rimmonim,* which had been ordered to replace a pair that had been dropped and severely damaged. The *Matir Asurim* Confraternity, the recipient of the gift, was devoted to the task of ransoming Jews imprisoned for debt in the grand-ducal prison beginning in the early eighteenth century. The confraternity's oratory was then located in a room adjacent to the Scuola Italiana. Gaetano Coppini, one of the most renowned silversmiths in Florence during the first half of the century, was employed to produce these objects. Although still anchored in the eclecticism that was typical of the Florentine production of this period, his style retains a high level of craftsmanship. Indeed Jewish art, which differed substantially in its forms and decoration from contemporaneous Christian and profane works, compelled him to invent new solutions. The musical instruments inserted on the convex medallions among the vegetal motifs stand out like bright gems, displaying inventiveness in comparison with the other objects produced at his workshop. The presence of the hallmark of the *marzocco* on the letter F, which began to be used in Florence in 1832, confirms that the crown was made close to the date provided by the inscription.

DLB

Unpublished

Torah Shields

212. **Torah Shield with Musical Insignia** (fig. 43)

Padua, 1740–1741

Silver: repoussé, chiseled, engraved, grained ground

6¾ × 10½ in. (17.2 × 26.8 cm) (shield); 3¹⁵⁄₁₆ × 4³⁄₁₆ in. (10 × 10.6 cm) (small shield)

Padua, Comunità Israelitica

This piece is one of the earliest Torah shields still preserved in its original location. Its rectangular form is typical of Padua and is a cross between the "crown" type used in Venice and the "heraldic shield" form, typical of communities that experienced a greater Ashkenazic influence. The decorative repertory—acanthus leaves (around which are wound long vine shoots), flowers (particularly tulips), and splayed scallop shells—and the lower cartouche, with its large, rich volutes—are characteristic of Paduan silver. The addition of groups of musical instruments, found very frequently on synagogal furnishings, must have been made at the request of those who commissioned the piece:

נדבה לכבוד התורה כמר משה ספורוני יצו ואשתו
ברוניטה מ״נת / שנת תק״א לפק

(Donated in honor of the Torah [by] Moses Soforni and his wife Barontina . . . the year [5]501 [1740–1741]).

DLB

Unpublished

213. **Torah Shield**

Urbino(?), 1791–1792

Silver, repoussé and engraved

Hallmark: *VR*

8½ × 4¾ in. (21.6 × 12.0 cm)

New York, The Moldovan Family Collection

The use of crown-shaped shields, such as this one, is unique to Italian Judaica.[1] This example is decorated with acanthus and shell forms and bears an inscription:

כתר תורה שנ׳ התקכב
מתנה נתונה מהגבי׳ הנע׳ כ״הר שמשון בכמ״ר אברהם אלקוסטנטיני מאנקונא יעא לאורבינו יעא לכבוד ה׳ ולתורתו׳

(Crown of the Torah [Ethics of the Fathers 4:17] [the] y[ear] 5522 [1791–1792] a gift given by the treas[urer] . . . Samson, s[on of] . . . Abraham Alcostantini from Ancona . . . to Urbino . . . In honor of God and his Torah.)

GMG

Unpublished

1. For other examples of this type, see Palazzo dei Diamanti, Palazzo Paradiso, *Arte e cultura ebraiche in Emilia-Romagna* (Ferrara, 1988), nos. 44–49.

214. **Torah Shield** (fig. 99)

Venice, second half of the eighteenth century (amulet), second quarter of the nineteenth century (shield)

Silver: repoussé, chiseled, engraved; granite

Hallmarks: comet and LF in an oval field (above the right cornucopia)

6¼ × 4⁵⁄₁₆ in. (16 × 11 cm) (amulet); 13⅜ × 10 in. (34 × 25.5 cm) (shield); H (overall): 26⅜ in. (67 cm)

Venice, Comunità Israelitica (no. 162)

This shield is the result of a curious fusion: an amulet has been inserted at the center of a shield, framed by cornucopias at the bottom and at the side and at top by vines. The amulet has been divided in half along the soldering that joins the two sides; it belongs to a rather rich group of almost identical objects, produced mainly in Venice during the second half of the eighteenth century (see cat. no. 225). Some of them were used in Italian synagogues as Torah shields (in Genoa and in Bologna, for example). In this case, however, the object was substantially reworked, for the amulet has been camouflaged within a shield, as were many others produced in the city, thus skillfully concealing its earlier function. Although the silversmith's hallmark is not identifiable at present, the "comet" was used after 1811, a date supported by the shape of the object and by the eclectic references to earlier historical periods. According to the inscription,

מאיר בר מרדכי מורפורגו שבעות

the shield was the "gift of Meir, son of Mordecai Morpurgo, on the Shavuot festival."

DLB

Bibliography: International Fund for Monuments, New York, *Jewish Art Treasures in Venice* (Venice, [1973 ?]), pp. 38–39.

215. **Torah Shield**

Ferrara, 1800

Silver, embossed, chiseled, and engraved

6⁷⁄₁₆ × 7¼ in. (16.3 × 18.5 cm) (without chain)

Ferrara, Comunità Israelitica

According to the inscription, this shield was dedicated in 1799–1800:

נדבת הילד אליהו ה״י בר כמר משה מרדכי סינגאלא יצ׳ו בשנת קס״ת / הסופר

(The donation of the youth Eliyahu . . . the son of Moses Mordecai Senigallia . . . in the year [5]560 [1799–1800], the scribe).

Although the inscribed date corresponds to the neoclassical period, this piece is executed in rococo style. In fact, the asymmetrical shield is flanked by splayed half shells and conjoined volutes typical of a style favored thirty years earlier. It is not unusual for Italian ecclesiastical silver to retain earlier shapes and decorative motifs, however, particularly in pieces of inferior quality, and one may assume that this Torah shield was fashioned after an earlier model. It is possible that the use of bells on shields, unknown in most other Italian communities yet common in Ferrara, reflects an Ashkenazic influence.

DLB

Unpublished

216. **Torah Shield**

Ferrara, 1808–1809

Silver, embossed, chiseled, engraved, and incised

8¼ × 8⅝ in. (21 × 22 cm)

Ferrara, Comunità Israelitica

This Torah shield, like most produced in Ferrara, was once provided with bells hanging from short chains. Without these decorative and functional elements, the shield has been deprived of much of its aesthetic balance, already compromised by the disproportionately large smooth central area relative to the decorated edge. Still marked by an ornamental repertory typical of the preceding century, the decoration is nonetheless stiffly executed, suggesting that the date of the shield's production was concurrent with that of its donation, as indicated by the inscription:

כתר תורה / חדש מהכבודה מרת דיאמנטא אלמנת / המנוח כ' ידידיה ח' הלוי ע' ס'ת' / שקנתה בכסף מלא על מצות השי' / בתודה בשנת התקסט ליצירה קדש ולמ'ב'י לה'

(Crown of Torah / Renewed by . . . Signora Diamanta the widow of / the deceased . . . Jedidiah Ḥai ha-Levi on the T[orah] S[croll] / that she bought "at the full price" [Gen. 23:9] fulfilling the commandment of G[od] M[ay He] b[e blessed] / in t[hanks] t[o] G[od] in the year 5569 (1808–1809) of the creation / Holy: A[nd] f[or the] q[uorum of the] c[hildren of] I[srael]: F[or] G[od]).

Torah shields of this type continued to be produced at least until the middle of the nineteenth century, as evidenced by other examples preserved in Ferrara.

DLB

Unpublished

217. **Torah Shield**

Pacifico Levi (active after 1818)

Turin, after 1818

Silver, repoussé and engraved

Hallmarks: Bargoni L62; Pl. III, 5 (assay mark of Giuseppe Vernoni, active 1778–1824); Pl. X, 1 (Turin city mark after 1814)

14⅛ × 10⅝ in. (36 × 27 cm)

Ramat Aviv, Gross Family Collection

This shield is a more elaborate version of one in the collection of the Comunità Israelitica of Turin (cat. no. 218) and should probably be dated somewhat later on stylistic grounds. It includes the same overlaying of cartouches whose shapes play against one another and the same richness of surface textures. The outline of this shield is, however, more complex, and the crown form at top is more developed. Like the shield in Turin, this one hung from the staves by means of a suspension device shaped like eyeglasses.

VBM

Unpublished

218. **Torah Shield**

Pacifico Levi (active after 1818)

Turin, 1832 (inscription date)

Silver, repoussé and engraved

Shield: 11$\frac{1}{16}$ × 7½ in. (28 × 19 cm); H: (with chain): 21⅝ in. (55 cm)

Turin, Comunità Israelitica (inv. no. C 57 T0)

Pacifico Levi was one of twelve Jewish silversmiths nominated for membership in the Turin guild, the Università degli Orefici ed Argentieri, in the years 1817–1818. He registered as his mark a hand holding a pouring pitcher, symbolic of his Levite status within the Jewish community. The records for the commission of this shield are still extant in the Turin city archives. According to the inscription on the shield, it was:

נדבת חברת / ילידי אל / והדור בית / הכנסת / התקצ'ב

(donated by the Society of Sons of the Lord and Those who Beautify the Synagogue 5592 [1832]). The unusual name of the society suggests that it encompassed two previously independent groups.[1]

VBM

Bibliography: P. Gaglia, *L'arredo in argento,* in *Ebrei a Torino,* exh. cat. (Turin, 1984), pp. 142–143, no. 9.

1. I would like to thank Dr. Elliott Horowitz for this suggestion.

219. **Torah Shield**

Venice (?), second quarter of the nineteenth century

Silver, repoussé, chiseled, and engraved; the musical instruments are gilt and appliquéd

Hallmarks: *VG* within a heart-shaped field

8½ × 13⅝ in. (21.5 × 34.7 cm)

Venice, Comunità Israelitica (no. 192)

Lacking the city mark and an identifiable silversmith's mark, this Torah shield cannot be securely attributed to Venice. The form is unusual, a crown seen in perspective from below; it is also used on a Florentine shield. In his *Riti* (cat. no. 79), the Venetian rabbi Leone Modena calls a Torah shield a *hatarah,* the term generally used to refer to a crown; he may have had an object like this one in mind. The wealth of decorative motifs on it reflects the rococo exuberance that characterized Venetian silver until the end of the eighteenth century, although the presence of rosettes, stylized vine shoots, and rigid scalloping reflects a neoclassical taste, filtered through nineteenth-century historicism.

נדבת כ״ר שמשון מנחם מורפורגו מעיר אנקונה יצ״ו

According to the inscription, it was donated by Samson Menaḥem Morpurgo of Ancona.

DLB

Unpublished

Torah Pointers

220. **Torah Pointer**

Italy, 1783–1784

Silver, cast, chased, and engraved

10 × ¾ in. (25.5 × 0.8 cm)

New York, The Moldovan Family Collection

This delicately modeled pointer features bud-form knops, a rope-twist handle, and an acanthus leaf–shaped cuff. On the rectangular shaft of the pointer is an inscription stating that it was dedicated in honor of the recovery of a child from illness.

להודות ל״ה על רפואת הבן יקיר ילד שעשועים ה״ה הנער המכובד יהושע הבבא אוקיליו שנת התקמד לפק או סיליו

(To thank God for the healing of the dear son, a cherished child . . . the honored youth Joshua . . . Anquilio the year 5544 [1783–1784] . . .)

GMG

Unpublished

Etrog Containers

221. ***Etrog* Container**

Padua, 1754–1755

Silver, repoussé, chiseled, and engraved

Hallmarks: A. S.; illegible mark

8½ × 13¾ × 8⅞ in. (21.5 × 35 × 22.5 cm)

Padua, Comunità Israelitica

The inscription reads:

קערת בה״כ איטליאני / אשר הבחור יהודה / בכמ״ר יעקב משולם / ז״ל הניח בעדה נ׳ דוקאטין / להזכיר נשמתו בכל / שבת שנת התקיה לפ״ג

(The container of the I[talian] S[ynagogue] that the youth Judah, son of Jacob Meshullam, of blessed memory, donated for fifty ducats in order to remember his soul on every Sabbath, the year 5515 [1754–1755]).

This *etrog* container represents the height of the rococo style in its shape and in the exuberance and expansiveness of its decoration, which relates to Venetian types. The date of donation indicated by the inscription therefore corresponds to that of the object's execution. Since one of the hallmarks is illegible (perhaps a stylized angel), an exact date is impossible to determine. It is missing its lid, which would have had fruit and vegetal motifs like those visible on the body. For an etrog container, the shape is extremely unusual and indeed without parallel.

DLB

Unpublished

222. ***Etrog* Container**

Venice, late eighteenth century (lid), 1853 (container)

Silver, gilt, repoussé, chiseled, and engraved; granite; applied decorative motifs

Hallmarks: comet and globe with stars (in the vessel)

6¾ × 8⅜ × 5⅛ in. (17.2 × 21.2 × 13 cm)

Venice, Comunità Israelitica (no. 163),
Gift of Shlomo Aboaf de Flandes on the first day of Passover, in the year 5613 (no. 163)

שלמה בכר יואל אבוהף די פלאנדיס: יום א׳ של פסח התר״יא 5613

Both hallmarks on the vessel point to its manufacture in Venice after 1811 at a factory that maintained a monopoly over the production of Jewish ceremonial objects in Italy as late as the mid-nineteenth century.

This object, along with its identical companion piece, is extremely original compared with others meant for similar use. The oblong form and the downturned edges of the container were probably modeled after older objects, as the covers are made out of a much thinner and more finely repoussé silver with fruit and leaf motifs and are cut along the edges, interrupting the decorations. The donor, a descendent of one of the most celebrated families in Venice, may have adapted an older object in his possession and offered it for public religious use. The container itself seems heavier, and its structure is closely tied to nineteenth-century stylistic trends (for example, the foot that is raised on a rather high cornice and the lively corner treatment of the surfaces). The floret and vine decoration hints at the neo-Renaissance revivals typical of the second half of the century.

DLB

Bibliography: International Fund for monuments, New York, *Jewish Art Treasures in Venice* (Venice, [1973 ?]), pp. 37, 80–81, no. N 32.

Amulets

223. **Amulet** (fig. 114)

Master: VF(?)

Rome, c. 1650–1700

Silver, cast, openwork, and engraved

4¾ × 2⅜ in. (12.1 × 6 cm)

New York, The Jewish Museum, Gift of Abraham Bornstein through Dr. Harry G. Friedman (JM 16–51)

This amulet bears a low-relief scene of the Binding of Isaac flanked by columns of pinecones. Two cutout lions flanking an open book are at top, surmounted by ornamental scrollwork that forms a hanging loop. Below the scene is a triangle with engraved scrolls with a cutout ogee at its apex. The incorporation of the Binding of Isaac iconography indicates the amulet's use as protection for an infant during circumcision. A similar example is in the collection of the Musée de Cluny, Paris (Cl. 13084).

GMG

Bibliography: S. Kayser and Schoenberger, *Jewish Ceremonial Art* (Philadelphia, 1959), no. 159; The Jewish Museum, *Celebrating Rites of Passage: Judaic Treasures from The Jewish Museum* (New York, 1983), no. 16.

224. **Amulet and Amulet Case**

Venice?, eighteenth century

Ink on Parchment; Silver: filigree

4⅝ × 3½ × ⅝ in. (11.8 × 8.9 × 1.6 cm)

New York, The Jewish Museum,
Gift of Dr. and Mrs. Joseph Epstein, JM 34–78

The rectilinear architectural form of this amulet case is constructed of fancifully scrolling filigree. A central rectangular area contains the folded parchment amulet, the first two paragraphs of the *Shema* (Deut. 6:4–9 and Deut. 11:13–21). This area is flanked by columns of stacked balls and petaled flowers. The case is topped by two small gothic spires flanking filigree scrolls suggesting a cupola. Comparable amulet cases are in the collection of The Jewish Museum, New York (F2164, F2165), the Wolfson Museum, Hechal Shlomo, Jerusalem[1] and the Furman Collection, Santiago.[2]

GMG

Bibliography: New York, The Jewish Museum, *The Jewish Patrons of Venice,* by S. J. Makover, exhibition brochure, 1985, no. 46.

1. See Yehuda L. Bialer, *Jewish Life in Art and Tradition* (New York, 1976), p. 60.
2. See New York, The Jewish Museum, *Personal Vision: The Jacobo and Asea Furman Collection of Jewish Ceremonial Art* by Susan L. Braunstein, exhibition catalogue, 1985, no. 33.

225. **Amulet Case** (fig. 114)

Italy, eighteenth-nineteenth century

Silver, cast, chased, and parcel-gilt

5¼ × 3¾ × 1½ in. (13.4 × 9.8 × 3.8 cm)

New York, The Jewish Museum (F 2097)

This bulbous amulet case is a common Italian type.[1] It is composed of scrolling tendrils and acanthus leaves, with a pentafoil loop at top and a grape cluster at bottom. Added gilt symbols decorate the case: Tablets of the Law (engraved with the abbreviated text of the Decalogue), the high priest's miter, the menorah and a censer. Similar stock gilt Temple implements can be found on other Italian Judaica, such as Torah crowns (see cat. no. 205). Heart-shaped cartouches inscribed with the divine name in relief are placed at center. At bottom are cartouches surmounted by eagles with outstretched wings. One such element features a screw and nut so that it could be removed in order to insert a parchment amulet scroll into the case.

GMG

Bibliography: S. Kayser and Schoenberger, *Jewish Ceremonial Art,* no. 160; Maurice Spertus Museum of Judaica, *Magic and Superstition in the Jewish Tradition* (Chicago, 1975), no. 179.

1. Comparable examples include New York, The Jewish Museum (1983–230); Jerusalem, Israel Museum (103/427, 103/962); Paris, Musée de Cluny (Cl. 13083). See also R. D. Barnett, *Catalogue of the Permanent and Loan Collections of the Jewish Museum, London* (London, 1974), nos. 593–595, 603–605.

226. **Amulet** (fig. 114)

Filipo Grimaldi(?) (c. 1782–1848)

Rome, first half of the nineteenth century

Silver, cast and engraved

4¼ × 1¹³⁄₁₆ × ⅛ in. (10.7 × 4.4 × 0.4 cm)

New York, The Jewish Museum (S 654a)

This amulet consists of an inscribed rectangular shield framed by a columned archway with scrollwork above and below. An oval cartouche above the arch is inscribed with a divine name, and the central rectangular shield contains the Hebrew text of the priestly blessing (Num. 6:24–26) and names of angels. A seven-branched menorah and a divine name are engraved on the back of the amulet.

Many examples of this Roman amulet type are known. An almost identical marked example by Filippo Grimaldi, cast from a different mold than this one, is in the collection of the Jewish Museum, New York (S 654b), as is a similar brass amulet (S 734). A gilt example is in the Furman collection, Santiago (JF 113),[1] and an early eighteenth-century silver amulet is in the collection of the Israel Museum, Jerusalem (103/964).[2]

GMG

Unpublished

1. See Jewish Museum, *Personal Vision: The Jacobo and Asea Furman Collection of Jewish Ceremonial Art* exh. cat., by S. L. Braunstein (New York, 1985), no. 32.
2. See Israel Museum, *The Stieglitz Collection: Masterpieces of Jewish Art,* by C. Benjamin (Jerusalem, 1987), no. 271.

227. **Amulet and Amulet Case** (fig. 114)

Italy, nineteenth century

Ink on parchment; silver, cast and engraved

3⅜ × 2¹⁄₁₆ × ⅛ in. (8.6 × 5.2 × 0.4 cm)

New York, The Jewish Museum, Gift of Dr. Harry G. Friedman (F 2083)

The bottom of this case pulls out in order to insert the amuletic manuscript, a folded text of selections from Ps. 72. The case itself is based on an architectural form, a common feature of some Italian amulets (see cat. nos. 223, 224). A windowed gable surmounted by a hanging loop is placed atop a rectangular frame of engraved tendrils, which is flanked by cast vegetal scrolls. The centers of both sides of the case are engraved with circular cartouches surrounded by spirals and fans. On one side of this case the cartouche contains a six-pointed star with a divine name in its center and a hexagram, six letters arranged one in each point of the star in order to create a magical inscription. A coat of arms of a rampant lion flanking a tower beneath a star, possibly the shield of the Abrabanel family, is in the cartouche on the opposite side of the case.

GMG

Unpublished

228. **Amulet**

Italy, nineteenth to twentieth century

Red gold, cast and engraved

1¼ × ⅞ in. (3.2 × 2.2 cm)

Collection of the descendants of Elia Treves

Small circular amulets of this type were probably worn as pendants (see also cat. no. 229). On the front of this amulet is a divine name, and on the back an engraved Italian inscription:

Il Signore / ti dia / lunga vita
(The Lord give you a long life).

GMG

Unpublished

229. **Amulet**

Italy, 1917

Gold, cast and engraved

1¹⁄₁₆ × ¾ in. (2.7 × 1.9 cm)

Collection of the descendants of Elia Treves

This disk-shaped amulet is engraved with a divine name on its front and with a blessing for a long life on its back. It was presented as a gift to a newborn child in 1917:

Gino / Il Signore / Ti / Dia Lunga Vita / 6 – 4 – 1917

(Gino, The Lord give you a long life 4 – 6 – 1917).

GMG

Unpublished

Miscellaneous Ceremonial Silver

230. **Pair of Sconces in the Form of Cornucopias** (fig. 102)

Venice, second half of the eighteenth century

Silver plate, repoussé, chiseled, engraved; wood core

Hallmarks: lion of San Marco on the initials *NP*; another illegible hallmark *DO*

31½ × 3⅞ in. (80 × 10 cm); H: (crown): 7⅞ in. (20 cm)

Venice, Comunità Israelitica (nos. 202, 202 *bis*)

The surface of this pair of sconces shows signs of repeated reworkings, necessitated by the pressure of the heavy wood core against the thin, fragile plates that cover the lamps. The inscriptions, separated from each other by a few years, testify to the restorations:

השני המאורות האלו ניתנו כתורת פיקדון בבית הכנסת קהל קדוש

ליואנטיני יצ״ו פה ויניציאה יע״א מאת האשה יראת ה׳ היא תתהלל הבנות מרת בילה מב״ת אלמנת המנוח כה׳ר יצחק מימון ויואנטי ז״ל הובאו של הקדש פנימה ביום הכפורים שנת ל׳ר׳י׳ח נ׳יחח אשה ל״ה לפרט קטן

"These two lamps were given as a loan to the Levantine Synagogue here in Venice by . . . Bilah . . . the widow of Rabbi Isaac Maimun Vivante . . . "brought into the sanctuary within" (Lev. 10:18) on Yom Kippur in the year "a pleasing odor, an offering by fire for the Lord" (Ex. 29:18) (5566 = 1805)

In Italian:

"Gift of Giacomo and Lazzaro Tedesco, sons of the late Sabato of Corfu, August 1890"

"Gift of Massimo Tedesco, son of the late Lazzaro, 1912"

The lion of San Marco on the letters *NP,* the initials of the assayer, were used after the mid eighteenth century.[1] Stylistic evidence also points to that date: the hatched background, the rigid acanthus leaves that frame the upper cornice, and the oval medallions. Unfortunately it is impossible to read the second mark made by the silversmith. The scrolls with the oldest inscription were clearly attached some years after the lamps were made. Indeed, in 1805, which corresponds to the year 5566 engraved on them, the stamp of the lion of San Marco had already been abolished for eight years. The surname of one of the donors, Vivante, suggests that the two lamps were made for this family's study hall. The second inscription includes the date 1890, perhaps the year when the sconces passed to the Levantine synagogue, where they are now. Clearly the third date, 1912, pertains to the execution of the two bobeches in the form of crowns. While these attempt to imitate the leaves that embellish the upper part of the cornucopia, their workmanship and the quality of the metal are typical of the early twentieth century.

DLB

Bibliography: International Fund for Monuments, New York, *Jewish Art Treasures in Venice* (Venice, [1973 ?]), p. 39.

1. G. Mariacher, *Oreficeria sacra nel Friuli occidentale* (Pordenone, 1976), p. 9.

231. **Spice Container**

Venice, seventeenth to eighteenth century

Silver, filigree, parcel-gilt; cloisonné enamels

16½ × 4⅜ dm in. (41.9 × 11.1 cm)

New York, The Jewish Museum, Gift of Dr. Harry G. Friedman (F 3140)

The earliest extant spice containers are of tower shape, no doubt inspired by their functional relationship to reliquaries, which were often based on architectural models.[1] The form of the tower used for a particular spice container depended on local artistic and architectural traditions. This example features niches filled with urns of flowers, a common motif in Italian baroque art. The technique used, filigree, was a specialty of Venetian goldsmiths, its renown indicated by the medieval name *opus venetum.* In Venice and surrounding areas during the Middle Ages, filigree was often used to fashion reliquaries and monstrances of architectural form. These earlier examples probably inspired later works such as this spice container, filigree Torah finials, and amulets still found in Italian collections.[2]

VBM

Bibliography: Jewish Museum, *The Jewish Patrons of Venice,* exh. brochure, by S. J. Makover, (New York, 1985), no. 56; Kleeblatt and Mann, *Treasures,* pp. 74–75.

1. For a full discussion of this point, see V. B. Mann, "The Golden Age of Jewish Ceremonial Art in Frankfurt: Metalwork of the Eighteenth Century," in *The Leo Baeck Institute Yearbook,* vol. 31 (1986), pp. 390–391.
2. G. R. Sullam, *Il ghetto di Venezia: Le sinagoghe e il museo* (Rome, 1985), p. 89.

232. **Laver and Basin from the Catalan Synagogue** (figs. 100–101)

German-Flemish manufacture, second half of the seventeenth century

Silver, repoussé, carved, engraved; cast and chased; gilt; granite

Laver: 13⅜ × 5 in. (34 × 12.8 cm); Basin: 20½ × 5¾ in. (52 × 14.5 cm)

Rome, Comunità Israelitica (125 *bis*/67, 125/67)

On the back of the laver is the following inscription:

קודש לכנסת האטאלאני ואראגונניסי יעא נדבת האחים
ה׳ה ר׳ שלמה ור׳ מרדכי ור׳ אברהם מבית אשכנזי זל
בשנת התק ליצירה

(Dedicated to the Lord, to the Catalan and Aragonese Synagogue, offered by the brothers Solomon, Mordecai, and Abraham from the Ashkenazi [Tedeschi] family, in the year 5500 [1739–1740] of the creation).

Clearly the year of the donation, 1739–1740, doesn't correspond to the date of execution. The composition and decoration of both the lion-shaped laver and the basin seem far from the rococo style that dominated eighteenth-century silversmiths' work. The basin widens into a broadly curved rim, while the symmetrical composition of the decoration sets up a contrast between the shininess of the shells, borders, and pod forms and the background, made opaque by a dense series of parallel marks. These forms are closely tied to the whimsical and pictorial taste of the baroque period. The persistence of traces of the "auricular" style, particularly in the soft bulging of the border motifs, suggests that the goldsmith was from a non-Italian background. A German attribution is also suggested by the form of the laver, a rampant lion, which was unknown in Italy, and by the surname of the donors, who had perhaps recently arrived in Rome. In all probability these objects were originally intended for domestic use and were later donated to the Catalan Synagogue. It is less likely that the Tedeschi family, whose crest is affixed to both the shield held by the lion and to the medallion at the bottom of the basin, had commissioned the work from one of the numerous German artists working in Rome beginning in the second half of the seventeenth century.

DLB

Bibliography: F. Pitigliani, *Permanent Exhibition of the Jewish Community of Rome* (Rome, [1962]), pp. 19–20, figs. 5, 6; *Tesori d'arte sacra* (Rome, 1975), p. 180; A. Milano, *Il ghetto di Roma* (Rome, 1964), p. 224, fig. 47; S. Servi, *The Jewish Museum of Rome* (Rome, 1985), p. 5.

233. **Eternal Light**

Rome, 1777–1778

Pietro Zappati (active 1759–1781)

Silver: repoussé, carved, and engraved; granite

Hallmarks: state stamp; insignia of San Bernardino (stamped on the support); Bulgari vol. 2, p. 555, no. 1091

15⅛ × 11 in. (38.5 × 28 cm); 37¾ in. (96 cm) (with the chains)

Rome, Comunità Israelitica (inv. no. 232/457)

The record of the donation is engraved on the ornamental cartouches:

קדש אל לכנ׳ יראי ה״ יעא נ״ד כמר יהושע יצ׳ו ב׳
אליהו סרמוניטא ז״ל לז״כ אביו ואמו ואשתו ולז׳כ אליהו
ושמחה

בניו ולז״כ אליהו רינאני ואשתו ובניו ז״ל שהדלק תמיד
זו בעוד בחיים ייתר ואף כי אחרי מותו לכך נדב

ונתן די ספוק לצאת ממנו כדי להעלות נר תמיד לזכרם
בש ואש״ר הוא עשה ה׳ מצליח לפ״ק

([1] Dedicated to the Lord. To the community of those in awe of the Lord. Gi[ft of] Joshua . . . son of Eliahu Sermonneta of blessed memory, in m[emory] of his father and of his mother, and of his wife, and in memory of Eliahu and Simḥah

[2] his sons, and in mem[ory] of Eliahu Rignani and of his wife and his sons of blessed memory, who gave this Eternal [Light] when he was still alive and even after his death

[3] he donated and gave to acquire what was necessary to light the lamp eternally in their memory in the y[ear] "and whatever he did the Lord made successful" [Gen. 39:23] [5538 = 1777–1778]).

Pietro Zappati, who made pyriform lamps of this type, was the descendant of a famous family of Roman silversmiths. He took over the workshop mark with the insignia of San Bernardino, which appears on this work.[1] The lamp was made during his late period, as can be seen by the attempt to reconcile the traditional spread-out form of the object with stiffer rococo motifs such as the schematic cornices in very low relief. The use of such motifs presages neoclassicism, which developed earlier in Rome than in other Italian cities. The date of the donation coincides roughly with the date of execution.

DLB

Unpublished

1. C. Bulgari, *Argentieri, gemmari e orafi d'Italia,* vol. 2 (Rome, 1958), p. 555.

234. **Kiddush Goblet** (fig. 117)

Bartolomeo Bernardi (active 1778–1816)

Turin, 1778–1816

Silver, cast

Hallmarks: Bargoni Pls. III, 10; V, 8

15 15/16 × 5 13/16 dm in. (40.5 × 14.8 cm)

New York, Private Collection of a Jewish Family from Turin

Large goblets for kiddush were fashionable among Turinese Jewish families of the nineteenth century.[1]

VBM

Unpublished

1. See *Ebrei a Torino,* exh. cat. (Turin, 1984), p. 147; a similar example is in the collection of the Comunità Israelitica, Ferrara.

235. **Menorah**

Italy, c. 1930

Silver, cast and chased

17 3/8 × 11 1/4 in. (44.1 × 28.5 cm)

Private collection

Seven-branched menorot were frequently used in the decoration of Italian synagogues. Since this menorah featuring a twelve-sided base and gadrooning is seven-branched, it was probably based on synagogue models.

GMG

Unpublished

Domestic Objects

236. ***Cofanetto* (Casket)** (fig. 171)

Jeshurum Tober(?)

Northern Italy, fifteenth century

Silver, cast, engraved, nielloed, parcel-gilt, and appliquéd

2 7/16 × 4 7/8 × 2 7/8 in. (6.2 × 12.3 × 7.3 cm)

Jerusalem, The Israel Museum, Gift of Mrs. Astorre Mayer, Milan (131/20)

This unique work is a small casket created for the mistress of a Jewish household in northern Italy, probably to hold keys to various linen chests.[1] The front is covered with a nielloed plate on which appear three female figures, each engaged in one of the three commandments incumbent upon a woman: (from right to left) the separation of dough, immersion in a *mikveh* or ritual bath, and kindling of the Sabbath lights (Babylonian Talmud: Shabbat 31:b). Each figure is accompanied by a scroll on which is inscribed the blessing recited on performing the commandment. The order of the acts has been changed from that written in the Talmud in order to form a mnemonic device, *ḥ"annah,* equivalent to the name Hannah.

The top of the casket is unusual; it is appliquéd with eight dials set in two rows of four each and labeled with varying sequences of Hebrew letters, the equivalent of the numbers one through twelve. Each dial is labeled in Judeo-Italian with the name of a type of linen:

לינצולי / מנטיל / טוואיי / קמיזי מאיש / קמיזי מאשה /
פצולי / גרמיאלי / מכנסים /

(transliteration and translation: *lenzoli* [sheets], *mantil* [tablecloths], *tovaglie* [towels], *camicia me-ish* [men's shirts], *camicia me-ishah* [women's chemises], *fazzoli* [handkerchiefs], *mikhnasayim* [knickers], *grembiale* [aprons or cloths for menstruation]). Below the last dial is the artist's name Jeshurum Tober.

Mordekhai Narkiss suggested that the unique function of the casket is related to the prohibition against carrying on the Sabbath and the requirement to transform whatever keys a woman needed outside the home on that day into a piece of jewelry.[2] By placing all her keys to linen chests into this *cofanetto* and locking it, the owner would secure her linen against thievery. He also suggested that the use of Hebrew letters in place of Arabic numerals on the dials was an added security device, since presumably the servants could not decipher how many pieces of each type of linen were in the various chests.

Since the transliterated words are written in Venetian dialect, northern Italian origin is suggested for the casket. It is dated to the fifteenth century on stylistic grounds. Recently Elliot Horowitz noted that the casket is an illustration of the emphasis on immersion in the *mikveh* among the Jews in northern Italy, in contrast to the lax observance of the commandment among the Jews of Palermo, as narrated by Rabbi Obadiah da Bertinoro (c. 1450–before 1516), who traveled there.

VBM

Bibliography: M. Narkiss, "A Silver Niello Casket from the Fifteenth Century in Italy," in *Scritti in Memoria di Sally Mayer* (Jerusalem, 1956), pp. 167–195 (Hebrew); idem, "An Italian Niello Casket of the Fifteenth Century," *Journal of the Warburg and Courtauld Institutes* 21 (1958): 288–295; idem, "The Secret of the Italian Casket of the Fifteenth Century," *Rimmonim* 2 (1985): 32–36 (Hebrew); E. Horowitz, "On Jewish Religious Observance at the End of the Fifteenth Century according to the Letters of Rabbi Obadiah from Bertinoro," *Pa'amim* 37 (1988): 34 (Hebrew).

1. This discussion is based on the work of Mordekhai Narkiss (see the Bibliography for the relevant articles). I would like to thank Rafi Grafman for examining the casket at the Israel Museum.
2. Narkiss, "An Italian Niello Casket," pp. 289–290.

237. **Book Cover**

Rome, eighteenth century

Maker: EB

Silver repoussé, hammered, and chased

Hallmarks: *EB*; Rome city mark

12¾ × 9¾ in. (32.5 × 24.8 cm)

New York, The Jewish Museum,
Gift of Mr. and Mrs. Albert A. List (JM 3–72)

This book cover is an outstanding example of the wedding gift customarily exchanged by Italian-Jewish families. On one side is the coat of arms of the Portaleone family, a closed gate surmounted by a crouching lion, and on the other, the emblem of the Grassini family, a tower flanked by rampant lions.

The decorative motifs and composition of the cover are comparable to those of dated works of the eighteenth century.[1] Two silversmiths of the period could have used the hallmark on this piece: Ercole Baldelli (b. 1741, active through 1806) and Eusebio Bertoni (b. 1750, active through 1794).[2]

VBM

Bibliography: The Jewish Museum, *The Book and Its Cover: Manuscripts and Bindings of the Twelfth through the Eighteenth Centuries,* exh. brochure, by V. B. Mann (New York, 1981), no. 34.

1. See S. Fornari, *Gli argenti romani* (Rome, 1968), pp. 105, 130, 162.
2. C. G. Bulgari, *Argentieri, gemmari e orafi d'Italia: Parte prima—Roma* (Rome, 1958), pp. 90, 158.

238. **Covered Bonbon Dish from the Wedding of Elia Emanuelle Treves and Ines Cassin in 1910**

Turin, 1910

Silver, cast and parcel-gilt

Hallmark: indistinguishable Turin mark

5$^{11}/_{16}$ × 10 in. (14.5 × 25.3 cm)

Private Collection

VBM

Unpublished

239. **Candelabra**

Turin, c. 1900

Silver, cast and chased

23 × 9 in. (58.4 × 22.8 cm)

Collection of the grandchildren of Elia Treves (1877–1943)

VBM

Unpublished

240. **Set of Cutlery for Passover**

Venice, late nineteenth to early twentieth century

Silver, cast; leather, tooled and gilt

Knife: 8⅝ × ¾ in. (21.9 × 1.9 cm); spoon: 7⅛ × 1$^{7}/_{16}$ in. (18.1 × 3.7 cm); fork: 7 × ⅞ in. (17.8 × 2.2 cm); leather case: 10¼ × 2⅛ in. (26 × 5.4 cm)

Hallmarks (on knife): Rosenberg 3 7488; *R* (crowned); illegible mark

New York, ASB Collection

The set consists of a knife, a fork, and a spoon that fit into a tooled leather case that is inscribed with the initials *S.A.N.* and the Hebrew phrase

של פסח

(for Passover). The case bears a sticker that reads: *Dominici.Giusepe / Venise . . . Magasin / Antiquités et Objets d'Art.*

Although the cutlery is now a set, each piece is of a different pattern. The knife is the only one with hallmarks; it also bears the initials *F.P.* on the handle. The spoon is engraved on the back with the initials *D A S.*

VBM

Unpublished

Jewelry

241. **Wedding Ring**

Italy, sixteenth century

Gold, hammered, engraved, and cut out

1⅜ × ¾ dm in. (3.5 × 1.8 cm)

New York, The Jewish Museum, Rose and Benjamin Mintz Collection (M 45)

The earliest extant Jewish marriage ring—a piece excavated in Weissenfels (Halle), Germany, that is dated to the first quarter of the fourteenth century—is remarkably similar in form to this example.[1] Its bezel is in the form of a house with cutout apertures and a crocketed roofline. Whereas the openings on the Weissenfels ring are Gothic in shape, the apertures in the building on this ring form a colonnade along all four sides, creating a classicizing effect that is somewhat at odds with the Gothic roofline. This mix of German and Italian stylistic elements finds its parallel in fifteenth-century manuscript illumination, for example, in the work of Joel ben Simeon of Cologne, who was active in Italy (see the essay by Evelyn M. Cohen above). Both phenomena are attributable to the immigration of Ashkenazic Jews to Italy from the late thirteenth century on.

VBM

Unpublished

1. V. B. Mann, "'New' Examples of Jewish Ceremonial Art from Medieval Ashkenaz," *Artibus et Historiae* 17 (1988): 14, fig. 2.

242. **Wedding Ring**

Venice(?), eighteenth century

Gold, hammered, engraved, and filigree

7⁄16 × 1¼ dm in. (1.1 × 3.2 cm)

New York, The Jewish Museum, Gift of Mrs. Arthur Miller (JM 9–47)

The wish customarily expressed on festive occasions, *mazel tov* (good luck), is inscribed in Hebrew letters on a flat plate affixed to the outer surface of the ring.

VBM

Bibliography: NYJM, *Jewish Patrons,* no. 32.

The Modern Period: From the Risorgimento to the Resistance

243. **Locket and Chain with Matching Earrings**

Turin, c. 1878

Gold, diamonds, and onyx; photograph

Locket: 2 5⁄16 × 1½ in. (5.9 × 3.9 cm); Chain: 15⅞ in. (40.3 cm); Earrings: 2 × ⅝ in. (5 × 1.5 cm)

Private collection

The photograph within the locket depicts Anna Treves holding her grandson Samuele (1835–1905).

VBM

Unpublished

244. **Watch Fob with Miniature of Lucia Ricolo Vitalevi (1891–1948)**

Turin(?), c. 1916

Gold, engraved; enamel; diamonds; photograph

Locket: Diam: 1⅛ in. (2.9 cm); Chain: 14¼ in. (36.2 cm)

Private collection

The inscription within the locket reads *1891 / 17 settembre / 1916.* It probably refers to the dates of the subject's birth and of her marriage to Moise Vitalevi.

VBM

PAINTINGS

245. ***Martyrdom of Simon of Trent*** (fig. 10)

Gandolfino di Roreto d'Asti (active c. 1493)

Piedmont, late fifteenth century

Tempera on panel

6⅞ × 24⅞ in. (17.5 × 63 cm)

Jerusalem, Israel Museum (503/134)
Gift of Jacob Rothschild, London

In 1475 the Franciscan friar Bernardino of Feltre delivered a Lenten sermon in Trent against Jews, predicting that their sins would soon be evident to all. Shortly thereafter a Christian infant, Simon, son of Andreas Unverdosben, disappeared. His body was discovered near the house of the head of the Jewish community of Trent. Subsequently the entire Jewish community was arrested. Following fifteen days of torture, seventeen Jews "confessed" to ritually murdering the child. Six Jews were burnt at the stake, two converted to Christianity and were strangled, and one died in prison.

Pope Sixtus IV intervened in the affair, sensing impropriety and illegality. He sent a papal commissary, who was forced to leave Trent when his investigations challenged the results of the local trial. In 1478 a papal court of inquiry affirmed the legality of the trial. The saintliness of the child martyr was used as a pretext for anti-Semitic persecutions, including expulsions, the closing of loan banks, and other measures, throughout Italy and beyond its borders. Bernardino of Feltre continued to instigate anti-Semitism, using the death of Simon of Trent as a catalyst for further expulsions and destruction. Both Simon and Bernardino were beatified.

Gandolfino di Roreto d'Asti is known to have painted many panels for Piedmontese churches. This scene depicts the murder and bloodletting of the martyred child, and alludes to parallels between Simon's martyrdom at the hands of the Jews and the Crucifixion. Simon's attributes, the pliers and scarf used in his supposed torture, are included. This scene is probably based on woodcut prints of the Trent episode.[1] The use of such virulently anti-Semitic iconography, coupled with inflammatory sermons, encouraged anti-Semitic attitudes and persecution among illiterate segments of the Italian populace.

GMG

Unpublished

1. For a study of the iconography of Simon of Trent see Eric M. Zafran, *The Iconography of Anti-Semitism: A Study of the Representation of the Jews in the Visual Arts of Europe 1400–1600.* Unpublished Ph.D. Dissertation, New York University, Institute for Fine Arts, 1973, pp. 54–90.

246. ***Portrait of Jacob de Joseph Barukh Caravalho*** (fig. 191)

Anonymous

Venice, 1687

Oil on canvas

81 × 74 in. (205.7 × 188 cm)

New York, The Daniel M. Friedenberg Collection

In the seventeenth century Venetian Jews frequently commissioned portraits. For example, Rabbi Leone Modena is known to have sat for three portraits (see cat. no. 79).[1] Surviving examples of portraits of Jews are rare, however. This one was probably painted in honor of the sitter's wedding, as is indicated by the ring held in his right hand. Since the illuminated marriage contract for Jacob, son of Joseph Barukh Caravalho, and Esther, daughter of Dr. Aaron Habib, is dated 1687, this portrait can be dated to that year.

The Barukh Caravalho family originally lived in Portugal, where they converted to Christianity. The family moved to Italy in the seventeenth century, probably to avoid persecution by the Inquisition, and returned to their ancestral faith. The tombstone of Samuel Barukh Caravalho, a relative of Jacob de Joseph, tells of his return to Judaism in 1644 and of his death a year later.

Jacob ben Joseph Barukh Caravalho is dressed in an elegant white shirt with ruffled cuffs and cravat, a lavishly embroidered waistcoat, black cloak, breeches, hose, and buckled shoes. He wears a fine powdered wig set back on his head. It has been suggested that the wig may be placed in this position to emphasize that Jacob ben Joseph was also wearing a skullcap. Lavish clothing, such as that depicted in this painting, was commonly worn by seventeenth-century Venetian Jews, leading to the passage of sumptuary laws in 1696–1697 forbidding the wearing of brocade and of lace made of gold, silver, or silk and placing a limit of twelve ducats on the price that a man could pay for his wig.

GMG

Provenance: Giuseppe Pardo Roques, Pisa.

Bibliography: D. M. Friedenberg, "Now Rest in Peace Jacob Baruch Caravalho: The Three-Century Diaspora of a Jewish Portrait," *Jewish Art* 14 (1988): 56–63; NYJM, *Jewish Patrons* no. 30; C. Roth, "New Notes on Pre-Emancipation Jewish Artists," in *Hebrew Union College Annual,* vol. 17 (1942–1943), p. 500.

1. See M. Cohen, ed. and trans., *The Autobiography of a Seventeenth-Century Venetian Rabbi: Leon Modena's Life of Judah* (Princeton, 1988), p. 258.

Fig. 191. Anonymous, *Portrait of Jacob de Joseph Barukh Caravalho,* Venice, 1687, Daniel M. Friedenberg Collection, New York (cat. no. 246)

247. ***Il matrimonio ebraico***

Master of the Reflections (school of Pietro Longhi)

Venice, c. 1750

Oil on canvas

25 × 34¼ in. (63.5 × 87 cm)

Jerusalem, Israel Museum, Gift of
Dr. and Mrs. Astorre Mayer, Milan (503/116)

Elements of this painting depict traditional Jewish wedding customs, for example, the two cups and lighted torches. This work thus appears to document actual eighteenth-century weddings in the ghetto, and similar depictions of lavishly costumed and wigged participants celebrating among numerous musicians can be found on contemporary marriage contracts. The composition, however, appears to have been based on the print by Bernard Picart *Ceremonie nuptiale des juives portugais* (Amsterdam, 1723) or possibly on Francesco Novelli's engraving after Picart (Venice, 1789). Furthermore, although the painting probably depicts the veiling of the bride prior to the actual wedding, the exact subject is difficult to determine. The prospective bride and groom are seated on a dais with a rabbi standing before them. A woman, probably the mother of the bride or groom, appears to be blessing the couple. The identities and actions of the other participants are unclear.

This painting is similar to Longhi's work in that it portrays the richness and elegance of eighteenth-century Venetian interiors, costume, and entertainment. Its ambiguity of action and of relationships within a narrative setting is also typical of Longhi, suggesting that this painting was made by a follower.

GMG

Provenance: Probably Gino Fogolari, Venice; Vittorio Forti, Rome; Barozzi, Venice; Dr. and Mrs. Astorre Mayer, Milan.

Bibliography: G. Fiocco, "Una pittura di Pietro Longhi," *Arte Veneta* 10, (1956): 206–207; T. Pignatti, *Pietro Longhi: Paintings and Drawings,* trans. Pamela Waley (London, 1969), pp. 30, 120.

248. ***Isaac Ḥayyim de Medina*** (fig. 45)

Anonymous

Italy, second half of the eighteenth century

Oil on canvas

39⅜ × 33 in. (100 x 84 cm)

Livorno, Comunità Israelitica

In this portrait the sitter is portrayed dressed in stylish cloak and wig, with attributes indicating his musical interests. On a nearby table is a musical score on which is placed a recorder and a second woodwind instrument, probably an oboe. It is likely that this composition was based on contemporary popular prints of well-known composers such as Telemann or Vivaldi.

Isaac Ḥayyim de Medina served as coeditor of *Seder Zemirot ve-Limmud,* the publication of the cantata libretto composed by Volunio Gallichi for the inauguration of the new Siena synagogue in 1786. A pendant portrait of the sitter's wife, similarly shown with musical attributes, is also in the collection of the Comunità Israelitica di Livorno.

GMG

Unpublished

249. ***Funeral Procession***

Anonymous

Italy, late eighteenth century

Oil on canvas

16⅛ × 31⅞ in. (41 × 81 cm)

Jerusalem, Israel Museum, Gift of Maurice Rheims, Paris (513/20)

This painting depicts a group of men in a funeral procession in an Italian streetscape. The men surround the coffin, and it is possible that the scene depicts the custom of walking around the deceased seven times.[1] The men wear hats and scarves, which were required distinctive dress for Jews.

The artist has conveyed a convincing Italian street scene, complete with cobblestones, a running dog, palazzo-like architecture, and a genre vignette of a boy struggling with a calf. The spirited jocularity of street life contrasts greatly with the somber mourners of the funeral procession.

The identity of the patron who commissioned this work and its pendant (see cat. no. 250) and the reason for this commission are unknown. The patron may have wanted a general study of Jewish customs, or the painting may depict a specific event. Contemporary Italian prints of Jewish funeral scenes were issued in this period, attesting to the popularity of this iconography (see cat. no. 89).

GMG

Unpublished

1. For an example of the practice of this custom in Italy, see M. R. Cohen, ed. and trans., *The Autobiography of a Seventeenth-Century Venetian Rabbi: Leon Modena's Life of Judah* (Princeton, 1988), p. 178.

250. ***Jewish Funeral***

Anonymous

Italy, late eighteenth century

Oil on canvas

16⅜ × 32 in. (41.5 × 81.3 cm)

Jerusalem, Israel Museum, Gift of Maurice Rheims, Paris (503/21)

This scene depicts a Jewish funeral in Italy. Ten men with mournful expressions, forming a minyan,[1] surround the coffin containing a shrouded corpse. They stand beneath a portico beside the cemetery. A rabbi, wearing a tallit on his head and holding a book, leads the funeral service. The ten men are all dressed in capes, breeches, boots, and wide-brimmed hats with attached scarves. The hats and scarves were distinctive clothing, which Jews were required to wear. The rabbi wears a black cloak with a white collar and a brimmed hat. In the distance can be seen the expanse of the cemetery, where a group of men stand beside an open grave.

It is unclear for whom this painting and its pendant (see cat. no. 249) were painted. It is likely that it was commissioned by a Jewish patron. The painting probably presents a general impression of Jewish funeral customs, or it may be a portrait of particular individuals.

GMG

Bibliography: A. Rubens, *A History of Jewish Costume* (New York, 1973), pl. 197.

1. A minyan, ten males over the age of thirteen, is the quorum necessary for the recitation of kaddish, the mourner's prayer.

251. ***Sukkah* Decoration: *The Song of the Sea***

Anonymous

Venice, 6 June 1826

Oil on panel

24⅝ × 14¾ in. (62.5 × 37.5 cm)

Venice, Comunità Israelitica (221)

Italian sukkot were elaborately decorated with wall hangings, as can be seen from extant examples (see also cat. nos. 108–109) and from descriptions in diaries and halakhic literature.[1] This panel depicts the drowning of the Egyptian armies following the splitting of the Red Sea and the celebration of the Israelites following their miraculous escape (Exod. 14:21–15:21).

Moses, his arms outstretched, as in the biblical narrative (Exod. 14:27), is the central figure in the composition, with Aaron behind him. Miriam is depicted kneeling beneath a tree, with a timbrel in her hand, as described in the text (Exod. 15:20). The panel is topped by the blessings recited when dwelling in a sukkah.

The second blessing inscribed on this panel, the *she-heḥiyanu,* which thanks God for life and sustenance, may be linked to the representation of the celebration of the miracle at the Red Sea. This event is a paradigm of a wonder that makes life possible, and it relates to an individual's recitation of the *she-heḥiyanu* blessing upon dwelling in a sukkah for the first time in a given year. A pendant panel, also in the collection of the Comunità Israelitica, Venice, depicts the Israelites in the wilderness and includes a dated poem. Elaborate tents are depicted in that scene, representing the booths that the Israelites built in the wilderness, the biblical origin of the custom of dwelling in sukkot.

Elongated trees frame the central action, along with a foreground repoussoir of greenery and figures on either side. The background, with its low horizon and trees, is rendered in a painterly style, in accordance with Venetian tradition. The figures are defined by a dramatic play of light and shade, and with particular attention to the folds of their classicizing drapery.

GMG

Unpublished

1. See S. Makover, "The Iconographic Program of a Series of Italian Sukkah Decorations," in *The Proceedings of the Ninth World Congress of Jewish Studies* (Jerusalem, 1985), p. 38.

Fig. 193. Portrait of Rabbi Vivante with his Circumcision Implements, late nineteenth century, Private Collection, Venice

252. ***The Feast of the Rejoicing of the Law at the Synagogue in Leghorn, Italy,* 1850** (fig. 175)

Solomon Alexander Hart (English, 1806–1881)

London, 1850

Oil on canvas

55⅝ × 68¾ in. (141.3 × 174.6 cm)

New York, The Jewish Museum, Gift of Mr. and Mrs. Oscar Gruss (JM 28–55)

The Jewish community of Livorno (Leghorn) was established by Spanish Jews and by Marranos who were invited to settle there by the duke of Tuscany in 1591. Their ducal charter provided that Livornese Jews would never be forced to reside in a ghetto. The community grew rapidly, necessitating successive enlargements and refurbishing of the synagogue, which was renowned for its beauty and spaciousness.[1]

Most depictions of the synagogue's interior emphasize its size and grandeur (see cat. no. 89; fig. 184). In contrast, Hart focuses on one area, that surrounding the reader's desk, at the moment the scrolls of the Torah are carried in procession. Some of the figures, such as the father and son at extreme left, are exotically dressed. They probably represent Jews of Ottoman origin, who formed a significant segment of the Italian-Jewish population from the sixteenth century on.

Hart's accuracy in rendering the scene before him may be seen by comparing objects in the painting with works in this exhibition.

VBM

Bibliography: A. Ziegler, "Jewish Artists in England," *Studio* 153 (1957): 1–12; R. Ormond, "The Diploma Paintings from 1840 Onwards," *Apollo* 89 (1969): 56–57; Kleeblatt and Mann, *Treasures,* pp. 150–151.

1. The synagogue of Livorno depicted in Hart's painting was destroyed by the Nazis. Some of its furnishings remain, stored in the modern synagogue.

The Modern Period: From the Risorgimento to the Resistance

253. Serafino De Tivoli
***L'Arno* (The Arno)**
1860–1861
Oil on canvas
19¾ × 23⅝ in. (50 × 60 cm)
Private Collection

254. Serafino De Tivoli
***La questua* (Begging for Alms)** (fig. 121)
1856
Oil on canvas
13 × 16½ in. (33 × 42 cm)
Private Collection, Bologna

255. Vito D'Ancona
***Signora in giardino* (Lady in the Garden)** (fig. 120)
c. 1861–1862
Oil on Canvas
14⅞ × 10 in. (37.9 × 25.3 cm)
Private Collection, Montecatini

256. Vito D'Ancona
***Veduta di Volognano* (View of Volognano)** (fig. 124)
1878
Oil on canvas
15 × 10¼ in. (38 × 26 cm)
Private Collection

257. Vito D'Ancona
***La finestra sul pomaio* (Window on the Orchard)** (fig. 122)
1873
Oil on canvas
13⅜ × 10⅝ in. (34 × 27 cm)
Private Collection, Florence

258. Vito D'Ancona
***Nudo* (Nude)** (fig. 123)
1873
Oil on Canvas
10⅜ × 16¼ in. (26.5 × 41 cm)
Civica Galleria d'Arte Moderna, Milan

259. Vito D'Ancona
***Signora in conversazione* (Woman in Conversation)**
c. 1875
Oil on canvas
14¼ × 8¼ in. (36 × 21 cm)
Private Collection, Montecatini

260. Vito D'Ancona
***Ritratto di donna con lo scialle* (Portrait of a Woman in a Shawl)**
1866
Oil on canvas
33 × 26½ in. (84 × 67.5 cm)
The Israel Museum, Jerusalem,
Gift of Prof. Paolo D'Ancona, Milan

261. Vito D'Ancona
***Donna dormiente* (Sleeping Woman)** (fig. 47)
c. 1870s
Oil on canvas
34½ × 45 in. (87.5 × 114.5 cm)
The Israel Museum, Jerusalem,
Gift of Prof. Paolo D'Ancona, Milan

262. Telemaco Signorini
***Il Ghetto a Firenze* (The Ghetto in Florence)** (fig. 125)
1882
Oil on canvas
37½ × 25⅝ in. (95 × 65 cm)
Galleria Nazionale d'Arte Moderna, Roma

263. Ulvi Liegi
***Lo studio del pittore* (The Studio of the Painter)**
1885
Oil on canvas
17¾ × 23⅝ in. (45 × 60 cm)
Private Collection

264. Ulvi Liegi
***Terrazza al Pian dei Giullari* (The Terrace at Pian dei Giullari)**
c. 1894
Oil on panel
17¾ × 10¾ in. (27.5 × 17 cm)
Private Collection

265. Ulvi Liegi
***La modellina* (The Young Model)** (fig. 129)
1889
Oil on canvas
18½ × 15 in. (47 × 38 cm)
Galleria d'Arte Moderna, Palazzo Pitti, Florence

266. Ulvi Liegi
***Interno della sinagoga* (Interior of the Synagogue at Livorno)** (fig. 130)
c. 1935
Oil on panel
10¾ × 19½ in. (27.5 × 49.5 cm)
Museo Civico "G. Fattori," Livorno

267. Vittorio Corcos
***Ritratto di Yorik* (Portrait of Yorik)** (fig. 127)
1889
Oil on canvas
78⅝ × 55½ in. (200 × 141 cm)
Museo Civico "G. Fattori," Livorno

268. Vittorio Corcos
***Sogni* (Dreams)** (fig. 126)
1896
Oil on canvas
74⅜ × 64⅛ in. (189 × 163 cm)
Galleria Nazionale d'Arte Moderna, Rome

269. Vittorio Corcos
***Strada di Parigi* (Paris Street Scene)**
c. 1882
Oil on canvas
25½ × 24¼ in. (65.5 × 64.5 cm)
Private Collection

270. Vittorio Corcos
***Ritratto di Emilio Treves* (Portrait of Emilio Treves)** (fig. 128)
1907
Oil on canvas
53½ × 31½ in. (136 × 80 cm)
Studio Paul Nicholls, Milan

271. Mario Nunes Vais
Photographs
Istituto Centrale per il Catalogo e la Documentazione, Gabinetto Fotografico Nazionale, Collection Nunes Vais, Rome
All archive numbers beginning with N are prints made from original positives. All other archive numbers are prints made from original glass plate negatives. Photographs and enlargements processed by Roberto Galasso, I.C.C.D., Rome.

a) *Sabatino Lopez*
c. 1909
12 × 9¼ in. (30.5 x 23.5 cm)
Archive no. E98799

b) *Angiolo Orvieto* (fig. 135)
1912
12 × 9¼ in. (30.5 x 23.5 cm)
Archive no. E97996

c) *Luigi Luzzatti*
1909
12 × 9¼ in. (30.5 x 23.5 cm)
Archive no. E98383

d) *Ugo Piperno*
1909
12 × 9¼ in. (30.5 x 23.5 cm)
Archive no. F36374

e) *Alessandro D'Ancona with his son Paolo* (fig. 119)
1908
9¼ × 12 in. (23.5 × 30.5 cm)
Archive no. E98125

f) *Claudio Treves*
1910
12 × 9¼ in. (30.5 × 23.5 cm)
Archive no. E98834

g) *Felice Boghen with Moritz Rosenthal*
1913
9¼ × 12 in. (23.5 × 30.5 cm)
Archive no. E98246

h) *Amelia Rosselli* (fig. 132)
c. 1929
12 × 9¼ in. (30.5 × 23.5 cm)
Archive no. E104687

i) *Gabriele D'Annunzio with Alberto Franchetti* (fig. 131)
1905
12 × 9¼ in. (30.5 × 23.5 cm)
Archive no. F34630

j) *Sidney Sonnino*
1917
12 × 9¼ in. (30.5 × 23.5 cm)
Archive no. D11419

k) *Benito Mussolini*
c. 1925
12 × 9¼ in. (30.5 × 23.5 cm)
Archive no. D11348

l) *Margherita Sarfatti* (fig. 149)
c. 1915
12 × 9¼ in. (30.5 × 23.5 cm)
Archive no. F37140

m) *The Families of Alberto Nunes Vais and Alberto Issel, Villa Nunes Vais, Pian dei Giullari, Florence*
c. 1890
12 × 9¼ in. (30.5 × 23.5 cm)
Archive no. N24284

n) *Sofia Nunes Vais Feeding the Chickens at the Uzielli Farm, Sensano (Sienna)* (fig. 133)
c. 1895
9¼ × 12 in. (23.5 × 30.5 cm)
Archive no. N24088

o) *The Nunes Vais Family with the painter, Ulvi Liegi, his wife Paola Levi and the publisher, Piero Barbera, Villa Nunes Vais, Pian dei Giullari, Florence* (fig. 134)
c. 1890
9¼ × 12 in. (23.5 × 30.5 cm)
Archive no. N24069

p) *Group Portrait with Mario Nunes Vais and Man Identified as Vittorio Corcos*

c. 1895

12 × 9¼ in. (30.5 × 23.5 cm)

Archive no. N26284

q) *Giuseppe Uzielli in his Hunting Outfit, Uzielli Farm, Sensano (Sienna)*

c. 1887

12 × 9¼ in. (30.5 × 23.5 cm)

Archive no. N24074

r) *Sofia Nunes Vais and the Staff of the Uzielli Household in the Garden, Uzielli Farm, Sensano (Sienna)*

c. 1890

9¼ × 12 in. (23.5 × 30.5 cm)

Archive no. N25992

s) *Procession of the Feast of the Madonna, Pian dei Giullari, Florence*

c. 1890

12 × 9¼ in. (30.5 × 23.5 cm)

Archive no. N24504

t) *Peasant Bride and Groom, Uzielli Farm, Sensano (Sienna)*

c. 1885

12 × 9¼ in. (30.5 × 23.5 cm)

Archive no. N24403

u) *The Viterbo Family in the Garden, Entrance to the Villa Nunes Vais, Pian dei Giullari, Florence*

c. 1891

9¼ × 12 in. (23.5 × 30.5 cm)

Archive no. N24145

272. Mario Cavaglieri

***Piccola russa* (The Little Russian)** (fig. 136)

1913

Oil on canvas

51½ × 60 in. (131 × 152 cm)

Private Collection, Bassano del Grappa

273. Mario Cavaglieri

***Il baule e i vasi cinesi* (The Trunk and the Chinese Vases)** (fig. 137)

1915

Oil on canvas

61 × 45¼ in. (155 × 115 cm)

Collection Ermes Drago, Marostica

274. Mario Cavaglieri

Elena e Cecilia (fig. 138)

1917

Oil on canvas

59 × 47¼ in. (150 × 120 cm)

Collection Ermes Drago, Marostica

275. Amedeo Modigliani

***L'amazzone* (The Amazon)** (fig. 139)

1909

Oil on canvas

36¼ × 25⅝ in. (92 × 64.5 cm)

Mrs. Alexander Lewyt, New York

276. Amedeo Modigliani

***Portrait de Joseph Levi* (Portrait of Joseph Levi)** (fig. 141)

1910

Oil on canvas

21¼ × 19¾ in. (54 × 50 cm)

Private Collection

277. Amedeo Modigliani

***Tête* (Head)**

1911–1912

Limestone

19¼ × 5 × 7 in. (48.8 × 12.5 × 17.5 cm), base 4 × 6 × 6 in. (10.2 × 15.4 × 15.4 cm)

Henry and Rose Pearlman Foundation, Inc.

278. Amedeo Modigliani
***Tête* (Head)** (fig. 140)
1911–1912
Stone
27¾ × 9¼ × 6½ in. (70.5 × 23.5 × 16.5 cm)
The Philadelphia Museum of Art.
Gift of Mrs. Maurice J. Speiser in memory of her husband

279. Amedeo Modigliani
***Tête* (Head)**
1911–1912
Stone
19⅝ × 7¼ × 9 in. (50 × 15 × 20 cm); base: 6 × 9 × 9 in. (15.3 × 22.8 × 22.8 cm)
Hirshhorn Museum and Sculpture Garden, Smithsonian Institution. Gift of Joseph H. Hirschhorn, 1966

280. Amedeo Modigliani
***Cariatide* (Caryatid)**
1912–1913
Stone
36¼ × 16⅜ × 16⅞ in.
(92 × 41.7 × 42.4 cm)
Museum of Modern Art, New York

281. Amedeo Modigliani
***Portrait de Manuello* (Portrait of Manuello) [Manuel Humbert]** (fig. 142)
1916
Oil on canvas
26 × 20¼ in. (66 × 51.4 cm)
Los Angeles County Museum of Art.
Gift of Mr. William Wyler

282. Amedeo Modigliani
Haricot rouge
1917
Oil on canvas
21⅝ × 15 in. (54.9 × 38.1 cm)
Private Collection

283. Gino Parin
***Armonia in bianco e rosso* (Harmony in Red and White)** (fig. 145)
1914
Oil on canvas
39½ × 35¾ in. (100.5 × 91 cm)
Museo Civico Revoltella-Galleria d'Arte Moderna, Trieste

284. Gino Parin
***Sera* (Evening)** (fig. 195)
c. 1920s
Oil on canvas
15¾ × 18½ in. (40 × 47 cm)
Museo Civico Revoltella-Galleria d'Arte Moderna, Trieste

285. Isidoro Grünhut
***Ritratto del Pittore Umberto Veruda* (Portrait of the Painter Umberto Veruda)** (fig. 143)
1886
Oil on canvas
28½ in. (100.5 × 72 × 57.5 cm)
Museo Civico Revoltella-Galleria d'Arte Moderna, Trieste

286. Vittorio Bolaffio
***Il Poeta Umberto Saba* (The Poet Umberto Saba)** (fig. 177)
c. 1924
Oil on canvas
29½ × 39½ in. (75 × 100.5 cm)
R.A.I., Radiotelevisione Italiana, Sede Regionale, Friuli-Venezia Giulia, Trieste

Fig. 195. Gino Parin, *Sera* (Evening), c. 1920s, Museo Civico Revoltella–Galleria d'Arte Moderna, Trieste (cat. no. 284)

287. Arturo Rietti
***Contessa Sordina* (The Countess Sordina)** (fig. 194)
1907
Pastel on cardboard
41 × 27¼ in. (104 × 69 cm)
Museo Civico Revoltella-Galleria d'Arte Moderna, Trieste

288. Arturo Rietti
***Ritratto del Maestro Barbasetti* (Portrait of the Maestro Barbasetti)** (fig. 144)
c. 1907
Pastel on cardboard
20⅜ × 16¾ in. (51.9 × 42.7 cm)
Museo Civico Revoltella-Galleria d'Arte Moderna, Trieste

289. Arturo Nathan
***Statua naufragata* (Shipwrecked Statue)** (fig. 147)
1930
Oil on canvas
25½ × 36 in. (65 × 91.5 cm)
Museo Civico Revoltella-Galleria d'Arte Moderna, Trieste

290. Arturo Nathan
***Scoglio incantato* (Enchanted Rock)**
1931
Oil on canvas
25½ × 35⅜ in. (65 × 90 cm)
Museo Civico Revoltella-Galleria d'Arte Moderna, Trieste

291. Arturo Nathan
***Autoritratto* (Self-Portrait)**
1925
Oil on canvas
20½ × 17¾ in. (52 × 45 cm)
Daisy Nathan Margadonna, Rome

292. Arturo Nathan
***Autoritratto* (Self-Portrait)** (fig. 146)
1927
Oil on panel
21¼ × 17¾ in. (54 × 45 cm)
Museo Civico Revoltella-Galleria d'Arte Moderna, Trieste

Fig. 194. Arturo Rietti, *Contessa Sordina* (The Countess Sordina), 1907, Museo Civico Revoltella–Galleria d'Arte Moderna, Trieste (cat. no. 287)

293. Umberto Boccioni

***Ritratto di Margherita Sarfatti* (Portrait of Margherita Sarfatti)** (fig. 21)

1912

Tempera on canvas

27¾ × 24¾ in. (70.5 × 53 cm)

Private Collection

294. Mario Sironi

***Ritratto di Margherita Sarfatti* (Portrait of Margherita Sarfatti)**

c. 1914

Pastel on canvas

28¼ × 20 in. (72 × 51 cm)

Private Collection

295. **Books and Texts by Margherita Sarfatti**

a) *Storia della pittura moderna,* 1st edition

Cremona: Rome

1930

164 pages, plus illustrations

7 × 5 × ¾ in. (17.8 × 12.7 × 1.9 cm)

Private Collection

b) *Segni, Colori e Luci: Note d'Arte*

Bologna: Nicola Zanichelli

1925

260 pages

9 × 6 × ½ in. (22.7 × 15.6 × 1.3 cm)

Philippe Daverio Gallery, New York

c) Exhibition Catalogue

Novecento Italiano. Catalogo della mostra d'arte

Milan, Palazzo della Permanente

February–March 1926

113 pages including illustrations

8½ × 6¼ × 3¼ in. (21.6 × 15.9 × 8.3 cm)

Philippe Daverio Gallery, New York

d) Exhibition Catalogue

Il Novecento Italiano. Seconda mostra del Novecento Italiano Catalogo

Milan, Palazzo della Permanente

2 March–30 April, 1929

115 pages including illustrations

9½ × 7 × ¾ in. (24.1 × 17.8 × 1.9 cm)

Philippe Daverio Gallery, New York

e) *Tunisiaca*
Mondadori: Milan and Rome
1924
109 pages
9½ × 6¾ × ½ in. (24.1 × 17.1 × 1.3 cm)
Private Collection

f) *Storia della pittura moderna,* 1st edition
Cremona: Rome
1930
164 pages, plus illustrations
7 × 5 × ¾ in. (17.8 × 12.7 × 1.9 cm)
Private Collection

g) *Segni, Colori e Luci: Note d'Arte*
Bologna: Nicola Zanichelli
1925
260 pages
9 × 6 × ½ in. (22.7 × 15.6 × 1.3 cm)
Philippe Daverio Gallery, New York

h) "L'Americano come lo si parla"
Nuova Antologia (reprint)
Rome
December 1, 1934
pp. 416–434
9½ × 6¾ in. (24.1 × 17.1 cm)
Private Collection

i) Exhibition Catalogue
Novecento Italiano. Catalogo della mostra d'arte
Milan, Palazzo della Permanente
February–March 1926
113 pages including illustrations
8½ × 6¼ × 3¼ in. (21.6 × 15.9 × 8.3 cm)
Philippe Daverio Gallery, New York

j) Exhibition Catalogue
Il Novecento Italiano. Seconda mostra del Novecento Italiano Catalogo
Milan, Palazzo della Permanente
2 March–30 April, 1929
115 pages including illustrations
9½ × 7 × ¾ in. (24.1 × 17.8 × 1.9 cm)
Philippe Daverio Gallery, New York

296. **Margherita Sarfatti: Documentary Photographs**
Private Collection

a) Roberto Sarfatti with Alpine Soldiers at the Front
1917
7 × 5 in. (17.8 × 12.7 cm)

b) Palazzo Bembo (16th century), Venice, Fondamenta del Carbon
1985
5 × 7 in. (12.7 × 17.8 cm)

c) Giuseppe Terragni, Monument to Roberto Sarfatti
1935
5 × 7 in. (12.7 × 17.8 cm)

d) Cesare Sarfatti sitting at his desk
c. 1923
5 × 7 in. (12.7 × 17.8 cm)

e) Margherita Sarfatti sitting on deck of ship from Lisbon to Buenos Aires
1939
5 × 7 in. (12.7 × 17.8 cm)

f) Tomb of Cesare Sarfatti in the Jewish section of the Cimitero Monumentale, Milan
1924
7 × 5 in. (17.8 × 12.7 cm)

g) Margherita Sarfatti about ten years old
c. 1890
7 × 5 in. (17.8 × 12.7 cm)

h) Margherita Sarfatti sitting on deck of ship from Lisbon to Buenos Aires
1939
5 × 7 in. (12.7 × 17.8 cm)

i) Il Soldo, villa of Margherita Sarfatti in Cavallasca (Como)
c. 1935
5 × 7 in. (12.7 × 17.8 cm)

297. Roberto Melli

***Signora dal cappello nero* (Woman with a Black Hat)**

1913

Bronze

14½ × 15¾ × 11¾ in. (37 × 40 × 30 cm)

Galleria Nazionale d'Arte Moderna, Rome

298. Roberto Melli

***Composizione con oggetti* (Composition with Objects)**

1918

Oil on canvas

17¾ × 24 in. (45 × 61 cm)

Galleria Nazionale d'Arte Moderna, Rome

299. Roberto Melli

***Interno* (Interior)** (fig. 150)

1919

Oil on canvas

39⅜ × 27½ in. (100 × 70 cm)

Private Collection, Rome

300. Roberto Melli

***Terrazze a sera* (Terraces in the Evening)**

1936

Oil on canvas

28¼ × 32 in. (72 × 81 cm)

Private Collection, Rome

301. Roberto Melli

***Scenografia* (Scenography)** (fig. 151)

1936

Oil on canvas

56¾ × 42½ in. (144 × 108 cm)

Private Collection, Rome

302. Roberto Melli

***Il pastore* (The Shepherd)**

1937

Oil on canvas

43¼ × 26¾ in. (110 × 68 cm)

Galleria Civica d'Arte Moderna, Palazzo dei Diamanti, Ferrara

303. Roberto Melli

***Autoritratto con guanto bianco* (Self-Portrait with White Glove)** (fig. 162)

1944

Oil on canvas

20 × 16½ in. (51 × 42 cm)

Private Collection, Rome

304. Corrado Cagli

***Guerrieri* (Warriors)** (fig. 152)

1933

Encaustic on plywood

16¼ × 19¾ in. (41.4 × 50 cm)

Private Collection, Rome

305. Corrado Cagli

***I neofiti* (The Neophytes)**

1934

Encaustic on plywood

24 × 24 in. (61 × 61 cm)

Collection Franco Muzzi, Rome

306. Corrado Cagli

***Veduta di Roma* (View of Rome) or *Trionfo di Roma* (Triumph of Rome)** (fig. 24)

1937

Oil and encaustic on plywood

94½ × 78¾ in. (240 × 200 cm)

Eredi Cagli, Rome

307. Corrado Cagli
***Veduta di Roma* (View of Rome)**
1937
Oil and encaustic on plywood
94½ × 78¾ in. (240 × 200 cm)
Eredi Cagli, Rome

308. Corrado Cagli
***I fratelli Rosselli* (The Rosselli Brothers)**
1937
Oil on paper
9¾ × 12¾ in. (25 × 32.5 cm)
Eredi Cagli, Rome

309. Antonietta Raphaël Mafai
***Natura morta con chitarra* (Still-Life with Guitar)**
1928
Oil on panel
15 × 17¾ in. (39 × 45 cm)
Private Collection, Rome

310. Antonietta Raphaël Mafai
***Autoritratto con violino* (Self-Portrait with Violin)** (fig. 118)
1928
Oil on panel
20½ × 21¼ in. (52.3 × 54 cm)
Private Collection, Rome

311. Antonietta Raphaël Mafai
***Veduta dalla terrazza di via Cavour* (View from the Terrace of via Cavour)** (fig. 153)
1930
Oil on panel
13¾ × 16½ in. (35 × 42 cm)
N. M. de' Angelis, Rome

312. Antonietta Raphaël Mafai
***Yom Kippur nella sinagoga* (Yom Kippur in the Synagogue)** (fig. 154)
1931
Oil on canvas
18⅞ × 25 in. (48 × 64 cm)
Private Collection, Rome

313. Antonietta Raphaël Mafai
***La fuga da Sodoma* (Flight from Sodom)** (fig. 155)
1935–1936
Bronze (cast: 1968)
94½ × 42 × 26 in. (240 × 107 × 66 cm)
Private Collection, Turin

314. Antonietta Raphaël Mafai
***Tramonto su Genova Quarto* (Sunset in Genoa Quarto)**
1940
Oil on canvas
16 × 13¾ in. (41 × 35 cm)
Private Collection, Rome

315. Antonietta Raphaël Mafai
***Mosè* (Moses with Ritual Shawl)**
c. 1944
Painted terracotta
H: 20¼ in. (51.5 cm); base: 1¼ × 10¼ × 12½ in. (3 × 26 × 31.5 cm)
Collection Giuseppe Selvaggi, Rome

316. Antonietta Raphaël Mafai
***La sognatrice* (The Dreamer)** (fig. 166)
1946
Bronze (cast: 1988)
56 × 21½ × 25 in. (142 × 54.5 × 63.5 cm)
Private Collection, Rome

317. Antonietta Raphaël Mafai
***Tre sorelle* (Three Sisters)**
1947
Bronze
34½ × 38½ × 15¾ in. (87.5 × 97.5 × 40 cm)
Private Collection, Turin

318. Antonietta Raphaël Mafai
***La fuga* (The Flight)** (fig. 163)
1958
Bronze
63¾ × 25½ × 19¼ in. (162 × 65 × 49 cm)
Private Collection, Rome

319. Antonietta Raphaël Mafai
***Il quarto giorno della creazione* (The Fourth Day of Creation)** (back cover)
1963
Oil on canvas
55 × 37¾ in. (140 × 96 cm)
Private Collection, Turin

320. Paola Levi Montalcini
***Estate* (Summer)**
c. 1935
Oil on paper
32⅜ × 27¼ in. (82.2 × 69 cm)
Galleria Civica d'Arte Moderna, Turin

321. Carlo Levi
***Il fratello e la sorella* (Brother and Sister)** (fig. 156)
1925
Oil on canvas
48½ × 39⅜ in. (123 × 100 cm)
Fondazione Carlo Levi, Rome

322. Carlo Levi
***Ritratto del padre convalescente seduto con il braccio al collo* (Portrait of the Artist's Father Convalescing with his Arm in a Sling)**
1928
Oil on canvas
51¼ × 43¼ in. (130 × 110 cm)
Fondazione Carlo Levi, Rome

323. Carlo Levi
***Ritratto di Nello Rosselli* (Portrait of Nello Rosselli)**
1929
Oil on canvas
18 × 15 in. (46 × 38 cm)
Fondazione Carlo Levi, Rome

324. Carlo Levi
***L'eroe cinese* (The Chinese Hero)**
1930
Oil on canvas
36¼ × 28⅞ in. (92 × 73 cm)
Fondazione Carlo Levi, Rome

325. Carlo Levi
***Ritratto di Alberto Moravia* (Portrait of Alberto Moravia)** (fig. 176)
1932
Oil on cardboard mounted on canvas
24 × 19¾ in. (60 × 50 cm)
Fondazione Carlo Levi, Rome

326. Carlo Levi
***Ritratto di Carlo Rosselli* (Portrait of Carlo Rosselli)**
1932
Oil on canvas
24 × 19¾ in. (61 × 50 cm)
Fondazione Carlo Levi, Rome

327. Carlo Levi

***Ritratto di Leone Ginzburg* (Portrait of Leone Ginzburg)** (fig. 157)

1933

Oil on canvas

25½ × 19¾ in. (65 × 50 cm)

Fondazione Carlo Levi, Rome

328. Carlo Levi

***Nudo piccolo* (Small Nude)** (fig. 160)

1935

Oil on canvas

28¾ × 36¼ in. (73 × 92 cm)

Fondazione Carlo Levi, Rome

329. Carlo Levi

***Il figlio della Parroccola* (The Son of the Parroccola)** (fig. 159)

1936

Oil on canvas

24 × 19¾ in. (61 × 50 cm)

Fondazione Carlo Levi, Rome

330. Adriana Pincherle

***Autoritratto* (Self Portrait)**

c. 1931

Oil on canvas

65 × 27⅛ in. (165 × 69 cm)

Galleria degli Uffizi, Florence

331. ***La Difesa della Razza***

Printed journal

11⅞ × 9⅜ in. (30.2 × 23.9 cm)

Library of The Jewish Theological Seminary of America, New York

a) Volume I, no. 1, 5 August 1938
b) Volume I, no. 4, 20 September 1938
c) Volume I, no. 6, 20 October 1938 (fig. 161)
d) Volume IV, no. 19, 5 August 1941
e) Volume IV, no. 23, 5 October 1941
f) Volume VI, no. 6, 20 January 1943

332. ***Legislazione per la difesa della razza* (Legislation for the Defence of the Race)**

(Tito Staderini)

Rome: Carlo Colombo

1938

135 pages

8½ × 6¼ × ⅜ in. (21.5 × 15.5 × 1 cm)

Piero and Naomi Foà, Detroit

333. Aldo Carpi

The Gusen Diary

1945

Ink on paper

8⅞ × 6$\frac{1}{16}$ × 3⅜ in. (22.5 × 15.5 × 8.5 cm)

Biblioteca Apostolica Vaticano, Vatican City

334. Aldo Carpi

***Carpi dammi da bere* (Carpi Give Me Something to Drink)**

1945

Ink on paper

10¼ × 7$\frac{7}{16}$ in. (26 × 20 cm)

Collection Carpi Family, Milan

335. Aldo Carpi

***Il dottor Toni Goscinski mentre suona il violino* (Doctor Toni Goscinski Playing the Violin)** (fig. 164)

1945

Pencil on paper

7⅞ × 5½ in. (20 × 14 cm)

Collection Carpi Family, Milan

336. Aldo Carpi

***L'ultimo compagno nel forno crematorio di Gusen* (The Last Companion in the Gusen Crematorium)**

1945

Pencil on paper

11⅜ × 7⅞ in. (26.3 × 20 cm)

Collection Carpi Family, Milan

337. Aldo Carpi

***Cadaveri davanti al crematorio* (Cadavers in Front of the Crematorium)** (fig. 165)

1945

Pencil on paper

10¼ × 8⅝ in. (26 × 22 cm)

Collection Carpi Family, Milan

338. Aldo Carpi

***Questo russo, come ha fatto ad arrivare fin qui?* (How Did This Russian Get This Far?)**

1945

Pencil on paper

7⁵⁄₁₆ × 9 in. (16.6 × 23 cm)

Collection Carpi Family, Milan

339. Aldo Carpi

Dante Alighieri

1945

Pencil on paper

7⅞ × 4¾ in. (16 × 12 cm)

Collection Carpi Family, Milan

BIOGRAPHIES OF PAINTERS AND SCULPTORS

Vito D'Ancona

(1825–1884)

Vito D'Ancona was born in Pesaro to a large, wealthy family. He began his art studies in Florence with the engraver Samuele Jesi. In 1844 he studied at the Accademia di Belle Arti in Florence with Giuseppe Bezzuoli, becoming a close friend of Serafino De Tivoli, with whom he often painted in the Tuscan countryside. In 1848, during the First War of Independence, he and De Tivoli participated as volunteers in the battles of Curtatone and Montanara. In 1855 he began frequenting the Caffè Michelangiolo and met Telemaco Signorini, then just twenty years old. Signorini introduced D'Ancona to literature, both Italian and foreign, especially the French naturalists, and also urged D'Ancona to free himself from his academic background. In 1856 the two artists traveled together to Bologna, Mantua, Modena, and Venice. While Signorini painted some views of the city, D'Ancona studied in the museums, showing particular interest in the work of Palma il Vecchio. Despite his new artistic interests, for some years D'Ancona's painting still showed the influence of his training in romantic history painting for example, *Savonarola che rifusa di assolvere il morente Lorenzo de' Medici* (Savonorola Who Refuses to Absolve the Dying Lorenzo de' Medici), acquired by King Carlo Alberto, and *Dante e Beatrice,* 1859. For the latter, in 1861 he won the gold medal at the Esposizione Nazionale in Florence but refused the prize, maintaining that the jury was incompetent. From the mid-1860s until 1875 he lived in Paris, where he became interested in the new realist school. Signorini recalled that D'Ancona also knew Gustave Courbet quite well and that he frequented both Italian and French art circles, where he met Giovanni Boldini, Giuseppe de Nittis, De Tivoli, and Michele Gordigiani. According to his letters, he often painted *all'aperto* in the Fontainebleau forest, but none of these landscapes remains. Following the outbreak of the Franco-Prussian War in 1870, D'Ancona moved for a time to Boulogne-sur-Mer and London. In 1875 his health deteriorated further, and he returned to Florence, where he died in the villa that his brother Sansone had built for the family in the Piazza d'Azeglio.

FM

Selected Exhibitions

Prima Esposizione Italiana, Florence, 1861.

Esposizione Nazionale di Belle Arti, Naples, 1877.

Selected Bibliography

E. Cecchi, "Vito D'Ancona," *Bollettino d'arte* 4 (1926–1927): 291–304.

T. Signorini, "Vito D'Ancona," in *Storia dei pittori italiani dell'Ottocento* (Milan, 1928), pp. 86–91.

Lettere dei Macchiaioli, ed. L. Vitali (Turin, 1953).

D. Durbé, *I Macchiaioli,* exh. cat. (Florence, 1976).

Vittorio Bolaffio

(1883–1931)

Vittorio Bolaffio was born in the former Jewish quarter of Gorizia, the son of a successful wine wholesaler. He studied with Giovanni Fattori at the Accademia di Belle Arti in Florence and traveled to Paris, where he met Amedeo Modigliani and was influenced by the work of the postimpressionists. In 1912 he sailed for the Orient, working as a stoker for the Lloyd's line. It was there that he began to sketch his characteristic scenes of the lower classes, port scenes, and workers. Upon his return to Italy in 1913, he settled in Trieste. He served in the Austrian armed forces (1914–1918) during World War I. His early work was influenced by Fattori and certain social themes characteristic of the divisionist painter Pelizza da Volpedo. He was also an accomplished portraitist, painting members of his family and other members of the Jewish community.

After the war he led an isolated existence, limiting his social contacts to the circle of artists and writers of the Caffè Garibaldi. He became a close friend of the poet Umberto Saba, whose poems *La brama* and *Canzoniere* were inspired by the figure of the shy, withdrawn painter. The poet in turn was immortalized in Bolaffio's best-known painting, *Ritratto di Umberto Saba* (c. 1924). Much of his mature work was devoted to the bustling activities of the port of Trieste, often depicted in triptych formats with allegorical overtones. His refined chromatic sense, the subtle play of colors, and rhythmic use of line betray his artistic origins in the central European culture of Trieste.

FM

Selected Exhibitions

Esposizione del Sindacato delle Belle Arti e del Circolo Artistico di Trieste, 1927, 1928.

"Mostra d'arte d'avanguardia," Padiglione Municipale, Trieste, 1931.

Biennale Internazionale d'Arte, Venice, 1948.

"Vittorio Bolaffio, 1883–1931," Palazzo Attems, Gorizia, 1975.

Selected Bibliography

U. Saba, "Io sono alla retroguardia," *Corriere della Sera,* 3 October 1946.

S. Benco, "Vittorio Bolaffio," in *XXIV Biennale di Venezia,* exh. cat. (1948), pp. 50–51.

Vittorio Bolaffio, 1883–1931, exh. cat. (Gorizia, 1975).

Corrado Cagli

(1910–1976)

Corrado Cagli was born in Ancona; in 1915 his family moved to Rome. Largely self-taught, he began to paint murals at the age of seventeen. In 1929–1930 he worked as the artistic director of a ceramics factory in Umbertide in Umbria. In 1933 Cagli exhibited with Giuseppe Capogrossi and Emanuele Cavalli at the Galleria del Milione, Milan, as the Gruppo dei Nuovi Pittori Romani (Group of New Roman Painters). Later that year they exhibited at the Galerie Bonjean, Paris, and were dubbed the "Ecole de Rome" by the critic Waldemar George. Soon after, the group dissolved over logistical problems and ideological differences, such as Cagli's desire to pursue his interest in large-scale didactic painting.

Cagli was a regular contributor to the magazine of Rationalist aesthetics, *Quadrante,* directed by his uncle the writer Massimo Bontempelli and Pier Maria Bardi. There he expounded his personal interpretation of the *primordio* (origins): painting based on pure formal relationships of tone and mythic subject matter. Cagli was the charismatic central figure of a group of young artists (Afro and Mirko Basaldella, Alberto Ziveri, Pericle Fazzini, and Renato Guttuso) who gravitated around the Galleria Sabatello in Rome.

With his interest in historical and allegorical subjects, Cagli enjoyed numerous public commissions, including the decoration of the entrance rotunda of the II Quadriennale in Rome. In 1936 he painted the monumental *Battaglia di San Martino* for the VI Milan Triennale and became a leading protagonist in the mural painting movement begun by the artists of the Novecento.

Between 1935 and 1938 he was associated with the activities of the Galleria della Cometa, which opened with a show of his drawings. In 1937 Cagli and the gallery were the focus of anti-Semitic, antimodernist attacks by the critic Giuseppe Pensabene. The same year Cagli was chosen to decorate the Italian pavilion at the Universal Exhibition in Paris; the large cycle on the history of Rome and great Italians was ordered destroyed by Galeazzo Ciano, minister of foreign affairs, but Cagli managed to salvage the completed panels. With the Racial Laws of 1938 he took refuge in Paris and then in New York. He became an American citizen, enrolled in the armed forces in 1941, and participated in the liberation of Buchenwald in 1944. He returned to New York and in 1948 designed the sets and costumes for Balanchine's *Triumph of Bacchus and Ariadne,* with music by Vittorio Rieti. He moved back to Rome in 1948.

In the postwar period Cagli experimented with a variety of styles, including abstraction, and continued his involvement with stage and costume design. In 1973 he completed a commemorative sculpture in Göttingen West Germany, on the site of the town's synagogue, which was destroyed on Kristallnacht. He died in Rome.

FM

Selected Exhibitions

"Corrado Cagli e Adriana Pincherle," Galleria di Roma, Rome, 1932.

Quadriennale d'Arte Nazionale, Rome, 1935.

Galleria della Cometa, Rome, 1937.

Julien Levy, New York, 1941.

Galleria del Secolo, Rome, 1950.

Biennale Internazionale d'Arte, Venice, 1965.

Selected Bibliography

E. Crispolti, *Il Cagli romano,* exh. cat. (Siena, 1985).

H. Wurm and C. Benincasa, *Corrado Cagli: La notte dei cristalli* (Rome, 1975).

Cagli: La Battaglia di S. Martino, exh. cat. (Florence, 1979).

E. Crispolti, *I percorsi di Cagli,* exh. cat. (Naples, 1982).

Aldo Carpi

(1886–1973)

Aldo Carpi was born in Milan, where he studied at the Liceo Classico and frequented the studio of Stefano Bersani. In 1906 he attended the Brera Academy. In 1912 he won a national prize for his painting *Il battesimo* (The Baptism), which was part of a mystical-religious series of works marked by a chromatic lyricism. During World War I Carpi fought on the Albanian front, where he participated in the tragic retreat of the Serbian forces. This experience inspired a series of drawings, collected in the volume *Serbia eroica* (1917). He then concentrated on self-portraits. He had individual exhibitions in 1920 and 1926 with Lino Pesaro, a Jewish dealer who played a central role in the Milanese art world. Through Pesaro he came into contact with the critic Margherita Sarfatti and the Novecento. He participated in the first Novecento exhibition of 1926 and in a few of the group's exhibitions abroad but for the most part was not aligned with Sarfatti's critical platform. In the 1920s Carpi concentrated on his Maschere (Masquerade) cycle, paintings of Pierrot and Harlequin tinged with surrealism and melancholy. Beginning in the late 1920s, he created large public works, including windows for the Milan Cathedral, works for the Vatican, and mosaics for the basilica of Nazareth. In 1944 he was arrested and sent to the camp at Mauthausen, and then to Gusen, where he kept a diary of letters and drawings. After the war he resumed his teaching position at the Brera Academy. In the 1950s he painted his Carabinieri (Police) series, which reflected the horror of his arrest and persecution. He died in Milan.

FM

Selected Exhibitions

"Aldo Carpi," Galleria Pesaro, Milan, 1920.

"Fiorentina primaverile," Parco di S. Gallo, Florence, 1922.

Biennale Internazionale d'Arte, Venice, 1932.

"Aldo Carpi," Rotonda della Besana, Milan, 1972 (organized by M. De Micheli).

Selected Bibliography

A. Bucci, *Aldo Carpi,* exh. cat. (Milan, 1921), pp. 29–30.

A. Sassu, "Visite ad artisti: Carpi," in *L'Italia letteraria* (Milan), 12 February 1928.

M. De Micheli, *Aldo Carpi* (Milan, 1963).

P. Carpi, ed., *Aldo Carpi: Diario di Gusen Lettere a Maria* (Milan, 1971).

Mario Cavaglieri

(1887–1969)

Mario Cavaglieri was born in the former Jewish quarter of Rovigo. From 1900 to 1917 he lived in Padua, making brief visits to Rome, Bologna, and Verona, where he painted small-scale views. Between 1900 and 1907 he studied first with the painter Giovanni Vianello and then in Venice with Cesare Laurenti. There he came into contact with the lively artistic circle around the Ca' Pesaro; the painter Ugo Valeri, brother of the poet Diego, was a particular influence on Cavaglieri.

In 1911 Cavaglieri went to Paris, where he became interested in the painting of Edouard Vuillard and Henri Matisse. By 1914, after a period during which he absorbed many influences (from old Venetian painting to post-impressionism, from Giovanni Boldini to the Spanish "naturalism" of Ignacio Zuloaga), he found his own style of exuberant brushwork and brilliant colors. He specialized in interiors of a highly refined sensibility, brimming with luxurious objects and art (which perhaps unwittingly hid a fear of the frailty of the human condition). He coarsely applied the paint directly on the canvas, so that the pigments retained an intense luminosity—an effect that was further heightened by the strong gestural quality of the brush strokes. In 1919 the critic Roberto Longhi saw Cavaglieri's one-man exhibition at the Casa d'Arte Cagiati in Rome, bought his painting *Sala di campagna* (Florence, Longhi Foundation), and wrote an article on the artist's work for the newspaper *Il Tempo.*

In 1921 Cavaglieri married Giulietta Catellini, a member of a noble family from Ferrara. They moved to Piacenza, where they stayed until 1924; the following year they moved to Auch, France. During this period he was often visited by

Filippo de Pisis, and the two artists painted together in the countryside. He worked prodigiously between 1929 and 1939, when the outbreak of war forced him to return to Italy until 1946. He then returned to France, where he died in 1969.

FM

Selected Exhibitions

Esposizione Internazionale di Belle Arti, Società Amatori e Cultori, Rome, 1907.

Esposizione Internazionale, Rome, 1911.

Ca' Pesaro, Venice, 1912.

Kunstverein, Munich, 1913.

Terza Esposizione Internazionale d'Arte della "Secessione," Rome, 1915.

Mostra d'Arte Italiana, Zurich, 1919.

Casa d'Arte Cagiati, Rome, 1919.

Galleria Caminati, Milan, 1923.

Esposizione Internazionale d'Arte Italiana, Budapest, 1936.

Galleria d'Arte "La Strozzina," Florence, 1953.

"Arte moderna in Italia, 1915–1935," Palazzo Strozzi, Florence.

Musée des Augustins, Toulouse, 1974.

Selected Bibliography

R. Longhi, "Cavaglieri," *Il Tempo* (Rome), 28 May 1919.

Mario Cavaglieri, 1887–1969, exh. cat., ed. G. Perrocco et al. (Florence, 1978).

Mario Cavaglieri, exh. cat., ed. G. Sangiorgi et al. (Rome, 1980).

Vittorio Matteo Corcos

(1859–1933)

Vittorio Matteo Corcos was born in Livorno to a family of modest means. He studied drawing and painting with Enrico Pollastrini at the Accademia di Belle Arti in Florence, and from 1878 to 1879 he trained under Domenico Morelli in Naples. In Paris from 1880 to 1886 he studied with Léon Bonnat and painted under contract with the dealer Goupil. Corcos was highly successful with his delicate female portraits and sporting and society scenes. He also illustrated French and English magazines, book covers, and posters. Through Edmond de Goncourt he was introduced to a circle of writers and painters, among them Émile Zola, Gustave Flaubert, Giuseppe de Nittis, and the impressionists.

Returning to Italy for military service, Corcos settled in Florence in 1886, where he painted the leading cultural figures of his time such as Giosuè Carducci (1892), Pietro Mascagni (1895), and Yorik (Pietro Ferragni; 1889). At the same time he continued to travel to Paris and London for portrait commissions. He wrote for the Florentine journal *Il Marzocco,* which also published his collection of short stories, *Mademoiselle Leprince* (1901), and was close to the writers Gabriele D'Annunzio, Giovanni Pascoli, and Renato Fucini. In 1904 Corcos went to Potsdam, Germany, for two years, where he painted the Emperor William II and numerous German society figures; he also painted royalty in Portugal and Italy.

Corcos's son, also a painter, was killed in World War I. In the 1920s he participated in the Gruppo Labronico, a cultural organization in Livorno that included Plinio Nomellini and Ulvi Liegi among its members. He continued to receive commissions, including a portrait of Mussolini in 1928. Corcos divided his time between his villa in Castiglioncello, built for him by a wealthy patron, and Florence, where he died in 1933.

FM

Selected Exhibitions

Prima Esposizione di Belle Arti, Livorno, 1886.

Esposizione Annuale della Società delle Belle Arti, Florence 1891.

"Festa dell'Arte e dei Fiori," Florence, 1896–1897.

Selected Bibliography

A. De Gubernatis, *Artisti italiani viventi* (Florence, 1889), pp. 140–141.

U. Ojetti, "Vittorio Corcos," in *Illustrazione Italiana,* vol. 1 (1907), pp . 377–380.

Vittorio Corcos, exh. cat., ed. D. Durbé (Livorno, 1965).

Isidoro Grünhut

(1862–1896)

Born in Trieste, Isidoro Grünhut demonstrated artistic talent at a very young age and left home at sixteen to pursue his vocation. He earned his livelihood as a caricaturist and portraitist, traveling throughout Italy. In 1880 he enrolled in the Accademia in Venice. From 1882 to 1886 he studied at the Munich Academy, along with Umberto Veruda and Carlo Wostry, and the three artists established a studio together. Grünhut's early style was inspired by seventeenth-century Italian painting and by Wilhelm Leibl; this was modified by his studies of the loose and luminous brushwork of Lovis Corinth and Max Slevogt. In 1886 he returned to Trieste, where he became active in artistic and bohemian circles, executing many portraits and caricatures. That same year he won the Rittmeyer competition, along with Wostry and

Veruda, but the prize itself went to Wostry. With the help of a patron he moved to Rome, where he stayed from 1887 to 1888, painting portraits. He then moved to Florence; during this phase his painting reached its full expressive maturity, free from all academic style and characterized by broad, free brush strokes. In 1891 he moved to Mantua and in the following year spent time in both Trieste and Rome. Although he was gravely ill during this period, he developed a romantic, exuberant style similar to that of Antonio Mancini, as seen in his final work, *Ritratto di bambino* (Portrait of a Young Boy, 1895), now in the Civico Museo Revoltella, Trieste. He died in Florence.

FM

Selected Exhibitions

Kunstverein, Munich, 1883.

Concorso Rittmeyer, Trieste, 1886.

Esposizione Annuale della Società delle Belle Arti, Florence, 1890–1891.

Triennale di Brera, Milan, 1891.

Selected Bibliography

A. De Gubernatis, *Dizionario degli artisti viventi* (Florence, 1892), pp. 241–242.

C. Wostry, *Storia del Circolo Artistico di Trieste* (Udine, 1934), pp. 61–92.

R. Da Nova, "Isidoro Grünhut," in *Arte nel Friuli-Venezia Giulia, 1900–1950,* exh. cat. (Trieste, 1981), pp. 16–17.

Carlo Levi

(1902–1975)

Carlo Levi was born in Turin; his uncle Claudio Treves was a dominant figure in the Italian Socialist party. Around 1922 he became friendly with the political activist Piero Gobetti, who invited him to collaborate on his journal *Rivoluzione Liberale*; Gobetti wrote the first review of Levi's painting in *Ordine Nuovo* in 1923. Through Gobetti, he began to study under Felice Casorati, whose salon was the focal point for the younger avant-garde in Turin. Levi's early work consisted mainly of family portraits, such as *Arcadia* (1923) and *Il fratello e la sorella* (Brother and Sister, 1925), which reflect the influence of Casorati as well as his awareness of German Neue Sachlichkeit (New Objectivity) painting. During this period Levi was an active participant in the vibrant cultural life of Turin and also earned a degree in medicine.

Levi traveled to Paris for the first time in 1923 and maintained a studio there from 1925 to 1927. Around 1927 his work underwent the first of several stylistic changes, influenced at first by the Fauves and the School of Paris and, in 1929–1930, by Modigliani. In 1929 he formed the Sei di Torino (Turin Six) group along with Gigi Chessa, Nicola Galante, Francesco Menzio, Enrico Paulucci, and Jessie Boswell, who were supported by the critics Lionello Venturi and Edoardo Persico. They exhibited regularly until 1931 in Milan, Genoa, Rome, London, and Paris. In 1930 Levi developed a dramatic expressionist painting style, as exemplified by *L'eroe cinese* (The Chinese Hero), which would continue to characterize his portraits and landscapes in the following decade.

In 1931 he joined the anti-Fascist movement Giustizia e Libertà, founded three years earlier by Carlo Rosselli. In March 1934 he was arrested for suspected anti-Fascist activities. After his second arrest in 1935, Levi was sent into political exile in Lucania. His nine months among the southern peasants inspired *Cristo si è fermato a Eboli* (Christ Stopped at Eboli, 1945), his most famous literary work. Several paintings from the period of confinement were included in his solo exhibition at the Galleria del Milione in Milan in 1936.

Levi traveled to New York in 1937 and fled Italy after the enactment of the Racial Laws. He lived in Paris from 1939 to 1941. He then returned to Italy and participated in the Resistance. In 1947 he moved to Rome and began painting in a more realistic mode with existential overtones. Much of his subject matter reflected his involvement in the socioeconomic problems of the *mezzogiorno,* or the Italian south.

Levi's painting underwent further changes in the 1960s, and his work became more poetic and universal (as seen in the *Carrubo* series of the following decade), provoking renewed interest on the part of the public and critics both in Italy and abroad. He was elected senator in 1963 and again in 1968. Levi published numerous political and literary works, including *Paura della pittura* (1942), *L'orologio* (1950), and *Le parole sono pietre* (1955).

FM

Selected Exhibitions

Galerie-Librairie Jeune Europe, Paris, 1931 (cat. essay by A. Aniante).

Galleria della Cometa, Rome, 1937 (cat. essay by S. Solmi).

Cometa Art Gallery, New York, 1938.

Biennale Internazionale d'Arte, Venice, 1954.

Selected Bibliography

C. L. Ragghianti, *Carlo Levi* (Florence, 1948) (with a previously unpublished essay by Levi, "Paura di volare," 1942).

Archivio Centrale dello Stato, *Carlo Levi disegni dal carcere 1934: Materiale per una storia,* exh. cat. (Rome, 1983).

Carlo Levi: Opere dal 1923 al 1973, exh. cat. (Perugia, 1988).

Ulvi Liegi (Luigi Mosè Levi)

(1858–1939)

Ulvi Liegi was born in Livorno to a wealthy banking family. He studied painting with Adolfo Tommasi, Carlo Markò, and then with Giuseppe Ciaranfi at the Accademia di Belle Arti in Florence. He developed a close friendship with the Macchiaiolo painter Telemaco Signorini, who encouraged him to paint *all'aperto* and influenced the atmospheric effects of his early work. Liegi's knowledge of contemporary French currents was already apparent in works such as *Lo studio del pittore* (The Studio of the Painter, 1885).

After establishing his reputation in Tuscany, he traveled in 1886 to Paris, where he met Claude Monet, Edgar Degas, and Alfred Sisley and became friendly with Maurice Utrillo. He also went to London, where he became acquainted with James McNeill Whistler and the pre-Raphaelite circle. His work of the 1890s, beginning with *La modellina* (The Young Model, 1889), reveals his direct contact with postimpressionism. In the following decades he applied this style to an interpretation of the Tuscan landscape and, along with Oscar Ghiglia, bridged the generations of the Macchiaioli and the twentieth-century avant-garde.

After 1895 he moved to Florence, where he became friendly with Giovanni Fattori and joined the circle of artists and writers of the Caffè Michelangiolo. In 1906 he spent nearly a year in Val Sugana, where he painted with John Singer Sargent. In 1920 he was elected president for life of the Gruppo Labronico, which promoted Livornese art through exhibitions and cultural activities. Later he helped organize a museum of Jewish art in the Livorno synagogue. Liegi's comfortable economic situation allowed him to acquire a fine collection of Macchiaioli paintings, especially works by Fattori. In 1932 he received a gold medal for his artistic achievement and cultural activities from the province of Livorno, where he spent the final years of his life.

FM

Selected Exhibitions

Esposizione Solenne della Società d'Incoraggiamento delle Belle Arti, Florence, 1882.

Prima Esposizione di Belle Arti, Livorno, 1886.

Slade School of Art, London, 1889.

"Mostre personali Luigi Levi, Benvenuto Benvenuti, R. D. M. Ferenzona," Bottega d'Arte, Livorno, 1923.

Esposizione del Gruppo Labronico, Galleria Pesaro, Milan, 1924.

Biennale Internazionale d'Arte, Venice, 1934.

"Ulvi Liegi," Galleria Apollo, Rome, 1937 (cat. essay by M. Biancale).

Selected Bibliography

R. Franchi, "Ulvi Liegi," in *Illustrazione Toscana* (Florence, 1930).

P. Caprile, *Ulvi Liegi,* exh. cat. (Livorno, 1958).

G. Matteucci, *Ulvi Liegi* (Florence, 1970), with an essay by M. Borgiotti.

Antonietta Raphaël Mafai

(c. 1895–1975)

Antonietta Raphaël Mafai was born in Kovno, Lithuania. Following the death of her father, a rabbi, she moved with her mother to London. She received her diploma in piano from the Royal Academy, and began to pursue a career in music. Later she developed an interest in drawing and spent the winter of 1919 in Paris. Raphaël arrived in Rome in 1924, and the following year she enrolled in the Scuola Libera del Nudo, where she met Scipione (Gino Bonichi) and Mario Mafai. She and Mafai soon found living quarters together in a studio on the via Cavour, near the Colosseum, which became the center of a lively bohemian circle.

In 1929 she exhibited in the First Fascist Syndicate Exhibition of Lazio. The expressionist quality of her work received favorable comments from the critic Roberto Longhi, who first referred to Raphaël and Mafai as the "school of the via Cavour." This term was soon extended to include Scipione and Renato Marino Mazzacurati. In 1930 Raphaël and Mafai went to Paris, where she remained for almost four years, traveling intermittently to London and Rome. It was in Paris that she began to study sculpture. While in London between 1931 and 1932, she was in contact with Jacob Epstein. Upon her return to Rome, she began her first major sculptural piece, *La fuga da Sodoma* (The Flight from Sodom), which reflected the influences of Aristide Maillol, Antoine Bourdelle, and Auguste Rodin.

In 1939, with the onslaught of racial persecution, Raphaël, Mafai, and their three daughters sought refuge in Genoa with the help of the collectors Alberto della Ragione and Emilio Jesi. She lived in Rome from 1943 to 1945, then moved to Genoa, returning to the Italian capital only in 1952. As Raphaël rarely exhibited during the Fascist period, her role in bringing the style of the School of Paris to Rome in the 1920s and her influence on the Scuola romana were recognized only after World War II, in particular, with the exhibition "La Scuola romana dal 1930 al 1945," organized as part of the VIII Quadriennale in Rome in 1959–1960. During the 1960s she made bronze castings of her most important works and later took up lithography. She died in Rome.

FM

Selected Exhibitions

I Mostra del Sindacato Laziale Fascista, Rome, 1929.

Mostra del Sindacato Fascista Belle Arti del Lazio, Rome, 1937, 1938.

"Raphaël Mafai," Galleria dello Zodiaco, Rome, 1952.

Biennale Internazionale d'Arte, Venice, 1948, 1950, 1952, 1954.

Quadriennale d'Arte Nazionale, Rome, 1951, 1959, 1965, 1972.

"Raphaël," Galleria Narciso, Turin, 1960.

"Raphaël," Centro Culturale Olivetti, Ivrea, 1960.

Selected Bibliography

V. Martinelli, *Antonietta Raphaël* (Rome, 1960).

A. Mezio, *Raphaël,* exh. cat. (Ivrea, 1960).

M. Pinottini, *Scultura di Raphaël* (Milan, 1971).

M. Fagiolo dell' Arco and E. Coen, *Raphaël: Scultura lingua viva* (Rome, 1978).

F. D'Amico, *Antonietta Raphaël. Sculture,* exh. cat. (Rome-Milan, 1985).

Roberto Melli

(1885–1958)

Roberto Melli was born in Ferrara; during his teens he frequented the studios of Nicola Laurenti and the sculptor Arrigo Minerbi. In 1902 he moved to Genoa and created his first sculptures, which were influenced by Medardo Rosso.

In 1911 he settled in Rome, with his wife and frequent model, Anna Meotti. He became an important figure in the capital, developing an innovative style of modeling and organizing a group of young artists known as the Gruppo Moderno Romano. They participated in the Rome Secession exhibition of 1914. Shortly thereafter he gave up sculpture to concentrate on painting, convinced that this was the medium best suited to modern artistic expression. In 1918 he founded the journal *Valori Plastici* with the critic Mario Broglio, participating in exhibitions organized under its auspices in Germany (1921) and in the "Fiorentina primaverile" (1922).

Melli underwent an artistic crisis in the mid-1920s, during which time he worked as an illustrator and poster designer and experimented with set design. His earlier paintings, such as *Interno* (Interior, 1919), contributed to the general climate of "return to order" in the postwar period in Rome. They also anticipated the style of *pittura tonale* (tonal painting), which Melli further developed later in the mid-1930s with the younger painters Giuseppe Capogrossi and Emanuele Cavalli. They outlined the theory of tonalism in the *Manifesto del primordialismo plastico* (Manifesto of Plastic Primordialism). Melli began to exhibit again in 1932. Associated with the artists of the Scuola romana, he was also active as an art critic and published numerous articles in *Quadrivio* and *Il Tevere* before they became anti-Semitic journals under the direction of Telesio Interlandi.

With the enactment of the Racial Laws in 1938, Melli was forced into hiding. During this period Giuseppe Bottai, minister of national education, secretly acquired some of his works. After the war Melli began to teach painting at the Accademia di Belle Arti in Rome and founded the Istituto di Solidarietà Artistica, an artists' rights organization. In 1957 he published a collection of poetry, *Lunga favolosa notte.* He died in Rome the following year.

FM

Selected Exhibitions

"Fiorentina primaverile," Parco di S. Gallo, Florence, 1922.

Galleria della Cometa, Rome, 1936.

Galleria del Secolo, Rome, 1947.

Biennale Internazionale d'Arte, Venice, 1950, 1954.

Galleria Nazionale d'Arte Moderna, Rome, 1958.

Palazzo dei Diamanti, Ferrara, 1975.

Selected Bibliography

L. De Libero, *Pitture di Roberto Melli,* exh. cat. (Rome, 1936).

M. Calvesi, *Roberto Melli* (Rome, 1954), preface by C. G. Argan.

P. Bucarelli and N. Ponente, *Roberto Melli,* exh. cat. (Rome, 1958).

R. Bossaglia, *Roberto Melli,* exh. cat. (Ferrara, 1975).

F. R. Morelli, "Roberto Melli," in *Le pagine di pietra,* ed. A. Masi (Marino [Rome], 1987).

Amedeo Modigliani

(1884–1920)

Amedeo Modigliani was born in Livorno. His brother Giuseppe Emanuele became a prominent Socialist and member of Parliament. From 1890 to 1898 he studied philosophy and classical literature. After being stricken with typhus and pleurisy, he left school to study with the landscape painter Guglielmo Micheli, a follower of the Macchiaioli master Giovanni Fattori. In the winter of 1901 his health declined further, and he traveled with his mother to the south to convalesce, subsequently touring Rome, Florence, and Venice. In 1902 he enrolled at the Scuola Libera del Nudo in Florence and continued his studies the following year in Venice.

In 1906 Modigliani moved to Montmartre and became friendly with Pablo Picasso, Max Jacob, André Salmon, Maurice Utrillo, and Gino Severini. The following year he met Dr. Paul Alexandre, who became his first patron, encouraging him to exhibit in the Salon des Indépendents of 1908. In 1909 he moved to Montparnasse and was introduced to Constantin Brancusi, who inspired him to begin sculpting in stone. Modigliani devoted himself to sculpture until 1913. Although the dealer Paul Guillaume began to purchase his works in 1914 and the Polish poet Leopold Zborowski became his dealer two years later, his economic situation remained precarious.

In 1917 Modigliani began a series of paintings of nudes that caused a scandal in his first one man show at the Galerie Berthe Weill. In April of that year he met Jeanne Hébuterne, whom he married in the fall. With Modigliani's ill health aggravated by drug and alcohol abuse and Hébuterne's pregnancy, friends and family collected funds to send them to the Côte d'Azur, where he painted his four known landscapes. In November their daughter, Jeanne, was born in Nice. In May 1919, Modigliani returned to Paris, where he continued to paint portraits of his family and a close circle of friends; he also executed his only self-portrait. He died in January 1920; Hébuterne committed suicide immediately afterward.

FM

Selected Exhibitions

Salon des Indépendents, Paris, 1908, 1910, 1911.

Salon d'Automne, Paris, 1912.

Lyre et Palette, Paris, 1915.

Galerie Berthe Weill, Paris, 1917.

Galerie Bernheim-Jeune, Paris, 1922.

Galerie Bing, Paris, 1925.

Biennale Internazionale d'Arte, Venice, 1930.

Palais des Beaux-Arts, Brussels, 1933.

Museum of Modern Art, New York, 1951.

Palazzo Reale, Milan, 1958.

Galleria Nazionale d'Arte Moderna, Rome, 1959.

Tate Gallery, London, 1963.

Perls Galleries, New York, 1963, 1966.

Acquavella Galleries, New York, 1971.

Daimuru, Tokyo, Osaka, 1979.

Musée d'Art Moderne de la Ville de Paris, Paris, 1981.

Centro Cultural de la Caixa de Pensions, Barcelona, 1983.

National Gallery of Art, Washington, D.C. 1984.

Selected Bibliography

A. Ceroni and F. Cachin, *Tout l'oeuvre peint de Modigliani,* (Paris, 1972).

Amedeo Modigliani, 1884–1920, exh. cat. (Paris, 1981).

O. Patani, ed., *Modigliani dipinti e disegni, incontri italiani 1900–1920,* exh. cat. (Milan, 1984).

K. Silver and R. Golan, *The Circle of Montparnasse: Jewish Artists in Paris, 1905–1945,* exh. cat. (New York, 1985).

Paola Levi Montalcini

(b. 1909)

Paola Levi Montalcini was born in Turin into a cultured Jewish family; her twin sister, Rita, studied medicine (winning the Nobel Prize in 1986) and her brother Gino became an engineer and architect. In the late 1920s she studied under Felice Casorati. She first received critical attention in 1934 at the Primo Raduno d'Arte Contemporanea (First Assembly of Contemporary Art; Galleria Arbiter, Catania), followed by the II Quadriennale in 1935. In 1939 Giorgio de Chirico wrote the first monograph on Levi Montalcini, noting her preferences for solid construction, large surfaces (she also worked in fresco painting), and the tendency to draw attention to the fantastic aspect of reality.

During the postwar period, after experimenting with an abstract-concrete style, she studied engraving with Stanley William Hayter, who introduced her to the surrealist aesthetics of automatic writing and gestural abstraction. Later, in a third phase of artistic activity, she produced luminous and kinetic sculpture related to her investigation of scientific principles. She has lived in Rome since the 1970s, and her studies have been directed toward the use of language and its expressive implications. This includes fragments of written scripts, composed and transformed according to the rhythmic intervals of intersecting spirals and spatial trajectories. Graphics form an important part of her artistic production.

FM

Selected Exhibitions

Prima Quadriennale d'Arte Nazionale, Rome, 1931.

Premio Modena, Modena, 1947.

Biennale Internazionale d'Arte. Venice, 1950.

"Paola Levi Montalcini et Filippo Scroppo," Musée d'Art et d'Histoire, Neuchâtel, 1962.

"Paola Levi Montalcini," Calcografia Nazionale, Rome, 1980.

Selected Bibliography

G. de Chirico, *Paola Levi Montalcini* (Turin, 1939).

G. Dorfles, *Paola Levi Montalcini* (Turin, 1962).

Turin, Foyer del Piccolo Regio *Paola Levi Montalcini,* exh. cat. (Rome, 1981).

Arturo Nathan

(1891–1944)

Arturo Nathan was born in Trieste. His father's family was from Bombay, and his mother came from a prominent Jewish family in Trieste. He moved to London in 1911. A British citizen, he completed military service there and then departed for Genoa, where he studied philosophy. Nathan returned to Trieste following the war in 1918 and worked for an insurance company. A self-taught artist, he began to draw while undergoing psychoanalysis with Edoardo Weiss, a disciple of Freud. He subsequently attended informal drawing classes at the Circolo Artistico. He was close to Carlo Sbisà, Linuccia Saba, Boby Bazlen, and Leonor Fini.

Most of Nathan's highly refined images were self-portraits, conceived as mystical or surreal, oneiric visions. In 1925 he traveled to Rome to meet Giorgio de Chirico. From this time on, his painting was characterized by elements of metaphysical painting: desolate landscapes, often devoid of human presence, filled with fragments of classical statues. The main subject of his art was his intimate psychological life, represented by a repertory of idiosyncratic symbols often set within the port or surrounding landscape of Trieste. Later Nathan began to study painting of the past (Claude Lorrain, J. M. W. Turner, the German romantics), and he learned to prepare his own paints, applying multiple layers on wood panels to achieve a heightened luminosity.

From 1940 to 1943 Nathan was interned in the Marches. In September of 1943 he was arrested in Trieste and sent to the concentration camp in Carpi. From there he was deported to Bergen-Belsen, where he was gravely injured in hard labor. He was transferred to Biberach and found dying when the Allies liberated the camp in 1944. Nathan was the subject of a commemorative retrospective at the Venice Biennale of 1948.

FM

Selected Exhibitions

Esposizione Biennale Internazionale d'Arte, Venice, 1924–1934.

"Arturo Nathan," Galleria Milano, 1929 (cat. essay by S. Benco).

Quadriennale d'Arte Nazionale, Rome, 1931, 1935.

Esposizione Internazionale d'Arte, Barcelona, 1929.

Jahresausstellung moderne italienische Kunst, Vienna, 1933.

"Arturo Nathan," Civico Museo Revoltella, Trieste, 1976.

Selected Bibliography

J. Girmounsky, *Arturo Nathan* (Paris, 1935).

G. de Chirico, "Arturo Nathan pittore e poeta," *Domenica* (Rome), 3 June 1945.

U. Apollonio, *Arturo Nathan,* exh. cat. (Venice, 1948), pp. 36–37.

Gino Parin

(1876–1944)

Gino Parin was born in Trieste. He began his artistic training under the painter Eugenio Scomparini. He then studied with Gerolamo Navarra in Venice and took courses with Karl Raupp at the Munich Academy. He was enthralled by the cultural climate of Munich and became interested in the realism of Franz von Lenbach and the secession style of Franz von Stuck. He was also familiar with the symbolism of Fernand Khnopff, the pre-Raphaelite movement, and Aubrey Beardsley; these influences were evident primarily in his graphic work. He became a member of and active participant in the Münchner Künstler Genossenschaft.

Upon his return to Trieste following the outbreak of World War I, he began to teach painting. His portraits and landscapes continued to reflect the influence of the Munich Academy. During the 1920s he was extremely active, exhibiting in important Italian shows abroad and maintaining close ties with Germany. He concentrated on portraiture, in particular portraits of women in interiors. The 1938 Racial Laws prohibited him from exhibiting, and although he had obtained Swiss citizenship, he was deported to Germany in 1944. He became ill during the voyage and died shortly after arriving at Bergen-Belsen.

FM

Selected Exhibitions

Hagenbund, Vienna, 1904.

Glaspalast, Munich, 1913 (gold medal), 1919.

La Quadriennale, Turin, 1923.

Biennale Romana, Rome, 1923, 1925.

Prima Esposizione Fiumana Internazionale di Belle Arti, Fiume, 1925.

Biennale Internazionale d'Arte, Venice, 1928.

Esposizione d'Arte Triveneta, Padua, 1929.

Esposizione Internazionale d'Arte, Barcelona, 1929.

Selected Bibliography

R. da Nova, "Gino Parin," in *Arte nel Friuli-Venezia Giulia, 1900–1950,* exh. cat. (Trieste, 1981), pp. 28–29, 314–315.

Adriana Pincherle

(b. 1906)

Pincherle was born in Rome to an upper-class family; her father was a Jewish engineer of Venetian origins, and her Catholic mother claimed noble descent. Pincherle was particularly close to her brother, the novelist Alberto Moravia.

After completing her secondary schooling, Pincherle studied at the Accademia di Francia and the Scuola Libera del Nudo. In 1932 she had her first major exhibition with Corrado Cagli at the Galleria d'Arte di Roma. Her paintings drew the keen interest of Roberto Longhi, who likened them to "plasticine forms soaked in violent colors." Her early works, such as *Autoritratto* (Self-Portrait), looked to Modigliani and the artists of the Scuola romana, notably Scipione (Gino Bonichi) and Antonietta Raphaël Mafai. Pincherle and Moravia participated in the intellectual milieu of the Caffè Rosati in the Piazza del Popolo, along with Massimo Bontempelli, Libero De Libero, Tomaso Landolfi, G. B. Angioletti, and others. In 1933 Pincherle made her first trip to Paris, accompanied by her cousin Carlo Rosselli. She studied the works of Pierre-Auguste Renoir and Henri Matisse and subsequently developed a new freedom of brushwork and coloristic vivacity.

At the end of the 1930s Pincherle was arrested for reasons related to her friendship with the anti-Fascist Mario Levi (brother of the writer Natalia Ginzburg) but was immediately released. In 1941 she married the painter Onofrio Martinelli in Rome and settled in Florence. Because of the Racial Laws, she and Martinelli fled to Bernard Berenson's Tuscan villa for protection (Berenson, a Jew, had taken refuge in the Vatican). At the end of 1943 they went into hiding in the cellars of the Palazzo Strozzi in Florence, where they remained until the American forces liberated Tuscany.

In 1950 she settled in Florence and became part of a literary circle that included Carlo Emilio Gadda, Eugenio Montale, and Arturo Loria. She continues to work in a figurative style informed by developments in abstraction and infused with a bold colorism.

FM

Selected Exhibitions

"Exhibition of Contemporary Italian Art," traveling exhibition in the United States, 1935.

"Caterina Castellucci e Adriana Pincherle," Galleria della Cometa, Rome, 1936.

"Renato Guttuso e Adriana Pincherle," Galleria Genova, Genoa, 1940.

Galleria del Vantaggio, Rome, 1955.

Complesso del S. Michele, Rome, 1989.

Selected Bibliography

Adriana Pincherle (Florence, 1987), with an essay by V. Sgarbi and an interview conducted by R. Guerrichio.

Arturo Rietti

(1863–1943)

Arturo Rietti was born in Trieste to a family of financiers. In 1879 he enrolled at the Accademia di Belle Arti in Florence, where he studied with Giovanni Fattori. During this period he became a great admirer of the work of Arnold Böcklin, and he studied painting with Nikolas Gysis and Franz von Defregger in Munich from 1884 to 1886. He was also interested in the work of Max Liebermann and Franz von Lenbach. Returning to Trieste, he lived a reclusive existence; one of his few friends was the young poet Silvio Benco. Rietti traveled to Rome and Milan and again to Germany. His work had a stylistic affinity with the Milanese painters Mosè Bianchi, Paolo Troubetzkoi, and Emilio Gola; he also looked to the portraits of Leonardo for their suggestive quality of chiaroscuro. While in Milan he became devoted to the music of Arrigo Boito and the novels of Tolstoi. In 1889 he went to Paris, where he discovered the work of Eugène Carrière; returning there in 1908, he discovered the more intense colors contrasts of James McNeill Whistler. The year 1890 marked the beginning of his most creative period; he participated in many exhibitions and received official recognition. In 1904 he moved to Milan, where he became well known for his portraits, nearly always executed in pastel. Some of his most famous subjects were Boito, Giacomo Puccini, Arturo Toscanini, Gabriele D'Annunzio, Lino Pesaro, Rabindranath Tagore, and the Princess Trivulzio della Somaglia. He began to travel again, visiting Strasbourg, Budapest, Vienna, and Paris. After the 1920s his painting was embellished by a colorful impasto that imparted an ephemeral quality to his compositions. He died in Padua.

FM

Selected Exhibitions

Universal Exhibition, Paris, 1889.

Biennale Internazionale d'Arte, Venice, 1897, 1910.

Esposizione Universale, Milan, 1906.

"Antonio Mancini, Arturo Rietti," Galleria Pesaro, Milan, 1925.

80° Esposizione Nazionale, Palazzo Pitti, Florence, 1927.

Quadriennale d'Arte Nazionale, Rome, 1931.

Selected Bibliography

U. Ojetti, *L'arte nella esposizione di Milano* (Milan, 1906), p. 43.

R. Giolli, *Antonio Mancini, Arturo Rietti,* exh. cat. (Milan, 1925), pp. 20–44.

S. Benco, "Ricordo del pittore Arturo Rietti," *L'Italia Letteraria* (Rome), 27 June 1946.

L. Borghese, "L'orso dei salotti dipingeva belle donne," *Corriere della Sera,* 21 October 1948.

R. da Nova, "Arturo Rietti," in *Arte nel Friuli-Venezia Giulia, 1900–1950,* exh. cat. (Trieste, 1981), pp. 18–19.

Serafino De Tivoli

(1826–1892)

Serafino De Tivoli was born in Livorno but moved to Florence with his family at the age of twelve. He showed an early interest in art and, with his younger brother Felice, became a student of Carlo Markò. In 1848, during the First War of Independence, he fought as a volunteer with his friend Vito D'Ancona in the battles of Curtatone and Montanara. The following year he participated in the defense of the Roman republic and was taken a prisoner of war. During this period in Rome, he met Domenico Induno, Nino Costa, and Eleuterio Pagliano. He returned in 1854 to Florence, where he formed the so-called Staggia school of painters, who sketched in the countryside around Siena. A cultivated individual who knew several languages, De Tivoli was among the first habitués of the Caffè Michelangiolo in Florence. In 1855 De Tivoli and Saverio Altamura went to Paris (where De Tivoli probably met Domenico Morelli), to visit the Universal Exhibition. He became interested in the Barbizon school of landscape painting and for some time frequented the studios of Constant Troyon, Alexandre-Gabriel Decamps, and Rosa Bonheur. He returned to Florence around 1856, where he imparted the new techniques to his contemporaries, giving rise to the Macchiaioli movement in Italy; indeed he was considered the movement's founding father. De Tivoli's style, however, did not progress beyond this initial innovative stage; indeed, in 1862 Telemaco Signorini, while recognizing the innovative character of De Tivoli's art, pointed out the limitations of his work shown at the Promotrice Fiorentina exhibitions. In 1864 De Tivoli joined his brother in London; from 1873 to 1890 he lived in Paris, where he was close to Giuseppe Palizzi, Giovanni Boldini, Giuseppe de Nittis, and D'Ancona. He worked energetically and also established "La polenta," an art club where Edgar Degas was often present. He returned to Florence, where he again painted the Tuscan countryside; ill and impoverished, he died in Florence in 1892.

FM

Selected Exhibitions

Prima Esposizione Italiana, Florence, 1861.

Esposizione Nazionale di Belle Arti, Turin, 1880.

Prima Esposizione di Belle Arti, Livorno, 1886.

Selected Bibliography

A. De Gubernatis, *Dizionario degli artisti italiani viventi* (Florence, 1889), pp. 179–180.

E. Somarè, *Storia dei pittori italiani dell'Ottocento* (Milan, 1928), pp. 82–85.

Lettere dei Macchiaioli, ed. L. Vitali (Turin, 1953).

I Macchiaioli, ed. D. Durbé (Florence, 1976).

Mario Nunes Vais

(1856–1932)

Mario Nunes Vais was born in Florence to a well-to-do bourgeois family, and following their expectations, he worked as an agent in currency exchange. Members of his social set shared a general interest in the new field of photography, but Nunes Vais was particularly drawn to it through his friendships with many pioneers in the field, and around 1885 he began to dedicate himself to the medium. His early work was limited to images of everyday life, from the most representative public events (popular holidays, demonstrations, trips) to private activities of the Tuscan countryside and Florentine milieu.

In the early years of the twentieth century, Nunes Vais turned to portraiture. Through an increasingly accurate study of light and an increasingly intimate psychological penetration of the sitter, he achieved results that led him to be one of the most sought-after portrait photographers of his time. In 1890 he joined the Italian Photographic Society of Florence, becoming an active member. He sat on various competition juries held in Italy from the turn of the century onward and achieved a position of some authority as one of the great amateur practitioners. He viewed photography exclusively as a hobby, never depending on it for economic support, which liberated him from the obligations of patronage and allowed him to work in complete freedom.

Nunes Vais was involved only marginally with the developing and printing processes, and although he supervised each phase, he entrusted this work to the Alvino laboratory in Florence and later to the Bencini and Sardoni laboratories.

Fig. 192. *Plans for the Tempio Maggiore Israelitica in Reggio Emilia,* Reggio, 1859, Archivio di Stato, Reggio Emilia (cat. no. 95)

He used negatives from national companies, such as Dringoli, La Luminosa, and Cappelli, as well as from the more famous firms of Lumière, Monckoven, and Lomberg. The formats of the negatives ranged from 4.5 × 6 cm to 50 × 65 cm. It was recently discovered that in 1904 Nunes Vais made several images using a three-color process directly on plates sensitized by Alinari, with a photocollogram system (see *Bullettino della Società Fotografica Italiana* [Florence, 1904], p. 141).

His grand plan, to realize a "photographic pantheon" of Italians for the Laurentian Library in Florence, resulted in what can be considered a definitive collection of portraits, with almost sixty thousand negative plates of various sizes. More than thirty thousand of these are now at the Istituto Centrale per il Catalogo e la Documentazione of the Ministero per i Beni Culturali e Ambientali in Rome, thanks to a donation by his daughter, Laura Weil, who wanted to protect the collection from any form of commercialization. The remaining plates were destroyed in the 1966 flood in Florence, with the exception of about one thousand, which were sold to Alinari after Weil's death.

Nunes Vais's remarkable production documents every aspect of art, culture, and public life in Italy between the end of the nineteenth century and the third decade of the twentieth, bearing witness to a solitary commitment that has rarely been matched in the history of Italian photography.

MTC

Selected Exhibitions

Palazzo Vecchio, Sala d'Armi, Florence, 1974.

Istituto Italiano di Cultura, Tel Aviv, 1976.

Palazzo Venezia, Sala Barbo, Rome, 1979.

"Aspetti ed immagini della cultura fotografica in Italia," Venice, 1979; Florence, 1980.

"Mostra del Liberty italiano e ticinese," Villa la Malpensata, Lugano, 1981.

Selected Bibliography

Mario Nunes Vais fotografo, exh. cat. (Florence, 1974).

M. Vannucci and AA.VV., *Mario Nunes Vais, gentiluomo fotografo* (Florence, 1975).

D'Annunzio nel suo tempo (Milan, 1977).

I.C.C.D., Gabinetto Fotografico Nazionale, *Gli italiani nelle fotografie di Mario Nunes Vais,* exh. cat. (Rome, 1978).

M. T. Contini, *I fiorentini di Nunes Vais* (Rome, 1978).

I. Zannier, *70 anni di fotografia in Italia* (Modena, 1978), p. 21.

M. T. Contini, "Mario Nunes Vais," in *Fotografia pittorica 1889/1911* (1979), p. 58.

G L O S S A R Y

Amulet—an object believed to serve a protective function. The efficacy of Jewish amulets is considered to depend on their being inscribed with one or more names of God or of His angels.

Ashkenazi—in medieval Hebrew lit. "German"; conventional term used to designate Jews of West or East European origin.

Atarah—in Hebrew lit. "crown"; see TORAH CROWN.

Baroque—a period whose art is marked by three-dimensionality, by the interaction between the space of the work and the space surrounding it, and by a heightened sense of drama; largely in the seventeenth century.

Bemah—see READER'S DESK.

Chronogram—the writing of a date by means of words or biblical verses, based on the numerical value assigned to each letter in the Hebrew alphabet.

Curtain for the Torah Ark—a curtain hung in front of the Torah ark in synagogues.

Diaspora—Jewish settlement outside the land of Israel.

Eternal Light—a continuously burning lamp that hangs before the Torah ark in a synagogue.

Etrog—citron, a fruit resembling a lemon; it is one of the four species of plants used during the liturgy of the Sukkot holiday.

Gruppo dei Sei or I Sei di Torino—founded by the painters Carlo Levi, Enrico Paulucci, Nicola Galante, Jesse Boswell, Francesco Menzio, and Gigi Chessa in 1929. They followed French post-impressionism and fauvism rather than the neoclassical or archaic revivals prominent in Italy during the fascist period.

Haggadah—the liturgical order of service for the seder; also the term for the book containing the service.

Halakhah—generic term for Jewish law based on the Torah, the Talmud, and rabbinic exposition.

Hanukkah—a Jewish holiday commemorating the victory of the Hasmoneans over their Greco-Syrian overlords in 165 B.C.E. and the establishment of religious freedom in ancient Israel.

Havdalah—in Hebrew lit. "separation"; a ceremony held to mark the end of the Sabbath and holy days and the beginning of the workday week.

Ḥuppah—a canopy under which the bride and groom stand during the wedding ceremony.

Il Novecento italiano—in Italian lit. "twentieth century"; began in 1922 as a group of seven painters in Milan and grew to a national movement by 1926 under the leadership of the critic Margherita Sarfatti. Although the Novecento claimed to be the art of the new Fascist state, it was never officially recognized as such by Mussolini, and it dissolved by 1933.

Kabbalah—in Hebrew lit. "that which has been received" or "tradition"; generic term for the Jewish mystical tradition and the esoteric teachings of Judaism; certification of a ritual slaughterer and inspector of kosher meat.

Kedushtah—a type of poem sequence embellishing the *amidot* of Sabbaths and holy days, which includes the *kedushah* or "Prayer of Sanctification."

Ketubbah—in Hebrew lit. "that which is written"; a Jewish marriage contract.

Kiddush—prayer of sanctification over wine recited on Sabbaths and holy days.

Kinah—in Hebrew lit. "lament"; dirges recited during a time of mourning.

Kohen—priest; a descendant of Aaron, the biblical High Priest.

Levite—a descendant of the tribe of Levi, aides to the priests of the ancient Temple.

Macchiaioli—refers to the group of eleven painters active in the years 1855–1862; derives from the word *macchia* meaning patch or stain and refers to the bold effects of chiaroscuro which the painters incorporated into their canvases.

Maḥzor—in Hebrew lit. "cycle"; a prayer book including the prayers and *piyyutim* for special Sabbaths and annual holy days.

Makama—[Arabic]; rhymed prose narrative, interspersed with metered poems.

Mappah—see Torah Cover.

Matzah—unleavened bread eaten during Passover.

Megillah—a scroll, e.g., *Megillat Esther,* the book of Esther written on a scroll.

Me'il—see Torah Mantle.

Menorah—a seven-branched candelabrum found in the biblical sanctuary and Jerusalem Temple; a similar candelabrum found in a synagogue; an eight-branched candelabrum used during the Hanukkah festival (plural: *menorot*).

Mishnah—body of Jewish oral law or *halakhah* edited by Rabbi Judah ha-Nasi around the beginning of the third century C.E.

Mitzvah—in Hebrew lit. "commandment"; a good deed.

Omer—49 day period between the second day of Passover and the first day of Shavuot, originally a sacrifice brought on the second day of Passover.

Passover—the spring pilgrimage festival commemorating the Exodus from Egypt (Heb. *Pesach*).

Pinkas—Hebrew from the Greek *pinaxes,* "register" or "list"; a book of minutes or records of a society within the Jewish community.

Piyyut—Hebrew liturgical poetry.

Rahit—a genre of Hebrew liturgical poetry.

Reader's Desk—desk on which the Torah is placed for reading; in Hebrew *tevah* or *bemah.*

Reader's Desk Cover—a textile used to cover the table on which the Torah is placed for reading.

Renaissance—a period beginning in the fourteenth and fifteenth centuries marked by a revival of classical texts, forms, structures, and artistic style.

Reshut—poetic prelude to a prayer.

Rimmon(im)—in Hebrew lit. "pomegranate(s)"; adornment for the staves of the Torah scroll; also called finials.

Risorgimento—in Italian lit. "rebirth or resurrection"; the movement for the unification of Italy under a single government free of foreign domination; it began in 1848 in Piedmont and was completed with the freeing of Rome in 1870.

Rococo—a decorative style of the eighteenth century characterized by a lightness and playfulness of forms and iconography whose quintessential motif is the shell (*rocaille* in French).

Rosh ha-Shanah—the New Year; holy days occurring on the first and second days of the Hebrew month of Tishri.

Sarcophagus—a stone coffin.

Scuola romana—in Italian lit. "Roman school"; refers to two groups of artists active in Rome between the world wars. Also called the school of Via Cavour and the *Tonalisti.*

Seder—in Hebrew lit. "order"; term given to the fourteen-part order of liturgical home service for the first two nights of Passover, which includes recitation of the story of the Exodus from Egypt, accompanied by ritual eating and drinking.

Sefer—in Hebrew lit. "book."

Seliḥah—penitential verse in Hebrew.

Sephardi—in medieval Hebrew lit. "Spanish" or "of Spain"; conventional term used to designate Jews of Spanish and Portuguese ancestry.

Shammash—in Hebrew lit. "servant" or "one who ministers"; used to designate a synagogue functionary (sexton) and the candle or light on the Hanukkah lamp that kindles (serves) the eight other lamps.

Shavuot—Feast of Weeks; a two-day festival commemorating the giving of the Torah at Sinai and the bringing of offerings to the Temple in Jerusalem, which occurs seven weeks after the second day of Passover.

Sheḥitah—the ritual slaughter of kosher animals.

Shofar—a ram's horn sounded during the services on Rosh Hashanah and Yom Kippur as a call to repentance.

Siddur—a daily prayer book.

Spice Container—a container for spices used during the *havdalah* service.

Sukkah—in Hebrew lit. "booth"; a temporary shelter erected during the Festival of Sukkot (Feast of Tabernacles) to recall the homes inhabited by the ancient Israelites during their wanderings in the desert.

Sukkot—Feast of Tabernacles; in Hebrew lit. "booths"; festival which falls four days after Yom Kippur, at the time of the autumnal harvest.

Tallit—a prayer shawl.

Tallit Katan—a fringed four-cornered ritual garment.

Talmud—in Hebrew lit. "study" or "learning"; rabbinic commentary on the Mishnah. The Babylonian Talmud was compiled circa 500 C.E., the Jerusalem Talmud circa 400 C.E.

Tefillin—two leather boxes enclosing parchment inscribed with passages from the Torah that are worn during morning prayer, except on Sabbaths and Festivals.

Tevah—see READER'S DESK.

Tik—cylindrical case for the Torah scroll.

Torah—a parchment or leather scroll inscribed with the first five books of the Hebrew Bible.

Torah Ark—a cabinet set in or against one wall of a synagogue. It holds the Torah scrolls and is the focus of prayer.

Torah Binder—a band that holds the two staves of a Torah scroll together when the Torah is not being read.

Torah Cover—a textile used to cover the Torah between readings.

Torah Crown—adornment for the staves of a Torah scroll.

Torah Curtain—see CURTAIN FOR THE TORAH ARK.

Torah Mantle—a cover of silk or other precious fabric that encases the Torah scroll and is removed for reading.

Torah Pointer—a small rod of wood or precious metal used by the reader of the Torah to follow the text.

Torah Shield—an ornamental metal plaque hung from the staves of a Torah.

Valori Plastici—an art and literary journal founded in Rome in 1918 by the critic Mario Broglio and the painter Roberto Melli. It also refers to the group of artists associated with the publication.

Yeshivah—an academy or school for Jewish learning.

Yom Kippur—in Hebrew lit. "Day of Atonement"; a day of fasting and prayer that falls on the tenth day of the Hebrew month of Tishri, and is the culmination of the Days of Awe that begin on Rosh ha-Shanah (the New Year).

Yotzer—a poem sequence inserted in the *Shema* prayers during the morning service.

Frequently cited works are abbreviated and are indicated by brackets.

History

Bonfil, R. "Change in Cultural Patterns of Jewish Society in Crisis: The Case of Italian Jewry at the Close of the Sixteenth Century." *Jewish History* (forthcoming).

———. *Ha-Rabbanut be-Italyah bi-Tekufat ha-Renasance.* Jerusalem, 1979.

———. "The Historian's Perception of the Jews in the Italian Renaissance: Towards a Reappraisal." *Revue des études juives* 143 (1984): 59–82.

Cacioli, M., L. De Courten, L. Moro, and A. Mule, eds. *Italia Judaica: Gli ebrei in Italia tra Rinascimento ed età barocca.* Rome, 1986.

Calimano, R. *The Ghetto of Venice.* Venice, 1987.

Canepa, A. "Cattolici ed ebrei nell'Italia liberale (1870–1915)." *Comunità* 32 (April 1978): 43–109.

———. "Emancipation and Jewish Response in Mid-Nineteenth-Century Italy." *European History Quarterly* 16 (1986): 403–439.

———. "Emancipazione, integrazione, e antisemitismo in Italia: Il caso Pasqualigo." *Comunità* 29 (June 1975): 166–203.

———. "L'immagine dell'ebreo nel folclore e nella letteratura del postrisorgimento." *Rassegna mensile di Israel* 44 (May–June 1978): 389–399.

Carpi, D. *Peulat 'K' K' Italiani' she-be-Venezia le-ma'an a'neyei Eretz Yisrael.* Tel Aviv, 1978–1979.

Centro di documentazione ebraica contemporanea. *Ebrei in Italia: Deportazione, resistenza.* Florence, 1975.

Cohen, M. R., ed. and trans. *The Autobiography of a Seventeenth-Century Venetian Rabbi: Leon Modena's Life of Judah.* Princeton, 1988.

Cozzi, G., ed. *Gli ebrei e Venezia, secoli XIV–XVIII: Atti del convegno.* Milan, 1987.

De Felice, R. *Storia degli ebrei italiani sotto il fascismo.* 2 vols. Turin, 1977.

Del Canuto, F., ed. *Israel: Saggi sulli-ebraismo italiano.* Rome, 1984.

Della Pergola, S. *Anatomia dell'ebraismo italiano.* Assisi and Rome, 1976.

Dubin, L. C. "Trieste and Berlin: The Italian Role in the Cultural Politics of the Haskalah." In *Toward Modernity: The European Jewish Model,* edited by J. Katz, pp. 189–224. New Brunswick, N.J., and Oxford, 1987.

Foa, S. *Gli ebrei nel Risorgimento italiano.* Rome, 1978.

Fornari, S. *La Roma del ghetto.* Rome, 1984.

Fubini, G. *La condizione giuridica dell'ebraismo italiano.* Florence, 1974.

SELECTED BIBLIOGRAPHY

Gentile, E. *Le origini dell'ideologia fascista, 1918–1925.* Bari, 1975.

Goldenberg, R. "The Jewish Sabbath in the Roman World up to the Time of Constantine the Great." *Aufstieg und Niedergang der römischen Welt* II.19.1 (1979): 414–447.

Horowitz, E. "On Jewish Religious Observance at the End of the Fifteenth Century according to the Letters of Rabbi Obadiah from Bertinoro." *Pa'amim* 37 (1988): 31–41 (Hebrew).

Hughes, H. S. *Prisoner of Hope: The Silver Age of the Italian Jews, 1924–74.* Cambridge, Mass., 1983.

Leon, H. J. *The Jews of Ancient Rome.* Philadelphia, 1960. [Leon, *Jews of Ancient Rome*]

Levi, P. *Survival in Auschwitz and The Reawakening: Two Memoirs.* Translated by S. Woolf. New York, 1986.

Marcus, J. R. *The Jew in the Medieval World.* Philadelphia, 1960. [Marcus, *The Jew*]

Michaelis, M. *Mussolini and the Jews: German-Italian Relations and the Jewish Question in Italy, 1922–1945.* Oxford, 1978.

———. *Mussolini e la questione ebraica.* Milan, 1982.

A. Milano. *Il Ghetto di Roma.* Rome, 1964.

———. *Storia degli ebrei in Italia.* Turin, 1963.

Roth, C. *History of the Jews of Italy.* Philadelphia, 1946.

———. *The Jews in the Renaissance.* New York, 1959.

———. *Venice.* Philadelphia, 1930.

Segre, D. V. *Memoirs of a Fortunate Jew: An Italian Story.* Bethesda, Md., 1987.

Sermoneta, G. "Considerazioni frammentarie sul giudeo italiano." Parts 1, 2. *Italia* 1, no. 1 (1976): 1–29; 1, no. 2 (1978): 62–106.

Simonsohn, S. *History of the Jews in the Duchy of Mantua.* Jerusalem, 1983.

Sonne, I. *Ha-yahadut ha-italkit: Demutah u-mekomah be-toldat am yisrael.* Jerusalem, 1961.

Stow, K. R. *Catholic Thought and Papal Jewry Policy, 1555–1593.* New York, 1977.

Tas, L. *Storia degli ebrei italiani.* Rome, 1987.

Tortorelli, G. "L'affaire Dreyfus e i socialisti italiani." *Societa e storia* 9 (January–March 1986): 105–132.

Toscano, M. "Fermenti culturali ed esperienze organizzative della gioventu ebraica italiana (1911–1925)." *Storia contemporanea* 13 (December 1982): 915–961.

———. "Gli ebrei in Italia dall'emancipazione alla persecuzione." *Storia contemporanea* 17 (October 1986): 905–954.

———. "Tra identità culturale e partecipazione politica: Aspetti e momenti di vita ebraica italiana (1956–1976)." *Annuario di studi ebraici 1985–1987,* vol. 2, pp. 293–325.

Turin, Archivi d'Arte e Cultura Piedmontesi. *Ebrei a Torino*. Exhibition catalogue. Turin, 1984.

Zucotti, S. *The Italians and the Holocaust*. New York, 1987.

The Art of Antiquity

Avi-Yonah, M. "Places of Worship in the Roman and Byzantine Periods." *Antiquity and Survival* 2 (1957): 260–275.

Barag, D. "Glass." In *Encyclopaedia Judaica,* vol. 7, cols. 604–614.

Eitan, A. "The Menora as a Symbol." *The Israel Museum News* 3 (1968): 45–49.

Frey, J.-B. *Corpus Inscriptionum Iudaicarum*. Rome, 1938. Reprint. New York, 1975. [Frey, *Corpus Inscriptionum Iudaicarum*]

Garrucci, R. *Dissertazioni archeologiche di vario argomento*. Rome, 1865.

Goodenough, E. R. *Jewish Symbols in the Greco-Roman Period*. 13 vols. New York, 1953–1968. [Goodenough, *Jewish Symbols*]

———. *The Archaeological Evidence from the Diaspora*. New York, 1953.

Konikoff, A. *Sarcoghagi from the Jewish Catacombs of Ancient Rome*. Stuttgart, 1986.

Momigliano, A. "I nome delle prime 'synagoghe' romane e la condizione giuridica delle comunità in Roma sotto Augusto." *Rassegna mensile di Israel,* 2d ser., 6, no. 7 (1931): 283–292.

New York, The Jewish Museum, *Israel in Antiquity*. Exhibition catalogue. By A. Ackerman and S. Braunstein. New York, 1982.

Paribeni, R. *Le Terme di Diocleziano e il Museo Nazionale Romano*. Rome, 1928–1932.

Reifenberg, A. *Ancient Hebrew Arts*. New York, 1950.

Revel-Neher, E. "L'alliance et la promesse: Le symbolisme d'Eretz-Israël dans l'iconographie juive du moyen âge." *Jewish Art* 12–13 (1987).

———. *L'arche d'alliance dans l'art juif et chrétien du second au dixième siècles*. Paris, 1984.

St. Clair, A. "God's House of Peace in Paradise: The Feast of Tabernacles on a Jewish Gold Glass." *Journal of Jewish Art* 11 (1985): 6–15.

Schuler, I. "A Note on Jewish Gold Glass." *Journal of Glass Studies* 8 (1966): 48–61.

Squarciapino, M. F. "Plotius Fortunatus Archisynagogus." *Rassegna mensile di Israel* 36 (1970): 183–191.

———. "La Sinagoga di Ostia." *Bolletino d'arte,* 4th ser., 46 (1961): 326–337.

———. "The Synagogue at Ostia." *Archaeology* 16 (1963): 194–203.

Manuscripts and Documents

Adler, E. N. *Catalogue of Hebrew Manuscripts in the Collection of Elkan Nathan Adler*. Cambridge, 1921.

Beit Arie, M. "Joel Ben Simeon's Manuscripts: A Codicologer's View." *Journal of Jewish Art* 3–4 (1977): 25–39.

Cohen, E. M. "The Illustrations in Abraham Farissol's Haggadah of 1515." *Jewish Art* 12–13 (1986–1987): 89–95.

Edmunds, S. "The Place of the London *Haggadah* in the Work of Joel ben Simeon." *Journal of Jewish Art* 7 (1980): 25–34.

Fooner, M. "Joel ben Simeon, Illuminator of Hebrew Manuscripts in the Fifteenth Century." *Jewish Quarterly Review* 27 (1937): 217–232.

Goldstein, D. *The Ashkenazi Haggadah*. New York, 1985.

Grassi, L., ed. *Ketubbot italiane: Antichi contratti nuziali ebraici miniati*. Milan, 1984.

Gutmann, J. *Hebrew Manuscript Painting*. New York, 1978.

———. "Thirteen Manuscripts in Search of an Author: Joel ben Simeon, Fifteenth-Century Scribe-Artist." *Studies in Bibliography and Booklore* 9 (1970): 76–95.

Jerusalem, Jewish National and University Library. *Manuscripts and Rare Books: An Exhibition from the Collections of the Jewish National and University Library*. Exhibition catalogue. Jerusalem, 1970.

———. *Selected Manuscripts and Prints: An Exhibition from the Treasures of the Jewish National and University Library*. Exhibition catalogue. Jerusalem, 1985. [JNUL, *Selected*]

Landsberger, F. "Illuminated Marriage Contracts with Special Reference to the Cincinatti Ketubahs." *Hebrew Union College Annual* 26 (1955): 503–542.

———. "The Washington Haggadah and Its Illuminator." *Hebrew Union College Annual* 21 (1948): 73–103.

Martelli, V. A., and L. Mortara Ottolenghi. *Manoscritti biblica ebraici decorati*. Milan, 1966.

Metzger, M. *La Haggadah enluminée; Étude iconographique et stylistique des manuscrits enluminés et decorés de la Haggada du XIII au XVI siècle*. Leiden, 1973.

———. "The John Rylands Megillah and Some Other Illustrated Megilloth of the Fifteenth to Seventeenth Centuries." *Bulletin of the John Rylands Library* 45 (1962): 148–184.

———. "Un mahzor italien enluminé du XVe siècle." *Mitteilungen des Kunsthistorischen Instituts in Florenz* 20 (1976): 159–196.

———. "A Study of Some Unknown Hand-Painted Megilloth of the Seventeenth and Eighteenth-Centuries." *Bulletin of the John Rylands Library* 46 (1963): 84–126.

Metzger, T. "Les illustrations d'un psautier hebreu italien de la fin du XII siècle. Le Ms. Parm 1870–de Rossi 510 de la Bibliothèque Palatina de Parma." *Cahiers archéologiques* 26 (1977): 145–162.

Metzger, T. and M. *Jewish Life in the Middle Ages*. New York, 1982.

Nahon, U., and G. Sarfatti, eds. *Sefer Ha-Maftir di Urbino: Manuscritto ebraico del 1704*. Jerusalem, 1964.

Narkiss, B. *Hebrew Illuminated Manuscripts*. Jerusalem, 1978.

Narkiss, M. "The Oeuvre of the Jewish Engraver Salom ben Mordecai Italia." Parts 1, 2. *Tarbiz* 25 (1956): 441–451; 26 (1957): 87–101.

New York, The Jewish Museum, *Illuminated Hebrew Manuscripts from the Library of The Jewish Theological Seminary of America*. Exhibition catalogue. By T. Freudenheim. New York, 1965.

———. "Manuscripts and Printed Books from the Collection of The Royal Library, Copenhagen." In *Kings and Citizens: The History of the Jews in Denmark, 1622–1983*. Vol. 2. Exhibition catalogue. By U. Haxen. New York, 1983.

New York, The Library of The Jewish Theological Seminary of America. *The Rothschild Mahzor: Florence 1492*. Introduction by E. M. Cohen and M. Schmelzer. New York, 1983.

Ottolenghi, L. Mortara. "Manoscritto ebraici miniati in Italia settentrionale." *Arte Lombarda* 60 (1981): 41–48.

Panofsky, E. "Giotto and Maimonides in Avignon: The Story of an Illustrated Hebrew Manuscript." Parts 1, 2. *Journal of the Walters Art Gallery* 4 (1941): 27–44; 5 (1942): 124–127.

Sabar, S. "The Beginnings and Flourishing of Ketubbah Illustration in Italy: A Study in Popular Imagery and Jewish Patronage during the Seventeenth and Eighteenth Centuries." Ph.D. diss., University of California, Los Angeles, 1987.

———. "The Beginnings of *Ketu'bbah* Decoration in Italy: Venice in the Late Sixteenth to the Early Seventeenth Centuries." *Jewish Art* 12–13 (1987): 96–110.

———. "The Use of Christian Motifs in Illustrations of Jewish Marriage Contracts in Italy and Its Meaning." *Journal of Jewish Art* 10 (1984): 47–63.

Sed-Rajna, G. *The Hebrew Bible in Medieval Illuminated Manuscripts*. New York, 1987.

Swarzenski, G., and R. Schilling. *Die illuminierten Handschriften und Einzelminiaturen des Mittelalters und der Renaissance in Frankfurter Besitz*. Frankfurt, 1929.

Printing and Printed Books

Amram, D. W. *The Makers of Hebrew Books in Italy*. London, 1963. [Amram, *Makers*]

Berkowitz, D. S. *In Remembrance of Creation*. Waltham, Mass., 1968.

Berlin, C., ed. *Hebrew Printing and Bibliography*. New York, 1976.

Carmilly-Weinberger, M. *Censorship and Freedom of Expression in Jewish History*. New York, 1977. [Carmilly-Weinberger, *Censorship*]

Epstein, M. "Simon Levi Ginzburg's Illustrated Customal of Venice, 1593, and Its Travels." In *The Proceedings of the Fifth World Congress of Jewish Studies, Jerusalem* 4 (1973): 197–218.

Habermann, A. M. "The Jewish Art of the Printed Book." In *Jewish Art,* edited by B. Narkiss, pp. 163–174, 1971.

———. *Ha-Madpisim B'nei Soncino.* Vienna, 1932–1933. [Habermann, *Ha-Madpisim*]

Jerusalem, Jewish National and University Library, *Manuscripts and Rare Books: An Exhibition from the Collections of the Jewish National and University Library.* Exhibition catalogue. Jerusalem, 1970.

———. *Selected Manuscripts and Prints: An Exhibition from the Treasures of the Jewish National and University Library.* Exhibition catalogue. Jerusalem, 1985. [JNUL, *Selected*]

London, British Library, Department of Oriental Manuscripts and Printed Books. *Illustration in Early Hebrew Printing, 1474–1700.* Exhibition brochure. London, 1979–1980. [British Library, *Illustration*]

Marx, A. *Bibliographical Studies and Notes on Rare Books and Manuscripts in the Library of The Jewish Theological Seminary.* New York, 1977. [Marx, *Bibliographical Studies*]

Marx, M. "On the Date of Appearance of the First Printed Hebrew Books." In *Alexander Marx Jubilee Volume,* edited by S. Lieberman, pp. 481–501. New York, 1950.

The New York Public Library, *The People and the Book: The Background of Three Hundred Years of Jewish Life in America.* Exhibition catalogue. By J. Bloch. New York, 1954.

———. *Treasures from the New York Public Library.* New York, 1985.

———. *A Sign and a Witness: Two Thousand Years of Hebrew Books and Illuminated Manuscripts.* L. S. Gold, ed. Exhibition Catalogue. New York and Oxford, 1988. [NYPL, *A Sign*]

Ottawa, National Library of Canada. *Incunabula, Hebraica, and Judaica: Five Centuries of Hebraica and Judaica, Rare Bibles, and Hebrew Incunables from the Jacob M. Lowy Collection.* Exhibition catalogue. By B. S. Hill. Ottawa, 1981. [Hill, *Lowy*]

Popper, W. *The Censorship of Hebrew Books.* Introduction by M. Carmilly-Weinberger. New York, 1969.

Rabinowitch, R. N. N. *Ma'amar al ha-dfasat ha-Talmud.* Munich, 1876–1877.

Roth, C. *Studies in Books and Booklore.* Farnborough, England, 1972.

Schmeruk, H. "D'fusei Yiddish Be-Italia." *Italia* 3, nos. 1–2 (1982): 112–175.

Steinschneider, M. *Catalogus Librorum Hebraeorum in Bibliotheca Bodleiana.* Hildesheim, 1964. [Steinschneider, *Bodleiana*].

Wischnitzer-Bernstein, R. "Passover in Art." In *The Passover Anthology,* edited by P. Goodman. pp. 295–324, Philadelphia, 1961.

———. "Von der Holbeinbibel zur Amsterdamer Haggadah." *Monatsschrift für Geschichte und Wissenchaft des Judentums.* 7 (1931): 269–286.

Yaari, A. *Bibliographia shel haggadot pesaḥ.* Jerusalem, 1960.

———. "Ha-Madpisim B'nei Foa." *Kiryat Sefer* 17 (1940): 222–238, 393–412.

Yerushalmi, Y. H. *Haggadah and History: A Panorama in Facsimile of Five Centuries of the Printed Haggadah from the Collections of Harvard University and The Jewish Theological Seminary of America.* Philadelphia, 1974.

Zedner, J. *Catalogue of the Hebrew Books in the Library of the British Museum.* London, 1964. [Zedner, *British Museum*]

Ceremonial and Decorative Arts

Adler, C., and I. M. Casanowicz. "The Collection of Jewish Ceremonial Objects in the Collection of the United States National Museum." *Proceedings of the U.S. National Museum* 34, no. 1630 (1908).

Armand, A. *Les medailleurs italiens des quinzième et seizième siècles.* Bologna, 1966.

Avery, C. "A Bronze Founder and Sculptor of the Late Sixteenth Century, Giuseppe de Levis of Verona: New Discoveries," *Connoisseur* 194 (February 1977): 114–121.

———. "Giuseppe de Levis of Verona, Bronze Founder and Sculptor." In *Studies in European Sculpture,* pp. 45–78. London, 1981.

———. "Giuseppe de Levis of Verona, Bronze Founder and Sculptor: 2—Figurestyle." *Connoisseur* 182 (February 1973): 87–97.

———. "Giuseppe de Levis of Verona, Bronze Founder and Sculptor: 3—Decorative Utensils and Domestic Ornaments." *Connoisseur* 185 (February 1974): 123–129.

Balletti, A. *Il Tempio Maggiore Israelitico di Reggio nell'Emilia.* Reggio Emilia, 1908.

Bemporad, D. Liscia. "Atarot fiorentine." *MCM,* no. 3 (1985): 46.

———. "I ricami datati della Sinagoga di Firenze." In *I tessili antichi e il lora uso.* Turin, 1986.

———. "La Scuola italiana e la Scuola levantina nel ghetto di Firenze: Prima ricostruzione." *Revista d'arte* 38, 4th ed., vol. 2 (1964): 3–48.

Bialer, Y. L. *Jewish Life in Art and Tradition: Based on the Collection of the Sir Isaac and Lady Edith Wolfson Museum, Hechal Shlomo, Jerusalem.* New York, 1976.

Blair, C. "Cesare Borgia's Sword-Scabbard." *Victoria and Albert Museum Bulletin* 2, no. 4 (1966).

Bondoni, S. M., and G. Busi, eds. *Cultura ebraica in Emilia-Romagna.* Rimini, 1987.

Boralevi, A. "Un tappeto ebraico italo-egiziano." *Critica d'arte* 49, no. 2 (1984): 34–47.

———. "Three Egyptian Carpets in Italy." In *Oriental Carpet and Textile Studies.* Vol. 2, *Carpets of the Mediterranean Countries,* pp. 211–220. London, 1986.

Chicago, The Maurice Spertus Museum of Judaica. *Magic and Superstition in the Jewish Tradition.* Exhibition catalogue. By M. R. Josephy. 1975.

Ferrara, Palazzo dei Diamanti, Palazzo Paradiso. *Arte e cultura ebraiche in Emilia-Romagna.* Exhibition catalogue. Ferrara, 1988–1989.

Fishof, Iris. "Renaissance Hanukah Lamps from Italy." *Israel Museum News* 8 (1970): 65–76.

Franzoni, L., ed. *Fonditori di campane a Verona dal XI al XX secolo.* Verona, 1979.

Friedenberg, D. M. *Jewish Medals from the Renaissance to the Fall of Napoleon (1503–1815).* New York, 1970.

Geiger, A. "Eine mittelalterliche jüdische Medaille." Parts 1, 2. *Zeitschrift der deutschen Morgenlandischen Gesellschaft* 12 (1858): 680–693; 12 (1859): 272–275.

Gramberg, W. "Der Veroneser Bildhauer Giuseppe de Levis und Guglielmo della Porta." *Jahrbuch der Kunsthistorischen Sammlungen in Wien,* n.s., 11 (1937): 184–186.

Grossman, C. "Womanly Arts: A Study of Italian Torah Binders in the New York Jewish Museum Collection." *Journal of Jewish Art* 7 (1980): 35–43.

Gutmann, J. *Jewish Ceremonial Art.* New York and London, 1964.

Jerusalem, Israel Museum. *The Stieglitz Collection: Masterpieces of Jewish Art.* Exhibition catalogue. By C. Benjamin. Jerusalem, 1987.

Kayser, S. S., and G. Schoenberger, eds. *Jewish Ceremonial Art.* Philadelphia, 1959. [Kayser and Schoenberger, *Jewish Ceremonial Art*]

Klagsbald, V. *Catalogue raisonné de la collection juive du Musée de Cluny.* Paris, 1981.

Kottek, S. S. "Humilitas: On a Controversial Medal of Benjamin, Son of Elijah Beer the Physician (1497?–1503?)." *Journal of Jewish Art* 11 (1985): 41–46.

Landsberger, F. *A History of Jewish Art.* Cincinnati, 1946.

Lazar, H. "Jonah, the Tower, and the Lions: An Eighteenth-Century Italian Silver Book Binding." *Journal of Jewish Art* 3–4 (1977): 58–73.

Loewe, L. "Memoir on the Lemlein Medal." *Numismatic Chronicle* 19 (April 1856–January 1857): 237–270.

London, Jewish Museum. *Catalogue of the Permanent and Loan Collections of the Jewish Museum, London.* Edited by R. D. Barnett. London, 1974.

Mann, V. B. "Forging Judaica—The Case of the Italian Majolica Seder Plates." *Studies in Contemporary Jewry* 6 (1990). In press.

———. "Jewish-Muslim Acculturation in the Ottoman Empire: The Evidence of Ceremonial Art." In *Proceedings of the Brandeis Conference on the Jews of the Ottoman Empire.* In press.

———. "The Recovery of a Known Work." *Jewish Art* 12–13 (1986–1987): 269–278.

Nahon, U. *Ornamenti del Sefer Tora.* Jerusalem, 1966.

Narkiss, M. *The Hanukkah Lamp.* Jerusalem, 1939.

———. "An Italian Niello Casket of the Fifteenth Century." *Journal of the Warburg and Courtauld Institutes* 21 (1958): 288–295.

———. "The Secret of the Italian Casket of the Fifteenth Century." *Rimmonim* 2 (1985): 32–36 (Hebrew).

———. "A Silver Niello Casket from the Fifteenth Century in Italy." In *Scritti in memoria di Sally Mayer,* pp. 167–195. Jerusalem, 1956 (Hebrew).

New York, The Jewish Museum. *The Book and Its Cover: Manuscripts and Bindings of the Twelfth through the Eighteenth Centuries.* Exhibition brochure. By V. B. Mann and M. Schmelzer. New York, 1981.

———. *Coins Reveal.* Exhibition catalogue. By Y. Meshorer. New York, 1983.

———. *Danzig 1939: Treasures of a Destroyed Community.* Exhibition catalogue. By V. B. Mann and J. Gutmann. New York, 1980.

———. *Fabric of Jewish Life: Textiles from the Jewish Museum Collection.* Exhibition catalogue. By B. Kirshenblatt-Gimblett. New York, 1977. [NYJM, *Fabric of Jewish Life*]

———. *The Jewish Patrons of Venice.* Exhibition brochure. By S. J. Makover. New York, 1985. [NYJM, *Jewish Patrons*]

———. *Loan Exhibit of Antique Ceremonial Objects and Paintings from the Collection of Mr. M. Zagayski.* Exhibition brochure. New York, 1951.

———. *Personal Vision: The Jacobo and Asea Furman Collection of Jewish Ceremonial Art.* Exhibition catalogue. By S. L. Braunstein. New York, 1985.

———. *The Silver and Judaica Collection of Mr. and Mrs. Michael M. Zagayski.* Exhibition catalogue. By G. Schoenberger and T. Freudenheim. 1963.

———. *A Tale of Two Cities: Jewish Life in Frankfurt and Istanbul, 1750–1870.* Exhibition catalogue. By V. B. Mann. 1982.

———. *Treasures of the Jewish Museum.* Exhibition catalogue. By N. L. Kleeblatt and V. B. Mann. 1986. 1986. [Kleeblatt and Mann, *Treasures*]

Pinkerfeld, J. *The Synagogues of Italy: Their Architectural Development since the Renaissance.* Jerusalem, 1954 (Hebrew).

Pisa, F. "Parnassim: Le grandi famiglie ebraiche italiane dal secolo XI al XIX." *Annuario di studi ebraici* 10 (1984): 291–491.

Pitigliani, F. *Permanent Exhibition of the Jewish Community of Rome.* Rome, 1962.

Planiscig, L. *Venezianische Bildhauer der Renaissance.* Vienna, 1924.

Roth, C. *Arte nella tradizione ebraica.* Milan, 1963.

Rubens, A. *A History of Jewish Costume.* New York, 1973.

San Francisco, Jewish Community Museum. *Fifty Treasures: Judaica and Hebraica from Bay Area Collections.* Exhibition catalogue. By J. R. Goldyne. San Francisco, 1984.

Servi, S. *The Jewish Museum of Rome.* Rome, 1985.

Sullam, G. R. *Jewish Art Treasures in Venice.* New York, 1973.

———. "Catalogo delle opere." In *Oggetti del culto ebraico,* edited by Franco Faranda, pp. 32–33. Bertinoro, 1988.

Toaff, A. S. "Cenni storici sulla Comunità ebraica e sulla Sinagoga di Livorno." *Rassegna mensile di Israel* 21 (1955): 423–424.

———. "Il Museo dell Comunità Israelitica." *Libvrni Civitas* 9 (1931).

———. "Vita artistico-letteraria degli ebrei a Livorno nel '700." *Rassegna mensile di Israel* 8 (1933).

Washington, D.C., Smithsonian Institution. *The Precious Legacy: Judaic Treasures from the Czechoslovak State Collections.* Exhibition catalogue. Edited by D. Altshuler. Washington, D.C., 1983.

Weisberg, G. P. *Stile Floreale: The Cult of Nature in Italian Design.* Exhibition catalogue. Miami, 1988.

Yaniv, B. "Sixteenth–Eighteenth Century Bohemian and Moravian Parochot with an Architectural Motif." Ph.D. diss., The Hebrew University, Jerusalem, 1987 (Hebrew).

Zunz, L. "Eine merkwürdige Medaille." *Gesammelte Schriften* 3 (1876): 87–97.

Literature

Carmi, T. *Penguin Book of Hebrew Verse.* New York, 1981.

Haberman, A. M. *A History of Hebrew Liturgical and Secular Poetry in the Middle Ages.* Ramat Gan, 1970 (Hebrew).

———. *Topics in Poetry and Piyyut of the Middle Ages.* Jerusalem, 1972.

Jarden, D., ed. *The Cantos of Immanuel of Rome.* Jerusalem, 1957.

Lazzeri, G. *Antologia dei primi secoli della letteratura italiana.* Milan, 1940.

Lopez, G. "Infanzias e giovinezza di un grande editore: Emilio Treves." *Rassegna mensile di Israel* 36 (July–September 1970): 213–231.

Pagis, D. *Change and Tradition in the Secular Poetry: Spain and Italy.* Jerusalem, 1976 (Hebrew).

Ruderman, D. B. "The Italian Renaissance and Jewish Thought." In *Renaissance Humanism: Foundations and Forms,* edited by A. Rabil, Jr.. Vol. 1, pp. 382–433. Philadelphia, 1988.

———. *Kabbalah, Magic, and Science: The Cultural Universe of a Sixteenth-Century Jewish Physician.* Cambridge, Mass., and London, 1988.

Schirmann, J. "The Beginning of Hebrew Poetry in Italy and Northern Europe, 1: Italy." In *The World History of the Jewish People.* Tel Aviv, 1966.

Wardy, B. "Jewish Religion in Pagan Literature during the Late Republic and Early Empire." *Aufstieg und Niedergang der römischen Welt* II.19.1 (1979): 592–644.

Zinberg, I. *The History of Jewish Literature.* Translated by B. Martin. Philadelphia, 1972–1978. [Zinberg, *Jewish Literature*]

Music and Dance

Adler, I. "Hebrew Writings Concerning Music." In *Répertoire internationale des sources musicales.* Vol. 9, pt. 2, Munich, 1975.

———. Practique Musicale Savante dans quelques communantés juives en Europe aux 17 et 18 siècle. Paris, 1966.

———. "The Rise of Art Music in the Italian Ghetto." In *Jewish Medieval and Renaissance Studies,* edited by A. Altmann. Cambridge, Mass., 1967.

Newman, J. "The Madrigals of Salamon de' Rossi." Ph.D. diss., Columbia University, 1962.

Newman, J., and F. Rikko. *A Thematic Index to the Works of Salamon Rossi.* Hackensack, N.J., 1972.

Pesaro, Palazzo Lazzarini. *Mesura et arte del danzare: Guglielmo Ebreo da Pesaro e la danza nelle corti italiane del XV secolo.* Exhibition catalogue. Pesaro, 1987.

Rikko, F., ed. *Ha shirim asher li shlomo.* New York, 1975.

Painting and Sculpture

Bassani, G. "Un inedito di Mario Cavaglieri." *Paragone,* no. 39 (March 1953): 51–53.

Bossaglia, R. *Il "Novecento italiano."* Milan, 1979.

Braun, E., ed. "The Scuola Romana: Fact or Fiction?" *Art in America* 76 (March 1988): 128–136.

Broude, N. *The Macchiaioli: Italian Painters of the Nineteenth Century.* New Haven and London, 1987.

Camesasca, E. *Mario Sironi: Scritti editi e inediti.* Milan, 1980.

Carpi, P., ed. *Aldo Carpi: Diario di Güsen.* Milan, 1971.

Crispolti, E. *Il mito della macchina e altri temi del futurismo.* Trapani, 1969.

D'Amico, F. *Antonietta Raphaël sculture.* Exhibition catalogue. Rome, Milan 1985.

D'Ancona, F. Aghib Levi. *La giovinezza dei fratelli D'Ancona.* Rome, 1982.

D'Ancona, P. *Modigliani, Chagall, Soutine, Pascin: Aspetti dell'espressionismo.* Milan, 1952.

———. "Quattro maestri ebrei della pittura moderna italiana." In *Scritti in memoria di Sally Mayer (1875–1953).* Milan, 1956.

De Donato, C. *Carlo Levi: Coraggi dei miti: Scritti contemporanei, 1922–1974.* Bari, 1975.

Fagiolo dell'Arco, M. *Scuola romana: Pittura e scultura a Roma dal 1919 al 1943.* Rome, 1986.

Fagiolo dell'Arco, M., and V. Rivosecchi. *Scuola romana: Artisti tra le due guerra.* Exhibition catalogue. Milan, 1988.

Fiocco, G. "Una pittura di Pietro Longhi." *Arte veneta* 10 (1956): 206–207.

Florence, Palazzo Strozzi. *Cagli: La battaglia di San Martino per Firenze.* Exhibition catalogue. Florence, 1979.

Friedenberg, D. M. "Now Rest in Peace Jacob Baruch Caravalho: The Three-Century Diaspora of a Jewish Portrait." *Jewish Art* 14 (1988): 56–63.

George, W. *Exposition des peintures romains: Capograssi, Cavalli, Cagli, Scalvi.* Paris, 1933.

Imhof, Johann Jacob. *Der Historienmaler Hieronymous Hess von Basel.* Basel, 1887.

Landsberger, F. "Jewish Artists before the Period of Emancipation." *Hebrew Union College Annual* 16 (1941): 321–414.

Levi-Montalcini, R. *Elogio dell'imperfezione.* Milan, 1987.

London, Bloomsbury Gallery. *Exhibition of New Italian Painting by Carlo Levi, Francesco Menzio, Enrico Paulucci.* Exhibition catalogue. London, 1930.

London, Royal Academy of Arts, *Italian Art in the Twentieth Century.* London and Munich, 1989.

Los Angeles, Frederick S. Wight Art Gallery, University of California. *The Macchiaioli: Painters of Italian Life 1850–1900.* Exhibition catalogue. Edited by E. Tonelli and K. Hart. Los Angeles, 1986.

New York, The Jewish Museum. *Circle of Montparnasse.* Exhibition catalogue. New York, 1985.

New York, Museum of Modern Art. *De Chirico.* Exhibition catalogue. Edited by W. Rubin. New York, 1982.

Pignatti, T. *Pietro Longhi: Paintings and Drawings.* Translated by P. Waley. London, 1969.

Rome, Archivio dello Stato. *Carlo Levi: Disegni dal carcere 1934: Materiali per una storia.* Exhibition catalogue. Rome, 1983.

Rubens, A. *A Jewish Iconography.* London, 1981.

Rubinstein-Bloch, S. *Catalogue of the Collection of George and Florence Blumenthal.* Paris, 1926.

Signorini, T. *Caricaturisti e caricaturati al Caffè Michelangiolo.* Florence, 1952.

Tempesti, R. *Arte dell'Italia fascista.* Milan, 1976.

Toulouse, Musée des Augustins. *Hommage à Mario Cavaglieri.* Exhibition catalogue. Toulouse, 1974.

Trieste, Civico Museo Revoltella–Galleria d'Arte Moderna. *Umberto Veruda: Pittore di "Senilità".* Exhibition catalogue. Trieste, 1962.

Trieste, Palazzo Revoltella. *Arturo Nathan, 1891–1944.* Exhibition catalogue, Trieste, 1976.

Trieste, Stazione Marittima. *Arte nel Friuli-Venezia Giulia 1900–1950.* Exhibition catalogue 1981.

Venturi, L. "The Collection of Modern Art of Signor Gualino and the Modigliani Room at the Venice Biennial Exhibition." *Formes* 7 (July 1930): 9–10.

Wostry, C. *Storia del Circolo Artistico di Trieste.* Udine, 1934.

Wurm, H., and Benincasa, C. *Corrado Cagli: La notte dei cristalli.* Rome, 1975.

CONTRIBUTORS TO THE CATALOGUE

Dora Liscia Bemporad is a Researcher in the Dipartimento di Studi sul Medioevo e il Rinascimento at the University of Florence. She has published several studies on Italian Judaica and serves as the Director of the Jewish Museum of Florence.

Emily Braun is an art historian who specializes in modern art. She is the author of *Thomas Hart Benton: The America Today Murals* and most recently edited *Italian Art in the Twentieth Century*.

Richard Brilliant is Professor of Art History and Archaeology at Columbia University. He has written extensively on the art of Greco-Roman antiquity.

Evelyn M. Cohen is Curator of Jewish Art at The Jewish Theological Seminary of America and a specialist in illuminated Hebrew manuscripts. She is the recipient of the 1985 National Jewish Book Award for *The Rothschild Maḥzor: Florence 1492.*

Maria Teresa Contini is curator of the Fondi Storici Fotografici dell'I.C.C.D. di Roma. She has written numerous catalogues on photography and a book on Italian theater.

Primo Levi (1919–1987), renowned Italian novelist is the author of numerous short stories and novels including *The Periodic Table* and *Survival in Auschwitz,* which draws upon his experiences in the Holocaust. The preface that appears in this volume was written on the occasion of an exhibition marking the 100th anniversary of the Turin Synagogue. Dr. Levi granted the Jewish Museum permission to publish the English translation shortly before his untimely death.

Allen Mandelbaum, literary historian, poet, and noted translator of Dante, is Kenan Professor of Humanities at Wake Forest University. His most recent work is *The Savantasse of Montparnasse.*

Vivian B. Mann is Curator of Judaica at The Jewish Museum, New York. She serves as director of the Bernard Manekin Institute for Jewish Art, a joint project of the Museum and The Jewish Theological Seminary of America. She has written numerous articles on Jewish ceremonial art and medieval art.

Francesca Morelli is Curator of the Archivio della Scuola romana, Rome and specializes in the history of Italian art between the world wars.

David B. Ruderman is Frederick P. Rose Professor of Jewish History at Yale University. He received the National Jewish Book Award in 1982 for his publication, *The World of a Renaissance Jew: The Life and Thought of Abraham B. Farissol.*

Mario Toscano is on the Faculty of Political Science at the University of Rome and writes on Italian Jewry, particularly the cultural revival at the beginning of the twentieth century.

Tullia Zevi, a journalist by profession, is President of the Unione Comunità Ebraiche Italiane.

Additional catalogue entries were prepared by:

Charles Avery, Christie, Manson and Woods, Ltd., London

Marina Bertinetti, Soprintendenza Archeologica di Roma, Rome

Maria L. Cabielli, Soprintendenza Archeologica di Roma, Rome

Silvia Allegro Dayan, Soprintendenza Archeologica di Roma, Rome

Gabriel M. Goldstein, The Jewish Museum, New York

Sam Gruber, World Monuments Fund, New York

Laura Martelli, Soprintendenza Archeologica di Roma, Rome

Cecilia Ricci, Soprintendenza Archeologica di Roma, Rome

Marina Sapelli, Soprintendenza Archeologica di Roma, Rome

Maria Floriana Squarciapino

Lucina Vattuone, Soprintendenza Archeologica di Roma, Rome